I/S 11/10

Fodor's

D1334936

Newcastle College
Library Services

To be returned by the date stamped below
If you wish to renew your books please call 0191 200 4020

Fodor's Travel Publications   New York, Toronto, London, Sydney, Auckland
www.fodors.com

FODOR'S SCOTLAND

Editor: Linda Cabasin (lead project editor), Mike Nalepa, Mark Sullivan

Writers: Duncan Forgan, Michael Gonzalez, Shona Main, Fiona Parrott, Elizabeth Reeder

Production Editor: Evangelos Vasilakis

Maps & Illustrations: David Lindroth, *cartographer;* Bob Blake, Rebecca Baer, *map editors;* William Wu, *information graphics*

Design: Fabrizio La Rocca, *creative director;* Guido Caroti, Siobhan O'Hare, *art directors;* Tina Malaney, Chie Ushio, Ann McBride, Jessica Walsh, *designers;* Melanie Marin, *senior picture editor*

Cover Photo: (Sweetheart Abbey, Dumfries and Galloway): Wysocki Pawel/Hemis/age fotostock

Production Manager: Amanda Bullock

22nd Edition

ISBN 978-1-4000-0432-4

ISSN 0743-0973

SPECIAL SALES

This book is available at special discounts for bulk purchases for sales promotions or premiums. Special editions, including personalized covers, excerpts of existing books, and corporate imprints, can be created in large quantities for special needs. For more information, write to Special Markets/Premium Sales, 1745 Broadway, MD 6-2, New York, New York 10019, or e-mail specialmarkets@randomhouse.com.

AN IMPORTANT TIP & AN INVITATION

Although all prices, opening times, and other details in this book are based on information supplied to us at press time, changes occur all the time in the travel world, and Fodor's cannot accept responsibility for facts that become outdated or for inadvertent errors or omissions. So **always confirm information when it matters,** especially if you're making a detour to visit a specific place. Your experiences—positive and negative—matter to us. If we have missed or misstated something, **please write to us.** We follow up on all suggestions. Contact the Scotland editor at editors@fodors.com or c/o Fodor's at 1745 Broadway, New York, NY 10019.

PRINTED IN THE UNITED STATES OF AMERICA

10 9 8 7 6 5 4 3 2 1

Be a Fodor's Correspondent

Your opinion matters. It matters to us. It matters to your fellow Fodor's travelers, too. And we'd like to hear it. In fact, we need to hear it.

When you share your experiences and opinions, you become an active member of the Fodor's community. That means we'll not only use your feedback to make our books better, but we'll publish your names and comments whenever possible. Throughout our guides, look for "Word of Mouth," excerpts of your unvarnished feedback.

Here's how you can help improve Fodor's for all of us.

Tell us when we're right. We rely on local writers to give you an insider's perspective. But our writers and staff editors—who are the best in the business—depend on you. Your positive feedback is a vote to renew our recommendations for the next edition.

Tell us when we're wrong. We're proud that we update most of our guides every year. But we're not perfect. Things change. Hotels cut services. Museums change hours. Charming cafés lose charm. If our writer didn't quite capture the essence of a place, tell us how you'd do it differently. If any of our descriptions are inaccurate or inadequate, we'll incorporate your changes in the next edition and will correct factual errors at fodors.com immediately.

Tell us what to include. You probably have had fantastic travel experiences that aren't yet in Fodor's. Why not share them with a community of like-minded travelers? Maybe you chanced upon a beach or bistro or B&B that you don't want to keep to yourself. Tell us why we should include it. And share your discoveries and experiences with everyone directly at fodors.com. Your input may lead us to add a new listing or highlight a place we cover with a "Highly Recommended" star or with our highest rating, "Fodor's Choice."

Give us your opinion instantly at our feedback center at www.fodors.com/feedback. You may also e-mail editors@fodors.com with the subject line "Scotland Editor." Or send your nominations, comments, and complaints by mail to Scotland Editor, Fodor's, 1745 Broadway, New York, NY 10019.

You and travelers like you are the heart of the Fodor's community. Make our community richer by sharing your experiences. Be a Fodor's correspondent.

Happy Traveling!

Tim Jarrell, Publisher

CONTENTS

MAPS

ABOUT
THIS BOOK

Our Ratings

Sometimes you find terrific travel experiences and sometimes they just find you. But usually the burden is on you to select. That's where our ratings come in.

As travelers we've all discovered a place so wonderful that its worthiness is obvious. And sometimes that place is so unique that superlatives don't do it justice. These sights, properties, and experiences get our highest rating, **Fodor's Choice** indicated by orange stars throughout this book. Black stars highlight sights and properties we deem **Highly Recommended** places that our writers, editors, and readers praise again and again for consistency and excellence.

By default, there's another category: any place we include in this book is by definition worth your time, unless we say otherwise. And we will.

Disagree with any of our choices? Care to nominate a place or suggest that we rate one more highly? Visit our feedback center at www. fodors.com/feedback.

Budget Well

Hotel and restaurant price categories from £ to £££££ are defined in the opening pages of each chapter or in Where to Eat and Where to Stay sections in city chapters. For attractions, we always give standard adult admission fees; reductions are usually available for children, students, and senior citizens. Want to pay with plastic? **AE, DC, MC, V** following restaurant and hotel listings indicate whether American Express, Diner's Club, MasterCard, and Visa are accepted.

Restaurants

Unless we state otherwise, restaurants are open for lunch and dinner daily. We mention dress only when there's a specific requirement and reservations only when they're essential or not accepted—it's always best to book ahead.

Hotels

Hotels have private bath, phone, TV, and air-conditioning and operate on the European Plan (aka EP, meaning without meals), unless we specify that they use the Continental Plan (CP, with a continental breakfast), Breakfast Plan (BP, with a full breakfast), or Modified American Plan (MAP, with breakfast and dinner). We always list facilities but not whether you'll be charged an extra fee to use them.

Many Listings	
★	Fodor's Choice
★	Highly recommended
⊠	Physical address
✛	Directions or Map coordinates
⌂	Mailing address
☎	Telephone
🖷	Fax
⊕	On the Web
✉	E-mail
☜	Admission fee
☉	Open/closed times
▭	Credit cards
Hotels & Restaurants	
⌂	Hotel
⌂⊃	Number of rooms
⌂	Facilities
⍾⊙⍾	Meal plans
✕	Restaurant
⌂	Reservations
⌂	Dress code
↘	Smoking
⏃⏁	BYOB
Outdoors	
⍓	Golf
⚠	Camping
Other	
ℭ	Family-friendly
⊠	Branch address
☞	Take note

1

Experience Scotland

WORD OF MOUTH

"We had a great 15-day holiday. The weather, in general, was super. It would have been nicer to watch the Tattoo in Edinburgh without rain dripping off our hoods, but what can you do? You take what you get, plus the show was still wonderful. For people who love Scotland, Skye is almost a necessity to visit. Words can barely describe the beauty of this island. The best parts of the trip were the scenery and the people—I love how many great people we got to meet and speak with. It makes a wonderful trip even better."

—twina49

WHAT'S WHERE

Numbers correspond to chapter numbers.

2 Edinburgh and the Lothians. Scotland's captivating capital is the country's most popular city, famous for its high-perched castle, Old Town and 18th-century New Town, ultramodern Parliament building, and Georgian and Victorian architecture. Among the city's highlights are superb museums, including the National Museum of Scotland, and the most celebrated arts festival in the world, the International Festival. If Edinburgh's crowds are too much, escape to the Lothians and visit coastal towns, beaches, ancient chapels, and castles.

3 Glasgow. The country's largest city has evolved from prosperous Victorian hub to depressed urban center to thriving modern city with a strong artistic, architectural, and culinary reputation. Museums and galleries such as the Kelvingrove and Burrell are here, along with the Arts and Crafts architecture of Charles Rennie Mackintosh and iconic institutions such as Glasgow University. Glasgow is also the place to shop in Scotland.

4 The Borders and the Southwest. Scotland's southern gateway from England, the Borders with its moors and gentle hills and river valleys is rustic but historically rich. It's known for being the home of Sir Walter Scott and has impressive stately homes such as Floors Castle and ruined abbeys including Melrose. The Southwest, or Dumfries and Galloway region, is perfect for scenic drives, castles, and hiking.

5 Fife and Angus. The "kingdom" of Fife is considered the sunniest and driest part of Scotland, with sandy beaches, fishing villages, and stone cottages. St. Andrews has its world-famous golf courses, but this university town is worth a stop even for nongolfers. To the north in Angus is Glamis Castle, the legendary setting of Shakespeare's *Macbeth*, as well as the reviving city of Dundee.

6 The Central Highlands. This area convenient to both Edinburgh and Glasgow encompasses some of Scotland's most beautiful terrain, with rugged, dark landscapes broken up by lochs and fields. Not to be missed is Loch Lomond and the Trossachs, Scotland's first national park. Perth and Stirling are the main metropolitan hubs and worth a stop; Stirling Castle has epic views that stretch from coast to coast.

Loch Linnhe

Oban

Firth of Lorn

Arduaine

Inveraray

Lochgilphead

Rothesay   Largs

Ardrossan

Brodick

Kintyre

Arran   Firth of Clyde

0   20 miles

0   20 kilometers

Girvan

North Channel

Stranraer

Luce Bay

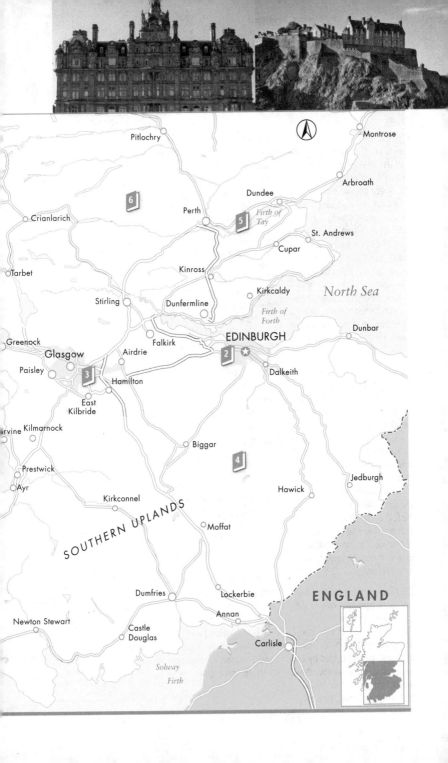

Pitlochry

Montrose

Arbroath

Crianlarich

Dundee

Perth

6

5

Firth of Tay

St. Andrews

Cupar

Kinross

Tarbet

Kirkcaldy

North Sea

Stirling

Dunfermline

Firth of Forth

Greenock

Falkirk

EDINBURGH ★

Dunbar

Glasgow

Airdrie

2

Paisley

3

Dalkeith

Hamilton

East Kilbride

Irvine Kilmarnock

Biggar

Prestwick

4

Jedburgh

Ayr

Hawick

Kirkconnel

SOUTHERN UPLANDS

Moffat

Lockerbie

ENGLAND

Dumfries

Annan

Newton Stewart

Castle Douglas

Carlisle

Solway Firth

WHAT'S WHERE

7 **Aberdeen and the Northeast.** Malt-whisky buffs can use the prosperous port city of Aberdeen, known for its silvery granite buildings, as a base for exploring the region's Malt Whisky Trail, with its excellent selection of distilleries large and small. Aberdeen also makes a good starting point for touring Royal Deeside, with its purple moors and piney hills as well as the notably rich selection of castles built over many centuries, including the queen's Balmoral.

8 **Argyll and the Isles.** Remote and picturesque, this less-visited region of the southwestern coastline has excellent gardens, religious sites, and distilleries. To experience the region in full, catch a ferry from adorable Oban to Mull and the southern isles. If you like whisky, go to Islay; if it's mountains you're after, try Jura; if a Christian site strikes a chord, head to Iona. Arran is the place to see Scotland's diversity shrunk down to more intimate size.

9 **Around the Great Glen.** An awe-inspiring valley laced with rivers and streams defines this part of the country. A top spot for hikers, this Highland glen is ringed by tall mountains, most notably Ben Nevis, Britain's tallest mountain. Glencoe and Culloden

are historic sites not to miss; those who believe in Nessie, Scotland's famous monster, can follow the throngs to Loch Ness. Inverness, the capital of the Highlands, is mostly useful as a base for exploring.

10 **The Northern Highlands and the Western Isles.** This rugged land is home to the lore of clans, big moody skies, and wild rolling moors. It's also the place to see one of Scotland's most picturesque castles, Eilean Donan, which you pass on the way to the beautiful, popular Isle of Skye. The stark, remote Outer Hebrides, or Western Isles, offer ruined forts and chapels. This is where you go for real peace and quiet.

11 **Orkney and Shetland Islands.** Remote and austere, these isles at the northern tip of Scotland require tenacity to reach but have an abundance of intriguing prehistoric sites including standing circles, *brochs* (circular towers), and tombs, as well as wild, open landscapes. A Scandinavian heritage gives them a unique flavor. The Shetland Isles, with their barren moors and vertical cliffs, are well-known for bird-watching and diving opportunities. Both Orkney and Shetland host numerous festivals throughout the year.

TO SHETLAND ISLANDS

ORKNEY ISLANDS

Mainland 11 Kirkwall
Hoy South Ronaldsay
Pentland Firth
Cape Wrath Thurso John o'Groats
Port of Ness Wick
Latheron

OUTER HEBRIDES
Isle of Lewis
The Minch
Harris 10
North Uist Ullapool Bonar Bridge Dornoch
Dornoch Firth
The Little Minch Cromarty Tain Moray Firth Elgin Fraserburgh
South Uist Dingwall Inverness Keith Peterhead
Barra Inner Sound 9 Ellon
North Uist Isle of Skye Kyle of Lochalsh Invermoriston Loch Ness HIGHLANDS 7 Aberdeen
Rhum Invergarry Aviemore Banchory Stonehaven
Mallaig Braemar GRAMPIAN MOUNTAINS
Coll Fort William Pitlochry Montrose
Loch Linnhe Dundee Arbroath
Tire Mull Oban Crianlarich Perth St. Andrews
Iona Firth of Lorn Firth of Tay
ATLANTIC Colonsay Inveraray Tarbet Kinross North Sea
OCEAN Lochgilphead Stirling Dunfermline Firth of Forth
Port Askaig Greenock Glasgow Falkirk EDINBURGH Dunbar
Jura Rothesay Paisley Hamilton Dalkeith
Islay 8 Ardrossan Berwick
Brodick Biggar
Kintyre Arran Firth of Clyde Jedburgh
Ayr Hawick The Cheviot Hills
Girvan Moffat
NORTHERN IRELAND SOUTHERN UPLANDS Lockerbie
North Channel Newton Stewart Dumfries Annan
Stranraer Castle Douglas ENGLAND
Luce Bay Solway Firth Carlisle

0 ___ 20 miles
0 ___ 20 kilometers

SCOTLAND PLANNER

When to Go

Peak tourist season runs from mid-May through mid-September. City museums stay open year-round, but some tourist sites such as castles close from November through to Easter. You can get some excellent deals in spring and fall; weather can be pleasant and crowds are not as intense.

The Scottish climate is extreme; there is often a combination of all four seasons in a 24-hour period. Winter nights are very long, as are summer days. Summer temperatures can linger in the 60s, sometimes the 70s or 80s, with dry spells lasting a week or two. Winter sees lots of rain, snow depending on latitude, and icy sharp winds. Spring and fall are on the cool side; again expect rain. Below are average daily maximum and minimum temperatures.

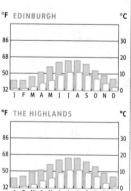

Getting Here and Around

You can arrive in Scotland by plane, train, or boat, and there are many places to disembark. Most international flights arrive at Glasgow International Airport (GLA). Edinburgh (EDI), and Prestwick (PIK) Airports are much smaller and handle mainly European and charter flights.

Scotland is not a large country: the entire United Kingdom (including England, Scotland, Wales, and Northern Ireland) is about the size of Oregon, so you're less likely to fly. The country's train and bus systems are extensive and relatively well maintained; for major towns and cities, there is generally no need to rent a car. To see castles and historic houses—which may be far from towns—you may have to rent a car or join a tour. Driving is on the left, and gas (petrol) is expensive at $7–$8 a U.S. gallon. ⇨ *For more details, see Getting Here and Around in Travel Smart Scotland.*

Distances and Travel Times

Edinburgh to Glasgow	51 mi; 1 hr by car; 1 hr by train
Edinburgh to Stirling	36 mi; 1 hr by car; 50 min by train
Edinburgh to Aberdeen	127 mi; 2 hrs by car; 2½ hrs by train
Edinburgh to Inverness	158 mi; 3¼ hrs by car; 3½ hrs by train
Edinburgh to Dumfries	73 mi; 2 hrs by car; ¾ hrs by train
Glasgow to Stirling	27 mi; 45 mins by car; 40 mins by train
Glasgow to Aberdeen	145 mi; 3¼ hrs by car; 2¾ hrs by train
Glasgow to Inverness	170 mi; 3½ hrs by car; 3¼ hrs by train
Glasgow to Dumfries	77 mi; 1½ hrs by car; 2 hrs by train
Aberdeen to Dumfries	215 mi; 4 ¼ hrs by car; 5¼ hrs by train
Inverness to Dumfries	235 mi; 4½ hrs by car; 6 hrs by train

Restaurants: The Basics

Scotland has a great variety of restaurants, both casual and formal, in both urban and country areas. Overall, food has improved substantially over the past decade, and the country has become a good destination for foodies interested in fresh seasonal and local fare. All major cities have more than a handful of good Scottish and international restaurants to choose from, but some rural pubs are also known for serving fresh hearty meals and scrumptious baked goods. Sandwich shops, tearooms, cafés, and places serving familiar fast foods round out the options.

Along the coasts, and up north in Inverness and Aberdeen, fish and seafood dominate the menus: salmon, shellfish, and trout are among the favorites. Stirling, Edinburgh, and Glasgow are well known for their love of beef, lamb, and venison; Indian and French restaurants are popular in these regions as well. In the Borders and Southwest, lamb and seafood are staples. ⇨ *For details and a price-category chart, see Eating Out in Travel Smart Scotland.*

Lodging: The Basics

Edinburgh and Glasgow have a wide range of hotels, from cutting edge to basic chain establishments, as well as inns and bed-and-breakfasts, but prices can change dramatically from one season to the next. Hotel prices in particular fluctuate when concerts, sporting events, and festivals come to town. It's a good idea to book online and well in advance to get the best rates and secure your room. Off-season deals can also be promising.

In the smaller cities and towns you have more options than in rural areas, where hotels are harder to find. In all these places, you may want to stay in a small bed-and-breakfast in a family's home. B&Bs are popular with British travelers and can be a great way to meet locals. Prices can be half of what an inn or hotel might charge. Some B&Bs give discounts for extended stays.

Other options include old country inns with a traditional Scottish pub underneath bedrooms. There are modern inns, too, but they don't have the same character, although amenities can be better. Some older inns can be old-fashioned, but they're usually less pricey. House and apartment rentals can be an excellent option, too. ⇨ *For details and a price-category chart, see Accommodations in Travel Smart Scotland.*

Visitor Information

Both VisitScotland and Visit-Britain have extensive Web sites that are useful for basic planning.

VisitScotland (⊕ *www.visitscotland.com*). **VisitBritain** (⊕ *www.visitbritain.com*).

Saving Money

Throughout this book and in Travel Smart Scotland you'll find advice for pinching your pence. Here are more tips for saving.

■ Take advantage of free breakfasts if your hotel, inn, or B&B offers them.

■ Many pubs serve lunches for less than £10; most restaurants offer cheap lunch deals.

■ Make one meal a prepared sandwich from a grocery store.

■ Carry your own water.

■ In the larger cities, consider staying in a house or apartment.

■ Outside the cities, stay in a B&B or small guesthouse.

■ Check the Web sites of major chains for deals.

■ Ask about family tickets at major sights.

■ Spend time in the free national museums.

■ Check out sightseeing passes such as the Great British Heritage Pass.

■ Use the exceptional public transportation system.

SCOTLAND
TOP ATTRACTIONS

Edinburgh Castle

(A) Looming from its craggy perch atop an ancient volcano, this iconic castle dates back to the 11th century and defines the city's skyline even today. Take in a royal view of Edinburgh and the surrounding countryside from its battlements, and see storied treasures such as the Honours of Scotland—the crown, scepter, and sword that once graced the Scottish monarch. *(See Chapter 2.)*

Kelvingrove Art Gallery and Museum

(B) Scotland has some of Britain's most spectacular museums, including Edinburgh's National Museum of Scotland (undergoing a major renovation at the time of this writing). Glasgow's Kelvingrove, a city favorite, fills a vast, castlelike building with international and Scottish art, local and natural history displays, and much more—in modern, engaging displays. *(See Chapter 3.)*

Mackintosh Trail

(C) In the late 19th century, architect Charles Rennie Mackintosh turned pompous Victorian style on its head with sleekly distinctive designs influenced by the art nouveau style. Glasgow is the best place to see his enticing designs such as the Glasgow School of Art. *(See Chapter 3.)*

Glencoe

(D) In this dramatic region of countryside between rugged mountains and rolling valleys, the Campbell clan massacred the MacDonald clan under English orders in 1692. Besides rich local history and chilling wild beauty, Glencoe has superb hiking and climbing. *(See Chapter 9.)*

Isle of Skye

(E) With the misty Cuillin Mountains and aged stone crofts, Skye is a place to linger over sunsets, explore meadows of heather, and savor fresh-caught seafood. The island's romantic past is linked to the saga of Bonnie Prince Charlie. On your way,

visit the most famous of Scottish castles, Eilean Donan. *(See Chapter 10.)*

Floors Castle

(F) Sweeping turrets and fanciful towers distinguish palatial Floors, built in 1721 for the duke of Roxburghe and now Scotland's largest inhabited castle. Sprawling along the banks of the River Tweed, the castle has magnificent interiors and grounds to explore. *(See Chapter 4.)*

Melrose Abbey

(G) Scotland's ruined abbeys recall the country's brilliant but turbulent monastic past. Melrose, an elegant but commanding red-sandstone structure, was begun in the 12th century. The abbey's ruins retain their power in well-preserved decorative carvings including a bagpipe-playing pig. *(See Chapter 4.)*

Loch Lomond and the Trossachs

(H) Sparkling clear water, lush woodlands, jagged mountains, and open skies make Loch Lomond a coveted—and easily accessible from Glasgow and Edinburgh—weekend retreat for visitors and locals alike. Loch Lomond and the Trossachs, Scotland's first national park, is ideal for hiking, biking, and more. *(See Chapter 6.)*

Malt Whisky Trail

(I) Aficionados of malt whisky can explore distilleries around Scotland, but many will head to this northeastern region. The Malt Whisky Trail in the scenic River Spey valley is renowned for its single-malt distilleries. The nine sights include distilleries large and small and a historic cooperage. *(See Chapter 7.)*

St. Andrews

(J) Famous first for its golf course and second for its university, the town of St. Andrews is also historic, prosperous, and charming. The ruined castle and cathedral are atmospheric, and this is a perfect destination for an idyllic stroll by the shore or in town, with its adorable shops and bakeries and restaurants. *(See Chapter 5.)*

QUINTESSENTIAL SCOTLAND

The Kettle's On

Scots are always eager to stop for a cup of tea and catch up with the local gossip. Tea is still the most popular refreshment, but the spread of café culture has introduced a new generation of coffeehouses—and not just in the cities but in the countryside. The Willow Tearooms in Glasgow and the Balmoral Hotel in Edinburgh are perhaps the most gentrified places to enjoy an afternoon pot of tea, tiny sandwiches with the crusts removed, and a slice of cake; they are well worth the stop. City coffeehouses are becomingly increasingly popular; they offer a different but equally worthwhile atmosphere. But if you're looking to taste a little of what life has to offer in smaller towns and villages, there is always some local haven that can offer you tea and delicious scones, probably with homemade jam.

It's Your Round

Going to the pub is a pastime enjoyed by men and women of all ages and backgrounds; you can find out why when you explore a few. The no-smoking laws mean that the pub environment is fresher now. In the cities you can take your pick of every kind of bar; traditional favorites are now joined by Australian, Cuban, and even wacky theme bars. In more rural areas, options may be fewer, but the quality of the experience, which may include pub quizzes or local folk bands, may be better. There isn't a pub in Scotland that doesn't sell whisky, but if you seek to sample a wee dram of the more obscure malts, ask someone to point you in the right direction. Fans of whisky will want to go beyond the pubs and head for a distillery or two for a tour and a tasting—on or off the Malt Whisky Trail.

If you want to get a sense of contemporary Scottish culture, and indulge in some of its pleasures, start by familiarizing yourself with the rituals of daily life. These are a few highlights—things you can take part in with relative ease.

It's Only a Game

Listening to Scots talk about football—please don't call it soccer—gives a fine insight into the national temperament. "Win, lose, or draw, you go home to your bed just the same," sang Scottish singer Michael Marra, and the Scots will try to make you believe it's only a game. But go to a match or be in a pub when a game is on the TV, and you can see plenty of grown men (and women) having a vigorous emotional workout. The main league, the Scottish Premiership, is dominated by the Rangers and Celtic; the battle for the title is usually between them. However, other teams, such as Aberdeen, delight in slaying, or at least tripping up, these giants. The state of the national team is debated everywhere, but although Scotland loses out in collecting trophies, the Tartan Army is consistently applauded as the most agreeable and entertaining traveling fans.

Who Ate All the Pies?

Although the treats may not perhaps be as elegant as those produced in an Italian *panificio* or a French patisserie, Scots love their bakeries. Go beyond shortbread and oatcakes and sample local favorites during your travels. From the Aberdeen buttery (a melting, salty *bap*, or soft morning roll) to the Selkirk bannock (a sweet, raisin-strewn scone, perfect when buttered and served with tea) to Forfar bridies (an Angus specialty, similar to a meat pasty), regional specialties are abundant. Most areas have their own interpretations of the popular Scotch pie (with beef mince, mutton, bean, and macaroni among the varieties available). There's even a Scotch Pie Championship each year. The rise of large supermarkets is putting many establishments out of business, but it's worth seeking out an independent bakery and trying the delicacies.

IF YOU LIKE

Castles

Whether a jumble of stones or a fully intact fortress, whether in private ownership or under the care of a preservation group—such as Historic Scotland (a government agency) or the National Trust for Scotland (a private, charitable organization)—Scotland's castles powerfully demonstrate the country's lavish past and its once-uneasy relationship with its southern neighbor.

Scotland has every type of castle imaginable, from triangular 13th-century fortresses such as **Caerlaverock,** to picturesque stereotypes like **Eilean Donan,** surrounded by lakes. Royal Deeside, west of Aberdeen, has an eclectic group strung together along a series of roadways called the **Castle Trail.** Here you can find Drum, Crathes, Balmoral, Braemar, Corgarff, Glenbuchat, Kildrummy, and Dunnottar, all within a 100-mi radius. **Glamis Castle,** northeast of Dundee, is one of Scotland's most beautiful castles, connecting Britain's royalty from Macbeth to the late Princess Margaret. Farther south, in the Borders, are several stunning castles—all good representations of medieval architecture and lifestyle. Among these, the **Hermitage Castle,** where Mary, Queen of Scots, traveled to visit her lover, the earl of Bothwell, is dark and foreboding; **Floors Castle** has grand turrets and towers; and **Neidpath Castle** has dungeons carved out of solid rock.

Scottish castles are not restricted to country roads or seaside cliffs; most are, however, on the mainland. Of the castles in cities and towns, majestic **Edinburgh Castle** has dramatic views of Fife, and **Stirling Castle** is a must for anyone interested in Scottish history.

Mountains and Lochs

For the snowcapped mountains and glassy lochs (lakes) for which Scotland is famous, you have to leave the south and the cities behind you—though some Lowland lakes are beautiful. Wherever you go in Scotland, nature is at your fingertips.

Among the loveliest Lowland lakes is **Loch Lomond,** 20 minutes from Glasgow, which has shimmering shores and plenty of water-sport options. **Loch Leven,** in Fife, is famed for its birdlife and fighting trout. It was also where Mary, Queen of Scots, signed the deed of abdication in her island prison. **Loch Katrine,** in the heart of the Trossachs in the Central Highlands, was the setting of Walter Scott's narrative poem "The Lady of the Lake." In summer you can take the steamer SS *Sir Walter Scott* across it. From the parking lot of **Loch Achray** you begin the climb to **Ben An,** the sheer-faced mountain with fabulous views of the Trossachs.

Half of Scotland's highest peaks are in **Cairngorms National Park,** east of the Great Glen and an excellent place for hiking, skiing, and reindeer sightings. In the Great Glen, monumental **Ben Nevis** hovers over Fort William; no matter when you visit, you'll probably see snow on the summit plateau. **Glen Torridon,** east of Shieldaig in the Northern Highlands, has the finest mountain scenery in the country. **Loch Maree,** also in the Northern Highlands and one of Scotland's most scenic lochs, is framed by Scots pines and Slioch Mountain.

Fabulous Festivals

Cultural festivals of all kinds thrive in Scotland; no matter where you are, you can probably find one to suit you. The **Edinburgh International Festival** is the spectacular flagship of Scotland's cultural events, with everything from orchestral music to comedy skits. Indeed, the capital suffers from festival overkill in August, partly because of the size of the **Fringe,** the official festival's less formal, rowdier offshoot. Adding to the August pileup in Edinburgh are the **Military Tattoo, International Book Festival,** and **Jazz and Blues Festival.**

If crowds and famous faces aren't your thing, plenty of other festivals take place year-round, predominantly in and around the major cities and islands. Edinburgh and other cities prepare for and celebrate the New Year in grand style with **Hogmanay,** which may include fireworks, music, and other revels. In the last two weeks of January Glasgow presents **Celtic Connections,** during which musicians from all over the world gather to play Celtic-inspired music. During October and November Glasgow also hosts **Glasgay,** a cultural festival focusing on gay and lesbian themes.

One popular festival is **Up-Helly-Aa,** held in Shetland at the end of January; food, drink, and dressing up come to a spectacular end with the burning of a replica Viking ship. April's **Shetland Folk Festival** and October's **Shetland Accordion and Fiddle Festival** draw large numbers of visitors at times of year when the weather is a bit more temperate. Orkney hosts music festivals in spring and summer, including the **St. Magnus Festival** in June, the **Jazz Festival** in April, and the **Folk Festival** in May.

Perfect Links

Some of the most scenic, established, and challenging courses in the world are in Scotland, the home of 550 golf courses and, arguably, the game itself. A few clubs are exclusive, but most are affordable and accessible, even to beginners; the cost of a round can go from £35 on a good course to well over £100. Just make reservations in advance, and you won't be disappointed.

Many golf pilgrimages to Scotland begin with a visit to the legendary **St. Andrews,** now so popular that reservations for summer play are required a year in advance. **Nairn,** on the Moray Coast, is the regular home of Scotland's Northern Open and has breathtaking views across the Moray Firth; **Rosemount, Blairgowrie Golf Club,** in Perthshire, is laid out on rolling land with wide fairways and large greens; and **Western Gailes,** in Ayrshire, is the finest natural links course in the country.

Don't limit yourself to the expensive, well-known greens. Off the beaten track are some good-value classic courses with striking views, particularly in the Stewartry, at **Powfoot** and **Southerness.** The Northeast has more than 50 courses, many with exceptional reputations, such as the reasonably priced **Boat of Garten,** Scotland's greatest "undiscovered" course, at Speyside. Western Scotland has nearly two dozen golf courses; **Machrihanish,** near Campbeltown, is one of the most popular. Keep in mind that attractive courses can be found in or near the urban centers; there are 30 in or close to Edinburgh and 7 courses in Glasgow.

Island Havens

A remote, windswept world of white-sand beaches, forgotten castles, and crisp, clear rivers awaits you in the Scottish isles. Out of the hundreds of isles (islands), only a handful are actually inhabited, and here ancient culture and tradition remain alive and well. Each island has its own distinct fingerprint; getting to some might be awkward and costly, but the time and expense are worth your while.

Near Glasgow, the **Isle of Bute** is one of the more affordable and accessible, drawing celebrities to its estates for lavish weddings and Glaswegians to its rocky shores for summer holidays. Like Bute, **Arran** is not too costly and mirrors the mainland, with activities from golf to hiking, but on a smaller, more intimate scale. **Islay,** near the Kintyre Peninsula, is where you go to watch rare birds, buy woolen goods, and taste the smoothest malt whiskies. Spiritual and spectacular **Iona** was the burial place of Scottish kings until the 11th century. Smaller isles like Rum, Eigg, Muck, and Canna are isolated and atmospheric but offer nothing in the way of lodgings or eateries. Although more populated and touristy, **Skye,** with its legends, hazy mountains, hidden beaches, and glens, is unsurpassed. It also has good hotels, B&Bs, and restaurants.

Orkney and **Shetland,** two remote island groups collectively known as the Northern Isles, have a Scandinavian heritage that adds color to their severe landscapes. If you're after remarkable prehistoric artifacts and festivals, go to Orkney; if you prefer something with more sophistication, Shetland is your isle.

Hiking

People who have hiked in Scotland often return to explore the country's rural landscape of loch-dotted glens and forested hills.

From Edinburgh's **Arthur's Seat** to **Ben Nevis,** Britain's tallest peak, the country holds unsurpassed hiking possibilities, no matter what your ambitions. Moderate hikes can be found in places like **Glen Nevis,** with footpaths leading past waterfalls, croft ruins, and forested gorges. Even parts of the **Southern Upland Way,** the famous 212-mi coast-to-coast journey from Portpatrick to Cockburnspath, can be comfortably walked in sections. A local's favorite, the **West Highland Way,** from Milngavie to Fort William, is a well-marked 95-mi trek with various hotels to stay in along the way. Other popular Highland trails are on **Ben Lawers, Ben Ledi,** and **Ben Lomond.**

Scotland has two national parks, **Loch Lomond and the Trossachs National Park** in the Central Highlands, and **Cairngorms National Park** east of the Great Glen. Some park trails are unmarked, so check with area tourist information centers before you set out. In the **Great Glen** area, some of the best routes can be found near **Glen Nevis, Glencoe,** and on the mighty **Ben Nevis.**

As you would for all outdoor activities, be sure you're properly equipped with appropriate shoes and clothing. Keep in mind that weather conditions can and do change rapidly in the Scottish hills, even at low altitude. The best time for hiking is from May to September, the same time the country's native insect, the midge, makes an unfavorable appearance (no amount of repellent will deter it).

Megalithic Monuments

Scattered throughout the Scottish landscape are prehistoric standing stones, stone circles, tombs, and even stone houses that provide a tantalizing glimpse into the country's remarkable past and people. If you're interested in ancient remains, leave the mainland and head for the isles, where the most impressive and important are found.

Arran's **Machrie Moor Stone Circles,** a mixture of granite boulders and tall redsandstone circles, are in the middle of an isolated moor 11 mi north of Lagg. **Calanais Standing Stones,** on the Isle of Lewis in the Outer Hebrides, are reminiscent of those at Stonehenge; it's believed they were used in astronomical observations. Tiny Colonsay in the Western Isles has the standing stones at Kilchattan Farm, called **Fingal's Limpet Hammers** after Fingal MacCoul, the larger-than-life warrior in Celtic mythology.

Orkney, however, has the greatest concentration of these types of prehistoric structures. Between Loch Harray and Loch Stennes is the **Ring of Brodgar,** a magnificent circle made up of 36 Neolithic stones. **Maes Howe** (circa 2500 BC) is an enormous burial mound measuring 115 feet in diameter, with an imposing burial chamber. The Vikings raided the site in the 12th century and Norse crusaders used the area for shelter; you can still see the runic inscriptions they left behind. Orkney's Neolithic village of **Skara Brae,** first occupied around 3000 BC, was well preserved in sand until it was discovered in 1850. Here the houses are joined by covered passages, with stone beds, fireplaces, and cupboards—more intriguing remnants from the distant past.

Retail Therapy

No longer is Scotland simply the land of whisky and wool. International names from Louis Vuitton to Versace have all set up shop here, and top British department stores like John Lewis, Harvey Nichols, and Debenhams, as well as stylish boutiques, are peppered throughout the major cities. Prices may not be cheap, but quality is first class and products are fashionable and long-lasting.

Glasgow claims the best shopping in Britain, outside of London's Oxford Street; **Buchanan Street** is the best place to start. **Edinburgh** is popular for crystal and clusters of antique shops, especially on St. Stephen and Dundas streets. Just outside of **Perth** is Caithness Glass, a factory renowned for its attractive glassware. **Aberdeen** and the **Northeast** are good places for trying and buying malt whisky.

If your shopping agenda favors the traditional, head to the islands of **Shetland, Skye,** and **Arran** for tweeds, knitwear, woolens (including knits), tartan blankets, Celtic silver, and pebble jewelry; these items can often be found in urban specialty shops as well. The **Scottish Highlands** bristle with old bothies (farm buildings) that have been turned into small crafts workshops selling handmade pottery and wood, leather, and glass items.

Rich chocolates (often with whisky fillings), marmalades, heather honeys, and the traditional petticoat-tail shortbread are easily portable gifts. So, too, are the boiled sweets (hard candies) in jars from particular localities—**Berwick** cockles, **Jethart** snails, **Edinburgh** rock, and more. **Dundee** cake, a rich fruit mixture with almonds on top, is among the other prize edibles on sale in the city they're named after.

FLAVORS OF SCOTLAND

Locally Sourced, Seasonally Inspired

A new focus of culinary interest, in Scotland as elsewhere, is on local and seasonal foods. Whether restaurants are riding the green wave or just following good food sense, they are trying their best to buy from local suppliers; many proudly advertise their support. Farmers' markets, too, seem to be popping up on every other street corner.

From meats and fish to fruits and vegetables, most urban and many country restaurants are now designing their menus around seasonal foods. In the winter, look for Angus beef, venison, rabbit, and pigeon on menus; in the spring, summer, and fall, langoustines, crab, halibut, and trout appear. The rotating array of (often organic) blackberries, raspberries, strawberries, apples, rhubarb, carrots, and potatoes offers choices so fat and flavorful that they could in themselves make any meal memorable. When in season, asparagus and green beans are tender but fresh enough that you can actually taste their snap. Scottish pies, puddings, and jams are also inspired by the land and time of year. Throughout the year, there are memorable tastes for all palates.

Superb Fish and Seafood

Some of the most coveted fish and seafood in the world lives in the rivers and lakes, as well as off the coasts, of Scotland. Fortunately, restaurants and markets all around the country showcase this local bounty. Treats not to miss include wild salmon, trout, haddock, mackerel, herring (often served as cold-smoked kippers), langoustines (small lobsters with slender claws), scallops, mussels, oysters, and crabs.

Fish is prepared in a tantalizing variety of ways in Scotland, but smoked fish is the national specialty—so much so that the process of both hot and cold smoking has developed to a fine art. Scots eat smoked fish for breakfast and lunch, and as an appetizer with their evening meal. The fish is often brushed with cracked pepper and a squeeze of lemon, and accompanied by thin slices of hearty bread or oat crackers. Places like Arbroath as well as the isles of North Uist and Skye have won international praise for locally smoked haddock, salmon, and trout, which are synonymous with delicacy.

Other seafood to try includes the traditional fish-and-chips, *the* Scottish favorite not to be overlooked. The fish is either cod or haddock, battered and deep fried until it's crispy and golden. Another classic preparation is Cullen skink, a creamy fish stew thick with smoked haddock, potatoes, and onions. It's perfect on cold winter nights as a tasty hot appetizer. For a special treat, grilled, sautéed, or baked langoustines offer the ultimate seafood indulgence, succulent and tasty.

Tempting Baked Goods

The Scots love their cakes, biscuits, breads, and pies. There's always something sweet and most likely crumbly to indulge in, whether after a meal or with a nice cup of tea. Bakeries are the perfect place to sample fresh goodies.

Some of the local favorites range from conventional butter-based shortbreads to Border biscuits (chocolate, ginger, and hazelnut cookies dipped in chocolate or nuts), empire biscuits (two shortbread cookies with jam in between, glazed in white icing and topped with a bright red cherry), whisky cake, mince pies (small pies filled with brandy, stewed dried fruits, and nuts), and scones. Treacle tarts, gingerbread, butterscotch apple pie, and oatcakes (more a savory cracker than a sweet

cake) are also popular as late morning or early afternoon temptations.

Not to be missed are the many treats named after their locations of origin: Balmoral tartlets (filled with cake crumbs, butter, cherries, and citrus peel), Dornoch creams (little buns bursting with raspberries and flavored with honey and Drambuie), Abernathy biscuits (cookies with extra sugar and caraway seeds), Islay loaves (sweet bread with raisins, walnuts, and brown sugar) and Dundee cakes (full of cherries, raisins, sherry, and spices).

Traditional Scottish Fare

Food in Scotland is steeped in history, and a rich story lies behind many traditional dishes. Once the food of peasants, haggis—a mixture of sheep's heart, lungs, and liver cooked with onions, oats, and spices, and then boiled in a sheep's stomach—has made a big comeback in more formal Scottish restaurants. If the dish's ingredients turn you off, there's often an equally flavorful vegetarian option. You'll find "neeps and tatties" alongside haggis; the three are inseparable. Neeps are yellow turnips, potatoes are the tatties, and both are boiled and then mashed.

Black pudding is another present-day delicacy (and former peasant food) that you can find just about everywhere, from breakfast table to local fish-and-chip shop to formal dining establishment. It's made from cooked sheep's- or goat's blood that congeals and is mixed with such ingredients as oats, barley, potato, bread, and meat. Black pudding can be grilled, boiled, or deep-fried. The Scottish prefer it for breakfast with fried eggs, bacon, beans, square sausages, toast, and potato scones. These fried, triangular-shape scones have the consistency of a dense pancake and are an intimate part of the Scottish breakfast,

aptly called a fry-up because—apart from the beans and toast—everything else on the plate is fried. Another popular breakfast dish is porridge with salt instead of sugar, cinnamon, or honey. Sweet porridge doesn't go down well in Scotland.

Whiskies and Real Ales

"Uisge beatha," translated from Scottish Gaelic, means "water of life," and in Scotland it most certainly is. Whisky helps weave together the country's essence, capturing the aromas of earth, water, and air in a single sip.

Whiskies differ greatly between single malts and blends. This has to do with the ingredients, specialized distillation processes, and type of oak cask. Whisky is made predominantly from malted barley that, in the case of blended whiskies, can be combined with grains and cereals like wheat or corn. Malts or single malts can come only from malted barley.

The five main whisky regions in Scotland produce distinctive tastes, though there are variations even within a region: the Lowlands (lighter in taste), Speyside (sweet with flower scents), the Highlands (fragrant, smooth, and smoky), Campbeltown (full-bodied and slightly salty), and Islay (strong peat flavor). Do sample these unique flavors; distillery tours are a good place to begin.

Real ales—naturally matured, cask-conditioned beer made from traditional ingredients—are making their mark in the United Kingdom. These ales are not, at present, as popular as whisky but are quickly making their mark on the Scottish beverage scene. Good brews to try include Arran Blonde (Arran Brewery), Dark Island (Orkney Brewery), Duechars (Caledonian Brewery) and Red Cuillin (Skye Brewery).

GREAT ITINERARIES

BEAUTIFUL SCOTLAND: CASTLES, LOCHS, GOLF, AND WHISKY

10 Days
Edinburgh

Days 1 and 2. The capital of Scotland is loaded with iconic sights in its Old Town and New Town. Visit Edinburgh Castle and the National Gallery of Scotland, and take tours of the National Museum of Scotland and the modern Scottish Parliament building. Walk along Old Town's Royal Mile and New Town's Princes Street for some fresh air and retail therapy. When the sun goes down, feast on the food of your choice and seek out a traditional pub with live music that will keep your toes tapping.

Logistics: Fly into Edinburgh Airport if you're flying via London and take a taxi or bus to the city center. If you're flying directly into Glasgow from overseas, make your way from Glasgow Airport to Queen Street Station (if traveling by train) or Buchanan Bus Station (if traveling by bus) via taxi or bus. It takes an hour to travel from Glasgow to Edinburgh by car or bus, about 45 minutes by train. Once in the city, explore by foot, public transportation, or taxi. There's no need to rent a car.

Stirling to St. Andrews

Day 3. Rent a car in Edinburgh and drive to the historic city of Stirling. Spend the day visiting Stirling Castle and the National Wallace Monument. If you're eager to tour a distillery, make time for a stop at the Famous Grouse Experience in Crieff. Then drive to the legendary seaside town of St. Andrews, famous for golf. Have dinner at one of the city's exceptional seafood restaurants.

Logistics: Leave Edinburgh after 9 AM to miss the worst of the rush-hour traffic. It's 35 mi or a one-hour drive to Stirling from Edinburgh, and 50 mi and 90 minutes from Stirling to St. Andrews. You can easily take a train or bus to these destinations.

St. Andrews to Inverness

Day 4. Spend the morning exploring St. Andrews, known for its castle and the country's oldest university as well as its famous golf courses. The British Golf Museum is here, too. If you've booked well in advance (the time varies by season), play a round of golf. After lunch, drive to Inverness. Along the way, stretch your legs at one of Scotland's notable sights, Blair Castle (just off the A9 and 10 mi north of Pitlochry), a turreted white treasure with a war-torn past. Head to Inverness in the Highlands for the night.

Logistics: It's 150 mi from St. Andrews to Inverness via the A9, a drive that will take 3½ hours. This is a scenic journey, so do stop along the way. You can also take a train or bus.

Around Inverness and Castle Country

Day 5. Use Inverness as a base for exploring the Northeast, a region known for tempting castles and whisky distilleries. Don't visit too many sights or your day may become a forced march; two to three castles or distilleries is a good number. Some of the region's most interesting castles are Kildrummy, a 13th-century architectural masterpiece, and Balmoral, popular because of its royal connection to Queen Elizabeth. Castle Fraser has beautiful gardens. End your day with a visit to Culloden Moor, where Bonnie Prince Charlie's forces were destroyed by the Duke of Cumberland's army. Keep Inverness as your base because of the number of restaurants and entertainment venues.

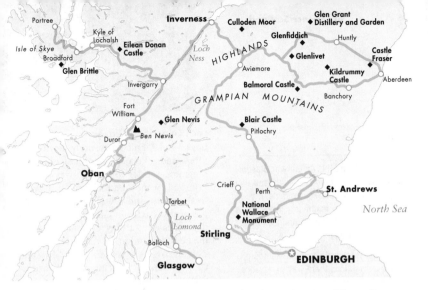

Alternatives: Prefer whisky to castles? Explore the Malt Whisky Trail in Speyside, near Inverness. Glenfiddich, Glenlivet, and Glen Grant are good choices. Another option for the day is to visit Loch Ness, though it's not one of Scotland's prettiest lakes; still, perhaps you'll spot Nessie. It's a 20-minute drive from Inverness.

Logistics: A car is best for this part of your journey. Rent one in Inverness or sign up for an organized tour; public transportation is not a viable option. Castles are open seasonally, so many close in winter; check in advance. It's about 2 hours from Inverness to Kildrummy. Some sample distances are 30 mi (1 hour) from Balmoral Castle to Kildrummy Castle; 20 mi (30 minutes) from Kildrummy Castle to Castle Fraser; and Castle Fraser to Balmoral, 40 mi (90 minutes). The distilleries are about 90 minutes from Inverness. Some distances between distilleries are 18 mi (50 minutes) from Glenfiddich to Glenlivet; 17 mi (30 minutes) from Glenlivet to Glen Grant; and 13 mi (30 minutes) from Glen Grant to Glenfiddich.

The Isle of Skye

Day 6. Leave Inverness early and head south to Skye. The drive to the island is peaceful, full of raw landscapes and big,

open horizons. Stop at Eilean Donan Castle on the way; go in, walk around, and take a few photos. This castle set on an island among three lochs is the stuff postcards are made of. Explore Skye; Glen Brittle is the perfect place to enjoy mountain scenery, and Armadale is a good place to go craft shopping. End up in Portree for dinner and the night.

Logistics: It's 80 mi (a 2-hour drive) from Inverness to Skye. You can take public transportation, but it's best to have the freedom of a car.

Oban via Ben Nevis

Day 7. Leave Skye no later than 9 AM and head for Fort William. The town isn't worth stopping for, but the view of Britain's highest mountain, the 4,406-foot Ben Nevis, is. If time permits, take a hike in Glen Nevis. Continue on to Oban, a traditional Scottish resort town on the water. Outside Oban, stop by the Scottish Sealife Sanctuary. At night, feast on fish-and-chips in a local pub.

Logistics: It's nearly 100 mi from Skye to Oban; the drive is 3½ hours without stopping. Public transportation is an option but a challenging one.

TIPS

■ You can begin this itinerary in Glasgow and finish in Edinburgh, or adjust the timing to your interests. For example, if you enjoy castles, you might stay in Inverness longer; if you like golf, St. Andrews may deserve more time.

■ August is festival season in Edinburgh; make reservations there well in advance during that month.

■ Remember to drive on the left side of the road and keep alert, especially on small, narrow country roads. Travel will take longer on smaller roads.

■ Weather is unpredictable; always dress in layers. Hikers should carry a cell phone and tell someone where they're going. Golfers and everyone else should carry rain gear.

■ Pack bug repellent for the midges (small, biting insects that travel in swarms). These insects breed in stagnant water; their season is May through September.

■ When visiting distilleries, choose a designated driver or take a bus tour. Drunken drivers aren't tolerated.

Loch Lomond to Glasgow

Days 8 and 9. Enjoy a leisurely morning in Oban and take a waterfront stroll. Mid-morning, set off for Glasgow via Loch Lomond. Stop in Balloch on the loch for fresh oysters and a walk along the bonnie banks. Arrive in Glasgow in time for dinner; take in a play or concert. Spend the next day and night visiting the sights: Kelvingrove Art Gallery and Museum, Charles Rennie Mackintosh's Glasgow School of Art, and the city's imposing cathedral are a few highlights.

Logistics: It's 127 mi (a three-hour drive) from Oban to Glasgow via Balloch. Traveling by train is a possibility, but you won't be able to go via Balloch. Return your rental car in Glasgow; it's easy to travel around the city by foot, subway, or train.

Glasgow

Day 10. On your final day, leave your suitcases at your hotel and hit Buchanan and Sauchiehall Streets for some of Britain's best shopping. Clothes, whisky, and tartan items are good things to look for.

Logistics: It's less than 10 mi (15 minutes) by taxi to Glasgow's international airport in Paisley but over 30 mi (40 minutes) to the international airport in Prestwick. Be sure you have the correct airport information.

Edinburgh and the Lothians

WORD OF MOUTH

"Edinburgh is amazingly beautiful with Edinburgh Castle rising above the city, and I could never see it and not feel stirred by its majesty. The whole of central Edinburgh is as dramatic as a film set and very evocative of all the history it embodies."

— KERRYAJS1

"Edinburgh during the festivals, with my then-15-year-old daughter, was an excellent destination. If I had the opportunity to go again, I would definitely consider it. You have to decide your tolerance for crowds, though."

—WillTravel

Updated
by Duncan
Forgan

Edinburgh is to London as poetry is to prose, as Charlotte Brontë once wrote. One of the world's stateliest cities and proudest capitals, it's built—like Rome—on seven hills, making it a striking backdrop for the ancient pageant of history. In a skyline of sheer drama, Edinburgh Castle watches over the capital city, frowning down on Princes Street as if disapproving of its modern razzmatazz. Its ramparts still echo with gunfire each day when the traditional one-o'clock gun booms out over the city, startling unwary shoppers.

Nearly everywhere in Edinburgh (the *burgh* is always pronounced *burra* in Scotland) there are spectacular buildings, whose Doric, Ionic, and Corinthian pillars add touches of neoclassical grandeur to the largely Presbyterian backdrop. The most notable examples perch amid the greenery of Calton Hill, which overlooks the city center from the east. Large gardens and greenery are a strong feature of central Edinburgh, where the city council is one of the most stridently conservationist in Europe. Conspicuous from Princes Street is Arthur's Seat, a mountain of bright green and yellow furze rearing up behind the spires of the Old Town. This child-size mountain jutting 822 feet above its surroundings has steep slopes and little crags, like a miniature Highlands set down in the middle of the busy city. Appropriately, these theatrical elements match Edinburgh's character—after all, the city has been a stage that has seen its fair share of romance, violence, tragedy, and triumph.

PARLIAMENT AND POWER

Three centuries after the Union of Parliaments with England in 1707, Edinburgh is once again the seat of a Scottish parliament. A new parliament building, designed by the late Spanish architect Enric Miralles, stands adjacent to the Palace of Holyroodhouse, at the foot of the Royal Mile. The first-time visitor to Scotland may be surprised that the country still has a capital city at all; perhaps believing the seat of government was drained of its resources and power after the union with England, but far from it. The Union of Parliaments brought with it a set of political partnerships—such as separate legal, ecclesiastical, and educational systems—that Edinburgh assimilated and integrated with its own surviving institutions.

Scotland now has significantly more control over its own affairs than at any time since 1707, and the 129 Members of the Scottish Parliament (MSPs), of whom 40% are women, have extensive powers in Scotland over education, health, housing, transportation, training, economic development, the environment, and agriculture. Foreign policy, defense, and economic policy, however, remain under the jurisdiction of the U.K. government in London.

TOP REASONS TO GO

Kaleidoscope of culture: Edinburgh covers it all, from floor-stomping ceilidhs to avant-garde modern dance, from traditional painting and sculpture to cutting-edge installations, from folksy fiddlers to the latest rock bands. The city's calendar of cultural festivals, including the famous Edinburgh International Festival, is outstanding.

The power and the glory: History plays out before your eyes in this centuries-old capital, along the Royal Mile or farther afield. Edinburgh Castle and the Palace of Holyroodhouse were the locations for some of the most important struggles between Scotland and England.

Awe-inspiring architecture: From the Old Town's labyrinthine medieval streets to the neoclassical orderliness of the New Town to imaginative modern developments like the Scottish Parliament, the architecture of Auld Reekie spans the ages.

Food, glorious food: Edinburgh has sophisticated restaurants serving cuisines from around the world. Perhaps the most exotic, however, is genuine Scottish cuisine, with its classic dishes like Cullen skink and haggis with neeps and tatties.

Retail therapy: Scotland has a strong tradition of distinctive furniture makers, silversmiths, and artists. Look to the "villages" of Edinburgh—such as Stockbridge—for exclusive designer clothing, edgy knitwear, and other high-end items.

EDINBURGH TODAY

Today the city is the second most important financial center in the United Kingdom, and the fifth most important in Europe. The city regularly is ranked near the top in quality-of-life surveys. Accordingly, New Town apartments on fashionable streets sell for considerable sums. In some senses the city is showy and materialistic, but Edinburgh still supports learned societies, some of which have their roots in the Scottish Enlightenment. The Royal Society of Edinburgh, for example, established in 1783 "for the advancement of learning and useful knowledge," remains an important forum for interdisciplinary activities.

Even as Edinburgh moves through the 21st century, its tall guardian castle remains the focal point of the city and its venerable history. Take time to explore the streets—peopled by the spirits of Mary, Queen of Scots; Sir Walter Scott; and Robert Louis Stevenson—and pay your respects to the world's best-loved terrier, Greyfriars Bobby. In the evenings you can enjoy candlelit restaurants or a folk *ceilidh (*a traditional Scottish dance with music, pronounced *kay-lee),* though you should remember that you haven't earned your porridge until you've climbed Arthur's Seat. Should you wander around a corner, say, on George Street, you might see not an endless cityscape, but blue sea and a patchwork of fields. This is the county of Fife, beyond the inlet of the North Sea called the Firth of Forth—a reminder, like the mountains to the northwest that can be glimpsed from Edinburgh's highest points, that the rest of Scotland lies within easy reach.

ORIENTATION AND PLANNING

GETTING ORIENTED

For all its steep roads and hidden alleyways, Edinburgh is not a difficult place to navigate. Most newcomers gravitate to two areas, the Old Town and the New Town. The former funnels down from the castle on either side of the High Street, better known as the Royal Mile. Princes Street Gardens and Waverly Station separate the oldest part of the city from the stately New Town, known for its neoclassical architecture and verdant gardens. To the north, the city sweeps down to the Firth of Forth. It is here you will find the port of Leith with its trendy pubs and fine restaurants. The southern and western neighborhoods are mainly residential, but are also home to such attractions as Edinburgh Zoo.

Old Town. The focal point of Edinburgh for centuries, the Old Town is picturesque jumble of medieval tenements. Here you will find prime attractions such as Edinburgh Castle and the newer symbol of power, the Scottish Parliament. Amid the historic buildings you will find everything from buzzing nightclubs and bars to ghostly alleyways where the spirits of the past often make their presence felt.

New Town. Built in the 18th and 19th century to prevent the residents of overcrowded Old Town from decamping to London, the neoclassical sweep of the New Town is a masterpiece of city planning. Significant sights include the National Gallery of Scotland and Calton Hill, which offers some of the best views of the city from its summit. The city's main shopping thoroughfares, Princes Street and George Street, are also found here.

Side Trips from Edinburgh. The historic houses and castles in the green countryside outside Edinburgh—Midlothian, West Lothian, and East Lothian, collectively called the Lothians—can be reached quickly by bus or car, welcome day-trip escapes from the festival crush at the height of summer.

PLANNING

WHEN TO GO

Scotland's reliably inclement weather means that you could visit at the height of summer and be forced to wear a scarf. Conversely, conditions can be balmy in early spring and late autumn. You may want to avoid the crowds during July and August, but you'd also miss the famed Edinburgh International Festival and other summer celebrations. May, June, and September are probably the most hassle-free months in which to visit. Short days and grim conditions make winter less appealing, but Edinburgh's New Year celebrations are justly renowned.

PLANNING YOUR TIME

One of Edinburgh's greatest virtues is its compact size, which means that it is possible to pack a fair bit into even the briefest of visits. The two main areas of interest are the Old Town and the New Town, where you'll find Edinburgh Castle, the Scottish Parliament, Princes Street

Gardens, and the National Gallery of Scotland. You can cover all four attractions in one day, but two days is more realistic. If you have a few more days you can take in the fantastic architecture of the New Town and explore the Royal Botanic Gardens and Holyrood Park.

GETTING HERE AND AROUND
AIR TRAVEL

Airlines serving Edinburgh include Aer Arann (⊕ *www.aerarann.com*), Aer Lingus (⊕ *www.aerlingus.com*), British Airways (⊕ *www.britishairways.com*), British Midland (⊕ *www.flybmi.com*), Continental (easyJet (⊕ *www.easyjet.com*), flybe (⊕ *www.flybe.com*), KLM (⊕ *www.klm.com*), Lufthansa (⊕ *www.lufthansa.com*), Ryanair (⊕ *www.ryanair.com*), Air France (⊕ *www.airfrance.com*), and Jet2 (⊕ *www.jet2.com*).

A few transatlantic flights come through Edinburgh (Continental has service from Newark Liberty, near New York City). Except for these flights, you'll probably have to fly into Glasgow, 50 mi away. Ryanair and easyJet have sparked a major price war on the Anglo-Scottish routes. They offer unbeatable, no-frills airfares on routes connecting Edinburgh Airport, Glasgow International, Prestwick Airport (30 mi south of Glasgow), and London's major airports.

AIRPORTS Edinburgh Airport, 7 mi west of the city center, offers only a few transatlantic flights. It does, however, have air connections throughout the United Kingdom—London (Heathrow, Gatwick, Stansted, Luton, and City), Birmingham, Bristol, East Midlands, Humberside, Jersey, Kirkwall (Orkney), Inverness, Leeds–Bradford, Manchester, Norwich, Sumburgh (Shetlands), Southampton, Wick, and Belfast (in Northern Ireland)—as well as with a number of European cities, including Amsterdam, Brussels, Copenhagen, Cork, Dublin, Frankfurt, Paris, Rome, Stockholm, and Zurich. Flights bound for Edinburgh depart virtually every hour from London's Gatwick and Heathrow airports; it's usually faster and less complicated to fly through Gatwick, which has excellent rail service from London's Victoria Station.

Glasgow Airport, 50 mi west of Edinburgh, serves as the major point of entry into Scotland for transatlantic flights. Prestwick Airport, 30 mi southwest of Glasgow, after some years of eclipse by Glasgow Airport, has grown in importance, not least because of the activities of Ryanair.

Airport Information Edinburgh Airport (☎ 0844/481–8989 ⊕ www. edinburghairport.com). **Glasgow Airport** (☎ 0844/481–5555 ⊕ www. glasgowairport.com). **Prestwick Airport** (☎ 0871/223–0700 ⊕ www.gpia.co.uk).

TRANSFERS There are no rail links to the city center, even though the airport sits
FROM between two main lines. By bus or car you can usually make it to Edin-
EDINBURGH burgh in a half hour, unless you hit the morning (7:30 to 9) or evening
AIRPORT (4 to 6) rush hours. Lothian Buses runs between Edinburgh Airport and the city center every 15 minutes daily from 9 to 5 and roughly every hour during off-peak hours. The trip takes about 40 minutes, or up to an hour during peak traffic times. A single-fare ticket costs £1.20. Lothian Buses runs an Airlink express service to Waverley Station via Haymarket that takes 25 minutes. Buses run every 10 minutes and single-fare tickets cost £3.50.

You can arrange for a chauffeur-driven limousine to meet your flight at Edinburgh Airport through Transvercia Chaffeur Drive, Little's Chauffeur Drive, or W L Sleigh Ltd., for about £50.

Taxis are readily available outside the terminal. The trip takes 20 to 30 minutes to the city center, 15 minutes longer during rush hour. The fare is roughly £20. Note that airport taxis picking up fares from the terminal are any color, not the typical black cabs.

Airport Transfer Contacts Little's Chauffeur Drive (✉ 1282 Paisley Rd. W, Paisley ☎ 0141/883–2111 ⊕ www.littles.co.uk). **Transvercia Chaffeur Drive** (✉ 6/19 Pilrig Heights, Leith ☎ 0131/555–0459 ⊕ www.transvercia.co.uk). **W L Sleigh Ltd.** (✉ 6 Devon Pl., West End ☎ 0131/337–3171 ⊕ www.sleigh.co.uk).

TRANSFERS FROM GLASGOW AIRPORT Scottish Citylink buses leave Glasgow Airport every 15 minutes to travel to Glasgow's Buchanan Street (journey time is 25 minutes), where you can transfer to an Edinburgh bus (leaving every 20 minutes). The trip to Edinburgh takes 70 minutes and costs £8.50 one-way. ■ TIP→ **A far more pleasant option is to take a cab from Glasgow Airport to Glasgow's Queen Street train station (20 minutes and costs about £18) and then take the train to Waverley Station in Edinburgh.** Trains depart about every 30 minutes; the trip takes 50 minutes and costs about £9. Another, less-expensive alternative—best for those with little luggage—is to take the bus from Glasgow Airport to Glasgow's Buchanan bus station, walk five minutes to the Queen Street train station, and catch the train to Edinburgh. Taxis from Glasgow Airport to downtown Edinburgh take about 70 minutes and cost around £100.

Glasgow Transfer Contacts Scottish Citylink (☎ 08705/505050 ⊕ www.citylink.co.uk).

BUS TRAVEL

National Express provides bus service to and from London and other major towns and cities. The main terminal, St. Andrew Square bus station, is a short walk north of Waverley station, immediately east of St. Andrew Square. Long-distance coaches must be booked in advance from the booking office in the terminal. Edinburgh is approximately eight hours by bus from London.

Lothian Buses provides much of the service between Edinburgh and the Lothians and conducts day tours around and beyond the city. First runs buses out of Edinburgh into the surrounding area. Megabus offers dirt-cheap fares if you book in advance.

Bus Contacts First (☎ 0870/872–7271 ⊕ www.firstgroup.com). **Lothian Buses** (☎ 0131/555–6363 ⊕ www.lothianbuses.com). **Megabus** (☎ 0900/160–0900 ⊕ www.megabus.com). **National Express** (☎ 08717/818181 ⊕ www.nationalexpress.co.uk).

TRAVEL WITHIN EDINBURGH Lothian Buses is the main operator within Edinburgh. You can buy tickets on the bus. The Day Ticket (£3), allowing unlimited one-day travel on the city's buses, can be purchased in advance or from the driver on any Lothian bus (exact fare is required when purchasing on a bus). The Ridacard (for which you'll need a photo) is valid on all buses for seven days (Sunday through Saturday night) and costs £15; the four-

2

week Rider costs £37. ■TIP→ Buses are great for cheap daytime travel, but in the evening you'll probably want to take a taxi.

Information **Lothian Buses** (✉ *Waverley Bridge, Old Town* ☎ *0131/555–6363* ⊕ *www.lothianbuses.co.uk*).

CAR TRAVEL

Driving in Edinburgh has its quirks and pitfalls, but don't be intimidated. Metered parking in the city center is scarce and expensive, and the local traffic wardens are a feisty, alert bunch. Note that illegally parked cars are routinely towed away, and getting your car back will be expensive. After 6 PM the parking situation improves considerably, and you may manage to find a space quite near your hotel, even downtown. If you park on a yellow line or in a resident's parking bay, be prepared to move your car by 8 the following morning, when the rush hour gets under way. Parking lots are clearly signposted; overnight parking is expensive and not always permitted.

TAXI TRAVEL

Taxi stands can be found throughout the downtown area. The following are the most convenient: the west end of Princes Street; South St. David Street and North St. Andrew Street (both just off St. Andrew Square); Princes Mall; Waterloo Place; and Lauriston Place. Alternatively, hail any taxi displaying an illuminated FOR HIRE sign.

TRAIN TRAVEL

Edinburgh's main train hub, Waverley Station, is downtown, below Waverley Bridge and around the corner from the unmistakable spire of the Scott Monument. Travel time from Edinburgh to London by train is as little as 4½ hours for the fastest service.

Edinburgh's other main station is Haymarket, about four minutes (by rail) west of Waverley. Most Glasgow and other western and northern services stop here. Haymarket can be more convenient if you're staying in hotels beyond the west end of Princes Street.

Train Contacts **National Rail Enquiries** (☎ *08457/484950* ⊕ *www.nationalrail. co.uk*). **ScotRail** (☎ *0845/601–5929* ⊕ *www.scotrail.co.uk*).

TRAM TRAVEL

After an absence of 65 years, trams are set to return to the streets of Edinburgh in early 2012. The plan has been quite controversial, with many feeling that the estimated £512 million cost is too high. Supporters hope that the network, which will be integrated with buses, will finally provide the city with a world-class public transport system.

Tram Contact **Edinburgh Trams** (☎ *0800/328—3934* ⊕ *www.edinburghtrams. co.uk*).

VISITOR INFORMATION

The Edinburgh and Scotland Information Centre, next to Waverley Station (follow the TIC signs in the station and throughout the city), offers an accommodations-booking service in addition to the more typical services. Complete information is also available at the information desk at the Edinburgh Airport.

SIGHTSEEING TOURS

ORIENTATION TOURS

The best way to get oriented in Edinburgh is to take a bus tour, most of which are operated by Lothian Buses. Its "City Sightseeing" open-top bus tours (£9) include multilingual commentary; its "MacTours" (£9) are conducted in vintage open-top vehicles. All tours take you to the main attractions, including Edinburgh Castle, the Royal Mile, Palace of Holyroodhouse, and museums and galleries. Buses depart from Waverley Bridge, and are hop-on/hop-off services, with tickets lasting 24 hours. Lothian Buses' 60-minute Majestic Tour (£12) operates with a professional guide, and takes you from Waverly Bridge to the New Town, past Charlotte Square, the Royal Botanic Garden, and Newhaven Heritage Museum until it reaches the royal yacht *Britannia* moored at Leith. Tickets for all tours are available from ticket sellers on Waverley Bridge or on the buses themselves.

Orientation Tours Contacts Lothian Buses (☎ *0131/555–6363* ⊕ *www.edinburghtour.com*).

PERSONAL GUIDES

Scottish Tourist Guides can supply guides (in 19 languages) who are fully qualified and will meet clients at any point of entry into the United Kingdom or Scotland. They can also tailor tours to your interests.

Personal Guide Contacts Scottish Tourist Guides (*Contact Doreen Boyle* ⊠ *18b Broad St., Stirling* ☎ *01786/451953* ⊕ *www.stga.co.uk*).

WALKING TOURS

Cadies and Witchery Tours, a member of the Scottish Tourist Guides Association, has built a reputation for combining entertainment and historical accuracy in its lively and enthusiastic Ghosts & Gore Tour and Murder & Mystery Tour (£7.50 each), which take you through the narrow Old Town alleyways and closes. Costumed guides and other theatrical characters show up en route. The Scottish Literary Tour Company takes you around Edinburgh's Old Town or New Town (£10 each), with guides invoking Scottish literary characters.

Walking Tour Contacts Cadies and Witchery Tours (⊠ *84 W. Bow, Edinburgh* ☎ *0131/225–6745* ⊕ *www. witcherytours.com*). **Scottish Literary Tour Company** (⊠ *5 Wellington Pl., Edinburgh* ☎ *0131/226–6665* ⊕ *www.edinburghliterarypubtour. co.uk*).

Visitor Info Edinburgh and Scotland Information Centre (⊠ *3 Princes St., East End* ☎ *08457/550033* ⊕ *www.edinburgh.org*).

EXPLORING EDINBURGH

Edinburgh's Old Town, which bears a great measure of symbolic weight as the "heart of Scotland's capital," is a boon for lovers of atmosphere and history. In contrast, if you appreciate the unique architectural heritage of the city's Enlightenment, then the New Town's for you. If you belong to both categories, don't worry—the Old and New towns are only yards apart. Princes Street runs east–west along the north edge of the Princes Street Gardens. Explore the main thoroughfares but also don't forget to get lost among the tiny *wynds* and *closes*: old medieval alleys that connect the winding streets.

Like most cities, Edinburgh incorporates small communities within its boundaries, and many of these are as rewarding to explore as Old Town and New Town. Dean Village, for instance, even though it's close to the New Town, has a character all of its own. Duddingston, just southeast of Arthur's Seat, has all the feel of a country village. Then there's Corstorphine, to the west of the city center, famous for being the site of Murrayfield, Scotland's international rugby stadium. Edinburgh's port, Leith, sits on the shore of the Firth of Forth, and throbs with smart bars and restaurants.

OLD TOWN

East of Edinburgh Castle, the historic castle esplanade becomes the street known as the Royal Mile, leading from the castle down through Old Town to the Palace of Holyroodhouse. The Mile, as it's called, is actually made up of one thoroughfare that bears, in consecutive sequence, different names—Castlehill, Lawnmarket, Parliament Square, High Street, and Canongate. The streets and passages winding into their tenements, or "lands," and crammed onto the ridge in back of the Mile really *were* Edinburgh until the 18th century saw expansions to the south and north. Everybody lived here, the richer folk on the lower floors of houses, with less well-to-do families on the middle floors—the higher up, the poorer.

Time and progress (of a sort) have swept away some of the narrow closes and tall tenements of the Old Town, but enough survive for you to be able to imagine the original profile of Scotland's capital. There are many guided tours of the area, or you can walk around on your own. The latter is often a better choice in summer when tourists pack the area and large guided groups have trouble making their way through the crowds.

TIMING An exploration of the Old Town could be accomplished in a day, but to give the major sights—Edinburgh Castle, the Palace of Holyroodhouse, and the Royal Museum—their due, you should allow more time. ■TIP➜ **Don't forget that some attractions have special hours during the Edinburgh International Festival. If you want to see something special, check the hours ahead of time.**

TOP ATTRACTIONS

❶ **Edinburgh Castle.** The crowning glory of the Scottish capital, Edinburgh Castle is popular not only because it's the symbolic heart of Scotland but also because of the views from its battlements: on a clear day the vistas—stretching to the "kingdom" of Fife—are breathtaking. ■TIP➜ **There's so much to see that you need at least three hours to do the site justice, especially if you're interested in military sites.**

Fodor'sChoice
★

You enter across the **Esplanade**, the huge forecourt built in the 18th century as a parade ground. The area comes alive with color and music each August when it's used for the Military Tattoo, a festival of magnificently outfitted marching bands and regiments. Heading over the drawbridge and through the gatehouse, past the guards, you can find the rough stone walls of the **Half-Moon Battery,** where the one-o'clock gun is fired every day in an impressively anachronistic ceremony; these curving ramparts give Edinburgh Castle its distinctive appearance from miles away. Climb up through a second gateway and you come to the oldest surviving building in the complex, the tiny 11th-century **St. Margaret's Chapel,** named in honor of Saxon queen Margaret (1046–93), who had persuaded her husband, King Malcolm III (circa 1031–93), to

> **SAVE ON SIGHTS**
>
> The money-saving **Edinburgh Pass** (☎ 0131/473–3600 ⊕ www.edinburghpass.org) gives you city bus transport (including a return ticket on the airport bus), access to more than 30 attractions, and other exclusive offers. A one-day pass costs £24; a two-day pass £36, and a three-day pass £48. Passes are available from the tourist information centers in Princes Street, at Edinburgh Airport, or online.

move his court from Dunfermline to Edinburgh. Edinburgh's environs—the Lothians—were occupied by Anglian settlers with whom the queen felt more at home, or so the story goes (Dunfermline was surrounded by Celts). The **Crown Room,** a must-see, contains the "Honours of Scotland"—the crown, scepter, and sword that once graced the Scottish monarch. Upon the **Stone of Scone,** also in the Crown Room, Scottish monarchs once sat to be crowned. In the section now called **Queen Mary's Apartments,** Mary, Queen of Scots, gave birth to James VI of Scotland. The **Great Hall** displays arms and armor under an impressive vaulted, beamed ceiling. Scottish parliament meetings were conducted here until 1840.

Military features of interest include the **Scottish National War Memorial,** the **Scottish United Services Museum,** and the famous 15th-century Belgian-made cannon *Mons Meg.* This enormous piece of artillery has been silent since 1682, when it exploded while firing a salute for the duke of York; it now stands in an ancient hall behind the Half-Moon Battery. Contrary to what you may hear from locals, it's not *Mons Meg* but the battery's gun that goes off with a bang every weekday at 1 PM, frightening visitors and reminding Edinburghers to check their watches. ⊠ *Castle Esplanade and Castlehill, Old Town* ☎ *0131/225–9846 Edinburgh Castle, 0131/226–7393 War Memorial* ⊕ *www.edinburghcastle. gov.uk* ☑ *£13* ⊙ *Apr.–Oct., daily 9:30–6; Nov.–Mar., daily 9:30–5; last entry 45 mins before closing.*

NEED A BREAK? You can have lunch or afternoon tea with panoramic views of the city at the **Red Coat Café** (⊠ *Edinburgh Castle, Old Town* ☎ *0131/225–9746).* Baked sweets, sandwiches, soup, tea, and Starbucks coffee are all available at reasonable prices.

⑮ High Kirk of St. Giles. Sometimes called St. Giles's Cathedral, this is one of the city's principal churches. However, anyone expecting a rival to Paris's Notre Dame or London's Westminster Abbey will be disappointed: St. Giles is more like a large parish church than a great European cathedral. There has been a church here since AD 854, although

Edinburgh's Castle Fit for a King

Archaeological investigations have established that the rock on which Edinburgh Castle stands was inhabited as far back as 1000 BC, in the latter part of the Bronze Age. There have been fortifications here since the mysterious people called the Picts first used it as a stronghold in the 3rd and 4th centuries AD. Anglian invaders from northern England dislodged the Picts in AD 452, and for the next 1,300 years the site saw countless battles and skirmishes. In the castle you'll hear the story of how Randolph, Earl of Moray and nephew of freedom fighter Robert the Bruce, scaled the heights one dark night in 1313, surprised the English guard, and recaptured the castle for the Scots. During

this battle he destroyed every one of the castle's buildings except for St. Margaret's Chapel, dating from around 1076, so that successive Stewart kings had to rebuild the castle bit by bit.

The castle has been held over time by Scots and Englishmen, Catholics and Protestants, soldiers and royalty. In the 16th century Mary, Queen of Scots, gave birth here to the future James VI of Scotland (1566–1625), who was also to rule England as James I. In 1573 it was the last fortress to support Mary's claim as the rightful Catholic queen of Britain, causing the castle to be virtually destroyed by English artillery fire.

most of the present structure dates from either 1120 or 1829, when the church was restored. The tower, with its stone crown towering 161 feet above the ground, was completed between 1495 and 1500. The most elaborate feature is the **Chapel of the Order of the Thistle,** built onto the southeast corner of the church in 1911 for the exclusive use of Scotland's only chivalric order, the Most Ancient and Noble Order of the Thistle. It bears the belligerent national motto NEMO ME IMPUNE LACESSIT ("No one provokes me with impunity"). Inside the church stands a life-size statue of the Scot whose spirit still dominates the place—the great religious reformer and preacher John Knox, before whose zeal all of Scotland once trembled. The church lies about one-third of the way along the Royal Mile from Edinburgh Castle. ✉ *High St., Old Town* ☎ *0131/225–9442* ⊕ *www.stgilescathedral.org.uk* 🎫 *£3 suggested donation* ☉ *May–Sept., weekdays 9–7, Sat. 9–5, Sun. 1–5; Oct.–Apr., Mon.–Sat. 9–5, Sun. 1–5.*

⓭ **High Street (Royal Mile).** Some of Old Town's most impressive buildings and sights are on High Street, one of the five streets making up the Royal Mile. Also here are other, less obvious historic relics. Near Parliament Square, look on the west side for a **heart** set in cobbles. This marks the site of the vanished Tolbooth, the center of city life from the 15th century until the building's demolition in 1817. The ancient civic edifice housed the Scottish parliament and was used as a prison—it also inspired Sir Walter Scott's novel *The Heart of Midlothian.*

Just outside Parliament House is the **Mercat Cross** (*mercat* means "market"), a great landmark of Old Town life. It was an old mercantile center, where in the early days executions were held, and where royal

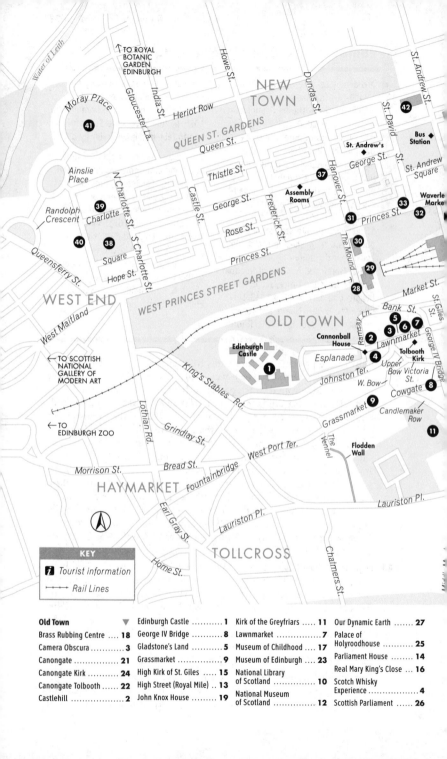

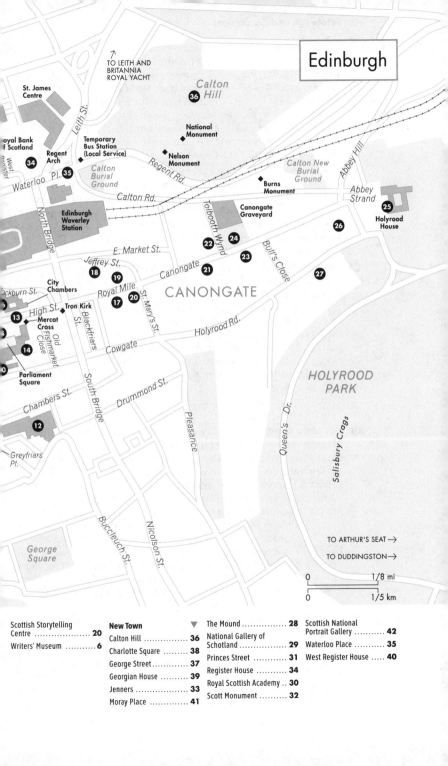

Edinburgh

To Leith and Britannia Royal Yacht

St. James Centre

Royal Bank of Scotland

Regent Arch

Leith St.

Calton Hill — **36**

National Monument

Nelson Monument

Calton Burial Ground

Regent Rd.

Waterloo Pl. — **34** **35**

Calton Rd.

Burns Monument

Calton New Burial Ground

Abbey Hill

Abbey Strand

Canongate Graveyard

Holyrood House — **25**

North Bridge

Edinburgh Waverley Station

E. Market St.

Tolbooth Wynd — **22** **24**

23

26

Jeffrey St.

Canongate — **21**

Bull's Close

27

City Chambers

18 **19**

Royal Mile

St. Mary's St.

CANONGATE

Cockburn St.

High St. — Tron Kirk

17 **20**

13

Mercat Cross

Old Fishmarket Close

Blackfriars St.

Holyrood Rd.

14

Cowgate

Parliament Square

Chambers St.

South Bridge

Drummond St.

HOLYROOD PARK

12

Pleasance

Queen's Dr.

Salisbury Crags

Greyfriars Pl.

George Square

Buccleuch St.

Nicolson St.

To Arthur's Seat →

To Duddingston →

0 — 1/8 mi

0 — 1/5 km

proclamations were—and are still—read. Most of the present cross is comparatively modern, dating from the time of William Ewart Gladstone (1809–98), the great Victorian prime minister and rival of Benjamin Disraeli (1804–81). Across High Street from the High Kirk of St. Giles stands the **City Chambers,** now the seat of local government. Built by John Fergus, who adapted a design of John Adam in 1753, the chambers were originally known as the Royal Exchange and intended to be where merchants and lawyers could conduct business. Note how the building drops 11 stories to Cockburn Street on its north side.

A *tron* is a weigh beam used in public weigh houses, and the **Tron Kirk** was named after a salt tron that used to stand nearby. The kirk itself was built after 1633, when St. Giles's became an Episcopal cathedral for a brief time. In this church in 1693, a minister offered an often-quoted prayer for the local government: "Lord, hae mercy on a' [all] fools and idiots, and particularly on the Magistrates of Edinburgh." ⊠ *Between Lawnmarket and Canongate, Old Town.*

⑲ **John Knox House.** It's not certain that Scotland's severe religious reformer John Knox ever lived here, but there's evidence to show that he died here in 1572. Mementos of his life are on view inside, and the distinctive dwelling gives you a glimpse of what Old Town life was like in the 16th century. The projecting upper stories were once commonplace along the Royal Mile, darkening and further closing in the already narrow passage. Look for the initials of former owner James Mossman and his wife, carved into the stonework on the marriage lintel. Mossman was goldsmith to Mary, Queen of Scots, and was hanged in 1573 for his allegiance to her. ⊠ *45 High St., Old Town* ☎ *0131/556–2647* ⊕ *www. scottishstorytellingcentre.co.uk* ⊡ *£3* ⊙ *Mon.–Sat. 10–6; last admission ½ hr before closing.*

⑪ **Kirk of the Greyfriars.** Greyfriars Church, built circa 1620 on the site of a medieval monastery, was where the National Covenant, declaring that the Presbyterian Church in Scotland was independent of the monarch and not Episcopalian in government, was signed in 1638. The covenant plunged Scotland into decades of civil war. Informative panels tell the story, and there's a visitor center on-site. Be sure to search out the graveyard—one of the most evocative in Europe. Its old, tottering, elaborate tombstones mark the graves of some of Scotland's most respected heroes and despised villains. Nearby, at the corner of George IV Bridge and Candlemaker Row, stands one of the most photographed sites in Scotland, the Greyfriars Bobby statue. ⊠ *Greyfriars Pl., Old Town* ☎ *0131/225–1900* ⊕ *www.greyfriarskirk.com* ⊡ *Free* ⊙ *Easter–Oct., weekdays 10:30–4:30, Sat. 10:30–2:30; Nov.–Easter, Thurs. 1:30–3:30.*

⑫ **National Museum of Scotland.** This museum traces the country's fascinating story from the oldest fossils to the most recent popular culture, making it a great stop for first-time visitors to Scotland or anyone interested in history. One of the most famous treasures is the Lewis Chessmen, 11 intricately carved ivory chess pieces found in the 19th century on one of Scotland's Western Isles, other pieces are in London's British Museum. At this writing, part of the museum is slated to be closed for renovations

THE BUILDING OF EDINBURGH

Towering over the city, Edinburgh Castle was actually built over the plug of an ancient volcano. Many thousands of years ago, an eastward-grinding glacier encountered the tough basalt core of the volcano and swept around it, scouring steep cliffs and leaving a trail of matter. This material formed a ramp gently leading down from the rocky summit. On this *crag* and *tail* would grow the city of Edinburgh and its castle.

CASTLE, WALLED TOWN, AND HOLYROODHOUSE

By the 12th century Edinburgh had become a walled town, still perched on the hill. Its shape was becoming clearer: like a fish with its head at the castle, its backbone running down the ridge, and its ribs leading briefly off on either side. The backbone gradually became the continuous thoroughfare now known as the Royal Mile, and the ribs became the closes (alleyways), some still surviving, that were the scene of many historic incidents.

By the early 15th century Edinburgh had become the undisputed capital of Scotland. The bitter defeat of Scotland at Flodden in 1513, when Scotland aligned itself with France against England, caused a new defensive city wall to be built. Though the castle escaped destruction, the city was burned by the English earl of Hertford under orders from King Henry VIII (1491–1547) of England. This was during a time known as the "Rough Wooing," when Henry was trying to coerce the Scots into allowing the young Mary, Queen of Scots (1542–87) to marry his son Edward. The plan failed and Mary married Francis, the Dauphin of France.

By 1561, when Mary returned from France already widowed, the guesthouse of the Abbey of Holyrood had grown to become the Palace of Holyroodhouse, replacing Edinburgh Castle as the main royal residence. Mary's legacy to the city included the destruction of most of the earliest buildings of Edinburgh Castle; she was eventually executed by Elizabeth I.

ENLIGHTENMENT AND THE CITY

In the trying decades after the union with England in 1707, many influential Scots, both in Edinburgh and elsewhere, went through an identity crisis. Out of the 18th-century difficulties, however, grew the Scottish Enlightenment, during which educated Scots made great strides in medicine, economics, and science.

Changes came to the cityscape, too. By the mid-18th century it had become the custom for wealthy Scottish landowners to spend the winter in the Old Town of Edinburgh, in town houses huddled between the high Castle Rock and the Royal Palace below. Cross-fertilized in coffeehouses and taverns, intellectual notions flourished among a people determined to remain Scottish despite their parliament's having voted to dissolve itself. One result was a campaign to expand and beautify the city, to give it a look worthy of its future nickname, the Athens of the North. Thus was the New Town of Edinburgh built, with broad streets and gracious buildings creating a harmony that even today's throbbing traffic cannot obscure.

2

until 2011. The redevelopment will free up more space for exhibitions, but the architectural character of the complex—including the impressive main hall, with its soaring roof and bird-cage design—will remain intact. There is still plenty to see before the complex reopens, including Viking brooches, Pictish stones, Jacobite relics, machinery, and Queen Mary's *clarsach* (harp). ⊠ *Chambers St., Old Town* ☎ *0131/225–7534* ⊕ *www.nms.ac.uk* ⌨ *Free* ⊙ *Daily 10–5.*

㉗ Our Dynamic Earth. Using state-of-the-art technology, the 11 theme galleries at this interactive science gallery educate and entertain as they explore the wonders of the planet, from polar regions to tropical rain forests. Geological history, from the big bang to the unknown future, is also examined. ⊠ *Holyrood Rd., Holyrood, Old Town* ☎ *0131/550–7800* ⊕ *www.dynamicearth.co.uk* ⌨ *£9.50* ⊙ *Apr.–June, Sept., and Oct., daily 10–5; July and Aug., daily 10–6; Nov.–Mar., Wed.–Sun. 10–5; last admission 1 hr before closing.*

㉕ Palace of Holyroodhouse. Once the haunt of Mary, Queen of Scots, and the setting for high drama—including at least one notorious murder, several major fires, and centuries of the colorful lifestyles of larger-than-life, power-hungry personalities—this is now Queen Elizabeth's official residence in Scotland. A doughty and impressive palace standing at the foot of the Royal Mile in a hilly public park, it's built around a graceful, lawned central court at the end of Canongate. When the queen or royal family is not in residence you can take a tour. The free audio guide is excellent.

Many monarchs, including Charles II, Queen Victoria, and George V, have left their mark on its rooms, but it's Mary, Queen of Scots, whose spirit looms largest. For some visitors, the most memorable room here is the little chamber in which David Rizzio (1533–66), secretary to Mary, Queen of Scots, met an unhappy end in 1566. In part because Rizzio was hated at court for his social-climbing ways, Mary's second husband, Lord Darnley (Henry Stewart, 1545–65), burst into the queen's rooms with his henchmen, dragged Rizzio into an antechamber, and stabbed him more than 50 times; a bronze plaque marks the spot. Darnley himself was murdered the next year, which made way for the queen's marriage to her lover, the Earl of Bothwell.

■ TIP→ There's plenty to see here, so make sure you have at least two hours to tour the palace, gardens (in summer), and the ruins of the 12th-century abbey. The **King James Tower** is the oldest surviving section, containing the rooms of Mary, Queen of Scots, on the second floor, and Lord Darnley's rooms below. Though much has been altered, there are fine fireplaces, paneling, plasterwork, tapestries, and 18th- and 19th-century furnishings throughout. At the south end of the palace front you can find the **Royal Dining Room,** and along the south side are the **Throne Room** and other drawing rooms now used for social and ceremonial occasions.

At the back of the palace is the **King's Bedchamber.** The 150-foot-long **Great Picture Gallery,** on the north side, displays the portraits of 110 Scottish monarchs. These were commissioned by Charles II, who was eager to demonstrate his Scottish ancestry—some of the royal figures here are fictional and the likenesses of others imaginary. All the portraits

2

were painted by a Dutch artist, Jacob de Witt, who signed a contract in 1684 with the queen's cash keeper, Hugh Wallace. The contract bound him to deliver 110 pictures within two years, for which he received an annual stipend of £120.

The Queen's Gallery (separate admission), in a former church and school at the entrance to the palace, holds rotating exhibits from the Royal Collection.

Holyroodhouse has its origins in an Augustinian monastery founded by David I (1084–1153) in 1128. In the 15th and 16th centuries, Scottish royalty, preferring the comforts of the abbey to the drafty rooms of Edinburgh Castle, settled into Holyroodhouse, expanding and altering the buildings until the palace eventually eclipsed the monastery. You can still walk around some ruins though.

After the Union of the Crowns in 1603, when the Scottish royal court packed its bags and decamped for England, the building fell into decline. It was Charles II (1630–85) who rebuilt Holyrood in the architectural style of Louis XIV (1638–1715), and this is the style you see today.

In 1688 an anti-Catholic faction ran riot within the palace, and in 1745, during the last Jacobite campaign, Charles Edward Stuart occupied the palace, followed a short while later by the duke of Cumberland, who defeated Charles at Culloden. After the 1822 visit of King George IV (1762–1830), at a more peaceable time, the palace sank into decline once again. But Queen Victoria (1819–1901) and her grandson King George V (1865–1936) renewed interest in the palace: the buildings were once more refurbished and made suitable for royal residence. Behind the palace lie the open grounds and looming crags of Holyrood Park, the hunting ground of early Scottish kings. From the top of Edinburgh's mini mountain, **Arthur's Seat** (822 feet), views are breathtaking. ⊠ *Abbey Strand, Holyrood, Old Town* ☎ *0131/556–5100* ⊕ *www.royalcollection.org.uk* 🎫 *£10 £5.50 Queen's Gallery, £14.30 joint ticket* ☉ *Apr.–Oct., daily 9:30–6; Nov.–Mar., daily 9:30–4:30; last admission 1 hr before closing. Closed during royal visits.*

⑯ **Real Mary King's Close.** Hidden beneath the City Chambers, this nar-
Ⓒ row, cobbled *close,* or lane, named after a former landowner, is said
★ to be one of Edinburgh's most haunted sites. The close was sealed off in 1645 to quarantine residents who became sick when the bubonic plague swept through the city, and many victims were herded there to die. After the plague passed, the bodies were removed and buried, and the street was reopened. A few people returned, but they soon reported ghostly goings-on and departed, leaving the close empty for decades. In 1753 city authorities built the Royal Exchange (later the City Chambers) directly over the close, sealing it off and, unwittingly, ensuring it remained intact, except for the buildings' upper stories, which were destroyed. Today you can walk among the remains of the shops and houses. People still report ghostly visions and eerie sounds, such as the crying of a young girl. Over the years visitors have left small offerings for her, such as dolls, pieces of ribbon, or candy. ■TIP➡ **Although kids like the spookiness of this attraction, it's not for the youngest ones. In fact, children under age five are not admitted.** ⊠ *Writers' Court, Old*

A GOOD WALK IN THE OLD TOWN

A perfect place to start your stroll through the Old Town is Edinburgh Castle. After exploring its extensive complex of buildings and admiring the view from the battlements, set off down the first part of the Royal Mile. The Camera Obscura's Outlook Tower affords more splendid views of the city. The six-story tenement known as Gladstone's Land, a survivor of 16th-century domestic life, is on the left as you head east. Near Gladstone's Land, down another close, stands the Writers' Museum, in a fine example of 17th-century urban architecture called Lady Stair's House. Farther down on the right are the Tolbooth Kirk (a *tolbooth* was a town hall or prison, and *kirk* means "church") and Upper Bow.

Turn right down George IV Bridge to reach the historic Grassmarket, where parts of the old city walls still stand. Turn left up Candlemaker Row and you can see the Kirk of the Greyfriars, and the little statue of faithful Greyfriars Bobby. On Chambers Street, at the foot of George IV Bridge, are the impressive galleries of the National Museum of Scotland.

Returning to the junction of George IV Bridge with the Royal Mile, turn right (east) down High Street to visit the old Parliament House; the High Kirk of St. Giles; the Mercat Cross; and the elegant City Chambers, bringing a flavor of the New Town's neoclassicism to the Old Town's severity. Beneath the chambers is the eerie Real Mary King's Close, a lane that was closed off in the 17th century when the bubonic plague struck the city.

A short distance down Canongate on the left is Canongate Tolbooth. The Museum of Edinburgh stands opposite, and the Canongate Kirk and Acheson House are nearby. This walk draws to a close, as it started, on a high note, at the Palace of Holyroodhouse, full of historic and architectural interest and some fine paintings, tapestries, and furnishings to admire, in Holyrood Park.

Town ☎ *0845/070–6244* ⊕ *www.realmarykingsclose.com* ✉ *£10.50* ⊙ *Apr.–July, Sept., and Oct., daily 10–9; Aug., daily 9–9; Nov.–Mar., daily 10–5.*

NEED A BREAK?   **Always Sunday** (✉ *170 High St., Old Town* ☎ *0131/622–0667*), in a white-walled, light-filled space near the cathedral and opposite the City Chambers, offers fresh, flavorful fare including great breakfasts (salmon and eggs), lunches (hearty soups, meat pies, salads), and cakes and coffee or tea. It's open daily until 6.

㉖ **Scottish Parliament.** Scotland's somewhat controversial Parliament build-
★ ing is dramatically modern, with irregular curves and angles that mirror the twisting shapes of the surrounding landscape. The structure's artistry is most apparent when you step inside, where the gentle slopes, forest's worth of oak, polished concrete and granite, walls of glass, water features, and subtle imagery create an understated magnificence appropriate to the modest but proud Scots. It's worth taking the 45-minute tour to see the main hall and debating chamber, a committee room, and

other areas. Another option is to call well in advance to get a free ticket to view Parliament in action. Originally conceived by the late Catalan architect Enric Mirales, who often said the building was "growing out of the ground," the design was completed by his widow, Bernadette Tagliabue, in August 2004. ⊠ *Horse Wynd, Old Town* ☏ *0131/348–5200* ⊕ *www.scottish.parliament.uk* ⊠ *Free; £5.85 for tour* ⊙ *Tours Nov.–Mar., daily 10–4; Apr.–Oct., daily 10–6; no tours when Parliament is sitting, generally Tues.–Thurs.*

WORTH NOTING

18 **Brass Rubbing Centre.** No experience is necessary for you to make your own souvenirs of Scotland at this center. You can explore the past by creating do-it-yourself replicas from original Pictish stones and markers, rare Scottish brasses, and medieval church brasses, or you can buy them in the shop for anywhere between £1.50 and £20. All the materials are here, and children find the pastime quite absorbing. The center occupies the surviving piece of a Gothic church down a close opposite the Museum of Childhood. ⊠ *Trinity Apse, Chalmers Close, Old Town* ☏ *0131/556–4364* ⊕ *www.cac.org.uk* ⊠ *Free* ⊙ *Apr.–Sept., Mon.–Sat. 10–5.*

3 **Camera Obscura and World of Illusions.** Want to view Edinburgh as Victorian travelers once did? Then head for the 17th-century Outlook Tower's camera obscura, where an optical instrument—a sort of projecting telescope—affords bird's-eye views of the whole city (on a clear day, that is) illuminated onto a concave table. The tower was significantly altered in the 1840s and 1850s with the installation of the telescopic "magic lantern." ⊠ *Castlehill, Old Town* ☏ *0131/226–3709* ⊕ *www.camera-obscura.co.uk* ⊠ *£8.50* ⊙ *Apr.–June, Sept., and Oct., daily 9:30–6; July–Aug., daily 9:30–7:30; Nov.–Mar., daily 10–5.*

21 **Canongate.** This section of the Royal Mile takes its name from the canons who once ran the abbey at Holyrood. Canongate—in Scots, *gate* means "street"—was originally an independent town, or *burgh,* another Scottish term used to refer to a community with trading rights granted by the monarch. Here you'll find **Canongate Kirk** and its graveyard, **Canongate Tolbooth,** and the **Museum of Edinburgh** *(see below).* ⊠ *Section of Royal Mile from end of High St. to Abbey Strand at entrance to Palace of Holyroodhouse, Old Town.*

24 **Canongate Kirk.** This unadorned building, built in 1688, is run by the Church of Scotland and has an interesting graveyard. Although you can find information about the graveyard in the church, local authorities actually oversee it. This is the final resting place of some notable Scots, including economist Adam Smith (1723–90), author of *The Wealth of Nations* (1776), who once lived in the nearby 17th-century Panmure House. Also buried here are Dugald Stewart (1753–1828), the leading European philosopher of his time, and the undervalued Scots poet Robert Fergusson (1750–74). That Fergusson's grave is even marked is the result of efforts by the much more famous Robert Burns (1759–96), who commissioned an architect—by the name of Robert Burn—to design one. Burns also designed the Nelson Monument, the tall column on Calton Hill to the north, which you can see from the graveyard.

Against the eastern wall of the graveyard is a bronze sculpture of the head of Mrs. Agnes McLehose, the "Clarinda" of the copious correspondence in which Robert Burns engaged while confined to his lodgings with an injured leg in 1788. Burns and McLehose—a highborn, talented woman who had been abandoned by her husband—exchanged passionate letters for some six weeks that year. The missives were dispatched across town by a postal service that delivered them within the hour for one penny. The curiously literary affair ended when Burns left Edinburgh in 1788 to take up a farm tenancy and to marry Jean Armour. ⊠ *Canongate, Old Town* ☎ *0131/556–3515* ⊕ *www.canongatekirk.com* ⊠ *Free* ⊙ *Daily.*

㉒ **Canongate Tolbooth.** Nearly every city and town in Scotland once had a tolbooth. Originally a customhouse where tolls were gathered, a tolbooth came to mean town hall and later prison because detention cells were in the basement. The building where Canongate's town council once met now has a museum, the **People's Story,** which focuses on the lives of "ordinary" people from the 18th century to today. Exhibits describe how Canongate once bustled with the activities of the tradespeople needed to supply life's essentials in the days before superstores. Special displays include a reconstruction of a cooper's workshop and a 1940s kitchen. ⊠ *163 Canongate, Old Town* ☎ *0131/529–4057* ⊕ *www.cac.org.uk* ⊠ *Free* ⊙ *Mon.–Sat. 10–5.*

NEED A BREAK?
You can get a good cup of tea and a scone, a quintessentially Scottish indulgence, at **Clarinda's** (⊠ *69 Canongate, Old Town* ☎ *0131/557–1888*). Like most tearooms, Clarinda's doesn't accept reservations. You may have to wait a short while for a table, but the experience is well worth it.

❷ **Castlehill.** In the late 16th century, alleged witches were brought to what is now a street in the Royal Mile to be burned at the stake, as a bronze plaque here recalls. The cannonball embedded in the west gable of Castlehill's **Cannonball House** was, according to legend, fired from the castle during the Jacobite Rebellion of 1745, led by Charles Edward Stuart (also known as Bonnie Prince Charlie, 1720–88), the most romantic of the Stuart pretenders to the British throne. Most authorities agree on a more prosaic explanation, however; they say it was a height marker for Edinburgh's first piped water-supply system, installed in 1681. Atop the Gothic **Tolbooth Kirk,** built in 1842–44 for the General Assembly of the Church of Scotland, stands the tallest spire in the city, at 240 feet. The church houses the Edinburgh Festival offices, the **Festival Centre.**

The **Upper Bow,** running from Lawnmarket to Victoria Street, was once the main route westward from the town and castle. Before Victoria Street was built in the late 19th century, the Upper Bow led down into a narrow dark thoroughfare coursing between a canyon of tenements. All traffic struggled up and down this steep slope from the Grassmarket, which joins the now-truncated West Bow at its lower end. ⊠ *East of Esplanade and west of Lawnmarket, Old Town.*

OFF THE
BEATEN
PATH

Duddingston. Tucked behind Arthur's Seat, and about an hour's walk from Princes Street via Holyrood Park, this little community, formerly of brewers and weavers, still seems like a country village. The Duddingston Kirk has a Norman doorway and a watchtower that was built to keep body snatchers out of the graveyard. The church overlooks Duddingston Loch, popular with bird-watchers, and moments away is an old-style pub called the Sheep's Heid Inn, which serves a wide selection of beers and has the oldest skittle (bowling) alley in Scotland. To get here, take Lothian Bus #42.

> ### GRASSMARKET GALLOWS
>
> Grassmarket's history is long and fabulous. The **cobbled cross** at the east end marks the site of the town gallows. Among those hanged here were many 17th-century Covenanters, members of the Church of Scotland who rose up against Charles I's efforts to enforce Anglican or "English" ideologies on the Scottish people. Judges were known to issue the death sentence for these religious reformers with the words, "Let them glorify God in the Grassmarket."

8 George IV Bridge. It's not immediately obvious that this is in fact a bridge, as buildings are closely packed most of the way along both sides. At the corner of the bridge stands one of the most photographed sculptures in Scotland, *Greyfriars Bobby*. This statue pays tribute to the famous Skye terrier who kept vigil beside his master John Gray's grave in the Greyfriar's churchyard for 14 years after Gray died in 1858. Bobby left only for a short time each day to be fed at a nearby coffee house. The 1961 Walt Disney film *Greyfriars Bobby* tells the story, though liberties were taken with the historical details. ⊠ *Bank St. and Lawnmarket, Old Town.*

5 Gladstone's Land. This narrow, six-story tenement, next to the Assembly Hall on Lawnmarket, is a survivor from the 17th century. Typical Scottish architectural features are evident on two floors, including an arcaded ground floor (even in the city center, livestock sometimes inhabited the ground floor). The house has magnificent painted ceilings and is furnished in the style of a 17th-century merchant's home. ⊠ *477B Lawnmarket, Old Town* ☎ *0131/226–5856* ⊕ *www.nts.org.uk/visits* ⊠ *£5* ☉ *Apr.–June, Sept., and Oct., daily 10–5; July and Aug., daily 10–6:30; last admission 30 mins before closing.*

9 Grassmarket. For centuries an agricultural marketplace, Grassmarket now is the site of numerous shops, bars, and restaurants, making it a hive of activity at night. Sections of the Old Town wall can be traced on the north (castle) side by a series of steps that run steeply up from Grassmarket to Johnston Terrace above. The best-preserved section of the wall can be found by crossing to the south side and climbing the steps of the lane called the Vennel. Here the 16th-century **Flodden Wall** comes in from the east and turns south at Telfer's Wall, a 17th-century extension.

From the northeast corner of the Grassmarket, **Victoria Street**, a 19th-century addition to the Old Town, leads up to George IV Bridge. Shops here sell antiques, designer clothing, and high-quality gifts.

7 **Lawnmarket.** The name *Lawnmarket* is a corruption of "land market," and is the second of the streets that make up the Royal Mile. It was formerly the site of the produce market for the city, with a once-a-week special sale of wool and linen. Now it's home to **Gladstone's Land** *(see above)* and the **Writers' Museum** *(see below)*. At different times the Lawnmarket Courts housed James Boswell, David Hume, and Robert Burns. In nearby Brodie's Close in the 1770s lived the infamous Deacon Brodie, pillar of society by day and a murdering gang leader by night. Robert Louis Stevenson (1850–94) may well have used Brodie as the inspiration for his *Strange Case of Dr. Jekyll and Mr. Hyde,* though the book isn't set in Edinburgh. ⊠ *Between Castlehill and High St., Old Town.*

NEED A BREAK? Several atmospheric pubs and restaurants bustle on this section of the Royal Mile. Try the friendly **Jolly Judge** (⊠ *7 James Ct., Old Town* ☎ *0131/225-2669*), where firelight brightens the dark-wood beams and a mixed crowd of university professors and students sip ale and eat light lunches of soup, pasta, quiche, or baked potatoes.

17 **Museum of Childhood.** Even adults tend to enjoy this cheerfully noisy museum—a cacophony of childhood memorabilia, vintage toys, and dolls, as well as a reconstructed schoolroom, street scene, fancy-dress party, and nursery. The museum claims to have been the first in the world devoted solely to the history of childhood. It's two blocks past the North Bridge–South Bridge junction on High Street. ⊠ *42 High St., Old Town* ☎ *0131/529–4142* ⊕ *www.cac.org.uk* ⊠ *Free* ☽ *Mon.–Sat. 9–6, Sun. during festival 2–5.*

23 **Museum of Edinburgh.** A must-see if you're interested in the details of Old Town life, this former home, dating from 1570, is a fascinating museum of local history, displaying Scottish pottery and Edinburgh silver and glassware. One of the museum's most impressive documents is the National Covenant, signed by Scotland's Presbyterian leadership in 1639. This "profession of faith" begins with not one, but three verses from the Bible. ⊠ *142 Canongate, Old Town* ☎ *0131/529–4143* ⊕ *www. cac.org.uk* ⊠ *Free* ☽ *Mon.–Sat. 10–5, Sun. during festival 10–5.*

10 **National Library of Scotland.** Founded in 1689, the library has a superb collection of books and manuscripts on the history and culture of Scotland, and also mounts regular exhibitions. Genealogists investigating family trees come here, and amateur family sleuths will find the staff helpful in their research. ⊠ *George IV Bridge, Old Town* ☎ *0131/623–3700* ⊕ *www.nls.uk* ⊠ *Free* ☽ *Library Mon., Tues., Thurs., and Fri. 9:30–8:30, Wed. 10–8:30, Sat. 9:30–1. Exhibitions weekdays 9:30–8, Sat. 9:30–5, Sun. 2–5.*

14 **Parliament House.** This was the seat of Scottish government until 1707, when the governments of Scotland and England were united, 104 years after the union of the two crowns. Partially hidden by the bulk of the High Kirk of St. Giles, it now houses the Supreme Law Courts of Scotland. ⊠ *11 Parliament Sq., Old Town* ☎ *0131/225-2595* ⊕ *www. scotcourts.gov.uk* ⊠ *Free* ☽ *Weekdays 9–4:30.*

④ Scotch Whisky Experience. The mysterious process that turns malted barley and springwater into one of Scotland's most important exports is revealed in this museum. Although whisky making is not in itself packed with drama, the center manages an imaginative presentation using models and tableaux viewed while riding in low-speed barrel cars. Explore Scotland's diverse whisky regions and the flavors they impart. Sniff the various aromas and decide whether you like fruity, sweet, or smoky; resident experts will then help you select your perfect dram. Your guide will then allow you access to a vault containing the Diageo Claive Vidiz Scotch Whisky Collection, the world's largest collection of Scotch whiskies. ✉ *354 Castlehill, Old Town* ☎ *0131/220–0441* ⊕ *www.whisky-heritage.co.uk* ✇ *Tour £11.50* ☉ *Tours Sept.–May, daily 10–6, last tour 5; June–Aug. daily 10–7, last tour 5:45.*

⑳ Scottish Storytelling Centre. This arts center is housed in a modern building that manages to blend seamlessly with the historic structures on either side. It hosts a year-round program of storytelling, theater, and literary events. A café serves lunch and tea. ✉ *43 High St., Old Town* ☎ *0131/556–9579* ⊕ *www.scottishstorytellingcentre.co.uk* ✇ *Free* ☉ *Sept.–June, Mon.–Sat. 10–6; July and Aug., Mon.–Sat. 10–6, Sun. noon–6.*

⑥ Writers' Museum. Down a close off Lawnmarket is Lady Stair's House, built in 1622 and a good example of 17th-century urban architecture. Inside, the Writer's Museum evokes Scotland's literary past with such exhibits as the letters, possessions, and original manuscripts of Sir Walter Scott, Robert Louis Stevenson, and Robert Burns. The Stevenson collection is particularly strong. ✉ *Lady Stair's Close, Old Town* ☎ *0131/529–4901* ⊕ *www.cac.org.uk* ✇ *Free* ☉ *Mon.–Sat. 10–5, last admission 4:45.*

NEW TOWN

It was not until the Scottish Enlightenment, a civilizing time of expansion in the 1700s, that the city fathers decided to break away from the Royal Mile's rocky slope and create a new Edinburgh below the castle. This was to become the New Town, with elegant squares, classical facades, wide streets, and harmonious proportions. Clearly, change had to come. At the dawn of the 18th century, Edinburgh's unsanitary conditions—primarily a result of overcrowded living quarters—was becoming notorious. The well-known Scots fiddle tune "The Flooers (flowers) of Edinburgh" was only one of many ironic references to the capital's unpleasant environment, which greatly embarrassed the Scot James Boswell (1740–95), biographer and companion of the English lexicographer Dr. Samuel Johnson (1709–84). In his *Journal of a Tour of the Hebrides,* Boswell recalled that on retrieving Johnson from his grubby inn in the Canongate, "I could not prevent his being assailed by the evening effluvia of Edinburgh . . . Walking the streets at night was pretty perilous and a good deal odoriferous."

To help remedy this sorry state of affairs, in 1767 James Drummond, the city's lord provost (the Scots term for mayor), urged the town council to hold a competition to design a new district for Edinburgh. The winner was an unknown young architect named James Craig (1744–95). His plan called for a grid of three main east–west streets, balanced at either end by two grand squares. These streets survive today, though some of the buildings that line them have been altered by later development. Princes Street is the southernmost, with Queen Street to the north and George Street as the axis, punctuated by St. Andrew and Charlotte squares. A look at the map will reveal a geometric symmetry unusual in Britain. Even the Princes Street Gardens are balanced by the Queen Street Gardens, to the north. Princes Street was conceived as an exclusive residential address, with an open vista facing the castle. It has since been altered by the demands of business and shopping, but the vista remains.

The New Town was expanded several times after Craig's death and now covers an area about three times larger than Craig envisioned. Indeed, some of the most elegant facades came later and can be found by strolling north of the Queen Street Gardens.

TIMING If you want to get the most out of the museums of the New Town, take a whole day and allow at least an hour for each one.

TOP ATTRACTIONS

OFF THE
BEATEN
PATH

Britannia. Moored on the waterfront at Leith, Edinburgh's port north of the city center, is the former Royal Yacht Britannia, launched in Scotland in 1953 and now retired to her home country. The Royal Apartments and the more functional engine room, bridge, galleys, and captain's cabin are all open to view. The land-based visitor center within the huge Ocean Terminal shopping mall has exhibits and photographs about the yacht's history. ⊠ *Ocean Terminal, Leith* ☎ *0131/555–5566* ⊕ *www.royalyachtbritannia.co.uk* 🎟 *£10* ☽ *Mar.–Oct., daily 10–4; Nov.–Feb., daily 10–3:30.*

39 ★ **Georgian House.** The National Trust for Scotland has furnished this house in period style to show the elegant domestic arrangements of an affluent family of the late 18th century. The hallway was designed to accommodate sedan chairs, in which 18th-century grandees were carried through the streets. ⊠ *7 Charlotte Sq., New Town* ☎ *0844/493–2188* ⊕ *www.nts.org.uk/visits* 🎟 *£5.50* ☽ *Mar., daily 11–4; Apr.–June, Sept., and Oct., daily 10–6; July and Aug., daily 10–7; Nov., daily 11–3; last admission ½ hr before closing.*

29
Fodor's Choice
★

National Gallery of Scotland. Opened to the public in 1859, the National Gallery presents a wide selection of paintings from the Renaissance to the postimpressionist period within a grand neoclassical building designed by William Playfair. Most famous are the old-master paintings bequeathed by the Duke of Sutherland, including Titian's *Three Ages of Man.* All the great names are here; works by Velázquez, El Greco, Rembrandt, Goya, Poussin, Turner, Degas, Monet, and Van Gogh, among others, complement a fine collection of Scottish art, including Sir Henry Raeburn's *Reverend Robert Walker Skating on Duddingston Loch* and other masterworks by Ramsay, Raeburn, and Wilkie. The Weston Link connects the National Gallery of Scotland to the Royal Scottish Academy and provides expanded gallery space as well as a restaurant, bar, café, information center, and shop. ⊠ *The Mound, New Town* ☎ *0131/624–6200 general inquiries, 0131/624–6336 recorded* *information ⊕ www.nationalgalleries.org ✉ Free ⊙ Fri.–Wed. 10–5, Thurs. 10–7.*

OFF THE BEATEN PATH

Royal Botanic Garden Edinburgh. Britain's largest rhododendron and azalea gardens are part of the varied and comprehensive collection of plant and flower species in this 70-acre garden, just north of the city center. An impressive Chinese garden has the largest collection of wild-origin Chinese plants outside China. There's a cafeteria, plus a gift shop that sells plants and books. A new visitors center with exhibits on biodiversity opened in late 2009. Take a taxi to the garden, or ride Bus 27 from Princes Street or Bus 23 from Hanover Street. To walk to the garden from the New Town, take Dundas Street, the continuation of Hanover Street, and turn left at the clock tower onto Inverleith Row (about 20 minutes). Guided tours are available. ✉ *23 Inverleith Row, Inverleith ☎ 0131/552–7171 ⊕ www.rbge.org.uk ✉ Free; greenhouses £3.50 ⊙ Nov.–Feb., daily 10–4; Mar.–May and Sept.–Oct., daily 10–6; June–Aug., daily 10–7.*

㉜ Scott Monument. What appears to be a Gothic cathedral spire chopped off and planted in the east end of the Princes Street Gardens is the nation's tribute to Sir Walter—a 200-foot-high monument looming over Princes Street. Built in 1844 in honor of Scotland's most famous author, Sir Walter Scott, the author of *Ivanhoe, Waverley,* and many other novels and poems, it's centered on a marble statue of Scott and his favorite dog, Maida. It's worth taking the time to explore the immediate area, Princes Street Gardens, one of the prettiest city parks in Britain. In the open-air theater, amid the park's trim flower beds, stately trees, and carefully tended lawns, brass bands occasionally play. Here, too, is the famous **monument to David Livingstone,** whose African meeting with H. M. Stanley is part of Scot-American history. ✉ *Princes St., New Town ☎ 0131/529–4068 ⊕ www.cac.org.uk ✉ £3 ⊙ Apr.–Sept., daily 10–7; Oct.–Mar., daily 10–3.*

OFF THE BEATEN PATH

Scottish National Gallery of Modern Art. This handsome former school building on Belford Road, close to the New Town, displays paintings and sculpture including works by Pablo Picasso, Georges Braque, Henri Matisse, and André Derain. The gallery also has an excellent restaurant in the basement. Across the street is the **Dean Gallery,** also part of the National Galleries of Scotland. It showcases modern art and changing exhibitions. ✉ *Belford Rd., Dean Village ☎ 0131/556–8921 ⊕ www.nationalgalleries.org ✉ Free ⊙ Daily 10–5; extended hrs during festival.*

㊷ Scottish National Portrait Gallery. A magnificent red-sandstone Gothic building dating from 1889 houses this must-visit institution. Currently under renovation, the gallery will reopen to visitors in November of 2011. Conceived as a gift to the people of Scotland, the new gallery will be curated under five broad themes: Reformation, Enlightenment, Empire, Modernity, and Contemporary. The refurbished complex will also feature a new photography gallery and increased exhibition space, which will allow the entirety of the existing collection to be shown alongside temporary exhibits. ✉ *1 Queen St., New Town ☎ 0131/624–6200 ⊕ www.nationalgalleries.org.*

CLOSE UP

Leith, Edinburgh's Seaport

Edinburgh's port has a rich history all of its own. While not as rambunctious as it used to be, Leith is still a good bet for an authentically Scottish night out. Ample restaurants and bars make this a good alternative to staying in the center of town.

Just north of the city, Leith sits on the south shore of the Firth of Forth and was a separate town until it merged with the city in 1920. After World War II and up until the 1980s, the declining seaport had a reputation for poverty and crime. In recent years, however, it has been revitalized with the restoration of commercial buildings as well as the construction of new luxury housing, bringing a buzz of trendiness. All of the docks have been redeveloped; the Old East and West docks are now the administrative headquarters of the Scottish Executive.

In earlier times, Leith was the stage for many historic happenings. In 1560 Mary of Guise, the mother of Mary,

Queen of Scots, ruled Scotland from Leith; her daughter landed in Leith the following year to embark on her infamous reign. A century later, Cromwell led his troops to Leith to root out Scots royalists. An arch of the Leith Citadel reminds all of the Scots' victory. Leith also prides itself on being a "home of golf" because official rules to the game were devised in 1744, in what is today Links Park. The rolling green mounds here hide the former field and cannon sites of past battles.

It's worth exploring the lowest reaches of the Water of Leith (the river that flows through the town), an area where restaurants, shops, and pubs proliferate. The major attraction for visitors here is the former royal yacht *Britannia,* moored outside the huge Ocean Terminal shopping mall. Reach Leith by walking down Leith Street and Leith Walk, from the east end of Princes Street (20 to 30 minutes) or take Lothian Bus 22 (Britannia Ocean Drive, Leith).

WORTH NOTING

㊱ Calton Hill. Robert Louis Stevenson's favorite view of his beloved city was from the top of this hill. The architectural styles represented by the extraordinary collection of monuments here include mock Gothic— the Old Observatory, for example—and neoclassical. Under the latter category falls the monument William Playfair (1789–1857) designed to honor his talented uncle, the geologist and mathematician John Playfair (1748–1819), as well as his cruciform **New Observatory.** The piece that commands the most attention, however, is the so-called **National Monument,** often referred to as "Edinburgh's [or Scotland's] Disgrace." Intended to mimic Athens's Parthenon, this monument for the dead of the Napoleonic Wars was started in 1822 to the specifications of a design by Playfair. But in 1830, only 12 columns later, money ran out, and the columned facade became a monument to high aspirations and poor fund-raising. The tallest monument on Calton Hill is the 100-foot-high **Nelson Monument,** completed in 1815 in honor of Britain's naval hero Horatio Nelson (1758–1805); you can climb its 143 steps for sweeping city views. The **Burns Monument** is the circular Corinthian temple below Regent Road. Devotees of Robert Burns may want to visit one other grave—that of Mrs. Agnes McLehose, or "Clarinda," in the Canongate Graveyard. ⊠ *Bounded by Leith St. to the west and Regent Rd. to the south, New Town* ☎ *0131/556–2716* ⊕ *www.cac. org.uk* 🎫 *Nelson Monument £3* ⊙ *Nelson Monument Apr.–Sept., Mon. 1–6, Tues.–Sat. 10–6; Oct.–Mar., Mon.–Sat. 10–3.*

38 **Charlotte Square.** At the west end of George Street is the New Town's centerpiece—an 18th-century square with one of the proudest achievements of Robert Adam, Scotland's noted neoclassical architect. On the north side, Adam designed a palatial facade to unite three separate town houses of such sublime simplicity and perfect proportions that architects come from all over the world to study it. Happily, the Age of Enlightenment grace notes continue within, as the center town house is now occupied by the **Georgian House** museum, and to the west stands **West Register House.** ⊠ *West end of George St., New Town.*

OFF THE BEATEN PATH

Edinburgh Zoo. Children love to visit the some 1,000 animals that live in Edinburgh Zoo. You can even handle some of the animals from April to September. The ever-popular Penguin Parade begins at 2:15 (but since penguin participation is totally voluntary, the event is unpredictable). The zoo spreads over an 80-acre site on the slopes of Corstorphine Hill. Take buses 12, 26, or 31. ⊠ *Corstorphine Rd., next to Holiday Inn Edinburgh, Corstorphine* ⊹ *3 mi west of city center* ☎ *0131/334–9171* ⊕ *www.edinburghzoo.org.uk* 🎫 *£14* ⊙ *Apr.–Sept., daily 9–6; Oct. and Mar., daily 9–5; Nov.–Feb., daily 9–4:30.*

37 **George Street.** With its upscale shops and handsome Georgian frontages, this is a more pleasant, less crowded street for wandering than Princes Street. The **statue of King George IV,** at the intersection of George and Hanover streets, recalls the visit of George IV to Scotland in 1822. He was the first British monarch to do so since King Charles II, in the 17th century. By the 19th century, enough time had passed since the Jacobite Uprising of 1745 for Scotland to be perceived at Westminster as being safe enough for a monarch to visit.

The ubiquitous Sir Walter Scott turns up farther down the street. It was at a grand dinner in the **Assembly Rooms,** between Hanover and Frederick streets, that Scott acknowledged having written the Waverley novels (the name of the author had hitherto been a secret, albeit a badly kept one). You can meet Scott once again, in the form of a plaque just downhill, at 39 Castle Street, his Edinburgh address before he moved to Abbotsford, in the Borders region, where he died in 1832. ⊠ *Between Charlotte and St. Andrew Squares, New Town.*

33 **Jenners.** Edinburgh's equivalent of London's Harrods department store, Jenners is noteworthy not only for its high-quality wares and good restaurants but also because of the building's interesting architectural detail—baroque on the outside, with a mock-Jacobean central well inside. It was one of the earliest department stores, established in 1838. The caryatids decorating the exterior were said to have been placed in honor of the store's predominantly female customers. ⊠ *48 Princes St., New Town* ☎ *0870/607–2841* ⊙ *Mon., Tues., Wed., Fri., and Sat. 9–6, Thurs. 9–8, Sun. 11–5.*

41 **Moray Place.** Moray Place—with its "pendants" of Ainslie Place and Randolph Crescent—was laid out in 1822 by the earl of Moray. From the start the homes were planned to be of particularly high quality, with lovely curving facades, imposing porticos, and a central secluded garden (for residents only). ⊠ *Between Charlotte Sq. and Water of Leith, New Town.*

28 **The Mound.** This rising street originated from the need for a dry-shod crossing of the muddy quagmire left behind when Nor' Loch, the body of water below the castle, was drained (the railway now cuts through this area). The work is said to have been started by a local tailor, George Boyd, who tired of struggling through the mud en route from his New Town house to his Old Town shop. The building of a ramp was under way by 1781, and by the time of its completion, in 1830, "Geordie Boyd's mud brig [bridge]," as the street was first known, had been built up with an estimated 2 million cartloads of earth dug from the foundations of the New Town. ⊠ *Running north–south from Princes St. to George IV Bridge, New Town.*

31 **Princes Street.** The south side of this well-planned street is occupied by the well-kept Princes Street Gardens, which act as a wide green moat to the castle on its rock. Unfortunately, the north side is now one long sequence of chain stores with unappealing modern fronts that can be seen in almost any large British town. ⊠ *Running east–west from Waterloo Pl. to Lothian Rd., East End to West End, New Town.*

34 **Register House.** Scotland's first custom-built archives depository, Register House, designed by the great Robert Adam, was partly funded by the sale of estates forfeited by Jacobite landowners after their last rebellion in Britain (1745–46). Work on the Regency-style building, which marks the end of Princes Street, started in 1774. The statue in front is of the first duke of Wellington (1769–1852). It's possible to conduct genealogical research here; check online and call ahead for more information. ⊠ *2 Princes St., New Town* ☎ *0131/535–1314* ⊕ *www.nas.gov. uk* ⊠ *Free* ⊙ *Weekdays 9–4:45.*

NEED A BREAK?

Café Royal (⊠ *19 W. Register St., New Town* ☎ *0131/5561884*) ⊕ *www. caferoyal.org.uk*), immediately west of Register House, serves good Scottish lagers and ales, and simple lunch items and, of course, oysters. The 18th-century building has plenty of character, with ornate tiles and stained-glass windows.

30 **Royal Scottish Academy.** The William Playfair–designed Academy hosts temporary art exhibitions (Monet paintings, for example), but is also worth visiting for a look at the imposing, neoclassic architecture. The underground Weston Link connects the museum to the National Gallery of Scotland. ⊠ *The Mound, New Town* ☎ *0131/225–6671* ⊕ *www. royalscottishacademy.org* ⊠ *Free* ⊙ *Mon.–Sat. 10–5, Sun. noon–5.*

35 **Waterloo Place.** The fine neoclassical architecture on this street was designed as a piece by Archibald Elliot (d. 1823) in 1815. Waterloo Place extends over Regent Bridge, bounded by the 1815 **Regent Arch**, a simple, triumphal Corinthian-column war memorial at the center of

Ancestor Hunting

Are you a Cameron or a Campbell, Mackenzie or Macdonald? If so, you may be one of the more than 25 million people of Scottish descent around the world. It was the Highland clearances of the 18th and 19th century, in which tenant farmers were driven from their homes and replaced with sheep, that started the mass emigration to North America and Australia. Before or during a trip, you can do a little genealogical research or pursue your family tree more seriously.

Start at VisitScotland's Web site, www.ancestralscotland.com, for information about clans and surnames, books, and family history societies.

The VisitScotland Web site may steer you to the Web site of the **General**

Register Office for Scotland (✉ *3 W. Register St., New Town* ☎ *0131/ 314–4300 for booking* ⊕ *www. scotlandspeople.gov.uk*), the official government source of genealogical data, which you can also visit in person. There's a charge for accessing information online and for on-site research (£17 per day, £65 per week). Space is limited, but some places are available each day on a first-come, first-served basis.

Willing to pay for help? Companies such as Scottish Ancestral Trail (www. scottish-ancestral-trail.co.uk) do the research and plan a trip around your family history. Throughout Scotland, you can check bookstores for information and visit clan museums and societies.

Ionic screens bordering the bridge. ✉ *Eastern extension of Princes St., New Town.*

40 West Register House. The former St. George's Church, in the middle of the west side of Charlotte Square, today fulfills a different role, as an extension of the original Register House on Princes Street. Much of the material is historical, with documents including clan maps and trial records. ✉ *17 Charlotte Sq., New Town* ☎ *0131/535–1400* ⊕ *www.nas. gov.uk* 🖼 *Free* ☉ *Weekdays 9–4:45.*

WHERE TO EAT

Edinburgh's eclectic restaurant scene has attracted a brigade of well-known chefs, including the award-winning trio of Martin Wishart, Tom Kitchin, and Paul Kitching. They and dozens of others have abandoned the tried-and-true recipes for more adventurous cuisine. Of course, you can always find traditional fare, which usually mean the Scottish-French style that harks back to the historical "Auld Alliance" of the 13th century. The Scots element is the preference for fresh and local foodstuffs; the French supply the sauces. In Edinburgh you can sample anything from Malaysian *rendang* (a thick, coconut-milk stew) to Kurdish kebabs, while the long-established French, Italian, Chinese, Pakistani, and Indian communities ensure that most of the globe's most treasured cuisines are well represented.

PRICES AND HOURS

It's possible to eat well in Edinburgh without spending a fortune. Multi-course prix-fixe options are common, and almost always less expensive than ordering à la carte. Even at restaurants in the highest price category, you can easily spend less than £30 per person. People tend to eat later in Scotland than in England—around 8 PM on average—or rather they finish eating and then drink on in leisurely Scottish fashion.

WHAT IT COSTS IN POUNDS					
	£	££	£££	££££	£££££
AT DINNER	under £10	£10–£14	£15–£19	£20–£25	Over £25

Prices are per person for a main course at dinner.

OLD TOWN

Use the coordinate (✛ B2) at the end of each listing to locate a site on the corresponding map.

The most historic part of the city houses the grander restaurants that many people associate with this city. It is also home to some of Edinburgh's oldest pubs serving informal meals.

££ · VEGETARIAN · ✕ **David Bann.** In the heart of the Old Town, this ultrahip vegetarian and vegan favorite attracts young locals with its light, airy, modern dining room and creative menu. Drinking water comes with mint and strawberries; dishes are sizable and extremely colorful. The food is so flavorful that carnivores may forget they're eating vegetarian. Try the spinach-and-smoked-cheese strudel and the malt-whisky *panna cotta.* ⊠ *56–58 St. Mary's St., Old Town* ☎ *0131/556–5888* ⊕ *www.davidbann.com* ▤ *AE, DC, MC, V* ✛ *H4.*

££ · BRITISH · ✕ **Doric Tavern.** Beyond the bar's grand entrance staircase is a languid bistro environment enhanced by the stripped wood floor, plain wood tables, and color scheme in subdued orange and terra-cotta. The menu lists a selection of fresh fish, meat, and vegetarian dishes, plus a daily special such as honey-baked salmon with oatcakes. Prix-fixe lunch and dinner options are an excellent value. ⊠ *15/16 Market St., Old Town* ☎ *0131/225–1084* ⊕ *www.the-doric.com* ⌂ *Reservations essential* ▤ *AE, MC, V* ✛ *G3.*

££ · MIDDLE EASTERN · ✕ **Hanam's.** A stone's throw from the castle, this enticing place transports you to the Middle East. Kurdish cuisine may not be as exalted others in that region, but the *bayengaan surocrau* (marinated eggplant) and the lamb *tashreeb* (a kind of casserole) will convince you that it's among the best. There's also a great range of kebabs and more familiar Lebanese options. It's possible to smoke a hookah pipe on the heated terrace, and you can bring your own alcohol. ⊠ *3 Johnston Terr., Old Town* ☎ *0131/225–1329* ⊕ *www.hanams.com* ▤ *AE, MC, V* ✛ *F4.*

£££ · BRITISH · ✕ **Howie's.** This chain consists of four stylish neighborhood bistros, each with its own character. The food is Scottish contemporary—lots of fresh local produce, fish, and game. The steaks are tender Aberdeen beef, and the Loch Fyne herring is sweet-cured to Howie's own recipe. ⊠ *10–14*

BEST BETS FOR EDINBURGH DINING

Where can you find the best food Edinburgh has to offer? Fodor's writers and editors have selected their favorite restaurants by price, cuisine, and experience in the lists below. In the first column, the Fodor's Choice properties represent the "best of the best" across price categories. You can also search by neighborhood for excellent eating experiences—just peruse our complete reviews on the following pages.

Fodor's Choice ★

Kalpna £, p. 64
The Kitchin, £££££, p. 66
Number One, £££££, p. 62
Wedgwood, £££, p. 58

By Price

£

Kalpna, p. 64
Kampong Ah Lee Malaysian Delight, p. 65
Mother India Cafe, p. 58

££

Al Dente, p. 65
David Bann, p. 56

£££

Merchants, p. 58
Wedgwood, p. 58

££££

Forth Floor, p. 59
Santini, p. 64
The Witchery, p. 59

£££££

The Kitchin, p. 66
Martin Wishart, p. 66
Number One, p. 62

By Cuisine

MODERN BRITISH

Howie's, £££, p. 56
21212, £££££, p. 63
Wedgwood, £££, p. 58

CHINESE

Chop Chop, ££, p. 63
Jasmine, ££, p. 64

FRENCH

La Garrigue, £££, p. 58
L'escargot Bleu, £££, p. 62
Martin Wishart, £££££, p. 66

INDIAN

Kalpna, £, p. 64
Mother India Cafe, £, p. 58

SPANISH

Rafael's, ££, p. 62

SEAFOOD

Fishers Bistro, £££, p. 65
Skippers Bistro, £££, p. 66

VEGETARIAN

David Bann, ££, p. 56
Henderson's, £, p. 59

By Experience

MOST KID-FRIENDLY

Al Dente, ££, p. 65
Howie's, £££, p. 56

BEST VIEW

Forth Floor, ££££, p 59
Oloroso, ££££, p. 62

HOTSPOTS

Forth Floor, ££££, p. 59
L'escargot Bleu, £££, p. 62

MOST ROMANTIC

Le Café St. Honoré, ££££, p. 62
The Witchery by the Castle, ££££, p. 59

BEST PRETHEATER EATS

Kampong Ah Lee Malaysian Delight, £, p. 65
La Garrigue, £££, p. 58

Victoria St., Old Town ☎ *0131/225–1721* ✢ *B3* ✉ *29 Waterloo Pl., East End* ☎ *0131/556–5766* ✢ *F4* ✉ *208 Bruntsfield Pl., South Side* ☎ *0131/221–1777* ✢ *G2* ✉ *1 Alva St., West End* ☎ *0131/225–9594* ▤ *AE, MC, V* ✢ *H6.*

£££

FRENCH

✕ **La Garrigue.** Edinburgh is blessed with several affordable French bistros, and this is one of the best. Although the modern decor evokes Paris, the food has the rustic flavor of the Languedoc region. Regional favorites include a starter of croquette of slow cooked pig's head and such main dishes as braised lamb shank and a casserole of shin of beef in a red wine sauce. Desserts such as a lavender crème brûlée offer a light finale to a heady dining experience. ✉ *31 Jeffrey St., Old Town* ☎ *0131/557–3032* ⊕ *www.lagarrigue.co.uk* ▤ *AE, DC, MC, V* ☉ *Closed Sun.* ✢ *G3*

£££

BRITISH

✕ **Merchants.** This is a bustling, cheery cavern with bright scarlet walls, mirrors, plants, and a nonstop jazz sound track, set beneath the dramatic arch of George IV Bridge. The menu ranges from simple haggis and beef to a mille-feuille of scallops and lamb chops with raspberry-and-mint sauce. Its more ambitious dishes are reminiscent of nouvelle cuisine, but Merchants really does the basics best. Prix-fixe lunches begin at £11, dinners from £22. ✉ *17 Merchant St., Old Town* ☎ *0131/225–4009* ⊕ *www.merchantsrestaurant.co.uk* ▤ *AE, DC, MC, V* ✢ *F5.*

£

INDIAN

✕ **Mother India Cafe.** Despite its popularity, good Indian food is hard to find in Scotland. Not so at this humble eatery, where the emphasis is on home-style cooking. Meals are served tapas-style, with lots of small, reasonably priced dishes, making it possible to sample a little of everything. The lamb *karahi* (a Pakistani curry made in a woklike pot) is particularly recommended, as are any of the fish dishes. The split-level dining area is smart and contemporary. ✉ *3–5 Infirmary St., Old Town* ☎ *0131/524–9801* ⊕ *www.motherindiaglasgow.co.uk* ▤ *AE, MC, V* ✢ *H4.*

££

THAI

✕ **Thai Orchid.** A golden Buddha greets you at the door of this stylish restaurant. Beautiful orchids and the traditionally dressed staff transport you to Thailand, if only for a few hours. To start, try the *todd mun kao pode* (deep-fried corn cakes with sweet-and-sour peanut-and-coriander dip). Good main courses include *pla priew wan* (monkfish poached with coconut milk) or *pedt Orchid,* duck stir-fried with mango, chili, garlic, and red peppers. The sticky rice with coconut milk and mango is a dessert not to be missed. ✉ *5A Johnston Terr., Old Town* ☎ *0131/225–6633* ⊕ *www.thaiorchid.uk.com* ▤ *MC, V* ✢ *F4.*

£££

Fodor'sChoice

★

BRITISH

✕ **Wedgwood.** Rejecting the idea that fine dining should be a stuffy affair, owners Paul Wedgwood and Lisa Channon opened this Royal Mile gem. The dining space is smart but informal, and the professional staff has mastered the tricky task of giving guests space to relax while remaining attentive. But Wedgwood's food is the standout. The best local produce is taken in some surprising directions with Asian, French, and traditional Scottish influences apparent in dishes such as sticky sesame beef and panfried pigeon with haggis, neeps (turnips), and tatties (potatoes), and red wine jus. ✉ *267 Canongate, Old Town* ☎ *0131/558–8737* ⊕ *www.wedgwoodtherestaurant.co.uk* ⌘ *Reservations essential* ▤ *AE, MC, V* ✢ *H3.*

2

££££ ✕**The Witchery.** The hundreds of "witches" who were executed on
FRENCH Castlehill, just yards from where you'll be seated, are the inspiration
for this outstanding and atmospheric restaurant. The cavernous interior,
complete with flickering candlelight, is festooned with cabalistic insignia
and tarot-card characters. Gilded and painted ceilings reflect the close
links between France and Scotland, as does the menu, which includes
roasted quail with braised endive and scallops with spiced pork belly
and carrot puree. Pre- and post-theater (5:30–6:30 and 10:30–11:30)
two-course specials are an inexpensive way to sample the exceptional
cuisine. ✉ *Castlehill, Royal Mile, Old Town* ☎ *0131/225–5613* ⊕ *www.
thewitchery.com* ▭ *AE, DC, MC, V* ✛ *F4.*

NEW TOWN

*Use the coordinate (✛ B2) at the end of each listing to locate a site on
the corresponding map.*

The New Town, with its striking street plan, ambitious architecture,
and professional crowd, has restaurants where you can get everything
from a quick snack to a more formal dinner.

£££ ✕**A Room in the Town.** At this relaxed, friendly bistro serving Scots-
BRITISH French fare, there's a strong emphasis on fresh local meat, with the
Scottish touch accounting for slightly sweeter-than-usual sauces. You
may bring your own bottle of wine—an excellent wine shop is just a
block away—to offset the somewhat high prices, although the restaurant serves wine, too, along with very nice brandy. Plain but cheerful
thanks to bright colors and wooden fixtures, it's perfect for a sociable
night out with friends. ✉ *18 Howe St., New Town* ☎ *0131/225–8204*
⊕ *www.aroomin.co.uk* ⌚ *Reservations essential* ▭ *MC, V* ✛ *D1.*

££££ ✕ **Forth Floor.** Harvey Nichols has become synonymous with chic shop-
MODERN BRITISH ping, so it stands to reason that the department store's restaurant is no
slouch when it comes to style. The decor pulls off the trick of being
minimalist without being too severe. Factor in a glorious view over
Princes Street Gardens and the Edinburgh Castle and it's a winner from
the moment you walk in the door. The imaginative menu devised by
chef Stuart Muir makes it clear that you are dining somewhere special indeed. Scallops wrapped in pancetta and enlivened with paprika,
capers, and horseradish makes for a great starter, while the Moroccan-
spiced lamb proves that you can have style with substance. ✉ *Harvey
Nichols, 30–34 St. Andrew Sq., New Town* ☎ *0131/524–8350* ⊕ *www.
harveynichols.com* ⌚ *Reservations essential* ▭ *AE, DC, MC, V* ✛ *F2.*

£ ✕**Henderson's.** This was a vegetarian restaurant long before it was fash-
VEGETARIAN ionable to serve healthful, meatless creations. The salad bar has more
than a dozen different offerings each day; a massive plateful costs less
than £7. Tasty hot options include Moroccan stew with couscous and
moussaka. Live mellow music plays six nights a week (seven during the
festival). Around the corner on Thistle Street is the Bistro, from the same
proprietors; it serves snacks, meals, and decadent desserts such as chocolate fondue. There's also an impressive organic wine list. ✉ *94 Hanover
St., New Town* ☎ *0131/225–2605* ⊕ *www.hendersonsofedinburgh.co.
uk* ▭ *AE, DC, MC, V* ☯ *Closed Sun.* ✛ *E2*

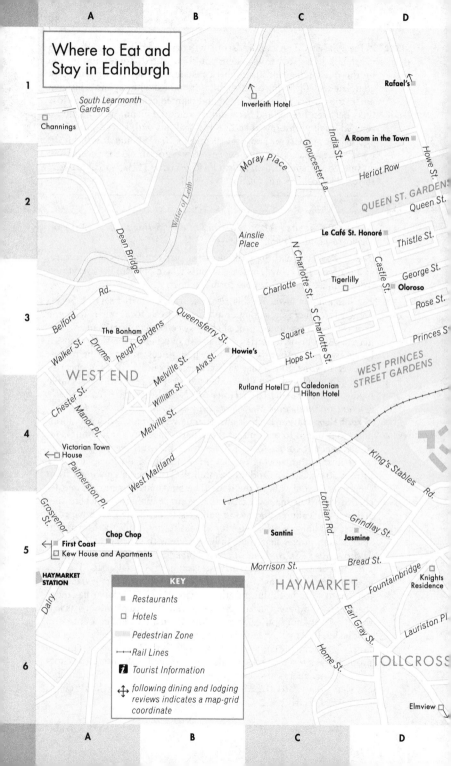

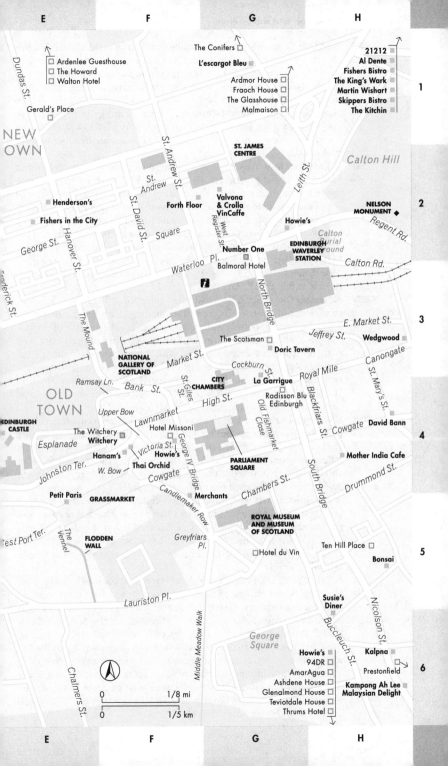

E   F   G   H

□ Ardenlee Guesthouse
□ The Howard
□ Walton Hotel

The Conifers □

L'escargot Bleu □

21212 ■
Al Dente ■
Fishers Bistro ■
The King's Wark ■
Martin Wishart ■
Skippers Bistro ■
The Kitchin ■

1

□ Gerald's Place

Ardmor House □
Fraoch House □
The Glasshouse □
Malmaison □

NEW
OWN

St. James
Centre

St. Andrew St.

Leith St.

Calton Hill

2

■ Henderson's

■ Fishers in the City

Forth Floor ■

Valvona
& Crolla
VinCaffe

Howie's ■

NELSON
MONUMENT ◆

St. Andrew Square

St. David St.

West Register St.

Regent Rd.

George St.

Hanover St.

Number One ■

Balmoral Hotel

EDINBURGH
WAVERLEY
STATION

Calton
Burial
Ground

Calton Rd.

Waterloo Pl.

North Bridge

ederick St.

The Mound

ℹ

3

E. Market St.

The Scotsman □

Jeffrey St.

Wedgwood ■

NATIONAL
GALLERY OF
SCOTLAND

Market St.

Doric Tavern □

Canongate

Cockburn St.

Ramsay Ln.

Bank St.

CITY
CHAMBERS

La Garrigue ■

Royal Mile

St. Mary's St.

St Giles St.

OLD
TOWN

Upper Bow

Lawnmarket

High St.

Radisson Blu
Edinburgh

Blackfriars St.

Cowgate

David Bann ■

EDINBURGH
CASTLE

The Witchery ■
Witchery

Hotel Missoni ■

Old Fishmarket Close

4

Esplanade

Hanam's ■

Victoria St.

George IV Bridge

South Bridge

Mother India Cafe ■

Johnston Ter.

Howie's ■
Thai Orchid ■

W. Bow

PARLIAMENT
SQUARE

Drummond St.

Cowgate

Petit Paris ■

GRASSMARKET

Candlemaker Row

Merchants ■

Chambers St.

est Port Ter.

The Vennel

FLODDEN
WALL

Greyfriars
Pl.

ROYAL MUSEUM
AND MUSEUM
OF SCOTLAND

Ten Hill Place □

5

□ Hotel du Vin

Bonsai ■

Chalmers St.

Lauriston Pl.

Middle Meadow Walk

Susie's
Diner

Nicolson St.

Buccleuch St.

George
Square

Howie's ■
94DR □
AmarAgua □
Ashdene House □
Glenalmond House □
Teviotdale House □
Thrums Hotel □

Kalpna ■

Prestonfield □

Kampong Ah Lee
Malaysian Delight ■

6

0   1/8 mi
0   1/5 km

E   F   G   H

££££   ✕ **Le Café St Honoré.** Quintessentially Parisian in style, this restaurant
FRENCH   reflects all that is charming about French café dining. From the moment
you enter the beautifully lighted room you're transported into the deca-
dently stylish belle epoque. A concise menu leaves more time for chat-
ting. You might start off with a warm salad of scallops, monkfish,
chorizo, and pine nuts, followed by lamb confit or panfried turbot
cooked with cider, green peppercorns, and prawns. ⊠ *34 N.W. Thistle
Street La., New Town* ☎ *0131/226–2211* ⊕ *www.cafesthonore.com*
☰ *AE, DC, MC, V* ✛ *D2.*

£££   ✕ **L'escargot Bleu.** Anyone still laboring under the misconception that
FRENCH   French cuisine is pretentious should pay a visit to this gem. In one of
the city's trendiest quarters, this venture from the former co-owner of
Petit Paris would make anyone from France feel at home. The welcome
is warm, the stripped wooden floors and period French posters add to a
convivial atmosphere that is loud and proud, and the food is as authentic as gendarme whistling La Marseillaise. Dishes like snails in parsley
butter and beef bourguignon fly the flag proudly. ⊠ *56A Broughton St.,
New Town* ☎ *0131/557–1600* ⊕ *www.lescargotbleu.co.uk* ⌂ *Reservations essential* ☰ *AE, DC, MC, V* ✛ *G1.*

£££££   ✕ **Number One.** Within the Edwardian splendor of the Balmoral Hotel,
Fodor'sChoice   this restaurant matches its grand surroundings with a menu that high-
★   lights the best of Scottish seafood and game. Try the roulade of organic
BRITISH   salmon with langoustine tortellini or the hazelnut-infused pork loin
with beetroot-and-chive *jus.* The wine list is extensive, the service
impeccable. All in all, this is the kind of stylish yet unstuffy restaurant that is perfect for an intimate dinner. ⊠ *Balmoral Hotel, Princes
St., New Town* ☎ *0131/557–2672* ⊕ *www.restaurantnumberone.com*
⌂ *Reservations essential* ☰ *AE, DC, MC, V* ✛ *G2.*

££££   ✕ **Oloroso.** In the heart of the New Town and close to the main shop-
MODERN BRITISH   ping streets, this is the perfect spot for a revitalizing lunch or dinner
after exploring the city. The contemporary international cooking reflects
influences from Europe and Asia, the service is efficient and friendly,
and the bar serves some of the best cocktails in Britain. Try the roasted
duck breast with braised red cabbage and apples, or the aubergine gal-
ette (eggplant tart) with a tomato-and-cinnamon sauce. The wine list
has about 230 selections, including champagne. The dining room and
roof terrace have stunning views across the Firth of Forth to the hills
of Fife on one side, and the castle and city rooftops on the other. ⊠ *33
Castle St., New Town* ☎ *0131/226–7614* ⊕ *www.oloroso.co.uk* ☰ *AE,
DC, MC, V* ✛ *D3.*

££   ✕ **Rafael's.** All great restaurants should be as laid back as Rafael's. Situ-
SPANISH   ated in a quaint pink-hued basement room replete with eccentric trinkets, the restaurant is clearly not in thrall to prevailing trends and is
all the better for it. Not only does chef/proprietor/all-round-good guy
Rafael Torrubia create affordably priced masterpieces with an Iberian
twist, he's also likely to deliver dishes such as a sea bass and salmon duo
with pesto or a wonderfully authentic tortilla with chorizo to your table
himself. Despite his Spanish background, Torrubia's use of ingredients
such as curry in his sauces shows that as well as being a man of the
people, he is also a man of the world. ⊠ *2 Deanhaugh St., New Town*
☎ *0131/332–1469* ☰ *MC, V* ✛ *D1.*

2

£££££ ✕ **21212.** Abandoning the Michelin-starred restaurant that made him
MODERN BRITISH famous might sound risky, but Paul Kitching didn't become known
as one of the region's most innovative chefs without being daring.
Housed in a grand old Georgian house, this restaurant is sumptuously
appointed, with prices to match; the five-course fixed-price dinner menu
is £65, though lunch is cheaper. The dining room combines boudoir-style
comfort with belle-epoque grandeur. Expect creative takes on old classics, such as his deconstructed fish-and-chips. Kitching's fearlessness is
apparent in dishes like turbot with chorizo, dates, vanilla, and rutabaga
puree—not to mention the cheesecake flavored with caraway seeds. ✉ *3
Royal Terr., New Town* ☎ *0845/222–1212* ⊕ *www.21212restaurant.
co.uk* ▭ *AE, DC, MC, V* ⊹ *H1.*

££ ✕ **Valvona & Crolla VinCaffe.** Every Scot with a passion for food knows
ITALIAN Valvona & Crolla, the country's first Italian delicatessen and wine merchant. This eatery of the same name may lack the old-world feel of the
original, but the food is as wonderful as you would expect. The fare is
relatively simple, but the quality of the ingredients ensure that treats
such as the white pizza with cured bacon do nothing to tarnish the
brand's reputation. ✉ *11 Multrees Walk, New Town* ☎ *0131/557–0088*
⊕ *www.vincaffe.com* ▭ *AE, D, MC, V* ⊹ *G2.*

HAYMARKET

*Use the coordinate (⊹ B2) at the end of each listing to locate a site on
the corresponding map.*

West of the Old Town and south of the West End is Haymarket, a district with its own down-to-earth character and well-worn charm. This
area has many restaurants that tend to be more affordable than those
in the center of town.

££ ✕ **Chop Chop.** Thank heavens for restaurants like this one, where the
CHINESE kitchen strives for authenticity. The chef is from the northern part of
China, and his flavorful creations are a far cry from the bland dishes
found elsewhere. Lamb with salt and cumin is a robust starter, while the
entrées inclues a huge array of noodle dishes. ✉ *248 Morrison St., Haymarket* ☎ *013/ 221–1155* ⊕ *www.chop-chop.co.uk* ▭ *MC, V* ⊹ *A5*

££ ✕ **First Coast.** This laid-back bistro, just a few minutes from Haymarket
BRITISH Station, is a favorite with locals. Hardwood floors, stone walls, soft blue
hues, and seaside paintings add to the coastal theme. Savory temptations include pumpkin stew and raisin couscous, panfried sea bass with
fennel, mustard, and ginger, and Aberdeen Angus sirloin steak with
tomato-and-red-onion salad. The international wine list is as varied as
the daily specials. ✉ *99–101 Dalry Rd., Haymarket* ☎ *0131/313–4404*
⊕ *www.first-coast.co.uk* ▭ *MC, V* ⊹ *A5.*

WEST END AND POINTS WEST

*Use the coordinate (⊹ B2) at the end of each listing to locate a site on
the corresponding map.*

Even after business hours, the city's commercial center is the place to
find a variety of international restaurants.

££   ✕ **Jasmine.** Seafood is the specialty of this small, friendly Cantonese res-
CHINESE   taurant. Delicious dishes include mixed seafood on a bed of lettuce, and
the chicken served inside the two halves of a mango. The staff doesn't
break a sweat as it serves a constant stream of customers. Flickering
candles add a relaxing feel to the interior, although tables are quite
closely spaced. Prix-fixe lunches, starting at £6.90 for three courses, are
a good value. A take-out menu is available. ⊠ *32 Grindlay St., West
End* ☎ *0131/229–5757* ▭ *AE, MC, V* ✛ *C5.*

££   ✕ **Petit Paris.** On a pleasant summer's day, the lively atmosphere of the
FRENCH   Grassmarket can be reminiscent of France. Even in more typically Scottish weather it's possible to get a taste of warmer climes at this little
bistro, cheerfully decorated with checked tablecloths, copper pots, and
bunches of garlic. The staff is predominantly French, and the emphasis is on casual dining, local produce, and home cooking. The two-
course lunch special for £9.95 is a real bargain. Try the traditional
French blood sausage and slow-baked rabbit with Dijon-mustard sauce.
⊠ *38/40 Grassmarket, Old Town* ☎ *0131/226–2442* ⊕ *www.petitparis-
restaurant.co.uk* ▭ *MC, V* ✛ *E5.*

££££   ✕ **Santini.** Its crisp decor isn't the only thing that makes Santini stand
ITALIAN   apart from the Italian eateries on Lothian Road. This trattoria also
serves you a mouthful of flavors. The chef cooks with real passion:
osso buco and steamed wild sea bass with mixed herbs and balsamic
vinegar are just two of the knee-tremblers on the menu. ⊠ *8 Conference Sq., West End* ☎ *0131/221–7788* ⊕ *www.santiniedinburgh.co.uk*
▭ *AE, DC, MC, V* ✛ *C5.*

SOUTH SIDE

*Use the coordinate (✛ B2) at the end of each listing to locate a site on
the corresponding map.*

The presence of university professors and students means eateries that
are both affordable and interesting.

££   ✕ **Bonsai.** Japanese food has taken ages to catch on in Edinburgh. As
JAPANESE   such, Bonsai is one of the very few sushi joints in town. The small
dining area may be a bit gloomy, but luckily the food is very good.
The succulent *gyoza* (steamed dumplings) are pliant and tasty, while
the wide variety of noodle and teriyaki dishes and the classy sushi are
also delicious. ⊠ *46 West Richmond St., Southside* ☎ *0131/668–3847*
▭ *MC, V* ✛ *H5.*

£   ✕ **Kalpna.** The facade of this vegetarian Indian restaurant, amid an ordi-
Fodor's Choice   nary row of shops, is unremarkable. But the food is unlike anything
★   you're likely to encounter elsewhere in the city. The *dam aloo kashmiri*
INDIAN   is a medium-spicy potato dish with a sauce made from honey, pista-
chios, and almonds. *Bangan mirch masala* is spicier, with eggplant and
red chili peppers. Thaali (a variety of dishes served in bowls on a tray),
a Gujarat specialty, is great value at £12.95. The low-key interior is
enlivened by a few colorful prints. ⊠ *2–3 St. Patrick Sq., South Side*
☎ *0131/667–9890* ⊕ *www.kalpnarestaurant.com* ▭ *MC, V* ☺ *Closed
Sun. Jan.–Mar.* ✛ *H6*

£   ✕ **Kampong Ah Lee Malaysian Delight.** Malaysian food tends to be over-
MALAYSIAN   looked when talking about the world's great cuisines. If you need evidence that it's among the best Southeast Asia has to offer, stop by this
place. The canteen-style dining area won't win any awards, but the food
deserves high praise. Almost everything here comes redolent with spices
and bursting with exotic flavors. Well-known dishes such as *laksa* (spicy
noodle soup with prawns) and beef *rendang* (a thick stew with coconut milk) are expertly prepared. Everything is so good you'll struggle
to pick out a favorite. ⊠ *28 Clerk St., Southside* ☎ *0131/662–9050*
☐ *MC, V* ✛ *H6*

£   ✕ **Susie's Diner.** While other restaurants have taken vegetarian food to
VEGETARIAN   the heady heights of fine dining, Susie's stays true to its roots as a
healthy hangout for bohemian students. There's nothing overly complicated about either the surrounds or the menu. Handmade fliers and
posters adorn the walls, and the kitchen serves up a hearty selection
of stews, pastas, and stir-fries. It may not be rocket science, but it's
been keeping its customers happy for years. ⊠ *51–53 W. Nicolson St.,*
Southside ☎ *0131/667–8729* ☐ *MC, V* ✛ *H6*.

LEITH

Use the coordinate (✛ B2) at the end of each listing to locate a site on
the corresponding map.

Seafood lovers are drawn to the old port of Leith to sample the freshest
seafood and to admire the authentic seafaring feel of the docklands.

££   ✕ **Al Dente.** This tiny neighborhood favorite is head and shoulders above
ITALIAN   the rest. Chef Graziano Spano, from the town of Puglia, knows the
freshness and flavors that typify food from southern Italy. He is equally
proficient with other regional styles, and frequently tackles dishes from
foodie havens like Tuscany and Liguria. During quiet times the jovial
Spano will often converse with his guests in a tiny dining area. ⊠ *139*
Easter Rd., Leith ☎ *0131/652–1932* ⊕ *www.aldente-restaurant.net*
⚜ *Reservations essential* ☐ *AE, MC, V* ✛ *H1.*

£££   ✕ **Fishers Bistro.** Locals and visitors flock to this laid-back pub-cum-
SEAFOOD   bistro down on the waterfront, and to its sister restaurant, **Fishers in**
the City, in the New Town. The menu is the same, but Fishers Leith
has the better reputation and vibe. Bar meals are served, although for
more comfort and elegance sit in the cozy blue-walled dining room.
Seafood is the specialty—the Loch Fyne oysters are wonderful. Watch
for the daily specials: perhaps a seafood or vegetarian soup followed by
North African prawns as big as your hand. It's a good idea to reserve
ahead for the bistro. ⊠ *1 The Shore, Leith* ☎ *0131/554–5666* ⊕ *www.*
fishersbistros.co.uk ✛ *H1* ⊠ *58 Thistle St., New Town* ☎ *0131/225–*
5109 ☐ *AE, MC, V* ✛ *E2.*

£££   ✕ **The King's Wark.** In Edinburgh, the emphasis at most bars remains
BRITISH   stolid pub grub. There are notable exceptions, however. The King's
Wark is arguably the best of them. At lunchtime, the dark-wood bar
does a roaring trade in simple fare such as gourmet burgers and fishcakes, but in the evening the kitchen ups the ante with such dishes as

sea trout stuffed with smoked mackerel risotto. ⊠ *36 The Shore, Leith* ☎ *0131/554–9260* ▭ *AE, MC, V* ✥ *H1*.

££££££   ✕ **The Kitchin.** One of the Edinburgh's most popular eateries, Tom
Fodor'sChoice   Kitchin's Michelin-starred venture has packed in the crowds since
★   opening in 2006. It's not difficult to see why. Kitchin, who trained
FRENCH   in France, runs a tight ship and his passion for utilizing seasonal and
locally sourced produce to his own creative ends shows no sign of dim-
ming. Unfashionable ingredients such as ox tongue, tripe, and pigs head
emerge heroic after Kitchin's alchemy, and he works his magic equally
dexterously on more familiar elements such as seafood and venison.
⊠ *78 Commercial Quay, Leith* ☎ *0131/555–1755* ⊕ *www.thekitchin.
com* ⌕ *Reservations essential* ▭ *AE, D, MC, V* ☺ *Closed Sun. and
Mon.* ✥ *H1*.

£££££   ✕ **Martin Wishart.** Slightly out of town but worth every penny of the
FRENCH   taxi fare and the cost (three ciurses for £60), this rising culinary star
woos diners with an impeccable and varied menu of beautifully presented, French-influenced dishes. Terrine of foie gras, compote of Agen
prunes, and sole Murat (glazed fillet of sole with baby onions, artichoke, parsley, and lemon) with *pommes en cocotte* (potatoes cooked
in a casserole) typify the cuisine. Reservations are essential on Friday
and Saturday night. ⊠ *54 The Shore, Leith* ☎ *0131/553–3557* ⊕ *www.
martin-wishart.co.uk* ▭ *AE, MC, V* ✥ *H1*. ☺ *Closed Sun. and Mon.
No lunch Sat.*

£££   ✕ **Skippers Bistro.** This superb seafood restaurant has a traditional,
SEAFOOD   snug, cluttered interior with dark wood, shining brass, and lots of pictures and seafaring ephemera. For a starter, try the fragrant Cullen
skink (a thick soup make with haddock). Main dishes change daily but
might include Finnan haddie, halibut, salmon, or monkfish in delicious
sauces. Reservations are essential on weekends. ⊠ *1A Dock Pl., Leith*
☎ *0131/554–1018* ▭ *AE, MC, V* ✥ *H1*.

WHERE TO STAY

From stylish boutique hotels to homey B&Bs, Edinburgh has a world-
class array of accommodation to suit every taste. While its status as one
of Britain's most attractive and fascinating cities ensures a steady influx
of visitors, the wealth of overnight options means there's no need to
compromise on where you stay. Grand old hotels such as the Balmoral
are rightly renowned for their regal bearing and old-world charm. If
your tastes are a little more contemporary, the city's burgeoning contin-
gent of chic design hotels offers an equally alluring alternative. For those
on a tighter budget, the town's B&Bs are the most likely choice.

Rooms are harder to find in August and September, when the Edinburgh
International Festival and the Fringe Festival take place, so reserve at
least three months in advance. Bed-and-breakfast accommodations may
be harder to find in December, January, and February, when some proprietors close for a few weeks. Scots are trusting people—many B&B
proprietors provide front-door keys and few impose curfews.

2

PRICES

Weekend rates in the larger hotels are always much cheaper than midweek rates, so if you want to stay in a plush hotel, come on the weekend. To save money and see how local residents live, stay in a B&B in one of the areas away from the city center, such as Pilrig to the north, Murrayfield to the west, or Sciennes to the south. Public buses can whisk you to the city center in 10 to 15 minutes.

WHAT IT COSTS IN POUNDS					
	£	££	£££	££££	£££££
FOR TWO PEOPLE	under £70	£70–£120	£121–£180	£181–£250	over £250

Prices are for two people in a standard double room in high season, usually including 17.5% V.A.T.

OLD TOWN

Use the coordinate (⊕ B2) at the end of each listing to locate a site on the corresponding map.

£££ 🏨 **Hotel Du Vin.** This is one of the U.K.'s most forward-thinking hotel chains, so it's no surprise that they haven't missed a trick here. Set in a former asylum, it retains a traditional feel despite its contemporary trappings. Situated right next to the university, the hotel is surrounded by pubs and restaurants, yet it's easy to find peace within the warrenlike recesses of the building. You can kick back in the hotel's whisky snug, where 270 different varieties of the "water of life" are ripe for sampling. The amply proportioned rooms are all individually designed, so it pays to do some research ahead of time, but all are stylishly appointed with luxe trimmings such as hand-sprung mattresses. **Pros:** trendy design; youthful feel. **Cons:** some rooms are better than others; in a noisy neighborhood. ⊠ *11 Bristo Pl., Old Town* ☎ *0131/247–4900* ⊕ *www. hotelduvin.com* ⇱ *37 rooms, 10 suites* ⚭ *In-room: no a/c, DVD, Wi-Fi. In-hotel: restaurant, room service, bar, Wi-Fi, parking (paid)* ▭ *AE, D, DC, MC, V* ⊕ *G5.* � *BP*

££££ 🏨 **Hotel Missoni.** Glasgow is regarded as Scotland's most stylish city, but the capital has beaten its rival by becoming the site of Italian fashion house Missoni's first boutique hotel. The daring—and to some tastes garish—delights to be found inside contrast with the Gothic surroundings, but the hotel pulls it off by being simultaneously chic and welcoming. Rooms and suites are decently sized and boldly designed, while the restaurant and the hotel's bar are fast becoming a magnet for the city's bright young things. **Pros:** perfect location; in the thick of the action; as far from staid as you can get. **Cons:** it's a little Austin Powers in places; some find it hard to relax in such chichi surrounds. ⊠ *1 George IV Bridge, Old Town* ☎ *0131/220–6666* ⊕ *www.hotelmissoni.com* ⇱ *129 rooms, 7 suites* ⚭ *In-room: no a/c, safe, DVD, Wi-Fi. In-hotel: restaurant, room service, bar, gym, Wi-Fi hotspot, parking (paid)* ▭ *AE, D, DC, MC, V* ❙❀❙ *BP* ⊕ *F4.*

BEST BETS FOR EDINBURGH LODGING

Fodor's Choice ★

Balmoral Hotel, £££££, p. 69

Rutland Hotel, ££££, p. 72

The Scotsman, £££££, p. 68

By Price

££

Elmview, p. 73

Gerald's Place, p. 70

£££

Channings, p. 72

Kew House and Apart-ments, p. 71

Hotel Du Vin, p. 67

Malmaison, p. 75

££££

The Bonham, p. 72

The Glasshouse, p. 70

The Howard, p. 70

Hotel Missoni, p. 67

Rutland Hotel, p. 72

£££££

Balmoral Hotel, p. 69

Prestonfield, p. 74

The Scotsman, p. 68

By Experience

BEST SPAS

Balmoral Hotel, £££££, p. 69

The Scotsman, £££££, p. 68

BEST HISTORIC HOTELS

Balmoral Hotel, £££££, p. 69

Elmview, ££, p. 73

BEST CONCIERGE

The Howard, ££££, p. 70

Malmaison, £££, p. 75

MOST ROMANTIC

Prestonfield, £££££, p. 74

The Witchery, £££££, p. 69

MOST KID-FRIENDLY

Caledonian Hilton Hotel, £££, p. 70

Knights Residence, £££, p. 68

£££   **Knights Residence.** Ten minutes from the Grassmarket, the Knights is made up of 19 different apartments. You are greeted by a concierge who will show you to your unit, which will be pleasingly furnished and filled with the things you need for a perfect stay, including a washer-dryer and a DVD library. Breakfast can be found in the fridge. **Pros:** comfortable apartments; secure location; good for families needing space and privacy. **Cons:** lack of staff won't suit everyone; better for stays of two or more nights. ⊠ *12 Lauriston St., Old Town* ☎ *0131/622–8120* ⊕ *www.theknightresidence.co.uk* ⤳ *19 apartments* ⌂ *In-room: no a/c, kitchen, Wi-Fi. In-hotel: parking (free)* ⎪⊙⎪ *CP* ✣ *D5.*

£££   **Radisson Blu Hotel, Edinburgh.** Although it was built in the late 1980s, this city-center hotel was designed to blend in among the 16th-, 17th-, and 18th-century buildings on the Royal Mile. Rooms are spacious and contemporary—practical rather than luxurious. **Pros:** central location; can-do staff. **Cons:** expensive breakfast; difficult to reach by car. ⊠ *80 High St., Royal Mile, Old Town* ☎ *0131/557–9797* ⊕ *www.radissonblu.co.uk/hotel-edinburgh* ⤳ *238 rooms, 10 suites* ⌂ *In-room: Internet, Wi-Fi. In-hotel: restaurant, bar, pool, gym, parking (paid)* ⊟ *AE, DC, MC, V* ⎪⊙⎪ *BP* ✣ *G4.*

£££££   **The Scotsman.** This magnificent turn-of-the-20th-century building,
Fodor's Choice   with a marble staircase and a fascinating history—it was once the head-
★   quarters of the *Scotsman* newspaper—now houses a modern, luxurious

hotel. Dark wood, earthy colors, tweeds, and contemporary furnishings decorate the rooms and public spaces. North Bridge, the casual-chic brasserie, serves shellfish and grill food. **Pros:** gorgeous surroundings; personalized service. **Cons:** no air-conditioning; spa is a bit noisy. ⊠ *20 N. Bridge, Old Town* ☎ *0131/556–5565* ⊕ *www.theetoncollection.com* ⤶ *56 rooms, 12 suites* ⏶ *In-room: no a/c, Internet, Wi-Fi. In-hotel: restaurant, bar, pool, gym, spa* ▭ *AE, DC, MC, V* ◐ *BP* ✢ *G1.*

££ 🏨 **Ten Hill Place.** This stylish hotel just around the corner from the Festival Theatre has impeccable service. The rooms are large, immaculate, and airy, filled with sleek furnishings covered in delectable colors ranging from oatmeal to mocha. The breakfasts are satisfying, and include plenty of top-notch coffee. **Pros:** well kept; close to everything but not in the midst of the brouhaha. **Cons:** rooms can be too dark; peekaboo glass doors on the bathrooms. ⊠ *10 Hill Pl., Old Town* ☎ *0131/662–2080* ⊕ *www.tenhillplace.com* ⤶ *78 rooms* ⏶ *In room: Internet. In hotel: bar, parking (paid)* ▭ *MC, V* ◐ *BP* ✢ *H5.*

£££££ 🏨 **The Witchery.** This lavishly theatrical lodging promises a night to remember. Each suite has a theme—choices include the Library, the Armory, and to the Inner Sanctum—and is decked out with jaw-droppingly grand antiques, champagne chilling in an immense bucket, and the finest quality bedding. Dining in the dark-paneled restaurant is just as dramatic, with old-world dishes such as saddle of rabbit and roast lobster. **Pros:** a Gothic treasure; sumptuous dining. **Cons:** can be noisy at night; ghost appearance not guaranteed. ⊠ *Castlehill, Royal Mile, Old Town* ☎ *0131/225–5613* ⊕ *www.thewitchery.com* ⤶ *8 suites* ⏶ *In-room: no a/c In-hotel: restaurant* ▭ *AE, DC, MC, V* ◐ *BP.*

NEW TOWN

Use the coordinate (✢ B2) at the end of each listing to locate a site on the corresponding map.

£ 🏨 **Ardenlee Guest House.** An exquisite Victorian-tile floor is one of many original features at this gem of a guesthouse tucked away from the hustle and bustle of the city center. A cast-iron staircase leads to simple but spacious rooms. The manager is friendly and helpful, and has plenty of information on the sights in and around Edinburgh. **Pros:** family-run establishment; good value for money. **Cons:** few amenities; uphill walk to the city center. ⊠ *9 Eyre Pl., New Town* ☎ *0131/556–2838* ⊕ *www.ardenlee.co.uk* ⤶ *9 rooms, 7 with bath* ⏶ *In-room: no a/c, no phone, Wi-Fi. In-hotel: Wi-Fi hotspot* ▭ *MC, V* ◐ *BP.* ✢ *E1.*

£££££ 🏨 **Balmoral Hotel.** The attention to detail in the elegant rooms—colors
Fodor's Choice were picked to echo the country's heathers and moors—and the sheer
★ élan that has re-created the Edwardian splendor of this grand, former railroad hotel make staying at the Balmoral a special introduction to Edinburgh. Here, below the landmark clock tower marking the east end of Princes Street, the lively buzz makes you feel as if you're at the center of city life. The hotel's main restaurant is the plush and stylish Number One, serving excellent Scottish seafood and game. If you overindulge, recuperate at the luxurious spa. **Pros:** big and beautiful building; top-hatted doorman; lovely touches in the rooms. **Cons:** small pool; spa books up fast; restaurants can be very busy. ⊠ *1 Princes St., New Town*

☎ *0131/556–2414* ⊕ *www.thebalmoralhotel.com* ⮩ *188 rooms, 20 suites* ⟁ *In-room: Internet. In-hotel: 2 restaurants, bar, pool, gym, spa, Internet terminal, parking (paid)* ⊟ *AE, DC, MC, V* ¦◯¦ *BP.* ✛ *G2.*

£££   ⊞ **Caledonian Hilton Hotel.** "The Caley," a conspicuous block of red sand-
⟳   stone beyond the west end of West Princes Street Gardens, was built between 1898 and 1902 as the flagship hotel of the Caledonian Rail-way, and its imposing Victorian decor has been faithfully preserved. The public area has marbled green columns and an ornate stairwell with a burnished-metalwork balustrade. Rooms and corridors are exceptionally large and well appointed. **Pros:** service with a smile; lots of choices at breakfast. **Cons:** Internet access is extra; rooms can be small. ⊠ *Princes St., New Town* ☎ *0131/222–8888* ⊕ *www.hilton.co.uk/caledonian* ⮩ *251 rooms, 20 suites* ⟁ *In-room: Internet, Wi-Fi. In-hotel: 2 restau-rants, 2 bars, pool, parking (paid)* ⊟ *AE, DC, MC, V* ¦◯¦ *BP* ✛ *C4.*

££   ⊞ **Gerald's Place.** Although he is not a native of the city, Gerald Della-Porta is one of those B&B owners to whom Edinburgh owes so much. Forget the clichés—you really are welcomed into his home and treated like a most honored guest. The rooms are furnished in classic style, with huge beds, fresh flowers, and original artwork (much of it for sale). A block beyond Queen Street, this lodging has a very central location. Breakfast around the big table is a communal affair, and the food is healthier than at most places. **Pros:** the advice and thoughtfulness of the owner; spacious rooms. **Cons:** stairs are difficult to manage; an uphill walk to the city center; cash only. ⊠ *21B Abercromby Pl.EH3 6QE* ☎ *0131/558–7017* ⊕ *www.geraldsplace.com* ⮩ *2 rooms* ⟁ *In-room: no a/c. In-hotel: Wi-Fi hotspot* ⊟ *No credit cards* ¦◯¦ *BP* ✛ *E1.*

££££   ⊞ **The Glasshouse.** Glass walls extend from the 19th-century facade of a former church, foreshadowing the daring interior of one of the city's chicest boutique hotels. Rooms are decorated in a minimalist style, with soft browns and beiges blending nicely with the wood and marble. The bathrooms were built in Denmark and shipped as intact "pods" that were then fitted into the rooms. A bedside control panel lets you control the drapes, and the flat-screen TV swivels to face the bed or the sitting area. Floor-to-ceiling windows overlook the New Town or the rooftop garden in back. The hotel's halls and rooms are adorned with female nude photographs by Scottish photographers Trevor and Faye Yerbury. **Pros:** near all the attractions; very modern and stylish. **Cons:** perhaps a little sterile for some; nightclub downstairs is noisy. ⊠ *2 Greenside Pl., New Town* ☎ *0131/525–8200* ⊕ *www.theetoncollection.com* ⮩ *65 rooms, 18 suites* ⟁ *In-room: safe, Internet, Wi-Fi. In-hotel: room ser-vice, bar* ⊟ *AE, MC, V* ¦◯¦ *BP* ✛ *G1.*

££££   ⊞ **The Howard.** This hotel is in a classic New Town building, elegant proportioned and superbly outfitted. Antique furniture and original art throughout make the Howard like a swank private club. You can expect the most upscale amenities, including private butlers. Some of the best rooms overlook the garden. **Pros:** small but grand building; staff has a great attitude. **Cons:** not for younger travelers; noisy neigh-borhood. ⊠ *34 Great King St., New Town* ☎ *0131/557–3500* ⊕ *www. thehoward.com* ⮩ *18 rooms, 5 suites* ⟁ *In-room: no a/c, Wi-Fi. In-hotel: restaurant, room service, laundry service, parking (free)* ⊟ *AE, MC, V* ¦◯¦ *BP* ✛ *E1.*

2

££ 🛏 **Inverleith Hotel.** Across from the Royal Botanical Gardens, this renovated Victorian town house has cozy, well-lighted rooms with velour bedspreads, dark wooden furniture, and pale-gold curtains. In winter, when the surrounding trees loose their leaves, a couple of the south-facing rooms have views of the castle. The reception doubles as a private bar for guests and sells a fine selection of malt whiskies. Several good restaurants and cafés are nearby. **Pros:** quiet surroundings; knowledgeable staff. **Cons:** some of the rooms are small; narrow passageways; uphill walk to the city center. ✉ *5 Inverleith Terr., New Town* ☎ *0131/556–2745* ⊕ *www.inverleithhotel.co.uk* 🛏 *12 rooms, 2 apartments* ♿ *In-room: no a/c, Wi-Fi. In-hotel: bar, parking (free)* ▭ *AE, MC, V* ⚭ *BP* ✚ *C1.*

££££ 🛏 **Tigerlilly.** On hip George Street, this boutique hotel has everything a girl could imagine—bowls of fresh fruit, designer candles, hair straighteners—for a night away from home. But there's plenty for the guys, too. Everyone will enjoy the little extras, like the iPod you can borrow. The restaurant serves confidently prepared pan-Asian fare. If you fancy a post-dinner snifter, the bar has a cocktail menu of biblical proportions. Don't worry if you overdo it—breakfast is served until noon. **Pros:** chic yet not intimidating; laid-back but efficient staff. **Cons:** no views; can be noisy. ✉ *125 George St., New Town* ☎ *0131/225–5005* ⊕ *www. tigerlilyedinburgh.co.uk* 🛏 *33 rooms* ♿ *In-room: Wi-Fi. In-hotel: restaurant, bar* ▭ *AE, MC, V* ⚭ *BP* ✚ *C3.*

££ 🛏 **Walton Hotel.** This B&B in a Georgian town house is a 10-minute walk from the city center. High-ceilinged, elegant rooms are furnished in an unfussy, traditional style, and there's a choice of breakfasts—traditional Scottish, continental, or American. Four of the rooms are on the ground floor, and six are in the basement (all have windows). **Pros:** top-class staff; bountiful breakfasts. **Cons:** limited parking; some rooms are below street level. ✉ *79 Dundas St., New Town* ☎ *0131/556–1137* ⊕ *www.waltonhotel.com* 🛏 *10 rooms* ♿ *In-room: no a/c, Internet, Wi-Fi. In-hotel: parking (free)* ▭ *MC, V* ⚭ *BP* ✚ *E1.*

HAYMARKET

Use the coordinate (✚ B2) at the end of each listing to locate a site on the corresponding map.

£££ 🛏 **Kew House and Apartments.** With such sumptuous rooms, you might think that Kew House was a full-service hotel. Inside the elegant 1860 terraced house are unfussy rooms with nice touches like hair dryers, coffeemakers, and pants presses. Welcome luxuries include fresh flowers, decadent chocolates, and a decanter of sherry on arrival. **Pros:** as clean as a whistle; thoughtful touches throughout. **Cons:** longish walk to the city center. ✉ *1 Kew Terr., Haymarket* ☎ *0131/313–0700* ⊕ *www. kewhouse.com* 🛏 *6 rooms, 2 apartments* ♿ *In-room: no a/c, Wi-Fi. In-hotel: Wi-Fi hotspot, parking (free)* ▭ *AE, DC, MC, V* ⚭ *BP* ✚ *A5.*

££ 🛏 **Victorian Town House.** In a leafy crescent, this house once belonged to David Alan Stevenson, cousin of Robert Louis Stevenson. The writer would doubtless be happy to lay down his head in this lovingly preserved home away from home. The bright yet calming rooms have beds that are piled with plump duvets. But those who don't sleep so easy will appreciate crystal decanter with just enough whisky to send you off. **Pros:** serene surroundings; gracious staff. **Cons:** no parking nearby. ⊠ *14 Eglinton Terr., Haymarket* ☎ *0131/337–7088* ⊕ *www. thevictoriantownhouse.co.uk* ⇌ *3 rooms* ⟡ *In-room: no a/c, Wi-Fi. In-hotel: Wi-Fi hotspot* ⊟ *MC, V* ⟠ *BP* ⊹ *A4.*

WEST END

> *Use the coordinate (⊹ B2) at the end of each listing to locate a site on the corresponding map.*

££££   ▦ **The Bonham.** This hotel in the elegant West End carries out a successful, sophisticated flirtation with modernity that makes it stand out from its neighbors. Bold colors and contemporary Scottish art set off its late-19th-century architecture and classic furniture. The good-size rooms are typical of an Edinburgh town house but offer peace and quiet without the noise often associated with this type of hotel. The chic, unadorned restaurant has oversize mirrors and a central catwalk of light; its focus is on beautifully presented contemporary cuisine. **Pros:** thorough yet unobtrusive service; excellent restaurant. **Cons:** not many common areas; can have a business-hotel feel. ⊠ *35 Drumsheugh Gardens, West End* ☎ *0131/226–6050* ⊕ *www.thebonham.com* ⇌ *42 rooms, 6 suites* ⟡ *In-room: no a/c, Wi-Fi. In-hotel: restaurant, parking (free)* ⊟ *AE, DC, MC, V* ⟠ *BP.* ⊹ *A3.*

£££   ▦ **Channings.** Five Edwardian terraced town houses make up this intimate, elegant hotel in an upscale West End neighborhood just minutes from Princes Street. Beyond the clubby, oak-paneled lobby lounge are quiet guest rooms with well-chosen antiques and marble baths. North-facing rooms have great views of Fife. Channings Restaurant offers excellent value in traditional Scottish and Continental cooking. **Pros:** romantic surroundings; inventive color schemes. **Cons:** not all rooms are equal; breakfasts are a bit meager. ⊠ *12–16 S. Learmonth Gardens, West End* ☎ *0131/315–2226* ⊕ *www.channings.co.uk* ⇌ *36 rooms, 5 suites* ⟡ *In-room: no a/c, Wi-Fi. In-hotel: restaurant, bar* ⊟ *AE, MC, V* ⟠ *BP* ⊹ *A1.*

££££   ▦ **Rutland Hotel.** The building may have once been the residence of Sir
Fodor's Choice   Joseph Lister—known as the "father of antiseptic surgery"—but there's
★   nothing clinical about this acclaimed boutique hotel at the west end of Princes Street. Nominated for several style awards, the design is chic without being intimidating. The restaurant is earning a fine reputation for itself. **Pros:** friendly staff; not pretentious; great bar and restaurant. **Cons:** the nearby taxi rank can harbor some unsavory characters on weekend evenings. ⊠ *1–3 Rutland St., West End* ☎ *0131/229–3402* ⊕ *www.therutlandhotel.com* ⇌ *12 rooms* ⟡ *In-room: no a/c, DVD, Wi-Fi. In-hotel: restaurant, room service, bar, Wi-Fi hotspot, parking (paid)* ⊟ *AE, D, DC, MC, V* ⟠ *BP* ⊹ *C4.*

SOUTH SIDE

Use the coordinate (✛ B2) at the end of each listing to locate a site on the corresponding map.

££ ⊡ **AmarAgua.** Deep-pile carpets, floral drapes with plenty of swags, and well-designed furniture create restrained opulence in this Victorian town house 10 minutes by bus from the city center. Many of the rooms look distinctly Asian, as the multilingual owners spent some time working in the Far East. Carry-out breakfasts are available for guests leaving early to catch a bus or plane. **Pros:** quiet setting; snug rooms. **Cons:** far from the city center; not all rooms have en-suite bathrooms. ✉ *10 Kilmaurs Terr., Newington* ☎ *0131/667–6775* ⊕ *www.amaragua. co.uk* ⥂ *7 rooms, 4 with bath* ♿ *In-room: no a/c* ⊟ *MC, V* ☾ *Closed Jan.* ❙◎❙ *BP* ✛ *H6.*

££ ⊡ **Ashdene House.** On a quiet residential street sits this Edwardian house, one of the city's first-class B&Bs. Country-style pine furniture and vividly colored fabrics decorate the guest rooms and common areas. The owners are particularly helpful in arranging tours and evening theater entertainment, and they will recommend local restaurants. There's ample parking on the street. The city center is 10 minutes away by bus. **Pros:** homemade breads at breakfast; spacious rooms. **Cons:** not within walking distance of the center. ✉ *23 Fountainhall Rd., The Grange* ☎ *0131/667–6026* ⊕ *www.ashdenehouse.com* ⥂ *5 rooms* ♿ *In-room: no a/c, Wi-Fi. In-hotel: parking (free)* ⊟ *AE, MC, V* ❙◎❙ *BP* ✛ *H6.*

££ ⊡ **Elmview.** Near Bruntsfield Links, the Elmview has a verdant location that completely justifies the name. Dating from the turn of the last century, the handsome stone house was designed by the celebrated architect, Sir Edwin Lutyens, as a "dignified holiday home." Guest rooms are spacious havens with furnishing that are homey but not too twee. The sociable breakfasts are great for sharing tips with your fellow travelers. They're healthy to boot, with refreshing organic and healthy alternatives. **Pros:** next to the historic golf course; superb breakfasts; helpful owners. **Cons:** books up in advance; doesn't cater to families with young children. ✉ *15 Glengyle Terr., Bruntsfield* ☎ *0131/228– 1973* ⊕ *www.elmview.co.uk* ⥂ *5 rooms* ♿ *In-room: no a/c, refrigerator, Wi-Fi. In-hotel: no children under 15* ⊟ *MC, V* ☾ *Closed Nov.–Apr.* ❙◎❙ *BP* ✛ *D6.*

££ ⊡ **Glenalmond House.** Longtime hoteliers Jimmy and Fiona Mackie are well schooled in making guests happy. There is nothing overly complicated about their latest venture, but the clean, spacious rooms, ample breakfasts, and friendly welcome are testament to the appeal of simplicity. **Pros:** knowledgeable owners; breakfast fit for champions. **Cons:** in a sleepy residential area that's a little bit of a walk to the New Town. ✉ *25 Mayfield Gardens, Southside* ☎ *0131/668–2392* ⊕ *www. glenalmondhouse.com* ⥂ *10 rooms* ♿ *In-room: no a/c, Wi-Fi (some). In-hotel: Wi-Fi hotspot, parking (free)* ⊟ *MC, V* ❙◎❙ *BP* ✛ *H6.*

££ ⊡ **94DR.** This is hardly your average guesthouse. Like owners Paul Lightfoot and John MacEwan—a self-described "high-octane" couple—94DR reaches for the stars with its stylish decor and contemporary trappings. Yet they never forget that their duty is making guests feel at home. Rooms are spacious and well appointed. The breakfasts are rightly famous. **Pros:** warm welcome; gay-friendly vibe; smashing breakfast. **Cons:** monochromatic color schemes; a long walk to the city center. ⊠ *94 Dalkeith Rd., SouthSide* ☎ *0131/662–9265* ⊕ *www.94dr. com* ↪ *7 rooms* ⚅ *In-room: DVD (some), Wi-Fi. In-hotel: Internet terminal, Wi-Fi hotspot, parking (free)* ▭ *AE, MC, V* ⏺ *BP* ✛ *H6.*

£££££   ⊡ **Prestonfield.** The cattle grazing on the hotel's 20-acre grounds let you know that you've entered a different world, even though you're five minutes by car from the Royal Mile. Inside this 1687 mansion, baroque opulence reigns in the well-restored public rooms; there are plenty of gilt treasures to relax among as you sip a whisky. Guest rooms are individually decorated, but mix antiques and the latest amenities for total indulgence. Borrow a laptop from the staff if you have to be in touch with the outside world. The romantic Rhubarb restaurant carries through the hedonistic note with superb Scottish fare, such as seared turbot with langoustine potatoes. **Pros:** eccentric grandeur; comfortable beds. **Cons:** slightly haphazard service; brooding decor can look gloomy. ⊠ *Priestfield Rd., Prestonfield* ☎ *0131/225–7800* ⊕ *www. prestonfield.com* ↪ *18 rooms, 5 suites* ⚅ *In-room: DVD, Wi-Fi. In-hotel: restaurant, bar, parking (free)* ▭ *AE, DC, MC, V* ⏺ *BP* ✛ *H6.*

££   ⊡ **Teviotdale House.** The lavish interior of this 1848 town house includes canopy beds and miles of festive fabrics. You'll be greeted at the door by the Thiebauds, your friendly hosts. This warm retreat sits on a tree-lined street away from the hustle and bustle of the city. If you need an urban fix, you can head downtown via a 10-minute bus ride. The hearty egg-and-sausage breakfasts are a pleasure. **Pros:** the kind of porridge that builds a nation; owners take pride in their hospitality. **Cons:** a long walk from the city center; not all bathrooms have tubs. ⊠ *53 Grange Loan, The Grange* ☎ *0131/667–4376* ⊕ *www.teviotdalehouse. com* ↪ *7 rooms* ⚅ *In-room: no a/c. In-hotel: Wi-Fi hotspot* ▭ *MC, V* ⏺ *BP* ✛ *H6.*

££   ⊡ **Thrums Hotel.** Inside this detached Georgian house are small, cozy rooms decorated with antique reproductions. Breakfast is served in a large, glass-enclosed conservatory. The staff is very welcoming and more than willing to advise you on what to see and do in and around Edinburgh. **Pros:** good value; neat and tidy. **Cons:** on a busy street; some rooms need refurbishing. ⊠ *14–15 Minto St., Newington,* ☎ *0131/667–5545* ⊕ *www.thrumshotel.com* ↪ *15 rooms* ⚅ *In-room: no a/c, Wi-Fi. In-hotel: parking (free)* ▭ *MC, V* ⏺ *BP* ✛ *H6.*

LEITH

Use the coordinate (✛ B2) at the end of each listing to locate a site on the corresponding map.

££   ⊡ **Ardmor House.** This low-key guesthouse combines the original features of a Victorian home with stylish contemporary furnishings. Rooms are fresh and modern, with an occasional antique adding some character. The friendly owner extends a warm welcome to all guests. There's a thoroughly efficient concierge service with a twist—lots of personal opinions and recommendations thrown in. **Pros:** warm and friendly owner; decorated with great style; gay-friendly environment. **Cons:** a bit out of the way; double room on the ground floor is tiny. ⊠ *74 Pilrig St., Leith*

☎ *0131/554–4944* ⊕ *www.ardmorhouse.com* ⇌ *5 rooms* ♿ *In-room: no a/c, Wi-Fi. In-hotel: Wi-Fi hotspot* ⊟ *AE, MC, V* ⍟⊙⍟ *BP* ✛ *G1.*

££ ⍟ **The Conifers.** This trim B&B in a red-sandstone town house north of the New Town offers simple, traditionally decorated rooms. Framed prints of old Edinburgh adorn the walls. The owner, Liz Fulton, has a wealth of knowledge about what to see and do in Edinburgh. **Pros:** nice mix of old and new; many original fittings; hearty breakfasts. **Cons:** a long walk to the city center; not all rooms have en-suite bathrooms. ⊠ *56 Pilrig St., Leith* ☎ *0131/554–5162* ⊕ *www.conifersguesthouse. com* ⇌ *4 rooms, 3 with bath* ♿ *In-room: no a/c. In-hotel: Wi-Fi hotspot* ⊟ *No credit cards* ⍟⊙⍟ *BP* ✛ *G1.*

££ ⍟ **Fraoch House.** This popular option manages to combine a homey feel and stylish decor without leaning too far in either direction. Traditional touches include complimentary tea and shortbread. The rooms, however, have a much more contemporary feel, meaning you can move from the old school to the new school without batting an eyelid. Breakfast is delicious, and you might find yourself addicted to the owner's porridge. **Pros:** a warm welcome; great DVD library. **Cons:** uphill walk to the city center. ⊠ *66 Pilrig St., Leith* ☎ *0131/554–1353* ⊕ *www.fraochhouse. com* ⇌ *9 rooms* ♿ *In-room: no a/c, DVD, Wi-Fi. In-hotel: Internet terminal, Wi-Fi hotspot, parking (free)* ⊟ *AE, MC, V* ⍟⊙⍟ *BP* ✛ *G1.*

£££ ⍟ **Malmaison.** Once a seamen's hostel, the Malmaison now draws a more refined clientele. A dramatic black and taupe color scheme prevails in the public areas. King-size beds, CD players, and satellite TV are standard in the bedrooms, which are decorated in a bold, modern style. The French theme of the hotel, which is part of a chic British chain, is emphasized in the bar and brasserie. **Pros:** impressive building; great location. **Cons:** bar can be rowdy at night; long way from the center of town. ⊠ *1 Tower Pl., Leith* ☎ *0131/468–5000* ⊕ *www. malmaison-edinburgh.com* ⇌ *100 rooms, 9 suites* ♿ *In-room: no a/c, Internet. In-hotel: restaurant, bar, gym, Wi-Fi hotspot, parking (free)* ⊟ *AE, DC, MC, V* ⍟⊙⍟ *BP* ✛ *G1.*

NIGHTLIFE AND THE ARTS

THE ARTS

Those who think Edinburgh's arts scene consists of just the elegiac wail of a bagpipe and the twang of a fiddle or two will be proved wrong by the hundreds of performing-arts options. The jewel in the crown, of course, is the famed Edinburgh International Festival, which now attracts the best in music, dance, theater, painting, and sculpture from all over the globe during three weeks from mid-August to early September. The *Scotsman* and *Herald*, Scotland's leading daily newspapers, carry listings and reviews in their arts pages every day, with special editions during the festival. Tickets are generally available from box offices in advance; in some cases they're also available from certain designated travel agents or at the door, although concerts by national orchestras often sell out long before the day of the performance.

DANCE

The Scottish Ballet performs at the **Festival Theatre** (⊠ *13–29 Nicolson St., Old Town* ☎ *0131/529–6000* ⊕ *www.eft.co.uk*) when in Edinburgh. Visiting contemporary dance companies perform in the **Royal Lyceum** (⊠ *Grindlay St., West End* ☎ *0131/248–4848* ⊕ *www.lyceum.org.uk*).

FESTIVALS

The **Edinburgh Festival Fringe** (⊠ *Edinburgh Festival Fringe Office, 180 High St., Old Town* ☎ *0131/226–0026* ⊕ *www.edfringe.com*) presents many theatrical and musical events, some by amateur groups (you have been warned), and is more of a grab bag than the official festival. Many events are free but some do require tickets; prices start at £2 and go up to £15. During festival time—roughly the same as the International Festival—it's possible to arrange your own entertainment program from morning to midnight and beyond, if you don't feel overwhelmed by the variety available.

☾ The **Edinburgh International Book Festival** (⊠ *Charlotte Sq. Gardens, New Town* ☎ *0131/718–5666* ⊕ *www.edbookfest.co.uk*), a two-week-long event in August, pulls together a heady mix of the biggest-selling and the most challenging authors from around the world and gets them talking about their work in a magnificent tent village. Workshops for would-be writers and children are hugely popular.

Fodor'sChoice The **Edinburgh International Festival** (⊠ *The Hub, Edinburgh Festival Cen-*
★   *tre, Castlehill, Old Town* ☎ *0131/473–2009 information, 0131/473–2000 tickets* ⊕ *www.eif.co.uk*), the flagship arts event of the year, attracts performing artists of international caliber to a celebration of music, dance, drama, and artwork. Advance information, programs, tickets, and reservations are available from the impressive Victorian Gothic church building renamed the Hub. Tickets range from £7 to £60, depending on the event. The festival runs from mid-August through early September.

The **Edinburgh International Film Festival** (⊠ *Edinburgh Film Festival Office, 88 Lothian Rd., West End* ☎ *0131/228–4051* ⊕ *www.edfilmfest. org.uk*) has grown into one of Europe's foremost film festivals. It is held in late June.

The **Edinburgh International Science Festival** (⊠ *The Hub, Castlehill, Edinburgh* ☎ *0131/553–0320* ⊕ *www.sciencefestival.co.uk*), held around Easter each year, aims to make science accessible, interesting, but above all fun. Children's events turn science into entertainment and are especially popular. Purchase tickets at the Hub.

★ The **Edinburgh Military Tattoo** (⊠ *Edinburgh Military Tattoo Office, 32 Market St., Old Town* ☎ *0131/225–1188 or 08707/555–1188* ⊕ *www. edintattoo.co.uk*) may not be art, but it is certainly Scottish culture. It's sometimes confused with the Edinburgh International Festival, partly because both events take place in August (though the Tattoo starts and finishes a week earlier). This celebration of martial music and skills with bands, gymnastics, and stunt motorcycle teams is on the castle esplanade, and the dramatic backdrop augments the spectacle. Dress warmly for late-evening performances. Even if it rains, the show most definitely goes on.

CLOSE UP

Festivals in Edinburgh

Walking around Edinburgh in late July, you'll likely feel the first vibrations of the earthquake that is festival time, which shakes the city throughout August and into September. You may hear reference to an "Edinburgh Festival," but this is really an umbrella term for five separate festivals all taking place around the same time. For an overview, check out ⊕ www.edinburghfestivals.co.uk.

Edinburgh International Festival. The best-known and oldest of the city's festivals is the Edinburgh International Festival, founded in 1947 when Europe was recovering from World War II. In recent years the festival has drawn as many as 400,000 people to Edinburgh, with more than 100 acts by world-renowned music, opera, theater, and dance performers, filling all the major venues in the city. Tickets for the festival go on sale in April, and many sell out within the month. However, you may still be able to purchase tickets, which range from £6 to £60, during the festival.

Edinburgh Festival Fringe. If the Edinburgh International Festival is the parent of British festivals, then the Edinburgh Festival Fringe is its unruly child. The Festival Fringe started in 1947 at the same time as the International Festival, when eight companies that were not invited to perform in the latter decided to attend anyway. Knowing there would be an audience,

these companies found small, local theaters to host them. By 2005 there were 1,800 shows and 27,000 performances of those shows at the Fringe, making it the largest festival of its kind in the world. Its events range from the brilliant to the impossibly mundane, badly performed, and downright tacky.

While the Fringe is going on, most of the city center becomes one huge performance area, with fire-eaters, sword swallowers, unicyclists, jugglers, string quartets, jazz groups, stand-up comics, and magicians all thronging into High Street and Princes Street. Every available theater and pseudo performance space is utilized—church halls, community centers, parks, sports fields, putting greens, and nightclubs. In 1954 the Edinburgh Festival Fringe Society was formed, and it oversees everything from ticket sales to publicity.

Festivals for all interests. Edinburgh festival time can fill almost any artistic need. Besides the International Festival and Festival Fringe, look for the Edinburgh Jazz and Blues Festival, the International Book Festival, and the Military Tattoo, which includes reenactments of historic events, military marching bands, Highland dancing, and more. The Edinburgh International Film Festival used to take place in August, but it moved to June when the calendar is less congested.

Edinburgh Jazz and Blues Festival (✉ 89 Giles St., Leith ☎ 0131/467–5200 ⊕ www.edinburghjazzfestival.co.uk), held in August, attracts international top performers and brings local enthusiasts out of their living rooms and into the pubs and clubs to listen and play.

FILM

The **Cameo** (✉ *38 Home St., Tollcross* ☎ *0131/228–4141*) has one large and two small auditoriums, which are extremely comfortable, plus a bar and late-night specials. Apart from cinema chains, Edinburgh has the excellent three-screen **Filmhouse** (✉ *88 Lothian Rd., West End* ☎ *0131/228–2688 box office*), the best venue for modern, foreign-language, offbeat, or simply less-commercial films.

MUSIC

The **Festival Theatre** (✉ *13–29 Nicolson St., Old Town* ☎ *0131/529–6000*) hosts performances by the Scottish Ballet and the Scottish Opera. The **Playhouse** (✉ *Greenside Pl., East End* ☎ *0131/524–3333*) leans toward popular artists and musicals. The intimate **Queen's Hall** (✉ *Clerk St., Old Town* ☎ *0131/668–2019*) hosts small recitals. **Usher Hall** (✉ *Lothian Rd., West End* ☎ *0131/229–7937*) is Edinburgh's grandest venue, and international performers and orchestras, including the Royal Scottish National Orchestra, perform here.

THEATER

MODERN   The **Theatre Workshop** (✉ *34 Hamilton Pl., Stockbridge* ☎ *0131/225–7942*) hosts fringe events during the Edinburgh Festival and modern, community-based theater year-round. It's wheelchair accessible. The **Traverse Theatre** (✉ *10 Cambridge St., West End* ☎ *0131/228–1404*) has developed a solid reputation for new, stimulating Scottish plays, performed in a specially designed flexible space.

TRADITIONAL   Edinburgh has three main theaters. The **Festival Theatre** (✉ *13–29 Nicolson St., Old Town* ☎ *0131/529–6000*) presents opera and ballet but also the occasional excellent touring play. The **King's** (✉ *2 Leven St., Tollcross* ☎ *0131/529–6000*) has a program of contemporary and traditional dramatic works. The **Royal Lyceum** (✉ *Grindlay St., West End* ☎ *0131/248–4848*) shows traditional plays and contemporary works, often transferred from or prior to their London West End showings.

On the eastern outskirts of Edinburgh, the **Brunton Theatre** (✉ *Ladywell Way, Musselburgh* ☎ *0131/665–2240*) presents a regular program of repertory, touring, and amateur performances. The **Church Hill Theatre** (✉ *Morningside Rd., Morningside* ☎ *0131/447–7597*) hosts productions by local dramatic societies that are of a high standard. The **Playhouse** (✉ *Greenside Pl., East End* ☎ *0131/524–3333*) hosts mostly popular artists and musicals.

NIGHTLIFE

The nightlife scene in Edinburgh is vibrant—whatever you're looking for, you'll most certainly find it here, and you won't have to go far. Expect old-style pubs as well as cutting-edge bars and clubs. Live music pours out of many watering holes on weekends, particularly folk, blues, and jazz. Well-known artists perform at some of the larger venues.

The List and *The Skinny* carry the most up-to-date details about cultural events. *The List* is available at newsstands throughout the city, while *The Skinny* is free and can be picked up at a number of pubs, clubs, and

CLOSE UP

Hogmanay: Hello, New Year

In Scotland, New Year's Eve is called Hogmanay, and celebrations continue the next day with customs such as "first-footing"—visiting your neighbors with gifts that include whisky, all with the purpose of bringing good fortune. It's so important that January 2 as well as January 1 is a holiday in Scotland; the rest of the United Kingdom settles for recuperating on January 1. Other places in Scotland have public celebrations, but Edinburgh's multiday event at sites in the heart of town is famous throughout Europe and beyond, with something for everyone. Yes, it's still winter and cold, but joining the festivities with up to 80,000 other people can be memorable.

Edinburgh's Hogmanay extends over five days with spectacles and performances (music, dance, and more); the yearly-changing lineup includes many free events. Festivities featuring fire add a dramatic motif; buildings may open for rare night tours; a ceilidh offers dancing outdoors to traditional music; and family concerts and serious discussions during the day round out the agenda. At the heart of Hogmanay, though, is the evening street party on New Year's Eve, with different music stages, food and drink (and people do drink), and the heart-lifting—despite the cold—sight of glowing fireworks over Edinburgh Castle and the singing of "Auld Lang Syne," written by Scotland's own Robert Burns.

A little planning is in order. Costs vary: entering the New Year's Eve street party costs around £10, and certain entertainments that night will cost more (a concert may be £30 or so, including the street party fee), but an outdoor fire installation on December 30, say, might be free. Book rooms ahead. Prices may go up, but look for multi-day packages; it's also easy to take buses outside the center. Obvious but essential is warmth: crazy hats and the bundled-up look are de rigueur. Check out ⊕ www.edinburghshogmanay.com for full details, and have a happy Hogmanay!

shops around town. The *Herald* and *Scotsman* newspapers are good for reviews and notices of upcoming events throughout Scotland.

BARS AND PUBS

Edinburgh's 400-odd pubs are a study in themselves. In the eastern and northern districts of the city you can find some grim, inhospitable-looking places that proclaim that drinking is no laughing matter. But throughout Edinburgh many pubs have deliberately traded in their old spit-and-sawdust images for atmospheric revivals of the warm, oak-paneled, leather-chaired howffs of a more leisurely age. Most pubs and bars are open weekdays and Saturday from 11 AM to midnight, and from 12:30 to midnight on Sunday.

OLD TOWN **Black Bo's** (⊠ *57–61 Blackfriars St., Old Town* ☎ *0131/557–6136*), one of the coziest places in town, has a decent selection of beers and an eclectic soundtrack.

★ The **Canons' Gait** (⊠ *232 Canongate, Old Town* ☎ *0131/556–4481*) sells Edinburgh's own special brew, Innis & Gunn, aged in American white-oak barrels. It also has live jazz and blues on Thursday and Saturday nights.

NEW TOWN **Abbotsford** (⊠ *3 Rose St., New Town* ☎ *0131/225–5276*) has lots of Victorian atmosphere, an ever-changing selection of five real ales, and bar lunches. **The Basement** (⊠ *10A–12A Broughton St., New Town* ☎ *0131/557–0097*), a longtime pre-club favorite, pumps out a great soundtrack for a young crowd. The Hawaiian-shirted bar staff adds to the general amiability. **Blue Blazer** (⊠ *2 Spittal St., West End* ☎ *0131/ 229–5030* has one of the city's finest selections of real ale and live folk music. **Café Royal Circle Bar** (⊠ *19 W. Regent St., New Town* ☎ *0131/ 556–1884*) has beautiful Victorian tiled murals, oysters on the half shell, and leather booths. **Cask and Barrel** (⊠ *115 Broughton St., New Town* ☎ *0131/556–3132*) is a spacious, busy pub in which to sample hand-pulled ales at the horseshoe bar, reflected in a collection of brewery mirrors. **Cumberland Bar** (⊠ *1–3 Cumberland St., New Town* ☎ *0131/558–3134*) has eight ales on tap, wood trim, typical pub mirrors, and a comfy sitting room.

★ **Guildford Arms** (⊠ *1 W. Register St., east end of Princes St., New Town* ☎ *0131/556–4312*) is worth a visit for its interior alone: ornate plasterwork, cornices, friezes, and wood paneling form the backdrop for some excellent draft ales, including Orkney Dark Island. **Joseph Pearce's** (⊠ *23 Elm Row, New Town* ☎ *0131/556–4140*, one of four Swedish-owned pubs, has a continental feel to it courtesy of the cosmopolitan staff and the varied selection of beers and spirits.

Kay's Bar (⊠ *39 Jamaica St., New Town* ☎ *0131/225–1858*), a friendly, comfortable spot, is a good place for a bar lunch. Don't miss the selection of 50 single-malt whiskies in addition to the real ales on draft. **Milne's Bar** (⊠ *35 Hanover St., New Town* ☎ *0131/225–6738*) is known as the poets' pub because of its popularity with the Edinburgh literati. Pies and baked potatoes go well with seven real ales and varying guest beers (beers not of the house brewery). Victorian advertisements and photos of old Edinburgh give the place an old-time feel. Tucked away but well worth seeking out, **Star Bar** (⊠ *1 Northumberland Pl., New Town* ☎ *0131/539–8070*) has a nice beer garden, table soccer, and a rarity—a good jukebox.

With more than 80 whiskies for sale, **Teuchters** (⊠ *26 William St., West End* ☎ *0131/225–2973)* is a fine place to sit back and enjoy a dram. **Tonic** (⊠ *34A Castle St., New Town* ☎ *0131/225–6431*), is a stylish basement bar with bouncy stools and comfy sofas, pale wood, and chrome—and more than 200 cocktails from which to choose.

SOUTH SIDE **Cloisters** (⊠ *26 Brougham St., Tollcross* ☎ *0131/221–9997*) prides itself on the absence of music, gaming machines, and any other modern pub gimmicks; it specializes instead in real ales, malt whiskies, and good food, all at reasonable prices. **Leslie's Bar** (⊠ *45 Ratcliffe Terr., South Side* ☎ *0131/667–7205*) is an unspoiled Victorian bar near the hotels and guesthouses of Newington, with a good range of traditional Scottish ales and whiskies. **Under The Stairs** (⊠ *3A Merchant St., South Side* ☎ *0131/466–8550*) is situated, as you might guess from the name, below street level. This cozy place does great bar food.

LEITH The **Cameo Bar** (⊠ *23 Commercial St., Leith* ☎ *0131/554–9999*), is a bright and airy haven for the young and hip. **Malt and Hops** (⊠ *45 The*

Shore, Leith ☎ *0131/555–0083*), more than 260 years old, has its own cask ales and ghost, and overlooks the waterfront. **Robbie's** (✉ *367 Leith Walk, Leith* ☎ *0131/554–6850*) is a classic pub and a great place for catching big sporting events.

CEILIDHS AND SCOTTISH EVENINGS

For those who feel a trip to Scotland is not complete without hearing the "Braes of Yarrow" or "Auld Robin Gray," several hotels present traditional Scottish-music evenings in the summer season. Head for the **Thistle King James Hotel** (✉ *107 Leith St., New Town* ☎ *0131/556–0111*) to see *Jamie's Scottish Evening,* an extravaganza of Scottish song, tartan, plaid, and bagpipes that takes place nightly. The cost is £53, including a three-course dinner.

COMEDY CLUBS

The Edinburgh Fringe Festival has become one of the world's most famous events for comedy. But throughout the year you can laugh until your sides split at the **Stand** (✉ *5 York Pl., East End* ☎ *0131/558–7272*), which hosts names, up-and-coming acts and, of course, central to any comedy performance, the audience.

FOLK CLUBS

You can usually find folk musicians performing in pubs throughout Edinburgh, although there's been a decline in the live-music scene because of dwindling profits and the predominance of popular theme bars.

The friendly "folk at the Oak" make the **Royal Oak** (✉ *1 Infirmary St., Old Town* ☎ *0131/557–2976*) so special. This cozy bar has live blues and folk most nights. **Whistle Binkies Pub** (✉ *4–6 South Bridge, Old Town* ☎ *0131/557–5114*), a friendly basement bar with great rock and folk music every night of the week, is the place for a bit of *wellie* (volume, energy).

GAY AND LESBIAN NIGHTLIFE

There's a burgeoning gay and lesbian scene in Edinburgh, and the city has many predominantly gay clubs, bars, and cafés. However, don't expect the scene to be as open as London, New York, or even Glasgow. The *List* and the *Skinny* have sections that focus on the gay and lesbian venues.

Blue Moon Café (✉ *36 Broughton St., New Town* ☎ *0131/556–2788*), Edinburgh's longest running gay café, is still the best. **CC Blooms** (✉ *23–24 Greenside Pl., New Town* ☎ *0131/556–9331*), modern, colorful, and open nightly, plays a mix of musical styles. Once a month there's an icebreaker evening for those new to the gay scene. More refined than the other gay spots, **GHQ** (✉ *4 Picardy Pl., New Town* ☎ *0845/166–6024*) hosts a number of the city's best DJs. The **Regent** (✉ *2 Montrose Terr., Abbeyhill* ☎ *0131/661–8198*) has a friendly vibe and a good selection of ales.

NIGHTCLUBS

For the young and footloose, many Edinburgh dance clubs offer reduced admission and/or less expensive drinks for early revelers. Consult the *List* for special events.

The **Bongo Club** (✉ *37 Holyrood Rd., Old Town* ☎ *0131/558–7604* ⊕ *www.thebongoclub.co.uk*) hosts some of the city's most acclaimed club nights and gigs by touring musicians.

Cabaret Voltaire (✉ *36–38 Blair St., Old Town* ☎ *0131/220–6176* ⊕ *www.thecabaretvoltaire.com*), one of the city's best loved clubs, hosts everything from cheesy rave-ups to cutting-edge bands and DJs.

The **Opal Lounge** (✉ *51A George St., New Town* ☎ *0131/226–2275*) is a casual but stylish nightspot favored by Prince William while he attended university.

Po Na Na Souk Bar (✉ *43B Frederick St., New Town* ☎ *0131/226–2224*) has a cool but cozy atmosphere, and a distinctly North African atmosphere, with its secluded booths and Bedouin furnishings. The music is a mix of funk, hip-hop, R&B, house, and disco.

SPORTS AND THE OUTDOORS

BICYCLING

Edinburgh is not the friendliest city for bikes; there's a lot of traffic, even on weekends. The tourist information center can point you toward some quieter routes just beyond the city center. Rentals cost £75 per week for a 21-speed or mountain bike. Daily rates (24 hours) are about £16, with half days costing £12. **Bike Trax** (✉ *11–13 Lochrin Pl., Tollcross* ☎ *0131/228–6633*) has a variety of rental bikes. **Edinburgh Cycle Tours** (☎ *0796/644–7206*) leads guided bicycle tours of the city. A three-hour tour runs twice a day and costs £15, which includes bike rental, a helmet, and waterproof gear.

GOLF

For the courses listed below, SSS indicates the "standard scratch score," the score a scratch golfer could achieve in ideal conditions. VisitScotland provides a free leaflet on golf in Scotland, available from the **Edinburgh and Scotland Information Centre** (✉ *3 Princes St., East End* ☎ *0131/473–3800* ⊕ *www.edinburgh.org*), or check online at http:// golf.visitscotland.com. *See Chapter 12 for an overview of the best golf near the capital.*

Braids. This 18-hole course was founded in 1897 and laid out over several small hills 3 mi south of Edinburgh. The 9-hole course opened in 2003. ✉ *Braids Hill Rd., Braidburn* ☎ *0131/447–6666* ⊕ *www.braidhillsgolf. co.uk* 🏌 *Course 1: 18 holes, 5,865 yds, SSS 67. Course 2: 9 holes.*

Bruntsfield Links. Several tournaments are held each year at this championship course, opened in 1898 a couple miles northwest of the city. ✉ *32 Barnton Ave., Davidson's Mains* ☎ *0131/336–4050* ⊕ *www. brruntsfieldlinks.co.uk* 🏌 *18 holes, 6,407 yds, SSS 71.*

Duddingston. You can find this public parkland course, founded in 1895, 2 mi east of the city. ✉ *Duddingston Rd. W, Duddingston* ☎ *0131/661–7688* ⊕ *www.duddingstongolfclub.co.uk 18 holes, 6,525 yds, SSS 72.*

Liberton. This public parkland course was built in 1920, 4 mi south of the city. ✉ *Kingston Grange, 297 Gilmerton Rd., Liberton* ☎ *0131/664–3009* ⊕ *www.libertongc.co.uk* 🏌 *18 holes, 5,344 yds, SSS 67.*

Lothianburn. You can see good views of the Midlothian countryside from this hillside course, founded in 1893, 6 mi south of the city. ✉ *Biggar Rd., Fairmilehead* ☎ *0131/445–2288* ⊕ *www.lothianburngc.co.uk* ⚑ *18 holes, 5,692 yds, SSS 69.*

Murrayfield. Only five minutes from the city center, this heathland-style course is kept in fine condition and commands outstanding views over Edinburgh ✉ *43 Murrayfield Rd., Murrayfield* ☎ *0131/337–3478* ⊕ *www.murrayfieldgolfclub.co.uk* ⚑ *18 holes, 5,551 yds, SSS 69.*

RUGBY

At **Murrayfield Stadium** (✉ *Roseburn Terr., Murrayfield* ☎ *0131/346–5000*), home of the Scottish Rugby Union, Scotland's international rugby matches are played in early spring and fall. During that time of year, crowds of good-humored rugby fans from all over the world add greatly to the sense of excitement in the streets of Edinburgh.

SOCCER

Like Glasgow, Edinburgh is soccer-mad, and there's an intense rivalry between the city's two professional teams. Remember, the game is called football in Britain. The **Heart of Midlothian ("Hearts") Football Club** (☎ *0871/663–1874*) plays in maroon and white and is based at Tynecastle. The green-bedecked **Hibernian ("Hibs") Club** (☎ *0131/661–2159*) plays its home matches at Easter Road.

SHOPPING

Despite its renown as a shopping street, **Princes Street** in the New Town may disappoint some visitors with its dull modern architecture, average chain stores, and fast-food outlets. One block north of Princes Street, **Rose Street** has many smaller specialty shops; part of the street is a pedestrian zone, so it's a pleasant place to browse. The shops on **George Street** tend to be fairly upscale. London names, such as Laura Ashley and Penhaligons, are prominent, though some of the older independent stores continue to do good business.

The streets crossing George Street—Hanover, Frederick, and Castle—are also worth exploring. **Dundas Street,** the northern extension of Hanover Street, beyond Queen Street Gardens, has several antiques shops. **Thistle Street,** originally George Street's "back lane," or service area, has several boutiques and more antiques shops. As may be expected, many shops along the **Royal Mile** sell what may be politely or euphemistically described as tourist-ware—whiskies, tartans, and tweeds. Careful exploration, however, will reveal some worthwhile establishments. Shops here also cater to highly specialized interests and hobbies.

Close to the castle end of the Royal Mile, just off George IV Bridge, is **Victoria Street,** with specialty shops grouped in a small area. Follow the tiny West Bow to **Grassmarket** for more specialty stores. North of Princes Street, on the way to the Royal Botanic Garden Edinburgh, is **Stockbridge,** an oddball shopping area of some charm, particularly on St. Stephen Street. To get here, walk north down Frederick Street and Howe Street, away from Princes Street, then turn left onto North West Circus Place. **Stafford and William streets** form a small, upscale shopping area in a Georgian setting. Walk to the west end of Princes Street and then along its continuation, Shandwick Place, then turn right onto Stafford Street. William Street crosses Stafford halfway down.

ARCADES AND SHOPPING CENTERS

Like most large towns, Edinburgh has succumbed to the fashion for under-one-roof shopping. **Cameron Toll** (⊠ *Bottom of Dalkeith Rd., Mayfield*), in the city's South Side, caters to local residents, with food stores and High Street brand names. The **Ocean Terminal** (⊠ *Ocean Dr., Leith*) houses a large collection of shops as well as bars and eateries. Here you can also visit the former royal yacht *Britannia*. The **St. James Centre** (⊠ *Princes St., East End*) has Dorothy Perkins, HMV, and numerous other chain stores. **Gyle Shopping Centre** (⊠ *Gyle Ave., near airport, Gyle*) is like a typical U.S.–style shopping mall. Here you can find the usual High Street brand names, including a huge Marks & Spencer.

DEPARTMENT STORES

In contrast to other major cities, Edinburgh has few true department stores. If you plan on a morning or a whole day of wandering from department to department, trying on beautiful clothes, buying crystal or china, or stocking up on Scottish food specialties, with a break for lunch at an in-store restaurant, Jenners is your best bet.

★ **Aitken and Niven** (⊠ *6 Selcon Rd., Morningside* ☎ *0131/477–3922*) is an Edinburgh institution: a small department store where the well-heeled come to buy upscale clothing, shoes, and accessories. **Harvey Nichols** (⊠ *30–34 St. Andrew Sq., New Town* ☎ *0131/524–8350*) is the local outpost of the high-style British chain. **Jenners** (⊠ *48 Princes St., New Town* ☎ *0131/225–2442*) specializes in traditional china and glassware, as well as Scottish clothing (upscale tweeds and tartans). Its justly famous food hall sells shortbreads and Dundee cakes (a light fruit cake with a distinctive pattern of split almonds arranged in circles on the top), honeys, and marmalades, as well as high-quality groceries. **John Lewis** (⊠ *69 St. James Centre, East End* ☎ *0131/556–9121*), part of a U.K.–wide chain, specializes in furniture and household goods but also stocks designer clothes. **Marks & Spencer** (⊠ *54 Princes St., New Town* ☎ *0131/225–2301*) sells well-priced, stylish everyday clothes and accessories. You can also buy food items and household goods here.

SPECIALTY SHOPS

ANTIQUES

Antiques dealers tend to cluster together, so it may be easiest to concentrate on one area—St. Stephen Street, Bruntsfield Place, Causewayside, or Dundas Street, for example—if you're short on time.

Courtyard Antiques (⊠ *108A Causewayside, Sciennes* ☎ *0131/662–9008*) stocks a mixture of high-quality antiques, toys, and militaria.

BOOKS, PAPER, MAPS, AND GAMES

As a university city and cultural center, Edinburgh is endowed with excellent bookstores.

Near the Grassmarket, **Armchair Books** (⊠ 72–74 W. Port, Old Town ☎ 0131/229–5927) is a chaotic secondhand bookshop heaving with tomes from your youth. **Beyond Words** (⊠ 42–44 Cockburn St., Old Town ☎ 0131/226–6636) has an awe-inspiring selection of photography books. **Carson Clark Gallery** (⊠ 181–183 Canongate, Old Town ☎ 0131/556–4710) specializes in antique maps, sea charts, and prints.

CLOTHING BOUTIQUES

Edinburgh is home to several top-quality designers—although, it must be said, probably not as many as are found in Glasgow, Scotland's fashion center—some of whom make a point of using Scottish materials in their creations.

Bill Baber (⊠ 66 Grassmarket, Old Town ☎ 0131/225–3249) is one of the most imaginative of the many Scottish knitwear designers, and a long way from the conservative pastel woolies sold at some of the large mill shops. The **Extra Inch** (⊠ 12 William St., West End ☎ 0131/226–3303) stocks a full selection of clothes in European sizes 16 (U.S. size 14) and up.

Herman Brown's (⊠ 151 W. Port, West End ☎ 0131/228–2589) is a secondhand clothing store where cashmere twinsets and classic luxe labels are sought and found. If you don't make it up to the main shop in Skye, **Ragamuffin** (⊠ 278 Canongate, Old Town ☎ 0131/557–6007) sells the funkiest and brightest knits produced in Scotland.

JEWELRY

Clarksons (⊠ 87 W. Bow, Old Town ☎ 0131/225–8141), a family firm, handcrafts a unique collection of jewelry, including Celtic styles. The jewelry here is made with silver, gold, platinum, and precious gems, with a particular emphasis on diamonds. **Hamilton and Inches** (⊠ 87 George St., New Town ☎ 0131/225–4898), established in 1866, is a silver- and goldsmith worth visiting not only for its modern and antique gift possibilities, but also for its late-Georgian interior, designed by David Bryce in 1834—all columns and elaborate plasterwork. **Joseph Bonnar** (⊠ 72 Thistle St., New Town ☎ 0131/226–2811), tucked behind George Street, has Scotland's largest collection of antique jewelry, including 19th-century agate jewels.

LINENS, TEXTILES, AND HOME FURNISHINGS

And So To Bed (⊠ 30 Dundas St., New Town ☎ 0131/652–3700) has a wonderful selection of embroidered and embellished bed linens, cushion covers, and the like. **In House** (⊠ 28 Howe St., New Town ☎ 0131/225–2888) sells designer furnishings and collectibles at the forefront of modern design for the home. **Studio One** (⊠ 10–16 Stafford St., New Town ☎ 0131/226–5812) has a well-established and comprehensive inventory of gift articles.

OUTDOOR SPORTS GEAR

Tiso (✉ *123–125 Rose St., New Town* ☎ *0131/225–9486* ✉ *41 Commercial St., Leith* ☎ *0131/554–0804*) stocks outdoor clothing, boots, and jackets ideal for hiking or camping in the Highlands or the islands.

SCOTTISH SPECIALTIES

If you want to identify a particular tartan, several shops on Princes Street will be pleased to assist. The **Clan Tartan Centre** (✉ *70–74 Bangor Rd., Leith* ☎ *0131/553–5516*) has a database containing details of all known tartans, plus information on clan histories. At the **Edinburgh Old Town Weaving Company** (✉ *555 Castlehill, Old Town* ☎ *0131/226–1555*), you can watch and even talk to the cloth and tapestry weavers as they work, then buy the products. The company can also provide information on clan histories, and, if your name is a relatively common English or Scottish one, tell you which tartan you're entitled to wear. **Geoffrey (Tailor) Highland Crafts** (✉ *57–59 High St., Old Town* ☎ *0131/557–0256*) can clothe you in full Highland dress, with kilts made in its own workshops.

SIDE TRIPS FROM EDINBURGH

If you stand on an Edinburgh eminence—the castle ramparts, Arthur's Seat, Corstorphine Hill—you can plan a few Lothian excursions without even the aid of a map. The Lothians is the collective name given to the swath of countryside south of the Firth of Forth and surrounding Edinburgh. Many courtly and aristocratic families lived here, and the region still has the castles and mansions to prove it. The rich arrived and with them came deer parks, gardens in the French style, and Lothian's fame as a seed plot for Lowland gentility. Although the region has always provided rich pickings for historians, it also used to offer even richer pickings for coal miners—for a century after the start of the industrial revolution, gentle streams in fairy glens (so the old writings describe them) steamed and stank with pollution. Although some black spots still remain, most of the rural countryside is once again a fitting setting for excursions. When the coal miners left, admirals came here to retire, and today the area happily holds many delights.

The 70-mi round-trip exploration of the historic houses and castles of West Lothian and the Forth Valley, and territory north of the River Forth, can be accomplished in a full day with select stops, or you can just pick one or two. Stretching east to the sea and south to the Lowlands from Edinburgh, Midlothian and East Lothian are no more than one hour from Edinburgh. The inland river valleys, hills, and castles of Midlothian and East Lothian's delightful waterfronts, dunes, and golf links offer a taste of Scotland close to the capital.

WHAT IT COSTS IN POUNDS					
	£	££	£££	££££	£££££
RESTAURANTS	under £10	£11–£14	£15–£19	£20–£25	over £25
HOTELS	under £70	£70–£120	£121–£160	£161–£220	over £220

Restaurant prices are for a main course at dinner. Hotel prices are for two people in a standard double room in high season, generally including 17.5% V.A.T. These are different from the Edinburgh city prices.

WEST LOTHIAN AND THE FORTH VALLEY

West Lothian comprises a good bit of Scotland's central belt. The River Forth snakes across a widening floodplain on its descent from the Highlands, and by the time it reaches the western extremities of Edinburgh, it has already passed below the mighty Forth bridges and become a broad estuary. Castles and stately homes sprout thickly on both sides of the Forth.

GETTING HERE AND AROUND

BUS TRAVEL First Bus services link most of this area, but working out a detailed itinerary by bus.

CAR TRAVEL What follows is a route for the main sights in this section. Leave Edinburgh by Queensferry Road—the A90—and follow signs for the Forth Bridge. At Cramond take the slip road, B924, for South Queensferry, watching for signs to Dalmeny House. After turning right onto A904, follow signs for Hopetoun House, House of the Binns, and Blackness Castle. Join the M9, which will speed you west, and look for signs leading to the Falkirk Wheel, southwest of the motorway. Then return to the M9 and cross the Forth.

At this point you'll leave the industrial northern shore of the Forth and enter the Ochil Hills, which you can explore by following the A91 east at Alva; the road continues to Dollar, where you should follow signs to Castle Campbell. From the castle, retrace your route to A91 and turn left. A few minutes outside Dollar, follow A823 through Powmill (follow the signs for Dunfermline); turn right off A823, following the signs for Saline, and then join the A907. Take the B9037 to Culcross and east to join the A994, which leads to Dunfermline. From here follow the Edinburgh signs to the A823 and return via North Queensferry and the Forth Road Bridge.

TRAIN TRAVEL Dalmeny, Linlithgow, and Dunfermline all have rail stations and can be reached from Edinburgh stations.

VISITOR INFORMATION

The Mill Trail Visitor Centre, at Alva, can provide information on the region's textile establishments as well as a Mill Trail brochure, which directs you to mill shops selling bargain woolen and tweed goods.

ESSENTIALS

Bus Contacts First (☎ 0870/872-7271 ⊕ www.firstgroup.com).

Train Contacts **National Rail Enquiries** (☎ 08457/484950 ⊕ www.nationalrail.co.uk).

Visitor Information **Mill Trail Visitor Centre** (✉ W. Stirling St., Alva ☎ 01259/763100).

CRAMOND
4 mi west of Edinburgh.

At this compact coastal settlement, you can watch summer sunsets upriver of where the Almond joins the Firth of Forth. The river's banks, once the site of mills and industrial works, now have pleasant, leafy walks.

WHERE TO EAT

££ ✕ **Cramond Inn.** After a bracing walk along the seaside promenade, stop
BRITISH by this dark, 17th-century village inn—once the haunt of Robert Louis Stevenson—for a pint at the bar or a selection from the small but varied pub menu. Among the options are staples such as homemade fish cakes and burgers. ✉ *Cramond Glebe Rd.* ☎ *0131/336–2035* ☰ *MC, V.*

DALMENY HOUSE
6 mi west of Edinburgh.

The first of the stately houses clustered on the western edge of Edinburgh, **Dalmeny House** is the home of the earl and countess of Rosebery. This 1815 Tudor Gothic mansion displays among its sumptuous contents the best of the family's famous collection of 18th-century French furniture. Highlights include the library, the Napoléon Room, the Vincennes and Sevres porcelain collections, and the drawing room, with its tapestries and intricately wrought French furniture. Admission is only by guided tour. ✉ *B924, by South Queensferry* ☎ *0131/331–1888* ⊕ *www.dalmeny.co.uk* 🎫 *£5* ☻ *May and June, Sun.–Tues. 2–5.*

SOUTH QUEENSFERRY
7 mi west of Edinburgh.

This pleasant little waterside community, a former ferry port, is completely dominated by the **Forth Bridges,** dramatic structures of contrasting architecture that span the Firth of Forth at this historic crossing point.

EXPLORING

★ The **Forth Rail Bridge** was opened in 1890 and at the time hailed as the eighth wonder of the world, at 2,765 yards long; on a hot summer's day it expands by about another yard. Its neighbor is the 1,993-yard-long **Forth Road Bridge,** in operation since 1964.

WHERE TO EAT

£££ ✕ **The Boat House.** Scotland's natural larder is used to sublime effect
SEAFOOD at this romantic restaurant on the banks of the Forth. Seafood is the star of the show, and chef Paul Steward lets it shine in all its glory in imaginative yet unfussy recipes. If you want a less formal affair, the bistro and bar next door has a friendly buzz and the food is predictably stellar. ✉ *22 High St., South Queensferry* ☎ *0131/331–5429* ⊕ *www.theboathouse-sq.co.uk* ☰ *AE, D, MC, V.*

2

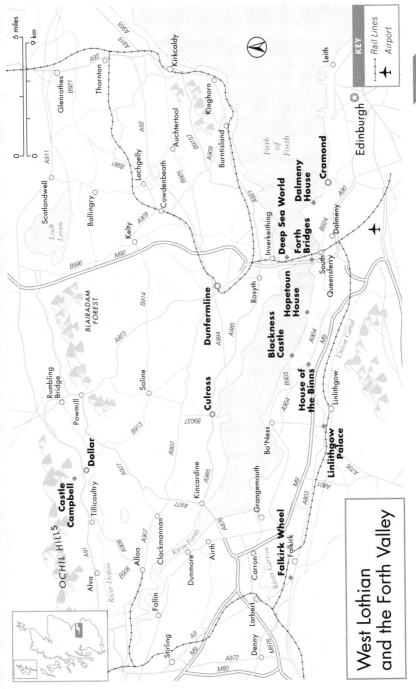

West Lothian and the Forth Valley

KEY
++ Rail Lines
✈ Airport

HOPETOUN HOUSE
10 mi west of Edinburgh.

★ The palatial premises of **Hopetoun House**, probably Scotland's grand-est courtly seat and home of the Marquesses of Linlithgow, are con-sidered to be among the Adam family's finest designs. The enormous house was started in 1699 to the original plans of Sir William Bruce (1630–1710), then enlarged between 1721 and 1754 by William Adam (1689–1748) and his sons Robert and John. There's a notable painting collection, and the house has decorative work of the highest order, plus all the trappings to keep you entertained: a nature trail, a restaurant in the former stables, and a museum. Much of the wealth that created this sumptuous building came from the family's mining interests in the surrounding regions. *⊠ Off A904, 6 mi west of South Queensferry ☎ 0131/331-2451 ⊕ www.hopetounhouse.com ⌦ £8 ⊙ Apr.–Sept., daily 10:30–5, last admission at 4.*

HOUSE OF THE BINNS
12 mi west of Edinburgh.

The 17th-century general "Bloody Tam" Dalyell (circa 1599–1685) transformed a fortified stronghold into a gracious mansion, the **House of the Binns** (the name derives from *bynn,* the old Scottish word for hill). The present exterior dates from around 1810 and shows a remodel-ing into a kind of mock fort with crenellated battlements and turrets. Inside, magnificent plaster ceilings are done in the Elizabethan style. The house is cared for by the National Trust for Scotland. *⊠ Off A904, 4 mi east of Linlithgow ☎ 01506/834255 ⊕ www.nts.org.uk/visits ⌦ £8.50 ⊙ June–Sept., Sat.–Wed. 2–5.*

BLACKNESS CASTLE
12 mi west of Edinburgh.

Blackness Castle stands like a grounded ship on the very edge of the Forth. A curious 15th-century structure, it has had a varied career as a strategic fortress, state prison, powder magazine, and youth hostel. The countryside is gently green and cultivated, and open views extend across the blue Forth to the distant ramparts of the Ochil Hills. *⊠ B903, 4 mi northeast of Linlithgow ☎ 01506/834807 ⊕ www.historic-scotland. gov.uk/places ⌦ £4.20 ⊙ Apr.–Sept., daily 9:30–5:30; Oct., daily 9:30–4:30; Nov.–Mar., Sat.–Wed. 9:30–4:30.*

LINLITHGOW PALACE
12 mi west of Edinburgh.

EXPLORING
On the edge of Linlithgow Loch stands the splendid ruin of **Linlithgow Palace,** the birthplace of Mary, Queen of Scots in 1542. Burned, perhaps accidentally, by Hanoverian troops during the last Jacobite rebellion in 1746, this impressive shell stands on a site of great antiquity, though it's not certain anything survived an earlier fire in 1424. The palace gatehouse was built in the early 16th century, and the central court-yard's elaborate fountain dates from around 1535. The halls and great rooms are cold, echoing stone husks now in Historic Scotland's care. *⊠ A706, south shore of Linlithgow Loch ☎ 01506/842896 ⊕ www.*

historic-scotland.gov.uk/places ⬜ *£5.20* ◷ *Apr.–Sept., daily 9:30–5:30;*
Oct.–Mar., daily 9:30–4:30.

FALKIRK WHEEL
25 mi west of Edinburgh.

EXPLORING

★ In 2002, British Waterways opened the **Falkirk Wheel,** the only rotating
boatlift in the world, linking two major waterways, the Forth and Clyde
Canal and the Union Canal, between Edinburgh and Glasgow. Considered an engineering marvel, the wheel transports eight or more boats at
a time overland from one canal to the other in about 45 minutes. The
boats float into a cradlelike compartment full of water; as the wheel
turns, they're transported up or down to meet the destination canal. You
can board tour boats at Falkirk to ride the Wheel, or you can take a multiday barge cruise between Edinburgh and Glasgow; book in advance.
At Falkirk, allow 30 minutes before your scheduled departure time
to pick up your tickets and choose your boat. There are limited daily
departures, so call ahead. ✉ *Lime Rd., Tamfourhill* ☎ *01324/619888,*
08700/500208 reservations ⊕ *www.thefalkirkwheel.co.uk* ⬜ *Boat trips*
£8 ◷ *Apr.–Oct., daily 11:10–4:10; Nov.–Mar., daily 10–3.*

OCHIL HILLS
24 mi northwest of Edinburgh.

The scarp face of the Ochil Hills looms unmistakably. It's an old fault
line that yields up hard volcanic rocks and contrasts with the quantities
of softer coal immediately around the River Forth. The steep Ochils provided grazing land and water power for Scotland's second-largest textile
area. Some mills still survive in the so-called Hillfoots towns, on the
scarp edge east of Stirling. The **Mill Trail Visitor Centre** (✉ *W. Stirling St.,*
Alva ☎ *01259/769696*), has information about the area's mill shops.

EXPLORING
Behind the town of Alva, on A91, sits **Alva Glen** (⊕ *www.alvaglen.org.*
uk), a park near the converted Strude Mill, at the top and eastern end
of the little town.

East of Alva Glen is the **Ochil Hills Woodland Park** (⊕ *www.clacksweb.org.*
uk/visiting/ochilhillswoodlandpark/), which provides access to lovely
Silver Glen.

The **Mill Glen,** behind Tillicoultry (pronounced tilly-*coot*-ree), with its
giant quarry, fine waterfalls, and interesting plants, is a good hiking
option for energetic explorers.

DOLLAR
30 mi northwest of Edinburgh.

This *douce* (Scots for well-mannered or gentle) and tidy town below
the Ochil Hills lies at the mouth of Dollar Glen.

EXPLORING
With green woods below, bracken hills above, and a view that on a
clear day stretches right across the Forth Valley to the tip of Tinto Hill
near Lanark, **Castle Campbell** is certainly the most atmospheric fortress
within easy reach of Edinburgh. Formerly known as Castle Gloom,
Castle Campbell stands out among Scottish castles for the sheer drama

of its setting. The sturdy square of the tower house survives from the 15th century, when the site was fortified by the first Earl of Argyll (died 1493). Other buildings and enclosures were subsequently added, but the sheer lack of space on this rocky eminence ensured that there would never be any drastic changes. John Knox, the fiery religious reformer, once preached here. In 1654 the castle was captured by Oliver Cromwell and garrisoned with English troops. It's now cared for by Historic Scotland. To get here, follow a road off the A91 that angles sharply up the east side of the wooded defile. ⊠ *Off A91, Dollar Glen ✛ 1 mi north of Dollar* ☎ *01259/742408* ⊕ *www.historic-scotland.gov.uk/places* 🎫 *£4.50* ☼ *Apr.–Sept., daily 9:30–5:30; Oct.–Mar., daily 9:30–4:30.*

CULROSS
17 mi northwest of Edinburgh.

★ With its Mercat Cross, cobbled streets, tolbooth, and narrow wynds (alleys), **Culross**, on the muddy shores of the Forth, is now a living museum of a 17th-century town and one of the most remarkable little towns in Scotland. It once had a thriving industry and export trade in coal and salt (the coal was used in the salt-panning process). It also had, curiously, a trade monopoly in the manufacture of baking *girdles* (griddles). As local coal became exhausted, the impetus of the industrial revolution passed Culross by, and other parts of the Forth Valley prospered. Culross became a backwater town, and the merchants' houses of the 17th and 18th centuries were never replaced by Victorian developments or modern architecture. In the 1930s the then-new and also poor National Trust for Scotland started to buy up the decaying properties. With the help of other agencies, these buildings were brought to life. Today ordinary citizens live in many of the National Trust properties. A few—the Palace, Study, and Town House—are open to the public. ⊠ *Off A985, 8 mi south of Dollar* ☎ *01383/880359* ⊕ *www.nts.org.uk/visits* 🎫 *Palace, Study, and Town House £8* ☼ *Palace, Study, and Town House June–Aug., daily 10–6; Apr. and May, Thurs.–Mon. noon–5; Sept.–late Oct., Thurs.–Mon. noon–4; last admission 1 hr before closing.*

DUNFERMLINE
16 mi northwest of Edinburgh.

Dunfermline was once the world center for the production of damask linen, but the town is better known today as the birthplace of millionaire industrialist and philanthropist Andrew Carnegie (1835–1919). Undoubtedly Dunfermline's most famous son, Carnegie endowed the town with a park, library, health and fitness center, and, naturally, a Carnegie Hall, still the focus of culture and entertainment.

EXPLORING

The 18th-century weaver's cottage where Carnegie was born in 1835 is now the **Andrew Carnegie Birthplace Museum.** Don't be misled by the cottage's simple exterior. Inside it opens into a larger hall, where documents, photographs, and artifacts relate Carnegie's fascinating life story. You can learn such obscure details as the claim that Carnegie was one of only three men in the United States then able to translate Morse code by ear as it came down the wire. ⊠ *Moodie St.* ☎ *01383/724302*

⊕ *www.carnegiebirthplace.com* ✉ *Free* ⊙ *Apr.–Oct., Mon.–Sat. 11–5, Sun. 2–5.*

The **Pittencrieff House Museum** tells the story of the town's damask linen industry. ⊠ *Pittencrieff Park* ☎ *01383/722935* ⊕ *www.scottishmuseums. org.uk* ✉ *Free* ⊙ *Apr.–Sept., daily 11–5; Oct.–Mar., daily 11–4.*

The **Dunfermline Abbey and Palace** complex was founded in the 11th century by Queen Margaret, the English wife of the Scots king Malcolm III. Some Norman work can be seen in the present church, where Robert the Bruce (1274–1329) lies buried. The palace grew from the abbey guesthouse and was the birthplace of Charles I (1600–49). Dunfermline was the seat of the royal court of Scotland until the end of the 11th century, and its central role in Scottish affairs is explored by means of display panels dotted around the drafty but hallowed buildings. ⊠ *Monastery St.* ☎ *01383/739026* ⊕ *www.historic-scotland.gov.uk/ places* ✉ *£3.70* ⊙ *Apr.–Sept., daily 9:30–5:30; Oct.–Mar., Mon.–Wed. and Sat. 9:30–4:30, Thurs. 9:30–noon and Sun. 2–4:30; last admission ½ hr before closing.*

DEEP SEA WORLD
9 mi northwest of Edinburgh.

EXPLORING
The former ferry port in North Queensferry dropped almost into oblivion after the Forth Road Bridge opened, but was dragged abruptly back into the limelight by the hugely popular **Deep Sea World**. This sophisticated aquarium—for want of a better word—on the Firth of Forth offers a fascinating view of underwater life. Go down a clear acrylic tunnel for a diver's-eye look at more than 5,000 fish, including 250 sharks (some over 9 feet long); and visit the exhibition hall, which has an Amazon-jungle display and an audiovisual presentation on local marine life. Ichthyophobes will feel more at ease in the adjacent café and gift shop. ⊠ *North Queensferry* ☎ *01383/411880* ⊕ *www.deepseaworld. com* ✉ *£11.75* ⊙ *Weekdays 10–5, weekends 10–6; last admission 1 hr before closing.*

MIDLOTHIAN AND EAST LOTHIAN

In spite of the finest stone carving in Scotland at Rosslyn Chapel, associations with Sir Walter Scott, outstanding castles, and miles of rolling countryside, Midlothian, the area immediately south of Edinburgh, for years remained off the beaten path. Perhaps a little in awe of sophisticated Edinburgh to the north and the well-manicured charm of the stockbroker belt of nearby upmarket East Lothian, Midlothian was quietly preoccupied with its own workaday little towns and dormitory suburbs.

As for East Lothian, it started with the advantage of golf courses of world rank, most notably Muirfield, plus a scattering of stately homes and interesting hotels. It's an area of glowing grain fields in summer and quite a few discreetly polite STRICTLY PRIVATE signs at the end of driveways. Still, it has plenty of interest, including photogenic villages, active fishing harbors, and vistas of pastoral Lowland Scotland, seemingly a world away (but much less than an hour by car) from bustling Edinburgh.

GETTING HERE AND AROUND

BUS TRAVEL City buses travel as far as Swanston and the Pentland Hills. First buses serve towns and villages throughout Midlothian and East Lothian. For details of all services, inquire at the St. Andrew Square bus station in Edinburgh.

CAR TRAVEL If traveling by car, here are the roads you'll need to know for visiting the region's main attractions. For Rosslyn Chapel, leave Edinburgh via the A701 (Liberton Road), then turn left to Roslin on the B7006. For a scenic route beneath the Pentland Hills, take the A766 and A702, which runs from Penicuik to West Linton. At the junction of B6372 with A7, just before Gorebridge, you can head to either the Scottish Mining Museum or Borthwick Castle.

West of Dunbar, on the way back to Edinburgh, the A1087 leads to the sandy reaches of Belhaven Bay, signposted from the main road, and to the John Muir Country Park. Beyond the park turn right onto the A1, then turn right onto the A198 to reach North Berwick, St. Mary's Parish Church at Whitekirk, Tantallon Castle, Dirleton Castle, and Gullane. A198 eventually leads to Aberlady, from which you can take the A6137 south to the former county town of Haddington and, by way of B6369, to Lennoxlove House.

TRAIN TRAVEL There is no train service in Midlothian. In East Lothian, the towns of North Berwick, Drem, and Dunbar have train stations with regular service from Edinburgh.

ESSENTIALS

Bus Contacts **First** (☎ 0870/872–7271 ⊕ www.firstgroup.com).

NEWHAILES

5 mi east of Edinburgh.

EXPLORING

This fine late-17th-century house (with 18th-century additions), owned and run by the National Trust for Scotland, was designed by Scottish architect James Smith (circa 1645–1731) in 1686 as his own home. He later sold it to Lord Bellendon, and in 1707 it was bought by Sir David Dalrymple (c. 1665–1721), first baronet of Hailes, who improved and extended the house, adding one of the finest rococo interiors in Scotland. The library played host to many famous figures from the Scottish Enlightenment, including inveterate Scot-basher Dr. Samuel Johnson, who dubbed the library "the most learned room in Europe." Most of the original interiors and furnishings remain intact, creating great authenticity. ⊠ *Newhailes Rd., Musselburgh* ☎ *0131/665–1546* ⊕ *www.nts.org.uk/visits* ☒ *House £10, grounds free* ☉ *House May–Oct., Thurs.–Mon. noon–5; grounds daily year-round.*

ROSLIN
7 mi south of Edinburgh.

EXPLORING

Fodor's Choice ★ **Rosslyn Chapel** has always beckoned curious visitors intrigued by the various legends surrounding its magnificent carvings, but today it pulses with tourists as never before. Dan Brown's bestselling novel *The Da Vinci Code* has made visiting this Episcopal chapel (services continue to be held here) an imperative stop for many of its enthusiasts. Whether you're a fan of the book or not—and of the book's theory that the chapel has a secret sign that can lead you to the Holy Grail—this is a site of immense interest. Originally conceived by Sir William Sinclair (circa 1404–80) and dedicated to St. Matthew in 1446, the chapel is outstanding for the quality and variety of the carving inside. Covering almost every square inch of stonework are human figures, animals, and plants. The meaning of these remains subject to many theories; some depict symbols from the medieval order of the Knights Templar and from Freemasonry. The chapel's design called for a cruciform structure, but only the choir and parts of the east transept walls were completed. ⊠ *Chapel Loan, Roslin* ☎ *0131/440–2159* ⊕ *www.rosslynchapel.com* 🎫 *£7.50* ⊘ *Apr.–Sept., Mon.–Sat. 9:30–5:30, Sun. noon–4:45; Oct.–Mar., Mon.–Sat. 9:30–4:30, Sun. noon–4:45*

SCOTTISH MINING MUSEUM
9 mi southeast of Edinburgh.

EXPLORING

The Scottish Mining Museum, in the former mining community of Newtongrange, provides a good introduction to the history of Scotland's mining industry. With the help of videos you can go on shift as a coal miner and experience life deep below the ground. There are also interactive displays and "magic helmets" that bring the tour to life and relate the power that the mining company had over the lives of the individual workers here, in Scotland's largest planned-mining village. This frighteningly autocratic system survived well into the 1930s—the company owned the houses, shops, and even the pub. The scenery is no more attractive than you would expect, though the green Pentland Hills hover in the distance. ⊠ *A7, Newtongrange* ☎ *0131/663–7519* ⊕ *www.scottishminingmuseum.com* 🎫 *£6.50* ⊘ *Apr.–Sept., daily 10–5; Oct.–Mar., daily 10–4; last admission 1½ hrs before closing.*

BORTHWICK CASTLE
12 mi southeast of Edinburgh.

EXPLORING

Set in green countryside with scattered woods and lush hedgerows, the village of Borthwick is dominated by **Borthwick Castle**, which dates from the 15th century and is still occupied. Mary, Queen of Scots, came to this stark, tall, twin-towered fortress on a kind of honeymoon with her ill-starred third husband, the Earl of Bothwell. Their already-dubious bliss was interrupted by Mary's political opponents, often referred to as the Lords of the Congregation, a confederacy of powerful nobles who favored the crowning of her young son, James. Rather insensitively, they laid siege to the castle while the newlyweds were there. Mary

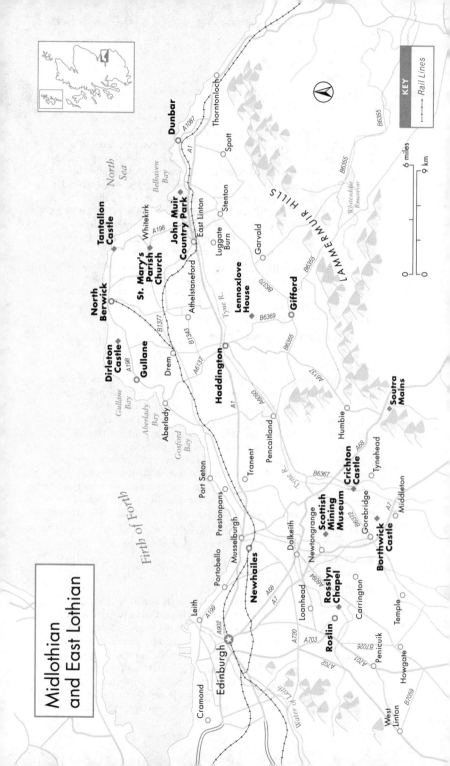

Midlothian and East Lothian

North Sea

Gullane Bay

Aberlady Bay

Gosford Bay

Belhaven Bay

Firth of Forth

LAMMERMUIR HILLS

KEY
+—+ Rail Lines

6 miles

9 km

Dunbar

Thorntonloch

Spott

Whitekirk

Tantallon Castle

St. Mary's Parish Church

John Muir Country Park

East Linton

Stenton

Luggate Burn

Garvald

Whiteadder Reservoir

B6355

B6355

B6355

B6355

North Berwick

Athelstaneford

Lennoxlove House

B6369

Gifford

B6370

Tyne R.

A1087

A1

A198

A198

B1377

B1343

B1343

A6137

Dirleton Castle

Gullane

Drem

Haddington

A1

A6093

Humbie

A6137

A68

Soutra Mains

Tynehead

Middleton

Pencaitland

Tranent

Tyne R.

B6367

Crichton Castle

Port Seton

Prestonpans

Portobello

Leith

A199

A902

A6094

A7

A68

A720

A702

A703

A701

B7026

B7059

Musselburgh

Dalkeith

Newtongrange

Gorebridge

Scottish Mining Museum

Borthwick Castle

Newhailes

Loanhead

Roslin

Rosslyn Chapel

Carrington

Temple

Penicuik

Howgate

Edinburgh

Cramond

Water of Leith

West Linton

subsequently escaped disguised as a man. She was not free for long, however. It was only a short time before she was defeated in battle and imprisoned. She languished in prison for 21 years before Queen Elizabeth I of England (1558–1603) signed her death warrant in 1587. Bothwell's fate was equally gloomy: he died insane in a Danish prison. The castle now functions as a hotel, but it's well worth a look around. ✉ *Borthwick* ✢ *1 mi south of Gorebridge* ☎ *01875/820514* ⊕ *www.borthwickcastlehotel.com* ✆ *Free* ⊙ *Tour hrs vary.*

CRICHTON CASTLE
11 mi southeast of Edinburgh.

EXPLORING
Crichton Castle stands amid rolling hills that are interrupted here and there by patches of woodland. Crichton was a Bothwell family castle; Mary, Queen of Scots, attended the wedding here of Bothwell's sister, Lady Janet Hepburn, to Mary's brother, Lord John Stewart. The curious arcaded range reveals diamond-faceted stonework; this particular geometric pattern is unique in Scotland and is thought to have been inspired by Renaissance styles on the Continent, particularly Italy. The oldest part of the work is the 14th-century keep (square tower). You can reach this castle from Borthwick Castle by taking a peaceful walk through the woods (there are signposts along the way). Do note that there are no toilets at the castle. ✉ *B6367, near Pathhead, 7 mi southeast of Dalkeith* ☎ *01875/320017* ⊕ *www.historic-scotland.gov.uk/places* ✆ *£3.70* ⊙ *Apr.–Sept., daily 9:30–5:30.*

DUNBAR
25 mi east of Edinburgh.

In the days before tour companies started offering package deals to the Mediterranean, Dunbar was a popular holiday beach resort. Now a bit faded, the town is still lovely for its spacious Georgian-style properties, characterized by the astragals, or fan-shape windows, above the doors; the symmetry of the house fronts; and the parapeted roof lines. Though not the popular seaside playground it once was, Dunbar has an attractive beach and a picturesque harbor.

EXPLORING
Taking in the estuary of the River Tyne winding down from the Moorfoot Hills, the **John Muir Country Park** encompasses varied coastal scenery: rocky shoreline, golden sands, and the mixed woodlands of Tyninghame, teeming with wildlife. Dunbar-born conservationist John Muir (1838–1914), whose family moved to the United States when he was a child, helped found Yosemite and Sequoia national parks in California. ✉ *Off A1087, 2 mi west of Dunbar.*

NORTH BERWICK
20 mi northeast of Edinburgh.

The pleasant little seaside resort of North Berwick manages to retain a small-town personality even when it's thronged with city visitors on warm summer Sunday afternoons. Eating ice cream, the city folk stroll on the beach and in the narrow streets or gaze at the sailing craft in the small harbor. The town is near a number of castles and other sights.

EXPLORING

An observation deck, exhibits, and films at the **Scottish Seabird Centre** provide a good introduction to the world of the gannets and puffins that nest on nearby Bass Rock. Live interactive cameras let you take an even closer look at the bird. ⊠ *The Harbour* ☎ *01620/890202* ⊕ *www.seabird.org* 🎫 *£7.95* ⊙ *Apr.–Sept., daily 10–6; Feb., Mar., and Oct., weekdays 10–5, weekends 10–5:30; Nov.–Jan., weekdays 10–4, weekends 10–5:30; last admission 45 mins before closing.*

In the center of tiny Dirleton sits the 12th-century **Dirleton Castle,** surrounded by a high outer wall. Within the wall you can find a 17th-century bowling green, set in the shade of yew trees and surrounded by a herbaceous flower border that blazes with color in high summer. Dirleton Castle, now in Historic Scotland's care, was occupied in 1298 by King Edward I of England as part of his campaign for the continued subjugation of the unruly Scots. ⊠ *A198, 2 mi west of North Berwick* ☎ *01620/850330* ⊕ *www.historic-scotland.gov.uk/places* 🎫 *£4.70* ⊙ *Apr.–Sept., daily 9:30–5:30; Oct.–Mar., daily 9:30–4:30; last admission ½ hr before closing.*

Rising on a cliff beyond the flat fields east of North Berwick, **Tantallon Castle** is a substantial ruin defending a headland with the sea on three sides. The red sandstone is pitted and eaten by time and sea spray, with the earliest surviving stonework dating from the late 14th century. The fortress was besieged in 1529 by the cannons of King James V (1512–42). Rather inconveniently, the besieging forces ran out of gunpowder. Cannons were used again, to deadlier effect, in a later siege during the Civil War in 1651. Twelve days of battering with the heavy guns of Cromwell's General Monk greatly damaged the flanking towers. Fortunately much of the curtain wall of this former Douglas stronghold, now cared for by Historic Scotland, survives. ⊠ *A198, 3 mi east of North Berwick* ☎ *01620/892727* ⊕ *www.historic-scotland.gov.uk/places* 🎫 *£4.70* ⊙ *Apr.–Sept., daily 9:30–5:30; Oct., daily 9:30–4:30; Nov.–Mar., Sat.–Wed. 9:30–4:30; last admission ½ hr before closing.*

The unmistakable red-sandstone **St. Mary's Parish Church,** with its Norman tower, stands in the village of Whitekirk, 6 mi south of North Berwick, on a site occupied since the 6th century. It was a place of pilgrimage in medieval times because of its healing well. Behind the kirk, in a field, stands a tithe barn. Tithe barns originated with the practice of giving to the church a portion of local produce, which then required storage space. In the 15th century, the church was visited by a young Italian nobleman, Aeneas Sylvius Piccolomini, after he was shipwrecked off the East Lothian coast. Two decades later, Piccolomini became Pope Pius II. At one end of the barn stands a 16th-century tower house, which at one point in its history accommodated visiting pilgrims. The large three-story barn was added to the tower house in the 17th century. ⊠ *A198, Whitekirk* 🎫 *Free* ⊙ *Daily 9 AM–sunset.*

WHERE TO STAY

££ 🏨 **Glebe House.** This dignified 18th-century manse sits amid its own secluded grounds, yet it's in the heart of town, a 10-minute walk east of the station. It's also close to the beach and 18 golf courses, including nearby Muirfield. The elegant bedrooms, one of which has a four-poster bed, are in keeping with the Georgian style of the house. Grand period furniture, paintings, and ornaments fill the sitting and dining rooms. **Pros:** peaceful atmosphere; interesting antiques; sociable breakfast around a mahogany table. **Cons:** books up well in advance; too twee for some. ⊠ *Law Rd.* ☎ *01620/892608* ⊕ *www.glebehouse-nb.co.uk* ⟿ *4 rooms* ♨ *In-room: no a/c, no TV* ⊟ *No credit cards* ◉ *BP.*

GULLANE

15 mi northeast of Edinburgh.

Noticeable along this coastline are the golf courses of East Lothian, laid out wherever there is available links space. Ultrarespectable Gullane is surrounded by them, and its inhabitants are typically clad in expensive golfing sweaters. Apart from golf, you can enjoy restful summer evening strolls at Gullane's beach, well within driving distance of the village.

HADDINGTON

15 mi east of Edinburgh.

One of the best-preserved medieval street plans in the country can be explored in Haddington. Among the many buildings of architectural or historical interest is the Town House, designed by William Adam in 1748 and enlarged in 1830. A wall plaque at the Sidegate recalls the great heights of floods from the River Tyne. Beyond is the medieval Nungate footbridge, with the Church of St. Mary a little way upstream.

EXPLORING

Just to the south of Haddington stands **Lennoxlove House,** the grand ancestral home of the very grand dukes of Hamilton since 1947 and the Baird family before them. A turreted country house, part of it dating from the 15th century, Lennoxlove is a cheerful mix of family life and Scottish history. The beautifully decorated rooms house portraits, furniture, porcelain, and items associated with Mary, Queen of Scots, including her supposed death mask. Sporting activities from falconry to fishing take place on the stunning grounds. ⊠ *B6369, 1 mi south of Haddington* ☎ *01620/823720* ⊕ *www.lennoxlove.com* 🎫 *£5* ☉ *Tours Apr.–Oct., Wed., Thurs, and Sun. 1:30–4.*

Glasgow

WORD OF MOUTH

"Don't rule out Glasgow, although every tourist tells you to go to Edinburgh. It's got a great buzz with friendlier people, great shops, and all the Charles Rennie Mackintosh architecture. The West End is great with lovely bars and restaurants, plus the Botanic Gardens. If you want museums and culture, visit the Kelvingrove; it's also free to enter. Glasgow is only a 45-minute drive from Loch Lomond, too."

—alihutch

"To add to ideas for things to do in Glasgow, the Burrell Collection is one of my favorites."

—historytraveler

Updated by
Fiona G.
Parrott

Currently undergoing an urban renaissance, Scotland's largest city has experienced both dramatic decline and upswing.
When Britain ruled over an empire, Glasgow pronounced
itself Second City of the Empire. Steamships were built here,
and great thinkers, such as Lord Kelvin and James Watt,
tested their groundbreaking theories. But by the middle of
the 20th century, the city's slums were notorious. "All Glasgow needs," said an architecture pundit, "is a bath and a little loving care." Today it has received both: trendy stores, a
booming cultural life, and stylish restaurants reinforce Glasgow's claim to be Scotland's most exciting city.

Glasgow first came into prominence in Scottish history around 1,400
years ago, and, as the story goes, it had to do with an argument between
a husband and wife. When the king of Strathclyde gave his wife a ring,
she was rash enough to present it to an admirer. The king, having sur-
reptitiously repossessed it, threw it into the Clyde before quizzing his
wife about its disappearance. In her distress, the queen turned to her
confessor, St. Mungo, for advice. He instructed her to fish in the river
and—surprise—the first salmon she landed had the ring in its jaws.
Glasgow's coat of arms is dominated by three salmon, one with a ring
in its mouth. Not surprisingly, Mungo became the city's patron saint.
His tomb lies in the mighty medieval cathedral that bears his name.

GROWTH AND DEVELOPMENT

As Glasgow prospered, its population grew. The "dear green place" (the
literal meaning of the Gaelic *glas cu,* from which the name "Glasgow"
purportedly derives) expanded beyond recognition, extending westward
and to the south of the original medieval city, which centered around
the cathedral and High Street. The 18th-century Merchant City, now
largely rejuvenated, lies just to the south and east of George Square,
where all but a few of the original merchants' houses remain in their
original condition. During the 19th century the population grew from
80,000 to more than 1 million, and along with this enormous growth
there developed a sense of exuberance and confidence reflected in the
city's public buildings. The City Chambers, built in 1888, are a proud
statement in marble and gold sandstone, a clear symbol of the wealthy
and powerful Victorian industrialists' hopes for the future.

Some of the city's development has been unashamedly commercial,
tied up with the wealth of its manufacturers and merchants, who constructed a vast number of civic buildings throughout the 19th century.
Among those who helped shape Glasgow's unique Victorian cityscape
during that great period of civic expansion was the local-born architect Alexander "Greek" Thomson (1817–75). Side by side with the

Victorian, Glasgow had an architectural vision of the future in the work of Charles Rennie Mackintosh (1868–1928). The Glasgow School of Art, the Willow Tearoom, the *Glasgow Herald* building (now home to the Lighthouse architecture and design center), and the churches and schools Mackintosh designed point clearly to the clarity and simplicity of the best of 20th-century design.

PRESENT AND FUTURE

Today, as always, Glasgow's eye is trained on the future. The city, with a metro area population of 2.3 million, is Scotland's major business destination, with the Scottish Exhibition and Conference Centre serving as the hub of activity. It's also a nexus of rail routes and motorways that can deliver you in less than an hour to Edinburgh, Stirling, Loch Lomond, the Burns country, and the Clyde coast golfing resorts. Still, Glasgow has learned to take the best of its past and adapt it for the needs of the present day. The dear green places still remain in the city-center parks; the medieval cathedral stands proud, as it has done for 800 years; the Merchant City is revived and thriving; the Victorian splendor has been cleansed of its grime; and the cultural legacy of museums and performing arts is stronger than ever.

ORIENTATION AND PLANNING

GETTING ORIENTED

Glasgow's layout is hard to read in a single glance. The city center is roughly defined by the M8 motorway to the north and west, the River Clyde to the south, and Glasgow Cathedral and High Street to the east. Glaswegians tend to walk a good deal, and the relatively flat and compact city center, most of which follows a grid plan, is designed for pedestrians. The West End has Glasgow University and lovely Kelvingrove Park. The River Clyde, on which Glasgow's trade across the Atlantic developed, runs through the center of the city—literally cutting it in two and offering intriguing views of South Side buildings.

Medieval Glasgow and the Merchant City. This central area includes some of Glasgow's most treasured and historic sights: the cathedral, the Necropolis, City Chambers, and the Gallery of Modern Art, as well as top-notch eateries. Most of the city's theaters are here too, along with many of the best shops.

The West End. In this quieter, slightly hillier western part of the city is Glasgow University and the often overlooked bohemian side of Glasgow. The West End's treasures include the Botanic Gardens, Kelvingrove Park, and the Kelvingrove Art Gallery and Museum. There are also plenty of well-priced restaurants and lively bars.

The South Side. Often overlooked, this less visited side of the city is home to the spectacular Burrell Collection. And if you want to sleep in a castle, try the stunning Sherbrooke Castle Hotel here.

TOP REASONS TO GO

Design and architecture: The ambitious Victorians left a legacy of striking architecture, and Glasgow's buildings manifest the city's enduring love of grand artistic statements—just remember to look up. The Arts and Crafts buildings and interiors by Charles Rennie Mackintosh are reason alone to visit the city.

Artistic treasures: Some of Britain's best museums and art galleries are in Glasgow. The Burrell Collection and the stunningly renovated Kelvingrove Art Gallery and Museum are definitely worth a visit even on a sunny day.

Gorgeous gardens: From the Kelvingrove to the Botanic Garden, Glasgow has more parks per square mile than any other in Europe. Stop by during one of the music festivals or outdoor theatrical productions in summer.

Pints and great grub: Whether you fancy a Guinness in a traditional old-man's pub like the Scotia or gin and tonic at one of Glasgow's many churches turned watering holes like Òran Mór, there's a pub to fit all thirsts. The city has restaurants for every palate and occasion. Locals love their cafés and tearooms; stop by the Willow Tearoom as a break from sightseeing.

Retail therapy: The city has become known for cutting-edge design. Look for everything from Scottish specialties to stylish fashions on the city center's hottest shopping streets, Buchanan and Sauchiehall, as well as in Princes Square.

Burns country: Outside the city are scenic landscapes from coastlines to cottages to castles. Here you can learn about the life and legacy of Robert Burns, Scotland's most renowned poet. Alloway and Ayr are the places to start.

PLANNING

WHEN TO GO

The best times to visit Glasgow are spring and summer. Although you may encounter crowds, the weather is more likely to be warm and dry. In summer the days are long and pleasant—that is, if the rain holds off—and festivals and outdoor events are abundant. Fall can be nice, although cold weather sets in after mid-September and the days begin to grow shorter. From November to February it is cold, wet, and dark. Although thousands of people flock to Glasgow for New Year's celebrations, the winter months are relatively quiet in terms of crowds.

PLANNING YOUR TIME

You could quite easily spend five comfortable days here, although in a pinch, two would do and three would be pleasant. The best strategy for seeing the city is to start in the center and work your way out. On the first day explore the core of historic Glasgow—the medieval area, dominated by Glasgow's cathedral, and Merchant City. Some fascinating museums are nearby, such as the St. Mungo Museum of Religious Life and Art and the Gallery of Modern Art. Shoppers should head for Buchanan Street. The Mackintosh sites can be seen one by one or as part of a full-day excursion on the Mackintosh Trail. Museum fans should make their way to West End to see the spectacular Kelvingrove Art Gallery and the Hunterian Art Gallery. Another option is to make a beeline to the Burrell Collection and the House for an Art Lover, on the south side of the city.

With an extra few days, head out to Burns country in Ayrshire. It's a scenic 45-minute drive from Glasgow, and you can use the city as a base. Most destinations on the Clyde Coast are easily accessible from Glasgow. Direct trains from Central Station take you to Paisley, Irvine, Largs, Troon, Kilmarnock, and Lanark in less than an hour. These small towns need no more than a day to explore. To get the flavor of island life, take the hour-long train ride to Wemyss Bay and then the ferry to the Isle of Bute.

GETTING HERE AND AROUND

AIR TRAVEL

Airlines flying from Glasgow Airport to the rest of the United Kingdom and to Europe include Aer Lingus, Air Malta, bmi/British Midland, British Airways, easyJet, Icelandair, and KLM. Several carriers fly from North America, including Air Canada, American Airlines, Continental, and Icelandair (service via Reykjavík).

Ryanair offers rock-bottom airfares between Prestwick and London's Stansted Airport. Budget-minded easyJet has similar services from Glasgow to London's Stansted and Luton airports.

Air Contacts Aer Lingus (☎ *0870/876–5000* ⊕ *www.aerlingus.com*). **Air Canada** (☎ *0871/220-1111* ⊕ *www.aircanada.com*). **Air Malta** (☎ *0845/607–3710* ⊕ *www.airmalta.com*). **American Airlines** (☎ *0845/778–9789* ⊕ *www.aa.com*). **bmi/British Midland** (☎ *0870/607–0555* ⊕ *www.flybmi.com*). **British Airways** (☎ *0844/493–0787* ⊕ *www.ba.com*). **Continental** (☎ *0845/607–6760* ⊕ *www.continental.com*). **easyJet** (☎ *0871/244–2366* ⊕ *www.easyjet.com*). **Icelandair** (☎ *0844/811–1190* ⊕ *www.icelandair.com*). **KLM** (☎ *0870/507–4074* ⊕ *www.klm.com*). **Ryanair** (☎ *0871/246–0000* ⊕ *www.ryanair.com*).

AIRPORTS   Glasgow Airport is about 7 mi west of the city center on the M8 to Greenock. The airport serves international and domestic flights, and most major European carriers have frequent and convenient connections (some via airports in England) to many cities on the Continent. There's frequent shuttle service from London, as well as regular flights from Birmingham, Bristol, East Midlands, Leeds/Bradford, Manchester, Southampton, Isle of Man, and Jersey. There are also flights from Wales (Cardiff) and Ireland (Belfast, Dublin, and Londonderry). Local Scottish connections can be made to Aberdeen, Barra, Benbecula, Campbeltown, Inverness, Islay, Kirkwall, Shetland (Sumburgh), Stornoway, and Tiree.

Prestwick Airport, on the Ayrshire coast about 30 mi southwest of Glasgow and for some years eclipsed by Glasgow Airport, has grown in importance, not least because of lower airfares from Ryanair.

Airport Contacts Glasgow Airport (☎ *0844/481-5555* ⊕ *www.glasgowairport.com*). **Prestwick Airport** (☎ *0871/223-0700* ⊕ *www.gpia.co.uk*).

TRANSFERS   **From Glasgow Airport:** Although there's a railway station about 2 mi from Glasgow Airport (Paisley Gilmour Street), most people travel to the city center by bus or taxi. It takes about 20 minutes, slightly longer at rush hour. Metered taxis are available outside domestic arrivals. The fare should be £15 to £18.

Express buses run from Glasgow Airport (outside departures lobby) to near the Central railway station, to Queen Street railway station, and to the Buchanan Street bus station. There's service every 15 minutes throughout the day. The fare is £3.30 on both Scottish Citylink and Fairline buses.

The drive from Glasgow Airport into the city center is normally quite easy, even if you're used to driving on the right. The M8 motorway runs beside the airport (Junction 29) and takes you straight into the Glasgow city center. Thereafter Glasgow's streets follow a grid pattern, at least in the city center. A map is useful—get one from the car-rental company.

Most companies that provide chauffeur-driven cars and tours will also do limousine airport transfers. Companies that are currently members of the Greater Glasgow and Clyde Valley Tourist Board are Charlton, Little's, and Peter Holmes.

From Prestwick Airport: An hourly coach service makes trips to Glasgow but takes much longer than the train. There's a rapid half-hourly train service (hourly on Sunday) direct from the terminal building to Glasgow Central. Strathclyde Passenger Transport and ScotRail offer an AirTrain discount ticket that allows you to travel for 50% off the standard rail fare. Just show a valid airline ticket (boarding cards are not accepted), for a flight to or from Prestwick Airport when you purchase your rail ticket from a booking office or conductor.

By car the city center is reached via the fast A77 in about 40 minutes (longer in rush hour). Metered taxi cabs are available at the airport. The fare to Glasgow is about £40.

Airport Transfer Contacts Charlton (☎ 0870/058–9500 ⊕ www.charltonlimo.com). **Little's** (☎ 0141/883–2111 ⊕ www.littles.co.uk). **Peter Holmes** (☎ 01389/830–688).

BUS TRAVEL

Transportation is required to go to either the West End or the South Side, and it's easy to use the city's integrated network of buses, subways, and trains.

Glasgow's bus station is on Buchanan Street at Argyle Street, not far from Central Station. The main intercity operators are National Express and Scottish Citylink, which serve numerous towns and cities in Scotland, Wales, and England, including London; there's also service to Edinburgh. Buchanan Street is close to the subway station of the same name and to the Queen Street station.

Bus service is reliable within Glasgow, and connections are convenient from buses to trains and the underground. Note that buses require exact fare, which varies by the destination, though it's usually around £1.50

Traveline Scotland can provide information on schedules and fares, as does the Strathclyde Passenger Transport Travel Centre, which has an information center.

Bus Contacts **Buchanan Street bus station** (☎ *0141/333–3708* ⊕ *www. spt.co.uk*). **National Express** (☎ *0871/781–8181* ⊕ *www.nationalexpress. co.uk*). **Scottish Citylink** (☎ *0870/550–5050* ⊕ *www.citylink.co.uk*). **Strathclyde Passenger Transport Travel Centre** (✉ *12 W. George St., City Center* ☎ *0141/332–6811* ⊕ *www.spt.co.uk*).**Traveline Scotland** (☎ *0871/200–2233* ⊕ *www.travelinescotland.com*).

CAR TRAVEL

If you come to Glasgow from England and the south of Scotland, you'll probably approach the city from the M6, M74, and A74. The city center is clearly marked from these roads. From Edinburgh the M8 leads to the city center and cuts straight across the city center. From the north either the A82 from Fort William or the A/M80 from Stirling also feed into the M8 in the Glasgow city center. From then on you only have to know your exit: Exit 16 serves the northern part of the city center, Exit 17/18 leads to the northwest and Great Western Road, and Exit 18/19 takes you to the hotels of Sauchiehall Street, and the Scottish Exhibition and Conference Centre.

You don't need a car in the city center, and you're probably better off without one; though most modern hotels have their own lots, parking here can be trying. More convenient are the park-and-ride operations at subway stations (Kelvinbridge, Bridge Street, and Shields Road), which will bring you into the city center in a few minutes. The West End museums and galleries have their own lots, as does the Burrell. Parking fines cost upward of £26 for parking illegally. Multistory garages are open 24 hours a day at the following locations: Anderston Centre, George Street, Waterloo Place, Mitchell Street, Cambridge Street, and Concert Square. Rates run between £1 and £2 per hour.

SUBWAY TRAVEL

Glasgow's subway, useful for all city center and West End attractions, is the most popular mode of transportation with locals. Signs and the Web site call it a subway, but Glaswegians refer to it as the underground or tube, and stations are marked with a U, for underground. You can choose between flat fares (£1.20) and the Discovery Ticket one-day pass (£3.50, after 9:30 AM). Trains run regularly from Monday through Saturday from early morning to late evening, with a limited Sunday service, and connect the city center with the West End (for the university) and the city south of the River Clyde. Look for the orange U signs marking the 15 stations. Note that the distance between many central stops is no more than a 5- to 10-minute walk. Further information is available from Strathclyde Passenger Transport Travel Centre.

Subway Contacts **National Rail** (☎ *0870/748–4950* ⊕ *www.nationalrail.co.uk*). **Strathclyde Passenger Transport Travel Centre** (✉ *12 W. George St., City Center* ☎ *0141/332–6811* ⊕ *www.spt.co.uk*).

TAXI TRAVEL

Taxis are a fast and money effective way to get around. You'll find metered taxis (usually black and of the London sedan type) at stands all over the city center. Most have radio dispatch. Some have also been adapted to take wheelchairs. You can hail a cab on the street if its FOR HIRE sign is illuminated. A typical ride from the city center to the West End or the South Side costs around £6.

Taxi Contacts **Glasgow Taxis** (☎ 0141/429–7070 ⊕ www.glasgowtaxisltd.co.uk).

TRAIN TRAVEL

Glasgow has two main rail stations: Central and Queen Street. Central is the arrival and departure point for trains from London's Euston station (five hours), which come via Crewe and Carlisle in England, as well as via Edinburgh from London's King's Cross station. It also serves other cities in the northwest of England and towns and ports in the southwest of Scotland: Kilmarnock, Dumfries, Ardrossan (for the island of Arran), Gourock (for Dunoon), Wemyss Bay (for the Isle of Bute), and Stranraer (for Ireland). The Queen Street station has frequent connections to Edinburgh (50 minutes) and onward by the east-coast route to Aberdeen or south via Edinburgh to Newcastle, York, and King's Cross. Other services from Queen Street go to Stirling, Perth, and Dundee; northward to Inverness, Kyle of Lochalsh, Wick, and Thurso; along the Clyde to Dumbarton and Balloch (for Loch Lomond); and on the scenic West Highland line to Oban, Fort William, and Mallaig. Oban and Mallaig have island ferry connections. For details contact National Rail.

A regular bus service links the Queen Street and Central stations. Both are close to stations on the Glasgow underground. At Queen Street go to Buchanan Street, and at Central go to St. Enoch. City taxis are available at both stations.

The Glasgow area has an extensive network of suburban railway services. Locals still call them the Blue Trains, even though most are now painted maroon and cream. Look for signs to LOW LEVEL TRAINS at the Queen Street and Central stations. For more information and a free map, call Strathclyde Passenger Transport Travel Centre or the National Rail Enquiry Line. Details are also available from the Greater Glasgow and Clyde Valley Tourist Board.

Train Contacts **National Rail** (☎ 0870/748–4950 ⊕ www.nationalrail.co.uk). **Strathclyde Passenger Transport Travel Centre** (✉ 12 W. George St., City Center ☎ 0141/332–6811 ⊕ www.spt.co.uk).

VISITOR INFORMATION

The Greater Glasgow and Clyde Valley Tourist Board provides information and has an accommodations-booking service, a currency-exchange office, a Western Union money-transfer service, city bus tours, guided walks, boat trips, and coach tours around Scotland. Books, maps, and souvenirs are also available. The tourist board has a branch at Glasgow Airport, too.

SIGHTSEEING TOURS

You can sign on for a sightseeing tour to get a different perspective on the city and the surrounding area.

BOAT TOURS

Cruises are available on Loch Lomond and to the islands in the Firth of Clyde; contact the Greater Glasgow and Clyde Valley Tourist Board for details. Contact the *Waverley* paddle steamer from June through August.

Contact Greater Glasgow and Clyde Valley Tourist Board (✉ *11 George Sq., near Queen Street station, City Center* ☎ *0141/204–4400* ⊕ *www.seeglasgow.com*). **Waverley** (☎ *0141/221–8152* ⊕ *www. waverleyexcursions.co.uk*).

BUS TOURS

The popular City Sightseeing bus tours leave daily from the west side of George Square. The Greater Glasgow and Clyde Valley Tourist Board can give information about city tours and about longer tours northward to the Highlands and Islands.

Day trips in minivans (16 people maximum) to the surrounding areas, including Loch Lomond and Oban are avaialble from Rabbie's Trail Burners.

Contact City Sightseeing (☎ *0141/204–0444* ⊕ *www. citysightseeingglasgow.co.uk*). **Greater Glasgow and Clyde Valley Tourist Board** (✉ *11 George Sq., near Queen Street station, City Center* ☎ *0141/ 204–4400* ⊕ *www.seeglasgow.com*). **Rabbie's Trail Burners** (☎ *0845/ 643–2248* ⊕ *www.rabbies.com*).

PRIVATE GUIDES

Little's Chauffeur Drive arranges personally tailored car-and-driver tours, both locally and throughout Scotland. The Scottish Tourist Guides Association also provides a private-guide service.

Taxi firms offer city tours. If you allow the driver to follow a set route, the cost is £16 per half-hour for up to five people, or 80 minutes for £34. If you wish the driver to follow your own route, the charge will be £16 an hour or the reading on the meter, whichever is greater. You can book tours in advance and be picked up and dropped off wherever you like. Contact Glasgow Taxis.

Contact Glasgow Taxis (☎ *0141/ 429–7070* ⊕ *www.glasgowtaxisltd. co.uk*). **Little's Chauffeur Drive** (☎ *0141/883–2111* ⊕ *www.littles. co.uk*). **Scottish Tourist Guides Association** (☎ *01786/451953* ⊕ *www.stga.co.uk*).

WALKING TOURS

The Greater Glasgow and Clyde Valley Tourist Board can provide information on special walks on a given day. Glasgow Walking Tours organizes specialized tours of the city's architectural treasures.

For spine-chilling tales about the city accompanied by costumed characters like Mary, Queen of Scots, contact Mercat Glasgow.

Contact Glasgow Walking Tours (☎ *01620/825722* ⊕ *www. glasgowarchitecture.co.uk/glasgow_ walking_tours.htm*). **Greater Glasgow and Clyde Valley Tourist Board** (✉ *11 George Sq., near Queen Street station, City Center* ☎ *0141/204–4400* ⊕ *www. seeglasgow.com*). **Mercat Glasgow** (☎ *0141/586–5378* ⊕ *www.w3serve. com/mercat*).

Contacts **Greater Glasgow and Clyde Valley Tourist Board** (⊠ *11 George Sq., near Queen Sreet Station, City Center* ☎ *0141/204–4400* ⊕ *www. seeglasgow.com*).

EXPLORING GLASGOW

As cities go, Glasgow is contained and compact. It's set up on a grid system, so it's easy to navigate and explore, and the best way to tackle it is on foot. In the eastern part of the city, start by exploring the highlights of Medieval Glasgow and the Merchant City. Next you can either walk (it takes a good 45 minutes) or take the subway to the West End. If you walk, go up Sauchiehall Street and visit Mackintosh's Glasgow School of Art. Once in the West End, visit the Botanic Gardens, Glasgow University and the Kelvingrove Art Gallery and Museum. Take a taxi to the South Side to experience the Burrell Collection. If you break your sightseeing up into neighborhoods and top sights, it's completely manageable. Distances between neighborhoods range from 3 mi (City Center to the West End) to 7 mi (West End to South Side). You need three full days to explore all three neighborhoods comfortably. Glasgow's pubs and clubs serve up entertainment until late in the evening; there's something for everyone.

MEDIEVAL GLASGOW AND THE MERCHANT CITY

In this central part of the city, alongside the relatively few surviving medieval buildings, are some of the best examples of the architectural confidence and exuberance that so characterized the burgeoning Glasgow of the turn of the 20th century. A lot of the city's most important historical buildings are found here, as well as plenty of trendy eateries and pubs.

GETTING HERE   Every form of public transportation can bring you here, from bus to train to subway. Get off at the stop or station closest to George Square and then walk from there.

TOP ATTRACTIONS

8 **Barras.** Scotland's largest indoor market—named for the barrows, or pushcarts, formerly used by the stall holders—is a must-see for anyone addicted to searching through piles of junk for bargains. The century-old institution, open weekends, consists of nine markets. The atmosphere is always good-humored, and you can find just about anything here, in any condition, from dusty model railroads to antique jewelry. Haggling is compulsory! You can reach the Barras by walking from the Argyle Street train station, or take any of the various buses to Glasgow Cross at the foot of the Gallowgate. ⊠ *Gallowgate, ¼ mi east of Glasgow Cross, Glasgow Cross* ☎ *0141/552–4601* ⊕ *www.glasgow-barras. com* ⊠ *Free* ⊗ *Weekends 10–5.*

2 **City Chambers.** Dominating the east side of George Square, this exuber-
★ ant expression of Victorian confidence, built by William Young in Italian Renaissance style, was opened by Queen Victoria (1819–1901) in 1888. Among the interior's outstanding features are the entrance hall's

vaulted ceiling, the marble-and-alabaster staircases, the banqueting hall, and Venetian mosaics. The debating chamber has gleaming oak panels and fixtures. Free guided tours lasting about 45 minutes depart week-days at 10:30 and 2:30. ■TIP➔ **Note that the building is closed to all visitors during occasional civic functions.** ✉ *80 George Sq., City Center* ☎ *0141/287–4020* ⊕ *www.glasgow.gov.uk* 🖅 *Free* ☉ *Weekdays 9–5.*

❶ **George Square.** The focal point of Glasgow's business district is lined with an impressive collection of statues of worthies: Queen Victoria; Scotland's national poet, Robert Burns (1759–96); the inventor and developer of the steam engine, James Watt (1736–1819); Prime Minister William Gladstone (1809–98); and towering above them all, Scotland's great historical novelist, Sir Walter Scott (1771–1832). The column was intended for George III (1738–1820), after whom the square is named, but when he was found to be insane toward the end of his reign, his statue was never erected. On the square's east side stands the magnificent Italian Renaissance–style **City Chambers**; the handsome **Merchants' House** fills the corner of West George Street.

Off and around George Square, several streets—Virginia Street, Miller Street, Glassford Street—recall the yesterdays of mercantile wealth. The French-style palaces, with their steep mansard roofs and cupolas, were once tobacco warehouses. Inside are shops and offices; here and there you may trace the elaborately carved mahogany galleries where auctions once took place. ✉ *Between St. Vincent and Argyle Sts., City Center.*

❸ **Glasgow Cathedral.** The most complete of Scotland's cathedrals (it would
Fodor's Choice have been more complete had 19th-century vandals not pulled down
★ its two rugged towers), this is an unusual double church, one above the other, dedicated to Glasgow's patron saint, St. Mungo. Consecrated in 1136 and completed about 300 years later, it was spared the ravages of the Reformation—which destroyed so many of Scotland's medieval churches—mainly because Glasgow's trade guilds defended it. A late-medieval open timber roof in the nave and lovely 20th-century stained glass are notable features. In the lower church is the splendid crypt of St. Mungo, who was originally known as St. Kentigern (*kentigern* means "chief word,") but who was nicknamed St. Mungo (meaning "dear one") by his early followers in Glasgow. The site of the tomb has been revered since the 6th century, when St. Mungo founded a church here. Mungo features prominently in local legends; one such legend is about a pet bird that he nursed back to life, and another tells of a bush or tree, the branches of which he used to miraculously relight a fire. Bird, tree, and the salmon with a ring in its mouth (from the famous tale related in the introduction to this chapter) are all to be found on the city of Glasgow's coat of arms, together with a bell that Mungo brought from Rome. ✉ *Cathedral St., City Center* ☎ *0141/552–6891* ⊕ *www. glasgow-cathedral.com* 🖅 *Free* ☉ *Apr.–Sept., Mon.–Sat. 9:30–5:30, Sun. 1–5; Oct.–Mar., Mon.–Sat. 9:30–4:30, Sun. 1–4:30.*

NEED A BREAK?
Peckham's ✉ *61–65 Glassford St., City Center* ☎ *0141/553–0666* ⊕ www. peckhams.co.uk, perfect for a quick little pick-me-up, has a gourmet café upstairs with glass walls, marble counters, and several tables. Choose among homemade cakes, pastries, and cookies as well as fresh soups,

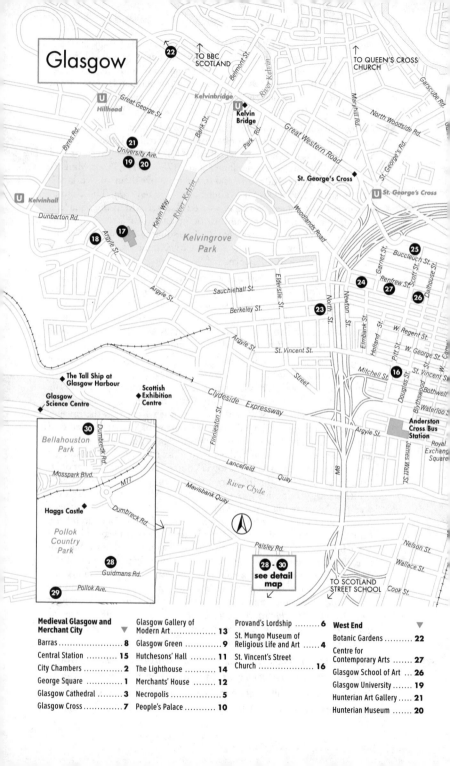

Glasgow

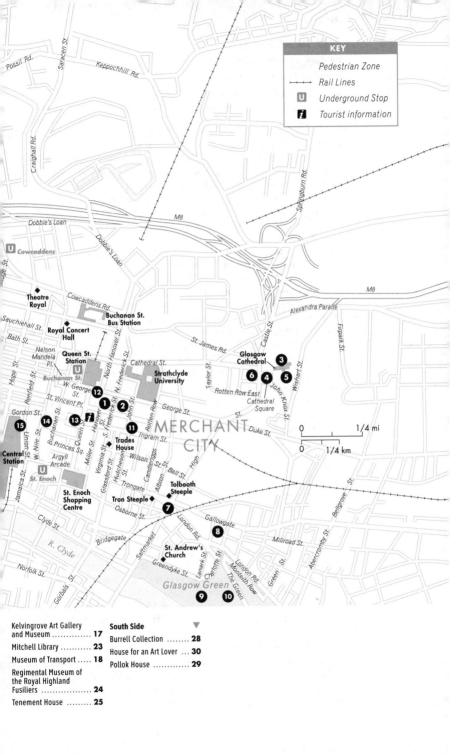

KEY

- Pedestrian Zone
- ⊢•⊣ Rail Lines
- Ⓤ Underground Stop
- 𝒊 Tourist information

Possil Rd.

Saracen St.

Keppochhill Rd.

Craighall Rd.

M8

Dobbie's Loan

Dobbie's Loan

Ⓤ Cowcaddens

Cowcaddens Rd.

M8

Alexandra Parade

Firpark St.

Springburn Rd.

Castle St.

Theatre Royal

Royal Concert Hall

Buchanan St. Bus Station

St. James Rd.

Glasgow Cathedral ③

⑥ ④ ⑤

Sauchiehall St.

Bath St.

Nelson Mandela Pl.

Queen St. Station

Cathedral St.

Strathclyde University

Rotten Row East

Cathedral Square

Hope St.

Renfield St.

Ⓤ Buchanan St.

W. George St.

⑫

North Hanover St.

N. Frederick St.

Taylor St.

Rotten Row

George St.

John Knox St.

Wishart St.

St. Vincent Pl.

① ②

John St.

Duke St.

St.

MERCHANT CITY

Gordon St.

⑭ ⑬ 𝒊

Miller St.

Virginia St.

Glassford St.

S. Frederick St.

⑪

Ingram St.

Ⓤ ⑮

W. Nile St.

Buchanan St.

Queen St.

Hutcheson St.

Candleriggs

Bell St.

High St.

Central Station

Princes Sq.

Argyll Arcade

Trades House

Wilson St.

Albion St.

Jamaica St.

Ⓤ St. Enoch

Trongate

Tolbooth Steeple

Gallowgate

St. Enoch Shopping Centre

Tron Steeple ◆

Osborne St.

⑦

⑧

Millroad St.

Clyde St.

Saltmarket

London Rd.

London Rd.

Bellgrove St.

Abercromby St.

R. Clyde

Bridgegate

St. Andrew's Church

Greendyke St.

Lanark St.

Charlotte St.

Monteith Row

Green St.

Norfolk St.

Gorbals

Glasgow Green

The Green

⑨

⑩

0 ————— 1/4 mi

0 ————— 1/4 km

hearty sandwiches, and frothy coffee drinks. Downstairs you can buy everything from international micobrews to European chocolates. It's a stone's throw from Argyle Street, and a good value.

MACKINTOSH TRAIL

If you're interested in the work of architect Charles Rennie Macintosh, you might purchase a £12 **Mackintosh Trail Ticket** at major sites, visitor centers, or online from the Mackintosh Society. It includes transportation and one-day admission to many sites. Strathclyde Passenger Transport (⊕ *www.spt.co.uk*) has more information.

⑬ **Glasgow Gallery of Modern Art.** One
★ of Glasgow's boldest, most innovative galleries occupies the neoclassical former Royal Exchange building. The modern art, craft, and design collections include works by Scottish conceptual artists such as David Mach, and also paintings and sculptures from around the world, including Papua New Guinea, Ethiopia, and Mexico. Each floor of the gallery reflects the elements—air, fire, earth, and water—which creates some unexpected juxtapositions and also allows for various interactive exhibits. The exchange building, designed by David Hamilton (1768–1843) and finished in 1829, was a meeting place for merchants and traders; later it became Stirling's Library. It incorporates the mansion built in 1780 by William Cunninghame, one of the wealthiest tobacco lords. ⊠ *Queen St., City Center* ☎ *0141/229–1996* ⊕ *www.glasgowmuseums.com* ⊠ *Free* ⊙ *Mon.–Wed. and Sat. 10–5, Thurs. 10–8, Fri. and Sun. 11–5.*

⑨ **Glasgow Green.** Glasgow's oldest park, on the north side of the River
ↂ Clyde, has a long history as a favorite spot for public recreation and political demonstrations. Note the Nelson Column, erected long before London's; the McLennan Arch, originally part of the facade of the old Assembly Halls in Ingram Street; and the Templeton Business Centre, a former carpet factory built in the late 19th century in the style of the Doge's Palace in Venice. The most significant building in the park is the **People's Palace.** ⊠ *Between Greendyke St. to north and River Clyde to south, and between Green to east and Saltmarket to west, Trongate and East End.*

⑭ **The Lighthouse.** Charles Rennie Mackintosh designed these former offices of the *Glasgow Herald* newspaper in 1893. Mackintosh's building now serves as a fitting setting for Scotland's **Centre for Architecture, Design and the City,** which celebrates all facets of the architectural profession. The **Mackintosh Interpretation Centre** is a great starting point for discovering more about his other buildings in the city. As you ascend the helical staircase you can take a look at Mackintosh's original designs for the building. ⊠ *11 Mitchell La., City Center* ☎ *0141/225–8414* ⊕ *www.thelighthouse.co.uk* ⊠ *£3 for Mackintosh Interpretation Centre* ⊙ *Mon. and Wed.–Sat. 10:30–5, Tues. 11–5, Sun. noon–5.*

Merchant City. Many of the city's most important Georgian and Victorian buildings, many built by the tobacco merchants, are found here, as well as elegant designer boutiques and trendy eateries and pubs. The City and County buildings on Ingram Street were built in 1842 to house

UNION AND GROWTH

Glasgow flourished quietly during the Middle Ages. Its cathedral was the center of religious life, its university a center of serious academia. Although the city was made a burgh (meaning that it was granted trading rights) in 1175 by King William the Lion, its population never numbered more than a few thousand people.

What changed Glasgow irrevocably was the Treaty of Union between Scotland and England, in 1707, which allowed Scotland to trade with the essentially English colonies in America. Glasgow, with its advantageous position on Scotland's west coast, prospered. In came cotton, tobacco, and rum; out went various Scottish manufactured goods and clothing. The key to it all was tobacco. The prosperous merchants known as tobacco lords ran the city, and their wealth laid the foundation for the manufacturing industries of the 19th century. You can still see some of the buildings they created in the renovated Merchant City.

civil servants; note the impressive arrangement of bays and Corinthian columns. To see more interesting architecture, explore the roads off Ingram Street—including Candleriggs, Wilson, and Glassford. It tends to be a little more rundown and remote toward the southeast. Stick to well-lit, well-traveled areas after sunset. ⊠ *Between George, Argyle, Buchanan, and High Sts., Merchant City.*

⑤ Necropolis. A burial ground since the beginning of recorded history, the
★ large Necropolis, modeled on the famous Père-Lachaise Cemetery in Paris, contains some extraordinarily elaborate Victorian tombs. A statue of John Knox (circa 1514–72), leader of the Scottish Reformation, watches over the cemetery, which includes the tomb of 19th-century Glasgow merchant William Miller (1810–72), author of the "Wee Willie Winkie" nursery rhyme. The city's Web site (⊕ *www.glasgow.gov. uk*) has a trail with a map; the main gates are behind the St.Mungo Museum of Religious Art and Life. ⊠ *Behind Glasgow Cathedral, City Center* ⊕ *www.glasgownecropolis.org* ☑ *Free* ☉ *Daily 7–dusk.*

⑩ People's Palace. An impressive Victorian red-sandstone building dating
☼ from 1894 houses an intriguing museum dedicated to the city's social history. Included among the exhibits is one devoted to the ordinary folk of Glasgow, called the *People's Story.* Also on display are the writing desk of John McLean (1879–1923), the "Red Clydeside" political activist who came to Lenin's notice, and the famous banana boots worn on stage by Glasgow-born comedian Billy Connolly. Behind the museum are the well-restored Winter Gardens, a relatively sheltered spot where you can escape the often chilly winds whistling across the green. ⊠ *Glasgow Green, Trongate and East End* ☎ *0141/271–2951* ⊕ *www.glasgowmuseums.com* ☑ *Free* ☉ *Mon.–Thurs. and Sat. 10–5, Fri. and Sun. 11–5.*

⑥ Provand's Lordship. Glasgow's oldest house was built in 1471 by Bishop Andrew Muirhead as a residence for churchmen. Mary, Queen of Scots (1542–87) is said to have stayed here. After her day, however, the house fell into decline and was used as a sweets shop, a soft-drink factory, the home of the city hangman, and a junk shop. The city finally rescued it and turned it into a museum. Exhibits show the house as it might have looked in its heyday, with period rooms and a spooky re-creation of the old hangman's room. ⊠ *3 Castle St., City Center* ☏ *0141/552–8819* ⊕ *www.glasgowmuseums.com* 🔲 *Free* ⊙ *Mon.–Thurs. and Sat. 10–5, Fri. and Sun. 11–5.*

❹ **St. Mungo Museum of Religious Life and Art.** An outstanding collection of artifacts, including Celtic crosses and statuettes of Hindu gods, reflects the many religious groups that have settled throughout the centuries in Glasgow and the west of Scotland. This rich history is depicted in the stunning Sharing of Faiths Banner, which celebrates the city's many different faiths. A Zen Garden creates a peaceful setting for rest and contemplation, and elsewhere stained-glass windows include a depiction of St. Mungo himself. ⊠ *2 Castle St., City Center* ☏ *0141/553–2557* ⊕ *www.glasgowmuseums.com* 🔲 *Free* ⊙ *Mon.–Thurs. and Sat. 10–5, Fri. and Sun. 11–5.*

WORTH NOTING

🅖 **Central Station.** The railway bridge supporting the tracks going into the station is known as the Highlandman's Umbrella because it was the traditional gathering place for immigrant Highlanders looking for work in Glasgow in the early 20th century. There are several interesting shops in the depot, which serves as the departure point for trains to England and the Ayrshire coast. ⊠ *Gordon St., bounded by Gordon, Union, Argyle, Jamaica, Clyde, Oswald, and Hope Sts., City Center.*

❼ **Glasgow Cross.** This crossroads was the center of the medieval city. The Mercat Cross (*mercat* means "market"), topped by a unicorn, marks the spot where merchants met, where the market was held, and where criminals were executed. Here, too, was the *tron*, or weigh beam, installed in 1491 and used by merchants to check weights. The Tolbooth Steeple dates from 1626 and served as the civic center and the place where travelers paid tolls. ⊠ *Intersection of Saltmarket, Trongate, Gallowgate, and London Rds., Glasgow Cross.*

⓫ **Hutchesons' Hall.** Now a visitor center and shop for the National Trust for Scotland, this elegant neoclassical building was designed by David Hamilton in 1802. The hall was originally a hospice founded by two brothers, George and Thomas Hutcheson; you can see their statues in niches in the facade. ⊠ *158 Ingram St., Merchant City* ☏ *0141/552–8391* ⊕ *www.nts.org.uk* 🔲 *Free* ⊙ *Mon., Tues., Thurs., and Fri. 10–5.*

⓬ **Merchants' House.** A golden sailing ship, a reminder of the importance of sea trade to Glasgow's prosperity, tops this handsome 1874 Victorian building, home to Glasgow's chamber of commerce. The interior isn't open to the public, but the exterior is impressive. ⊠ *West side of George Sq., Merchant City.*

⓰ **St. Vincent's Street Church.** Dating from 1859, this church, the work of Alexander Thomson, exemplifies his Greek Revival style, replete with Ionic temple, sphinx-esque heads, Greek ornamentation, and rich interior color. There are no tours; you can see the interior only by attending a service Sunday at 11 AM or 6:30 PM. ⊠ *Pitt and St. Vincent Sts., City Center* ⊕ *www.greekthomsonchurch.*

THE WEST END

Glasgow's West End is a neighborhood of museums and art galleries, having benefited from the generosity of industrial and commercial philanthropists and from the deep-seated desire of the city founders to place Glasgow at the forefront of British cities. The neighborhood is dominated by Glasgow University, founded in 1451, making it the third oldest in Scotland, after St. Andrews and Aberdeen, and at least 130 years ahead of the University of Edinburgh. It has thrived as a center of educational excellence, particularly in the sciences. The university buildings sit amid parkland, reminding you that Glasgow is a city with more green space per citizen than any other in Europe. ■TIP➔ **A good way to save money is to take a picnic lunch to the park (weather permitting, of course). You can buy sandwiches, salads, and other portable items at several shops on Byres Road.**

> **GETTING AROUND**
>
> A number of bus companies cooperate with the Underground and ScotRail to produce the **Family Day Tripper Ticket** (£15 for two adults), which gets you around the whole area, from Loch Lomond to Ayrshire. The tickets are a good value and are available from rail and bus stations and at Strathclyde Passenger Transport Travel Centre (⊠ *12 W. George St., City Center* ☎ *0141/332–6811*⊕ *www. spt.co.uk*).

GETTING HERE   The best way to get to the West End is by subway; get off at the Hillhead station. A taxi is another option.

TOP ATTRACTIONS

22 **Botanic Gardens.** The Royal Botanical Institute of Glasgow began to display plants here in 1842, and today the gardens include herbs, tropical plants, and a world-famous collection of orchids. The most spectacular building in the complex is the **Kibble Palace,** extensively renovated and reopened in 2006. Originally built in 1873, it was the conservatory of a Victorian eccentric named John Kibble. Its domed, interlinked greenhouses contain tree ferns, palm trees, temperate plants, and the Tropicarium, where you can experience the lushness of a rain forest. Elsewhere around the grounds are more conventional greenhouses, as well as immaculate lawns and colorful flower beds. ⊠ *730 Great Western Rd., West End* ☎ *0141/334–2422* ⊕ *www.glasgow.gov.uk* ✉ *Free* ⊙ *Gardens Mar.–mid-Oct., daily 7–dusk; mid-Oct.–Feb., daily 7–4:15. Kibble Palace and other greenhouses Mar.–mid-Oct., daily 10–6; mid-Oct.–Feb., daily 10–4:15.*

NEED A BREAK?   The Beanscene (⊠ *16 Cresswell La., West End* ☎ *0141/334–6776,* part of a Scottish coffeehouse chain, has comfy leather sofas and armchairs to help you enjoy the extra-large coffee drinks, toasted sandwiches, and triple-berry muffins. Homemade soups, paellas, and tapas are other options. This is a popular haunt among university professors and graduate students. Tall plants, laptops, and music complete the scene.

A GOOD WALK

This tranquil stroll, taking about an hour if you don't poke into the museums, showcases all of the beauty the West End has to offer. Start in Kelvingrove Park, at the junction of Sauchiehall (pronounced *socky*-hall) and Argyle streets, where the city's main art museum, Kelvingrove Art Gallery and Museum stands. The impressive red-sandstone building and its leafy surroundings are well worth a visit as is the Museum of Transport, on the opposite side of the street. From here stroll up tree-lined Kelvin Way; the skyline to your left is dominated dramatically by Glasgow University.

Turn left onto University Avenue and walk past the Memorial Gates. On the south side of University Avenue is the Hunterian Museum. Across University Avenue is the even more interesting Hunterian Art Gallery. From here make your way up to the Botanic Gardens, where 12 Victorian conservatories and their fragrant collections await you. To get there continue west along University Avenue, turn right at Byres Road, and walk as far as Great Western Road. The 40 acres of gardens are across the busy intersection. Its peaceful garden makes you feel a million miles away from the city center.

26 ★ **Glasgow School of Art.** The exterior and interior, structure, furnishings, and decoration of this art nouveau building, built between 1897 and 1909, form a unified whole, reflecting the inventive genius of Charles Rennie Mackintosh, who was only 28 years old when he won the competition for its design. Architects and designers from all over the world come to admire it, but because it's a working school of art, general access is sometimes limited. Guided tours beginning at the top of the hour are available; it's best to make reservations. You can always visit the four on-site galleries that host frequently changing exhibitions. The shop sells a good selection of Mackintosh prints, postcards, and books, plus a selection of contemporary art by the school's students and graduates. A block away at 217 Sauchiehall Street is Mackintosh's Willow Tearoom, perfect for a break. ⊠ *167 Renfrew St., City Center* ☎ *0141/353–4526* ⊕ *www.gsa.ac.uk* ⊠ *£7.75* ☉ *Tours Oct.–Mar., Mon.–Sat. 11 and 3; Apr.–Sept., daily 10–4.*

OFF THE BEATEN PATH

Glasgow Science Centre. Families with children love this museum, which has a fun-packed Science Mall, an IMAX theater, and the futuristic Glasgow Tower. The 417-foot spire—with an aerodynamic profile that twists 360 degrees—is a marvel. In the three-level Science Mall, state-of-the-art displays educate kids and adults about exploration, discovery, and the environment. The ScottishPower Planetarium has a fantastic Zeiss Starmaster projector, which allows visitors to gaze at the glittering stars. Set aside half a day to see everything. ⊠ *50 Pacific Quay, South Side* ☎ *0141/420–5000* ⊕ *www.gsc.org.uk* ⊠ *IMAX film, Science Mall, or Glasgow Tower £8.25; any two attractions £12* ☉ *Daily 10–6.*

19 **Glasgow University.** The architecture, grounds, and great views of Glasgow all warrant a visit to the university. The Gilbert Scott Building, the university's main edifice, was built more than a century ago and is a good example of the Gothic-revival style. **Glasgow University Visitor**

Centre, near the main gate on University Avenue, has exhibits on the university, a coffee bar, and a gift shop; it's the starting point for one-hour guided walking tours of the campus. A self-guided tour starts at the visitor center and takes in the east and west quadrangles, the cloisters, Professor's Square, Pearce Lodge, and the not-to-be-missed University Chapel. ⊠ *University Ave., West End* ☎ *0141/330–5511* ⊕ *www. glasgow.ac.uk* ⊡ *Tour £3.50* ⊙ *May–Sept., Mon.–Sat. 9:30–5.*

㉑ ★ Hunterian Art Gallery. This Glasgow University gallery houses William Hunter's (1718–83) collection of paintings (his antiquarian collection is housed in the nearby Hunterian Museum), together with prints and drawings by Tintoretto, Rembrandt, Sir Joshua Reynolds, and Auguste Rodin, as well as a major collection of paintings by James McNeill Whistler, who had a great affection for the city that bought one of his earliest paintings. Also in the gallery is a replica of **Charles Rennie Mackintosh's town house,** which once stood nearby. The rooms contain Mackintosh's distinctive art-nouveau chairs, tables, beds, and cupboards, and the walls are decorated in the equally distinctive style devised by him and his artist wife, Margaret. ⊠ *Hillhead St., West End* ☎ *0141/330–5431* ⊕ *www.hunterian.gla.ac.uk* ⊡ *Free* ⊙ *Mon.–Sat. 9:30–5.*

㉒ Hunterian Museum. Part of Glasgow University, the city's oldest museum (opened in 1807) showcases part of the collections of William Hunter, an 18th-century Glasgow doctor who assembled a staggering quantity of valuable material. (The doctor's art treasures are housed in the nearby Hunterian Art Gallery.) The museum displays Hunter's hoards of coins, manuscripts, scientific instruments, and archaeological artifacts in a striking Gothic building. ⊠ *University Ave., West End* ☎ *0141/330–4221* ⊕ *www.hunterian.gla.ac.uk* ⊡ *Free* ⊙ *Mon.–Sat. 9:30–5.*

⑰ Kelvingrove Art Gallery and Museum. Impressively remodeled in 2006, the Kelvingrove is a museum and gallery worthy of its world-class art Fodor's Choice collection and its other cultural and natural history holdings. This combination of cathedral and castle was designed in the Renaissance style and built between 1891 and 1901. The stunning red-sandstone edifice is an appropriate home for works by Botticelli, Rembrandt, Monet, and others; the museum has been hailed as "one of the greatest civic collections in Europe." The Glasgow Room houses extraordinary works by local artists. There's also a Mackintosh and the Glasgow Style room, a multimedia object cinema, a picture promenade, and a natural history exhibit on creatures of the past. Whether the subject is Scottish culture, design, or storytelling, every wall and room begs you to look deeper; labels are thought provoking and sometimes witty. You could spend a weekend here, but in a pinch three hours would do one level justice—there are three. ⊠ *Argyle St., Kelvingrove Park, West End* ☎ *0141/276–9599* ⊕ *www.glasgowmuseums.com* ⊡ *Free* ⊙ *Mon.–Thurs., and Sat. 10–5, Fri. and Sun. 11–5.*

Kelvingrove Park. A peaceful retreat, the park was purchased by the city in 1852 and takes its name from the River Kelvin, which flows through it. Among the numerous statues of prominent Glaswegians is one of Lord Kelvin (1824–1907), the Scottish mathematician and physicist

Charles Rennie Mackintosh

Not so long ago, the furniture of innovative Glasgow-born architect Charles Rennie Mackintosh (1868–1928) was broken up for firewood. Today art books are devoted to his distinctive, astonishingly elegant Arts and Crafts– and art nouveau–influenced interiors, and artisans around the world look to his theory that "decoration should not be constructed, rather construction should be decorated" as holy law. Mackintosh's stripped-down designs ushered in the modern age with their deceptively stark style.

AN ARCHITECT'S CAREER

Mackintosh trained in architecture at the Glasgow School of Art and was apprenticed to the Glasgow firm of John Hutchison at the age of 16. Early influences on his work included the Pre-Raphaelites, James McNeill Whistler (1834–1903), Aubrey Beardsley (1872–98), and Japanese art. But by the 1890s a distinct Glasgow style developed.

The building for the *Glasgow Herald* newspaper, which he designed in 1893 and which is now the Lighthouse Centre for Architecture, Design and the City, was soon followed by other major Glasgow buildings: Queen Margaret's Medical College; the Martyrs Public School; tearooms including the Willow Tearoom; the Hill House, in Helensburgh, now owned by the National Trust for Scotland; and Queen's Cross Church, completed in 1899 and now the headquarters of the Charles Rennie Mackintosh Society. In 1897 Mackintosh began work on a new home for the Glasgow School of Art, recognized as one of his major achievements.

Mackintosh married Margaret Macdonald in 1900, and in later years her decorative work enhanced the interiors of his buildings. In 1904 he became a partner in Honeyman and Keppie and designed Scotland Street School, now the Scotland Street School Museum, in the same year. Until 1913, when he left Honeyman and Keppie and moved to England, Mackintosh's projects included buildings over much of Scotland. He preferred wherever possible to include interiors as part of his overall design.

Commissions in England after 1913 included design challenges not confined to buildings, such as fabrics, furniture, and even bookbindings. Mackintosh died in London in 1928.

After 1904 architectural taste had turned against Mackintosh's style; his work was seen as strange. Mackintosh could not conform to the times; he lost commissions, drank heavily, and ended up poor and sick. His reputation revived only in the 1950s with the publication of his monographs.

HOW TO SEE HIS WORK

Glasgow is the best place in the world to admire Mackintosh's work: in addition to the buildings mentioned above, most of which can be visited, the Hunterian Art Gallery contains magnificent reconstructions of the principal rooms at 78 Southpark Avenue, Mackintosh's Glasgow home, and original drawings, documents, and records, plus the re-creation of a room at 78 Derngate, Northampton. To take it all in, purchase a £12 **Mackintosh Trail Ticket** at major sites, visitor centers, or online from the Mackintosh Society (⊕ www.crmsociety.com). It includes transportation and one-day admission to many sites.

who pioneered a great deal of work in electricity. The park also has a massive fountain commemorating a lord provost of Glasgow from the 1850s, a duck pond, a play area, a small open-air theater, and lots of exotic trees. ⊠ *Bounded roughly by Sauchiehall St., Woodlands Rd., and Kelvin Way, West End.*

㉓ Mitchell Library. The largest public reference library in Europe houses more than a million volumes, including what's claimed to be the world's largest collection about Robert Burns. A bust in the entrance hall commemorates the library's founder, Stephen Mitchell, who died in 1874. Minerva, goddess of wisdom, looks down from the library's dome, encouraging the library's users and frowning at the drivers thundering along the motorway just in front of her. The western facade (at the back), with its sculpted figures of Mozart, Beethoven, Michelangelo, and other artistic figures, is particularly beautiful. ⊠ *North St., City Center* ☎ *0141/287-2999* ⊕ *www.mitchelllibrary.org* ⊠ *Free* ☽ *Mon.– Thurs. 9–8, Fri. and Sat. 9–5.*

⑱ Museum of Transport. Here Glasgow's history of locomotive building is
ↄ dramatically displayed with impressive full-size exhibits. The collection of Clyde-built ship models is world famous. Anyone who knows what Britain was like in the 1930s will wax nostalgic at the re-created street scene from that era. ⊠ *Kelvin Hall, 1 Bunhouse Rd., West End* ☎ *0141/287-2720* ⊕ *www.glasgowmuseums.com* ⊠ *Free* ☽ *Mon.– Thurs. and Sat. 10–5, Fri. and Sun. 11–5.*

WORTH NOTING

㉗ Centre for Contemporary Arts. This arts, cinema, and performance venue is in a post–Industrial Revolution Alexander Thomson building. It has a reputation for unusual visual-arts exhibitions, from paintings and sculpture to new media, and has championed a number of emerging talents, including Toby Paterson, one of Scotland's most successful contemporary artists. The vibrant Tempus Bar Café is designed by Los Angeles–based artist Jorge Pardo. ⊠ *350 Sauchiehall St., City Center* ☎ *0141/352-4900* ⊕ *www.cca-glasgow.com* ⊠ *Free* ☽ *Tues.–Fri. 11–6, Sat. 10–6.*

**OFF THE
BEATEN
PATH**

Queen's Cross Church. Head for the Charles Rennie Mackintosh Society Headquarters, in the only church Mackintosh designed, to learn more about the famous Glasgow-born architect and designer. Although one of the leading lights in the turn-of-the-20th-century art nouveau movement, Mackintosh died in relative obscurity in 1928. Today he's widely accepted as a brilliant innovator. The church has beautiful stained-glass windows and a light-enhancing, carved-wood interior. The center's library and shop provide further insight into Glasgow's other Mackintosh-designed buildings, which include Scotland Street School, the Martyrs Public School, and the Glasgow School of Art. The church sits on the corner of Springbank Street at the junction of Garscube Road with Maryhill Road; a cab ride can get you here, or take a bus toward Queen's Cross from stops along Hope Street. It's a mile from the St. George's Cross subway stop. ⊠ *870 Garscube Rd., West End* ☎ *0141/946-6600* ⊕ *www.crmsociety.com* ⊠ *£2* ☽ *Mar.–Oct., week-days 10–5, Sun. 2–5; Nov.–Feb., weekdays 10–5.*

㉔ **Regimental Museum of the Royal Highland Fusiliers.** Exhibits of medals, badges, and uniforms relate the history of a famous, much-honored regiment and the men who served in it. ✉ *518 Sauchiehall St., City Center* ☎ *0141/332–0961* ⊕ *www.rhf.org.uk* ✉ *Free* ☉ *Mon.–Thurs. 9–4:30, Fri. 9–4, weekends by appointment only.*

OFF THE BEATEN PATH

The Tall Ship at Glasgow Harbor. This maritime attraction centers around the restored tall ship the *Glenlee*, a former cargo ship originally built in Glasgow in 1896, purchased by the Spanish navy, and bought back by the Clyde Maritime Trust in 1993. The ship itself is fascinating, but take time to explore the Pumphouse Exhibition and Gallery, which screens films of the restoration process and hosts interactive exhibits. A bus (No. 100) runs every half hour from the Buchanan Street bus station. ✉ *100 Stobcross Rd., West End* ☎ *0141/222–2513* ⊕ *www.thetallship.com* ✉ *£5.95* ☉ *Mar.–Oct., daily 10–5; Nov.–Feb., daily 11–4.*

㉕ **Tenement House.** This ordinary apartment building is anything but ordinary inside: it was occupied from 1911 to 1965 by Agnes Toward, who seems never to have thrown anything away. Her legacy is a fascinating time capsule, painstakingly preserved with her everyday furniture and belongings. The red-sandstone building dates from 1892 and can be found in the Garnethill area north of Charing Cross station. ✉ *145 Buccleuch St., City Center* ☎ *0141/333–0183* ⊕ *www.nts.org.uk* ✉ *£5.50* ☉ *Mar.–Oct., daily 1–5; last admission at 4:30.*

> **GLASGOW'S UNDERGROUND**
>
> Glasgow is the only city in Scotland with a subway—or underground, as it's called here. The system was built at the end of the 19th century and takes the simple form of two circular routes, one going clockwise and the other counterclockwise. All trains eventually bring you back to where you started, and the complete circle takes 24 minutes. The tunnels are small, and so are the trains. This, together with the affection in which the system is held and the bright orange paints of the trains, gave the system the nickname the "Clockwork Orange."

THE SOUTH SIDE: ART-FILLED PARKS

Just southwest of the city center in the South Side are two of Glasgow's dear green places—Bellahouston Park and Pollok Country Park—which have important art collections: Charles Rennie Mackintosh's House for an Art Lover, the Burrell Collection, and Pollok House. A respite from the buzz of the city can also be found in the parks, where you can have a picnic or ramble through greenery and gardens.

GETTING HERE Both parks are off Paisley Road, about 3 mi southwest of the city center. You can take a taxi or car, city bus, or a train from Glasgow Central Station to Pollokshaws West Station or Dumbreck.

TOP ATTRACTIONS

㉘ **Burrell Collection.** An elegant, ultramodern building of pink-sandstone

Fodor's Choice ★ and stainless steel houses thousands of items of all descriptions, from ancient Egyptian, Greek, and Roman artifacts to Chinese ceramics, bronzes, and jade. You can also find medieval tapestries, stained-glass windows, Rodin sculptures, and exquisite French-impressionist paintings—Degas's *The Rehearsal* and Sir Henry Raeburn's *Miss Macartney,* to name a few. Eccentric millionaire Sir William Burrell (1861–1958) donated the magpie collection to the city in 1944. The 1983 building's exterior and interior were designed with large glass walls so that the items on display could relate to their surroundings in Pollok Country Park: art and nature, supposedly in perfect harmony. You can get here via buses 45, 48, and 57 from Union Street. ⊠ *2060 Pollokshaws Rd., South Side* ☎ *0141/287–2550* ⊕ *www.glasgowmuseums.com* ☜ *Free* ⊗ *Mon.–Thurs. and Sat. 10–5, Fri. and Sun. 11–5.*

③⓪ House for an Art Lover. Within Bellahouston Park is a "new" Mackintosh house: based on a competition entry Charles Rennie Mackintosh submitted to a German magazine in 1901, the house was never built in his lifetime but took shape between 1989 and 1996. The building houses Glasgow School of Art's postgraduate study center and exhibits of designs for the various rooms and decorative pieces Mackintosh and his wife, Margaret, created. There's also a café and shop filled with artworks. Buses 9, 53, and 54 from Union Street will get you here. Call ahead, as the building is often closed for official functions. ⊠ *Bellahouston Park, 10 Dumbreck Rd., South Side* ☎ *0141/353–4770* ⊕ *www.houseforanartlover.co.uk* ☜ *£4.50* ⊗ *Apr.–Sept., Mon.–Wed. 10–4, Thurs.–Sun. 10–1; Oct.–Mar., weekends 10–1.*

WORTH NOTING

OFF THE BEATEN PATH **Holmwood House.** The National Trust for Scotland has undertaken the restoration of this large mansion house, designed by Alexander "Greek" Thomson for the wealthy owner of a paper mill. Its classical Greek architecture and stunningly ornamented wood and marble features are among his finest. You can witness the ongoing restoration process one or two days a week; call to check the dates. ⊠ *61–63 Netherlee Rd., South Side* ☎ *0141/637–2129* ⊕ *www.nts.org.uk* ☜ *£5.50* ⊗ *Apr.–Oct., Thurs.–Mon. noon–5:30; last admission at 5.*

②⑨ Pollok House. The classic Georgian Pollok House, dating from the mid-1700s, contains the Stirling Maxwell Collection of paintings, including works by El Greco, Murillo, Goya, Signorelli, and William Blake. Fine 18th- and early-19th-century furniture, silver, glass, and porcelain are also on display. The house has lovely gardens and looks over the White Cart River and Pollok Country Park, where, amid mature trees and abundant wildlife, the city of Glasgow's own cattle peacefully graze. Take buses 45, 47, or 57 to the Gate of Pollok County Park. ⊠ *2060 Pollokshaws Rd., South Side* ☎ *0141/616–6410* ⊕ *www.nts.org.uk* ☜ *£5.50* ⊗ *Daily 10–5.*

OFF THE BEATEN PATH **Scotland Street School Museum.** A former school designed by Charles Rennie Mackintosh, this building houses a fascinating museum of education. Classrooms re-create school life in Scotland during Victorian times and World War II, and a cookery room recounts a time when education for Scottish girls consisted of little more than learning how to become a housewife. An exhibition space and café are also here. The building sits opposite Shields Road underground station. ⊠ *225 Scotland St., South*

Side ☎ *0141/287–0500* ⊕ *www.glasgowmuseums.com* ✉ *Free* ⊙ *Apr.–Sept., Mon.–Thurs. and Sat. 10–5, Fri. and Sun. 11–5.*

WHERE TO EAT

The key to the latest trend in Glaswegian cuisine is fresh, local, often organic ingredients. In the past few years restaurants have been popping up that emphasize all the fine foods Scotland offers: grass-fed beef, wild seafood, free-range chicken, duck, and goose—not to mention superb fruits and vegetables. A flurry of foreign restaurants also line the streets—from casual late-night crepe stalls and *pakora* (Indian fried-chickpea cakes) bars to elegant restaurants with worldly menus. And because smoking isn't allowed in any enclosed space, many restaurants have decided to place tables outside under awnings during the warm(ish) summer months. With this type of outdoor dining comes fresher, more Mediterranean-style meals.

Although some celebrity chefs and chain restaurants have left their mark, it's the small, independent, Scottish-theme eateries like Cafezique, No. Sixteen Byres Road, the Sisters, Stravaigin, and the Ubiquitous Chip that are making all the waves. They focus on what's seasonal, and so the food scene is a far cry from the fried potatoes and black puddings of the past. Today's Glasgow is also a city with an appetite, so wherever you go be sure to make a reservation.

PRICES

Eating in Glasgow can be casual or lavish, with the same prices and variety as you'll find in Edinburgh. For inexpensive dining, consider the benefit of pretheater menus. Beer and spirits cost much the same as they would in a bar, but wine is relatively expensive in restaurants.

■ TIP→ **Many restaurants allow you to bring your own bottle of wine, charging just a small corkage fee. It's worth the effort.**

WHAT IT COSTS IN POUNDS				
£	££	£££	££££	£££££
AT DINNER	under £10	£10–£14	£15–£19	£20–£25	over £25

Prices are per person for a main course at dinner.

MEDIEVAL GLASGOW AND MERCHANT CITY

Use the coordinate (✛ B2) at the end of each listing to locate a site on the corresponding map.

This part of the city has restaurants catering to the 9-to-5 crowd, meaning there are a lot of fine dining establishments catching people as they leave work. You can however, always find a fish-and-chips shop on any busy street corner.

£££   ✕ **Amber Regent.** This may not be the cheapest Chinese restaurant in
CHINESE   town, but it's certainly one of the finest and most formal. For a start, the meticulously sculpted vegetables that accompany the hors d'oeuvres

BEST BETS FOR GLASGOW DINING

Where can you find the best food Glasgow has to offer? Fodor's writers and editors have selected their favorite restaurants by price, cuisine, and experience in the lists below. In the first column, the Fodor's Choice properties represent the "best of the best" across price categories. You can also search by neighborhood for excellent eating experiences—just peruse our complete reviews on the following pages.

Fodor's Choice ★

Balbir's, £ p. 132
Corinthian, £££ p. 127
Hotel du Vin Bistro, ££££ p. 133
No. Sixteen Byres Road, ££ p. 134
Rogano, £££££ p. 131
Ubiquitous Chip, £££££ p. 134

By Price

£

Balbir's, p. 132
Mother India Café, p. 133
Willow Tearoom, p. 131

££

Cafezique, p. 132
Café Cossachok, p. 126
Crabshakk, p. 132
Kool Ba, p. 130
No. Sixteen Byres Road, p. 134

£££

The Brasserie at Oran Mor, p. 132
Café Gandolfi, p. 126
Corinthian, p. 127
Two Fat Ladies, p. 131

££££

Hotel du Vin Bistro, p. 133
Khublai Khan Barbecue, p. 127
The Sisters, p. 134

£££££

Rogano, p. 131
Ubiquitous Chip, p. 134

By Cuisine

MODERN BRITISH

City Merchant, £££ p. 127
Stravaigin, p. 134

CHINESE

Amber Regent, £££ p. 124
Loon Fung, ££ p. 130

FRENCH

The Brasserie at Oran Mor, ££ p. 132
Brasserie, £££ p. 126
Hotel du Vin Bistro, ££££ p. 133

INDIAN

Balbir's, £ p. 132
Kool Ba, ££ p. 130
Mother India's Cafe, £ p. 133

ITALIAN

Fazzi, £ p. 127
Fratelli Sarti, ££ p. 127
La Parmigiana, £££ p. 133
Pavarotti Trattoria, ££ p. 130

SEAFOOD

Crabshakk, ££ p. 132
Mussel Inn, £££ p. 130
Rogano, £££££ p. 131
Two Fat Ladies, £££ p. 131

By Experience

MOST KID-FRIENDLY

Fratelli Sarti, ££ p. 127
Fressh, £ p. 127
Khublai Khan Barbecue, ££££ p. 127
Pancho Villa's, ££ p. 130

HOTSPOTS

Café Cossachok, ££ p. 126
Cafezique, ££ p. 132
The Left Bank, ££ p. 133
Stereo, £ p. 131

MOST ROMANTIC

Kool Ba, ££ p. 130
Hotel du Vin Bistro, ££££ p. 133
Rogano, £££££ p. 131

BEST PRETHEATER EATS

Corinthian, £££ p. 127
The Brasserie at Oran Mor, £££ p. 132
Hotel du vin Bistro, ££££ p. 133
No. Sixteen Byres Road, ££ p. 134

3

seem almost too artful to eat. Succulent king prawns or duck with mashed prawns in an oyster sauce readily attest to the kitchen's skill in preparing excellent Cantonese and Szechuan cuisine. Its reputation means that the restaurant can get very busy, so do make reservations, especially on weekends. For the best value, try the two- and three-course menus served between noon and 2:15. ⊠ *50 W. Regent St., City Center* ☎ *0141/331–1655* ⊕ *www.amberregent.com* ⊟ *AE, MC, V* ⊗ *No lunch Sun.* ✛ *F3.*

££ ✕ **Brasserie.** A hotel basement fitted with wooden booths and comfort-
FRENCH able seating makes for a quiet, relaxed environment in which to appreci-
ate a varied modern but local Scottish and French menu. The fish cakes are the traditional favorite here, but the chicken and haggis roulade and dry-aged, grass-fed sirloin are also good. Be sure to leave room for des-serts such as the warm chocolate and hazelnut pudding with Frangelico ice cream or passionfruit sorbet. The two-course lunch is an excellent deal at £13.50. ⊠ *Malmaison Hotel, 278 W. George St., City Center* ☎ *0141/572–1001* ⊕ *www.malmaison-glasgow.com* ⌂ *Reservations essential* ⊟ *AE, DC, MC, V* ✛ *E3.*

£ ✕ **The Butterfly and the Pig.** Down an innocuous-looking flight of stairs
BRITISH in the city center, this intimate restaurant is the type of place the locals love: warm colors, flickering candles, mix-and-match crockery, and food that is inventive, inexpensive, and original. The menu reads like a comedic narrative, with descriptions like "traditional fish and chips, battered to death place or soul [plaice or sole; kinds of fish] with mushy peas, kitchen-made tartar sauce and a slice of lemon, beans today as the peas don't want to cook." Worth trying are dishes such as hearty portobello-mushroom burgers with extra-thick potato chips or black pudding with bacon, Parmesan cheese, and apples. The chef uses only local ingredients, so the menu changes daily. ⊠ *153 Bath St., City Center* ☎ *0141/221–7711* ⊟ *DC, MC, V* ✛ *E3.*

££ ✕ **Café Cossachok.** In this willfully arty and collaborative restaurant in
EASTERN a trendy arts center, the tables are hand-carved, the lighting is courtesy
EUROPEAN of candles, and the decor is a sea of shawls. The Russian owner pays homage to his homeland with a menu that includes delicious blintzes and trout à la Pushkin (in a thirst-rousing salty sauce). Another wel-come touch is the nicely chilled selection of vodkas. This fun venue is fashionable among the fashionable, so it's best to book ahead. ⊠ *Tron-gate 103, Merchant City* ☎ *0141/553–0733* ⊕ *www.trongate103.com* ⊟ *AE, MC, V* ⊗ *Closed Mon. No lunch Sun.* ✛ *H5*

£££ ✕ **Café Gandolfi.** Occupying what were once the offices of a cheese mar-
BRITISH ket, this trendy café draws the style-conscious crowd. Wooden tables and chairs crafted by Scottish artist Tim Stead are so fluidly shaped it's hard to believe they're inanimate. The café opens early for breakfast, serving croissants, eggs *en cocotte* (casserole-style), and strong espresso. Don't miss the smoked venison or the finnan haddie (smoked haddock); pastas and salads are also on the menu. In 2007 the owners opened up an establishment next door, called Gandolfi Fish. Although the menu is more expensive, it's worth a visit if you enjoy seafood. ⊠ *64 Albion St., Merchant City* ☎ *0141/552–6813* ⊕ *www.cafegandolfi.com* ⊟ *AE, MC, V* ✛ *H5.*

£££ ✕ **City Merchant.** If you have a penchant for fresh and flavorful cuisine,
MODERN BRITISH this welcoming spot with simple but traditional furnishings, including white tablecloths, dark wood, soft lighting, and tartan carpets is a joy. The secret is the kitchen's use of only local ingredients. You can sample the tasty cuts of venison and beef (including fillet with a haggis mousse), but seafood remains the star attraction. The mussels and oysters from Loch Etive are wondrous, as is the sea bass. There's a relatively inexpensive selection of wines and a wonderful cheeseboard served, as the locals like it, with oatcakes, celery, and quince. Check out the fixed-price menus for good values. ⊠ *97–99 Candleriggs St., Merchant City* 🕾 *0141/553–1577* ⊕ *www.citymerchant.co.uk* ☰ *AE, DC, MC, V* ⊘ *Closed Sun.* ⊹ *H5*

£££ ✕ **Corinthian.** Built on the site of the Virginia Mansion erected by tobacco
Fodor's Choice merchant George Buchanan, this Victorian gem includes a 26-foot-high
★ glass central dome, classical statues, and gold-leaf paneling. Although
BRITISH it may feel more like a museum than a restaurant, Corinthian is a great place for a special night out. The menu constantly evolves but might include panfried sea bass that melts in your mouth and perfectly panseared Gressingham duck. Good wines add to the delight, and the summer berry bread pudding is a worthy indulgence for dessert. There are three stylish bars to check out as well. ⊠ *191 Ingram St., City Center* 🕾 *0141/559–6826* ⊕ *www.g1group.co.uk* ☰ *AE, MC, DC, V* ⊹ *G4.*

£ ✕ **Fazzi.** With its red tablecloths, tile floors, and bentwood chairs, this
ITALIAN inexpensive Italian café-bar is a cheerful place for a plateful of gnocchi *alla Emiliana* (with tomato, basil, and cheese sauce) or spinach-and-ricotta ravioli. The delicatessen here sells takeout. ⊠ *65–67 Cambridge St., City Center* 🕾 *0141/332–0941* ☰ *AE, DC, MC, V* ⊹ *F3.*

££ ✕ **Fratelli Sarti.** Glasgow's large Italian immigrant population is never
☾ more visible—or audible—than here. The cavernous surroundings are
ITALIAN cluttered and the tables are pressed close together, so this is not really the place for an intimate dinner, but the food is authentic, with Tuscan and Ligurian specialties as well as other classic dishes on an extensive menu. If you like seafood, try the wonderfully fresh and piquant pasta *vongole* (with small clams). Finish off with the light, creamy tiramisu. Note that the service can be a bit leisurely. The restaurant has two other locations with the same menu. ⊠ *121 Bath St., City Center* 🕾 *0141/204–0440* ⊕ *www.sarti.co.uk* ☰ *AE, DC, MC, V* ⊹ *F3.*

£ ✕ **Fressh.** Settle in at the counter or one of the tables and soft chairs of
☾ this airy café for a quick, healthy, and well- priced breakfast or lunch.
CAFÉ The food is simple but hearty and fresh. Warm baguettes come filled with Brie, grapes, and cranberries, and the seeded rolls stuffed with pastrami, cream cheese, and dill pickles hit the spot. Several homemade soups and salads are offered daily, as well as straight-from-the-blender low-fat smoothies. Coffee drinks and baked potatoes with a choice of toppings are available, too. ⊠ *51 Cochrane St., City Center* 🕾 *0141/552–5532* ⊕ *www.fressh.com* ⚒ *No reservations* ☰ *MC, V* ⊘ *No dinner* ⊹ *G4.*

££££ ✕ **Khublai Khan Barbecue.** Wild boar, ostrich, shark, and other exotic
☾ flavors feature prominently at this eclectic, mostly Asian eatery. Odds
ASIAN are you'll devour the legendary Mongolian Feast, which includes an

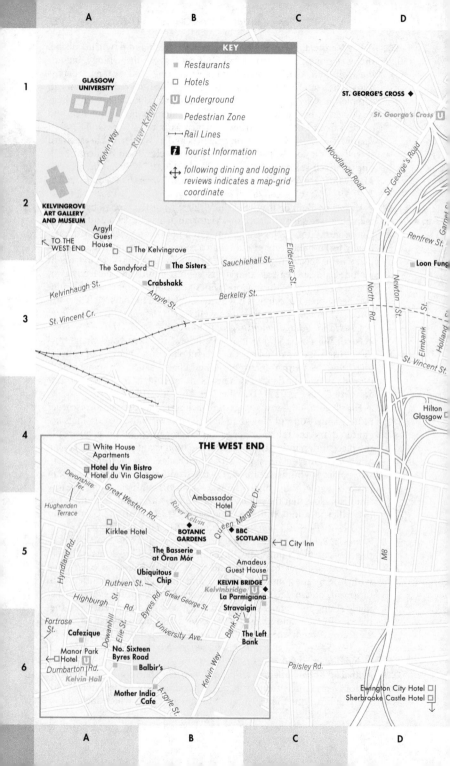

KEY

- Restaurants
- ☐ Hotels
- Ⓤ Underground
- Pedestrian Zone
- Rail Lines
- 🅸 Tourist Information
- ⬌ following dining and lodging reviews indicates a map-grid coordinate

A · B · C · D

1

GLASGOW UNIVERSITY

ST. GEORGE'S CROSS ◆

St. George's Cross Ⓤ

Kelvin Way

River Kelvin

Woodlands Road

St. George's Road

Garnet

2

KELVINGROVE ART GALLERY AND MUSEUM

← TO THE WEST END

Argyll Guest House ☐

☐ The Kelvingrove

The Sandyford ☐ ■ The Sisters

■ Crabshakk

Kelvinhaugh St.

Argyle St.

Sauchiehall St.

Berkeley St.

Elderslie St.

North St.

Newton St.

Renfrew St.

■ Loon Fung

St.

Holland

3

St. Vincent Cr.

St. Vincent St.

Elmbank St.

Hilton Glasgow

4

THE WEST END

☐ White House Apartments

■ Hotel du Vin Bistro / Hotel du Vin Glasgow

Devonshire Ter.

Great Western Rd.

Hughenden Terrace

River Kelvin

Ambassador Hotel ☐

Queen Margaret Dr.

☐ Kirklee Hotel

BOTANIC GARDENS ◆

◆ BBC SCOTLAND

←☐ City Inn

M8

5

Hyndland Rd.

■ The Basserie at Òran Mór

Ubiquitous Chip

Ruthven St. —

Highburgh Rd.

Byres Rd.

Great George St.

Amadeus Guest House

KELVIN BRIDGE Ⓤ
Kelvinbridge Ⓤ ◆

◆ La Parmigiana

■ Stravaigan

6

Fortrose St.

■ Cafezique

Manor Park ←☐ Hotel

Dumbarton Rd.

Kelvin Hall

Dowanhill St.

Elie St.

University Ave.

No. Sixteen Byres Road

■ Balbir's

Mother India Cafe

Bank St.

■ The Left Bank

Kelvin Way

Argyle St.

Paisley Rd.

Ewington City Hotel ☐
Sherbrooke Castle Hotel ☐
↓

A · B · C · D

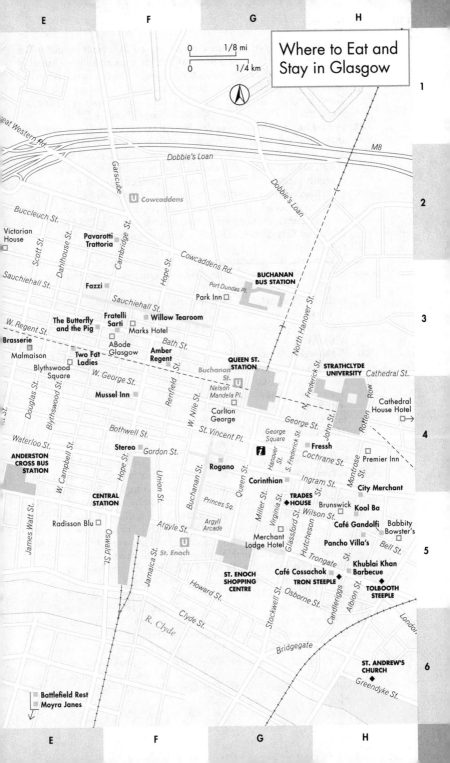

Where to Eat and Stay in Glasgow

E F G H

1

0   1/8 mi
0   1/4 km

Great Western Rd.

Dobbie's Loan

M8

U Cowcaddens

Dobbie's Loan

2

Buccleuch St.

Victorian
House

Scott St.

Dalhouse St.

Pavarotti
Trattoria

Cambridge St.

Sauchiehall St.

Cowcaddens Rd.

BUCHANAN
BUS STATION

North Hanover St.

Fazzi

Hope St.

Port Dundas Pl.

Park Inn

3

Sauchiehall St.

Willow Tearoom

The Butterfly
and the Pig

W. Regent St.

Fratelli
Sarti

Marks Hotel

Bath St.

QUEEN ST.
STATION

STRATHCLYDE
UNIVERSITY   Cathedral St.

Brasserie

Malmaison

ABode
Glasgow

Amber
Regent

Buchanan
St.

Frederick St.

Cathedral
House Hotel

Blythswood
Square

Two Fat
Ladies

W. George St.

U

Nelson
Mandela Pl.

N. Hanover St.

John St.

Rotten Row

4

Douglas St.

Blythswood St.

Mussel Inn

Renfield St.

Carlton
George

St. Vincent Pl.

George St.

Frederick St.

Premier Inn

Waterloo St.

W. Campbell St.

Stereo

Gordon St.

Hope St.

George
Square

i

Hanover St.

S. Frederick St.

Cochrane St.

Fressh

Montrose St.

City Merchant

ANDERSTON
CROSS BUS
STATION

Bothwell St.

CENTRAL
STATION

Union St.

Buchanan St.

Rogano

Queen St.

Corinthian

Miller St.

Virginia St.

Ingram St.

TRADES
HOUSE

Brunswick
St.

Wilson St.

Kool Ba

Café Gandolfi

Babbity
Bowster's

James Watt St.

Radisson Blu

Oswald St.

Princes Sq.

Argyll
Arcade

Glassford St.

Hutcheson St.

Pancho Villa's

Bell St.

5

Jamaica St.

Argyle St.

U
St. Enoch

Merchant
Lodge Hotel

Trongate

Candleriggs

Khublai Khan
Barbecue

Albion St.

Howard St.

ST. ENOCH
SHOPPING
CENTRE

Café Cossachok

Stockwell St.

TRON STEEPLE

Osborne St.

TOLBOOTH
STEEPLE

London

Clyde St.

R. Clyde

Bridgegate

ST. ANDREW'S
CHURCH

6

Battlefield Rest

Moyra Janes

Greendyke St.

E F G H

unlimited supply of barbecued meats cooked on a giant hotplate. The massive space is festooned with handwoven rugs and a huge mural of Mongolian warriors advancing threateningly. Don't worry: the service is friendly. This place is popular with groups, and it can get noisy. ⊠ *26 Candleriggs St., Merchant City* ☎ *0141/552–5646* ⊕ *www.khublaikhan. co.uk* ⊟ *AE, DC, MC, V* ⊗ *No lunch Sun.–Thurs.* ⊕ *H5*

££
ECLECTIC
✕ **Kool Ba.** Thick wooden tables, Persian tapestries, and soft candlelight make you feel, somehow, relaxed and at home in this small yet atmospheric haven that serves an intriguing mix of Indian and Persian fare. It's all about healthy, flavorful cooking here: chicken tikka masala in a yogurt sauce or lamb korma with coconut cream and fruit are good picks. Accompany your meal with bowls of basmati saffron rice and fluffy naan bread. This popular place continues to win award after award; reserve ahead on Friday and Saturday. ⊠ *109–113 Candleriggs, Merchant City* ☎ *0141/552–2777* ⊕ *www.koolba.com* ⊟ *AE, MC, V* ⊕ *H5.*

££
CHINESE
✕ **Loon Fung.** The pleasant, enthusiastic staff at this popular Cantonese eatery guides you through the house specials, including the famed dim sum. If you like seafood, try the deep-fried wonton with prawns, crispy stuffed crab claws, or lobster in garlic-and-cheese sauce. The first-rate three-course business lunch, available until 6:30 PM, is a bargain at £9. ⊠ *417 Sauchiehall St., City Center* ☎ *0141/332–1240* ⊟ *AE, MC, V* ⊕ *D3.*

£££
SEAFOOD
✕ **Mussel Inn.** West coast shellfish farmers own this restaurant and feed their customers incredibly succulent oysters, scallops, and mussels. The kilo pots of mussels, beautifully steamed to order and served with any of a number of sauces, are revelatory. The surroundings are simple but stylish, with cool ceramic tiles, wood floors, and plenty of sleek wooden furniture. Another plus is the staff, who are helpful yet unpretentious. This is the type of place locals take their friends, family, and favorite out-of-towners. ⊠ *157 Hope St., City Center* ☎ *0141/572–1405* ⊕ *www.mussel-inn.com* ⊟ *AE, MC, V* ⊗ *No lunch Sun.* ⊕ *F4*

££
☺
MEXICAN
✕ **Pancho Villa's.** Bright and festive, this is a fun place to dine; and if you have a craving for margaritas, look no further. References to the man and to Mexico are everywhere; the authentic masks and statues, as well as the bold blue, yellow, and pink walls. The locals can't get enough of the cocktails or the food, which includes all the traditional favorites—enchiladas, burritos, tacos, and fajitas—and some untraditional dishes. For something different, try the *barbacoa,* flour tortillas filled with marinated garlic and chili lamb or the mole poblano, chicken with a spicy and savory chocolate sauce. ⊠ *26 Bell St., Merchant City* ☎ *0141/552–7737* ⊕ *www.panchovillas.co.uk* ⊟ *AE, MC, V* ⊕ *H5.*

££
ITALIAN
✕ **Pavarotti Trattoria.** Despite the somewhat silly name, no doubt arising from the restaurant's proximity to Scottish Opera's Theatre Royal, this is not a kitschy affair, but a very good Italian restaurant. The menu changes regularly because the kitchen uses only the freshest ingredients, so the standard meat and fish dishes are unusually succulent. Lunch and pretheater set menus—£8.50 and £12—are an exceptionally good value. ⊠ *91 Cambridge St., City Center* ☎ *0141/332–9713* ⊟ *AE, DC, MC, V* ⊗ *Closed Sun.* ⊕ *F2*

3

££££££ ✕**Rogano.** The spacious art deco interior, modeled after the style of the
Fodor's Choice *Queen Mary* ocean liner—maple paneling, chrome trim, and dramatic
★ ocean murals—is enough to recommend this restaurant. Portions are
SEAFOOD generous in the main dining area, where impeccably prepared favorites
include classic seafood dishes like pan-seared seared scallops or lobster Thermidor as well as roast rack of lamb. Downstairs in the less-
expensive Café Rogano, the brasserie-style food is more modern and
imaginative. The theater menu provides early evening and late-night
bargains, and the fixed-price lunch menu is popular with locals. You
can also order one of the fabulous cocktails and linger at the swank
oyster bar. ✉ *11 Exchange Pl., City Center* ☎ *0141/248–4055* ⊕ *www.
roganoglasgow.com* ☰ *AE, DC, MC, V* ✛ *G4.*

£ ✕ **Stereo.** Down a quiet lane, this ultracool vegetarian restaurant dishes
VEGETARIAN up a fantastic range of vegan food from paella to gnocchi to a colorful
mezze platter with hummus, red-pepper pâté, and home-baked flatbread. Roasted sweet-potato chips are the perfect side dish. There's also
a good list of organic juices and wines. The hip decor includes modern
oil paintings, black and red chairs, and wood floorboards, which all
contrast with the building, designed by Charles Rennie Mackintosh.
The adjoining music venue downstairs can get a little loud after 9 and
service can be on the slow side, but wholesome food and friendly staff
make it all worthwhile. ✉ *20–28 Renfield La., City Center* ☎ *0141/222–
2254* ⊕ *www.stereocafebar.com* ⊜ *No reservations* ☰ *MC, V* ✛ *F4.*

£££ ✕**Two Fat Ladies.** A Glasgow institution, this spot has the same name
BRITISH as the owner's other restaurants at 88 Dumbarton Road (the original
location) and 652 Argyle Road, but this branch on Blythswood Street
deserves a visit because it has more space, more light, and a better
location than its oldest sister. The menu is predominantly fish, from
the delicate smoked salmon, crab, and asparagus salad to the fresh
whole sea bream stuffed with red pepper, oregano, and garlic salsa.
But if fish doesn't rock your boat, then choices such as fillets of Angus
beef with wild mushrooms and spinach jus are also delicious. The trio
of berry crème brûlées is the perfect dessert. Reservations are a good
idea. ✉ *118A Blythswood St., City Center* ☎ *0141/847–0088* ⊕ *www.
twofatladiesrestaurant.com* ☰ *AE, DC, MC, V* ✛ *E3.*

£ ✕**Willow Tearoom.** There are two branches of this restaurant (the other,
BRITISH opened in 1997, is at 97 Buchanan), but the Sauchiehall Street location
is the real deal even though you enter through a street-level jewelry and
souvenir store. Designed by the great Charles Rennie Mackintosh, the
Room De Luxe (the original tearoom) is kitted out with his trademark
furnishings, including highback chairs with elegant lines and subtle
curves. You can also eat in the airy Gallery. The St. Andrew's Platter is
an exquisite selection of trout, salmon, and prawns. Scottish and continental breakfasts are available throughout the day, and the scrambled
eggs with salmon is traditional Scots food at its finest. The in-house
baker guarantees fresh scones, cakes, and pastries. ✉ *217 Sauchiehall
St., City Center* ☎ *0141/332–0521* ⊕ *www.willowtearooms.co.uk*
☰ *MC, V* ☽ *No dinner* ✛ *F3.*

WEST END AND ENVIRONS

Use the coordinate (✛ B2) at the end of each listing to locate a site on the corresponding map.

Because of the Glasgow University, the food in this area was once just for students. That has changed in recent years. You can still find fast food at any hour of the day, but you'll discover some of the best Scottish food served at some of the city's most respected restaurants.

£   ✕ **Balbir's.** Don't let the tinted windows discourage you: this place is a temple for pure, healthy Indian food that's impressive in taste and presentation, and it's always busy. Twinkling chandeliers, grand ceilings, immaculate white tablecloths, and perfectly polished silverware set the stage, and the waitstaff tend to your every need. All food is prepared with cholesterol-free rapeseed oil; no artificial food colors or additives are used. Try the chicken tikka chasni (a mild, cream dish with mango chutney, lemon juice, and mint) or lamb Ceylonese korma (with coconut, cream, and mild spices). The tandoori salmon is also a good bet. ⊠ *7 Church St., West End* ☎ *0141/339–7711* ⊕ *www. balbirsrestaurants.co.uk* ⊟ *AE, DC, MC, V.* ✛ *A6*

Fodor's Choice
★
INDIAN

£££   ✕ **The Brasserie at Òran Mór.** This is the more formal eatery (the other being the bistro-style Conservatory) within this handsome church-turned-cultural-center. There's lots of elegantly curved dark wood and high-backed bench seating, as well as some Alasdair Gray murals to savor. The food is equally well crafted. Expect contemporary treats using Angus beef, Gressingham duck, and sea bass. ⊠ *731–735 Great Western Rd., West End* ☎ *0141/357–6226* ⊕ *www.oran-mor.co.uk* ⚞ *Reservations essential* ⊟ *AE, MC, V* ✛ *B5.*

BRITISH

££   ✕ **Cafezique.** Small but inviting, this West End magnet has a vibrant, changing breakfast, lunch, and dinner menu that is always fresh and exciting. The food is divided on the dinner menu into "wee things," "big things," and "sweet things." Try the roasted globe artichoke as your wee thing (if it's in season), the roast lamb with Mediterranean vegetables as your big thing, and fruit crumble with custard as your sweet thing. The curved wooden bar that snakes around the belly of the restaurant allows you to watch your food being prepared. Soft music, twinkling lights, and sepia photographs of seaside scenes help create a cozy but lively scene. ⊠ *66 Highland St., West End* ☎ *0141/339–7180* ⊟ *MC, V* ✛ *A6.*

BRITISH

££   ✕ **Crabshakk.** It's anything but a shack: the intimate dining space has heavy wooden tables and chairs, and a bar so shiny and inviting that it seems to almost insist you have a drink. The lamps are like half-moons, and the ceiling is elegantly ornate. Mirrors make the place feel bigger, though it doesn't need to. The food comes from the sea: oysters, langoustines, lobster, and squid—you can have your choice served iced, grilled, roasted, or battered. Other options are a smoked fish plate, shellfish chowder, and a fish club sandwich. Only local and sustainably sourced Scottish seafood is featured. ⊠ *1114 Argyle St., West End* ☎ *0141/334–6127* ⊕ *www.crabshakk.com* ⚞ *Reservations essential* ⊟ *AE, DC, MC, V* ✛ *B3.*

SEAFOOD

££££ ✕ **Hotel du Vin Bistro.** A kilted door-
Fodor'sChoice man, crystal chandeliers, stylish
★ blue-and-green tartan carpets, and
FRENCH oak paneling beckon you into the
city's most elegant eatery. The service is impeccable from beginning
to end, and all the food is locally
sourced from a 35-mi radius. It's
the perfect place for cold, wet
days, as romantic fires flicker in
the background and stained-glass
murals twist the natural light into
colorful new shades. From the
menu of French and Scottish fare,
try the monkfish poached in squid
oil with fennel confit, or the roast
breast of squab with a passionfruit
sauce. The coffee and chocolate
soufflé with caramel ice cream is a
truly indulgent dessert. Ask for a tour of the superb wine cellar on
the premises. ✉ *1 Devonshire Gardens, West End* ☎ *0141/339–2001*
⊕ *www.hotelduvin.com* ▭ *AE, DC, MC, V* ✛ *A4.*

> **TAKE TIME FOR TEA**
>
> In the Victorian tradition, while
> men went to pubs, Glasgow
> women's social interaction would
> take place in the city's many tea-
> rooms and cafés. Today *everyone*
> goes to the café. Glaswegians
> have succumbed to the worldwide
> love for Italian-style, espresso-
> based coffees, but they'll never
> give up the comfort of a nice cup
> of tea, so you'll find both at most
> tearooms, along with scones, Scot-
> tish pancakes, other pastries, and
> light lunch fare like sandwiches
> and soup.

£££ ✕ **La Parmigiana.** The refreshing elegance of the surroundings is mir-
ITALIAN rored by the consistently exquisite fare at this longtime favorite. The
Giovanazzis pride themselves on using the freshest of ingredients—this
means you may be able to enjoy simply prepared sea bass or veal one
day, guinea fowl or scallops the next. This expertise in the kitchen is
reflected in the well-balanced wine list and the impeccable attentive-
ness of the black-jacketed waiters. ✉ *447 Great Western Rd., West
End* ☎ *0141/334–0686* ⊕ *www.laparmigiana.co.uk* ▭ *AE, DC, MC,
V* ☉ *Closed Sun.* ✛ *C5*

££ ✕ **The Left Bank.** Close to Glasgow University and Kelvingrove Park, this
ECLECTIC popular hangout attracts a more mature student crowd. It's an airy spot
with high ceilings, leather sofas, and wood floors, and the specialty is
good, eclectic food at reasonable prices. Breakfast is your best bet with
thick-sliced French toast, maple syrup, and bacon; or eggs Mornay
served with an English muffin, spinach, and smoked salmon. Tapas-
style plates are an option: try roasted eggplant and wild garlic hummus
with wholegrain flatbread, or sticky pork ribs cooked in maple syrup
and sesame. Moroccan spiced free-range chicken with walnut and beet
quinoa salad carries you across the sea to Africa. This is also a nice
place for a beer after walking around Kelvingrove Park. ✉ *33–35 Gibson St., West End* ☎ *0141/339–5969* ⊕ *www.theleftbank.co.uk* ▭ *AE,
DC, MC, V* ✛ *C6.*

£ ✕ **Mother India Cafe.** Overlooking the Kelvingrove Art Gallery and
INDIAN Museum, this quaint, casual eatery has a spectacular view as well as a
spectacular menu. Food is served tapas-style in small dishes, so you're
encouraged to share. The idea is that you get to try lots of different
flavors. Chili king prawns, chicken *achari* (cooked with lime and chili
pickle) and *aloo saag dosa* (potato and spinach stuffed in a rice and

lentil pancake) are all rich in flavor and presentation. ⊠ *1355 Argyle St., West End* ☎ *0141/339–9145* ⊕ *www.motherindiaglasgow.co.uk* ▤ *AE, DC, MC, V* ✛ *B6.*

££ ✕ **No. Sixteen Byres Road.** The knowledgeable staff make you feel at home in this intimate restaurant serving only the freshest of ingredients, superbly prepared. There's room for only 40 patrons here, and the result is cozy but not cramped, cute but classy. Roast fillet of pollock and warm salad of white beans and citrus fruits melt in your mouth; the risotto of spring peas, mint and oregano, Parmesan, and crème fraîche is a good choice, too. A good deal here is the pretheater, three-course deal at £11.50. For dessert, sticky toffee pudding with butterscotch sauce and cream is a must. Reservations are essential on weekends. ⊠ *16 Byres Rd., West End* ☎ *0141/339–2544* ⊕ *www.number16.co.uk* ▤ *AE, DC, MC, V* ✛ *A6.*

*Fodor's*Choice
★
BRITISH

££££ ✕ **The Sisters.** Walk up the smooth sandstone steps to this restaurant
BRITISH that inspires both your palate and heart. Douglas Gray tartan pads the pristine room, and polished floorboards reflect the natural light shining in from the long windows around the unusual oval-shaped room. Wild seascape paintings are a nice touch in a space that feels both wide open and contained. The food is locally sourced and ever changing: all meat comes from Smitten Farm (in Galloway) and is prepared using seasonal vegetables. A typical dish is the Ullapool salmon, cucumber, mussel, and dill salad with mustard dressing. For vegetarians, wild Scottish mushrooms and thyme with light butter pastry and creamed celeriac is a tasty main course. The homegrown Arran gooseberry fool is the ultimate Scottish pudding. ⊠ *36 Kelvingrove St., West End* ☎ *0141/564–1157* ⊕ *www.thesisters.co.uk* ▤ *AE, DC, MC, V* ✛ *B3.*

£££ ✕ **Stravaigin.** The busy bar on street level draws people in with its
MODERN BRITISH sweetly strong cocktails and ultracool scene; you wouldn't know a restaurant was downstairs unless someone pointed it out. Stairs lead to a dining room, an underground cavern with leather chairs and shiny tables in neat, orderly rows. Locals favor the mix of Scottish fare with Italian, Mexican, Thai, and French. Try the Shetland crab with roast corn blinis and black-bean salsa, or Aberdeen Angus rump steak with ham and Gruyère gratin, wild mushroom duxelles, and port gravy. For dessert, the Andalusian lemon and mascarpone tart with brown-bread ice cream is a unique treat. ⊠ *28 Gibson St., West End* ☎ *0141/334– 2665* ⊕ *www.stravaigin.com* ▤ *AE, DC, MC, V* ✛ *C6.*

£££££ ✕ **Ubiquitous Chip.** Occupying a converted mews stable behind the
*Fodor's*Choice Hillhead underground station, this restaurant is an institution among
★ members of Glasgow's media and thespian communities. The service is
BRITISH friendly, and the interior very outdoorsy, with a glass roof, much greenery, and a fishpond. The menu specializes in game but has something for everyone (even vegetarian haggis); smoked salmon in Darjeeling tea is typical of the chef's clever blending of authentic Scots fare with unusual elements. For a more casual and inexpensive experience, try the brasserie and pub area upstairs (££). ⊠ *12 Ashton La., West End* ☎ *0141/334– 5007* ⊕ *www.ubiquitouschip.co.uk* ▤ *AE, DC, MC, V* ✛ *B5.*

SOUTH SIDE

Use the coordinate (✛ B2) at the end of each listing to locate a site on the corresponding map.

££ ✕ **Battlefield Rest.** Built in 1915, this old tram station has been lovingly
ITALIAN restored into an authentic, very popular Italian restaurant where the walls of windows are framed by heavy cream drapes. The food is rich, honest, and full of flavor; try chicken stuffed with goat cheese and then wrapped in Parma ham, or panfried duck with figs. There are plenty of pastas and pizzas to choose from, too. Take the train from Central Station to Mt. Florida or the number 66 bus from St. Enoch underground station; the restaurant is near Queen's Park. ⊠ *55 Battlefield Rest, South Side* ☎ *0141/636–6955* ⊕ *www.battlefieldrest.co.uk* ▤ *AE, DC, MC, V* ⊗ *Closed Sun.* ✛ *E6.*

££ ✕ **Moyra Janes.** Pull up a chair to one of the marble-topped tables in
BRITISH this former bank building and soak up the genteel Scots charm. This South Side favorite serves a splendid tea with mouthwatering cakes. There's a healthy dash of cosmopolitan flair to boot: alongside the all-day breakfast menu are Thai fish cakes and Italian pasta creations. The two-course all-night special for £10.95 is a real bargain. ⊠ *20 Kildrostan St., South Side* ☎ *0141/423–5628* ▤ *MC, V* ⊗ *No dinner Sun. and Mon.* ✛ *E6.*

WHERE TO STAY

Over the next few years, tourism officials say, the city will add about 2,400 rooms. New on the horizon is the Hamilton Hotel, a luxury property in the West End, just behind the Botanic Gardens. For now, the city has a wide spectrum of excellent hotels, bed-and-breakfasts, guesthouses and inns, and apartments to choose from in different neighborhoods.

Central Glasgow never sleeps, so downtown hotels will be noisier than those in the leafy and genteel West End. Downtown hotels are within walking distance of all the main sights; the West End is convenient for museums and art galleries. Although big hotels are spread out all around the city, B&Bs are definitely a more popular, personal, and cheaper option. For country-house luxury you should look beyond the city—try Mar Hall, near Paisley. Regardless of the neighborhood, hotels are about the same in price. Some B&Bs as well as the smaller properties may also offer discounts for longer stays.

Make your reservations in advance, especially when there's a big concert, sporting event, or holiday (New Year's Eve is very popular). Glasgow is most busy during summer, but it can fill up when something special is going on. If you arrive in town without a place to stay, contact the Glasgow Tourist Board.

PRICES AND MONEY-SAVING OPTIONS

There are some excellent hotels, B&Bs, and inns in Glasgow that won't break the bank, and many these days are willing to take an offer on a room if you contact them within a day or two of your arrival if they have availability. It never hurts to ask.

Another money-saving option is to an apartment. The White House Apartments have kitchens and dining tables; they have affordable weekly and monthly rates. B&Bs are the best priced short-term accommodation option overall, and you're sure to get breakfast.

Most smaller hotels and all guesthouses include breakfast in the room rate. Larger hotels usually charge extra for breakfast. Also note that for V.A.T. (Value Added Tax, the sales tax), the most expensive hotels often exclude the 17.5% charge in the initial price quote but budget places include it.

WHAT IT COSTS IN POUNDS					
	£	££	£££	££££	£££££
FOR TWO PEOPLE	under £70	£70–£120	£121–£180	£181–£250	over £250

Hotel prices are for two people in a standard double room in high season, generally including the 17.5% V.A.T.

MEDIEVAL GLASGOW AND MERCHANT CITY

Use the coordinate (✛ B2) at the end of each listing to locate a site on the corresponding map.

This is a good area to stay in if you want to be close to the pulse of the city. You're close to everything—the main sights, shops, theaters, restaurants and bars. You don't have to worry about transportation in the center of town, but it can get a little noisy on weekend nights. Also included here are places in the center city west of the Merchant City; these can be more than a mile from the Merchant City restaurants and shops.

££   **ABode Glasgow.** Part of the stylish ABode mini-chain, this 1829 building near the boutiques of Buchanan Street has retained and embellished its best features, like the wrought-iron elevator and gold-leaf lions, while modernizing the spaces to meet today's sense of luxury. Guest rooms have dramatic yet tasteful decor highlighted by leaded-glass windows and contemporary artwork. Noted chef Michael Caines supervises the chain's restaurants: the Café Bar has a modish, international menu, and the Bar MC downstairs is one of Glasgow's hot spots. **Pros:** stylish rooms; great location; nice mix of old and new in public areas. **Cons:** some front rooms can be a little noisy; parking is a pricey £12 a day. ⊠ *129 Bath St., City Center* ☎ *0141/221–6789* ⊕ *www. abodehotels.co.uk* ⌘ *60 rooms, 1 suite* ⌂ *In-room: DVD, Internet. In-hotel: restaurant, room service, bar, parking (paid)* ▤ *AE, DC, MC, V* ❢⊙❘ *CP* ✛ *F3.*

Fodor's Choice
★

£   **Babbity Bowster's.** The popular on-site restaurant and bar make this restored 18th-century Robert Adam town house a lively place to stay. The rooms have modern furniture and beds with starched, white linens. A first-floor gallery displays many works by Glaswegian artists. **Pros:** centrally located; quiet street; great downstairs bar and restaurant. **Cons:** can get noisy on weekends; no elevator; no computer hook-ups or Wi-Fi. ⊠ *16–18 Blackfriars St., Merchant City* ☎ *0141/552–5055*

BEST BETS FOR GLASGOW LODGING

🛏 *6 rooms* ❧ *In-room: no a/c. In-hotel: restaurant, bar* ▭ *AE, MC, V* ⭍ *BP* ✢ *H5.*

££££ 🏛 **Blythswood Square.** History and contemporary luxury come together at this smart conversion of the former Royal Automobile Club of Scotland headquarters, occupying a classical building on peaceful Blythswood Square. A sense of place (acres of marble, huge chandeliers, the stylish Salon with its lovely views) blends happily with sleek design (fancy showers and faucets; the latest entertainment systems). The fairly masculine bedrooms are mainly a calming gray and white, with Harris tweed on the floor and chairs; some are wallpapered with an enlarged photo of the 1955 Monte Carlo auto rally, which started here. At the time of this writing the expansive spa was not open, but it should increase the pleasant air of escape and pampering. **Pros:** indulgent Spanish marble bathrooms; great restaurants nearby; spectacular public areas. **Cons:** room lighting may be too dim for some; minor street noise. ✉ *11 Blythswood Sq., City Center* ☎ *0141/248–8888* ⊕ *www.townhousecompany.com/blythswoodsquare* 🛏 *93 bedrooms, 7 suites* ❧ *In-room: a/c, safe, refrigerator (some), Wi-Fi. In-hotel: restaurant, room service, 2 bars, gym, spa, laundry service, parking (paid).* ▭ *AE, DC, MC, V.* ⭍ *BP.*

£   ⊡ **Brunswick.** In a contemporary town house, this small six-story hotel showcases quintessential Glasgow style and ambition. The guest rooms, which have ceiling fans, are done in a mostly modern, minimalist style, but squared-off wall fixtures and occasional splashes of color make bold statements. The three-bedroom penthouse suite has a separate kitchen and a sauna. The downstairs Brutti ma Buoni (meaning "ugly but good" in Italian) café/restaurant-bar has an eclectic menu, a compact but complete wine list, and a selection of draft lagers. **Pros:** excellent value for money; hip downstairs café scene; apples on pillows; free Wi-Fi. **Cons:** neighborhood can get loud on weekends; some rooms are on the small side. ⊠ *106–108 Brunswick St., Merchant City* ☎ *0141/552–0001* ⊕ *www.brunswickhotel.co.uk* ⌁ *18 rooms, 1 suite* ᗌ *In-room: no a/c. In-hotel: restaurant, bar, Wi-Fi hotspot* ▤ *AE, MC, V* |◎| *CP* ⊹ *H5.*

££   ⊡ **Carlton George.** The narrow revolving doorway, a step back from busy West George Street, creates the illusion of a secret passageway into this lavish boutique hotel. Local artwork hangs from the lobby's walls, and Charles Rennie Macintosh–inspired furniture fills the lobby. Guest rooms are Scottish theme, with subtle tartan tones in the carpets and bathroom tiles. There are decanters of gin, sherry, and whisky in every room, as well as complimentary minibars and bathrobes. The location couldn't be better: minutes away from Queen Street Station, Buchanan Street, and George Square. Windows, the cutting-edge restaurant, has a 180-degree view of Glasgow's rooftops and surrounding hills. **Pros:** near city center attractions; complimentary in-room drinks; executive lounge with library and fireplace. **Cons:** breakfast is an additional £14 per person; you must upgrade your room (£20) to use the lounge facilities. ⊠ *44 W. George St., City Center* ☎ *0141/353–6373* ⊕ *www. carltonhotels.co.uk/george* ⌁ *64 rooms* ᗌ *In-room: a/c, safe, refrigerator, DVD, Wi-Fi. In-hotel: restaurant, room service, Wi-Fi hotspot, parking (paid)* ▤ *AE, DC, MC, V* ⊹ *G4.*

££   ⊡ **Cathedral House Hotel.** Adjacent to Glasgow Cathedral, this Scottish Baronial–style building dating to 1867 once served as the church's ecclesiastical headquarters—hence the name of this small hotel. It's suitably grand, with crow-stepped gables and towering turrets. The rooms, accessed by a spiraling stone staircase, are of varying size, but all are smartly decorated with dark-wood furnishings. Rooms 4 and 7 have perfect views of the cathedral and Necropolis across the street. The downstairs bar is popular but far enough from the rooms that the noise won't disturb you. A full Scottish breakfast—or a vegetarian option—is served in the private café. **Pros:** historic atmosphere; quiet location; good views. **Cons:** no elevator; a long 10-minute walk to the center of town. ⊠ *28–32 Cathedral Sq., Merchant City* ☎ *0141/552–3519* ⊕ *www.cathedralhouse.org* ⌁ *7 rooms* ᗌ *In-hotel: bar, Wi-Fi hotspot, parking (free)* ▤ *AE, MC, V* |◎| *BP* ⊹ *H4.*

£   ⊡ **City Inn.** Overlooking the River Clyde and a just a few minutes from the Scottish Exhibition and Conference Center, this is a good choice for travelers who are in town for concerts or business by the river. Guest rooms are bright and contemporary, dressed in white, red, and gold. The furniture has a gentle softness to it. Rooms overlooking the river have lovely views, and the City Café restaurant has an inviting terrace. **Pros:** bargain prices; a relaxing lounge area. **Cons:** 30-minute walk to the city center; 10-minute walk to accessible public transportation; breakfast is an additional £10. ✉ *Finnieston Quay, City Center* ☎ *0141/240–1002* ⊕ *www.cityinn.com* 🛏 *164 rooms* ♿ *In-room: DVD, Wi-Fi. In-hotel: 2 restaurants, room service, bar, gym, Wi-Fi hotspot, parking (free)* ▭ *AE, DC, MC, V* ✚ *E5.*

£££   🏨 **Hilton Glasgow.** On first impression this is a typical international hotel, but Glasgow friendliness permeates its professional facade. The rooms are spacious, but lack individuality, although the fittings and furniture are high quality. There are two restaurants: Cameron's is designed to resemble a Highland shooting lodge, and Minsky's is a New York–style deli. Raffles bar, with its colonial Singapore theme, is a popular hangout for local and visiting celebrities. **Pros:** fabulous service; great pool; interesting bar. **Cons:** uninspiring room decor; mediocre location beside motorway and over a mile from Merchant City shops. ✉ *1 William St., City Center* ☎ *0141/204–5555* ⊕ *www.hilton.com* 🛏 *319 rooms* ♿ *In-room: safe, refrigerator, Internet. In-hotel: 2 restaurants, bar, pool, gym, laundry service, Wi-Fi hotspot, parking (paid)* ▭ *AE, DC, MC, V* ❙◯❙ *BP* ✚ *D4.*

£££   🏨 **Malmaison.** Housed in a converted church, this modern boutique
Fodor's Choice   hotel, part of a stylish mini-chain, prides itself on personal service and
★   outstanding amenities: each room has nice touches like plasma televisions and music systems. The art deco interior employs bold colors in playful prints and geometric shapes all balanced out by traditional fabrics and furnishings. The lobby's splendid staircase has a wrought-iron balustrade illustrating Napoléon's exploits (the hotel chain takes its name from his home). The warm Brasserie offers British-French cooking. Champagne Bar serves savory pasta dishes in an airy terracotta-hue room with iron fixtures and a spiral staircase. **Pros:** stunning lobby; staff pays great attention to detail; five-minute walk to Sauchiehall Street. **Cons:** bland views; dark hallways; no on-site parking. ✉ *278 W. George St., City Center* ☎ *0141/572–1000* ⊕ *www.malmaison.com* 🛏 *72 rooms, 8 suites* ♿ *In-room: refrigerator, Wi-Fi. In-hotel: restaurant, bar, gym, Wi-Fi* ▭ *AE, DC, MC, V* ❙◯❙ *CP* ✚ *E3.*

££   🏨 **Marks Hotel.** This elegant hotel has a lot to recommend it, not the least of which is its location, just a stone's throw away from Sauchiehall Street. The rooms are spacious and have nice touches such as plasma televisions and fresh cut flowers. The One Ten Bar and Grill serves breakfast, lunch, and dinner, including specialties such as mushroom bruschetta and grilled rib-eye steak. **Pros:** good location; lively downstairs restaurant and bar; free Wi-Fi. **Cons:** very busy wallpaper in rooms and corridors not to all tastes; parking garage is a brisk five-minute walk away and charges £10 per day. ✉ *110 Bath St., City Center* ☎ *0141/353–0800* ⊕ *www.markshotels.com* 🛏 *102 rooms* ♿ *In-room: no a/c, Wi-Fi. In-hotel: restaurant, bar, Wi-Fi hotspot* ▭ *AE, MC, V* ❙◯❙ *CP* ✚ *F3.*

££   🏨 **Merchant Lodge Hotel.** This sturdy-looking sandstone lodge bears the marks of time but is well cared for. Some guests return annually; some stay long term because, they say, they feel as if they're "coming home." Stones and wine barrels bursting with pansies lead to the door of this

300-year-old building, which has a turret with a spiral staircase to the top. The welcoming reception area soothes even the most tired traveler, and Peter, who works the reception desk, is happy to help with whatever you need. Guest rooms are spacious and have original pine floorboards and simple pine furniture, with taupe, moss, and cream-color decorative accents. The location is ideal; although central, it's very quiet. **Pros:** romantic and historic setting; great breakfast; long-stay discounts. **Cons:** no elevator; doesn't accept American Express. ⊠ *52 Virginia St., Merchant City* 🕾 *0141/552–2424* ⊕ *www.merchantlodgehotel.com* ⤵ *40 rooms* ⚲ *In-room: no a/c, Wi-Fi. In-hotel: Wi-Fi, parking (paid)* ☰ *DC, MC, V* ⦿ *BP.* ⊹ *G5.*

££   🛏 **Park Inn.** The minimalist look here extends from the sleek wood reception desk to the sophisticated platform beds in the bright bedrooms; suites on the top floor come in three styles, ranging from monochrome to pop art. Contemporary Scottish cooking is the forte of the Oshi restaurant, which serves three-course pretheater meals. The downtown location puts you close to Glasgow Royal Concert Hall and the Buchanan Galleries shopping mall. **Pros:** perfectly situated for downtown outings; modern rooms; relaxing waterfall and fireplace in lobby. **Cons:** next door to bus station; fees for Wi-Fi and parking; some rooms have disappointing views. ⊠ *2 Port Dundas St., City Center* 🕾 *0141/333–1500* ⊕ *www.parkinn.com* ⤵ *70 rooms, 30 suites* ⚲ *In-room: no a/c, Wi-Fi. In-hotel: restaurant, room service, bar, gym, Wi-Fi hotspot* ☰ *AE, DC, MC, V* ⦿ *CP* ⊹ *G3.*

£   🛏 **Premier Inn.** It may be a chain hotel, but the bright rooms and low prices appeal to savvy travelers. The guest rooms are larger than most in this 1,400-year-old city, and have nice touches like coffeemakers. Rooms facing the street can be noisy at night, so ask for one that looks out onto the graveyard, where rabble-rousers are highly unlikely. **Pros:** great location; bargain price; spacious, modern rooms. **Cons:** some front rooms are noisy; extra charges for parking (£12 per day), Wi-Fi (£9 per 24 hours) and breakfast (£8). ⊠ *187 George St., Merchant City* 🕾 *0870/238–3320* ⊕ *www.premierinn.com* ⤵ *239 rooms* ⚲ *In-room: no a/c. In-hotel: restaurant, bar, Wi-Fi, parking (paid)* ☰ *AE, MC, V* ⊹ *H4.*

££££   🛏 **Radisson Blu.** You can't miss this eye-catching edifice behind Central Station in the city's up-and-coming financial quarter. Its glass front makes the interior, particularly the lounge, seem as though it were part of the street. Rooms are decorated in several styles—the Nordic rooms, for example, are done up in an icy shade of blue. Both restaurants—the pop-art-inspired Collage, serving Continental cuisine, and Tapaell'Ya, the tapas bar—are popular with business and artist types, as is the sleek street-level bar. **Pros:** kilted doorman; great gym; free Wi-Fi; impeccable service. **Cons:** neighborhood can get noisy; most rooms have poor views; constant traffic on the doorstep. ⊠ *301 Argyle St., City Center* 🕾 *0141/204–3333* ⊕ *www.radissonblu.com* ⤵ *247 rooms, 3 suites* ⚲ *In-room: safe, refrigerator, Wi-Fi. In-hotel: restaurant, room service, bar, pool, gym, Wi-Fi, parking (paid)* ☰ *AE, DC, V* ⦿ *CP* ⊹ *E5.*

£   🛏 **Victorian House.** Compared with the bright-yellow entrance hall, the rooms in this hotel are rather plain. But its location—on a quiet residential street only a block from the Charles Rennie Mackintosh–designed Glasgow School of Art—is prime. There are plenty of restaurants and bars on nearby Sauchiehall Street, and the friendly staff is more than happy to help you choose one. **Pros:** next to the Glasgow School of Art; great front patio; basement rooms very spacious. **Cons:** some rooms need to be freshened up; no elevator; on-street parking can be difficult to find. ✉ *212 Renfrew St., City Center* ☏ *0141/332–0129* ⊕ *www.thevictorian.co.uk* ⇨ *58 rooms* ⌂ *In-room: no a/c. In-hotel: Wi-Fi hotspot* ▤ *MC, V* ‖◎‖ *BP* ⊹ *E2.*

WEST END AND ENVIRONS

Use the coordinate (⊹ B2) at the end of each listing to locate a site on the corresponding map.

£ 🏨 **Amadeus Guest House.** This adorable, newly remodeled Victorian town house is on a leafy residential street overlooking the River Kelvin. Rooms are comfortable and have plenty of natural light. Flickering candles and Mozart playing in the background add a nice touch to the breakfast buffet. **Pros:** near West End attractions; two-minute walk from subway; kids under six stay free. **Cons:** some rooms are small; finding parking can be difficult. ✉ *411 N. Woodside Rd., West End* ☏ *0141/339–8257* ⊕ *www.amadeusguesthouse.co.uk* ⇨ *9 rooms* ⌂ *In-room: no a/c. In-hotel: Wi-Fi hotspot* ▤ *AE, MC, V* ‖◎‖ *CP* ⊹ *C5.*

££ 🏨 **Ambassador Hotel.** Opposite the West End's peaceful Botanic Gardens, the Ambassador is part of a string of elegant town houses on the banks of the River Kelvin. The interior echoes the peacefulness of the location and the Victorian ethos of the spacious former family home. The rooms have a contemporary look, with rich red-and-gold fabrics and beech furniture. **Pros:** views of Botanical Gardens; great for kids; five-minute walk to public transportation and West End amenities. **Cons:** no elevator; on-street parking can be difficult after 6 PM. ✉ *7 Kelvin Dr., West End* ☏ *0141/946–1018* ⊕ *www.glasgowhotelsandapartments. co.uk* ⇨ *17 rooms* ⌂ *In-room: no a/c, safe, refrigerator, In-hotel: bar, laundry facilities Wi-Fi hotspot, parking (free)* ▤ *MC, V* ‖◎‖ *BP* ⊹ *B5.*

£ 🏨 **Argyll Guest House.** At this small but cozy hotel, all the rooms are spacious and plainly furnished with prints and modern pieces. The full Scottish breakfast is deliciously hearty, and you're welcome to have dinner at the restaurant in the Argyll Guest House's sister hotel, the Argyll Hotel, across the street. The best attraction, however, is the caring staff. **Pros:** close to Kelvingrove Park; near public transportation; bargain prices. **Cons:** front rooms noisy on weekends; decor is bland and uninspiring; no elevator. ✉ *966–970 Sauchiehall St., West End* ☏ *0141/357–5155* ⊕ *www.argyllguesthouseglasgow.co.uk* ⇨ *19 rooms* ⌂ *In-room: no a/c, Wi-Fi. In-hotel: bar, laundry service, Wi-Fi, parking (free)* ▤ *AE, MC, V* ‖◎‖ *BP* ⊹ *A2.*

£££ 🏨 **Hotel du Vin Glasgow.** Once the legendary One Devonshire Gardens, frequented by such celebrities as Luciano Pavarotti and Elizabeth Taylor, the Hotel Du Vin Glasgow is still a destination for those in search of luxury. Made up of a group of Victorian houses on a tree-lined street, the hotel is all about elegance, from the sophisticated drawing room to the individually decorated guest rooms with flowing draperies,

Fodor's Choice
★

Egyptian linens, and mahogany furnishings like four-poster beds. The Bistro restaurant is equally stylish; expect such delights as poached lobster and air-dried duck followed by a warm chocolate tart with pear sorbet. The beverage menu is also impressive: there are more than 600 wines and 300 whiskies. **Pros:** stunning Scottish rooms; doting service; complimentary whisky upon arrival. **Cons:** no elevator; on-street parking can be difficult after 6 PM. ⊠ *1 Devonshire Gardens, West End* ☎ *0141/339–2001* ⊕ *www.hotelduvin.com/glasgow* ⤳ *49 rooms, 7 suites* ⚭ *In-room: refrigerator, no a/c, Wi-Fi. In-hotel: restaurant, room service, bar, spa, gym, Wi-Fi hotspot, parking (free)* ☰ *AE, DC, MC, V* ⦿ *BP* ✢ *A4.*

££ 🏠 **The Kelvingrove.** Family run and friendly, this small hotel has some-
☼ thing for everyone. The walled garden is tenderly cared for by grand-
Fodor's Choice mother Muriel, whose loving touch keeps flowers blooming. It's a nice
★ place to sit with a cup of tea. Guest rooms are generous in size and comfortable; creams and browns are the color scheme, set off by shiny hardwood floors. The rooms are on the ground and basement levels; those at the back are quiet and overlook a tranquil garden. Many front rooms have large bay windows. All needs are seen to with TLC; breakfast is massive, and the family rooms are a steal at £120 per night. **Pros:** close to West End amenities; 24-hour reception; informative guest pack in every room. **Cons:** street noise can be a problem for front rooms on Friday and Saturday nights; 15-minute walk to nearest subway station. ⊠ *944 Sauchiehall St., West End* ☎ *0141/339–5011* ⊕ *www.kelvingrovehotel.com* ⤳ *22 rooms* ⚭ *In-room: no a/c, kitchen (some), Wi-Fi. In-hotel: Internet terminal, public Wi-Fi hotspot, parking (free), some pets allowed* ☰ *AE, DC, MC, V* ⦿ *BP* ✢ *A2.*

££ 🏠 **Kirklee Hotel.** This West End B&B occupies a small and cozy Edwardian town house filled with home-away-from-home comforts. A bay window in the lounge overlooks a garden, and the old-fashioned morning room is adorned with embroidered settees and silk-wash wallpapers. Engravings on the walls and shelves of books in the library offer touches that any university don would appreciate. The owners are friendly and helpful. A neighboring gym charges guests £7.50 per session. **Pros:** friendly service; quiet street; close to West End attractions. **Cons:** on-street parking is challenging; city center is 2 mi away. ⊠ *11 Kensington Gate, West End* ☎ *0141/334–5555* ⊕ *www.kirkleehotel.co.uk* ⤳ *9 rooms* ⚭ *In-room: no a/c. In-hotel: Wi-Fi hotspot* ☰ *AE, DC, MC, V* ⦿ *BP* ✢ *A5.*

££ 🏠 **Manor Park Hotel.** On a quiet street close to Victoria Park, one of Glasgow's most idyllic public spaces, this stately terraced town house combines urban spaciousness with proximity to city action. Each of the neat and airy bedrooms, even the bright attic ones, bears the name in Gaelic of a Scottish island. The friendly owners themselves are Gaelic speakers, and tartan plays its part subtly in the homey interior. **Pros:** quiet residential area; helpful staff; delicious breakfast. **Cons:** an hour walk to the city center; close to motorway. ⊠ *28 Balshagray Dr., West End* ☎ *0141/339–2143* ⊕ *www.manorparkhotel.com* ⤳ *10 rooms* ⚭ *In-room: no a/c, Wi-Fi. In-hotel: Wi-Fi hotspot, parking (free)* ☰ *AE, MC, V* ⦿ *BP* ✢ *A6.*

£ 🏨 **The Sandyford.** The Victorian exterior of this hotel anticipates the colorful interior. Each room is freshly decorated with basic pine furnishings. On the western end of famous Sauchiehall Street, the hotel is convenient to all city-center sights, including the Scottish Exhibition Centre and many art museums. **Pros:** on the doorstep of Kelvingrove Park; minutes from several good West End eateries; newly refurbished rooms. **Cons:** front rooms can get late-night street noise; popular with stag parties; no elevator. ⊠ *904 Sauchiehall St., West End* ☎ *0141/334–0000* ⊕ *www. sandyfordhotelglasgow.com* 📲 *63 rooms* ♿ *In-room: no a/c, Wi-Fi. In-hotel: Internet terminal, Wi-Fi hotspot* ▭ *MC, V* ⦿⏐*BP* ✢ *B3.*

£–££ 🏨 **The White House Apartments.** On a tranquil Victorian crescent just
☺ west of the Botanical Gardens, this well-managed group of town houses has more than 30 apartments—studios to two bedrooms—that can be rented from a night to a week to as long as a year. Apartments are spacious and individually decorated; all have kitchens, tables, chairs, and even little living areas, along with beds and dressers. Some are more contemporary than others, but it's hard to beat the space, views, location, or peace and quiet—not to mention the value. The lobby is very Scottish, with tartan carpets, and elaborate chandeliers pepper the corridors. Helpful staff can point you in any direction you need to go. **Pros:** large rooms; fully equipped kitchens; courtyard gardens; larger units good for families or groups. **Cons:** some carpets are a little shabby; rooms that haven't been renovated look drab. ⊠ *11–13 Cleveden Crescent, West End* ☎ *0141/339–9375* ⊕ *www.whitehouse-apartments.com* 📲 *32 apartments* ♿ *In-room: no a/c, kitchen, refrigerator, Wi-Fi. In-hotel: laundry service, Internet terminal, Wi-Fi hotspot, parking (free)* ▭ *AE, DC, MC, V* ✢ *A4.*

SOUTH SIDE

Use the coordinate (✢ B2) at the end of each listing to locate a site on the corresponding map.

£ 🏨 **Ewington City Hotel.** This quiet row of town houses opposite Queen's Park is known for its traditional demeanor. Victorian-style furniture, ornately decorated bedrooms with heavy and elaborate pink-and-green floral fabrics, and an open fire in the spacious lobby all add to the relaxed, elegant character. Downtown Glasgow is only a short bus or train ride away. **Pros:** lovely reception area; nice views of Queens's Park; most rooms are spacious and stylish. **Cons:** service can be slow; rear-facing rooms can be noisy. ⊠ *132 Queen's Dr., South Side* ☎ *0141/423–1152* ⊕ *www.mckeverhotels.co.uk* 📲 *42 rooms* ♿ *In-room: no a/c, Wi-Fi. In-hotel: restaurant, bar, Wi-Fi hotspot, parking (free)* ▭ *AE, DC, MC, V* ⦿⏐*BP* ✢ *D6.*

£££ 🏨 **Sherbrooke Castle Hotel.** At this architectural flight of fantasy, the
Fodor'sChoice cavernous rooms hark back to grander times when the South Side of
★ Glasgow was home to the immensely wealthy tobacco barons whose homes boasted turrets and towers. The spacious grounds are far from the noise and bustle of downtown yet only a 10-minute drive from the city center. The hotel's proprietor insists on tasteful interior styling and good traditional cooking using fresh ingredients. Everything is prepared on the premises, including the breads. Locals flock to the

busy bar. **Pros:** great atmosphere; top-notch service; exceptional food. **Cons:** some rooms are small; some distance from center of town; weekends functions can get very loud; no elevator. ⊠ *11 Sherbrooke Ave., Pollokshields, South Side* ☎ *0141/427–4227* ⊕ *www.sherbrooke.co.uk* ⟋ *14 rooms* ⚷ *In-room: no a/c. In-hotel: restaurant, bar, Wi-Fi hotspot* ⊟ *AE, DC, MC, V* ⫮⊙⫵ *BP* ✛ *D6.*

NIGHTLIFE AND THE ARTS

Home to Scotland's national orchestra, and opera and dance companies, Glasgow is truly the artistic hub of the country. The city's mix of university students, artists, and professionals has created a spirited pub-and-club scene at night.

THE ARTS

Because Glasgow is home to the Royal Scottish Academy of Music and Drama, there is always a pool of impressive young talent that's pressing the city's artistic boundaries in theater, music, and film. Glasgow is known for vibrant theater, with everything from cutting-edge one-act plays to over-the-top pantomines. And the arts don't end with theater, as Glasgow's music scene is eclectic and constantly growing. Most bars host live bands whose music ranges from traditional Scottish to the blues to rock and roll. There are, of course, plenty of places to enjoy classical music.

ARTS CENTER

Trongate 103 (⊠ *Trongate 103, Merchant City* ☎ *0141/276–8380* ⊕ *www.trongate103.com*), a contemporary visual arts center in a converted Edwardian warehouse, is home base for diverse groups producing prints, film, photography, painting, and more, all reflecting the city's artistic energy. Exhibits, concerts, readings, and more are scheduled; the center is open Tuesday through Sunday.

CONCERTS

The **Glasgow Royal Concert Hall** (⊠ *2 Sauchiehall St., City Center* ☎ *0141/353–8000*) has 2,500 seats and is the main venue of the Royal Scottish National Orchestra, which performs in winter and spring. The **Royal Scottish Academy of Music and Drama** (⊠ *100 Renfrew St., City Center* ☎ *0141/332–4101*) is one of the most important small venues for concerts, recitals, and theater productions. The **Scottish Exhibition and Conference Centre** (⊠ *Exhibition Way, Finnieston St., West End* ☎ *0141/248–3000*) regularly hosts large-scale pop concerts.

St. Andrew's in the Square (⊠ *1 St. Andrew's in the Square, Trongate and East End* ☎ *0141/559–5902*) is a glorious 18th-century church, restored as an arts and Scottish dancing venue; call to check about Thursday tours. Drop in to see fiddle players on Monday evenings or take a *ceilidh* (traditional Scottish dance) class on Wednesday nights. The downstairs café is a nice resting place.

DANCE AND OPERA

★ Glasgow is home to the Scottish Opera and Scottish Ballet, both of which perform at the **Theatre Royal** (✉ *282 Hope St., City Center* ☎ *0141/332–9000*). Visiting dance companies from many countries appear here as well.

FESTIVALS

Celtic Connections (✉ *Glasgow Royal Concert Hall, 2 Sauchiehall St., City Center* ☎ *0141/353–8000* ⊕ *www.celticconnections.com*) is an ever-expanding Celtic music festival held in the second half of January. Musicians from Africa, France, Canada, Ireland, and Scotland perform and conduct hands-on workshops on topics such as how to make a harp. **Glasgay** (☎ *0141/552–7575* ⊕ *www.glasgay.co.uk*), held between October and November, is the United Kingdom's largest multiarts festival focusing on gay and lesbian issues. The international and Scottish line-up is always impressive and draws a huge audience.

FILM

The **Center for Contemporary Arts** (✉ *350 Sauchiehall St., City Center* ☎ *0141/352–4900*) screens classic, independent, and children's films. The **Glasgow Film Theatre** (✉ *12 Rose St., City Center* ☎ *0141/332–8128*), an independent public cinema, screens the best new-release films from all over the world.

★ The **Grosvenor** (✉ *Ashton La., West End* ☎ *0141/339–8444*) is a popular, compact cinema with leather sofas and a bar in Glasgow's trendy West End. **UGC** (✉ *7 Renfrew St., City Center* ☎ *0871/200–2000*), an 18-screen multilevel facility, is Glasgow's busiest movie complex. At 170 feet tall, it's also the world's tallest cinema building.

THEATER

Tickets for theatrical performances can be purchased at theater box offices or online through **Ticketmaster** (⊕ *www.ticketmaster.co.uk*).

★ The **Arches** (✉ *253 Argyle St., City Center* ☎ *0870/240–7528*) stages challenging yet accessible drama from around the world.

★ Some of the most exciting theatrical performances take place at the internationally renowned **Citizens' Theatre** (✉ *119 Gorbals St., South Side* ☎ *0141/429–0022*), where productions, and their sets, are often of hair-raising originality. Behind the theater's striking contemporary glass facade is a glorious Victorian red-and-gilded auditorium. Contemporary works are staged at **Cottier's Arts Theatre** (✉ *93 Hyndland St., West End* ☎ *0141/357–5825*), in a converted church.

The **King's Theatre** (✉ *297 Bath St., City Center* ☎ *0141/240–1111*) puts on dramas, variety shows, and musicals.

★ **Òran Mór** (✉ *731 Great Western Rd., West End* ☎ *0141/357–6200*) puts on a variety of plays during lunch- and dinnertime. The "Play, Pie and Pint" and "Dinner, Drama and Dram" run in 10-week blocks. Both sell out quickly, so book in advance. The **Pavilion** (✉ *121 Renfield St., City Center* ☎ *0141/332–1846*) hosts family variety entertainment along with rock and pop concerts.

The **Ramshorn Theatre** ✉ *98 Ingram St., Merchant City* ☎ *0141/552–3498*) an impressive converted church, is home to the Strathclyde

Theatre Group. You can take a tour on Saturday from mid-July to mid-September. Some of Glasgow's most famous dead lie buried in the spooky graveyard. The **Royal Scottish Academy of Music and Drama** (✉ *100 Renfrew St., City Center* ☎ *0141/332–4101*) stages international and student performances.

The **Theatre Royal** (✉ *282 Hope St., City Center* ☎ *0141/332–1133*) hosts performances of major dramas, as well as opera and ballet. The **Tron Theatre** (✉ *63 Trongate, Merchant City* ☎ *0141/552–4267*) puts on contemporary theater from Scotland and around the world.

NIGHTLIFE

Glasgow's nightlife scene is impressive and there's something here for everyone. Bars and pubs often close at midnight on the weekends, but nightclubs often stay open until 3 or 4 AM. Traditional ceilidh (a mix of country dancing, music, and song; pronounced *kay*-lee) is not as popular as it used to be (unless you're at a wedding), but you can still find it at many establishments. Consult the biweekly magazine the *List*, available at newsstands and bookstores, and the *Scotsman, Herald,* and *Evening Times* newspapers for up-to-date performance and event listings.

BARS AND PUBS

Glasgow's pubs were once hangouts for serious drinkers who demanded few comforts. Times have changed, and many of these gritty establishments have been transformed into trendy cocktail bars. Bars and pubs vary according to location: those in the city center tend to cater to business types, although some still cater to a more traditional clientele. The bars and pubs in the West End were once favored by students; however, that is slowly changing as thirty-, forty-, and even fiftysomething crowds have moved in.

First-timers to Glasgow's pub scene should order a pint, meaning a pint of lager. Bottled beers are available, but draft beer is the most popular beverage for men; women tend to drink wine or cocktails (yes, this gender difference is extremely obvious). Most bars and pubs are open daily from 11 AM to midnight (some are open until 2 AM) and also serve food. Keep in mind opening hours are often extended by an hour on weekends.

CITY CENTER Many of the most popular bars are in the center of the city. **Babbity Bowster's** (✉ *16–18 Blackfriars St., Merchant City* ☎ *0141/552–5055*), a busy, friendly spot, serves interesting beers and good food. The **Black Sparrow** (✉ *241 North St., City Center* ☎ *0141/221–5530*, a cool Charles Bukowski theme bar named after the American writer's publishing company, has plenty of tall plants and cocktails as well as sophisticated bar food; there's a great outdoor beer garden. At **Bloc** (✉ *117 Bath St., City Center* ☎ *0141/574–6066*), you can step behind a curious version of the Iron Curtain where Tex-Mex diner food mixes with an eclectic musical mash of DJs and live rock and folk bands. **King Tut's Wah Wah Hut** (✉ *227a St. Vincent St., City Center* ☎ *0141/221–5279*), which hosts live music most nights, claims to have been the venue that discovered the U.K. pop band Oasis. It's a favorite with students, but the cozy and traditional pub setting draws people of all ages.

For a splash of Mediterranean style, head to **Moskito** (⊠ *200 Bath St., City Center* ☎ *0141/331–1777*). Amid the cool, aquatic hues you can see people dancing to laid-back tunes Thursday to Sunday nights.

★ **Sloans** (⊠ *62 Argyle Arcade, 108 Argyle St., City Center* ☎ *0141/221–8886)* is one of Glasgow's oldest and most beautiful pubs, with mahogany wood paneling, vaulted ceilings, and a marble fireplace. It hosts dinner cabarets and ceilidhs every Friday night. There's a good selection of beers and spirits, and the outdoor area is always lively on a dry night.

★ The **Riverside Club** (⊠ *33 Fox St., off Clyde St., City Center* ☎ *0141/248–3144*) hosts traditional bands on Friday and Saturday evenings; get there early, as it's popular. **Rogano** (⊠ *11 Exchange Pl., City Center* ☎ *0141/248–4055*) is famous for its champagne cocktails and general air of 1920s decadence.

Fodor'sChoice The **Scotia Bar** (⊠ *112 Stockwell St., Merchant City* ☎ *0141/552–8681*)
★ serves up a taste of an authentic Glasgow pub, with some traditional folk music occasionally thrown in.

WEST END There's also a thriving scene in the West End. **Ben Nevis** (⊠ *1147 Argyle St., West End* ☎ *0141/576–5204*) is an eccentric pub full of Highland artifacts. There's more than 180 whiskies to choose from and traditional live music just about every night. Despite its former austere existence as a church, the always-busy **Cottiers** (⊠ *Hyndland St., West End* ☎ *0141/357–5825*) is a famous haunt of the young. The best seat is outside in the popular beer garden. There's often a good lineup of established and up-and-coming rock groups at the **Halt** (⊠ *160 Woodlands Rd., West End* ☎ *0141/564–1527*), which attracts an older clientele. **Òran Mór** (⊠ *731 Great Western Rd., West End* ☎ *0141/357–6200*), at the top of Byres Road, is popular with all ages. Situated in a massive church, the bar has beautiful stained-glass windows. The beer garden fills up quickly in good weather.

★ **Tennents** (⊠ *191 Byres Rd., West End* ☎ *0141/341–1021*), a spacious street-corner bar, prides itself on a comprehensive selection of beers, lively conversation, and a refreshing lack of loud music. The best Gaelic pub in Glasgow is **Uisge Beatha** (⊠ *232–246 Woodlands Rd., West End* ☎ *0141/564–1596*). The name, pronounced *oos*-ki *bee*-ha, means "water of life" and is said to be the origin of the word "whisky." The bar serves *fraoch* (heather beer) in season and has live music on Wednesday and Sunday. The **78** (⊠ *10–14 Kelvinhaugh St., West End* ☎ *0141/576–5018*) has cozy sofas, vegan food, and a real coal fire. There's live music every night, with jazz on Sunday.

NIGHTCLUBS

As elsewhere in Britain, electronic music—from house to techno to drum and bass—is par for the course in Glasgow's dance clubs. Much of the scene revolves around Center City.

★ The **Arches** (⊠ *253 Argyle St., City Center* ☎ *0901/022–0300*) is one of the city's largest arts venues, but on Friday (11 PM to 3 AM) and Saturday (10:30 PM to 4 AM) it thumps with house and techno. The club welcomes big music names like Colours and Inside Out at legendary parties. A few times a month it holds dressed-up gay nights.

Oozing with Edwardian style, the **Polo Lounge** (✉ *84 Wilson St., Merchant City* ☎ *0141/553–1221*) is Glasgow's largest gay club. Upstairs is a bar that resembles an old-fashioned gentlemen's club; downstairs two dance floors play something for everyone. The festivities run Monday through Thursday from 5 PM to 1 AM, Friday from 5 PM to 3 AM, and weekends from noon to 3 AM.

Stereo (✉ *20–28 Renield La., City Center* ☎ *0141/222–2254*) has a wide range of live music Sunday through Thursday (9 PM to 11:30 PM) and DJ club nights Friday and Saturday (11 PM to 3 AM). The small downstairs music venue gets crowded quickly, but that only adds to the electric atmosphere. Upstairs, a café/bar serves tasty vegan food and organic drinks.

The **Sub Club** (✉ *22 Jamaica St., City Center* ☎ *0141/248–4600*) is an atmospheric underground venue that has staged cutting-edge music events since its jazz club days in the '50s. Legendary favorites like Saturday's SubCulture (House) and Sunday's Optimo (a truly eclectic mix for musical hedonists) pack in friendly and sweaty crowds.

SPORTS AND THE OUTDOORS

Until recently, Glasgow wasn't a city known for its exercise enthusiasts. Times have most definitely changed, as you can't go far these days without seeing a runner or cyclist. Because of the city's numerous parks, there is plenty of space. Rarely is the weather conducive for outdoor exercise; it rains a lot in Glasgow, but don't let that deter you. It doesn't deter the locals who play soccer, tennis, hike, bike, run, swim and walk in the rain. Alternatively, there are plenty of indoor gyms for those who prefer to stay dry.

GOLF

Several municipal courses are operated within Glasgow proper by the local authorities. Bookings are relatively inexpensive and should be made directly to the course 24 hours in advance to ensure prime tee times (courses open at 7 AM). A comprehensive list of contacts, facilities, and greens fees of the 30 or so other courses near the city is available from the tourist board. The abbreviation SSS means standard scratch score, which is often used here instead of par.

Douglas Park. North of the city near Milngavie, Douglas Park is a long, attractive course set among birch and pine trees with masses of rhododendrons blooming in early summer. ✉ *Hillfoot, Bearsden* ☎ *0141/942–0985* ⊕ *www.douglasparkgolfclub.co.uk* 🏌 *18 holes, 5,962 yds, par 69.*

Lethamhill. The fairways of this city-owned parkland course overlook Hogganfield Loch. To get here, take the M8 north to Junction 12, and drive up the A80 about a quarter mile. ✉ *1240 Cumbernauld Rd., North City* ☎ *0141/770–6220* 🏌 *18 holes, 5,836 yds, SSS 68.*

Littlehill. Level fairways and greens make this municipal course not too difficult to play. It's about 4 mi north of the city center. ✉ *Auchinairn Rd., North City* ☎ *0141/772–1916* 🏌 *18 holes, 6,240 yds, SSS 70.*

FOOTBALL

The city has been sports mad, especially for football (soccer), for more than 100 years. The rivalry between its two main football clubs, the Rangers and the Celtic, is legendary. Matches are held usually on Saturday in winter. Admission prices start at about £20. Don't go looking for a family-day-out atmosphere; football remains a fiercely contested game attended mainly by males, though the stadiums at Ibrox and Celtic Park are fast becoming family-friendly. The Rangers wear blue and play at **Ibrox** (✉ *150 Edmiston Dr., South Side* ☎ *0871/702–1972*), pronounced *eye*-brox, on the south side of the Clyde. The Celtic wear white and green stripes and play in the east at **Celtic Park** (✉ *18 Kerrydale St., East End* ☎ *0845/671–1888*). The game in Glasgow isn't just blue or green, nor is it dominated by international players and big money. Partick Thistle (the Jags) wear red and yellow and their ground is **Firhill Park** (✉ *80 Firhill Rd., West End* ☎ *0141/579–1971*).

SHOPPING

Glaswegians love to dress up, and you'll find the mark of the fashion industry on the city center's hottest shopping streets, Buchanan and Sauchiehall, as well as in Princes Square. Glasgow is the biggest and most popular British retail center outside London. Besides straight-off-the-runway couture, Glasgow has an impressive number of antiques stores, and Scottish specialty shops selling woolen, cashmere, and tartan dress.

Should the weather turn *dreich* (dismal) you can avoid getting *drookit* (wet) by sheltering in one of the many covered arcades in the city center. For more unusual items, head to the West End's Byres Road and Great Western Road. ■TIP→ If you're here in late June and early July, there are always big sales. You can pick up some fantastic bargains.

ARCADES AND SHOPPING CENTERS

The **Buchanan Galleries** (✉ *220 Buchanan St., City Center* ☎ *0141/333–9898*), at the top end of Buchanan Street next to the Glasgow Royal Concert Hall, is packed with high-quality shops; its magnet attraction is the John Lewis department store.

Fodor'sChoice ★ By far the best complex is the art nouveau **Princes Square** (✉ *38–42 Buchanan St., City Center* ☎ *0141/221–0324*), with high-quality shops alongside pleasant cafés and a tony restaurant or two. Look for the Scottish Craft Centre, which carries an outstanding collection of work created by some of the nation's best craftspeople. **St. Enoch's Shopping Centre** (✉ *55 St. Enoch Sq., City Center* ☎ *0141/204–3900*) is eye-catching if not especially pleasing—it's a modern glass building that resembles an overgrown greenhouse. It houses various stores, but most are also found elsewhere. **Silverburn** (✉ *Barrhead Rd., Pollock* ☎ *0141/880–3200*) is enormous; it's Europe's largest shopping mall and a good option on a rainy day. The interior feels like a village with streams, waterfalls, and restaurants galore, plus shops from retail giants like Marks & Spencer to small purse stalls. Direct buses from Buchanan Street Station leave every 20 minutes.

SHOPPING DISTRICTS

On the main, often-crowded pedestrian area of **Argyle Street,** you'll find chain stores such as Debenham's. An interesting diversion off Argyle Street is the covered **Argyll Arcade,** which has the largest collection of jewelers under one roof in Scotland. The L-shape arcade, built in 1904, houses several locally based jewelers and a few shops specializing in antique jewelry. **Buchanan Street,** off the Argyll Arcade, is Glasgow's premier shopping street and almost totally a pedestrian area. The usual suspects are here: Monsoon, Topshop, Burberry, Jaeger, and other household names, some with premises in Buchanan Galleries, at the top end of the street. **St. Enoch Square,** which is also the main underground station, houses the St. Enoch Shopping Centre.

The huge **Barras** indoor market, on London Road in the Glasgow Cross neighborhood east of the city center, prides itself on selling everything "from a needle to an anchor." Stalls hawk antique (and not-so-antique) furniture, bric-a-brac, good and not-so-good jewelry, and textiles—you name it, it's here. Many of Glasgow's young and upwardly mobile make their home in **Merchant City,** on the edge of the city center. Shopping here is expensive, but the area is worth visiting if you're seeking the youthful Glasgow style. The university dominates the area around **West End,** and the shops cater to local and student needs. The easiest way to get here is by the underground system to Hillhead. If you're an antiques connoisseur and art lover, a walk along **West Regent Street,** particularly its **Victorian Village,** is highly recommended, as there are various galleries and shops, some specializing in Scottish antiques and paintings.

DEPARTMENT STORES

Debenham's (⊠ *97 Argyle St., City Center* ☎ *0844/561–6161*) is one of Glasgow's principal department stores, with fine china and crystal as well as women's and men's clothing.

Fodor'sChoice **House of Fraser** (⊠ *21–45 Buchanan St., City Center* ☎ *0141/221–3880*),
★ a Glasgow institution, stocks wares that reflect the city's material aspirations—leading European designer clothes and fabrics combined with home-produced articles, such as tweeds, tartans, glass, and ceramics. The magnificent interior, set off by the grand staircase rising to various floors and balconies, is itself worth a visit.

★ **John Lewis** (⊠ *Buchanan Galleries, 220 Buchanan St., City Center* ☎ *0141/353–6677*) is a favorite for its stylish mix of clothing and household items. **Marks & Spencer** (⊠ *2–12 Argyle St., City Center* ☎ *0141/ 552–4546* ⊠ *172 Sauchiehall St., City Center* ☎ *0141/332–6097*) sells sturdy, practical clothes and accessories at moderate prices; you can also buy food items and household goods here.

SPECIALTY SHOPS

Scotland has fantastic specialty shops, and Glasgow is home to many of them. Antiques shops are a big draw, as are bookstores and gourmet food emporiums. And don't forget kilts! Glasgow has plenty of kilt shops, especially in the city center.

ANTIQUES AND FINE ART

★ The **Compass Gallery** (✉ *178 W. Regent St., City Center* ☎ *0141/221–6370*) hosts exhibitions focusing on abstract and expressionist art. **Cyril Gerber Fine Art** (✉ *148 W. Regent St., City Center* ☎ *0141/221–3095 or 0141/204–0276*) specializes in British paintings from 1880 to the present; they will ship your purchase for you, as will most galleries. **De Courcys** (✉ *5–21 Cresswell La., West End*), an antiques and crafts arcade, has quite a few shops to visit, and lots of goods, including paintings and jewelry, are regularly auctioned. It's on one of the cobblestone lanes to the rear of Byres Road.

BOOKS, PAPER, AND MUSIC

Fopp (✉ *19–27 Union St., City Center* ☎ *0141/285–7190* ✉ *358 Byres Rd., West End* ☎ *0141/337–7490*) is a funky, three-level extravaganza of music, books, and DVDs. Prices are a lot more reasonable than those at most mainstream stores.

The **Glasgow School of Art** (✉ *167 Renfrew St., City Center* ☎ *0141/353–4526*) sells books, cards, jewelry, and ceramics. Students often display their work during the degree shows in June.

For the latest literature on the city's ever-thriving music scene, try **Monorail Music** (✉ *12 Kings Ct., King St., City Center* ☎ *0141/552–9458*). You can also find rare soundtracks and eclectic grooves, listen to occasional live music, or grab a microbrew beer and veggie burger at the city's only vegan restaurant.

Both branches of **Papyrus** (✉ *374 Byres Rd., West End* ☎ *0141/334–6514* ✉ *10 Sauchiehall St., City Center* ☎ *0141/332–6788*) carry designer cards, as well as a good selection of books.

CLOTHING BOUTIQUES

Male and female fashionistas must not miss **Cruise** (✉ *180 Ingram St., City Center* ☎ *0141/572–3232*), which stocks hot labels at cool prices. An eclectic array of designer clothing and accessories for women fills **Moon** (✉ *10 Ruthven La., off Byers Rd., West End* ☎ *0141/339–2315*). **Mr. Ben** (✉ *6 King's Ct., King St., City Center* ☎ *0141/553–1936*) has a funky selection of vintage clothing. **Strawberry Fields** (✉ *517 Great Western Rd., West End* ☎ *0141/339–1121*) sells colorful children's wear.

FOOD

Demijohn (✉ *382 Byres Rd., West End* ☎ *0141/337–3600*) specializes in infused wines, spirits, oils, and vinegars; it calls itself a "liquid deli."

★ **Iain Mellis Cheesemonger** (✉ *492 Great Western Rd., West End* ☎ *0141/339–8998*) has a superb, seemingly endless selection of fine Scottish cheeses. **Peckham's Delicatessen** (✉ *124–126 Byres Rd., West End* ☎ *0141/357–1454* ✉ *43 Clarence Dr., West End* ☎ *0141/357–2909* ✉ *61–65 Glassford St., Merchant City* ☎ *0141/553–0666*) is *the* place for Continental sausages, cheeses, and anything else you'd need for a delicious picnic.

HOME FURNISHINGS AND TEXTILES

Linens Fine (✉ *The Courtyard, Princes Sq., City Center* ☎ *0141/248–7082*) carries wonderful embroidered and embellished bed linens and other textiles. **Nancy Smillie** (✉ *53 Cresswell St., West End* ☎ *0141/334–4240*), ultracontemporary and local to the floorboards, is a one-of-a-kind boutique that sells unique glassware, jewelry, and furnishings.

SCOTTISH SPECIALTIES

For high-quality gifts in Charles Rennie Mackintosh style, head to **Catherine Shaw** (✉ *24 Gordon St., City Center* ☎ *0141/204–4762* ✉ *32 Argyll Arcade, City Center* ☎ *0141/221–9038*). **Hector Russell Kiltmakers** (✉ *110 Buchanan St., City Center* ☎ *0141/221–0217*) specializes in Highland outfits, wool and cashmere clothing, and women's fashions. **MacDonald MacKay Ltd.** (✉ *161 Hope St., City Center* ☎ *0141/204–3930*) makes, sells, and exports Highland dress and accessories.

SPORTS GEAR

You'll find good-quality outerwear at **Tiso Sports** (✉ *129 Buchanan St., City Center* ☎ *0141/248–4877* ✉ *50 Couper St., West End* ☎ *0141/559–5450*), handy if you're planning some Highland walks.

TOBACCO

Much of Glasgow's wealth was generated by the tobacco lords during the 17th and 18th centuries. At **Robert Graham** (✉ *71 St. Vincent St., City Center* ☎ *0141/221–6588*) you'll experience a little of that colorful history. The shop carries a tremendous variety of tobaccos and pipes.

SIDE TRIPS: AYRSHIRE, CLYDE COAST, AND ROBERT BURNS COUNTRY

The jigsaw puzzle of firths and straits and interlocking islands that you see as you fly into Glasgow Airport harbors numerous tempting one-day excursion destinations. You can travel south to visit the fertile farmlands of Ayrshire—Robert Burns country—or west to the Firth of Clyde, or southeast to the Clyde Valley, all by car or by public transportation. You may want to begin with the town of Paisley. Now part of the Glasgow suburbs, it has plenty of gritty character from its industrial heritage; it was once famous for paisley shawl manufacturing; a museum displays a fine collection of these garments. Besides the Burns sites, key treasures in this area include the Marquess of Bute's Mount Stuart House on the Isle of Bute, and Culzean Castle, as famous for its Robert Adam (1728–92) design as it is for its spectacular seaside setting and grounds.

For many people, a highlight of this region is Robert Burns country, a 40-minute drive from Glasgow. The poet was born in Alloway, beside Ayr, and the towns and villages where he lived and loved make for an interesting day out. English children learn that Burns (1759–96) is a good minor poet. But Scottish children know that he's Shakespeare, Dante, Rabelais, Mozart, and Karl Marx rolled into one. As time goes by, it seems that the Scots have it more nearly right. As poet and humanist, Burns increases in stature. When you plunge into Burns country, don't forget that he's held in extreme reverence by Scots of all backgrounds. They may argue about Sir Walter Scott and Bonnie Prince Charlie, but there's no disputing the merits of the author of "Bonnie Doon."

On your way here you travel beside the estuary and firth of the great River Clyde and will be able to look across to Dumbarton and its Rock, a nostalgic farewell point for emigrants leaving Glasgow. The river is surprisingly narrow here, considering that the *Queen Elizabeth II* and the other great ocean liners sailed these waters from the place of their birth.

GETTING HERE AND AROUND

From Glasgow, you can take the bus to Ayr for the Burns Heritage Trail; and Troon, Prestwick, and Ayr to play golf. Bus companies also operate one-day guided excursions; for details, contact the tourist information center in Glasgow or the Strathclyde Passenger Transport Travel Centre. Traveline Scotland has a helpful Web site.

If you were making a circuit of the sights, you could begin your trip from Glasgow westbound on M8, signposted for Glasgow Airport and Greenock, and join A8. Head south on A78 to the old Victorian village of Wemyss Bay and take the ferry over to Bute to see Mount Stuart (leave your car behind: a bus service takes you there from the ferry). Then continue down the A78 through Irvine, Troon, and on to Ayr and Alloway. Head to Culzean Castle, then return to Ayr and turn eastward on the B743, the Mauchline Road; but before you get here, turn left on a little road to Tarbolton and the Bachelors' Club. Glasgow is less than an hour away on the fast A77.

You can travel via train to Ayr for the Burns Heritage Trail; and Troon, Prestwick, and Ayr to play golf.

WHAT IT COSTS IN POUNDS					
	£	££	£££	££££	£££££
RESTAURANTS	under £10	£11–£14	£15–£19	£20–£25	over £25
HOTELS	under £70	£70–£120	£121–£160	£161–£220	over £220

Restaurant prices are for a main course at dinner. Hotel prices are for two people in a standard double room in high season, generally including 17.5% V.A.T. These are different from the Glasgow city prices.

PAISLEY

7 mi south of Glasgow.

The industrial prosperity of Paisley came from textiles and, in particular, from the woolen paisley shawl. The internationally recognized paisley pattern is based on the shape of a palm shoot, an ancient Babylonian fertility symbol brought from Kashmir. Today you can explore this history at several attractions.

GETTING HERE AND AROUND

Paisley-bound buses depart from the Buchanan Street bus station in Glasgow. Traveline Scotland provides information on schedules and fares. Trains to Paisley depart daily every 5 to 10 minutes from Glasgow Central Station. If you're driving, take the M8 westbound and turn off at Junction 27, which is clearly signposted to Paisley.

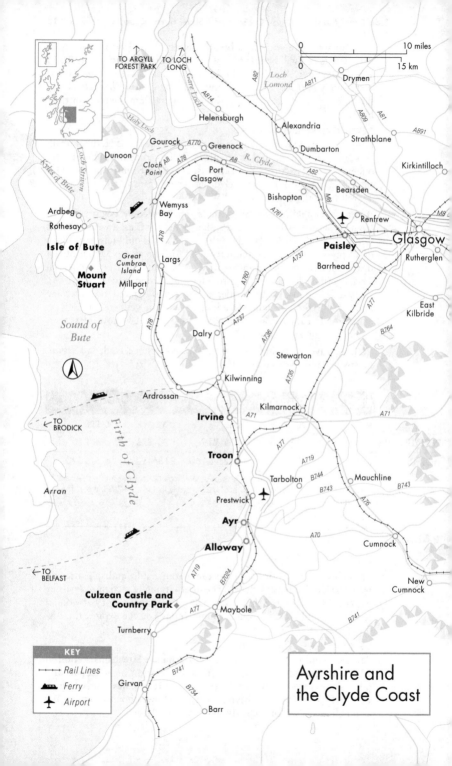

ESSENTIALS

Visitor Information **Paisley** (⊠ *9A Gilmour St.PA1 1DD* ☎ *0141/889–0711* ⊕ *www.seeglasgow.com*).

EXPLORING

★ The full story of the pattern and of the innovative weaving techniques introduced in Paisley is told in the **Paisley Museum & Art Gallery,** which has a world-famous shawl collection. ⊠ *High St.* ☎ *0141/889–3151* 🎫 *Free* ⊙ *Tues.–Sat. 10–5, Sun. 2–5.*

To get an idea of the life led by textile industry workers, visit the **Sma' Shot Cottages.** These re-creations of mill workers' houses contain displays of linen, lace, and paisley shawls. An 18th-century weaver's cottage is also open to visitors. ⊠ *11–17 George Pl.PA1 2HZ* ☎ *0141/ 889–1708* 🎫 *Free* ⊙ *Apr.–Sept., Wed. and Sat. noon–4; Oct.–Mar. by appointment.*

Paisley's 12th-century Cluniac **Abbey** dominates the town center. Almost completely destroyed by the English in 1307, the abbey was not totally restored until the early 20th century. It's associated with Walter Fitzallan, the high steward of Scotland, who gave his name to the Stewart monarchs of Scotland (Stewart is a corruption of "steward"). Outstanding features include the vaulted stone roof and stained glass of the choir. Paisley Abbey is today a busy parish church; if you're visiting with a large group you should call ahead. ⊠ *13 High St.* ☎ *0141/889–7654* ⊕ *www.paisleyabbey.org.uk* 🎫 *Free* ⊙ *Mon.–Sat. 10–3:30, Sun. services at 11, 12:15, and 6:30.*

WHERE TO STAY

££££ 🏨 **Mar Hall.** Set amid 240 acres of formal gardens and woodlands, this
★ neo-Gothic manor on the River Clyde seems isolated from the bustle of daily life, even though it's only 20 minutes from Glasgow. Mar Hall is one of Scotland's most dramatic lodgings, with stone steps that sweep up to the massive, mid-19th-century stone house. The guest rooms continue the romance, with four-poster beds draped in silks and satins; you may prefer a room that overlooks the gardens rather than one in the spa annex. Dining choices include afternoon tea in the Grand Hall and sophisticated Scottish fare at Cristal. **Pros:** spacious rooms; fantastic pool; Aveda spa is excellent. **Cons:** you need to drive to city center; public transportation is difficult; service can be patchy if there's a large function. ⊠ *Earl of Mar Estate, Mar Hall Dr. Bishopton* ☎ *0141/812– 9999* ⊕ *www.marhall.com* ⇆ *53 rooms* ⅏ *In-room: refrigerator, DVD, Internet. In-hotel: 2 restaurants, bar, pool, gym, spa, golf course, laundry service, Wi-Fi hotspot* ⊟ *AE, DC, MC, V* ⊚| *BP.*

ISLE OF BUTE

75 mi west of Glasgow.

The Isle of Bute affords a host of relaxing walks and scenic vistas. Mount Stuart, a stately home, is a popular attraction. Like the nearby Isle of Arran *(see Chapter 8),* the Isle of Bute was a Victorian holiday favorite convenient for Glaswegians.

In the old Victorian village of Wemyss Bay there's ferry service to the island. The many handsome buildings, especially the station, are a reminder of the Victorian era's grandeur and style.

ESSENTIALS

Visitor Information **Rothesay** (✉ *The Winter Gardens* ☎ *08452/255121* ⊕ *www.isle-of-bute.com*).

EXPLORING

Rothesay, a faded but appealing resort, is the main town. Some of the ornate Victorian architecture is striking.

Bute's biggest draw is spectacular **Mount Stuart,** ancestral home of the marquesses of Bute. The massive Victorian Gothic palace, built in red sandstone, has ornate interiors, including the Marble Hall, with a star-studded vault, stained glass, arcaded galleries, and magnificent tapestries woven in Edinburgh in the early 20th century. The paintings and furniture throughout the house are equally outstanding. Even if you don't like Victorian style, you may appreciate the lovely gardens and grounds here. Call to check opening times, as corporate events or weddings may cause closures. ✉ *5 mi south of Rothesay* ☎ *01700/503877* ⊕ *www.mountstuart.com* 🎟 *Gardens £4; house and gardens £8* ⊙ *Gardens May–Sept., daily 10–6; house May–Sept., Sun.–Fri. 11–5, Sat. 10–2:30.*

WHERE TO STAY

££ ▣ **Munro's Bed and Breakfast.** Surrounded by colorful gardens, this small B&B in a peaceful residential area has a home-away-from-home feel. The newly refurbished rooms are stylish with all the modern touches like flat-screen TVs and under-floor heating in the bathrooms. Muted dark purples and browns give the spacious rooms an elegant, warm feel. Room number 2 is the best as it has a small lounge area attached. Downstairs, an open fire welcomes guests. **Pros:** beautiful location; freshly remodeled; environmentally aware. **Cons:** hilltop location a problems for those with trouble walking; no dinner facilities on-site. ✉ *Ardmory Rd., Ardbeg* ☎ *01700/502346* ⊕ *www.visitmunros.co.uk* 🛏 *6 rooms* ♿ *In-room: no a/c, Wi-Fi* ▤ *MC, V* ⦿ *BP.*

IRVINE

24 mi south of Glasgow.

Beyond Irvine's cobbled streets and grand Victorians, look for a peaceful crescent-shape harbor and fishermen's cottages huddled in solidarity against the Atlantic winds. The town has links to Robert Burns, who lived here in 1781.

ESSENTIALS

Visitor Information **Irvine** (✉ *New St.* ☎ *08452/255121*).

EXPLORING

Founded in 1826, the **Irvine Burns Club** is one of the oldest Burns clubs in the world. Today its gallery displays a collection of original manuscripts, plus murals and stained-glass windows that narrate Burns's life and work. The author lived in Irvine when he was 22. ✉ *28 Eglinton*

St.KA12 8AS ☎ *01294/274511* ⊕ *www.irvineayrshire.org* ✉ *Free* ☉ *Apr.–Sept., Mon., Wed., Fri., and Sat. 2:30–4:30; Oct.–Mar., Sat. 2:30–4:30.*

The **Vennel Art Gallery** occupies the 18th-century cottage where Burns came to live and the shed where he learned to heckle—or dress—flax (the raw material for linen). Both buildings have on display paintings, photographs, and sculpture by mainly Scottish artists. ✉ *10 Glasgow VennelKA12 0BD* ☎ *01294/275059* ✉ *Free* ☉ *Thurs.–Sat. 10–1 and 2–5.*

3

TROON

4 mi south of Irvine, 30 mi south of Glasgow, 7 mi north of Ayr.

The small coastal town of Troon is famous for its outstanding golf course, Royal Troon. You can easily see that golf is very popular here and in this area: at times, the whole 60-mi-long Ayrshire coast seems one endless course. *(For more about the best courses in this area, see Chapter 12.)* The town's several miles of sandy beaches provide other diversions. It's easy to get to Troon by train or bus from both Glasgow and Ayr.

WHERE TO EAT AND STAY

£££ ✕ **MacCallums Oyster Bar.** The main ingredients at MacCallums come
★ straight from the sea, and the menu varies depending on the day's catch.
SEAFOOD You can usually count on lobster in garlic butter, seared scallops, or grilled langoustines. Excellent light white wines match the freshness of the food. Solid wooden tables and other simple furniture add a rustic touch to the dining room. Hidden among the boatyards and customs buildings of Troon Harbour, this top-class restaurant is easy to miss, but you can find it next to the Seacat Ferry Terminal. ✉ *Harbour Rd.* ☎ *01292/319339* ▭ *DC, MC, V* ☉ *Closed Mon. No dinner Sun.*

£££ ⌂ **Piersland House Hotel.** A late-Victorian mansion on the southern edge of town, formerly the home of a whisky magnate, is now a country-house hotel. All the bedrooms in the half-timbered main house are furnished in traditional style, and many have romantic four-poster or canopy beds. Oak paneling and log fires in the restaurant provide a warm backdrop for Scottish cuisine, including specialties such as beef medallions in pickled walnut sauce. **Pros:** gorgeous gardens and grounds; close to golf courses; near Prestwick Airport. **Cons:** helps to have a car to get around; can get crowded with private functions. ✉ *15 Craigend Rd.* ☎ *01292/314747* ⊕ *www.piersland.co.uk* ⇗ *30 rooms* ♨ *In-room: no a/c, Wi-Fi. In-hotel: restaurant, bar, Wi-Fi hotspot* ▭ *AE, DC, MC, V* ⧆⧆ *BP.*

GOLF

Founded in 1878, **Royal Troon** has two 18-hole courses: the Old, or Championship, Course and the Portland Course. The views are magnificent, but the courses can get windy. Access for nonmembers is limited between May and mid-October to Monday, Tuesday, and Thursday only; day tickets cost £220 and include two rounds, morning coffee, and a buffet lunch, but there are cheaper options. ✉ *Craigend Rd.*

☎ *01292/311555* ⊕ *www.royaltroon.co.uk* ⌇. *Old Course: 18 holes,
7,150 yds, SSS 74. Portland Course: 18 holes, 6,289 yds, SSS 70.*

SHOPPING

Many Glaswegians frequent **Regalia Fashion Salon** (⊠ *44 Church St.*
☎ *01292/312162*) for its unusual collection of designer clothing for
women. For a fascinating look at local antiquities, visit **Tantalus Antiques**
(⊠ *79 Templehill* ☎ *01292/315999*).

AYR AND ALLOWAY

6 mi south of Troon, 34 mi south of Glasgow.

The commercial port of Ayr is Ayrshire's chief town, a peaceful and
elegant place with an air of prosperity. Poet Robert Burns was baptized
in the Auld Kirk (Old Church) here and wrote a humorous poem about
the Twa Brigs (Two Bridges) that cross the river nearby. Burns described
Ayr as a town unsurpassed "for honest men and bonny lasses." If he
were to visit today, he might also mention the good shopping.

If you're on the Robert Burns trail, head for Alloway, on B7024 in Ayr's
southern suburbs. A number of sights here are part of the **Burns National
Heritage Park** (⊕ *www.burnsheritagepark.com*). At the time of this writing, exciting plans that include the National Trust for Scotland are under-
way to redevelop the area as the Robert Burns Birthplace Museum.

GETTING HERE AND AROUND

From Glasgow you can take the bus or train to Ayr; travel time is
about an hour (a bit less by train). Drivers can use the A78 and A77
near the coast; a car would provide more flexibility to see the Burns
sites around Alloway.

ESSENTIALS

Visitor Information Ayr (⊠ *22 The Sandgate, Ayr* ☎ *08452/255121* ⊕ *www.
ayrshire-arran.com*).

EXPLORING

★

In Alloway, among the middle-class residences, you'll find the one-room
thatched and freshly restored **Burns Cottage**, where Scotland's national
poet was born in 1759 and which his father built. Not many outside
Scotland appreciate the depth of affection Scotland has for Burns. To
his fellow Scots he's more than a great lyric bard; he's the champion
of the underdog, the lover of noble causes, the hater of pomposity and
cant, the prophet of social justice. "A man's a man for a' that"—such
phrases have exalted the Scottish character, while his love songs warm
the coldest hearts. January 25, Burns Night, is an anniversary of importance in Scotland. An **education pavilion** next to the cottage contains an
original manuscript of "Auld Lang Syne" and other important Burns
manuscripts and artifacts. ⊠ *Murdoch's La., Alloway* ☎ *01292/441215*
⊕ *www.burnsheritagepark.com* ☞ *£5 ticket includes admission to Tam
o' Shanter Experience and Burns Monument* ☉ *Apr.–Sept., daily 9:30–
5:30; Oct.–Mar., daily 10–5.*

Find out all about Burns at the **Tam o' Shanter Experience.** Here you
can enjoy a 10-minute audiovisual journey through his life and times,

then watch as one of Burns's most famous poems, "Tam o' Shanter," is brought to life on a three-screen theatrical set. It's down the road from Burns Cottage and around the corner from Alloway's ruined church. ✉ *Murdoch's La., Alloway* ☎ *01292/443700* ⊕ *www.burnsheritagepark.com* 🎫 *£5 ticket includes Burns Cottage and Burns Monument* ⊙ *Apr.–Sept., daily 10–5:30; Oct.–Mar., daily 10–5.*

Auld Kirk Alloway is where Tam o' Shanter, in Burns's eponymous poem, unluckily passed a witches' revel—with Old Nick himself playing the bagpipes—on his way home from a night of drinking. Tam, in flight from the witches, managed to cross the medieval **Brig o' Doon** (*brig* is Scots for *bridge*; you can still see the bridge) just in time. His gray mare, Meg, lost her tail to the closest witch. (Any resident of Ayr will tell you that witches cannot cross running water.) The church is in ruins, but the graveyard includes the tomb of Burns's father, William. ✉ *Murdoch's La., Alloway* ⊕ *www.burnsheritagepark.com*

The **Burns Monument,** a tall neoclassical structure built in 1823, overlooks the Brig o' Doon. ✉ *Murdoch's La., Alloway* ☎ *No phone* ⊕ *www.burnsheritagepark.com* 🎫 *£1; £5 ticket includes Burns Cottage and Tam o' Shanter Experience* ⊙ *Apr.–Sept., daily 9:30–5; Nov.–Mar., daily 10–4.*

At Tarbolton, 8 mi northeast of Ayr and 28 mi southwest of Glasgow, is the **Bachelors' Club,** the 17th-century house where Robert Burns learned to dance, founded a debating and literary society, and became a Freemason. ✉ *Sandgate St., Tarbolton* ☎ *01292/541940* ⊕ *www.nts.org.uk* 🎫 *£5* ⊙ *Apr.–late Sept., Fri.–Tues. 1–5.*

WHERE TO EAT

££

★

BRITISH

✕ **Brig o' Doon House.** Originally built in 1827 and later upgrade, this attractive white building with a restaurant and five guest rooms is a popular site for weddings; it's quite common to be greeted at the door by a piper. The setting is very Scottish, with tartan carpets, dark wood paneling, and buck heads mounted on the walls. The bar is a shrine to Robert Burns, and the surrounding gardens overlook the Brig o' Doon as well as a small, rushing river. The food keeps to the Scottish theme too: try panfried scallops with citrus butter to start, and venison casserole with juniper berries and creamed potatoes or haggis with neeps and tatties (served with a dram) as a main course. ✉ *High Maybole Rd., Alloway* ☎ *01292/442466* 💳 *AE, DC, MC, V.*

£££ ✕ **Fouter's Bistro.** In the center of Ayr, Fouter's is in a long and narrow
★   cellar that was an 18th-century bank vault, yet its white walls and deco-
BRITISH rative stenciling create a sense of airiness. The cuisine is also light and
skillful—no heavy sauces here. Try the roast Ayrshire lamb with pan
juices, red wine, and mint, or sample the Taste of Scotland appetizer—
smoked salmon, trout, and other goodies. This is modern Scottish and
French cooking at its best. ⊠ *2A Academy St., Ayr* ☎ *01292/261391*
🗀 *DC, MC, V* ⊗ *Closed Sun. and Mon.*

SHOPPING

Ayr has a good range of shops. The **Begg & Co.** (⊠ *Viewfield Rd., Ayr*
☎ *01292/267615*) sells a good selection of scarves, stoles, plaids, and
travel rugs handmade on the premises. You can watch craftspeople at
work at the jewelry workshop **Diamond Factory** (⊠ *26 Queen's Ct., Ayr*
☎ *01292/280476*). Particularly coveted are the handmade Celtic wedding bands. The store will export your purchases if you don't have time
to wait for the work to be completed.

CULZEAN CASTLE AND COUNTRY PARK

12 mi south of Ayr, 50 mi south of Glasgow.

GETTING HERE AND AROUND

Stagecoach buses run from Ayr to the park entrance; the nearest train
station from Glasgow is at Maybole, 4 mi to the east, but there is Stagecoach bus service to the park entrance. Note that the park entrance is
a mile walk from the castle visitor center.

EXPLORING

★   The dramatic cliff-top **Culzean Castle and Country Park** (pronounced ku-
Ⓒ   *lain*) is the National Trust for Scotland's most popular property, yet it
remains unspoiled. Robert Adam designed the neoclassical mansion,
complete with a walled garden, in 1777. A tour includes an armory display, the library, dining room, several drawing rooms, and the kitchen.
In addition to its marvelous interiors, the house contains the National
Guest Flat, donated by the people of Scotland in appreciation of General Eisenhower's (1890–1969) services during World War II; as presi-
dent he stayed here once or twice. The rooms on the approach to this
apartment evoke the atmosphere of World War II: mementos of Glenn
Miller (1904–44), Winston Churchill (1874–1965), and other personalities of the era all help create a suitably 1940s mood. On the estate
grounds (which are as memorable as the house), shrubberies reflect the
essential mildness of this coast, though some visitors, meeting the full
force of a westerly gale, might think otherwise. Culzean's perpendicular
sea cliff affords views across the Firth of Clyde to Arran and the Irish
coast. Not a stone's throw away, it seems, the pinnacle of Ailsa Craig,
a rock, rears from mid-channel. There are guided tours of the castle
from July to September at 11 and 3 and from October to June at 3. It's
easy to spend a day here. ⊠ *A719, Maybole* ☎ *01655/884400* ⊕ *www.
culzeanexperience.org* 🗀 *Park £8.50, park and castle £13* ⊗ *Park, daily
9:30–sunset; castle, Mar.–Oct., daily 10:30–5; last admission at 4.*

SIDE TRIPS: THE CLYDE VALLEY

The River Clyde is (or certainly was) famous for its shipbuilding and heavy industries, yet its upper reaches flow through some of Scotland's most fertile farmlands, rich with tomato crops. It's an interesting area with some museums, most notably at New Lanark, that tell the story of manufacturing and mining prosperity.

GETTING HERE AND AROUND

To make a circuit of the area by car, take the (not very pretty) A724 east out of Glasgow, south of the river through Rutherglen toward Hamilton. In Blantyre look for signs to the David Livingstone Centre. Travel on A72 toward Lanark. You pass lots of greenhouses, nurseries, and gnarled old orchards running down to the Clyde. Before reaching Lanark, follow the signs down a long winding hill to New Lanark. The A72 continues south of Lanark to join the A702 near Biggar. You can return to Glasgow the quick way by joining the M74 from the A744 west of Lanark (the Strathaven road). Or take a more scenic route through Strathaven (pronounced *stra*-ven) itself, A726 to East Kilbride, and enter Glasgow from south of the river.

Train service runs from Glasgow Central Station to Hamilton (near Blantyre) and Lanark; for details check National Rail. There are no trains to Biggar, but there's a connecting bus from Hamilton to Biggar.

BLANTYRE

8 mi southeast of Glasgow.

Blantyre, a suburb of Hamilton, is not a pretty town. The explorer David Livingstone was born here.

EXPLORING

The **David Livingstone Centre** includes a museum and the tiny tenement apartment where the great explorer of Africa (1813–73) was born. Displays tell of his journeys, of his meeting with Stanley ("Dr. Livingstone, I presume"), of Africa, and of the area's industrial heritage. There are 20 acres of parkland and garden to explore at the site. ⊠ *165 Station Rd.* ☎ *01698/823140* ⊕ *www.nts.org.uk* ✉ *£5.50* ⏱ *Apr.–late Dec., Mon.–Sat. 10–5, Sun. 12:30–5.*

LANARK

19 mi east of Glasgow.

Set in pleasing, rolling countryside, Lanark is a typical old Scottish town. It's now most often associated with its unique neighbor New Lanark, a model workers' community about a mile to the south.

ESSENTIALS

Visitor Information Lanark (⊠ *Horsemarket, Ladyacre Rd.* ☎ *01555/661661*).

EXPLORING

Fodor's Choice ★ **New Lanark,** now a World Heritage Site, was home to a social experiment during the Industrial Revolution—a model community with well-designed workers' homes, a school, and public buildings. The River

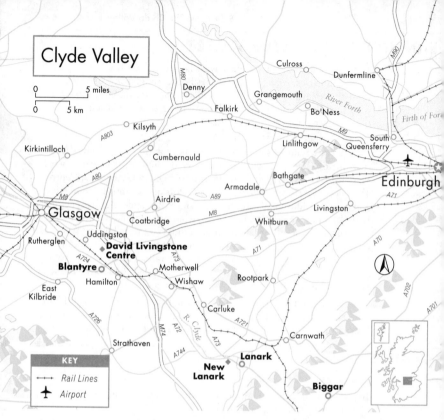

Culross
Dunfermline
Denny
Grangemouth
Bo'Ness
Falkirk
River Forth
Firth of For
Kilsyth
Linlithgow
South
Queensferry
Kirkintilloch
Cumbernauld
Bathgate
Edinburgh
Armadale
Airdrie
Livingston
Glasgow
Coatbridge
Whitburn
Rutherglen
Uddingston
David Livingstone
Centre
Blantyre
Motherwell
East
Kilbride
Hamilton
Wishaw
Rootpark
Carluke
Carnwath
Strathaven
R. Clyde
Lanark
New
Lanark
Biggar

KEY
Rail Lines
Airport

Clyde powers its way through a beautiful wooded gorge here, and its waters were harnessed to drive textile-mill machinery before the end of the 18th century. The owner, David Dale (1739–1806), was noted for his caring attitude toward the workers, unusual for that era. Later, his son-in-law, Robert Owen (1771–1858), took this attitude even further, founding a benevolent doctrine known as Owenism and eventually crossing the Atlantic to become involved in a similar planned-community project in Indiana, called New Harmony, which, unlike New Lanark, failed. Robert Owen's son Robert Dale Owen (1801–77) helped found the Smithsonian Institution.

After many changes of fortune, the mills eventually closed and were converted into a hotel and private residential properties. As a result, residents have moved in, and New Lanark has maintained its unique environment, where those leading normal everyday lives mix easily with the tourists.

One of the mills has been converted into a visitor and interpretive center that tells the story of this brave social experiment. You can also explore Robert Owen's house, the school, and a mill worker's house. Other restored mills hold various shops and eateries; one has a rooftop garden with impressive views of the entire site.

Upstream, the Clyde flows through some of the finest river scenery anywhere in Lowland Scotland, with woods and spectacular water-falls; the falls are nearby, and it's easy to explore these. ✉ *New Lanark Rd., New Lanark* ☎ *01555/665876* ⊕ *www.newlanark.org* ☜ *£6.95* ⊙ *Oct.–Mar., daily 11–5; Apr.–Sept., daily 10:30–5.*

WHERE TO STAY

££ 🖥 **New Lanark Mill Hotel.** Housed in a converted cotton mill at the 18th-century model village of New Lanark, this hotel is decorated in a spare, understated style that allows the impressive architecture of barrel-vaulted ceilings and elegant Georgian windows to speak for itself. Right next to the river in the heart of the village, the hotel has all the attractions—visitor center, shops, Falls of Clyde Wildlife Reserve—at its doorstep. **Pros:** beautiful views of the river; large rooms; impressive spa. **Cons:** bland bar; some rooms can get cold. ✉ *New Lanark Rd., New Lanark* ☎ *01555/667200* ⊕ *www.newlanark.org* ⬗ *38 rooms, 8 cottages* ⬙ *In-room: no a/c. In-hotel: restaurant, pool, gym, Wi-Fi hotspot* ▭ *AE, DC, MC, V* ⧀ *BP.*

SHOPPING

Lanark has an interesting selection of shops within walking distance of each other; there are also some shops such as the Edinburgh Woollen Mill at New Lanark. **McKellar's** (✉ *41 High St.* ☎ *01555/661312*) sells Charles Rennie Mackintosh–inspired designs in gold and silver. **Strands** (✉ *8 Bloomgate* ☎ *01555/665757*) carries yarns and knitwear, including Arran designs and one-of-a-kind creations by Scottish designers.

BIGGAR

34 mi southeast of Glasgow.

A pleasant town built of stone, Biggar is a rewarding place to spend an hour or two, out of all proportion to its size, thanks to an excellent collection of small, specialized museums. At Biggar you are near the headwaters of the Clyde, on the moors in the center of southern Scot-land. The Clyde flows west toward Glasgow and the Atlantic Ocean, and the Tweed, only a few miles away, flows east toward the North Sea. There are fine views around Biggar to Culter Fell and to the Border Hills in the south.

ESSENTIALS

Visitor Information Biggar (✉ *155 High St.* ☎ *01899/221066*).

EXPLORING

Gladstone Court Museum paints a fascinating picture of life in the town in years past, with reconstructed Victorian-era shops, a bank, a phone exchange, and a school. ✉ *Northback Rd.* ☎ *01899/221050* ⊕ *www. biggarmuseumtrust.co.uk* ☜ *£2* ⊙ *Easter weekend and Apr.–Oct., Mon.–Sat. 11–4:30, Sun. 2–4:30.*

For a look at Biggar's geology and prehistory, plus an interesting embroi-dery collection (including samplers and fine patchwork coverlets), visit the **Moat Park Heritage Centre,** also in the town center, in a former church.

⊠ *Kirkstyle* ☎ *01899/221050* ⊕ *www.biggarmuseumtrust.co.uk* ✉£2 ⊙ *May–Sept., Mon.–Sat. 11–4:30, Sun. 2–5.*

The **Biggar Gasworks,** built in 1839, is a fascinating reminder of the efforts once needed to produce gas for light and heat. ⊠ *Gasworks Rd.,* ☎ *01899/221050* ⊕ *www.biggarmuseumtrust.co.uk* ✉£1.50 ⊙ *June–Sept., daily 2–5.*

The **Greenhill Covenanters' House** is a farmhouse filled with 17th-century furnishings, costume dolls, and rare farm breeds. The Covenanters were breakaway supporters of Presbyterianism in the 17th century. ⊠ *Burn Braes* ☎ *01899/221050* ⊕ *www.biggarmuseumtrust.co.uk* ✉£1 ⊙ *May–Sept., weekends 2–4:30.*

⟳ **Biggar Puppet Theatre** regularly presents performances by Purves Puppets. Before and after performances, two half-hour hands-on tours led by the puppeteers are available. One tour goes backstage as the puppets being demonstrated on stage; the other tours the puppet museum. The theater also has games and a picnic area. ⊠ *Broughton Rd.* ☎ *01899/220631* ⊕ *www.purvespuppets.com* ✉ *Tours £3; performances £7* ⊙ *Call ahead for tours.*

The Borders and the Southwest

WORD OF MOUTH

"There are some wonderful old houses in the Borders. Mellerstain and Floors Castle come to mind. Both are near Kelso and, to my mind, are much better to visit than yet another ruined abbey. Manderston house is another great place. It is near Duns and has a silver-plated staircase."

—almcd

"The southwest and the Borders are terrific. A good Borders base would be in the Selkirk/Galashiels/Kelso triangle. You could vsit the Border abbeys, Abbotsford, Traquair House, Floors Castle, and other castles/houses. In the southwest you might stay near Dumfries, by Sweetheart Abbey, Cael-averlock Castle, and Threave."

—janisj

Updated by
Fiona G.
Parrott

If you're coming to Scotland by road or rail from England, you'll first encounter either the Borders area or the southwest (also known as Dumfries and Galloway) depending on the route you take. These regions have more stately homes, fortified castles, and medieval monastic houses than any other part of Scotland. This is also Sir Walter Scott territory, and it is here that you'll find his pseudo-baronial home at Abbotsford, the most visited of Scotland's literary landmarks.

The Borders region embraces the whole 90-mi course of one of Scotland's greatest rivers, the Tweed, and its tributaries. Passing mill chimneys, peel towers (small fortified towers), ruined abbeys, stately homes, and woodlands luxuriant with game birds, the rivers flow in a series of fast-rushing torrents and dark serpentine pools through landscapes that have witnessed the history of two nations. At different times, parts of the region have been in English hands, just as slices of northern England (Berwick-upon-Tweed, for example) have been in Scottish hands.

All the main routes from London to Edinburgh traverse the Borders region, whose hinterland of undulating pastures, woods, and valleys is enclosed within three lonely groups of hills: the Cheviots, the Moorfoots, and the Lammermuirs. Innumerable hamlets and towns dot the land, giving valley slopes a lived-in look, yet the total population is still relatively sparse. Sheep outnumber human beings by 14 to 1.

To the west is the region of Dumfries and Galloway, on the shores of the Solway Firth. It might appear to be an extension of the Borders, but the southwest has a history all its own. Inland, the earth rises toward high hills, forest, and bleak but captivating moorland, whereas nearer the coast you can find pretty farmlands, small villages, and unassuming towns. The shoreline is washed by the North Atlantic Drift (Scotland's answer to the Gulf Stream), and first-time visitors are always surprised to see palm trees and exotic plants thriving in gardens and parks along the coast.

ORIENTATION AND PLANNING

GETTING ORIENTED

Once a battleground region separating Scotland and England, today the Borders area is a gateway between the two countries. This is a place of upland moors and hills, fertile farmland, and forested river valleys. It's rustic and peaceful, with century-old textile mills, abbeys, castles, and gardens. The area is a big draw for hikers and walking enthusiasts, too. The Borders region is also steeped in history; the area was once home to Sir Walter Scott and Mary Queen of Scots.

TOP REASONS TO GO

Ancient abbeys: The region's four ruined abbeys—Melrose, Dryburgh, Jedburgh, and Kelso—tell of a long history of struggle. Vestiges of intricately carved capitals, decorative gargoyles, and painstakingly exquisite tracery reveal a flicker of the abbeys' former brilliance.

Country biking: Away from busy roads, the Borders area is ideal for bicycling. In the southwest, once you're off the beaten track, you'll discover quiet roads and country lanes that beg to be explored. There are bike-rental shops in many towns, including Peebles, Dumfries, and Castle Douglas.

Stately homes and castles: Transport yourself back to a more gracious time. Paxton and Manderston houses hold well-preserved treasures

from a bygone era, and you can sip ale on the grounds of the 12th-century Traquair House. Splendid Floors Castle is the largest inhabited castle in Scotland.

Scott's Scotland: This part of the country has enough monuments and sites dedicated to Sir Walter Scott to make his life and works a theme of your visit. Don't miss the epic Abbotsford House, Smailholm Tower, Dryburgh Abbey, and Scott's View.

Sweaters and sweets: The Borders is well known for its knitwear industry, and mill shops are abundant. Throughout the region also look for specialty peppermint or fruit-flavor boiled sweets (hard candies), tablet (a sugary caramel-like candy), and fudges. Don't worry; you won't go home empty-handed.

The Borders. Borders towns cluster around and between two great rivers—the Tweed and its tributary, the Teviot. These are mostly textile towns with plenty of personality, filled with residents with fierce pride in their local municipalities. The area's top attractions include Jedburgh Abbey, Floors Castle in Kelso, and Abbotsford House just outside Melrose.

Dumfries and Galloway. Easygoing and peaceful, towns in this region are usually very attractive, with wide streets and colorful buildings. Highlights here include Caerlaverock Castle, Threave Castle, Castle Kennedy, and Logan Botanic Gardens.

PLANNING

WHEN TO GO

Because many lodgings and some sights are privately owned and shut down from early autumn until early April, the area is less suited to off-season touring than some other parts of Scotland. The best time to visit is during the summer months. The region does look magnificent in autumn, however, especially along the wooded river valleys of the Borders. Late spring is the time to see the rhododendrons in the gardens of Dumfries and Galloway.

PLANNING YOUR TIME

Dumfries is one of the biggest, most intriguing towns of the region; it's a good base for seeing nearby sights like Caerlaverock Castle (9 mi away), Threave Gardens (20 mi away), and Sweetheart Abbey (8 mi away).

Another good place to seek accommodations is Kirkcudbright, midway between Dumfries and western towns like Newton Stewart, Portpatrick, and Glen Trool (where you will not find as many lodging options). It's 25 mi from Kirkcudbright to Newton Stewart, and another 10 mi to Glen Trool. Three days should be ample time to comfortably explore this area.

From Glen Trool it's a scenic three-hour drive to Jedburgh, and another 13 mi to Melrose Abbey. Two days in Jedburgh and Melrose (with a detour to Abbotsford House) is plenty of time. It's 36 mi from Jedburgh to Peebles, where you can finish up your journey with a long afternoon of shopping.

GETTING HERE AND AROUND

AIR TRAVEL

The nearest Scottish airports are at Edinburgh, Glasgow, and Prestwick (outside of Glasgow).

BOAT AND FERRY TRAVEL

P&O European Ferries runs a service from Larne, in Northern Ireland, to Cairnryan, near Stranraer, several times daily. The crossing takes 1 hour on the Superstar Express, 1¾ hours on other ferries. Stena Line operates a ferry service between Stranraer and Belfast.

Boat and Ferry Contacts P&O European Ferries (☎ 0870/2424777 ⊕ www. poirishsea.com). **Stena Line** (☎ 08705/707070 ⊕ www.stenaline.co.uk).

BUS TRAVEL

If you're approaching from the south, contact Scottish Citylink or National Express. For buses from Edinburgh and Glasgow, First and Stagecoach Western are two good choices. Stagecoach Western also serves towns and villages in Dumfries and Galloway.

Bus Contacts First (☎ 08708/727271 ⊕ www.firstgroup.com). **National Express** (☎ 08705/808080 ⊕ www.nationalexpress.com). **Scottish City-link** (☎ 08705/505050 ⊕ www.citylink.co.uk). **Stagecoach Western** (☎ 01387/253496 in Dumfries, 01563/525192 in Kilmarnock, 01776/704484 in Stranraer ⊕ www.stagecoachbus.com).

CAR TRAVEL

Traveling by car is the best way to explore the area. The main route into both the Borders and Galloway from the south is the M6, which becomes the M74 at the border. Or you can take the scenic and leisurely A7 northeastward through Hawick toward Edinburgh or the A75 and other parallel routes westward into Dumfries and Galloway and to the ferry ports of Stranraer and Cairnryan.

There are, however, several other routes: starting from the east, the A1 brings you from the English city of Newcastle to the border in about an hour. The A1 has the added attraction of Berwick-Upon-Tweed, on the English side of the border, but traffic on the route is heavy. Moving west, the A697, which leaves the A1 north of Morpeth (in England)

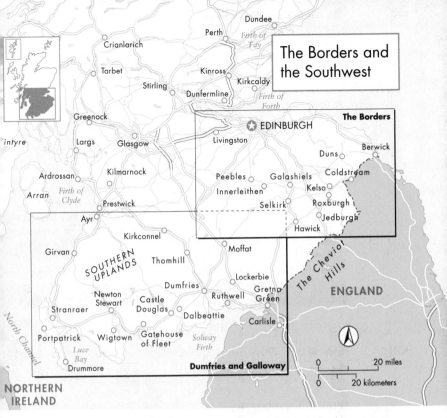

The Borders and the Southwest

and crosses the border at Coldstream, is a leisurely back-road option. The A68 is probably the most scenic route to Scotland: after climbing to Carter Bar, it reveals a view of the Borders hills and windy skies before dropping into the ancient town of Jedburgh.

The best way to explore the region is to get off the main, and often crowded, arterial roads and onto the little back roads. You may occasionally be delayed by a herd of cows on their way to the milking parlor, but this is often far more pleasant than, for example, tussling on the A75 with heavy-goods vehicles rushing to make the Irish ferries.

TRAIN TRAVEL

There is no train service in the Borders, apart from the Edinburgh–London King's Cross line. Trains stop at Berwick-Upon-Tweed, just south of the border. First Edinburgh has a bus service linking Hawick, Selkirk, and Galashiels with rail services at Carlisle, Edinburgh, and Berwick.

There is only limited service in the southwest. Trains from London's Euston to Glasgow stop at Carlisle, just south of the border, and some also stop at Lockerbie. There are direct trains from Carlisle to Dumfries and the Nith Valley, stopping at Gretna Green and Annan. From Glasgow, there are services to Stranraer, the Nith Valley, and Dumfries.

Train Contacts First Edinburgh (☎ 0131/663–9233 or 0871/200–2233 ⊕ www.firstgroup.com). **National Rail** (☎ 08457/484950 ⊕ www.nationalrail. co.uk). **ScotRail** (☎ 08457/550033 ⊕ www.scotrail.co.uk).

RESTAURANTS

In the past, most good restaurants in the region were located in hotels, but today things are changing. Good independent eateries are popping up in small (and sometime unlikely) towns and villages, and many of these new establishments specialize in fresh local ingredients. Seasonal menus are now very popular in the area.

HOTELS

From top-quality, full-service hotels to quaint 18th-century drovers' inns to cozy bed-and-breakfasts, the Borders has all manner of lodging options. Lodging choices in Dumfries and Galloway may be a little less expensive than in the Borders (with the same full range of services). These days many establishments have a shifting scale and are willing to lower their rates depending on availability, so it may be worth your while to ask if prices are negotiable when booking.

WHAT IT COSTS IN POUNDS					
	£	££	£££	££££	£££££
RESTAURANTS	under £10	£10–£14	£15–£19	£20–£25	over £25
HOTELS	under £70	£70–£120	£121–£160	£161–£220	over £220

Restaurant prices are for a main course at dinner. Hotel prices are for two people in a standard double room in high season, generally including the 17.5% V.A.T.

VISITOR INFORMATION

The Scottish Borders Tourist Board has offices in Jedburgh and Peebles, and the Dumfries & Galloway Tourist Board can be found in Dumfries and Stranraer. Seasonal information centers are at Castle Douglas, Coldstream, Eyemouth, Galashiels, Gretna Green, Hawick, Kelso, Kirkcudbright, Langholm, Melrose, Moffat, Newton Stewart, Sanquhar, and Selkirk.

Contacts Scottish Borders Tourist Board (✉ Murray's Green, Jedburgh ☎ 0870/6080404 ⊕ www.scot-borders.co.uk). **Dumfries & Galloway Tourist Board** (✉ 64 Whitesands, Dumfries ☎ 01387/253862 ⊕ www. dumfriesandgalloway.co.uk)

THE BORDERS

Although the Borders has many attractions, it's most famous for being the home base for Sir Walter Scott (1771–1832), the early-19th-century poet, novelist, and creator of *Ivanhoe*, who single-handedly transformed Scotland's image from that of a land of brutal savages to one of romantic and stirring deeds and magnificent landscapes. The novels of Scott are not read much nowadays—frankly, some of them are difficult to wade through—but the mystique that he created, the aura of historical romance, has outlasted his books and is much in evidence in the ruined abbeys, historical houses, and grand vistas of the Borders.

A visit to at least one of the region's four great ruined abbeys makes the quintessential Borders experience. The monks in these striking, long-abandoned religious orders were the first to work the fleeces of their sheep flocks, thus laying the groundwork for what is still the area's main manufacturing industry.

Borders folk take great pride in the region's fame as Scotland's main woolen-goods manufacturing area. To this day the residents possess a marked determination to defend their towns and communities. Changing times have allowed them to reposition their priorities: instead of guarding against southern raiders, they now concentrate on maintaining a competitive rugby team for the popular intertown rugby matches.

4

JEDBURGH

50 mi south of Edinburgh, 95 mi southeast of Glasgow.

The town of Jedburgh (*-burgh* is always pronounced *burra* in Scots) was for centuries the first major Scottish target of invading English armies. In more peaceful times it developed textile mills, most of which have since languished. The large landscaped area around the town's tourist information center was once a mill but now provides an encampment for the armies of modern tourists. The past still clings to this little town, however. The ruined abbey dominates the skyline and remains a reminder of the formerly strong, governing role of the Borders abbeys.

GETTING HERE AND AROUND

The best and easiest way to travel in this region is by car, although there are fairly good bus connections from all major Scottish cities to Jedburgh. From Edinburgh, direct routes to Melrose take about two hours. From Melrose you can connect to Jedburgh for less than £4 (20 minutes). From Glasgow it takes 3½ hours to reach Melrose. There is no direct train service (the closest station is in Dumfries). Driving is faster and much easier. From Edinburgh you can take the A68 (about 45 minutes) or the A7 (about an hour). From Glasgow take the M8 then the A68 direct to Jedburgh (about two hours).

ESSENTIALS

Visitor Information **Scottish Borders Tourist Board** (✉ *Murray's Green, Jedburgh* ☎ *0870/608–0404* ⊕ *www.scot-borders.co.uk*).

EXPLORING

TOP ATTRACTIONS

☾ **Harestanes Countryside Visitor Centre.** Housed in a former farmhouse 3 mi north of Jedburgh, this visitor center portrays life in the Scottish Borders through changing art exhibitions and interpretive displays on the natural history of the region. Crafts such as woodworking and tile-making are taught at the center, and finished projects are often on display. There's a gift shop and tearoom, and outside are paths for countryside walks, plus the biggest children's play area in the Borders. The quiet roads are suitable for bicycle excursions. ✉ *Ancrum, near*

junction of A68 and B6400, 4 mi north of Jedburgh ☎ *01835/830306*
✉ *Free* ⊙ *Apr.–Oct., daily 10–5.*

★ **Jedburgh Abbey.** The most impressive of the Borders abbeys was nearly destroyed by the English earl of Hertford's forces in 1544–45, during the destructive time known as the Rough Wooing. This was English king Henry VIII's (1491–1547) armed attempt to persuade the Scots that it was a good idea to unite the kingdoms by the marriage of his young son to the infant Mary, Queen of Scots (1542–87); the Scots disagreed and sent Mary to France instead. The full story is explained in vivid detail at the **Jedburgh Abbey Visitor Centre,** which also provides information on interpreting the ruins. Ground patterns and foundations are all that remain of the once-powerful religious complex. ⊠ *High St.* ☎ *01835/863925* ⊕ *www.historic-scotland.gov.uk/places* ✉ *£5.20* ⊙ *Apr.–Sept., daily 9:30–5; Oct.–Mar., daily 9:30–4:30.*

Mary, Queen of Scots House. This *bastel* (from the French *bastille*) was the fortified town house in which, as the story goes, Mary stayed before embarking on her famous 20-mi ride to Hermitage Castle to visit her wounded lover, the earl of Bothwell (circa 1535–78). Interpretative displays relate the tale and illustrate other episodes in her life. Some of her possessions are also on display, as are tapestries and furniture of the period. ⊠ *Queen St.* ☎ *01835/863331* ✉ *£3.50* ⊙ *Mar.–Nov., Mon.–Sat. 10–4:30, Sun. 11–4:30.*

WORTH NOTING

OFF THE
BEATEN
PATH

Hermitage Castle. To appreciate the famous 20-mi ride of Mary, Queen of Scots, to visit her wounded lover, the earl of Bothwell, travel southwest from Jedburgh to this, the most complete remaining example of the bare and grim medieval border castles, full of gloom and foreboding. Restored in the early 19th century, it was built in the 14th century to guard what was at the time one of the important routes from England into Scotland. The original owner, Lord Soulis, notorious for diabolical excess, was captured by the local populace, which wrapped him in lead and boiled him in a cauldron—or so the tale goes. ⊠ *On an unnamed road 2 mi west of B6399, about 15 mi south of Hawick near Liddesdale* ☎ *01387/376222* ⊕ *www.historic-scotland.gov.uk/places* ✉ *£3.70* ⊙ *Apr.–Sept., daily 9:30–5:30; last admission ½ hr before closing.*

Jedburgh Castle Jail. This was the site of the Howard Reform Prison established in 1820. Today you can inspect prison cells, rooms arranged with period furnishings, and costumed figures. Audiovisual displays recount the history of the Royal Burgh of Jedburgh. ⊠ *Castlegate* ☎ *01835/864750* ✉ *£2.20* ⊙ *Mar.–Oct., Mon.–Sat. 10–4:30, Sun. 1–4; last admission ½ hr before closing.*

WHERE TO EAT AND STAY

££
BRITISH
★

✕ **Cross Keys.** This cozy, traditional pub is a national treasure and preservation award winner (the aerial railway lines that once carried beer from cellar to bar still remain). The kitchen utilizes fresh, local ingredients; salmon, sausages, and lamb are perfectly cooked and come accompanied with a colorful array of seasonal vegetables. Local Broughton Brewery supplies Cross Keys with the finest microbrews this side of the border. This is the quintessential village inn, right down to the green outside the front door. ⊠ *The Green, Ancrum* ☎ *01835/ 830344* ⊕ *www.ancrumcrosskeys. co.uk* ▭ *DC, MC, V.*

£ 🏠 **Hundalee House.** This B&B in an 18th-century manor has richly decorated Victorian-style rooms with nice touches like four-poster beds and cozy fireplaces. Fifteen acres of gardens and woods surround the house, and there are splendid views across to the English border at Carter Bar and to the Cheviot hills in the southeast. **Pros:** fantastic views of apple orchards; hearty breakfasts with homemade jams and honey; good children's facilities. **Cons:** farm aromas; far from shops and restaurants. ⊠ *Off A68, 1 mi south of Jedburgh* ☎ *01835/863011* ⊕ *www.accommodation-scotland. org* ➥ *5 rooms* � *In-room: no a/c, no phone, Wi-Fi. In-hotel: Wi-Fi hotspot* ▭ *No credit cards* ⊘ *Closed Christmas, Jan.–Mar.* ⍾ *BP.*

RIDING THE MARCHES

Borders communities have reestablished their identities through the gatherings known as the Common Ridings. Long ago it was essential that each town be able to defend its area, and this need became formalized in mounted gatherings to "ride the marches," or patrol the boundaries. The Common Ridings possess much more authenticity than the concocted Highland Games, so often taken to be the essence of Scotland. You can watch the excitement of clattering hooves and banners proudly displayed, but this is essentially a time for native Borderers.

£ 🏠 **Spinney Guest House.** A converted farm cottage, this B&B offers simple but carefully decorated rooms. Additionally, there are two one-bedroom wood cabins that are perfect for couples who like privacy, and a two-bedroom cabin where three people can sleep comfortably. Each cabin has a kitchenette and a small patio. The common room in the main house has several welcoming armchairs. **Pros:** close to Jedburgh; plenty of peace and quiet; pristine cabins. **Cons:** 2 mi to nearest restaurant; dated decor; no Wi-Fi. ⊠ *The Spinney, Langlee* ☎ *01835/863525* ⊕ *www.thespinney-jedburgh.co.uk* ➥ *3 rooms, 3 cabins* � *In-room: no a/c, no phone, kitchen (some), refrigerator (some)* ▭ *MC, V* ⍾ *BP.*

BICYCLING

Christopher Rainbow Tandem & Bike Hire (⊠ *8 Timpendean Cottages* ☎ *01835/830326 or 07799/525123*) rents tandem bikes, mountain bikes, and touring bikes. It's on the A698 between Jedburgh and Ancrum, making it ideal for exploring the four abbeys as well as the Tweed Cycleway and Borderloop Cycleway. The company provides tour itineraries, as well as extra services such as luggage forwarding. ■TIP→ **Remember that cars drive on the left side of the road; this rule applies to cyclists as well.**

SHOPPING

Jedburgh Woollen Mill (⊠ *Bankend North, Edinburgh Rd.* ☎ *01835/863585*) has shelves bursting with sweaters, kilts, tartan knitwear, and scarves. It's a good place to stock up on gifts. **Scottish Tradition** (⊠ *New Bongate Mill, Bongate* ☎ *01835/863306*) sells beautiful cashmere items, as well as Scottish tartan goods. The knitwear and hats are of the finest quality.

KELSO

12 mi northeast of Jedburgh.

One of the most charming Borders burghs, Kelso is often described as having a Continental flavor—some people think its broad, paved square makes it resemble a Belgian market town. The community has some fine examples of Georgian and Victorian Scots town architecture.

GETTING HERE AND AROUND

There are direct bus routes from Jedburgh to Kelso. Edinburgh has direct buses to Jedburgh; buses from Glasgow aren't direct. Your best option is to travel by car. From Jedburgh to Kelso take the A698, which is 12 mi, or about 20 minutes. Alternatively, the A699 is a scenic half-hour drive.

ESSENTIALS

Visitor Information Kelso (✉ *The Square, Kelso* ☎ *01835/863170* ⊕ *www. scot-borders.co.uk*).

EXPLORING

Kelso Abbey is the least intact ruin of the four great abbeys—just a bleak fragment of what was once the largest of the group. It was here in 1460 that the nine-year-old James III was crowned king of Scotland. On a main invasion route, the abbey was burned three times in the 1540s alone, on the last occasion by the English earl of Hertford's forces in 1545, when the 100 men and 12 monks of the garrison were butchered and the structure all but destroyed. ✉ *Bridge St.* ☎ *0131/668–8800* ⊕ *www.kelso.bordernet.co.uk* ✉ *Free* ☼ *Apr.–Dec., daily 24 hrs.*

Fodor'sChoice ★ On the outskirts of Kelso stands the palatial **Floors Castle,** the largest inhabited castle in Scotland. The ancestral home of the dukes of Roxburghe, Floors is an architectural extravagance bristling with peppermill turrets and towers. It stands on the "floors," or flat terrain, on the banks of the River Tweed opposite the barely visible ruins of Roxburghe Castle. The enormous home was built in 1721 by William Adam (1689–1748) and modified by William Playfair (1789–1857), who added the turrets and towers in the 1840s. A holly tree in the deer park marks the place where King James II of Scotland (1430–60) was killed by a cannon that "brak in the shooting." ✉ *A6089* ☎ *01573/223333* ⊕ *www. floorscastle.com* ✉ *Grounds £3.50, castle and grounds £7.50* ☼ *Mid-Apr.–Oct., daily 11–5; last admission ½ hr before closing.*

One fine example of the Borders area's ornate country homes is **Mellerstain House.** Begun in the 1720s, it was finished in the 1770s by Robert Adam (1728–92) and is considered one of his finest creations. Sumptuous plasterwork covers almost all interior surfaces, and there are outstanding examples of 18th-century furnishings. The beautiful terraced gardens (open an hour before the house itself) are as renowned as the house. ✉ *Off A6089, Gordon, 7 mi northwest of Kelso* ☎ *01573/410225* ⊕ *www.mellerstain.com* ✉ *Gardens £4, house and gardens £7* ☼ *May, June, and Sept., Sun. and Wed. 12:30–5; July and Aug., Sun., Mon., Wed., and Thurs. 12:30–5; Oct., Sun. 12:30–5; last admission ½ hr before closing.*

The Borders

North Sea

Paxton House

R. Tweed

B6437

Manderston House

A6112

Swinton

B6461

Duns

A6105

Blackadder

A697

Eccles

A698

ENGLAND

Coldstream

B6350

Floors Castle

Kelso

Morebattle

Kale Wr.

CHEVIOT HILLS

Mellerstain House

A6089

Smailholm Tower

B6397

B6360

B6404

Dryburgh Abbey

A699

Roxburgh

B6400

B6397

B6356

Scott's View

Ancrum

A68

Lanton

Jedburgh

A68

Harestanes Countryside Visitor Centre

TO HERMITAGE CASTLE

A6088

Melrose

A6091

Galashiels

Abbotsford House

A707

Selkirk

A699

A7

Ashkirk

Hawick

A7

Roberton

A68

Lauder

A68

A7

Fala

A6093

A68

Heriot

A72

Bowhill

A708

Innerleithen

R. Tweed

Peebles

A703

A72

Penicuik

S. Esk

B709

Dalkeith

A7

Edinburgh

N. Esk

M9

A71

Kirkliston

Livingston

M8

A702

PENTLAND HILLS

A721

A702

R. Tweed

Haddington

Cockburnspath

Teviot

A6088

TO CRAIK FOREST

KEY

✈ Airport

10 miles

10 kilometers

0

The characteristic Borders structure **Smailholm Tower** stands uncompromisingly on top of a barren, rocky ridge in the hills south of Mellerstain. The 16th-century peel was built solely for defense, and its unadorned stones contrast with the luxury of Mellerstain House. If you let your imagination wander in this windy spot, you can almost see the flapping pennants and rising dust of an advancing raiding party and hear the anxious securing of doors and bolts. Sir Walter Scott found this spot inspiring. His grandfather lived nearby, and the young Scott visited the tower often during his childhood. A museum here displays costumed figures and tapestries relating to Scott's Borders folk ballads. ⌧ *Off B6404, 4½ mi south of Mellerstain House* ☎ *01573/460365* ⊕ *www. historic-scotland.gov.uk* ☙ *£3.70* ☉ *Apr.–Sept., daily 9:30–5:30; Oct., Sat.–Wed. 9:30–4:30; Nov.–Mar., weekends 9:30–4:30; last admission ½ hr before closing.*

WHERE TO EAT AND STAY

££ ✕**Oscar's Wine Bar and Restaurant.** Winner of numerous culinary and
MEDITERRANEAN entrepreneurial awards, this new(ish) establishment is a local favorite. The space is well-lit, with bright yellow walls and contemporary furniture. Service is attentive, and the staff is well-informed; there's a good balance here. In season, try the medallions of venison with black pudding or char-grilled monkfish and salmon kebabs. The homemade banoffee pie (with banana, toffee, and cream) is to die for. ⌧ *35–37 Horsemarket* ☎ *01573/224008* ☰ *AE, DC, MC, V.*

££ 🏠**Edenwater House.** This handsome stone house overlooks Edenwater, a
★ trout stream that runs into the River Tweed. Four well-appointed guest rooms afford superb views of the river and two of the Cheviot hills. The inn's restaurant is filled with antiques and serves what some connoisseurs regard as the best food in the Borders. Roast saddle of hare with foie gras and fillet of monkfish crusted with basil and coriander in beurre blanc are two of the dishes you might find on the menu. The restaurant, open to nonguests on weekends, offers a £35 three-course dinner. Children under 10 are not admitted to the restaurant. **Pros:** excellent food; romantic atmosphere; peaceful surroundings. **Cons:** not good for families with small children; far from urban amenities. ⌧ *Off B6461, Ednam* ☎ *01573/224070* ⊕ *www.edenwaterhouse.co.uk* ☙ *4 rooms* ⚭ *In-room: no a/c, no phone, Internet. In-hotel: restaurant, bar* ☰ *MC, V* ☉ *Closed Sun.–Tues. and Jan.* ⏍ *BP.*

£££ 🏠**Ednam House Hotel.** People return again and again to this large, stately
★ hotel on the banks of the River Tweed, close to Kelso's grand abbey and sprawling Market Square. The main hall, part of the original 1761 home, welcomes you with deep-seated armchairs, lovely paintings, and an open fire. The restaurant's three windowed walls overlook the garden and river, and its Scottish fare (£££££) includes Borders beef, Highland venison, smoked wild salmon, and homemade traditional puddings. **Pros:** great outdoor activities; atmospheric lobby; impressive restaurant. **Cons:** hunting is popular, so dead pheasants are a common sight; some rooms need a makeover. ⌧ *Bridge St.* ☎ *01573/224168* ⊕ *www.ednamhouse. com* ☙ *32 rooms* ⚭ *In-room: no a/c. In-hotel: restaurant, bars, Wi-Fi hotspot* ☰ *MC, V* ☉ *Closed late Dec. and early Jan.* ⏍ *BP.*

SHOPPING

John Moody (✉ *38 The Square* ☎ *01573/224400*) sells soft cashmere and lambs wool sweaters, along with purses, scarves, and gloves. It's a real treat for knitwear fanatics, or those simply looking for something Scottish to keep them warm.

COLDSTREAM

9 mi east of Kelso.

Three miles west of Coldstream, the England–Scotland border comes down from the hills and runs beside the Tweed for the rest of its journey to the sea. Coldstream itself, like Gretna Green, was once a Las Vegas of sorts, where runaway couples from the south could come to get married in a time when the marriage laws of Scotland were more lenient than those of England. A plaque on the former bridge tollhouse recalls this fact. The town is also celebrated in military history: in 1659 General Monck raised a regiment of foot guards here on behalf of his exiled monarch, Charles II of England (1630–85). Known as the Coldstream Guards, the successors to this regiment have become an elite corps in the British army. Today Coldstream is still a small town, with a mix of attractive 18th- and 19th-century buildings.

GETTING HERE AND AROUND

There is no direct bus service from Jedburgh or Kelso to Coldstream. Your best bet is to drive. From Jedburgh, take the A68/A698/A697 (30 minutes). From Kelso, take the A698 (15 minutes).

ESSENTIALS

Visitor Information Coldstream (✉ *68A High St.* ☎ *08706/080404* ⊕ *www.visitscottishborders.com*).

EXPLORING

The **Coldstream Museum,** in the Coldstream Guards' former headquarters, examines the history of the community. You can see 18th-century marriage contracts, pieces of masonry from the village's lost medieval convent, weapons, uniforms, and photographs. A children's play area has toys and costumes, including a child-size Coldstream Guard uniform and bearskin hat made by the Guards' regimental tailor. ✉ *12 Market Sq.* ☎ *01890/882630* ⊕ *www.scotborders.gov.uk* ✏ *Free* ⊙ *Mid-Apr.– Sept., Mon.–Sat. 10–4, Sun. 2–4; Oct., Mon.–Sat. 1–4.*

Dignified houses and gardens line the stretch of the Tweed near Coldstream. The best-known house is the **Hirsel,** where a complex of farmyard buildings now serves as a crafts center and museum, with interesting walks on the extensive grounds. It's a favorite spot for bird-watchers, and superb rhododendrons bloom here in late spring. The house itself is not open to the public. ✉ *A697, immediately west of Coldstream* ☎ *01890/882834* ⊕ *www.hirselcountrypark.co.uk* ✏ *House free, parking £2.50* ⊙ *Grounds daily sunrise–sunset; museum and crafts center weekdays 10–5, weekends noon–5.*

Stately **Paxton House** is a comely Palladian mansion designed in 1758 by James and John Adam, with interiors designed by their brother Robert. There's Chippendale and Trotter furniture, and the splendid Regency picture gallery, an outstation of the National Galleries of Scotland, has a magnificent collection of paintings. The garden is delightful, with a squirrel hide and a restored boathouse containing a museum of salmon fishing. The adjacent crafts shop and tearoom are open daily 9 to 5. ⊠ *15 mi northeast of Coldstream, take A6112 and B6461, Paxton* ☎ *01289/386291* ⊕ *www.paxtonhouse.co.uk* ⊠ *Grounds £4, house and grounds £7* ⊙ *Apr.–Oct., daily 11–5; last tour at 4.*

Manderston House is a good example of the grand, no-expense-spared Edwardian country house. The family that built it made its fortune selling herring to Russia. A Georgian house from the 1790s was completely rebuilt from 1903 to 1905 to the specifications of John Kinross. The silver-plated staircase was modeled after the one in the Petit Trianon, at Versailles. Look for the collection of late-19th- and early-20th-century cookie tins. There's much to see downstairs in the kitchens, and outside, among a cluster of other buildings, is the octagonal, one-of-a-kind marble dairy where lunch, dinner, or afternoon tea can be arranged for groups. You can reach the house by traveling northeast from Coldstream along the A6112 to Duns, then taking the A6105 east. ⊠ *Off A6105* ☎ *01361/882636* ⊕ *www.manderston.co.uk* ⊠ *Grounds £4.50, house and grounds £8.50* ⊙ *Mid-May–Sept., Thurs. and Sun. 1:30–5; last entry 4:15.*

WHERE TO EAT

£££

BRITISH

★
✕ **Wheatsheaf Hotel and Restaurant.** The Wheatsheaf is a dining establishment that also provides accommodation—an important distinction, according to the owner. You can have an outstanding casual meal in the black-beamed bar, but the real treat is the formal restaurant. Here, the sheer excellence of the Scottish cuisine, whether you order beef, salmon, or venison, has won widespread praise yet neither the food nor the small but carefully chosen wine list is overpriced. Extend your stay in one of the seven country-style bedrooms. The inn is on the main street of Swinton, 6 mi north of Coldstream. ⊠ *Main St., Swinton* ☎ *01890/860257* ▭ *DC, MC, V* ⊙ *Closed first 2 wks of Jan.*

MELROSE

24 mi west of Coldstream, 4 mi southeast of Galashiels.

Though it's small, there is nevertheless a bustle about Melrose, the perfect example of a prosperous Scottish market town and one of the loveliest in the Borders. It's set round a square lined with 18th- and 19th-century buildings housing myriad small shops and cafés. Despite its proximity to the much larger Galashiels, Melrose has rejected industrialization. You'll likely hear local residents greet each other by first name in the square.

GETTING HERE AND AROUND

Buses do go to Melrose. However, driving is the easiest, fastest, and most efficient way to travel here. From Coldstream, take the A699 (40 minutes). From Galashiels, take the A6091 (10 minutes).

ESSENTIALS

Visitor Information Scottish Borders Tourist Board (✉ *Abbey St., Melrose* ☎ *08706/080404* ⊕ *www.visitscottishborders.com*).

EXPLORING

TOP ATTRACTIONS

Fodor's Choice ★ **Abbotsford House.** In 1811 Sir Walter Scott, already an established writer, bought a farm on this site named Cartleyhole, which was a euphemism for the real name, Clartyhole (*clarty* is Scots for "muddy" or "dirty"). The name was surely not romantic enough for Scott, who renamed the property after a ford in the nearby Tweed used by the abbot of Melrose. Scott eventually had the house entirely rebuilt in the Scots baronial style. The result was called "the most incongruous pile that gentlemanly modernism ever devised" by art critic John Ruskin. That was Mr. Ruskin's idiosyncratic take; most people have found this to be one of the most fetching of all Scottish abodes. A gently seedy mansion chock-full of Scottish curios, paintings, and mounted deer heads, it seems an appropriate domicile for a man of such an extraordinarily romantic imagination. It's worth visiting just to feel the atmosphere that the most successful writer of his day created and to see the condition in which he wrote, driving himself to pay off his endless debts. To Abbotsford came most of the famous poets and thinkers of Scott's day, including Wordsworth and Washington Irving. With some 9,000 volumes in the library, Abbotsford is the repository for the writer's collection of Scottish memorabilia and historic artifacts. Scott died here in 1832, and the house is today owned by his descendants. Take the A6091 from Melrose. The journey is 2.3 mi, a 5-minute drive. ✉ *B6360, Galashiels* ☎ *01896/752043* ⊕ *www.scottsabbotsford.co.uk* ✉ *Grounds £3, house and grounds £7* ⊙ *Mid-Mar.–Oct., Mon.–Sat. 9:30–5, Sun., 2–5; Nov.– mid-Mar., weekdays by appointment only.*

★ **Melrose Abbey.** Just off the square, down Abbey Street, sit the ruins of Melrose Abbey, one of the four Borders abbeys. "If thou would'st view fair Melrose aright, go visit it in the pale moonlight," wrote Scott in *The Lay of the Last Minstrel*, and so many of his fans took the advice literally that a sleepless custodian begged him to rewrite the lines. Today the abbey is still impressive: a red-sandstone shell with slender windows, delicate tracery, and carved capitals, all carefully maintained. Among the carvings high on the roof is one of a bagpipe-playing pig. An audio tour is included in the admission price. ✉ *Abbey St.* ☎ *01896/822562* ⊕ *www.historic-scotland.gov.uk* ✉ *£5.20* ⊙ *Apr.–Sept., daily 9:30– 5:30; Oct.–Mar., daily 9:30–4:30; last entry ½ hr before closing.*

☾ **Thirlestane Castle.** This large, turreted, and castellated house, part of which was built in the 13th century and part in the 16th century, looks for all the world like a French château, and it brims with history. The former home of the Duke of Lauderdale (1616–82), one of Charles II's advisors, Thirlestane is said to be haunted by the duke's ghost. Exquisite 17th-century plaster ceilings and rich collections of paintings, porcelain, and furniture fill the rooms. In the nursery, children are invited to play with Victorian-style toys and to dress up in masks and costumes. Guided tours are available 11 to 2. ✉ *Off A68, 9 mi north of Melrose,*

Lauder ☎ *01578/722430* ⊕ *www.thirlestanecastle.co.uk* ✉ *Grounds £3, castle and grounds £8* ⊙ *May, June, and early Sept., Wed., Thurs., and Sun. 10–3; July and Aug., Sun.–Thurs., daily 10–3.*

WORTH NOTING

Dryburgh Abbey. The final resting place of Sir Walter Scott and his wife, and the most peaceful and secluded of the Borders abbeys, Dryburgh Abbey sits on gentle parkland in a loop of the Tweed. The abbey suffered from English raids until, like Melrose, it was abandoned in 1544. The style is transitional, a mingling of rounded Romanesque and pointed early English. The north transept, where the Haig and Scott families lie buried, is lofty and pillared, and once formed part of the abbey church. ⊠ *B6404, off A68* ☎ *01835/822381* ⊕ *www.historic-scotland. gov.uk/places* ✉ *£4.70* ⊙ *Apr.–Sept., daily 9:30–5:30; Oct.–Mar., daily 9:30–4:30; last entry ½ hr before closing.*

Priorwood Gardens. The National Trust for Scotland's Priorwood Gardens, next to Melrose Abbey, specializes in flowers for drying. Dried flowers are on sale in the shop. Next to the gardens is an orchard with some old apple varieties. ⊠ *Abbey St.* ☎ *0844/4932257* ⊕ *www.nts. org.uk* ✉ *£6* ⊙ *Jan.–Mar., Mon.–Sat. noon–4; Apr.–Dec., Mon.–Sat. 10–5, Sun. 1–5.*

OFF THE
BEATEN
PATH

Scott's View. There's no escaping Sir Walter in this part of the country: 3 mi north of Dryburgh on the B6356 is possibly the most photographed rural view in the south of Scotland. (Perhaps the only view used more often to summon a particular interpretation of Scotland is that of Eilean Donan Castle, far to the north.) The sinuous curve of the River Tweed and the gentle landscape unfolding to the triple peaks of the Eildons and then rolling out into shadows beyond are certainly worth seeking. You arrive at this peerless vista, where Scott often came to meditate, by taking the B6356 north from Dryburgh.

Three Hills Roman Heritage Centre. On exhibit here are such artifacts as tools, weapons, and armor retrieved from the largest Roman settlement in Scotland, which was at nearby Newstead. A blacksmith's shop, several examples of pottery, and scale models of the fort are also on display. A guided four-hour walk along the 5-mi trail to the site departs at 1:30 on Thursday (also on Tuesday in July and August). The cost is £3. ⊠ *The Ormiston, Melrose Sq.* ☎ *01896/822463* ⊕ *www.trimontium. org.uk/wb* ✉ *£2* ⊙ *Apr.–Oct., daily 10:30–4:30.*

WHERE TO EAT AND STAY

£££   ✕ **Hoebridge Inn.** Whitewashed walls, oak-beamed ceilings, and an open
BRITISH   fire welcome you into this converted 19th-century bobbin mill. The cui-
Fodor's Choice   sine is a blend of British and Mediterranean styles with occasional Asian
★   influences. You might have lamb served with rosemary mashed potatoes and red-currant sauce or panfried tiger prawns with chili and lime syrup, accompanied by a salad of bean sprouts and *mangetout* (peas in their edible pods). The inn lies in Gattonside, next to Melrose but a 2-mi drive along the B6360, thanks to the intervention of the Tweed; you can also reach the inn by a footbridge from the town. ⊠ *B360, Gattonside* ☎ *01896/823082* 🍴 *MC, V* ⊙ *Closed Mon. No dinner Sun.*

CLOSE UP

The World of Sir Walter Scott

Sir Walter Scott (1771–1832) was probably Scottish tourism's best propagandist. Thanks to his fervid "Romantik" imagination, his long narrative poems—such as "The Lady of the Lake"—and a long string of historical novels, including *Ivanhoe, Waverley, Rob Roy, Redgauntlet,* and *The Heart of Midlothian,* the world fell in love with the image of heroic Scotland. Scott wrote of Scotland as a place of Highland wilderness and clan romance, shaping outsiders' perceptions of Scotland in a way that to an extent survives even today.

Scott was born in College Wynd, Edinburgh. A lawyer by training, he was an assiduous collector of old ballads and tales. "The Lay of the Last Minstrel," a romantic poem published in 1805, brought him fame. In 1811 Scott bought the house that was to become Abbotsford, his Borders mansion near Melrose.

Scott started on his series of Waverley novels in 1814, at first anonymously, and by 1820 had produced *Waverley, Guy Mannering, The Antiquary, Tales of My Landlord* (three series), and *Rob Roy.* Between 1820 and 1825

there followed an additional 11 titles, including *Ivanhoe* and *The Pirate.* Many of his verse narratives and novels focused on real-life settings, in particular the Trossachs, northwest of Stirling, an area that rapidly became, and still remains, popular with visitors.

Apart from his writing, Scott is also remembered for rediscovering the Honours of Scotland—the crown, scepter, and sword of state of the Scottish monarchs—in 1819. These symbols had languished at the bottom of a chest in Edinburgh Castle since 1707, when Scotland lost its independence. Today they're on display in the castle.

Abbotsford can be visited in spring and summer, and other houses associated with Scott can be seen in Edinburgh: 25 George Square, which was his father's house, and 39 Castle Street, where he lived from 1801 to 1826. The site of his birthplace, in College Wynd, is marked with a plaque. The most obvious structure associated with Scott is the Scott Monument on Princes Street, which looks like a Gothic rocket ship with a statue of Scott and his pet dog as passengers.

4

£££ ⊞ **Burts Hotel.** This charming whitewashed building dating from the 18th century sits in the center of Melrose. Floral pastels fill the rooms and public areas. The bar is welcoming, with a cheerful open fire and a wide selection of fine malt whiskies; it's ideal for a quiet dram before or after a meal. The vast restaurant (££££) has high-back upholstered chairs and white-linen tablecloths. Lamb with applesauce and lentils or chicken breast with truffle foam are typical entrées on the prix-fixe, three-course menu costing £35. Fishing can be arranged. **Pros:** walking distance to restaurants and pubs; good menu in restaurant. **Cons:** some rooms are tiny; bland room decor. ⊠ *Market Sq.* ☎ *01896/822285* ⊕ *www.burtshotel.co.uk* ↪ *20 rooms* ♿ *In-room: no a/c, Wi-Fi (some). In-hotel: restaurant, bar, Wi-Fi hotspot* ⊟ *D, MC, V* ⌷ *BP.*

£££ ⊞ **Dryburgh Abbey Hotel.** Mature woodlands and verdant lawns surround this imposing, 19th-century mansion, which is adjacent to the abbey ruins on a sweeping bend of the River Tweed. Throughout the hotel you'll feel a sense of peace and quiet in keeping with the location. The rooms are large and sumptuous, with canopy beds and lace-trimmed curtains. The restaurant (££££) specializes in Scottish fare; a four-course meal is a bargain at £35. **Pros:** beautiful grounds; romantic setting. **Cons:** some rooms need to be freshened up; service can be on the slow side; not much nightlife. ✉ *Off B6404, St. Boswells* ☎ *01835/822261* ⊕ *www.dryburgh.co.uk* ⇆ *36 rooms, 2 suites* ⚐ *In-room: no a/c, Wi-Fi (some). In-hotel: restaurant, pool, Wi-Fi* ⊟ *AE, MC, V* � *BP.*

THE ARTS

The **Wynd Theatre** (✉ *3 Buccleuch St.* ☎ *01896/823854*) has a monthly program of four nights of drama from national touring companies, two concerts of folk, blues, jazz, or classical from touring national and international companies, plus screenings of classic films on two Fridays. There's an art gallery highlighting top contemporary Scottish artists. Tickets cost £10 to £12 for performances or £5 to £7 for films.

SHOPPING

Take a break from sightseeing at **Abbey Mill** (✉ *Annay Rd.* ☎ *01896/822 138*), where you'll find hand-woven knitwear as well as homemade jams and fudge. There's also a wee tearoom.

GALASHIELS

5 mi northwest of Melrose.

A busy gray-stone Borders town, Galashiels is still active with textile mills and knitwear factories (be aware that these mills and factories do not offer tours or have visitor centers or shops). Nearby Hawick (17.3 mi south of Galashiels along the A7) is less attractive but has far better shopping.

GETTING HERE AND AROUND

There is regular bus service from Melrose to Galashiels (20 minutes). You can also drive; from Melrose, take the B6374 or the A6091 (both 10 minutes).

EXPLORING

Dating from 1583, **Old Gala House** is the former home of the lairds (landed proprietors) of Galashiels. It now serves as a museum with displays on the building's history and the town of Galashiels, as well as a contemporary art gallery. You can trace your family history at a comprehensive genealogy facility. The house is a short walk from the town center. ✉ *Scott Crescent* ☎ *01750/20096* ⊕ *www.galashiels.bordernet.co.uk/ oldgalahouse* ⌑ *Free* ☉ *Apr., May, and Sept., Tues.–Sat. 10–4; June– Aug., Mon.–Sat. 10–4, Sun. 1–4; Oct., Tues.–Fri. 1–4, Sat. 10–4.*

SHOPPING

A fun place to get lost is **Books Plus** (✉ *2 Channel St.* ☎ *01896/752843*), which carries all forms of literature (from rare books to current best sellers), as well as toys and art supplies. **Hawick Factory Visitor Centre** (✉ *Arthur St., Hawick* ☎ *01450/371221*) is a good place to see knitwear in the making—literally. In the shop you can buy Hawick knitwear and cashmere goods for discounted prices. **White of Hawick** (✉ *Victoria Rd.,*

Hawick ☎ *01450/373206) sells an extensive range of cashmere, lamb-swood, and knitted garments. There's a room exclusively dedicated to cashmere, and it's a good place to stock up on warm outerwear.*

SELKIRK

6 mi south of Galashiels.

Selkirk is a hilly outpost with a smattering of antiques shops and an assortment of bakers selling Selkirk Bannock (fruited sweet bread) and other cakes. Sir Walter Scott was sheriff (judge) of Selkirkshire from 1800 until his death in 1832, and his statue stands in Market Place. The town is also near Bowhill, a stately home.

> **SELKIRK'S PRIDE**
>
> The little town of Selkirk claims its Common Riding is the largest mounted gathering anywhere in Europe. More than 400 riders take part in the event. It's also the oldest Borders festival, dating back to the Battle of Flodden in 1513.

GETTING HERE AND AROUND

If you're driving, take the A7 south to Galashiels. The scenic journey is less than 7 mi and takes around 10 minutes. First Edinburgh Bus offers a regular service between Galashiels and Selkirk.

ESSENTIALS

Visitor Information Selkirk (✉ *Halliwell's House, Market Pl.* ☎ *08706/080404*).

EXPLORING

Sir Walter Scott's Courtroom, where he presided, contains a display examining Scott's life, his writings, and his time on the bench, and it includes an audiovisual presentation. ✉ *Market Pl.* ☎ *01750/720096* ⊕ *www.scotborders.gov.uk* ✍ *Free* ☉ *Apr. and Sept., weekdays 10–4, Sat. 10–2; May–Aug., weekdays 10–4, weekends 10–2; Oct., Mon.–Sat. 1–4.*

Halliwell's House Museum, tucked off the main square, was once an iron-monger's shop, which is now re-created downstairs. Upstairs, an exhibit tells the town's tale, with useful background information on the Common Ridings. ✉ *Market Pl.* ☎ *01750/720096* ⊕ *www.scotborders.gov.uk* ✍ *Free* ☉ *Apr.–June and Sept., Mon.–Sat. 10–5, Sun. 10–noon; July and Aug., Mon.–Sat. 10–5:30, Sun. 10–noon; Oct., Mon.–Sat. 10–4.*

The **Lochcarron of Scotland Cashmere and Wool Centre** houses a museum where you can tour a mill and learn about the manufacture of tartans and tweeds. ✉ *Waverley Mill, Rodgers Rd.* ☎ *01750/726000* ⊕ *www.lochcarron.com* ✍ *Museum free, tour £2.50* ☉ *June–Sept., Mon.–Sat. 9–5, Sun. 11–4; Oct.–May, Mon.–Sat. 9–5. Guided tours Mon.–Thurs. at 10:30, 11:30, 1:30, and 2:30; Fri. at 10:30 and 11:30.*

Bowhill, one of the stately homes in the Borders, and home of the Duke of Buccleuch, dates from the 19th century and houses an outstanding collection of works by Gainsborough, Van Dyck, Canaletto, Reynolds, and Raeburn, as well as porcelain and period furniture. The house itself is only open in July; the grounds have more friendly hours. It's 3 mi west of Selkirk. ✉ *Off A708* ☎ *01750/22204* ⊕ *www.bowhill.org* ✍ *Grounds £3, house and grounds £7* ☉ *House July, daily 11–5;*

Aug., daily 2–3:30. Grounds May, and June, weekends 10–5; July and Aug., daily 10–5.

SHOPPING

Waverly Mill (✉ *Rodgers Rd.* ☎ *01750/726000*) has informative tours of its world-renowned mill. Here you can purchase of the best woolen goods on offer, from knitwear to tartans and tweeds. They also sell Scottish jewelry.

INNERLEITHEN

15 mi northwest of Selkirk.

Innerleithen is one of the larger Borders towns; you'll feel like you've entered a hub of activity when you arrive. It's also dramatically beautiful. Surrounded by hills and glens, the town is where the Tweed and Leithen rivers join then separate. Historically, Innerleithen dates back to pre-Roman times, and there are artifacts are all around for you to see. Once a booming industrialized town of wool mills, today it's a great destination for outdoor activities including hiking, biking, and fly-fishing.

GETTING HERE AND AROUND

To drive to Innerleithen, take the A707 northwest from Selkirk (about 30 minutes). Buses from Selkirk to Innerleithen are difficult (but not impossible) to find; there are no trains between the two towns.

EXPLORING

☺ A popular reason to come to Innerleithen is to see **Robert Smail's Printing Works.** The fully operational, restored print shop with a reconstructed waterwheel fascinates adults and older children, who can try their hand at old-fashioned typesetting. ✉ *7–9 High St.* ☎ *01896/830206* ⊕ *www.nts.org.uk/Visits* ✑ *£5.50* ☉ *Apr.–Oct., Thurs.–Sat. and Mon., noon–5, Sun. 1–5; last admission at 4:15.*

Fodor'sChoice Near the town of Innerleithen stands **Traquair House,** said to be the oldest
★ continually occupied home in Scotland. Inside you're free to discover secret stairways, a maze, more than 3,000 books, and a bed used by Mary, Queen of Scots, in 1566. The 18th-century brew house still makes highly recommended ale. You may even spend the night, if you wish. ✉ *B709, 1 mi from Innerleithen, Traquair* ☎ *01896/830323* ⊕ *www.traquair.co.uk* ✑ *Grounds £3.50, house and grounds £7* ☉ *Apr., May, and Sept. daily noon–5; June–Aug., daily 10:30–5; Oct., daily 11–4; Nov., weekends 11–3; last admission ½ hr before closing.*

WHERE TO STAY

££££ 🏨 **Traquair House.** To stay in one of the guest rooms in the 12th-century part of Traquair House is to experience a slice of Scottish history. Each spacious room is individually decorated with antiques and canopied beds. During your stay you may explore those parts of the house that are open to the public, or walk in the parkland and gardens. In the 18th-century lower drawing room you can savor a glass of the house ale before an open fire. Dinner can be arranged. **Pros:** stunning grounds; spacious rooms; great breakfast. **Cons:** nearly 2 mi to restaurants and shops; rooms fill up quickly in summer. ✉ *B709, Traquair*

☎ *01896/830323* ⊕ *www.traquair.co.uk* ⇥ *3 rooms* ⚷ *In-room: no a/c* ☰ *MC, V* ⏁⏁*BP.*

PEEBLES

6 mi west of Innerleithen.

Thanks to its excellent though pricey shopping, Peebles gives the impression of catering primarily to leisured country gentlefolk. Architecturally the town is nothing out of the ordinary, just a very pleasant burgh. Don't miss the splendid dolphins ornamenting the bridge crossing the River Tweed.

GETTING HERE AND AROUND

Because of its size and location, direct buses run from both Edinburgh and Glasgow to Peebles. There are also buses here from Innerleithen, though driving from here is more direct. (Take the A72; it's about a 10-minute drive.)

ESSENTIALS

Visitor Information Peebles ⊠ *High St.* ☎ *0870/608-0404* ⊕ *www.scot-borders. co.uk).*

EXPLORING

Neidpath Castle, a 15-minute walk upstream along the banks of the Tweed, perches artistically above a bend in the river. It comes into view as you approach through the tall trees. The castle is a medieval structure remodeled in the 17th century, with dungeons hewn from solid rock. You can return on the opposite riverbank after crossing an old, finely skewed railroad viaduct. ⊠ *Off A72* ☎ *01721/720333* ⊕ *www. discovertheborders.co.uk* ⌔ *£3* ⊗ *May–Sept., Mon.–Sat. 10:30–5, Sun. 12:30–5; last admission ½ hr before closing.*

The exotic, almost Moorish mosaics of the **Peebles War Memorial** (⊠ *Chambers Quadrangle, High St.*) are unique in Scotland, although most towns have a memorial to honor those killed in service. It's a remarkable tribute to the 225 Peebleans killed in World War II.

WHERE TO EAT

££££ ✕ **Bardoulet's Restaurant.** This is a good destination for special evenings.
FRENCH The color theme here is gold, and the inviting dining room has large gold-framed mirrors and heavy hanging drapes. A lot of care is put into the classic French food, which consists of local ingredients with rich sauces, perfectly presented. The Scottish lobster and Jersey potato salad and Gressingham duck breast with eggplant and foie gras are good choices. The bar-bistro also has top-notch food, but the prices are a little easier to swallow (about £10 cheaper per entrée). The crispy haggis with caramelized apple puree, sweet-potato gratin, and whisky sauce is a real treat. ⊠ *The Horseshoe Inn, Eddleston* ☎ *01721/730225* ⊕ *www.horseshoeinn.co.uk* ☰ *D, DC, MC, V.*

££ ✕ **The Sunfower Restaurant.** Quaint and bright, this unique little café has
ECLECTIC something for everyone. It serves fresh in-house baked breads, and uses only local meats, vegetables, and dairy products. The owner puts a lot of love into her establishment and cooking, whether it's breakfast, lunch, or dinner. The Thai fish cakes with coriander salad and lemon sauce

are full of flavor, as is the Moroccan lamb with couscous. The oatcakes and homemade chutney are a light and unusual way to end your meal. ⊠ *4 Bridgegate* ☏ *01721/722420* ⊟ *D, DC, MC, V* ⊗ *Closed Sun. No dinner Mon.–Wed.*

WHERE TO STAY

££££ ⚷ **Cringletie House.** With medieval-style turrets and crow-step gables,
★ this small-scale, peaceful retreat manages to be fancy *and* homey, Victorian (it was built in the 1860s) and modern (flat-screen TVs). A British-country-house style predominates. Some of the individually decorated bedrooms have fireplaces and four-posters, and all overlook the 28-acre grounds. From the drawing room there are views over the valley. A walled garden grows produce used in the excellent restaurant (£££££), which draws locals for Scottish fare. The afternoon tea, served in the conservatory, is especially recommended. **Pros:** elegant bedrooms; cozy fireplaces; decadent dining. **Cons:** some bedrooms have low ceilings; atmosphere can be almost too quiet. ⊠ *Edinburgh Rd., off A703* ☏ *01721/725750* ⊕ *www.cringletie.com* ⌂ *13 rooms* ☖ *In-room: no a/c, Wi-Fi. In-hotel: restaurant, bar, Wi-Fi hotspot, some pets allowed* ⊟ *AE, MC, V* ⋈ *BP.*

£££ ⚷ **Park Hotel.** An intimate retreat on the banks of the River Tweed at the northern tip of the Ettrick Forest, the Park Hotel offers tranquil, green surroundings and airy, modern rooms. The restaurant (£££££) serves superior Scottish cuisine; many of the dishes use locally caught salmon and trout. You are welcome to use the facilities at the Peebles Hydro Hotel, ½ mi away. **Pros:** homey feel; great views of golf course; complimentary sherry upon arrival. **Cons:** needs to be redecorated; some rooms have a slight doggy smell. ⊠ *Innerleithen Rd.* ☏ *01721/720451* ⊕ *www.parkpeebles.co.uk* ⌂ *24 rooms* ☖ *In-room: no a/c, Wi-Fi (some). In-hotel: restaurant, bar, some pets allowed, Wi-Fi hotspot* ⊟ *AE, DC, MC, V* ⋈ *BP.*

££££ ⚷ **Peebles Hydro.** Not only does the Hydro have something for everyone, but it has it in abundance: pony rides, a putting green, and a giant chess and checkers game are just a few of the diversions. The elegant Edwardian building stands on 30 acres of land, and you're welcome to explore every inch. The public areas and most rooms have lofty ceilings and elegant, antique-reproduction furnishings. The restaurant (£££££) has a Scottish menu that includes local salmon, lamb, and beef. **Pros:** plenty of activities; good children's programs; delicious breakfast. **Cons:** can feel impersonal; some rooms have bland decor; reception area in need of a makeover. ⊠ *Innerleithen Rd.* ☏ *01721/720602* ⊕ *www. peebleshotelhydro.com* ⌂ *132 rooms* ☖ *In-room: no a/c, Wi-Fi (some). In-hotel: restaurant, bar, tennis court, pool, gym, bicycles, children's programs (ages infant–16), laundry service, Wi-Fi hotspot* ⊟ *AE, DC, MC, V* ⋈ *BP.*

SHOPPING

Be prepared for temptations at every turn as you browse the shops on High Street and in the courts and side streets leading off it.

For all things Scottish, look no further than **Caledonia** (⊠ *61 High St.* ☏ *01721/722343*), where you'll find everything from kilts to throws, and jams to tablecloths. **Head to Toe** (✉ *43 High St.* ☎ *01721/722752*) stocks natural beauty products, handmade pine furniture, and handsome linens—from patchwork quilts to silk flowers. Among the many jewelers on High Street is **Keith Walter** (✉ *28 High St.* ☎ *01721/720650*), a gold- and silversmith who makes items on the premises. He also stocks jewelry made by other local designers.

DUMFRIES AND GALLOWAY

Galloway covers the southwestern portion of Scotland, west of the main town of Dumfries. Here a gentle coastline gives way to farmland and then breezy uplands that gradually merge with coniferous forests. Use caution when negotiating the A75—you're liable to find aggressive trucks bearing down on you as these commercial vehicles race for the ferries at Stranraer and Cairnryan. Trucks notwithstanding, once you're off the main roads, Dumfries and Galloway offer some of the most pleasant drives in Scotland—though the occasional herd of cows on the way to be milked is a potential hazard.

GRETNA GREEN

10 mi north of Carlisle, 87 mi south of Glasgow, 92 mi southwest of Edinburgh.

GETTING HERE AND AROUND

From Glasgow you can reach Gretna Glen via the M74 and A74; it's an hour and a half drive. From Edinburgh, take the A74 (about two hours). Buses and trains travel to Gretna Green from Glasgow and Edinburgh daily.

ESSENTIALS

Visitor Information **Gretna Green/Ruthwell** (✉ *Gretna Gateway Outlet Village, Unit 38, Glasgow Rd., Gretna Green* ☎ *01461/337834* ⊕ *www. visitdumfriesandgalloway.co.uk*).

EXPLORING

Gretna Green is tied to the reputation this community developed as a refuge for runaway couples from England, who once came north to take advantage of Scotland's more lenient marriage laws. This was the first place they reached on crossing the border. At one time anyone could perform a legal marriage in Scotland, and the village blacksmith (known as the "anvil priest") did the honors in Gretna Green. The blacksmith's shop is still standing, and today it contains a collection of blacksmithing tools, including the anvil over which many weddings were conducted. The town is highly commercialized rather than atmospheric, though, with plenty of shops.

RUTHWELL

21 mi west of Gretna, 83 mi south of Glasgow, 88 mi southwest of Edinburgh.

North of the upper Solway Firth the countryside is flat, fertile farmland. Progressing west, however, a pleasant landscape of low, round hills begins to take over. But there are historical features among the flatlands that should not be ignored.

GETTING HERE AND AROUND

There is no train station in Ruthwell; however, buses—both local and national—do frequent the town. But the best way to get here is via car. From Glasgow, take the M74 then A74; the trip is just under two hours. From Edinburgh take the A74; your journey will take just over two hours. Gretna Green is just under a half hour away via the A75.

EXPLORING

Inside **Ruthwell Parish Church** is the 8th-century Ruthwell Cross, a Christian sculpture admired for the detailed biblical scenes carved onto its north and south faces. The east and west faces have carvings of vines, birds, and animals, plus verses from an Anglo-Saxon poem called "The Dream of the Rood." Considered an idolatrous monument, it was removed and demolished by Church of Scotland zealots in 1642 but was later reassembled. ⊠ *6½ mi west of Annan* ☎ *No phone.*

Fodor'sChoice
★
The moated **Caerlaverock Castle** overlooks a nature reserve on a coastal loop of the B725. It's a pretty 7-mi (10-minute) drive from Ruthwell. Built in a triangular design unique to Britain, this 13th-century fortress has solid-sandstone masonry and an imposing double-tower gatehouse. King Edward I of England (1239–1307) besieged the castle in 1300, when his forces occupied much of Scotland at the start of the Wars of Independence. The castle suffered many times in Anglo-Scottish skirmishes, as the video presentation attests. ⊠ *Off B725, 5 mi west of Ruthwell* ☎ *01387/770244* ⊕ *www.historic-scotland.gov.uk/places* ⊠ *£5.20* ☉ *Apr.–Sept., daily 9:30–5:30; Oct.–Mar., daily 9:30–4:30.*

The **Caerlaverock National Nature Reserve** lets you observe wintering wild-fowl, including various species of geese, ducks, swans, and raptors. There are free guided walks throughout the year. ⊠ *Off B725, east of Caerlaverock Castle* ☎ *01387/770275* ⊠ *Free* ☉ *Daily 24 hrs.*

DUMFRIES

15 mi northwest of Ruthwell, 76 mi south of Glasgow, 81 mi southwest of Edinburgh.

Author J. M. Barrie (1860–1937) spent his childhood in Dumfries, and the garden of Moat Brae House is said to have inspired his boyish dreams in *Peter Pan*. The River Nith meanders through Dumfries, and the pedestrian-only town center makes wandering and shopping a pleasure. The town also contains the Globe Inn, a favorite *howff* (pub) of Scotland's national poet Robert Burns (1759–96), as well as one of the houses he lived in and his mausoleum.

GETTING HERE AND AROUND

Public transportation is a good option for reaching Dumfries—there's a good train station here, and most major Scottish cities have regular daily bus routes to the town. If you're driving from Ruthwell, take the B724 (12 mi/20 minutes). From Glasgow, take the M74 then A701 (77 mi/about 1½ hours). From Edinburgh, take the A701 (72 mi/about 2 hours).

ESSENTIALS

Visitor Information Dumfries & Galloway Tourist Board (⊠ *64 Whitesands* ☎ *01387/253862* ⊕ *www.dumfriesandgalloway.co.uk*).

EXPLORING

Not surprisingly, in view of its close association to the poet, Dumfries has a **Robert Burns Centre,** housed in a sturdy former mill overlooking the river. The center has an audiovisual program and an extensive exhibit on the life of the poet. During the Dumfries Festival, held late May to early June, films are screened in the theater. ⊠ *Mill Rd.* ☎ *01387/264808* 🖅 *Center free, audiovisual show £1.60* ⊗ *Apr.–Sept., Mon.–Sat. 10–8, Sun. 2–5; Oct.–Mar., Tues.–Sat. 10–1 and 2–5.*

At the center of the village of New Abbey, 7 mi south of Dumfries, is the red-tinted and roofless **Sweetheart Abbey.** The odd name is a translation of the abbey's previous name, St. Mary of the Dolce Coeur. The abbey was founded in 1273 by the Lady of Galloway, Devorgilla (1210–90), in memory of her husband, John Balliol (?–1269), who was buried in Bardard Castle in England. It's said Devorgilla had her husband's heart embalmed and placed in a tiny casket that she carried everywhere. After she died, Devorgilla was laid to rest before the High Altar of Sweetheart Abbey with the casket resting on her breast. The couple's son, also named John (1249–1315), was the puppet king installed in Scotland by Edward of England when the latter claimed sovereignty over Scotland. After John's appointment the Scots gave him a scathing nickname that would stay with him for the rest of his life: Toom Tabard (Empty Shirt). ⊠ *A710 at New Abbey* ☎ *01387/850397* 🖅 *£3* ⊗ *Apr.–Sept., Mon.–Sat. 9:30–5:30, Sun. 2–6:30; Oct.–Mar., Mon.–Wed. and Sat. 9:30–4:30, Thurs. 9:30–1, Sun. 2–4:30.*

The little community of Kirkbean (blink and you'll miss it), 12 mi south of Dumfries, is the backdrop for Arbigland Estate. It was in a cottage, now the **John Paul Jones Museum,** in this bright green landscape that John Paul (1747–92), the son of an estate gardener, was born. He eventually left Scotland, added "Jones" to his name, and became the founder of the U.S. Navy. The cottage where he was born is furnished as it would have been when John was a boy. An audio tour describes what life was like in the mid-18th century. John Paul Jones returned to raid the coastline of his native country in 1778. This exploit is described in an adjoining visitor center, where there's a replica of Jones's ship's cabin. ⊠ *Off A710 near Kirkbean* ☎ *01387/880613* 🖅 *£2.50* ⊗ *Apr.–June and Sept., Tues.–Sun. 10–5; July and Aug., daily 10–5.*

OFF THE
BEATEN
PATH

Drumlanrig Castle. This spectacular estate is as close as Scotland gets to the treasure houses of England—which is not surprising, since it's owned by the dukes of Buccleuch, one of the wealthiest British peerages. Resplendent with romantic turrets, this pink-sandstone palace

Dumfries and Galloway

KEY
— Rail Lines
—+— Ferry

ENGLAND

Solway Firth

Gretna Green
Carlisle
Langholm
Eskdalemuir
Davington
Boreland
Lockerbie
Moffat
Newton Wamphray
Lochmaben
Ruthwell
Annan
Caerlaverock National Nature Reserve
John Paul Jones Museum
Southerness
Durisdeer
FOREST OF AE
R. Nith
Dumfries
Caerlaverock Castle
New Abbey
Sweetheart Abbey
Sandyhills
Thornhill
Drumlanrig Castle
Colt Hill
DALMACALLAN FOREST
Crockefford
Crockerford
Rockcliffe
Abbey Head
Bogue
Edward
Castle Douglas
Threave Gardens
Dalbeattie
Kirkcudbright
R. Dee
Gatehouse of Fleet
CARSPHAIRN FOREST
New Galloway
Water of Fleet
Carsphairn
Creetown
Cairnsmore of Fleet
Eggerness Point
Isle of Whithorn
Wigtown Bay
Crosshill
GALLOWAY FOREST PARK
R. Cree
Glen Trool
Newton Stewart
Creetown Gem Rock Museum
The Moors
Wigtown
The Machars
Whithorn
Barr
R. Cree
B7067
Port William
Dailly
Pinwherry
New Luce
Glenluce
Maybole
Girvan
Cairnryan
Stranraer
Castle Kennedy Gardens
Sandhead
Ardwell
Drummore
Lendalfoot
Loch Ryan
Luce Bay
Mull of Galloway
B7041
Crammag Head
Ballantrae
Kirkcolm
Rhinns of Galloway
Logan Botanic Gardens
Portpatrick
North Channel
TO BELFAST, LARNE
TO ISLE OF MAN

10 miles
10 kilometers

was constructed between 1679 and 1691 by the first Duke of Queensbury, who, after nearly bankrupting himself building the place, found it disappointing on his first overnight stay and never returned. The Buccleuchs inherited the palace and soon filled the richly decorated rooms with French furniture from the period of Louis XIV, family portraits, and a valuable collection of paintings by Holbein, Rembrandt, and Murillo. Because of the theft of a Da Vinci painting in 2003, all visits are conducted by guided tour. There's also a playground, a gift shop, and a tearoom. ⊠ *Off A76 near Thornhill, about 18 mi northwest of Dumfries* ☎ *01848/600283* ⊕ *www.drumlanrig.com* ✉ *Park £4, castle and park £7.50* ☉ *Grounds Apr.–Sept., daily 11–5. Castle May and June, daily noon–4; July and Aug., daily 11–4.*

WHERE TO EAT AND STAY

££ ✕ **The Auld Alliance.** This is the place in Dumfries to enjoy good local
FRENCH food. The chef takes the greatest care in crafting his artful French-Scottish creations, which are almost too pretty to eat. The atmosphere is elegant and modern with dark walls, clear glass tables, and Rennie Macintosh–inspired furniture. The two-course and three-course options are inventive; try the seared Wester Ross scallops, Stornoway Black Pudding, and baby spinach to start, and loin of Lockerbie lamb with herb-crusted haricot bean stew and tomato-and-olive jus for your entrée. ⊠ *53 St. Michaels St.* ☎ *01387/255689* ⊟ *AE, DC, MC, V.*

£ ✕ **So You.** Bright and white with soft leather sofas, armchairs, tall bar
ECLECTIC stools, and smooth pine tables, this is a popular place for lighter fares and healthy fusion food. It can get crowded at night when there's music downstairs, so be sure to book in advance. Lunch is more casual but popular with shoppers in the know. The two-course, £13.95 option is a real bargain. Try the battered soy and ginger chicken strips with pineapple and jam or grilled mahimahi fish fillets with cucumber-and-mint dip. ⊠ *24 Castle St.* ☎ *01387/249911* ⊕ *www.soyoucafe.co.uk* ⊟ *AE, D, DC, MC, V.*

£ ⚇ **Ferintosh Guest House.** Ideally located directly across from the train station, this handsome sandstone guesthouse sits on a leafy street in a quiet part of town. The owners are very much involved, and this is more than just a place to sleep. Every room features original art and complimentary chocolates and drams of single-malt whisky; the proprietors host events such as local "kilted" historic pub tours and traditional Burns Suppers. You'll get a good taste of local culture here, and the breakfast isn't bad either. **Pros:** dog friendly; great complimentary robes; helpful owners. **Cons:** no children under 10 years of age; some rooms don't have en-suite bathrooms. ⊠ *30 Lovers Walk* ☎ *01387/252262* ⊕ *www.ferintosh.net* ⤳ *6 rooms* ⚇ *In-room: no a/c, no phone, safe, Wi-Fi. In-hotel: Wi-Fi hotspot, some pets allowed, no kids under 10* ⊟ *AE, DC, MC, V* ⊠⊟ *BP.*

THE ARTS

Gracefield Arts Centre (⊠ *28 Edinburgh Rd.* ☎ *01387/262084*) has galleries with constantly changing exhibits. The **Dumfries & Galloway Arts Festival** (☎ *01387/260447* ⊕ *www.dgartsfestival.org.uk*) is usually held at the end of May at several venues throughout the region.

BICYCLING

Bicycles can be rented from **G&G Cycle Centre** (⊠ *10–12 Academy St.* ☎ *01387/259483*). The staff gives good advice on where to ride. **7stanes** (⊠ *55/57 Moffat Rd.* ☎ *01387/272440* ⊕ *www.7stanes.gov.uk*) are seven different biking centers around the Borders and Dumfries/Galloway area that merge Scottish legend with riding. They've got a wealth of knowledge on the area.

SHOPPING

Dumfries is the main shopping center for the region, with all the big-name chain stores as well as specialty shops. For a souvenir that's easy to pack, try **David Hastings** (⊠ *Maryng, Shieldhill, near Amisfield* ☎ *01387/ 710451*), with more than 100,000 old postcards and postal history items. The store is open weekdays 10 to 3 or by appointment. The shop is in a house called Maryng in a group of houses called Shieldhill. **Grey-friars Crafts** (⊠ *56 Buccleuch St.* ☎ *01387/264050*) sells mainly Scottish goods, including glass, ceramics, and jewelry.

DALBEATTIE

14 mi southwest of Dumfries, 89 mi south of Glasgow, 95 mi southwest of Edinburgh.

Like the much larger Aberdeen far to the northeast, Dalbeattie contains buildings constructed with local gray granite from the town's quarry. The well-scrubbed gray glitter makes Dalbeattie atypical of Galloway towns, where house fronts are usually painted in pastels.

GETTING HERE AND AROUND

There are no direct bus routes from Dumfries to Dalbeattie; your best mode of transport is car. From Dumfries, take the A711 (about 25 minutes). From Glasgow take the M74, A74, then A701 (about two hours). From Edinburgh, take the A701 and A702 (about 2 hours, 15 minutes).

WHERE TO STAY

£ ▨ **Kerr Cottage.** This 165-year-old house is holding up quite well, thank you very much. Bedrooms are fresh, spacious, white, and newly renovated with contemporary wood furniture, comfy beds, and large, tiled bathrooms. For an extra £15 per person, the owners will cook you a hearty dinner made from fresh local ingredients that you can enjoy in their glass conservatory. Staying here feels like coming home. **Pros:** close to biking and hiking trails; great storage space for outdoor gear; comfortable lounge. **Cons:** no pets allowed; no children under 12. ⊠ *Port Rd.* ☎ *01556/612245* ⊕ *www.kerrcottage.co.uk* ▨ *3 rooms* ☖ *In-room: no a/c, no phone, DVD (some), Wi-Fi. In-hotel: Wi-Fi hotspot, no kids under 12* ▤ *AE, DC, MC, V.* ▮❂▮ *BP.*

SPORTS AND THE OUTDOORS

Barend Riding School and Trekking Centre (⊠ *A710, Sandyhills* ☎ *01387/ 780632*) helps you to a "horse-high" view of the beautiful coast and countryside. The school is 6 mi southeast of Dalbeattie.

CASTLE DOUGLAS

6 mi west of Dalbeattie, 84 mi south of Glasgow, 90 mi southwest of Edinburgh.

Castle Douglas is a quaint town that sits besides Carlingwark Loch. The Loch sets off the city perfectly, reflecting its dramatic architecture: sharp spires and soft sandstone arches. It's a popular base for experiencing the surrounding countryside. There are also some unique shops and eateries along the main shopping street, King Street.

GETTING HERE AND AROUND

There's no train station in Castle Douglas, and buses from Dumfries make several stops along the way. The best way to get to Castle Douglas is by car. From Dalbeattie, take the A711/A745 (10 minutes). From Glasgow, take the A713 (just under two hours). From Edinburgh, take the A70 (2 hours and 20 minutes).

ESSENTIALS

Visitor Information Castle Douglas (✉ *Market Hill* ☎ *01556/502611* ⊕ *www. visitdumfriesandgalloway.co.uk*).

EXPLORING

★ The main reason to come to this pleasant town is to visit **Threave Gardens**. The National Trust for Scotland cares for several garden properties, including the sloping parkland around the 1867 mansion built by William Gordon, a Liverpool businessman. Today a large section of the house has been converted into accommodations for students studying under the NTS's practical gardening program. The garden's horticultural undertaking demands the employment of many gardeners—and it's here that the gardeners train, thus ensuring there's always some fresh development or experimental planting here. There is also an on-site restaurant and visitor center. ✉ *South of A75, 1 mi west of Castle Douglas* ☎ *08444/932245* ⊕ *www.nts.org.uk/Visits* 🎟 *Gardens £6, house and gardens £10.50* ⊙ *House Apr.–Oct., Wed., Thurs., Fri., and Sun. 11–3:30. Visitor center Feb., Mar., Nov., and Dec., daily 10–4; Apr.–Oct. daily 10–5.*

Threave Castle, not to be confused with the mansion in Threave Gardens, was an early home of the Black Douglases, who were the earls of Nithsdale and lords of Galloway. The castle was dismantled in the religious wars of the mid-17th century, though enough of it remains to have housed prisoners from the Napoleonic Wars of the 19th century. It's a few minutes from Castle Douglas by car and is signposted from the main road. To get there, you must leave your car in a farmyard and walk the rest of the way. Make your way down to the reeds by the river on an occasionally muddy path. At the edge of the river you can then ring a bell, and, rather romantically, a boatman will come to ferry you across to the great stone tower looming from a marshy island in the river. ✉ *North of A75, 3 mi west of Castle Douglas* ☎ *07711/223101* 🎟 *£4.20, includes ferry* ⊙ *Castle Apr.–Sept., daily 9:30–5:30.*

WHERE TO EAT

£ ✕ **The Café at Designs Gallery.** For a good balance of art and food, look
CAFÉ no further. You'll find the freshest ingredients here, from bread to cakes,
soup to salads, sandwiches to quiches. Everything is made on-site,
including the bread, and it's all organic. The soup of the day is always a
good choice as are their seasonal fruit pies. The inside café is full of light
and wooden tables and chairs. You can also choose to sit in the well-
kept garden or sunny conservatory. ✉ *179 King St.* ☎ *01556/504552*
═ *MC, V* ☽ *No dinner. Closed Sun.*

SPORTS AND THE OUTDOORS

BICYCLING You can rent bicycles from **Castle Douglas Cycle Centre** (✉ *Church St.*
☎ *01556/504542*).

BOATING The **Galloway Sailing Centre** (✉ *Loch Ken* ☎ *01644/420626*) rents din-
ghies, kayaks, and canoes. It also offers sailing, windsurfing, canoeing,
mountain biking, archery, and rock-climbing courses.

SHOPPING

It's well worth the short drive north from Castle Douglas (A75 then
B794) to visit **Benny Gillies Books, Maps, and Prints** (✉ *31–33 Victoria St.,*
Kirkpatrick Durham ☎ *01556/650412*). The shop has an outstanding
selection of secondhand and antiquarian Scottish books, hand-color
antique maps, and prints depicting areas throughout Scotland.

Galloway Gems (✉ *130–132 King St.* ☎ *01556/503254*) sells mineral
specimens, polished stone slices, and a range of Celtic- and Nordic-
inspired jewelry. The **Posthorn** (✉ *26–30 St. Andrew St.* ☎ *01556/502531*)
is renowned for its display of figurines by Border Fine Art as well as
Scotland's biggest display of Moorcroft glazed and enamel pottery.

KIRKCUDBRIGHT

9 mi southwest of Castle Douglas, 89 mi south of Glasgow, 99 mi
southwest of Edinburgh.

Kirkcudbright (pronounced kirk-*coo*-bray) is an 18th-century town of
Georgian and Victorian houses, some of them washed in pastel shades
and roofed with the blue slates of the district. Since the early 20th century it has been known as a haven for artistic types, and its L-shape
main street is full of crafts and antiques shops.

GETTING HERE AND AROUND

Driving is your best and only real option. From Castle Douglas take the
A711 (15 minutes). From Glasgow, take the A713 (about two hours).
From Edinburgh, take the A701 (about 2½ hours).

ESSENTIALS

Visitor Information Kirkcudbright (✉ *Harbor Sq.* ☎ *01557/330494* ⊕ *www.*
visitdumfriesandgalloway.co.uk).

EXPLORING

The **Tolbooth Arts Centre,** in the old tollbooth (combination town hall/
courthouse/prison), gives a history of the town's artists' colony and
its leaders, E. A. Hornel, Jessie King, and Charles Oppenheimer. Some
of their paintings are on display, as are works by modern artists and

craftspeople. ✉ *High St.* ☎ *01557/ 331556* ⊕ *www.kirkcudbright. co.uk* ✆ *Free* ⊙ *Oct.–May, Mon.– Sat. 11–4; June–Sept., Mon.–Sat. 11–4, Sun. 2–5.*

The 18th-century **Broughton House** was once the home of the artist E. A. Hornel, one of the "Glasgow Boys" of the late 19th century. Many of his paintings hang in the house, which is furnished in period style and contains an extensive library specializing in local history. There's also a Japanese garden. ✉ *12 High St.* ☎ *01557/330437* ⊕ *www.nts. org.uk/Visits* ✆ *£5.50* ⊙ *House Apr.–Oct., daily noon–5; garden Feb. and Mar., weekdays 11–4; Apr.– Oct., daily noon–5.*

> ## GOLF GETAWAYS
>
> There are more than 30 courses in Dumfries and Galloway and 21 in the Borders. The Freedom of the Fairways Pass (five-day pass, £120; three-day pass, £88) allows play on all 21 Borders courses and is available from the Scottish Borders Tourist Board. The Gateway to Golf Pass (six-round pass, £115; three-round pass, £80) is accepted by all clubs in Dumfries and Galloway.

4

Conspicuous in the town center are the stone walls of **MacLellan's Castle**, a once-elaborate castellated mansion dating from the 16th century. You can walk around the interior, though the rooms are bare. There are lovely views over the town from the windows. ✉ *Off High St.* ☎ *01557/331856* ⊕ *www.historic-scotland.gov.uk* ✆ *£3.70* ⊙ *Apr.– Sept., daily 9:30–5:30.*

Stuffed with all manner of local paraphernalia, the delightfully old-fashioned **Stewartry Museum** allows you to putter and absorb as much or as little as takes your interest in the display cases. ✉ *St. Mary St.* ☎ *01557/331643* ✆ *Free* ⊙ *May, June, and Sept., Mon.–Sat. 11–5, Sun. 2–5; July and Aug., Mon.–Sat. 10–5, Sun. 2–5; Oct., Mon.–Sat. 11–4, Sun. 2–5; Nov.–Apr., Mon.–Sat. 11–4.*

WHERE TO EAT AND STAY

£££ ✕ **Artistas.** Paintings of Scotland, starched white tablecloths, and giant
BRITISH windows overlooking the well-kept garden beckon you into this highly praised eatery. Locals love it here, as they should; the food is locally sourced and full of imagination. You can choose from two courses for £21 or three courses for £26. In season, try the glove artichoke and asparagus salad, then the braised fillet of turbot over saffron-and-shrimp quinoa. The "posh" fish-and-chips is one of the best around. For a less expensive, more casual dining experience try the hotel's bistro: its à la cart menu is just as imaginative and delicious. ✉ *Selkirk Arms Hotel, High St.* ☎ *01557/330402* ▭ *AE, MC, V.*

££ 🛏 **Selkirk Arms.** Newly renovated and bursting with charm, this elegant 18th-century hotel has a lot going for it. Spacious rooms are decorated in cream and brown, with new beds, contemporary wood furniture, and soft lighting. The welcoming lobby, gracious staff, and first-class in-house restaurant make this hotel a destination in itself. **Pros:** attentive service; massive breakfast; lively traditional pub. **Cons:** rooms closest to bistro-restaurant-bar area get some noise; bar can get crowded during televised sporting events. ✉ *High St.* ☎ *01557/330402* ⊕ *www.*

selkirkarmshotel.co.uk ⌐⊐ *16 rooms* & *In-room: no a/c, Wi-Fi. In-hotel: 2 restaurants, room service, bar, Wi-Fi hotspot, some pets allowed* ▭ *AE, MC, V* ¦◎¦ *BP.*

NEWTON STEWART

18 mi northwest of Kirkudbright, 77 mi southwest of Glasgow, 105 mi southwest of Edinburgh.

The bustling town of Newton Stewart is a good place to stop in when touring the western region of Galloway.

GETTING HERE AND AROUND

Newton Stewart does not have a train station, but the town is served by regular buses from Glasgow and Edinburgh as well as local buses from neighboring towns. From Glasgow, take the A77 (about 2 hours). From Edinburgh, take the A702 (about 2 hours and 45 minutes).

ESSENTIALS

Visitor Information Newton Stewart (✉ *Dashwood Sq.* ☎ *01671/402431* ⊕ *www.newtonstewart.org*).

EXPLORING

The A712 heading northeast from town takes you to the **Galloway Forest Park,** where you can walk or bicycle along the paths. At the Clatteringshaws Visitor Centre there are exhibits about the region's wildlife and a reconstruction of an Iron Age dwelling. ✉ *A712, 7 mi northeast of Newton Stewart* ☎ *01644/420285* ⊕ *www.forestry.gov.uk/gallowayforestpark* ⌐ *Free* ⊙ *May–Sept., daily 10:30–5:30; Oct.–Apr., daily 10:30–4:30.*

Birders will love the **Wood of Cree Nature Reserve,** owned and managed by the Royal Society for the Protection of Birds. In the reserve you can see such species as the redstart, pied flycatcher, and wood warbler. To get there, take the minor road that travels north from Newton Stewart alongside the River Cree east of the A714. The entrance is next to a small parking area at the side of the road. ✉ *4 mi north of Newton Stewart* ☎ *01556/670464* ⊕ *www.rspb.org.uk* ⌐ *Donations accepted* ⊙ *Daily 24 hrs.*

The **Creetown Gem Rock Museum,** in the nearby village of Creetown, has an eclectic mineral collection, a dinosaur egg, an erupting volcano, and a crystal cave. There's also an Internet café, a tearoom, and a shop selling stones and crystals—both loose and in settings. ✉ *Chain Rd., off A75, Creetown* ☎ *01671/820357* ⊕ *www.gemrock.net* ⌐ *£3.75* ⊙ *Easter–Sept., daily 9:30–5:30; Sept.–Easter, daily 10–4; last admission ½ hr before closing.*

The **Machars** is the name given to the triangular promontory south of Newton Stewart. This is an area of pretty rolling farmlands, yellow-gorse hedgerows, rich grazing for dairy cattle, and stony prehistoric sites. Most of the glossy, green expanse is used for dairy farming. Fields are bordered by dry *stane dykes* (walls) of sharp-edge stones, and small hills and hummocks give the area its characteristic frozen-wave look, a reminder of the glacial activity that shaped the landscape.

GLEN TROOL

9 mi north of Newton Stewart, 86 mi southwest of Glasgow, 113 mi southwest of Edinburgh.

GETTING HERE AND AROUND

Driving is really the only way to get to Glen Trool. From Newton Stewart, take the A714 (about 15 minutes). From Glasgow, take the A77 (about 2 hours and 15 minutes). From Edinburgh, take the A702 (about three hours).

EXPLORING

★ **Glen Trool,** part of Galloway's Forest Park, is one of Scotland's best-kept secrets. With high purple-and-green hilltops shorn rock-bare by glaciers, and with a dark, winding loch and thickets of birch trees sounding with birdcalls, the setting almost looks more highland than the real Highlands. Note **Bruce's Stone,** just above the parking lot, marking the site where in 1307 Scotland's champion Robert the Bruce (King Robert I, 1274–1329) won his first victory in the Scottish Wars of Independence. To get here, follow the A714 north and turn right at the signpost for Glen Trool. This road leads you toward the hills that have thus far been the backdrop for the woodlands. Watch for another sign for Glen Trool. Follow this little road through increasingly wild woodland scenery to its terminus at a parking lot. Only after you have left the car and climbed for a few minutes onto a heathery knoll does the full, rugged panorama become apparent. ⊠ *Bargrennan* ☎ *01671/840302* ⊕ *www.forestry.gov. uk* ⊠ *Free* ⊙ *Visitor center Mar.–June, Sept.–Nov. 10:30–4:30; July and Aug. 10:30–5:30.*

WIGTOWN

7 mi south of Newton Stewart, 84 mi southwest of Glasgow, 111 mi southwest of Edinburgh.

More than 20 bookshops, mostly antiquarian and secondhand stores, have sprung up on the brightly painted main street of Wigtown, voted Scotland's national book town.

GETTING HERE AND AROUND

There is no train station in Wigtown, and you must make several transfers when traveling by bus to and from Scotland's larger cities. Driving is your best option. Take the A714 from Newton Stewart (15 minutes). From Glasgow, take the A77 (about two hours). From Edinburgh, take the A702 (about three hours).

EXPLORING

The 10-day **Wigtown Book Festival** (☎ *01988/402036* ⊕ *www.wigtown-booktown.co.uk*), held in late September and early October, has readings, performances, and other events around town.

The **Bookshop** (⊠ *17 N. Main St.* ☎ *01988/402499*), one of the country's largest secondhand bookstores, offers temptingly full shelves.

Wigtown's **Bladnoch Distillery** is Scotland's southernmost malt-whisky producer. It has a visitor center and a gift shop, and tours are available. Tours are given on the hour between 10 and 4. ⊠ *Wigtown* ☎ *01988/*

402605 or 01988/402235 ⊕ www.bladnoch.co.uk ✉ Distillery free, tours £3 ☉ Easter–June, Sept., and Oct., weekdays 9–5; July and Aug., weekdays 9–5, Sat. 11–5, Sun. noon–5.

WHITHORN

11 mi south of Wigtown, 94 mi southwest of Glasgow, 121 mi southwest of Edinburgh.

Whithorn is a tremendously historic town. The main street is notably wide, with cute pastel buildings nestled up against each other, their low doorways and small windows create images of years long past. It remains mainly a farming community, but is fast becoming a popular tourist destination. Its claim to fame is that several scenes from the original *Wicker Man* were shot in and around the area. During the summer months, it's a popular place for festivals.

GETTING HERE AND AROUND

There's no train station in Whithorn, and most of the buses are local (getting to main Scottish cities from Whithorn takes careful planning and several transfers). To drive from Wigtown, take the A746 (about 20 minutes). From Glasgow, take the A77 (about 2½ hours). From Edinburgh, take the A702 (about three hours).

EXPLORING

The road that is now the A746 was a pilgrims' path that led to the royal burgh of Whithorn, where sat **Whithorn Priory,** one of Scotland's great medieval cathedrals, now an empty shell. It was built in the 12th century and is said to occupy the site of a former stone church, the Candida Casa, built by St. Ninian in the 4th century. As the story goes, the church housed a shrine to Ninian, the earliest of Scotland's saints, and kings and barons sought to visit the shrine at least once in their lives. As you approach the priory, observe the royal arms of pre-1707 Scotland—that is, Scotland before the Union with England—carved and painted above the *pend* (covered walkway).

The **Whithorn Story and Visitor Centre** explains the significance of what is claimed to be the site of the earliest Christian community in Scotland. A museum has a collection of early Christian crosses. ⊠ 45–47 George St. ☎ 01988/500508 ⊕ www.whithorn.com ✉ £4.50 ☉ Apr.–Oct., daily 10:30–5; last tour at 4.

In the Isle of Whithorn (a small seaport, not an island) are the ruins of **St. Ninian's Chapel,** where pilgrims who came by sea prayed before traveling inland to Whithorn Priory. Some people claim that this, and not Whithorn Priory, is the site of the Candida Casa.

STRANRAER

31 mi northwest of Whithorn, 86 mi southwest of Glasgow via A77, 131 mi southwest of Edinburgh.

Stranraer has a lovely garden and is also the main ferry port to Northern Ireland—if you happen to make a purchase in one of its shops, you may wind up with some euro coins from Ireland in your change.

GETTING HERE AND AROUND

Stranraer has a busy train station that serves all major lines, and the buses are good as well (with many connections to smaller towns). If you're driving, take the A747 from Whithorn (about 45 minutes). From Glasgow, take the M77/A77 (two hours), and from Edinburgh, take the A77 (three hours).

ESSENTIALS

Visitor Information Stranraer (✉ *28 Harbour St.* ☎ *01776/702595* ⊕ *www. dumfriesandgalloway.co.uk.*

EXPLORING

★ The lovely **Castle Kennedy Gardens** surround the shell of the original Castle Kennedy, which was burned in 1716. The current 14th Earl of Stair lives on the grounds in Lochinch Castle, built in 1864 (not open to the public). Parks scattered

> **FISH TALES**
>
> The Solway Firth is noted for sea fishing, particularly at the Isle of Whithorn, Port William, Portpatrick, and Stranraer. The wide range of game-fishing opportunities extends from the expensive salmon beats of the River Tweed—sometimes known by its nickname, the Queen of Scottish Rivers—to undiscovered hill *lochans* (small lakes). You must have a fishing permit, available at tourist offices, tackle shops, newsstands, and post offices; and you should obtain permission from a landowner to fish on private property. Many hotels offer on-property fishing, or transportation and equipment so you can fish nearby.

around the property were built by the second Earl of Stair in 1733. The earl was a field marshal and used his soldiers to help with the heavy work of constructing banks, ponds, and other major landscape features. When the rhododendrons are in bloom, the effect is kaleidoscopic. There's also a pleasant tearoom. ✉ *North of A75, 3 mi east of Stranraer* ☎ *01776/702024* ⊕ *www.castlekennedygardens.co.uk* 🎫 *£4* 🕐 *Easter–Sept., daily 10–5.*

PORTPATRICK

8 mi southwest of Stranraer, 94 mi southwest of Glasgow, 139 mi southwest of Edinburgh.

The holiday town of Portpatrick lies across the Rhinns of Galloway from Stranraer. Once an Irish ferry port, Portpatrick's harbor eventually proved too small for larger vessels.

GETTING HERE AND AROUND

Direct buses travel between Portpartick to Stranraer and some of the neighboring towns, but travel to and from the larger Scottish cities can prove more difficult. There is no train station in Portpatrick (though there is one in Stranraer). Driving is probably your best bet. From Stranraer, take the A77; it's about a 15-minute journey. Take the M77/A77 from Glasgow (just over two hours) and the M8/A77 from Edinburgh (about three hours).

EXPLORING

Today the village is the starting point for Scotland's longest official long-distance footpath, the **Southern Upland Way,** which runs a switchback course for 212 mi to Cockburnspath, on the east side of the Borders.

The path begins on the cliffs just north of the town and follows the coastline for 1½ mi before turning inland.

Just south of Portpatrick are the lichen-yellow ruins of 16th-century **Dunskey Castle,** accessible from a cliff-top path off the B7042.

★ The spectacular **Logan Botanic Gardens,** one of the National Botanic Gardens of Scotland, are a must-see for garden lovers. Displayed here are plants that enjoy the prevailing mild climate, especially tree ferns, cabbage palms, and other Southern Hemisphere exotica. There are free guided walks every second Tuesday of the month at 10:30 AM. ✉ *Off B7065 at Port Logan* ☎ *01776/860231* 🖃 *£4* ☉ *Mar. and Oct., daily 10–5; Apr.–Sept., daily 10–6.*

If you wish to visit the southern tip of the Rhinns of Galloway, called the **Mull of Galloway,** follow the B7065/B7041 until you run out of land. The cliffs and seascapes here are rugged, and there's a lighthouse and a bird reserve.

Fife and Angus

WORD OF MOUTH

"You'll love Fife no matter what the weather. Much more to see and do than possible in your short stay, including St. Andrews Castle, St. Andrews Cathedral, Falkland Palace, Hill of Tarvit House, all the fishing villages, and great seafood."

—janisj

"In St. Andrews, I recommend staying in town if you are at all interested in the golf. There is quite a buzzing atmosphere, and St. Andrews has a brilliant seaside location and offers good access to nearby villages and even Edinburgh, at least if you have a car. You may want to book restaurant reservations well ahead. Almost all establishments that looked nice were completely booked."

—HSV

Updated by
Shona Main

Breezy cliff-top walkways, fishing villages, and open beaches characterize Fife and Angus. They sandwich Scotland's fourth-largest—and often overlooked—city, Dundee. Scotland's east coast has only light rainfall throughout the year; northeastern Fife, in particular, may claim the record for the most sunshine and the least rainfall in Scotland, which all adds to the enjoyment when you're touring the coast or the famous golf center of St. Andrews.

Fife proudly styles itself as a "kingdom," and its long history—which really began when the Romans went home in the 4th century and the Picts moved in—lends some substance to the boast. From medieval times its earls were first among Scotland's nobility and crowned her kings. For many, however, the most historic event in the region was the birth of golf, in the 15th century, which, legend has it, occurred in St. Andrews, an ancient university town with stone houses and seaside ruins. The Royal & Ancient Golf Club, the ruling body of the game worldwide, still has its headquarters here.

Not surprisingly, fishing and seafaring have also played a role in the history of the East Neuk coastal region. From the 16th through the 19th centuries, a large population lived and worked in the small ports and harbors that form a continuous chain around Fife's coast, which James V once called "a beggar's mantle fringed with gold." This golden fringe—today a series of waterfront villages darkened by the shrubbery of masts and rigging—is not all that golden in terms of sand or sunshine. The outlook of black rocks and seaweed may seem rather dreary to some, but the house in the villages have character, with brownstone or color-washed fronts, rusty charm, fishy weather vanes, outdoor stone stairways to upper floors, and crude carvings of anchors and lobsters on their lintels. All of the houses are crowded on steep *wynds* (narrow streets), hugging pint-size harbors that in the golden era supported village fleets of 100 ships apiece.

North, across the Firth of Tay, lies the region of Angus, whose charm is its variety: in addition to its seacoast and pleasant Lowland market centers, there's also a hinterland of lonely rounded hills with long glens running into the typical Grampian Highland scenery beyond. One of Angus's interesting features, which it shares with the eastern Lowland edge of Perthshire, is its fruit-growing industry, which includes raspberries. The chief fruit-growing area is Strathmore, the broad vale between the northwesterly Grampian Mountains and the small coastal hills of the Sidlaws behind Dundee. Striking out from this valley, you can make a number of day trips to uplands or seacoast.

TOP REASONS TO GO

Seeing St. Andrews: With its medieval streets, ruined cathedral and castle, and peculiarly posh atmosphere, St. Andrews is one of the most incongruous yet beguiling places in Scotland—even without its famous golf course.

Hitting the links: If you can't get on the Old Course in St. Andrews by ballot or by any other means, Fife and Angus have fabulous fairways aplenty, including the famous links course at Carnoustie (⇨ *see Chapter 12 for the best courses*).

Exploring East Neuk: As you take in crowstep-gabled fisherman's cottages, winding cobbled lanes, seaside harbor scenes, and lovely beaches, you can almost imagine

the harsh lives of the hard-working Fifers who lived in tiny hamlets such as Crail and Anstruther. Today artists and visitors make it all pleasantly picturesque.

Discovering Dundee: This formerly industrial city is becoming better known for its vibrant arts, music, theater, restaurant, and nightlife scenes. It's in a spectacular natural setting by Britain's most powerful river, the Tay.

Yen for the glens: The long Angus glens such as Glen Clova that run into the wild Grampian Mountains are magical places beloved of outdoors enthusiasts and those just wanting to rediscover nature.

ORIENTATION AND PLANNING

GETTING ORIENTED

Fife lies north of the Lothians, across the iconic bridges of the Firth of Forth. A headland, Fife's northeastern coast (or East Neuk) is fringed with golden sands, rocky shores, fishermen's cottages and, of course, the splendor of St. Andrews, home of golf. Northwest of Fife and across the glorious Firth of Tay, the city of Dundee is undergoing a post-industrial reinvention. Its rural hinterland, Angus, hugs the city which, stretching north toward the foothills of the Grampian Mountains, houses agricultural and fishing communities, and Glamis, one of Scotland's best-loved castles.

St. Andrews and Fife's East Neuk Villages. St. Andrews isn't just a playground for golfers. This religious and academic center is steeped in history and prestige, with grand buildings and a palpable air of prosperity. Beyond St. Andrews, the colorful fishing villages of the East Neuk are a day-tripper's (and fish eater's) delight.

Dundee and Angus. Dundee has a knockout setting beside Britain's mightiest river, historical sights—including Captain Scott's ship, RRS *Discovery*—and a vibrant social life. The tree-lined country roads of the Angus heartlands roll through strawberry- and raspberry fields, to busy market towns, wee villages, and Glamis Castle.

PLANNING

WHEN TO GO

Spring in the Angus glens can be quite captivating, with the hills along Angus' northernmost boundary still covered in snow. Similarly the moorland colors of autumn are appealing. However, Fife and Angus are really spring and summer destinations, when most of the sights are open to visitors. St. Andrews hosts a number of international golf tournaments that effectively take over the town. Non-duffers may become incredibly frustrated when searching for accommodations or places to eat during these times, so check ahead.

PLANNING YOUR TIME

St. Andrews, 52 mi from Edinburgh, is not to be missed, for its history and atmosphere as much as for the golf; allot an overnight stop and at least a whole day if you can. The nearby East Neuk of Fife has some of Scotland's finest coastline, now becoming gentrified by the Edinburgh second-home set but still evoking Fife's past. A day's drive along A917 (allow for exploring and stops for ice cream and fish) will take you through the fishing villages of Pittenweem, Anstruther, and Crail. Dundee, with a rich maritime history, is less visited but can be an ideal base for a drive round the Angus towns of Arbroath, Kirriemuir, and Alyth; if you make a three-hour stop at Glamis Castle, this trip will take about a day.

GETTING HERE AND AROUND

AIR TRAVEL

Dundee Airport is off A85, 2 mi west of the city center. Air France (⊕ *www.airfrance.com*) operates a popular direct flight from London City Airport. Flybe (⊕ *www.flybe.com*) flies here from Birmingham and Belfast.

BUS TRAVEL

Buses connect Edinburgh's St. Andrew Square bus station and Glasgow's Buchanan Street bus station to Fife and Angus. Scottish Citylink operates hourly service to Dundee from both Glasgow and Edinburgh. Stagecoach Fife serves Fife and St. Andrews, and Travel Dundee provides bus service in and around Dundee.

Stagecoach connects St. Andrews and Dundee to many of the smaller towns throughout Fife and Angus. A Day Rover ticket (£11.50 for Fife, Dundee, and Angus; £6.50 for Fife only) is a good value. However, a Super Dayrider ticket costs £10 and covers Fife and Angus, and will even take you as far as Edinburgh and Glasgow.

Traveline Scotland is a service that helps you plan all public transport journeys.

Bus Contacts Scottish Citylink (☎ *08705/505050* ⊕ *www.citylink.co.uk*). **Stagecoach Fife** (☎ *0871/2002233* ⊕ *www.stagecoachbus.com*). **Travel Dundee** (☎ *08706/082608* ⊕ *www.traveldundee.co.uk*). **Traveline Scotland** (☎ *08706/082608* ⊕ *www.travelinescotland.com*).

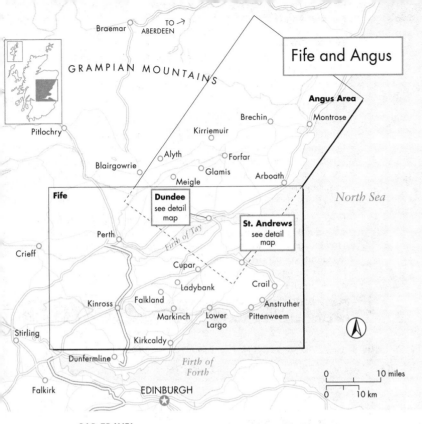

CAR TRAVEL

The fastest route to Angus and northeast Fife is the M90 motorway from Edinburgh. Exit onto the A90 at Perth (45 minutes), and travel an additional 20 minutes to reach Dundee; 15 minutes later, you'll arrive in St. Andrews. If you're coming from Fife, you can also take the A91 and the A914, and cross the Tay Bridge to reach Dundee. This is a slower route, but does take you through the heartland of Fife.

Fife and Angus cover a compact area, so getting around is straight-forward. You can visit everything via a series of excursions off the main north–south artery, the A90/M90, which leads from Edinburgh to Aberdeen. From here you can easily make day trips to Edinburgh, Glasgow, or Perthshire. Aberdeenshire and the Central Highlands are not too far away either.

Fife is easy to navigate—although it can be difficult to find a place to park in St. Andrews. The most interesting sights are in the east, which is served by a network of cross-country roads. Angus is also an easy region to explore. It's serviced by a fast main road (the A90), a gentler road (the A92), and several rural roads that run between the Grampians and the A90.

TRAIN TRAVEL

ScotRail stops at Kirkcaldy, Cupar, Leuchars (for St. Andrews), Dundee, Arbroath, and Montrose.

Train Contacts ScotRail (☎ 08457/550033 ⊕ www.scotrail.co.uk).

RESTAURANTS

With an affluent population, St. Andrews supports several stylish hotel restaurants. Because it's a university town and popular tourist destination, there are also many good cafés and bistro-style restaurants. Bar lunches are the rule in large and small hotels throughout the region, and in seaside places the carry-*oot* (to-go) meal of fish-and-chips is an enduring tradition.

HOTELS

If you're staying in Fife, the obvious choice for a base is St. Andrews, with ample accommodations of all kinds. Another good option is the Howe of Fife, between Strathmiglo and Cupar, where there are some excellent country-house hotels, many with their own restaurants. Dundee and its hinterlands have a number of diverse accommodations, all of which offer good value.

WHAT IT COSTS IN POUNDS					
	£	££	£££	££££	£££££
RESTAURANTS	under £10	£10–£14	£15–£19	£20–£25	over £25
HOTELS	under £70	£70–£120	£121–£160	£161–£220	over £220

Restaurant prices are for a main course at dinner. Hotel prices are for two people in a standard double room in high season, generally including the 17.5% V.A.T.

VISITOR INFORMATION

The Arbroath, Dundee, and St. Andrews tourist offices are open year-round. Smaller tourist information centers operate seasonally in Anstruther, Brechin, Crail, Forfar, Kirriemuir, and Montrose.

ST. ANDREWS AND FIFE'S EAST NEUK VILLAGES

In its western parts Fife still bears the scars of heavy industry, especially coal mining, but these signs are less evident as you move east. Northeastern Fife, around the town of St. Andrews, seems to have played no part in the Industrial Revolution; instead, its residents earned a living from the grain fields or from the sea. Fishing has been a major industry, and in the past a string of Fife ports traded across the North Sea. Today the legacy of Dutch-influenced architecture—crowstep gables (the stepped effect on the ends of the roofs) and distinctive town houses—gives these East Neuk villages a distinctive character.

St. Andrews is unlike any other Scottish town. Once Scotland's most powerful ecclesiastical center as well as the seat of the country's oldest university and then, much later, the very symbol and spiritual home

SIGHTSEEING TOURS

Travel Greyhound runs several general orientation bus tours of the main cities and the region from late July to early August. Fishers Tours has bus tours year-round both within and outside the region. Lochs and Glens operates bus tours of Scotland year-round.

Heritage Golf Tours Scotland specializes in golf vacations that include hotel and car rental and course reservations. Links Golf St. Andrews tailors tours to individual requirements.

Bus Tours Fishers Tours (⊠ 16 W. Port, Dundee ☎ 01382/227290 ⊕ www.fisherstours.co.uk). **Lochs and Glens** (⊠ Gartocharn, West Dunbartonshire ☎ 01389/713713 ⊕ www.lochsandglens.com). **Travel Greyhound** (Travel Dundee ⊠ 92 Commercial St., Dundee ☎ 01382/340006).

Golf Tours Heritage Golf Tours Scotland (⊠ Swilken House, 21 Loch Dr., Helensburgh ☎ 01436/674630 ⊕ www.golftours-scotland. co.uk). Links Golf St. Andrews (⊠ 7 Pilmour Links, St. Andrews ☎ 01334/478639 ⊕ www.linksgolf-standrews.com).

of golf, the town has a comfortable, well-groomed air, sitting almost smugly apart from the rest of Scotland.

ST. ANDREWS

52 mi northeast of Edinburgh, 83 mi northeast of Glasgow.

It may have a ruined cathedral and a grand university—the oldest in Scotland—but the modern claim to fame for St. Andrews is mainly its status as the home of golf. Forget that Scottish kings were crowned here, or that John Knox preached here, or that Reformation reformers were burned at the stake here. Thousands flock to St. Andrews to play at the Old Course, home of the Royal & Ancient Club, and to follow in the footsteps of Hagen, Sarazen, Jones, and Hogan.

The layout is pure Middle Ages: its three main streets—North, Market, and South—converge on the city's earliest religious site, near the cathedral. Like most of the ancient monuments, the cathedral ruins are impressive in their desolation—but this town is no dusty museum. The streets are busy, the shops are stylish, the gray houses sparkle in the sun, and the scene is particularly brightened during the academic year by bicycling students in scarlet gowns.

GETTING HERE AND AROUND

If you arrive by car, be prepared for an endless drive round the town as you look for a parking space. The parking lots around Rose Park (behind the bus station and a short walk from the town center) are your best bet. If you arrive by local or national bus, the bus station is a five-minute walk from into town. The nearest train station, Leuchars, is 10 minutes away by taxi (£10) or the same by bus (£2), both of which can be found outside the station. St. Andrews can be fully enjoyed on foot without too much exertion.

ESSENTIALS

Visitor Information St. Andrews (✉ *70 Market St.* ☎ *01334/472021* ⊕ *www. visitfife.com*).

EXPLORING

TOP ATTRACTIONS

⑤ British Golf Museum. This museum explores the centuries-old relationship between St. Andrews and golf and displays golf memorabilia from the 18th century to the 21st century. It's just opposite the Royal & Ancient Golf Club. ✉ *Bruce Embankment* ☎ *01334/460046* ⊕ *www. britishgolfmuseum.co.uk* 🎟 *£5.25* ⊙ *Apr.–Oct., Mon.–Sat. 9:30–5, Sun. 10–5; Nov.–Mar., Mon.–Sun. 10–4.*

③ St. Andrews Castle. On the shore north of the cathedral stands ruined St. Andrews Castle, begun at the end of the 13th century. The remains include a rare example of a cold and gruesome bottle-shape dungeon, in which many prisoners spent their last hours. Even more atmospheric is the castle's mine and countermine. The former was a tunnel dug by besieging forces in the 16th century; the latter, a tunnel dug by castle defenders in order to meet and wage battle below ground. You can stoop and crawl into this narrow passageway—an eerie experience, despite the addition of electric light. The visitor center has a good audiovisual presentation on the castle's history. ✉ *N. Castle St.* ☎ *01334/477196* ⊕ *www.historic-scotland.gov.uk* 🎟 *£5.20, with St. Rule's Tower and St. Andrews Cathedral £7.20* ⊙ *Apr.–Sept., daily 9:30–5:30; Oct.–Mar., daily 9:30–4.*

② St. Andrews Cathedral. Near St. Rule's Tower, St. Andrews Cathedral is a ruined, poignant fragment of what was once the largest and most magnificent church in Scotland. Work on it began in 1160, and after several delays it was finally consecrated in 1318. The church was subsequently damaged by fire and repaired, but fell into decay during the Reformation. Only ruined gables, parts of the nave's south wall, and other fragments survive. The on-site museum helps you interpret the remains and gives a sense of what the cathedral must once have been like. ✉ *Off Pends Rd.* ☎ *01334/472563* ⊕ *www.historic-scotland.gov.uk* 🎟 *£4.20, with St. Rule's Tower and St. Andrews Castle £7.20* ⊙ *Apr.–Sept., daily 9:30–5:30; Oct.–Mar., daily 9:30–4:30.*

① St. Rule's Tower. Local legend has it that St. Andrews was founded by one St. Regulus, or Rule, who, acting under divine guidance, carried relics of St. Andrew by sea from Patras in Greece. He was shipwrecked on this Fife headland and founded a church. The holy man's name survives in the cylindrical tower, consecrated in 1126 and the oldest surviving building in St. Andrews. You can enjoy dizzying views of town from the top of the tower, reached via a steep stairs. ✉ *Off Pends Rd.* ☎ *01334/477196* ⊕ *www.historic-scotland.gov.uk* 🎟 *£4.20, with St. Andrews Cathedral and St. Andrews Castle £7.20* ⊙ *Apr.–Sept., daily 9:30–5:30; Oct.–Mar., daily 9:30–4:30.*

WORTH NOTING

OFF THE
BEATEN
PATH

Leuchars. This small town has a 12th-century church with some of the finest Norman architectural features to be seen anywhere in Scotland. On the second Saturday of September, the Royal Air Force stages the **Leuchars Air Show** with dramatic performances by historic aircraft

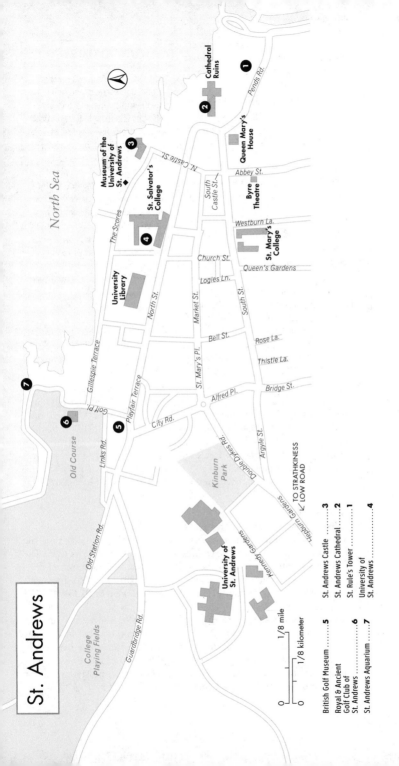

St. Andrews

North Sea

Cathedral Ruins ❶

❷

Pends Rd.

Museum of the University of St. Andrews ◆ ❸

St. Salvator's College

N. Castle St.

Queen Mary's House

South Castle St.

Abbey St.

Byre Theatre

The Scores

❹

Westburn La.

St. Mary's College

Church St.

Queen's Gardens

University Library

Logies Ln.

North St.

Market St.

South St.

Bell St.

Rose La.

Gillespie Terrace

St. Mary's Pl.

Thistle La.

❼

Golf Pl.

Playfair Terrace

Alfred Pl.

Bridge St.

❻

Links Rd.

❺

City Rd.

Argyle St.

Old Course

Kinburn Park

Double Dykes Rd.

Nelson Gardens

← TO STRATHKINESS / LOW ROAD

Old Station Rd.

University of St. Andrews

Kennedy Gardens

College Playing Fields

Guardbridge Rd.

0   1/8 mile

0   1/8 kilometer

British Golf Museum **5**

Royal & Ancient Golf Club of St. Andrews **6**

St. Andrews Aquarium **7**

St. Andrews Castle **3**

St. Andrews Cathedral **2**

St. Rule's Tower **1**

University of St. Andrews **4**

and their contemporary counterparts. ✉ *A919, 5 mi northwest of St. Andrews* ☎ *08700/130877* ⊕ *www.airshow.co.uk.*

⑥ Royal & Ancient Golf Club of St. Andrews. The ruling house of golf worldwide is the spiritual home of all who play or follow the game. Founded in 1754, its clubhouse on the dunes—open to members only, who must be male—is a mix of classical, Victorian, and neoclassical styles; it's adjacent to the famous Old Course. ✉ *The Scores, West Sands* ☎ *01334/460000* ⊕ *www. randa.org.*

⑦ St. Andrews Aquarium. This modest
☺ aquarium is run by real enthusiasts whose passion for all things oceanic is infectious. Seals, fish, crustaceans, and many other forms of marine life inhabit aquariums and pool gardens designed to simulate their natural habitats. The seals are fed at midday and 3 PM. ✉ *The Scores, West Sands* ☎ *01334/474786* ⊕ *www.standrewsaquarium.co.uk* 🎫 *£7.10* ☉ *Easter–Oct., daily 10–5:30; Nov.–Easter, hrs vary.*

> **A SWING HISTORY**
>
> The town of St. Andrews prospers on golf, golf schools, and golf equipment (the manufacture of golf balls is a local industry). Locals say that the game was first played with a piece of driftwood, a shore pebble, and a rabbit hole on the sandy, coastal turf. Residents of St. Andrews were playing golf on the town links as far back as the 15th century. Rich golfers eventually formed exclusive clubs. The world's first golf club was probably the Honourable Company of Edinburgh Golfers, founded in 1744. The Royal & Ancient Golf Club of St. Andrews was founded in 1754.

④ University of St. Andrews. St. Andrews is the site of Scotland's oldest university, and *alma mater* of John Knox (Protestant reformer), King James II of Scotland, Prince William, Scotland's First Minister Alex Salmond, and Chris Hoy, Scotland's Olympic cyclist. Founded in 1411, the university's buildings and residences pepper the town. The new **Museum of the University of St. Andrews** tells the history of this grand institution to the present day. ✉ *7a The Scores, West Sands* ☎ *01334/461660* ⊕ *www.st-andrews.ac.uk/musa* 🎫 *Free* ☉ *Apr.–Sept., Mon.–Sat. 10–5, Sun. noon–4; Oct.–Mar., Thurs.–Sun. noon–4.*

WHERE TO EAT

£££££
SEAFOOD
★
✗ **The Seafood Restaurant.** This glass-walled building is perched on the banks of the West Sands. Formerly the site of an open-air theater, the kitchen, visible to all diners, creates a sense of drama all its own. The food is adventurous without being flashy: start with lemon and coriander Pittenweem crab, then move on to the pan-seared scallops with beetroot and pancetta risotto. ✉ *Bruce Embankment* ☎ *01334/479475* ▭ *AE, MC, V.*

£
ECLECTIC
✗ **West Port Bar & Kitchen.** It's easy to forget that St. Andrews is a university town when the students are on summer break, but this modern bar and eatery remains vibrant and youthful year-round. The reasonably priced menu offers nicely prepared pub grub—everything from gourmet burgers to stuffed roasted aubergines—making this a satisfying stop for lunch or dinner. ✉ *170 South St.* ☎ *01334/473186* ▭ *AE, MC, V.*

WHERE TO STAY

££ 🖳 **Aslar Guest House.** This terraced town house dating from 1865 has large rooms with ornate cornicing and antique reproduction furniture. One room has a four-poster bed, another has a fireplace. St. Andrews's historic center is within walking distance. **Pros:** homey feel; good breakfast. **Cons:** slightly cluttered feel; books up quickly. ✉ *120 North St.KY16 9AF* ☎ *01334/473460* ⊕ *www.aslar.com* 🛏 *6 rooms* ⚅ *In-room: no a/c, no phone, DVD, Wi-Fi. In-hotel: Wi-Fi hotspot* ⊟ *MC, V* ⦿ *BP.*

££££–£££££ 🖳 **Fairmont St Andrews.** Just 2 mi from St. Andrews, this modern hotel
★ has spectacular views of the bay and superb golf. The rooms eschew swags and frills, opting instead for simple elegance. Look for thoughtful touches like luxurious linens on the beds and heated floors in the ample bathrooms. The restaurants are worth trying: Esperante (££££) offers an inventive menu that draws from the flavors of Tuscany, whereas the more casual Squire (£££) serves Scottish country-style dishes such as rump of lamb with a pea and mint puree. Golfers will find inspiration in the velvety fairways of two cliff-top courses: the Torrance Course, designed by the great Scottish player Sam Torrance, and the Kittock Course. **Pros:** spacious feel; excellent spa; golf at your doorstep. **Cons:** lacks character; paintings made to match the decor. ✉ *St. Andrews BayKY16 8PN* ☎ *01334/837000* ⊕ *www.fairmont.com/standrews* 🛏 *192 rooms, 17 suites* ⚅ *In-room: safe, refrigerator, DVD, Wi-Fi. In-hotel: 3 restaurants, room service, bars, golf courses, pool, gym, spa, laundry service* ⊟ *AE, DC, MC, V* ⦿ *BP.*

£££££ 🖳 **Old Course Hotel.** Taken over by Kohler Hotels in late 2007, the Old Course Hotel (regularly host to international golf stars and jet-setters) is experiencing a bit of renaissance. Many of the bedrooms and public spaces have been overhauled, and service has warmed up a bit. There are multiple dining choices; to work up an appetite, walk along the beach, and then have dinner in the chic Sands restaurant or the Jigger Inn, the hotels' famous pub. **Pros:** fabulous location and lovely views; unpretentious service; golfer's heaven. **Cons:** breakfast is not as lavish as you'd expect; patchy air-conditioning. ✉ *Old Station Rd.* ☎ *01334/474371* ⊕ *www.oldcoursehotel.co.uk* 🛏 *109 rooms, 35 suites* ⚅ *In-room: no a/c, refrigerator. In-hotel: 2 restaurants, bars, pool, gym, spa, laundry service, Wi-Fi hotspot* ⊟ *AE, MC, V* ⦿ *BP.*

£££££ 🖳 **Rufflets Country House Hotel.** Ten acres of formal and informal gardens
★ surround this creeper-covered country house just outside St. Andrews. All the rooms are beautifully decorated and have big, comfortable beds and light, well-designed bathrooms. Dinner is served in the roomy Garden Restaurant (£££££), famous for its use of local produce in memorable Scottish dishes. Try the East Neuk seafood bisque or the Fife lamb. Lighter fare is available at the bar. **Pros:** attractive gardens; cozy drawing room. **Cons:** too far to walk to St. Andrews; guest rooms too fussy for some tastes. ✉ *Strathkinness Low Rd.* ☎ *01334/472594* ⊕ *www. rufflets.co.uk* 🛏 *23 rooms, 4 suites* ⚅ *In-room: no a/c, refrigerator. In-hotel: restaurant, bar, Internet terminal* ⊟ *AE, DC, MC, V* ⦿ *BP.*

5

NIGHTLIFE AND THE ARTS

PUBS   Unlike a lot of local bars, the **Central Bar** (✉ *77 Market St.* ☎ *01334/ 478296*) hasn't gone down the minimalist-decor-and-cocktails road. You'll find a good range of beers (bottled and on tap) and decent pub food, including their sausage of the day.

THEATER   The **Byre Theatre** (✉ *Abbey St.* ☎ *01334/475000* ⊕ *www.byretheatre. com*) commissions and produces new works. Experimental and youth theater, small-scale operatic performances, contemporary dance, and Sunday night jazz (in the foyer) are also on the bill. There's an excellent café-bar and bistro.

GOLF

What serious golfer doesn't dream of playing at world-famous St. Andrews? Seven St. Andrews courses, all part of the St. Andrews Trust, are open to visitors, and more than 40 other courses in the region offer golf by the round or by the day. *For more information on courses in the Fife and Angus area, see Chapter 12.*

For information about availability—there's usually a waiting list, which varies according to the time of year—contact **St. Andrews Links Trust** (✉ *Pilmour House, St. Andrew* ☎ *01334/466666* ⊕ *www.standrews. org.uk*). Greens fees range from £64 to £130 for a round on the Old Course and from £8 to £65 for a round on the five other courses.

Balgove Course. Redesigned and reopened in 1993, Balgove is a beginner-friendly course at which you can turn up and tee off without prior reservation. ⚑ *9 holes, 1,520 yds, par 30* ✉ *£12 for two rounds.*

Castle Course. St. Andrews' newest course, designed by David McLay Kidd, opened in 2008. Located 2 mi from the town center, it hugs the coast and has jaw-dropping views. ⚑ *18 holes, 6,759 yds, par 71* ✉ *£120 per round.*

Eden Course. The inland and aptly named Eden, designed in 1914 by Harry S. Colt, has an easy charm compared to the other St. Andrews Links courses. ⚑ *18 holes, 6,250 yds, par 70* ✉ *£40 per round.*

Jubilee Course. This windswept course, opened in 1897, offers quite a challenge even for experienced golfers. ⚑ *18 holes, 6,742 yds, par 72* ✉ *£65 per round.*

★   **New Course.** Not exactly new—it opened in 1895—the New Course is rather overshadowed by the Old Course, but it has a firm following of golfers who appreciate the loop design. ⚑ *18 holes, 6,625 yds, par 71* ✉ *£65 per round.*

Old Course. Believed to be the oldest golf course in the world, the Old Course was first played in the 15th century. Each year, more than 44,000 rounds are teed off, and no doubt most get stuck in one of its 112 bunkers. A handicap certificate is required. ⚑ *18 holes, 6,721 yds, par 72* ✉ *£130 per round.*

Strathtyrum Course. Those with a high handicap will enjoy a toddle around this course, opened in 1993, without the worry or embarrassment of holding up more experienced golfers. ■ TIP➜ **This course is for novices, rather than serious golfers.** ⚑ *18 holes, 5,620 yds, par 69* ✉ *£25 per round.*

SHOPPING

Artery (⊠ *43 South St.* ☎ *01334/478221*) sells work by local, Scottish, and British artists, including jewelry, ceramics, paintings, and intriguing handmade clocks. **Di Gilpin** (⊠ *Burghers Close, 141 South St.* ☎ *01334/476193*) is a magnet for the knitters in the east coast of Scotland, where the finest wools are sold. The shop also sells fantastic one-off hand-knitted jumpers, cardigans, and accessories. **Mellis** (⊠ *149 South St.* ☎ *01334/471410*) is a cheese-lover's mecca. Look for a soft, crumbly local cheese called Anster.

CRAIL

Fodor'sChoice *10 mi south of St. Andrews.*

★ The oldest and most aristocratic of East Neuk burghs, pretty Crail is where many fish merchants retired and built cottages. The town landmark is a picturesque Dutch-influenced town house, or *tolbooth*, which contains the oldest bell in Fife, cast in Holland in 1520. Crail is an artists' colony but remains a working harbor; take time to walk the streets and beaches and to sample fish by the harbor. ■TIP➔ **As you head into East Neuk from this tiny port, look about for market crosses, merchant houses, and little** *doocots* **(dovecotes, where pigeons were kept)—typical picturesque touches of this region.**

GETTING HERE AND AROUND

Stagecoach bus number 63 operates between Crail and St. Andrews. However, the number 95 is more regular and also takes you to Anstruther, Pittenweem, and Lower Largo. Crail is about 15 minutes from St. Andrews by car via A917.

EXPLORING

The story of this trading and fishing town can be found in the **Crail Museum & Heritage Centre**, entirely run by local volunteers. There is a small Tourist Information Desk within the center. ⊠ *62–64 Marketgate* ☎ *01333/450869* ⊕ *www.crailmuseum.org.uk* ⊡ *Free* ☉ *June–Sept., Mon.–Sat. 10–1 and 2–5, Sun. 2–5.*

ANSTRUTHER

4 mi southwest of Crail.

Anstruther, locally called Ainster, has a lovely waterfront with a few shops brightly festooned with children's pails and shovels, a gesture to summer vacationers.

GETTING HERE AND AROUND

Strgecoach bus number 95 operates between St. Andrews, Crail, Anstruther, Pittenweem, and Lower Largo. Anstruther is 5 to 10 minutes from Crail by car via A917.

ESSENTIALS

Visitor Information Anstruther (⊠ *Scottish Fisheries Museum, Harbour Head* ☎ *01333/311073* ⊕ *www.visitfife.com*).

EXPLORING

★ Facing Anstruther harbor is the **Scottish Fisheries Museum,** in a colorful cluster of buildings, the earliest of which dates from the 16th century. The museum illustrates the life of Scottish fisherfolk through documents, artifacts, model ships, paintings, and displays (complete with the reek of tarred rope and net). There are also floating exhibits at the quayside. VisitFife has a small desk here with visitor information. ⊠ *Harbourhead* ☎ *01333/310628* ⊕ *www.scotfishmuseum.org* ⌨ *£6* ⊙ *Apr.–Sept., Mon.–Sat. 10–5:30, Sun. 11–5; Oct.–Mar., Mon.–Sat. 10–4:30, Sun. noon–4:30; last admission 1 hr before closing.*

NEED A BREAK?
Anstruther Fish Bar and Restaurant (⊠ *42–44 Shore St.* ☎ *01333/310518*) has space to eat, but most people order take-out at this popular fish-and-chip shop. Try Pittenweem-landed prawns in batter or the mackerel (line caught by the owners) for something a little different.

WHERE TO EAT

££££££ ✕ **The Cellar.** Entered through a cobbled courtyard, this unpretentious,
BRITISH old-fashioned restaurant is hugely popular. The low ceiling and exposed beams make for a cozy atmosphere. Specializing in seafood but serving a selection of local beef and lamb as well, the owner and chef, Peter Jukes, serves three-course meals cooked simply in modern Scottish style. The crayfish bisque served with Gruyère is known all over the region, as is the excellent wine list. ⊠ *24 E. Green* ☎ *01333/310378* ▱ *AE, DC, MC, V* ⊙ *Closed Sun. and Mon. Nov.–Easter.*

NIGHTLIFE

The **Dreel Tavern** (⊠ *16 High St.* W ☎ *01333/310727*) is a 16th-century coaching inn famous for its hand-drawn ales.

BICYCLING

The back roads of Fife make pleasant places for biking. You can rent bicycles from **East Neuk Outdoors** (⊠ *Cellardyke Park* ☎ *01333/311929*), which also has equipment for archery, climbing, orienteering, and canoeing.

PITTENWEEM

1½ mi southwest of Anstruther.

Many examples of East Neuk architecture serve as the backdrop for the working harbor at Pittenweem. Look for the crowstep gables, white *harling* (the rough mortar finish on walls), and red pantiles (roof tiles with an S-shape profile). The *weem* part of the town's name comes from the Gaelic *uaime,* meaning cave.

GETTING HERE AND AROUND

Stagecoach bus number 95 operates between St. Andrews, Crail, Anstruther, Pittenweem, and Lower Largo. Pittenweem is about five minutes from Anstruther by car via A917.

EXPLORING

This town's cavern is called **St. Fillan's Cave**, which contains the shrine of St. Fillan, a 6th-century hermit who lived here. It's up a *close* (alleyway) behind the waterfront. If the cave isn't open, ask at the Gingerbread House Café on the High Street. ⊠ *Cove Wynd* 🖃 *£1* ⊘ *Mon.–Sat. 10–5.*

Kellie Castle, dating from the 16th to 17th centuries and restored in Victorian times, stands among the grain fields and woodlands of northeastern Fife. Four acres of pretty gardens surround the castle, which is in the care of the National Trust for Scotland. In summer you can buy berries grown in their walled garden, and baked goods are sold in the tearoom. ⊠ *B9171, 3 mi northwest of Pittenweem* 🕾 *0844/4932184* ⊕ *www.nts.org.uk/Visits* 🖃 *£8.50* ⊘ *Castle Apr.–Oct., Fri.–Tues. 1–5; garden Apr.–Oct., Fri.–Tues. 10–5.*

The Cocoa Tree Shop & Café (⊠ *9 High St.* 🕾 *01333/311495*), open daily, is a former bakery that stocks the most imaginative and comprehensive range of fine chocolates you'll find in this part of the world. There is also a lovely café, with cakes and, of course, handmade chocolates.

There is nothing quite like the **Pittenweem Arts Festival** (🕾 *01333/313903* ⊕ *www.pittenweemartsfestival.co.uk*). Exhibitions, which involve hundreds of artists (local and international), take place in the town's public buildings and local's homes and gardens. It's a week of events, workshops, and live music.

WHERE TO EAT

££££££   ✕ **The Seafood Restaurant.** The big sister of the Seafood Restaurant in
SEAFOOD   St. Andrews (and a few pounds cheaper), this establishment put St. Monans on the culinary map of Scotland. The menu has vegetarian and meat options, but don't come here unless you want something fabulously fishy. Their smoked and kiln-roasted salmon is from St. Monan's smokehouse. ⊠ *16 West End, St. Monans, 2 mi west of Pittenweem* 🕾 *01333/730327* 🖚 *Reservations essential* ⊟ *AE, MC, V* ⊘ *Closed Mon. and Tues.*

FALKLAND

Fodor's Choice   *24 mi northwest of Pittenweem.*

★   One of the loveliest communities in Scotland, Falkland is a royal burgh of twisting streets and crooked stone houses.

GETTING HERE AND AROUND

Stagecoach bus number 64A connects Falkland to St. Andrews as well as Cupar and Ladybank (both of which are train stations on the Edinburgh to Dundee line). Falkland is about 15 minutes from Cupar and a half-hour from St. Andrews by car via A91 and A912, or A91 to A914 to A912.

EXPLORING

★   **Falkland Palace,** a former hunting lodge of the Stuart monarchs, dominates the town. The castle is one of the earliest examples in Britain of the French Renaissance style. Overlooking the main street is the palace's most impressive feature, the walls and chambers on its south side, all rich with Renaissance buttresses and stone medallions, built by French masons in the 1530s for King James V (1512–42). He died here, and the palace was a favorite resort of his daughter, Mary, Queen of Scots (1542–87). In the beautiful gardens, overlooked by the palace turret windows, you may easily imagine yourself back at the solemn hour when James on his deathbed pronounced the doom of the house of Stuart: "It cam' wi' a lass and it'll gang wi a lass." ⊠ *Main St.* ☎ *01337/857397 or 0844/4932186* ⊕ *www. nts.org.uk* ⬚ *£10.50* ☉ *Mar.–Oct., Mon.–Sat. 10–5, Sun. 1–5.*

> ### TENNIS, ANYONE?
>
> The gardens behind Falkland Palace contain a rare survivor: a royal tennis court, built in 1539. It's not at all like its modern counterpart. Look out for the four *Lunes* (holes in the wall) and the *ais* (a vertical green board), both of which feature in the *jeu quarré* (square-court) version of the game.

LOCH LEVEN

10 mi southwest of Falkland.

Scotland's largest Lowland loch, Loch Leven is famed for its fighting trout. The area is also noted for abundant bird life, particularly its wintering wildfowl. Mary, Queen of Scots, was forced to sign the deed of abdication in her island prison in the loch.

GETTING HERE AND AROUND

If you're driving from St. Andrews or Cupar, take A91 to Kinross and follow the signs from there. From Falkland, take A911.

EXPLORING

On the southern shore overlooking the lock, **Vane Farm Nature Reserve,** a visitor center run by the Royal Society for the Protection of Birds, provides information about Loch Leven's ecology. It's the best place in Britain to see lapwings, pink-footed geese, tufted ducks, and shovelers. ⊠ *Vane Farm, Rte. B9097, off M90 and B996* ☎ *01577/862355* ⊕ *www.rspb.org.uk* ⬚ *£3* ☉ *Daily 10–5.*

CUPAR

21 mi northwest of Loch Leven, 10 mi west of St. Andrews.

Cupar is a busy market town with several interesting sites, including a museum about Fife.

GETTING HERE AND AROUND

Cupar has a train station on the Edinburgh–Aberdeen line (which passes through Dundee), and there are trains almost every hour. Stagecoach buses serve the town as well. By car, you can reach Cupar from Loch Leven via M90 and A91; take A91 if you're traveling from St. Andrews.

EXPLORING

On rising ground near the town stands the National Trust for Scotland's **Hill of Tarvit House.** Originally a 17th-century mansion, the house was altered in the high-Edwardian style in the late 1890s and early 1900s by the Scottish architect Sir Robert Lorimer (1864–1929). Though the house is not open to the public, you can visit the extensive wood and parklands here; it's an enjoyable place for a picnic or stroll. Golfers will also want to play a round on the old Lorimer family course, the Hickory, which was brought back to life in 2008 after being ploughed up for agricultural use during World War II. The grounds are open from April to October (call 01334/653421 to book). ✉ *2 mi south of Cupar, off A916* ☎ *0844/4932185* ⊕ *www.nts.org.uk* ✉ ☉ *Gardens daily 9:30–sunset.*

To learn more about the history and culture of rural Fife, visit the **Fife Folk Museum.** The life of local rural communities is reflected in artifacts and documents housed in a former weigh house and adjoining weavers' cottages. The museum is 3 mi southeast of Cupar via A916 and B939, and 9 mi southwest of St. Andrews. ✉ *High St., Ceres* ☎ *01334/828180* ✉ *£3.50* ☉ *Ap.–Oct., daily 11:30–4:30.*

☺ At the **Scottish Deer Centre,** red deer can be seen at close quarters on ranger-guided tours. There are also nature trails, falconry displays, an adventure playground (a wood-and-tire fortress suitable for older children), a handful of shops, and a café. ✉ *Bow of Fife, outside Cupar on the A91* ☎ *01337/810391* ⊕ ✉ *£6.95* ☉ *May–Sept., daily 10–5; Oct.–Apr., daily 10–4.*

WHERE TO EAT AND STAY

£££££
BRITISH

✕ **Ostlers Close Restaurant.** It's thoroughly unpretentious, but this cottage-style restaurant with plain painted walls and stick-back chairs has earned a well-deserved reputation for top-quality cuisine that is imaginative without trying to be too trendy. The chef's light touch means the flavors are simple, with the shellfish and vegetables especially fresh-tasting. This longtime favorite is tucked away in an alley off the main street. It's a good idea to reserve ahead, particularly for lunch. ✉ *25 Bonnygate* ☎ *01334/655574* ▤ *AE, MC, V* ☉ *Closed Sun. and Mon. No lunch Tues.–Thurs.*

££££
Fodor'sChoice
★

▦ **The Peat Inn.** This popular inn is best known for its outstanding modern Scottish-style restaurant (£££), generally considered one of the finest in Scotland. Mouthwatering entrées might include cannelloni with langoustines and scallops, while main courses feature ingredients like belly of pork or wild halibut. A detached building houses eight bright and contemporary two-room suites. You'll start each day by enjoying an array of homemade breads and jams while gazing at the rolling pastures of Fife. **Pros:** exceptional restaurant; super-efficient but easygoing staff. **Cons:** you need a car to get here (a taxi costs £15 from St. Andrews); need to book well in advance. ✉ *At B940 and B941, 6 mi southwest of St. Andrews, 5 mi southeast of Cupar* ⌂ *Cupar, Fife KY15 5LH* ☎ *01334/840206* ⊕ *www.thepeatinn.co.uk* ⇄ *8 suites* ☖ *In-room: no a/c. In-hotel: restaurant, parking (free)* ▤ *AE, MC, V* ☉ *Closed Sun. and Mon.* ☉❘ *CP.*

DUNDEE AND ANGUS

The small city of Dundee sits near the mouth of the River Tay surrounded by the farms and glens of rural Angus and the coastal grassy banks and golf courses of northeastern Fife. A vibrant, industrious city that still isn't part of the main tourist track, Dundee plays a significant role in the biotech and computer-games industries. Dundee has a large student population, a lively arts, music, and nightlife scene, many smart restaurants, and several historical and nautical sights.

Angus combines coastal agriculture on rich, red soils with dramatic inland glens that pierce their way into the foothills of the Grampian mountain ranges to the northwest. ■TIP→ The main road from Dundee to Aberdeen—the A90—requires drivers to take special care, with its mix of fast cars, trucks, and unexpectedly slow farm traffic.

DUNDEE

14 mi northwest of St. Andrews, 58 mi north of Edinburgh, 79 mi northeast of Glasgow.

Dundee makes an excellent base for exploring Fife and Angus at any time of year. The West End—especially its main thoroughfare Perth Road—pulses with life, with intimate cafés and excellent bars. The Dundee Contemporary Arts center has gained the city some attention. As you walk the cobbled streets, you may glimpse the 1888 Tay Rail Bridge, and if you head southwest you can reach Magdalen Green, where landscape artist James McIntosh Patrick (1907–98) found inspiration from the views and ever-changing skyscapes. The popular comic strips *The Beano* and *The Dandy* were first published here in the 1930s, so statues depicting Desperate Dan, Dawg, and a catapult-wielding Minnie the Minx were erected in the City Square.

GETTING HERE AND AROUND

The East Coast Train line runs through the city, linking it to Edinburgh (and beyond, to London), Glasgow (and the West Coast of England), and Aberdeen, with trains to all every hour or half-hourly at peak times. Cheaper bus service is available to all of these locations, as well as St. Andrews and several other towns in Fife and Angus.

If you're traveling by car, the A92 will take you from Fife, over the road bridge, and north to Abroath and the Angus coast towns. The A90, from Perth, heads north to Aberdeen.

Most of the sights in Dundee are clustered together, so you can easily walk around the city. If the weather is bad or your legs are heavy, hail one of the many cabs on the easy-to-find taxi ranks for little more than a few pounds.

ESSENTIALS

Visitor Information Dundee (✉ *Discovery Point, Discovery Quay* ☎ *01382/ 527527* ⊕ *www.angusanddundee.co.uk*).

EXPLORING
TOP ATTRACTIONS

⑤ RRS *Discovery.* Dundee's urban-renewal program—the city is determined to shake off its industrial past—was motivated in part by the arrival of the RRS (Royal Research Ship) *Discovery,* the vessel used by Captain Robert Scott (1868–1912) on his polar explorations. The steamer was originally built and launched in Dundee; now it's a permanent resident. At Discovery Point, under the handsome cupola, the story of the

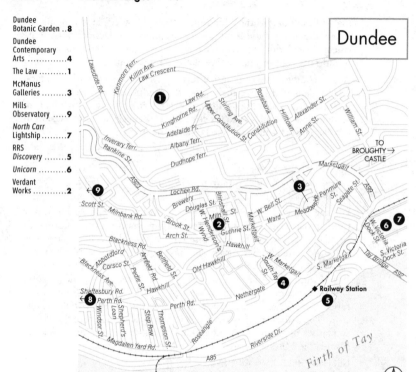

Dundee

ship and its famous expedition unfold; you can even feel the Antarctic temperature and the wind chill as if you were there. The ship, berthed outside, is the star: wander the deck, then explore the quarters to see the daily existence endured by the ship's crew and captain. ⊠ *Discovery Quay* ☏ *01382/201245* ⊕ *www.rrsdiscovery.com* ⊠ *£7.50, with Verdant Works £11.25* ☾ *Apr.–Sept., Mon.–Sat. 10–6, Sun. 11–6; Oct.–Mar., Mon.–Sat. 10–5, Sun. 11–5; last admission 1 hr before closing.*

❽ **Dundee Botanic Garden.** This renowned botanical garden contains an extensive collection of native and exotic plants outdoors and in tropical and temperate greenhouses. There are some beautiful areas for picnicking, as well as a visitor center, an art gallery, and a coffee shop. ⊠ *Riverside Dr.* ☏ *01382/381190* ⊕ *www.dundeebotanicgarden.co.uk* ⊠ *£3* ☾ *Mar.–Oct., daily 10–4:30; Nov.–Feb., daily 10–3:30.*

❹ **Dundee Contemporary Arts.** Between a 17th-century mansion and a cathe-
☾ dral, this strikingly modern building houses one of Britain's most excit-
★ ing artistic venues. The huge gallery houses up to six shows a year by internationally acclaimed contemporary artists. There are children's workshops and meet-the-artist events throughout the year. There are also two movie theaters showing mainly independent, revival, and children's films, a craft shop, and a buzzing café-bar called Jute that's open until midnight. ⊠ *152 Nethergate* ☏ *01382/909252* ⊕ *www.dca.org.uk*

⊠ *Free* ⊙ *Tues., Wed., Fri., and Sat. 10:30–5:30, Thurs. 10:30–8:30, Sun. noon–5:30.*

❸ **McManus Galleries.** Dundee's principal museum and art gallery, housed in a striking Gothic Revival–style building, has an engaging collection of artifacts that document the city's history and the working, social, and

> **ROYAL DISCOVERY PASS**
>
> With a Royal Discovery Pass, you can see the RRS *Discovery* and Glamis Castle in Angus for £13 (a saving of £3); you can purchase the pass at either site.

cultural lives of Dundonians throughout the Victorian period and the 20th century. Its varied fine art collection includes paintings by Rossetti, Raeburn, and Peploe as well as some thought-provoking yet accessible contemporary works. ⊠ *Albert Sq.* ☎ *01382/432350* ⊕ *www.mcmanus. co.uk* ⊠ *Free* ⊙ *Mon.–Wed., Fri., and Sat. 10–5, Thurs. 10–7, Sun. 12:30–4.*

❷ **Verdant Works.** In a former jute mill, Verdant Works houses a multi-faceted exhibit on the story of jute and the town's involvement in the jute trade. Restored machinery, audiovisual displays, and tableaux all bring to life the hard, noisy life of the jute worker. ⊠ *W. Hendersons Wynd* ☎ *01382/225282* ⊕ *www.verdantwork.co.uk* ⊠ *£7, with RRS Discovery £11.25* ⊙ *Apr.–Oct., Mon.–Sat. 10–6, Sun. 11–6; Nov.–Mar., Wed.–Sat. 10:30–4:30, Sun. 11–4:30.*

WORTH NOTING

OFF THE BEATEN PATH

Broughty Castle. Originally built to guard the Tay Estuary, Broughty Castle is now a museum focusing on fishing, ferries, and the history of the town of Broughty Ferry's whaling industry. The canons and ramparts make for fine photo opportunities, and inside (up a very narrow stairway) are four floors of displays, including the lovely art collection of the Victorian inventor and engineer Sir James Orchar. To the north of the castle lies beautiful Broughty Ferry Beach which, even in mid-winter, is enjoyed by the locals; there is regular bus service here from Dundee's city center. ⊠ *Broughty Ferry* ✛ *4 mi east of city center* ☎ *01382/436916* ⊕ *www.dundeecity.gov.uk/broughtycastle* ⊠ *Free* ⊙ *Apr.–Sept., Mon.–Sat. 10–4, Sun. 12:30–4; Oct.–Mar., Tues.–Sat. 10–4, Sun. 12:30–4.*

❶ **The Law.** For sweeping views of the city, the Angus Glens to the north, and Fife's coastline to the south, head here. This hill (*law* means hill in Scottish) is actually an extinct volcano whose summit reaches 1,640 feet above sea level. A World War II memorial, parking lot, and seating area are at the top. ⊠ *Law Rd.*

❾ **Mills Observatory.** At the top of a thickly forested hill, Mills Observatory is the only full-time public observatory in Britain. There are displays on astronomy, space exploration, scientific instruments, and a 12-inch refracting telescope for night viewing of the stars and planets. ⊠ *Balgay Hill, 2 mi west of city center* ☎ *01382/435967* ⊠ *Free* ⊙ *Oct.–Mar., weekdays 4–10 PM, weekends 12:30–4; Apr.–Sept., Tues.–Fri. 11–5, weekends 12:30–4.*

❼ ***North Carr* Lightship.** After playing a significant role in World War II, Scotland's only remaining lightship was wrecked on the Fife shore during a storm in 1959; seven crew members were lost. At this writing, the ship is closed for refurbishment. The Maritime Volunteer Service, which looks after the North Carr, runs exhilarating trips on its vessels, the *Badger* and *Marigold*. Excursions include a half-day boat trip along the River Tay to Perth or around the mouth of the delta, where pods of dolphins jump and play. ⊠ *Victoria Dock* ☎ *01382/542516* ⊕ *www.tayrivertrips.org* ☜ *Dolphin Watch £12.50, trip to Perth £36*

> **SEASIDE FLAVORS**
>
> You can't come to a great seaside town like Broughty Ferry, near Dundee, and not partake in the great institutions of ice cream and carry-out fish-and-chips. Close to the park benches that look out over the harbor, **Murray's Fish Bar** (⊠ 23 Gray St., Broughty Ferry ☎ 01382/738117) prides itself on having the crispiest batter and the chunkiest chips. **Visocchi** (⊠ 40 Gray St., Brought Ferry ☎ 01382/779297 ⊘ Closed Mon.) serves creamy cones and tubs to long lines.

6 **Unicorn.** Right next to the North Carr the frigate *Unicorn* is berthed, a 46-gun wood warship fronted by a figurehead of a white unicorn. The *Unicorn* has the distinction of being the oldest British-built warship afloat, having been launched in 1824 at Chatham, England. You can clamber right down into the hold, or see the models and displays about the Royal Navy's history. The ship's hours vary in winter, so call ahead. ⊠ *Victoria Dock, east of Tay Rd. bridge* ☎ *01382/200900 or 01382/200893* ⊕ *www.frigateunicorn.org* ☜ *£4* ⊘ *Apr.–Oct., daily 10–5; Nov.–Mar., Wed.–Fri. noon–4, weekends 10–4; last admission 20 mins before closing.*

WHERE TO EAT

££
ECLECTIC ✕ **Het Theatercafe.** At the lively Rep Theatre, you have a choice of the café-bar upstairs, which serves light fare and good coffee, or the restaurant downstairs. The international dishes always include scrumptious vegetarian dishes, such as vegetable *tagine* and mini *mezze* (appetizers), while puddings such as toffee apple crumble pie provide plenty of ballast. Theater posters of past productions and stills of actors decorate the walls. ⊠ *Tay Sq.* ☎ *01382/206699* ☰ *MC, V* ⊘ *Closed Sun.*

££
BRITISH ✕ **Jute.** Part of Dundee Contemporary Arts, this lively café-bar serves a
★ modish menu, including dishes like venison sausages served with creamy mashed potatoes and beet marmalade, or teriyaki salmon with spring-onion noodles. The pretheater dinner is a fabulous value: £13.95 for three courses. A glass wall separates the dining room from a printmaking studio. ⊠ *152 Nethergate* ☎ *01382/909246* ☰ *MC, V.*

££
ITALIAN ✕ **Piccolo.** This small basement eatery, with sound wooden tables and chairs and quirky staff, attracts a diverse clientele (including university staff). It serves surprisingly good pizzas, crepes, and a fine plate of pasta with an individual twist: think creamy ginger chicken with apricots served with *pappardelle* (broad fettuccine). ⊠ *21 Perth Rd.* ☎ *01382/201419* ☝ *Reservations essential* ☰ *MC, V* ⊘ *Closed Wed.*

£££
BRITISH ✕ **Playwright.** Opened in 2008, this stylish restaurant is one of the city's
★ more expensive, but it's worth the price. A glass floor looks into the wine cellar, and the staff is laid back but totally efficient. The menu is well put together, offering a range of flavors and textures and each dish,

such as seared salmon in a langoustine sauce. Portions are a decent size, and everything is perfectly presented. There's a beautiful bar, too, for pre- or post-dinner tippling. ✉ *11 Tay Sq.* ☎ *01382/223113* ⊕ *www. theplaywright.co.uk* ✍ *Reservations essential* ▤ *MC, V* ⊘ *Closed Sun.*

WHERE TO STAY

££–£££ ⌂ **Apex City Quay.** Sleek, Scandinavian-style rooms with easy chairs, satiny pillows, and CD/DVD players help you unwind at this contemporary quayside hotel. To relax further, or to exercise, head for the Japanese spa and fitness center. The restaurant (££) and brasserie (£), both with views of the harbor, have globally influenced menus with simple Italian and Asian dishes, as well as perfectly cooked steaks. **Pros:** stylish rooms; excellent brasserie. **Cons:** not an easy walk into town; often mobbed with conferences. ✉ *1 W. Victoria Dock Rd.* ☎ *01382/202404* ⊕ *www. apexhotels.com* ⇱ *145 rooms, 8 suites* ♿ *In-room: no a/c, DVD, Wi-Fi. In-hotel: 2 restaurants, bar, pool, gym, spa, laundry service, parking (free)* ▤ *MC, V* ⏐◯⏐ *CP.*

££ ⌂ **Duntrune House.** Situated just 5 mi to the northeast of Dundee and set among 8 acres of tidy lawns and rustling trees, this mansion house is a genteel contrast to the city. Those who appreciate antiques will find delight in each room; every piece of furniture tells a story (just ask the owners). Breakfast and dinners (book 24 hours in advance) are served downstairs in the dining room, which looks out over the gardens. **Pros:** owners are keen genealogists and can offer advice to ancestor-seekers; the house and gardens are full of interest. **Cons:** might be too cluttered for some tastes. ✉ *Duntrune* ☎ *01382/350239* ⊕ *www.duntrunehouse. co.uk* ⇱ *4 rooms* ♿ *In-room: no a/c. In-hotel: parking (free)* ▤ *MC, V* ⊘ *Closed Nov.–Feb.* ⏐◯⏐ *BP.*

££ ⌂ **Grampian Hotel.** This Georgian townhouse, right on the artery of the hip end of town, has undergone a few transformations over the years, but it has finally become the guesthouse it has always wanted to be. Fuss-free furnishings and quality bedding make for a restful night, and generous breakfasts prepare you for the day ahead. **Pros:** a few steps away from the lively West End; the loft room has wondrous views of the Tay. **Cons:** downstairs rooms feel rather tight. ✉ *295 Perth Rd.* ☎ *01382/667785* ⊕ *www.grampianhotel.com* ⇱ *10 rooms* ♿ *In-room: no a/c, Wi-Fi* ▤ *MC, V* ⏐◯⏐ *BP*

NIGHTLIFE AND THE ARTS

BARS AND Dundee's pub scene, centered in the West End–Perth Road area, is
PUBS one of the liveliest in Scotland. Better known as the bar at DCA, **Jute Café Bar** (✉ *152 Nethergate* ☎ *01382/909246*) is where west-enders, students, and the city's upwardly mobile go for cocktails, European beers, wine, spirits, or coffee. They also serve tasty bar snacks every night until 9:30. If you find yourself in Broughty Ferry, you can't leave without a tipple in the **Fisherman's Tavern** (✉ *10–16 Fort St., Broughty Ferry* ☎ *01382/775941*). The **Speedwell Bar** (✉ *165–168 Perth Rd.* ☎ *01382/667783*), called Mennie's by the locals, is in a mahogany-paneled building brimming with Dundonian character. It's renowned for its superb cask beers and its whalebonelike Armitage Shanks urinals.

DANCE CLUBS **Fat Sam's** (✉ *31 S. Ward Rd.* ☎ *01382/228181*) attracts clubbers of all ages to its various club nights, which feature DJs spinning everything from Indie to Deep House. It has now become Dundee's premier venue for gigs, hosting the likes of Franz Ferdinand, Pete Doherty, and local supergroup the View.

MUSIC **Caird Hall** (✉ *City Sq.* ☎ *01382/434451*) is one of Scotland's finest concert halls, staging a wide range of music.

THEATER The **Dundee Repertory Theatre** (✉ *Tay Sq.* ☎ *01382/223530*) is home to the nationally respected Dundee Rep Ensemble as well as Scotland's preeminent contemporary-dance group, Scottish Dance Theatre. Popular with locals, the restaurant and bar welcome late-night comedy shows and jazz bands. **Whitehall Theatre** (✉ *12 Bellfield St.* ☎ *01382/322684*) has mostly musical theater productions, including light opera.

SHOPPING

BOOKS There is no better place than **Big Bairn Books** (✉ *17 Exchange St.* ☎ *01382/ 220225*) to find old annuals of *The Beano, The Broons,* and *Oor Wullie*, all published by cult—and local—publisher D.C. Thomson.

COFFEE **J. Allan Braithwaite** (✉ *6 Castle St.* ☎ *01382/322693*) carries 13 types of
AND TEA freshly roasted coffees and more than 30 blended teas that you can pop into one of the quaint teapots you'll find here.

HOME The **Westport Gallery** (✉ *44 West Port* ☎ *01382/229707*) stocks contem-
FURNISHINGS porary designer housewares, including ceramics and glass, plus highly stylized clothing and jewelry.

JEWELRY The **Queen's Gallery** (✉ *160 Nethergate* ☎ *01382/220600*) has a compelling selection of jewelry, as well as paintings by Scottish artists.

ARBROATH

15 mi north of Dundee.

You can find traditional boatbuilding in the fishing town of Arbroath. It also has several small curers and processors, and shops sell the town's most famous delicacy, Arbroath smokies—whole haddock gutted and lightly smoked. A few miles north along the coast is the old fishing village of Auchmithie, with a beautiful little beach that you can walk to via a short path. The jagged, reddish cliffs and caves are home to a flourishing seabird population.

GETTING HERE AND AROUND

The East Coast train line stops at Arbroath. The Abbey and Signal Tower are all within walking distance, but you'll need a car to get to Auchmithie. If you're driving from Dundee, take A92.

ESSENTIALS

Visitor Information Arbroath (✉ *Fish Market Quay* ☎ *01241/872609* ⊕ *www. angusanddundee.co.uk*).

EXPLORING

Arbroath Abbey, founded in 1178, is an unmistakable presence in the town center; it seems to straddle whole streets, as if the town were simply ignoring the red-stone ruin in its midst. Surviving today are remains of the church, as well as one of the most complete examples in existence of an abbot's residence. From here in 1320 a passionate plea was sent by King Robert the Bruce (1274–1329) and the Scottish Church to Pope John XXII (circa 1245–1334) in far-off Rome. The pope had until then sided with the English kings, who adamantly refused to acknowledge Scottish independence. The Declaration of

> ### LIGHTHOUSE BUILDERS
>
> The name Stevenson is strongly associated with the building of lighthouses throughout Scotland. However, the family's most famous son was Robert Louis Stevenson (1850–94), who gravely disappointed his parents by choosing to be a writer instead of an engineer.

Arbroath stated firmly, "For as long as but a hundred of us remain alive, never will we on any conditions be brought under English rule. It is in truth not for glory, nor riches, nor honours that we are fighting, but for freedom—for that alone, which no honest man gives up but with life itself." Some historians describe this plea, originally drafted in Latin, as the single most important document in Scottish history. The pope advised English king Edward II (1284–1327) to make peace, but warfare was to break out along the border from time to time for the next 200 years. The excellent visitor center recounts this history in well-planned displays. ⊠ *Arbroath town center* ☎ *01241/878756* ⊕ *www. historic-scotland.gov.uk/places* ⊡ *£4.70* ⊙ *Apr.–Sept., daily 9:30–5:30; Oct.–Mar., daily 9:30–4:30.*

Arbroath was the base for the construction of the Bell Rock lighthouse on a treacherous, barely exposed rock in the early 19th century. A signal tower was built to facilitate communication with the builders working far from shore. That structure now houses the **Signal Tower Museum,** which tells the story of the lighthouse, built by Robert Stevenson (1772–1850) in 1811. The museum also houses a collection of items related to the history of the town, its customs, and the local fishing industry. ⊠ *Ladyloan, west of harbor* ☎ *01241/875598* ⊡ *Free* ⊙ *Sept.–June, Mon.–Sat. 10–5; July and Aug., Mon.–Sat. 10–5, Sun. 2–5.*

WHERE TO EAT AND STAY

£ ✕ **But 'n' Ben.** This homey restaurant offers a taste of quality Scottish
BRITISH home cooking, including smoked fish pâté, mince and tatties, and lemon drizzle cake, all at prices that make it an excellent value. After lunch, stroll down to the Auchmithie's lovely shingle beach. ⊠ *Auchmithie* ⊹ *Near Arbroath, 3 mi off A92* ☎ *01241/877223* ▬ *MC, V* ⊙ *Closed Tues.*

£ ✕ **Sugar and Spice** Peruse the sweets of your childhood and reminisce
BRITISH about the cakes your grandmother used to make in this combination café/sweet shop. Locals flock here to enjoy their tray bakes, meringues, and sponges (they also serve soups and sandwiches). At 5 PM it turns into a restaurant serving simple dishes like roast beef and Yorkshire pudding. ⊠ *9–13 High St.* ☎ *01241/437500*

£ 🏠 **Harbour Nights** An excellent and somewhat plush budget option, this B&B is right on the harbor, affording you the most authentic Arbroath stay possible. An interesting collection of ethnic and modern furniture show the thought that has gone into making the rooms attractive and comfortable. The shared bathrooms are kept absolutely spotless.

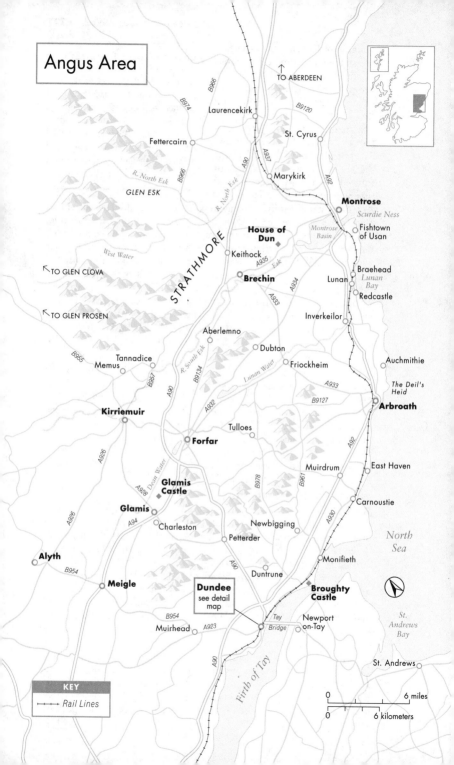

Pros: splendid seafront location; just-smoked Arbroath smokies are part of the delicious breakfast. Cons: only one room with own bath. ⊠ *4 Shore* ☎ *01421/434343* ⊕ *www.harbournights-scotland.com* ⇗ *5 rooms, 1 with bath* ⚲ *In-room: no a/c, DVD, In-hotel: parking (free), Wi-Fi* ⊟ *AE, D, DC, MC, V* |◎| *BP*

MONTROSE

14 mi north of Arbroath via A92.

An unpretentious and attractive town with a museum and a selection of shops, Montrose sits beside a wide estuary known as the Montrose Basin. The town's museum—housed in a neoclassical building that also contains the tourist information center—exhibits some fascinating bequests by the local gentry, including an early-19th-century ship carved from bone by French prisoners in the Napoleonic war.

GETTING HERE AND AROUND

On the main East Coast train line and local bus route (the Stagecoach Strathtay 39 and 73 from Dundee and Arbroath), the town is easily accessed by public transportation. However, you'll need a car to get to attractions outside town.

ESSENTIALS

Visitor Information **Montrose Museum and Tourist Information Centre** (⊠ *Panmure Pl.* ☎ *01674/673232* ⊕ *www.angusanddundee.co.uk* 🖾 *Free* ⊙ *Mon.– Sat. 10–5*).

EXPLORING

The **Montrose Basin Wildlife Centre,** run by the Scottish Wildlife Trust, is a nature reserve with geese, ducks, and swans. Several nature trails can take you up close to the reserve's residents if you're quiet. ⊠ *Rossie Braes* ☎ *01674/676336* ⊕ *www.montrosebasin.org.uk* 🖾 *£3.50* ⊙ *Visitor center Apr.–Oct., daily 10:30–5; Nov.–Mar., Fri.–Sun. 10:30–4.*

★ The National Trust for Scotland's leading attraction in this area is the **House of Dun,** which overlooks the Montrose Basin. The mansion was built in the 1730s for lawyer David Erskine, otherwise known as Lord Dun (1670–1755). Designed by architect William Adam (1689–1748), the house is particularly noted for its ornate plasterwork and curious Masonic masonry. Some of Lord Dun's heirlooms, including samples from the family's collection of embroidery, tell the story of the Seat of Dun and the eminent family's history. The sprawling grounds have restored workshops, plus an enchanting walled Victorian garden. The house is 4 mi west of Montrose via A935. ⊠ *A935* ☎ *01674/810264* ⊕ *www.nts.org.uk/Visits* 🖾 *House £8.50, garden and parking free* ⊙ *House July and Aug., daily 11–5; Sept. and Oct., Wed.–Sun. noon–5. Garden year-round, daily 9–sunset.*

BEAUTIFUL BEACHES

Scotland's east coast enjoys many hours of sunshine, compared with its west coast, and is blessed with lots of sandy beaches under the ever-changing backdrop of the sky. Take time to explore the beaches and walk along the coast for a change of pace whatever the time of year.

In Fife, Tentsmuir's Beach near St. Andrews is popular with kite flyers and horseback riders, and the famous and lovely West Sands in St. Andrews is where the running sequences in the movie *Chariots of Fire* were filmed. The small cove beach at Elie, just south of Crail, hosts local cricket matches in summer.

In Angus, the beach at Broughty Ferry, near the city of Dundee, fills with families and children on weekends and during school holidays—even on the most blustery of days you can find well-wrapped bairns (small children) making pictures in the sand.

North of Arbroath lies Auchmithie Beach, more shingly (pebbly) than the others and offering a bracing breath of North Sea air. And finally, near the Montrose Basin, you can discover the enchanting crescent of Lunan Bay, home to many species of seabirds.

BRECHIN

10 mi southwest of Montrose.

The small market town of Brechin has a cathedral that was founded around 1200 and contains an interesting selection of antiquities, including the Mary Stone, a Pictish relic.

GETTING HERE AND AROUND

Brechin is not on the East Coast train line but can be reached by bus from Montrose or Arbroath (the Stagecoach Strathtay number 30). It's on the A935, just off the main A90 road between Dundee and Aberdeen.

EXPLORING

Brechin Castle Centre and Tourist Information Centre has a dual function; while the town museum is being renovated, the tourist information center is located in the shop shared by Brechin Castle country park (with friendly alpacas) and the center for all things Pictish, Pictavia. ✉ *Haughmuir, A935* ☎ *01356/623050* ⊕ *www.angusanddundee.co.uk* 🖃 *Country park £3* 🕓 *Mon.–Sat. 9–5, Sun. 10–5.*

The town's 10th-century Brechin Cathedral and **Round Tower** is on the site of a former Celtic monastery (prior of the Culdee monks) and has some unusual examples of Medieval sculpture. The tower is one of only two on mainland Scotland (they're more frequently found in Ireland). ✉ *6 Church St.* ☎ *01356/629360* ⊕ *www.brechincathedral.org* 🖃 *Free* 🕓 *Daily 9–5.*

The first arrivals in this part of Scotland were the Picts, who came sometime in the first millennium AD. **Pictavia** explores what is known about this race of Celts using actual artifacts, replicas, and interactive exhibits. ⊠ *Brechin Castle Centre, off A90* ☎ *01307/626241* ⊕ *www. pictavia.org.uk* 🕮 *£3.25* ⊙ *Mon.–Sat. 9–5, Sun. 1–5.*

THE ANGUS GLENS

25 mi southwest of Brechin.

You can rejoin the hurly-burly of the A90 for the return journey south from Montrose or Brechin; the more pleasant route, however, leads southwesterly on minor roads (there are several options) that travel along the face of the Grampians, following the fault line that separates Highland and Lowland. The **Angus Glens** extend north from points on Route A90. Known individually as the glens of Isla, Prosen, Clova, and Esk, these long valleys run into the high hills of the Grampians and some clearly marked walking routes. Those in Glen Clova are especially appealing.

Be aware that Thursday is a half-day in Angus; many shops and attraction close at lunch.

GETTING HERE AND AROUND

You really need a car to reach the Angus Glens and enjoy the gentle (and not so gentle) inclines here. Glamis and Kirriemuir are both on the A928 (just off the A90), and the B955—which loops round at Glen Clova—is one of the loveliest Scottish roads to drive along, especially when the heather is blooming in late summer.

WHERE TO STAY

££ 🏨 **Glen Clova Hotel.** Since the 1850s, the hospitality of this hotel has lifted the spirits of many a bone-tired hill walker. The bedrooms are simply furnished but have comfortable, firm beds. The legendary Climbers Bar pours a fine pint—or glass of wine—and is often packed with walkers and climbers, many of whom are staying in the Hotel's bunkhouse. The restaurant (£) serves good home cooking; try the lamb casserole or the chicken breast stuffed with haggis in a whisky cream sauce. **Pros:** stunning location; great base for outdoor pursuits; spacious accommodations. **Cons:** lack of decent public transportation; rooms are booked well in advance. ⊠ *B955, Glen Clova* ☎ *01575/550350* ⊕ *www.clova. com* 🛏 *10 rooms* ☖ *In-room: no a/c. In-hotel: restaurant, bar* ▭ *MC, V* ⫿❶ *BP.*

KIRRIEMUIR

15 mi southeast of Brechin.

Kirriemuir stands at the heart of Angus's red-sandstone countryside and was the birthplace of the writer J. M. Barrie (1860–1937), best known abroad as the author of *Peter Pan* (a statue of whom you can see in the town's square).

GETTING HERE AND AROUND

A number of roads lead to Kirriemuir, but A928 (off A90), which also passes Glamis Castle, is one of the loveliest. Stagecoach Strathtay runs buses to this area; the 20 and 22 from Dundee are the most regular.

EXPLORING

Kirriemuir Gateway to the Glens Museum and Tourist Information Centre. As is the style in Angus, the local museum doubles as the visitor center, meaning you can get all the info you need and admire a few stuffed birds and artifacts at the same time. Rock fans will appreciate the exhibit celebrating local lad made good (or rather bad), the late Bon Scott, lead singer of ACDC. ⊠ *32 High St.* ☎ *01575/575479* ⊕ *www.angusanddundee. co.uk* ⊠ *Free* ☉ *Apr.–Sept., Mon.–Sat. 10–5; Oct.–Mar., Mon.–Wed., Fri., and Sat. 10–5, Thurs. 1–5.*

At **J.M. Barrie's Birthplace,** the National Trust has managed to pay tribute to the man who sought to preserve the ideal and magic of childhood more than any other writer of his age. The house's upper floors are furnished as they might have been in Barrie's time, complete with domestic necessities, while downstairs is his study, replete with manuscripts and personal mementos. The outside washhouse is said to have been Barrie's first theater. ⊠ *9 Brechin Rd.* ☎ *0844/4932142* ⊕ *www.nts.org.uk/ Visits* ⊠ *£5:50, includes Camera Obscura* ☉ *Apr.–June and Sept.–Oct., Sat.–Wed. noon–5; July–Aug., daily noon–5.*

NEED A BREAK? If you can endure the lackluster service, you'll enjoy the best coffee in town and temple-achingly sweet cakes and handmade chocolates at **88 Degrees** (⊠ *17 High St.* ☎ *01575/570888*).

J.M. Barrie donated the **Camera Obscura,** in a cricket pavilion on Kirriemuir Hill, just northeast of Kirriemuir, to the town. The device—a dark room with a small hole in one wall that projects an image of the outside world onto the opposite wall—is one of only three in the country. It affords magnificent views of the surrounding area on a clear day. ⊠ *Kirriemuir Hill* ☎ *0844/4932143* ⊠ *£3, with J.M. Barrie's birthplace £5.50* ☉ *Apr.–Sept. Mon.–Sat. 10–5, Sun. 1–5.*

FORFAR

7 mi east of Kirriemuir.

Forfar goes about its business of being the center of a farming hinterland without being preoccupied (or even that interested in) tourism.

GETTING HERE AND AROUND

Buses are slow here. The quickest route is by car: take the A90 north, then the A926 turnoff. Alternatively, the A932/A933 route from Arbroath takes you through farmland and Angus villages.

EXPLORING

A high point of the town is the **Meffan Museum & Art Gallery,** which displays an impressive collection of Pictish carved stones. Two galleries host frequently changing exhibitions by local and Scottish artists. The museum also houses a tourist information desk. ⊠ *20 W. High St.* ☎ *01307/464123* ⊠ *Free* ☉ *Mon.–Sat. 10–5.*

OFF THE BEATEN PATH **Aberlemno.** You can see excellent examples of Pictish stone carvings about 5 mi northeast of Forfar alongside the B9134. Carvings of crosses, angels, serpents, and other animals adorn the stones, which date from the 7th to the early 9th centuries. Note the stone in the nearby churchyard—one side is carved with a cross and the other side depicts the only known battle scene in Pictish art, complete with horsemen and foot soldiers.

GLAMIS

5 mi southwest of Forfar, 6 mi south of Kirriemuir.

Set in rolling countryside is the little village of Glamis (pronounced *glahms*).

GETTING HERE AND AROUND

The drive to Glamis Castle, along beech and yew lined roads, is as majestic as the castle itself. Take the A90 north from Dundee, then off onto the A928 (just of the A90). The village of Glamis can be reached by the Stagecoach Strathtay number 22, but service is rather infrequent.

EXPLORING

A row of 19th-century cottages with unusual stone-slab roofs makes up the **Angus Folk Museum,** whose exhibits focus on the tools of domestic and agricultural life in the region during the past 200 years. ⊠ *Off A94* ☎ *0844/4932141* ⊕ *www.nts.org.uk/Visits* 🎫 *£5.50* ☼ *Apr.–June and Sept.–Oct., weekends noon–5; July and Aug., daily noon–5*

Fodor's Choice
★

Glamis Castle, one of Scotland's best-known and most beautiful castles, connects Britain's royalty through 10 centuries, from Macbeth (Thane of Glamis) to the late Queen Mother and her daughter, the late Princess Margaret, born here in 1930 (the first royal princess born in Scotland in 300 years). The property of the earls of Strathmore and Kinghorne since 1372, the castle was largely reconstructed in the late 17th century; the original keep, which is much older, is still intact. One of the most famous rooms in the castle is Duncan's Hall, the legendary setting for Shakespeare's *Macbeth*. Guided tours allow you to see fine collections of china, tapestries, and furniture. Within the castle is the delightful Castle Kitchen restaurant; the grounds contain a huge gift shop, a food shop selling Glamis Castle produce, and a pleasant picnic area. ⊠ *A94, 1 mi north of Glamis* ☎ *01307/840393* ⊕ *www.glamis-castle. co.uk* 🎫 *Grounds £4.20, castle and grounds £8.50* ☼ *Mar.–Oct., daily 10–6; Nov. and Dec., daily 11–5.*

MEIGLE

7 mi southwest of Glamis, 11 mi northwest of Dundee.

The historic village of Meigle, nestled in the rich agricultural land of the Strathmore Valley, is well known to those with an interest in Pictish stones. Said to be built upon an 11th century Pictish monastery, the village has a number of interesting Victorian buildings.

GETTING HERE AND AROUND

Meigle is an easy and pleasant drive from Glamis on the A94 (or from Dundee on the B954). The hourly Stagecoach Strathtay from Dundee (number 57) stops here.

EXPLORING

The town of Meigle, in the wide swath of Strathmore, has one of the most notable collections of sculpted stones in western Europe, housed at the **Meigle Sculptured Stone Museum.** It consists of some 25 monuments from the Celtic Christian period (8th to 11th centuries), nearly all of which were found in or around the local churchyard. ⊠ *A94* ☎ *0131/ 640612* ⊕ *www.historic-scotland.gov.uk/places* 🎫 *£3.20* ⊙ *Apr.–Sept., daily 9:30–5:30; Oct.–Mar. daily 9:30–4:30.*

ALYTH

10 mi west of Glamis, 15 mi northwest of Dundee.

Dating back to the Dark Ages, this market town was completely transformed by the Industrial Revolution, which lined its streets with mills and factories. The 20th century saw the closing of most of these companies, but the town had never forgotten its agricultural heritage. To this day it holds on to its rural appeal.

GETTING HERE AND AROUND

Just 4 mi farther along the B954 from Meigle, Alyth is also served by Stagecoach Strathtay number 57.

EXPLORING

Alyth Museum, a small but intriguing museum about the town's history, displays nearly every type of tool and implement put to use by the resourceful and hardy locals. ⊠ *Commercial St.* ☎ *01828/632488* 🎫 *Free* ⊙ *May–Sept., Wed.–Sun. 1–5.*

WHERE TO STAY

££   🏠 **Tigh Na Leigh.** This grand house, now a B&B, was originally built by the Earl of Airlie for his doctor. Rooms are fresh and airy, with leather, brass or four-poster beds extravagantly dressed in Egyptian cotton. Evening meals (for guests only) are served in the Scandinavian-style conservatory. **Pros:** lovingly restored building; luxurious rooms; exceptional food. **Cons:** only five rooms; books up quickly. ⊠ *22–24 Airlie St.* ☎ *01828/632372* ⊕ *www.tighnaleigh.com* 🛏 *5 rooms* ⚒ *In-room: no a/c. In-hotel: Internet terminal* ⊟ *MC, V* ⌾ *BP.*

The Central Highlands

WORD OF MOUTH

"From Edinburgh, I'd visit Stirling instead of Inverness. More interesting, and much closer. There is so much to see. The castle, Bannockburn Heritage Center, the National Wallace Monument. If you have a car, there is more within half an hour's driving time, including Doune Castle, Loch Katrine, and Inchmahome."

—HollydaleK

"'If you don't like the weather here, wait five minutes.' I've decided the expression must have originated in Scotland! My son and I took the cruise on Loch Lomond. We had weather from fairly heavy rain to bright sunshine! Again, it was absolutely gorgeous."

—CAPH52

Updated
by Mike
Gonzalez

Central Scotland is a bridge between Highland Scotland and the cities of Glasgow and Edinburgh. From Stirling Castle, on a good day, you can see from coast to coast, before you travel north to the glens and the rising hills of the Trossachs. From there you can choose to seek out the tranquil waters of Loch Lomond to the west or the open country and darker peaks of Rannoch Moor to the north.

Central Scotland sits between the Glasgow–Edinburgh axis, marked by the M8 motorway and the dramatic natural divide that is the gateway to the Highlands—the Highland Boundary. The wide plain guarded by Stirling Castle was the scene of many of the important moments in Scotland's history—from the Roman invasion commemorated by the Antonine Wall, to the castles that mark the site of medieval kingdoms and the battles to preserve them.

North from Stirling, past Dunblane, are the highland hills and valleys of the Trossachs, whose high peaks attract walkers and a tougher breed of cyclist. From Callander, a neat tourist town, the hills stretch westward to the "bonnie bonnie banks" of Loch Lomond, a national park since 2001. From the peaks of the Trossachs, on a good day, you can see Edinburgh Castle to the east and the tower blocks of Glasgow's housing projects to the west.

Perth was once Scotland's capital; its wealthy mansions reflect the prosperous agricultural land that surrounds the city, and it is still an important market town today. Overlooking the River Tay, the city can reasonably claim to be the gateway to the Highlands, sitting as it does on the Highland Fault that divides Lowlands from Highlands. From Perth the landscape begins to change on the road to Pitlochry and the unforgiving moors of Rannoch.

For many years Stirling was the starting point for visitors from Edinburgh and Glasgow who were setting out to explore the Trossachs, with their lochs and hills hung with shaggy birch, oak, and pinewoods. Perhaps they were drawn by the lyrical descriptions of the area by Romantic poets like Sir Walter Scott (1771–1832), who set his dramatic verse narrative of 1810, "The Lady of the Lake," in the landscape of the Trossachs. Scott's poem was an immediate and huge success, and the poem is still a comprehensive guide to the area, though some bridges and farms have disappeared.

For those in search of more dramatic landscapes, the Highland fault line runs northeast above Perth, and into the old county of Angus and the high, rough country of Rannoch Moor and the towering Ben Lawers, near Killin, the ninth-highest peak in Scotland.

Loch Lomond, Scotland's largest loch in terms of surface area, lies just half an hour north of Glasgow. Its waters reflect the crags and dark woods that surround it, and attract those in search of a more romantic

TOP REASONS TO GO

Exploring Loch Lomond: You can see the sparkling waters of Scotland's largest loch by car, by boat, or on foot. A popular option is the network of bicycle tracks that creep over Loch Lomond and the Trossachs National Park, offering every conceivable terrain.

Take in a castle or two: Choosing among some of Scotland's most splendid fortresses and mansions is a challenge. Among the highlights are Stirling Castle, with its palace built by James V, and Scone Palace, near Perth, a residence displaying grand aristocratic acquisitions.

Bag a Munro: The way to experience the Central Highlands is to head out on foot. The fit and well-kitted-out can "bag a Munro" (hills over 3,000 feet, named after the mountaineer that listed them). The woodland paths and gentle rambles of the Trossachs will stir even the sedentary.

Whisky, the water of life: The Scots love their whisky, and what better way to participate in Scottish life and culture than to learn about the land's finest? There are some exceptional distilleries in this region, from the Edradour Distillery to Glenturret, home of the Famous Grouse.

Jump on a bike: This region claims excellent biking trails, ranging from a gentle pedal through Stirling to a wind-in-your-face journey on the Lowland/Highland Trail. Whatever your preference, biking is a beautiful way to tour the countryside.

6

and nostalgic Scotland enshrined in the verses of the famous song that bears its name. "The Banks of Loch Lomond," said to have been written by a Jacobite prisoner incarcerated in Carlisle, England, captures a particular style of Scottish sentimentality.

The region is full of reminders of heroic struggles, particularly against the English, from the monument to William Wallace to the field at Bannockburn (near Stirling), where Robert the Bruce took on the invader. In nearby Callander, Rob Roy MacGregor, the Scottish Robin Hood, lived (and looted and terrorized) his way into the storybooks.

ORIENTATION AND PLANNING

GETTING ORIENTED

The twin reference points for your trip are Stirling, an ancient historic town from whose castle you can see Central Scotland laid out before you, and Perth, 36 mi away, the gateway to the Highlands. North from Stirling, you cross the fertile open plain (the Carse of Stirling) dotted with historic cathedral towns like Dunblane and Doune. The Trossachs are the Scotland of the Romantic imagination, lochs and woodland glens, drovers' inns and grand country houses. The small towns of the region, like Callander, Aberfoyle, and Pitlochry, are bases from which to explore this changing countryside. To the west lies the beautiful and tranquil Loch Lomond, along whose banks the road leads from industrial Glasgow to the hills and glens of the Highlands.

Stirling. Stirling is a city vibrant with history. The old town is quite a small area on the hill, and is worth covering on foot. Look down from the Stirling Castle crag that dominates the plains below and you can see the stages of its growth descending from the hill. The town is compact and walkable, and a center from which to explore the changing landscape of Central Scotland.

The Trossachs and Loch Lomond. This area is small, but incredibly varied—from dramatic mountain peaks that attract walkers and climbers, to the gentler slopes and forests that stretch from Perth eastwards to Aberfoyle and the shores of Loch Lomond. The glens and streams that pepper the region create a romantic landscape that is a perfect habitat for the figure of Rob Roy McGregor—Robin Hood or bandit according to taste, but undeniably Scottish. Loch Lomond's western side is more accessible, if busier, but the views across the loch are always beautiful.

Perthshire. The prosperous air of Perth, once the capital of Scotland, testifies to its importance as a port exporting wool, salmon, and whisky to the world. Scone Palace serves as a monument to that era. The route northward leads across the Highland Boundary and into the changing landscapes beyond Pitlochry to Rannoch Moor, where the wind sweeps across the hardy heather.

PLANNING

WHEN TO GO

The Trossachs and Loch Lomond are in some ways a miniature Scotland, from the tranquil east shore of Loch Lomond to the hills and glens of the Trossachs and the mountains of the Arrochar Alps to the east—and all within a few hours' drive. In the summer, despite the erratic weather, the area is always crowded; this is a good time to go. However, the landscape is notably dramatic when the trees are turning red and brown in autumn or in a winter light. ■ TIP➔ Carry clothes for wet and dry weather, for rain and for sunshine.

PLANNING YOUR TIME

Scotland's beautiful interior is excellent touring country, though the cities of Stirling and Perth are worth your time too; Stirling in particular is worth a day. Two (slightly rushed) days would be enough to explore the Trossachs loop, to gaze into the waters of Loch Venachar and Loch Achray. The glens, in some places, run parallel to the lochs, including those along Lochs Earn, Tay, and Rannoch, making for satisfying loops and round-trips. Loch Lomond is easily accessible from either Glasgow or Stirling, and is well worth exploring. Don't miss the opportunity to take a boat trip on a loch, especially on Loch Lomond or on Loch Katrine in the Trossachs.

GETTING HERE AND AROUND
AIR TRAVEL

Perth and Stirling can be reached easily from the Edinburgh, Dundee, and Glasgow airports by train, car, or bus.

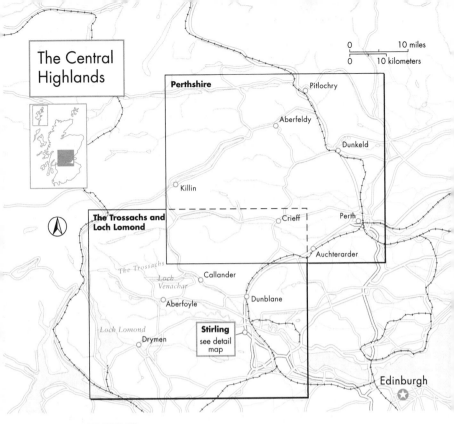

The Central Highlands

0   10 miles
0   10 kilometers

Perthshire

Pitlochry

Aberfeldy

Dunkeld

Killin

The Trossachs and Loch Lomond

Crieff

Perth

The Trossachs

Callander

Auchterarder

Loch Venachar

Aberfoyle

Dunblane

Loch Lomond

Drymen

Stirling see detail map

Edinburgh

BUS TRAVEL

A good network of buses connects with the central belt via Edinburgh and Glasgow. For more information contact Scottish Citylink or National Express. The Perth and Kinross Council supplies a map (available in tourist information centers) showing all public transport routes in Perthshire, marked with nearby attractions.

The following companies organize reliable service on routes throughout the Central Highlands: First, Scottish Citylink, and Stagecoach.

Bus Contacts First (☎ 08708/727271 ⊕ www.firstgroup.com). **National Express** (☎ 08705/808080 ⊕ www.nationalexpress.com). **Scottish Citylink** (☎ 08705/505050 ⊕ www.citylink.co.uk). **Stagecoach** (☎ 01738/629339 ⊕ www.stagecoachbus.com).

CAR TRAVEL

You'll find easy access to the area from the central belt of Scotland via the motorway network. The M9 runs within sight of the walls of Stirling Castle, and Perth can be reached via the M90 over the Forth Bridge. The A9 runs from Stirling to Perth, and onwards to Pitlochry; it is a good road but a little too fast for its own good (so take care). Two signed touring routes are useful: the Perthshire Tourist Route, and the Deeside Tourist Route, with a spectacular journey via Blairgowrie and

Glenshee to Deeside and Aberdeen. Local tourist information centers can supply maps of these routes.

TRAIN TRAVEL

The Central Highlands are linked to Edinburgh and Glasgow by rail, with through routes to England (some direct-service routes from London take fewer than five hours). Several discount ticket options are available, although in some cases on the ScotRail system the discount fares must be purchased before your arrival in the United Kingdom. Contact Trainline, National Rail, or ScotRail for details.

The West Highland Line runs through the western portion of the area. Services also run to Stirling, Dunblane, Perth, and Gleneagles, stops on the Inverness–Perth line include Dunkeld, Pitlochry, and Blair Atholl.

Train Contacts **National Rail Enquiries** (☎ 08457/484950 ⊕ www.nationalrail. co.uk). **ScotRail** (☎ 08457/550033 ⊕ www.scotrail.co.uk). **Trainline** (⊕ www. thetrainline.com).

RESTAURANTS

Regional country delicacies—loch trout, river salmon, lamb, and venison—appear regularly on even modest menus in Central Highlands restaurants. In all the towns and villages in the area you will find simple pubs, often crowded and noisy, many of them serving substantial food at lunchtime and in the early evening (eaten balanced on your knee, perhaps, or at a shared table).

HOTELS

There is a wide selection of accommodations available throughout the region, especially in Stirling and Callander. They range from the bed-and-breakfasts to private houses with a small number of rooms to rural accommodation (often on farms). The grand houses of the past—family homes to the landed aristocracy—have for the most part become country house hotels. Their setting, often in ample grounds, offers an experience of grand living—but there are also modern hotels in the area, for those who prefer their 21st-century amenities.

WHAT IT COSTS IN POUNDS					
	£	££	£££	££££	£££££
RESTAURANTS	under £10	£10–£14	£15–£19	£20–£25	over £25
HOTELS	under £70	£70–£120	£121–£160	£161–£220	over £220

Restaurant prices are for a main course at dinner. Hotel prices are for two people in a standard double room in high season and generally include the 17.5% V.A.T.

VISITOR INFORMATION

The tourist offices in Stirling and Perth are year-round, as are offices in larger towns; others are seasonal (generally from April to October).

STIRLING

26 mi northeast of Glasgow, 36 mi northwest of Edinburgh.

Stirling is one of Britain's great historic towns. An impressive proportion of the Old Town walls remain and can be seen from Dumbarton Road, as soon as you step outside the tourist information center. Its castle, built on a steep-sided plug of rock, dominates the landscape. From its esplanade there is a commanding view of the surrounding valley plain (called the Carse of Stirling). The guns on the castle battlements are a reminder of the military advantage to be gained from its position.

GETTING HERE AND AROUND

Stirling's central position in the area makes it an ideal point for travel to and from Glasgow and Edinburgh (or north to Perth and the Highlands) by rail, train, or bus. The town itself is compact and easily walkable, though a shuttle bus travels to and from the town center up the steep road to the castle every 20 minutes. The Back Walk takes the visitor on a circuit around the base of the castle walls.

TIMING

The historic part of town is tightly nestled around the castle—everything is within easy walking distance. The Bannockburn Heritage Centre (3 mi away) and the National Wallace Monument (2 mi away) are on the outskirts of the town and can be reached by taxi or, for the more energetic, on foot. ■ TIP→ **The weather is always changing in this part of the country. Bring sunscreen, a hat, and a waterproof jacket with you wherever you go.**

ESSENTIALS

Visitor Information Stirling (✉ *41 Dumbarton Rd.* ☎ *01786/479901* ✉ *Royal Burgh of Stirling Visitor Centre, Castle Esplanade* ☎ *01786/475019*).

EXPLORING STIRLING

TOP ATTRACTIONS

★ **Bannockburn Heritage Centre.** In 1298, the year after William Wallace's victory, Robert the Bruce (1274–1329) emerged as the nation's champion, and the final bloody phase of the Wars of Independence began. Bruce's rise resulted from the uncertainties and timidity of the great lords of Scotland (ever unsure of which way to jump and whether or not to bow to England's demands). The story is told at the Bannockburn Heritage Centre, hidden among the sprawl of housing and commercial development on the southern edge of Stirling. This was the site of the famed Battle of Bannockburn in 1314. In Bruce's day the Forth had a shelved and partly wooded floodplain, so he cunningly chose this site, where the heavy horses of the English would founder in the boggy ground. The events of this time have been re-created within the center by means of an audiovisual presentation, models and costumed figures, and an arresting mural depicting the battle in detail. ✉ *Glasgow Rd., Bannockburn* ☎ *0844/4932139* ⊕ *www.nts.org.uk/Visits* ✑ *£5* ☉ *Mar., daily 10:30–4; Apr.–Oct., daily 10–5:30.*

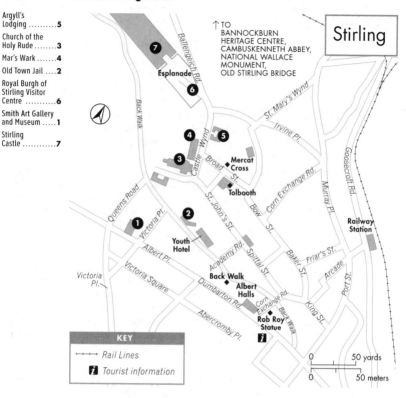

National Wallace Monument. It was near Old Stirling Bridge that the Scottish freedom fighter William Wallace (circa 1270–1305) and a ragged army of Scots won a major victory in 1297. The movie *Braveheart*, directed by and starring Mel Gibson, was based on Wallace's life. A more accurate version of events is told in an exhibition and audiovisual presentation at this pencil-thin museum on the Abbey Craig. Up close, this Victorian shrine to William Wallace, built between 1856 and 1869, becomes less slim and soaring, revealing itself to be a substantial square tower with a creepy spiral stairway. To reach the monument, follow the Bridge of Allan signs (A9) northward, crossing the River Forth by Robert Stephenson's (1772–1850) New Bridge of 1832, next to the historic old one. The National Wallace Monument is signposted at the next traffic circle. ⊠ *Abbey Craig* ☎ *01786/472140* ⊕ *www. nationalwallacemonument.com* ≦ *£6.50* ⊘ *Mar.–May and Oct., daily 10–5; June, daily 10–6; July and Aug., daily 9–6; Sept., daily 9:30–5:30; Nov.–Feb., daily 10:30–4.*

② **Old Town Jail.** The original town jail, now restored, has exhibitions ☾ about life in a 19th-century Scottish prison. Furnished cells, models, and staff—dressed as prisoners, wardens, and prison reformers—bring the gruesome prison regime to life. From October through March, these living-history performances take place only on weekends (9–4). Guided tours are offered every half hour. ⊠ *St. John's St.* ☏ *01786/450050* ⊕ *www.oldtownjail.com* ⊠ *guided tours only, £5.95* ☉ *Apr.–Sept., daily 9–6; Oct., daily 9:30–5; last admission 1 hr before closing.*

❼ Stirling Castle. Its magnificent strategic position made Stirling Castle the grandest prize in the Scots Wars of Independence in the late 13th and early 14th centuries. The Battle of Bannockburn in 1314 was fought within sight of its walls, and the victory by Robert the Bruce yielded both the castle and freedom from English subjugation for almost four centuries. Take time to visit the **Castle Exhibition** to get an overview of its long history and evolution as a stronghold and palace.

Fodor's Choice
★

The daughter of King Robert I (Robert the Bruce), Marjory, married Walter Fitzallan, the high steward of Scotland. Their descendants included the Stewart dynasty of Scottish monarchs (Mary, Queen of Scots, was a Stewart, though she preferred the French spelling, *Stuart*). The Stewarts were responsible for many of the works that survive within the castle walls today. They made Stirling Castle their court and power base, creating fine Renaissance-style buildings that were not completely obliterated, despite reconstruction for military purposes.

You can enter the castle through its outer defenses, which consist of a great curtained wall and batteries from 1708, built to bulwark earlier defenses by the main gatehouse. From this lower square the most conspicuous feature is the **Palace,** built by King James V (1512–42) between 1538 and 1542. The decorative figures festooning the ornately worked outer walls show the influence of French masons. At this writing, the Palace is closed, but check ahead; work is under way to re-create the furnishings and tapestries (including a copy of the Unicorn tapestries from New York's Metropolitan Museum) of the Palace during the reign of James V and his French queen, Mary of Guise. This will transform the empty rooms into the richly adorned living quarters of the kings and queens of Scotland. Overlooking the upper courtyard is the **Great Hall,** built by King James IV (1473–1513) in 1503. Before the Union of Parliaments in 1707, when the Scottish aristocracy sold out to England, this building had been used as one of the seats of the Scottish Parliament. It has since been restored to its original splendor, although it remains unfurnished.

Among the later works built for regiments stationed here, the **Regimental Museum** stands out; it's a 19th-century baronial revival on the site of an earlier building. Nearby, the **Chapel Royal** is unfurnished but was the site of a visit by Charles I in 1633. The oldest building on the site is the **Mint,** or **Coonzie Hoose,** perhaps dating as far back as the 14th century. Beside it are the kitchens, rebuilt with an orientation room and figures reenacting the hard lives lived below stairs. Below is an arched passageway leading to the westernmost section of the ramparts, the **Nether Bailey.** You'll have the distinct feeling here of being in the bow of a warship sailing up the *carselands* (valley plain) of the Forth Valley, which fans out before the great superstructure of the castle.

To the castle's south lies the hump of the Touch and the Gargunnock Hills (part of the Campsie Fells), which diverted potential direct routes from Glasgow and the south. For centuries all roads into the Highlands across the narrow waist of Scotland led to Stirling. If you look carefully northward, you can still see the Old Stirling Bridge, once the lowest and most convenient place to cross the river. ⌧ *Castlehill* ☎ *01786/450000* ⊕ *www.historic-scotland.gov.uk/places* 🎫 *£8.50, includes admission to Argyll's Lodging* ◷ *Apr.–Sept., daily 9:30–6; Oct.–Mar., daily 9:30–5.*

WORTH NOTING

❺ **Argyll's Lodging.** A nobleman's town house built in three phases from the 16th century onward, this building is actually older than the name it bears—that of Archibald, the ninth earl of Argyll (1629–85), who bought it in 1666. It was for many years a military hospital, then a youth hostel. It has now been refurbished to show how the nobility lived in 17th-century Stirling. Specially commissioned reproduction furniture and fittings are based on the original inventory of the house's contents at that time. Entry is by guided tour only. ⌧ *Castle Wynd* ☎ *01786/431319* ⊕ *www.historic-scotland.gov.uk/places* 🎫 *£8.50 for joint ticket with admission to Stirling Castle* ◷ *Tours daily every ½ hr, 9:30–3:45.*

❸ **Church of the Holy Rude.** The nave of this handsome church survives from the 15th century, and a portion of the original medieval timber roof can also be seen. This is the only Scottish church still in use to have witnessed the coronation of a Scottish monarch—James VI (1566–1625) in 1567. ⌧ *Top of St. John's St.*

❹ **Mar's Wark.** These distinctive windowless and roofless ruins are the stark remains of a Renaissance palace built in 1570 by Lord Erskine (died 1572), Earl of Mar and Stirling Castle governor. The name means "Mar's work," or building. Look for the armorial carved panels, the gargoyles, and the turrets flanking a railed-off *pend* (archway). During the 1745 Jacobite rebellion, Mar's Wark was laid siege to and severely damaged, but its admirably worn shell survives. The ruins are enclosed by a fence, you may view them from outside only. ⌧ *Castle Wynd* ☎ *01667/460232* ⊕ *www.historic-scotland.gov.uk/places.*

❻ **Royal Burgh of Stirling Visitor Centre.** This visitor center at the foot of the Castle Esplanade houses a shop and exhibition hall with an audiovisual presentation on the town and surrounding area. Groups perform Highland dancing on the Esplanade Tuesday evenings from mid-June through August. The Clan Centre allows you to trace your Scottish ancestry. ⌧ *Stirling Castle Esplanade* ☎ *01786/479901* 🎫 *Free* ◷ *Apr.–Oct., daily 9:30–6; Nov.–Mar., daily 9:30–5.*

❶ **Smith Art Gallery and Museum.** This community art gallery, founded in 1874 with the bequest of a local collector, showcases a varied exhibition program of paintings and sculpture. ⌧ *Albert Pl., Dumbarton Rd.* ☎ *01786/471917* ⊕ *www.smithartgallery.demon.co.uk* 🎫 *Free* ◷ *Tues.–Sat. 10:30–5, Sun. 2–5.*

WHERE TO EAT

£££
ECLECTIC

✕ **Hermann's Restaurant.** Run by Austrian Hermann Aschaber and his Glaswegian wife, the restaurant presents the cuisines of both countries. The Black Watch–tartan carpet and alpine murals are as successfully matched as the signature Scottish dishes like *cullen skink* (a fish and potato soup) and chicken with Stornaway black pudding and Drambuie cream, and Austrian staples like Wiener schnitzel and cheese spaetzle. ⊠ *58 Broad St.* ☎ *01786/450632* ▤ *AE, MC, V.*

£££   ✕ **River House.** At the foot of Stirling Castle, this restaurant sits by its
ECLECTIC   own tranquil little loch and is built in the style of a Scottish *crannog* (ancient loch dwelling). It's popular with both families and couples. Local produce dominates the menu, yet the food reflects Eastern and Mediterranean influences. Try the curried Scottish lamb with lime yogurt. ⊠ *The Castle Business Park, Craigforth* ☎ *01786/465577* ⊕ *www.riverhouserestaurant.co.uk* ▤ *AE, MC, V.*

WHERE TO STAY

£££   ⬚ **Barceló Stirling Highland Hotel.** This hotel occupies what was once the
★   Old High School, and several of the rooms preserve that history (the headmaster's study, for example). Other features of the original 1854 building that remain include the working observatory on the roof, but the extensions are more modern. Furnishings are old-fashioned, with solid wood, tartan, florals, and low-key, neutral color schemes. The Scholars Restaurant (£££££) serves modern-Scottish cuisine: outstanding seafood, game, and Aberdeen Angus beef. **Pros:** near train station; excellent restaurant; some rooms have views of the castle. **Cons:** slightly institutional feel. ⊠ *Spittal St.* ☎ *01786/272727* ⊕ *www.barcelo-hotels. co.uk* ⇆ *96 rooms* ⬚ *In-room: no a/c, Internet. In-hotel: restaurant, bar, pool, gym, Wi-Fi hotspot, some pets allowed* ▤ *AE, DC, MC, V* ⍾ *BP.*

£   ⬚ **Castlecroft.** Tucked beneath Stirling Castle, this warm and comfortable modern house is well situated for sightseeing in the Old Town. Guests enjoy fine views of the Trossachs and Grampian mountains to the north. People allergic to pets should be aware that the owners have three dogs and a cat. **Pros:** great location; lovely views; hearty breakfasts. **Cons:** rather old-fashioned decor; some rooms are small. ⊠ *Ballengeich Rd.* ☎ *01786/474933* ⊕ *www.castlecroft-uk.com* ⇆ *6 rooms* ⬚ *In-room: no a/c, no phone. In-hotel: Internet terminal, Wi-Fi hotspot* ▤ *MC, V* ⍾ *BP.*

£   ⬚ **Kilronan House.** In Bridge of Allan, close to the Wallace Monument and many shops and restaurants, this granite-walled B&B offers quality accommodation and good value. High ceilings and other details recall the house's genteel Victorian origins, and the well-tended gardens are a pleasant place to relax. **Pros:** lovely gardens; spacious rooms; close to bus stops. **Cons:** not all rooms have bathrooms; steep driveway. ⊠ *15 Kenilworth Rd.* ☎ *01786/831054* ⊕ *www.kilronan.co.uk* ⇆ *3 rooms* ⬚ *In-room: no a/c, no phone, no TV* ▤ *No credit cards* ⍾ *BP.*

££   ⬚ **Park Lodge Hotel.** This elegant 18th-century country-house hotel gives you a taste of French-inspired design and cuisine. It's run by a delightful French family who is only too willing to help. The interior is all fanlights, antique furniture, and candles. Rooms look out over Kings Park and Stirling Castle. The Heritage Restaurant (£££££) serves prix-fixe dinners that typically include French classics such as steak au poivre and *magret de canard* (duck breast). **Pros:** great views of park; homey feel; recently renovated. **Cons:** too many floral prints. ✉ *32 Park Terr.* ☎ *01786/474862* ⊕ *www.parklodge.net* ⇨ *9 rooms* ⟨⟩ *In-room: no a/c, In-hotel: restaurant, bar, some pets allowed* ⊟ *MC, V* ⦿ *BP.*

£   ⦿ **West Plean.** This handsome, rambling, early-Georgian house is part
★   of a working farm, with a walled garden and woodland walks. Well-prepared food and spacious rooms make this B&B an excellent bargain. **Pros:** beautiful gardens; plenty of peace and quiet; huge and hearty breakfast. **Cons:** long walk to Stirling; books up quickly. ✉ *Denny Rd.* ☎ *01786/812208* ⊕ *www.westpleanhouse.com* ⇨ *3 rooms* ⟨⟩ *In-room: no a/c. In-hotel: bar* ⊟ *MC, V* ⊘ *Closed Dec.* ⦿ *BP.*

THE ARTS

The **Macrobert Arts Centre** (✉ *Stirling University* ☎ *01786/466666* ⊕ *www.macrobert.org*) has a theater, art gallery, and studio with programs that range from films to pantomime.Built in 1705, the **Tolbooth** (✉ *Broad St.* ☎ *01786/274000* ⊕ *www.stirling.gov.uk/tolbooth*) has been many things: courthouse, jail, meeting place. At one time the city's money was kept here. It's undergone much remodeling over the years but has retained its traditional Scottish steeple and gilded weathercock. Today it serves as a popular music and arts venue with a 200-seat auditorium as well as a stylish restaurant and bar.

SHOPPING

The refurbished **Stirling Arcade** (✉ *King St.* ☎ *01786/474888*) was built in the 19th century, and today has about 20 shops. You'll find everything from toys and fine clothing to pizza here.

CERAMICS AND GLASSWARE

South of Stirling, in a farm setting at Larbert, and signposted off A9, is **Barbara Davidson's pottery studio** (✉ *Muirhall Farm, Larbert* ☎ *01324/554430* ⊕ *www.barbara-davidson.com*), run by one of the best-known potters in Scotland. You can make an appointment to paint a pot, which will be glazed, fired, and mailed to you, and in July and August you can even try throwing your own pot. **Village Glass** (✉ *14 Henderson St., Bridge of Allan* ☎ *01786/832137* ⊕ *www.villageglass. co.uk*) sells original glassware handblown on the premises.

CLOTHING

East of Stirling is **Mill Trail** country, along the foot of the Ochil Hills. A leaflet from any local tourist information center will lead you to the delights of a real mill shop and low mill prices—even on cashmere—at Tillicoultry, Alva, and Alloa.

In Stirling, **House of Henderson** (✉ *6–8 Friars St.* ☎ *01786/473681* ⊕ *www.houseofhenderson.co.uk*), a Highland outfitter, sells tartans, woolens, and accessories, and offers a made-to-measure kilt service.

GIFTS

Fotheringham Gallery (✉ *78 Henderson St., Bridge of Allan* ☎ *01786/ 832861*) has jewelry and paintings.

Stirling Bagpipes (✉ *8 Broad St.* ☎ *01786/448886*) has absolutely everything an aspiring piper could need.

Thomson's Tea and Coffee (✉ *4 Broad St.* ☎ *01786/475545*) has an extensive collection of teas and coffees.

THE TROSSACHS AND LOCH LOMOND

Immortalized by Wordsworth and Sir Walter Scott, the Trossachs (the name means "bristly country") may contain some of Scotland's loveliest forest, hills, and glens, well justifying the area's designation as a national park. The area has a special charm, combining the wildness of the Highlands with the prolific vegetation of an old Lowland forest. Its open ground is a dense mat of bracken and heather, and its woodland is of silver birch, dwarf oak, and hazel—trees that fasten their roots into the crevices of rocks and stop short on the very brink of lochs. There are also many small towns to visit along the way, some with their roots in a medieval world; others sprang up and expanded in the wake of the first tourists who came searching for wild country or seeking healing waters. Dunblane has a magnificent cathedral; Doune's castle will make you stare in awe.

When should you visit the Trossachs? The most colorful season is fall, particularly October, a lovely time when most visitors have departed, and the hares, deer, and game birds have taken over. Even in rainy weather the Trossachs of "darksome glens and gleaming lochs" are memorable: the water filtering through the rocks by Loch Lomond comes out so pure and clear that the loch is like a sheet of glass.

The best way to explore this area is by car, by bike, or on foot; the latter two depend, of course, on the weather. Keep in mind that roads in this region of the country are narrow and winding, which can make for dangerous conditions in all types of weather.

DUNBLANE

7 mi north of Stirling.

The small, quiet town of Dunblane, just 4 mi from Stirling, has long been an important religious center; it is dominated by its Cathedral, which dates mainly from the 13th century. The town also boasts one of Scotland's most impressive libraries, the Leighton Library.

GETTING HERE AND AROUND
Dunblane station is on the main line to Perth and Inverness, while a regular bus service links the town to Stirling. For drivers it is easily reached along the main A9 artery.

ESSENTIALS
Visitor Information **Dunblane** (✉ *Stirling Rd.* ☎ *01786/824428*).

EXPLORING
The oldest part of Dunblane—with its narrow winding streets—huddles around the Cathedral square. The **Cathedral** was built by Bishop Clement in the early 13th century on the site of St. Blane's tiny 8th-century cell; with the Reformation of the 16th century, it ceased to be a Cathedral. In 1996 it was the scene of a moving memorial service for

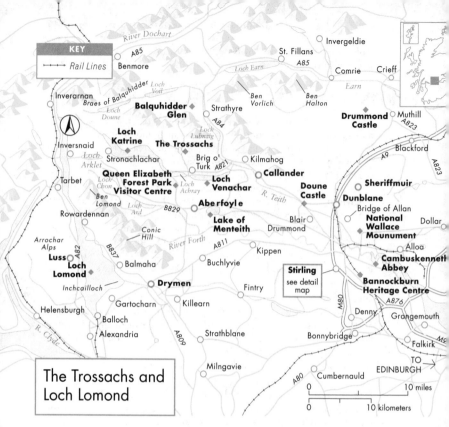

The Trossachs and
Loch Lomond

the 15 children killed in the local school by Thomas Hamilton. ⊠ *The Cross* ☎ *01667/460232* ⊕ *www.historic-scotland.gov.uk/places* 🎫 *Free* ⊙ *Apr.–Sept., Mon.–Sat. 9:30–12:30 and 1:30–5, Sun. 2–5; Oct.–Mar., Mon.–Sat. 9:30–4, Sun. 2–4*

The Highland-edge community of Doune, 5 mi west of Dunblane, was once a center for pistol making. No self-respecting Highland chief's attire was complete without a prestigious and ornate pair of pistols. Today Doune is more widely known for one of the best-preserved medieval castles in Scotland. It's also a place of pilgrimage for fans of Monty Python's *Holy Grail,* which was filmed here. **Doune Castle** is grim and high-walled, with echoing, drafty stone vaults. Construction of the fortress began in the early 15th century on a now-peaceful riverside tract. The best place to photograph this squat, walled fort is from the bridge, a little way upstream. Be sure to climb up to the curtain-wall walk for good views. The castle is signposted to the left as you enter the town from the Dunblane road. ⊠ *Off A84, Doune* ☎ *01786/841742* ⊕ *www.historic-scotland.gov.uk* 🎫 *£4* ⊙ *Apr.–Sept., daily 9:30–5:30; Oct.–Mar., Sat.–Wed. 9:30–4:30.*

WHERE TO EAT AND STAY

££ ╳ **Sheriffmuir Inn.** The road to Sheriffmuir from Dunblane is too nar-
ECLECTIC row to be numbered, and you may be concerned you have taken a
wrong turn . . . until you reach this splendidly isolated, whitewashed
inn. Inside there is a warm fire at a friendly bar filled with wooden
furniture that adds to the cozy feel. The restaurant is unpretentious,
with views onto the moor beyond. Owner and chef Geoff Cook keeps
to local produce wherever possible, but with an international touch;
try the monkfish with chili-crab crème and basmati rice. ⊠ *Sheriffmuir,
Dunblane* 🖻 ▭ *DC, MC, V* ☺ *Closed Tues.*

££££ 🏠 **Cromlix House Hotel.** A long, narrow drive leads to this mansion on a
2,000-acre estate just beyond the village of Kinbuck. The atmosphere
is quiet and relaxed, the furniture and decor reflect the style of a Victorian country house with its polished wood and floral patterns. Meals
are served in two elegant, country-house-style dining rooms with fixed-
price menus (£££££). Specialties include game and lamb from the estate.
Pros: beautiful and extensive grounds; comfortable large rooms; attentive staff. **Cons:** a little hard to find; not much for children; some old-
fashioned plumbing. ⊠ *B8033, 3 mi northeast of Dunblane, Kinbuck*
🖻 *01786/822125* ⊕ *www.cromlixhouse.com* ⇥ *6 rooms, 8 suites* ⅏ *In-
room: no a/c, Wi-Fi. In-hotel: restaurant, tennis court, Internet terminal*
▭ *AE, DC, MC, V* ⅋ *BP.*

CALLANDER

8 mi northwest of Doune.

A traditional Highland-edge resort, the little town of Callander bustles
throughout the year, even during off-peak times, simply because it's a
gateway to Highland scenery, and Loch Lomond and the Trossachs
National Park. As a result, there's plenty of window-shopping here, plus
nightlife in pubs and a good selection of accommodations.

GETTING HERE AND AROUND

The railway that brought visitors to Callander in the 19th century no
longer reaches the town. Today you can access Callander by bus from
Stirling, Glasgow, or Edinburgh; the Trossachs Trundler (£5.10) departs
Stirling at 9 AM for Callander, then travels in a circular route between
Callander and Aberfoyle via Loch Katrine, returning to Stirling from
Callander at 4:20 PM. If you're traveling by car from Stirling, take the
M8 to Dunblane, then the A820 (which becomes the A84) to Callander.
If you are coming from Glasgow, take the A81 through Aberfoyle to
Callander; an alternative route (longer but more picturesque) is to take
the A821 around Loch Venachar, then the A84 east to Callander.

ESSENTIALS

Bus Information Trossachs Trundler (🖻 *01786/442704* ⊕ *www.stirling.gov.
uk/trundler*).

Visitor Information Callander (⊠ *Ancaster Sq.* 🖻 *08707/200604* ⊕ *www.
visitscotland.com*).

EXPLORING

The **Hamilton Toy Collection** is one of the most extensive in Britain. Kids and adults can spend hours amid every conceivable toy from the Victorian age until the 1970s: teddy bears, porcelain dolls, toy soldiers, Matchbox cars, Thunderbirds memorabilia, and a wonderful selection of model railways. ⊠ *111 Main St.* ☎ *01877/330004* *£2* ☉ *Apr.–Oct., Mon.–Sat. 10–4:30, Sun. noon–4:30.*

WHERE TO EAT AND STAY

££
SCOTTISH ✕ **Lade Inn.** A traditional pub in Kilmahog (just a mile from Callander on the A85), the Lade Inn offers good solid pub fare in the bar. Steaks, burgers, and chicken are locally sourced, and there are elements of international cuisine, such as tagines. The establishment specializes in ales, and there's quite a selection. Staff are friendly and attentive, and traditional music (live or recorded) plays much of the time. ⊠ *Kilmahog* ☎ *01877/330152* *D, DC, MC, V.*

£
CAFÉ ✕ **Pip's Coffee House.** Come to this cheerful little place just off the main street for imaginative soups and salads, as well as exquisite Scottish home baking, including fresh scones. And then, of course, there's great coffee. ⊠ *Ancaster Sq.* ☎ *01877/330470* *No credit cards.*

£££ **Roman Camp.** Turn off the main street of Callander, and within a hundred yards you will find this pink-washed 17th-century hunting lodge, surrounded by ornate gardens. The drawing room and exquisite library recall the hotel's origins, and the rooms are furnished with the past in mind; comfortable and elegant, they have large and very modern bathrooms. The River Teith flows vigorously past the house, and guests enjoy fishing rights; for those with less vigorous activities in mind, there is a lovely walled garden and a riverside arbor. The restaurant has a prix-fixe menu (£££££). **Pros:** beautiful grounds; quite luxurious rooms. **Cons:** restaurant is quite expensive; no Internet facilities in rooms. ⊠ *Main St.* ☎ *01877/330003* ⊕ *www.romancamphotel. co.uk* ⌁ *12 rooms, 3 suites* ⚳ *In-room: no a/c. In-hotel: restaurant, room service, bar, Internet terminal, Wi-Fi hotspot, some pets allowed* *AE, DC, MC, V* ⍥ *BP.*

££ **Westerton B and B.** A large Victorian stone-built house with a large garden, the Westerton has gold, blue, and green rooms that are elegant and bright. All rooms have king-size beds and a comprehensive information pack provided by the friendly and attentive proprietors. The en-suite bathrooms are large and modern, and the thick towels are a thoughtful addition. You can select your choice the night before from an extensive breakfast menu. **Pros:** welcoming atmosphere; large comfortable rooms; in town center. **Cons:** awkward entrance and exit into the drive; no phones in room. ⊠ *Leny Rd.* ☎ *01877/330147* ⊕ *www. westerton.co.uk* ⌁ *13 rooms* ⚳ *In-room: no a/c, no phone, DVD, Wi-Fi. In-hotel: no children, some pets allowed* *D, DC, MC, V* ☉ *Closed Nov.–Feb.* ⍥ *BP.*

SPORTS AND THE OUTDOORS

BICYCLING **Wheels/Trossachs Backpackers** (⊠ *Invertrossachs Rd.* ☎ *01877/331100* ⊕ *www.scottish-cycling.com*) is a friendly firm that can help you find the best mountain-bike routes around the Trossachs and offers hostel accommodation for cyclists (£15 for a dorm bed).

TEEING OFF IN THE TROSSACHS

There is a wealth of beautiful golf courses within the Loch Lomond and the Trossachs National Park. The National Park Golf Pass (£50 for three days, £80 for five days) allows play at Callander, St. Fillans, Aberfoyle, Killin, and Buchanan Castle (£10 supplement).

Aberfoyle Golf Club (✉ *Braeval, Aberfoyle* ☎ *01877/382493* ⊕ *www. aberfoylegolf.com*).

Buchanan Castle Golf Club (✉ *A809, Drymen* ☎ *01360/660330*

⊕ *www.buchanancastlegolfclub. co.uk*).

Callander Golf Club (✉ *Aveland Rd., Callander* ☎ *01877/330975* ⊕ *www.callandergolfclub.co.uk*).

Killin Golf Club (✉ *Off A827, Killin* ☎ *01567/820312* ⊕ *www. killingolfclub.co.uk*).

St. Fillans Golf Club (✉ *S. Loch Earn Rd., St. Fillans* ☎ *01764/685312* ⊕ *www.st-fillans-golf.com*).

GOLF The course at the **Callander Golf Club,** designed by Tom Morris in 1890, has fine views and a tricky moorland layout. Keep between the trees on the 15th hole and you may end up with a hole in one. ✉ *Aveland Rd.* ☎ *01877/330090* ⊕ *www.callandergolfclub.co.uk* ⛳ *18 holes, 5,151 yds, par 66* 🏷 *£35 per round.*

HIKING Just north of Callander, the mountains squeeze both the road and rocky river into the narrow **Pass of Leny.** An abandoned railway—now a pleasant walking or biking path—also goes through the pass, past Ben Ledi and Loch Lubnaig.

A walk is signposted from the east end of the main street to the **Bracklinn Falls,** over whose lip Sir Walter Scott once rode a pony to win a bet.

It's a 1½-mi walk through the woods up to the **Callander Crags,** with views of the Lowlands as far as the Pentland Hills behind Edinburgh. The walk begins at the west end of the main street.

SHOPPING

The **Edinburgh Woollen Mill Group** operates three mill shops in and near Callander. All the stores have a vast selection of woolens on display, including luxurious cashmere and striking tartan throws, and will provide overseas mailing and tax-free shopping. *Callander Woollen Mill:* ✉ *7 Main St.* ☎ *01877/330612 Trossachs Woollen Mill:* ✉ *Kilmahog, 1 mi west of Callander* ☎ *01877/330268.*

BALQUHIDDER GLEN

12 mi north of Callander.

GETTING HERE AND AROUND

To reach Balquhidder Glen by car, take the A84 from Callander (signposted to Crianlarich). The road ends in the glen, so you will have to turn back and rejoin the A84 to continue your journey (but it's certainly worth the diversion).

EXPLORING

A 20-minute drive from Callander, through the Pass of Leny and beyond Strathyre, is **Balquhidder Glen** (pronounced *bal*-whidd-*er*), a typical Highland glen that runs westward. The glen has characteristics seen throughout the north: a flat-bottom U-shape profile, formed by prehistoric glaciers, extensive Forestry-Commission plantings replacing much of the natural woodlands above, a sprinkling of farms, and farther up the glen, hill roads bulldozed into the slopes to provide access for foresters. You may notice a boarded-up look of some of the area's houses, many of which are second homes for affluent residents of the south. The glen is also where Loch Voil and Loch Doune spread out, adding to the stunning vistas.

The area around Balquhidder Glen is known as the Braes (Slopes) of Balquhidder and was the home of the MacLarens and the MacGregors. The **grave of Rob Roy MacGregor,** the 18th-century Scottish outlaw hero and subject of Sir Walter Scott's novel *Rob Roy*, is signposted beside Balquhidder village. The site of his house, now a private farm, is beyond the parking lot at the end of the road up the glen. The glen has no through road, though there is a right-of-way (on foot) from the churchyard where Rob Roy is buried, through Kirkton Glen and on to open grasslands and a lake.

WHERE TO STAY

££££
Fodor's Choice
★

Monachyle Mhor. Set on 2,000 acres of forests and moorland, this beautifully converted farmhouse sits in splendid isolation against a backdrop of mountains and views over Lochs Voil and Doine. Rooms are striking and unique, with clean lines and touches of modern luxury, like plush animal-print throws and elegant toiletries. Known for its food, the hotel kitchen uses many homegrown ingredients, and everything is expertly prepared. There's a prix-fixe menu (£46), and if the weather is favorable you can eat on the patio. **Pros:** stunning scenery; delicious food; complimentary salmon- and trout fishing. **Cons:** you're pretty isolated; rooms are on the small side. ⊠ *Balquhidder* ☎ *01877/384622* ⊕ *www. monachylemhor.com* ⥅ *9 rooms, 2 suites* ⅃ *In-room: no a/c, DVD. In-hotel: restaurant, Wi-Fi hotspot* ▭ *MC, V* ⏅ *BP.*

THE TROSSACHS

10 mi west of Callander.

With its harmonious scenery of hill, loch, and wooded slopes, the Trossachs has been a popular touring region since the late 18th century, at the dawn of the age of the Romantic poets. Influenced by the writings of Sir Walter Scott, early visitors who strayed into the Highlands from the central belt of Scotland admired this as the first "wild" part of Scotland they encountered. Perhaps because the Trossachs represent the very essence of what the Highlands are supposed to be, the whole of this area, including Loch Lomond, is now protected as a national park. Here you can find birch and pine forests, vistas down lochs where the woods creep right to the water's edge, and, in the background, peaks that rise high enough to be called mountains, though they're not as high as those to the north and west.

GETTING HERE AND AROUND

To reach the Trossachs, take the A84 from Callander through the Pass of Leny, then on to Crianlarich; from here you can continue down the western shore of Loch Lomond or continue on toward Fort William.

EXPLORING

The A821 runs west together with the first and gentlest of the Trossachs lochs, **Loch Venachar.** A sturdy gray-stone building, with a small dam at the Callander end, controls the water that feeds into the River Teith (and, hence, into the Forth).

A few minutes after it passes Loch Venachar, the A821 becomes muffled in woodlands and twists gradually down to the village of **Brig o'**

SCOTLAND BY BIKE

The region's big attraction for cyclists is the **Lowland/Highland Trail,** which stretches over 60 mi and passes through Drymen, Aberfoyle, the Trossachs, Callander, Lochearnhead, and Killin. This route runs along former railroad-track beds, as well as private and minor roads, to reach well into the Central Highlands. Another almost completely traffic-free option is the roadway around Loch Katrine. Mountain bikes can tackle many of the forest roads and trails enjoyed by walkers. Avoid main roads, which can be busy with traffic.

Turk. (*Turk* is Gaelic for the Scots *tuirc,* meaning wild boar, a species that has been extinct in this region since about the 16th century.) ⊠ *A821.*

Loch Achray, stretching west of Brig o' Turk, dutifully fulfills expectations of what a verdant Trossachs loch should be: small, green, reedy meadows backed by dark plantations, rhododendron thickets, and lumpy hills, thickly covered with heather.

The parking lot by Loch Achray is the place to begin the ascent of steep, heathery **Ben An,** which affords some of the best Trossachs' views. The climb requires a couple of hours and good lungs. ⊠ *A821.*

★ At the end of Loch Achray, a side road turns right into a narrow pass, leading to **Loch Katrine,** the heart of the Trossachs. Sir Walter Scott traveled here in the early 19th century and was inspired to write "The Lady of the Lake." At that time, the road here was narrow and almost hidden by the overhanging crags and mossy oaks and birches. Today it ends at a slightly anticlimactic parking lot with a shop, café, and visitor center (there are brochures and restrooms, but don't make a special trip). To see the finest of the Trossachs lochs properly, you must—even for just a few minutes—walk or cycle further along the level, paved road beyond the parking lot (open only to Strathclyde Water Board vehicles). Loch Katrine's water is taken by aqueduct and tunnel to Glasgow—a Victorian feat of engineering that has ensured the purity of the supply to Scotland's largest city for more than 100 years. The steamer **Sir Walter Scott** (☎ *01877/332000* ☞ *£10 one-way, £12 round-trip*) embarks on cruises of Loch Katrine every day between April and late October. The boat leaves from Trossachs Pier at 10:30, 1:15, 2:30, 3:45, and 5.

■ TIP ➔ **Do take the cruise if time permits, as the shores of Katrine remain undeveloped and scenic.** ⊠ *Trossachs Pier* ☎ *01877/376316* ⊕ *www. lochkatrine.com* ☉ *Visitor center, Apr.–late Oct., daily 9–5.*

ABERFOYLE

11 mi south of Loch Katrine, in the Trossachs.

This small tourist town has a somewhat faded air, and several of its souvenir shops seem to have closed their doors. But the surrounding hills (some snowcapped) and the green slopes that surround the town are the reason so many visitors pause here before continuing up to Duke's Pass or on to Inversnaid.

GETTING HERE AND AROUND

The main route out of Glasgow, the A81, takes you through Aberfoyle and on to Callander and Stirling. There are regular buses from Stirling and Glasgow to Aberfoyle.

ESSENTIALS

Visitor Information Trossachs Discovery Centre (✉ *Main St., Aberfoyle* ☎ *08707/200604* ⊕ *www.visitscotland.com*).

EXPLORING

The **Scottish Wool Centre** stocks a vast range of woolen garments and knitwear and has a small café. Three times a day from April to September it presents the interactive 'Gathering' when dogs herd sheep and ducks in the large amphitheater, with a little help from the public. ✉ *Off Main St.* ☎ *01877/382850* 🎫 *Free* ⊙ *Feb.–Dec., daily 9:30–5:30; Jan., daily 10–4:30.*

The tiny island of **Inchmahome**, on the Lake of Menteith, was a place of refuge in 1547 for the young Mary, Queen of Scots. Between April and September, a ferry takes passengers from the lake's pier to the island. Now owned by the National Trust for Scotland, its ruined **priory** is a lovely place for a picnic. ■**TIP**→ **If the boat is not there when you arrive at the pier, turn the board so that the white side faces the island. The boat will come and collect you.** ✉ *Off A81, 4 mi east of Aberfoyle* ☎ *01786/450000* 🎫 *Ferry £4.70* ⊙ *Apr.–Sept., daily 9:30–5:30.*

OFF THE BEATEN PATH

Along the B829. From Aberfoyle you can take a trip to see the more enclosed northern portion of **Loch Lomond.** During the off-season the route has an untamed and windswept air when it extends beyond the shelter of trees. Take the B829 (signposted INVERSNAID and STRONACHLACHAR), which runs west from Aberfoyle and offers outstanding views of Ben Lomond, especially in the vicinity of Loch Ard. The next loch, where the road narrows and bends, is dark **Loch Chon.**

Beyond Loch Chon, the road climbs gently from the plantings to open moor with a breathtaking vista over **Loch Arklet** to the Arrochar Alps, the name given to the high hills west of Loch Lomond. Hidden from sight in a deep trench, Loch Arklet is dammed to feed Loch Katrine. Go left at the road junction (a right will take you to the town of Stronachlachar) and take the open road along Loch Arklet. These deserted green hills were once the rallying grounds of the Clan Gregor. Near the dam on Loch Arklet, on your right, **Garrison Cottage** recalls the days when the government had to billet troops here to keep the MacGregors in order. From Loch Arklet the road zigzags down to **Inversnaid,** where you can see a hotel, house, and parking lot, with **Loch Lomond** stretching out of sight above and below.

A QUEENLY PARK IN THE TROSSACHS

For exquisite nature, drive south from Aberfoyle on the A821 and turn right where signposts read **Queen Elizabeth Forest Park**; here you'll be heading toward higher moorland blanketed with conifers. The conifers hem in the views of Ben Ledi and Ben Venue, which can be seen over the spiky green waves of trees as the road snakes around heathery knolls and hummocks. There's another viewing area, and a small parking lot, at the highest point of the road. Soon the road swoops off the Highland edge and leads downhill.

Near the start of the descent, the **Queen Elizabeth Forest Park Visitor Centre** can be seen on the left. The center has displays on the life of the forest, a summer-only café, some fine views over the Lowlands to the south, and a network of footpaths. The Trossachs end here. ⌂ Off A821 ☎ 01877/382258 ⊕ www.forestry.gov.uk/qefp ☉ Park daily 24 hrs.

Visitor center Easter–Oct., daily 10–6; Nov.–Dec., weekends 10–6.

The **David Marshall Lodge** (⌂ A821 (Duke's Pass), 1 mi north of Aberfoyle, Queen Elizabeth Forest Park ☎ 01877/382383 ⊕ ☉ Mar.–Dec., daily 10–4; Feb., Thusr.–Sun. 10–4; closed Jan.) is the perfect starting point for walking or cycling through Queen Elizabeth Forest Park.

Go Ape High Wire Forest Adventure (⌂ A821, Duke's Pass, 1 mi north of Aberfoyle, Queen Elizabeth Forest Park ☎ 08704/445562 ⊕ www.goape.com ☁ £25 ☉ Apr.–Oct., daily 9–5; Nov.–Mar., weekends 9–5), by the David Marshall Lodge, is an exhilarating experience for thrill-seekers. Rope ladders and zip lines trace a route through the forest some 40 feet above the ground. You'll find the longest zip line in Britain (426 meters [1,398 feet]) here. When your heart has stopped racing, head to the lodge's Bluebell Café for some refreshment.

The only return to Aberfoyle is by retracing the same route. Right at the junction is the hamlet of **Stronachlachar,** on Loch Katrine, the outermost landing stage for the SS *Walter Scott*'s trips on the loch.

WHERE TO STAY

£££ ⌂ **Lake of Menteith Hotel.** This restful hotel emphasizes the peaceful air here with its muted colors and simple elegant rooms. Owner Ian Fleming says that its New England style is a response to the silent hills that ring the hotel and the tranquility of the nearby lake (no motorboats are allowed). Located in the tiny hamlet of Port of Menteith, beside the church, this is a year-round hotel; in winter, you'll find warm fires in the bar. Fishing and hunting trips can be arranged. The restaurant is so close to the lake that it feels as if you could reach out and touch the water. Lunch and dinner (prix-fixe £34) menus feature locally sourced produce and food (the owner catches his own fish). **Pros:** elegant unpretentious bedrooms; beautiful setting. **Cons:** not well signposted; not all rooms have lake views. ⌂ Port of Menteith ☎ 01877/385258 ⊕ www.lake-hotel.com ⇥ 16 rooms ⌂ In-room: no a/c. In-hotel: restaurant, room service, bar ▭ AE, D, DC, MC, V ⊠ BP.

£££ 🏠 **Macdonald Forest Hills Hotel.** A traditional Scottish-country-house theme pervades this hotel, from the rambling white building itself to the wood-paneled lounges, log fires, and numerous sporting activities. More than 20 acres of gardens and grounds surround the building, which sits on a grassy hillside overlooking Loch Ard. Chintz drapes and reproduction antiques fill the bedrooms. The restaurant (£31, fixed-price menu) has tartan decor that makes an appropriate backdrop for Scottish game, salmon, beef, and lamb. **Pros:** stunning views; log fires; good children's programs. **Cons:** restaurant is pricey and food is average; some of the building looks run down. ✉ *Kinlochard* ☎ *01877/387277* ⊕ *www. macdonaldhotels.co.uk/foresthills* 🛏 *56 rooms* ♿ *In-room: no a/c. In-hotel: 2 restaurants, tennis court, pool, gym, bicycles, children's programs (ages 5–12), no kids under 5* 🖃 *AE, DC, MC, V* 🍽 *BP.*

> ### HIKE THE HIGHLAND WAY
>
> The long-distance walkers' route, the **West Highland Way** (⊕ *www. west-highland-way.co.uk*), opened in 1980. It begins in Glasgow, running 95 mi from the lowlands of Central Scotland to the highlands at Fort William. Nearly 50,000 people discover the glens through which it passes each year, climbing the hills and listening to birds singing in the tree canopy. This is not a difficult walk, but travelers should keep Scotland's ever-changing weather in mind. From Milngavie, in Glasgow, the route passes along the banks of Loch Lomond before snaking northwards into the more demanding hills beyond.

SPORTS AND THE OUTDOORS

BICYCLING **Trossachs Cycle Hire** (✉ *Trossachs Holiday Park, near Aberfoyle* ☎ *01877/ 382614*) rents bicycles from March through October (£5 per hour) and will provide advice on routes.

LOCH LOMOND

14 mi west of Aberfoyle.

For the most outstanding Loch Lomond view from the south end, take the A831 to Balmaha and climb Conic Hill that rises behind it. Alternatively hire a boat and row (or you could take a motorboat) around the islands; the nearest is Inchcailloch, where you can tie up your craft and climb the small hill at the island's center. The view in every direction is spectacular. Note how Inchcailloch and the other islands line up with Conic Hill. This geographic line is indicative of the Highland boundary fault, which runs through Loch Lomond and the hill.

Drymen is 3 mi east of the loch via B837, which leads to Loch Lomond's eastern shore. It's a respectable and cozy town in the Lowland fields, with stores, tea shops, and pubs catering to the well-to-do Scots who have moved here from Glasgow.

GETTING HERE AND AROUND

To reach Loch Lomond, take the B837 from Drymen as far as it will take you. From Balloch the A82 hugs the bank all the way to Crianlarich, where the A85 will take you back to Callander and Stirling.

You can drive, cycle or walk along the 32 mi of Loch Lomond along its western shores, and watch the changing face of the loch as you go or look up towards the shifting slopes of Ben Lomond.

ESSENTIALS

Visitor Information Loch Lomond and the Trossachs National Park Headquarters (⊠ *The Old Station, Balloch* ☎ *01389/722600* ⊕ *www. lochlomond-trossachs.org*). **Loch Lomond Shores** (⊠ *Ben Lomond Way, Balloch* ☎ *01389/772199* ⊕ *www.lochlomondshores.com*).

SPORTS AND THE OUTDOORS

BOAT TOURS **Cruise Loch Lomond** (⊠ *Boatyard, Tarbet* ☎ *01301/702356*) runs tours all year from various ports around the loch. **Macfarlane and Son** (⊠ *Balmaha Boatyard, Loch Lomond* ☎ *01360/870214*) rents boats for £10 per hour or £30 per day (£20/£50 with an outboard motor). They also run cruises on the Loch.

WHERE TO EAT

££ ✕ **Coach House Coffee Shop.** This lively restaurant and café fits perfectly
BRITISH into its surroundings, with its cheerful over-the-top Scottishness. Long wooden tables, a large chimney with an open fire throughout the winter months, and a display cabinet full of mouthwatering cakes baked by the owner create the atmosphere. Rich homemade soups and stokies (large round rolls filled to overflowing) are served, as is the ubiquitous haggis, all in king-size quantities. It is worth asking for tea served in ceramic teapots representing everything from dining rooms to telephone boxes (the pots are for sale in the shop). ⊠ *Luss* ☎ *01436/860341* ▭ *AE, D, DC, MC, V.*

££ ✕ **Drovers Inn.** The portions at this noisy, friendly inn are enormous,
SCOTTISH which is just as well since many of the clientele have returned from a day's walking on the nearby West Highland Way. Scottish staples like sausage and mash, minced beef, and the ubiquitous haggis with mash and neeps (turnips) jostle for a place beside occasionally more adventurous dishes. The dining areas are hung with swords and some modern copies of old paintings. This is a genuine traveler's pub, with an appropriate range of whiskies (hearty rather than elegant). There is traditional music every weekend, and there are 26 rooms for rent. The bear at the door should not put you off (it is stuffed and very old). ⊠ *Inverarnan, just north of Ardlui* ☎ *01301/704234* ⊕ *www.thedroversinn. co.uk* ▭ *AE, D, MC, V.*

WHERE TO STAY

££ 🏨 **Balloch House Vintage Inn.** Cute, cozy, and very Scottish, this small hotel offers tasty breakfasts and hearty pub meals like fish-and-chips and local smoked salmon for reasonable prices (£–££). The tartan carpet and burning peat fires are nice touches, as are the low ceilings and flickering candles. Rooms upstairs are simple but clean and spacious. Some have great views of the loch. **Pros:** beautiful building; recently refurbished; near shopping. **Cons:** noisy pinball machine next to bar; not all rooms have views. ⊠ *Balloch Rd., Balloch, Alexandria* ☎ *01389/752579* ⊕ *www.vintageinn.co.uk* ➳ *12 rooms* ♿ *In-room: no a/c, Wi-Fi. In-hotel: restaurant, bar* ➾ *AE, DC, MC, V* ❑ *BP.*

£££££   🏨 **Cameron House.** There is very little that you cannot do at this luxury resort hotel beside Loch Lomond, including taking to the water in the hotel's own motorboat or riding a seaplane above the waters. Built around an old baronial house, the hotel echoes the dark hues and grand furniture of the original owners in the decor of the beautifully appointed rooms. There are several restaurants and elegant bars in the central complex and in the golf courses that form part of the estate. The newly opened spa and leisure club has pools, Jacuzzis, and game rooms. Noted chef Martin Wishart's restaurant offers a prix-fixe dinner, as does the Brasserie, while the enormous Great Scots bar celebrates national achievement in everything from soccer to literature. **Pros:** beautiful grounds; good dining. **Cons:** prices are high; slightly difficult access from the A82. ⊠ *A82* ☎ *01389/755565* ⊕ *www.devere. co.uk* ➳ *96 rooms, 7 suites* ♿ *In-room: no a/c, Wi-Fi, DVD. In-hotel: 3 restaurants, bars, golf courses, fishing, tennis courts, pools, gym, children's programs (ages 5–12)* ➾ *AE, D, DC, MC, V* ❑ *BP.*

££   🏨 **Culcreuch Castle Hotel.** The hand-painted wallpaper in the Chinese Bird Room dates from 1723, and has never been changed. It is the pride of this authentic castle, set in vast and beautiful grounds, with its own loch for those wanting to fish and hills for those who prefer walking. The bedrooms are furnished in 18th-century style, with en-suite shower rooms, some grander than others (the standard rooms are rather small). The restaurant is grand and baronial, while the downstairs bar still has arrow slits in the windows of what were once the castle kitchens. Original paintings line the stone stairways. The restaurant offers a four-course prix-fixe menu (£££££) of largely Scottish cuisine. **Pros:** historic building; expansive and beautiful grounds; good food at reasonable prices. **Cons:** a little remote from major tourist centers; steep stairways; rather small shower rooms. ⊠ *Fintry* ☎ *01360/860555* ⊕ *www. culcreuch-castle-hotel.com* ➳ *14 rooms* ♿ *In-room: no a/c, Wi-Fi. In-hotel: restaurant, room service, bar, Internet terminal* ➾ *AE, D, DC, MC, V* ❑ *BP.*

SHOPPING

Loch Lomond Shores (⊠ *Ben Lomond Way, Balloch* ☎ *01389/751035* ⊕ *www.lochlomondshores.com*) is a lakeside shopping complex that also contains restaurants, pubs, and a visitor center.

At **Thistle Bagpipe Works** (⊠ *Luss* ☎ *01436/860250*), on the western shore of Loch Lomond, you can commission your own made-to-order set of bagpipes. You can also order a complete Highland outfit, including kilt and jacket.

PERTHSHIRE

In some ways, Perthshire is a crossing point between different Scottish landscapes and histories. Perthshire itself is rural, agricultural Scotland, fertile and prosperous. Its woodlands, rivers, and glens (and agreeable

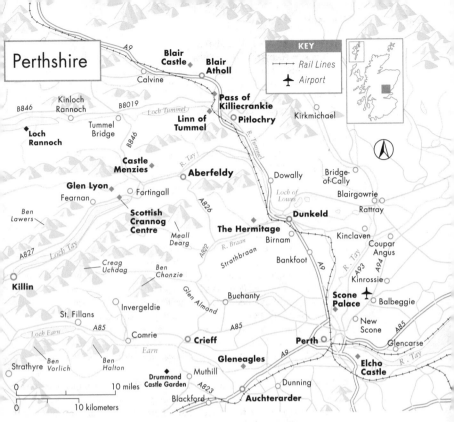

KEY

—★— Rail Lines

✈ Airport

Perthshire

A9 · Blair Castle · Blair Atholl · Calvine · Pass of Killiecrankie · Kinloch Rannoch · B846 · B8019 · Loch Tummel · Linn of Tummel · Pitlochry · Kirkmichael · Tummel Bridge · Loch Rannoch · B846 · R. Tay · Castle Menzies · Aberfeldy · Dowally · Bridge-of-Cally · Glen Lyon · Fortingall · Loch of Lowes · Blairgowrie · Fearnan · A826 · R. Tummel · Rattray · Ben Lawers · Scottish Crannog Centre · Dunkeld · Kinclaven · Meall Dearg · The Hermitage · Birnam · Coupar Angus · A827 · Loch Tay · A822 · R. Braan · Strathbraan · Bankfoot · A93 · A94 · Creag Uchdag · Ben Chonzie · A9 · Kinrossie · Killin · Glen Almond · Buchanty · Scone Palace · Balbeggie · Invergeldie · St. Fillans · A85 · A85 · New Scone · A85 · Loch Earn · Comrie · Earn · Crieff · Perth · Glencarse · Strathyre · Ben Vorlich · Ben Halton · Muthill · Gleneagles · A9 · R. Tay · Elcho Castle · Drummond Castle Garden · A823 · Dunning · Blackford · Auchterarder

0 ———— 10 miles

0 ———— 10 kilometers

climate and strategic position) drew the Romans and later the Celtic missionaries. In fact, the motto of the capital city, Perth, is "the perfect center." If Perthshire's castles invoke memories of past conflicts, the grand houses and spa towns here are testimony to the continued presence of a wealthy, landed gentry. This is also a place for walking, cycling, and water sports.

PERTH

36 mi northeast of Stirling, 43 mi north of Edinburgh, 61 mi northeast of Glasgow.

For many years, Perth was Scotland's capital, and central to its history. One king (James I) was killed here, and the Protestant reformer John Knox preached in St John's Kirk, where his rhetoric moved crowds to burn down several local monasteries. Perth's local whisky trade and the productive agriculture that surrounds the town have sustained it through the centuries. Its grand buildings, especially on either side of the River Tay, testify to its continued wealth. The open parkland within the city (the Inches) gives the place a restful air, and shops range from small craft boutiques to department stores.

GETTING HERE AND AROUND

Perth is served by the main railway line to Inverness, and regular and frequent buses run here from Glasgow, Edinburgh, and Stirling. The central artery, the A9, passes through the city en route to Pitlochry and Inverness, while a network of roads opens the way to the glens and hills around Glen Lyon, or the road to Loch Lomond (the A85) via Crianlarich.

ESSENTIALS

Visitor Information Perth (✉ Lower City Mills, W. Mill St. ☎ 01738/450600 ⊕ www.perthshire.co.uk).

EXPLORING PERTH

TOP ATTRACTIONS

Elcho Castle. From the tower battlements of Elcho Castle, you can see the River Tay stretching east and west. The castle marks a transition period when these structures began to be built as grand houses rather than fortresses, and it's easy to see that Elcho was built for both comfort and defense. The well conserved but uncluttered rooms let you imagine how life might have been here in the 17th century. The staircases still give access to all floors, and a torch is provided for the darker corners. Originally, the castle was only accessible via the river, but today it can be reached by road from Perth. ✉ Off A912, close to Rhynd ☎ 01738/639998 ⊕ www.historic-scotland.gov.uk/places 💷 £3.70 ⊙ Apr.–Sept., daily 9:30–5:30.

Ⓒ Scone Palace. About 2 mi from Perth, Scone Palace (pronounced skoon)
Fodor's Choice is much more cheerful and vibrant than the city's other castles. The
★ palace is the current residence of the Earl of Mansfield but is open to visitors. Although it incorporates various earlier works, the palace today has mainly a 19th-century theme, with mock castellations that were fashionable at the time. There's plenty to see if you're interested in the acquisitions of an aristocratic Scottish family: magnificent porcelain, furniture, ivory, clocks, and 16th-century needlework. A coffee shop, restaurant, gift shop, and play area are on site, and the extensive grounds have a pine plantation. The palace has its own mausoleum nearby, on the site of a long-gone abbey on Moot Hill, the ancient coronation place of the Scottish kings. To be crowned, they sat on the Stone of Scone, which was seized in 1296 by Edward I of England, Scotland's greatest enemy, and placed in the coronation chair at Westminster Abbey, in London. It was returned to Scotland in November 1996 and is now on view in Edinburgh Castle. Some Scots hint darkly that Edward was fooled by a substitution and that the real stone is hidden, waiting for Scotland to regain its independence. ✉ Braemar Rd. ☎ 01738/552300 ⊕ www.scone-palace.co.uk 💷 £8.50 ⊙ Apr.–Oct., daily 9:30–5:30, last admission at 5; Nov.–Mar., Fri. 10–4.

WORTH NOTING

Fergusson Gallery. The Round House, with its magnificent and newly restored dome and rotunda, contains this display of selections from a collection of 6,000 works—paintings, drawings, and prints—by the Scottish artist J.D. Fergusson (1874–1961). Fergusson was the longest lived member of the group called the Scottish Colourists, who took their inspiration from the French Impressionist painters in their use of color and light. ⊠ *Marshall Pl.* ☎ *01738/441944* ⊕ *www.scottishmuseums. org.uk* ⊴ *Free* ⊙ *Mon.–Sat. 10–5.*

Perth Art Gallery and Museum. The wide-ranging collection here includes exhibits on natural history, local history, archaeology, and art— including work by the great painter of animals Sir Edwin Landseer and some botanical studies of fungi by Beatrix Potter. ⊠ *78 George St.* ☎ *01738/632488* ⊴ *Free* ⊙ *May–Aug., Mon.–Sat. 10–5, Sun. 1–4:30; Sept.–Apr., Mon.–Sat. 10–5.*

Regimental Museum of the Black Watch. Some will tell you the Black Watch was a Scottish regiment whose name is a reference to the color of its tartan. An equally plausible explanation, however, is that the regiment was established to keep an undercover watch on rebellious Jacobites. The Gaelic word for black is *dubh,* meaning, in this case, "hidden" or "covert." A wide range of uniforms, weaponry, and marching banners are displayed. The castle is closed on the last Saturday in June. ⊠ *Facing North Inch Park, entrance from Hay St.* ☎ *0131/310–8530* ⊕ *www. theblackwatch.co.uk* ⊴ *Free* ⊙ *May–Sept., Mon.–Sat. 10–4:30; Oct.– Apr., weekdays 10–3:30.*

St. John's Kirk. This cruciform-plan church dates from the 12th century. It was internally divided into three parts at the Reformation, but was restored to something closer to its medieval state by Sir Robert Lorimer in the 1920s. ⊠ *St. John St.* ☎ *01738/626159* ⊕ *www.st-johns-kirk.co.uk* ⊴ *£1 donation* ⊙ *Weekdays 10–4, Sun. services at 9:30 and 11.*

WHERE TO EAT AND STAY

£££
BRITISH
✕ **Let's Eat.** The mixed clientele reflects noted chef Willie Deans' imaginative menu. Prix-fixe menus (lunch £15, dinner £21) combine some surprising dishes (sole with leek mash, broad beans, and bacon) with homelier, earthy dishes with a Scottish flavor (pork hough [hock] in pear cider or Blairgowrie beef fillet). The restaurant is airy and comfortable, merging warm colors and wood. ⊠ *77–79 Kinnoull St.* ☎ *01738/632377* ⊟ *AE, D, MC, V* ⊙ *Closed Sun. and Mon.*

£££
⊞ **Parklands.** This stylish Georgian town house overlooks lush woodland. It's perhaps best known for its pair of restaurants, Acanthus and No. 1 The Bank, serving Scottish fish, game, and beef. A sense of elegance permeates the low-key, contemporary interior. **Pros:** flat-screen TV in every room; superb restaurant. **Cons:** basic decor; some rooms have better views than others. ⊠ *2 St. Leonard's Bank,* ☎ *01738/622451* ⊕ *www.theparklandshotel.com* ⤴ *14 rooms* ⚬ *In-room: no a/c. In-hotel: 2 restaurants, Wi-Fi hotspot* ⊟ *AE, DC, MC, V* ⫟❕ *BP.*

££
★
⊞ **Sunbank House Hotel.** This early Victorian gray stone mansion near Perth's Branklyn Gardens overlooks the River Tay and the city of Perth. Unpretentious and comfortable, its front garden offers fine views. The owner (who is also the chef) takes great pride in his restaurant (£££££), which serves imaginatively prepared prix-fixe dinners that focus on locally raised meats and game. **Pros:** reasonably priced; friendly staff; delicious local cuisine. **Cons:** some rooms are very small; you can hear traffic from the main road. ⊠ *50 Dundee Rd.* ☎ *01738/624882* ⊕ *www.*

sunbankhouse.com ⤴ *9 rooms* ⚲ *In-room: no a/c, Wi-Fi. In-hotel: restaurant, bar* ⊟ *MC, V* ⦾ *BP.*

NIGHTLIFE AND THE ARTS

The Victorian **Perth Repertory Theatre** (✉ *185 High St.* ☎ *017384/727000*) stages plays and musicals. **Perth Concert Hall** (✉ *Mill St.* ☎ *01738 621031*) hosts musical performances of all types.

SHOPPING

The **Perthshire Visitor Centre** (✉ *A9, Bankfoot, 6 mi from Perth* ☎ *01738/ 787696*) is not so much an information center as a shopping complex and restaurant. The complex has a specialist whisky shop, a large delicatessen, a gift shop, and a clothes retail outlet.

CERAMICS Perth is an especially popular hunting ground for china and glass. **Caithness Glass** (✉ *Inveralmond, off A9 at northern Perth boundary* ☎ *01738/492320*) sells all types of silky-smooth glassware in its factory shop. You can watch glassblowers at work, and there's a small museum and a restaurant. **Watson of Perth** (✉ *163–167 High St.* ☎ *01738/639861*) has sold exquisite bone china and cut crystal since 1900 and can pack your purchase for shipment overseas.

CLOTHING **C & C Proudfoot** (✉ *104 South St.* ☎ *01738/632483*) sells a comprehensive selection of sheepskins, leather jackets, rugs, slippers, and handbags.

JEWELRY AND Perth proffers an unusual buy: Scottish freshwater pearls from the River
ANTIQUES Tay, in delicate settings. The Romans coveted these pearls. If you do, too, then you can make your choice at **Cairncross Ltd., Goldsmiths** (✉ *18 St. John's St.* ☎ *01738/624367*), where you can also admire a display of some of the more unusual shapes and colors of pearls. Some of the settings take their theme from Scottish flowers. Antique jewelry and silver, including a few Scottish items, can be found at **Timothy Hardie** (✉ *25 St. John's St.* ☎ *01738/633127*). **Whispers of the Past** (✉ *15 George St.* ☎ *01738/635472*) has a collection of jewelry, linens, and other items.

DUNKELD

14 mi north of Perth.

The ruined cathedral above the town of Dunkeld marks its historic beginnings. The present town grew up around the main square, built by the Atholl family in the wake of the 1689 defeat of the Jacobite army (following its earlier victory in the Battle of Killiecrankie). The National Trust for Scotland has helped to maintain the houses with its Little Houses Project; it has a small exhibition above the Dunkeld and Birnam Tourist Information Centre (ask for the Heritage Trail leaflet). Craft and interior design shops dominate Atholl Street, which leads down to the River Tay.

GETTING HERE AND AROUND

Dunkeld is on the A9 between Perth and Pitlochry. The town is also on the main train line to Inverness.

ESSENTIALS

Visitor Information Dunkeld and Birnam Tourist Information Centre (✉ *The cross in High St.* ☎ *01350/727688* ⊕ *www.visitscotland.com*).

EXPLORING

The bridge across the Tay, built by the great engineer Thomas Telford in 1809, connects Dunkeld to the village of Birnam. In the woods on Birnam Hill, some 500 yards from the town center, Macbeth met the three witches who foretold his death. Witty wooden notices lead the visitor to the right tree, a gnarled hollow oak. Less spooky is the **Beatrix Potter Garden,** which celebrates the life and work of this much loved children's writer who, for many years, spent her family holidays in the area. An enchanting garden walk allows you to peep into the homes of Peter Rabbit and Mrs. Tiggy Winkle, her best-known characters. The visitor center has a well-stocked shop, a small café, and an imaginative exhibition on the writer's life and work (entry £1). ⊠ *Birnam Arts Centre, Station Rd., Birnam* ☎ *01350/727674* ⊕ *www.birnaminstitute. com* ⊗ *Garden daily 10–4:30.*

At **Loch of Lowes,** a Scottish Wildlife Trust reserve near Dunkeld, the domestic routines of the osprey, one of Scotland's conservation success stories, can be observed in relative comfort. ⊠ *Off A923, about 2 mi northeast of Dunkeld* ☎ *01350/727337* ⊕ *www.swt.org.uk* ☜ *£3.50* ⊗ *Daily 10–5.*

★ On the outskirts of Dunkeld, the **Hermitage** is a woodland walk that follows the River Braan. In the 18th century, the dukes of Atholl constructed two follies (a fantasy building) here, **Ossian's cave** and the awesome **Ossian's Hall,** above a spectacular—and noisy—waterfall. (Ossian was a fictional Celtic poet invented by James MacPherson in the 19th century for a Victorian-era fascinated by the primitive past.) You'll also be in the presence of Britain's tallest tree, a Douglas fir measuring 214 feet. ⊠ *A9, 1 mi west of Dunkeld.*

WHERE TO EAT

££ ✕ **Taybank Hotel.** This hotel overlooking the river near the bridge is a
ECLECTIC musical meeting place owned by Scottish musical institution Dougie MacLean. There live music several nights a week. The bar serves good solid Scottish food; try the "stovies," a warming oven-cooked dish of onions, meat, and potatoes, or its speciality "Curly Skirlie Chicken Breast," cooked with bacon and kale. ⊠ *Tay Terrace* ☎ *01350/727340* 🖃 *AE, D, MC, V* ⊗ *Closed Sun. and Mon.*

SHOPPING

Dunkeld Antiques (⊠ *Tay Terr.* ☎ *01350/728832* ⊕ *www.dunkeldantiques. com.uniform.webhoster.co.uk*) is housed in a deconsecrated church facing the river. The shop stocks mainly 18th- and 19th-century items, from large furniture to ornaments, books, and prints. At the **Jeremy Law of Scotland's Highland Horn and Deerskin Centre** (⊠ *City Hall, Atholl St.* ☎ *01350/727569* ⊕ *www.moccasin.co.uk*), you can purchase stag antlers and cow horns shaped into walking sticks, cutlery, and tableware. Deerskin shoes and moccasins, small leather goods made from deerskin, and a specialty malt-whisky collection of more than 200 different malts are also sold.

PITLOCHRY

15 mi north of Dunkeld.

In the late 19th century, Pitlochry was an elegant Victorian spa town, famous for its mild microclimate and beautiful setting. Today it is a busy tourist town, with wall-to-wall gift shops, cafes and B&Bs, large hotels, and a huge golf course. The town itself is oddly nondescript and unimpressive, but it's a convenient base from which to explore the surrounding hills and valleys.

GETTING HERE AND AROUND

The main route through Central Scotland, the A9, passes through Pitlochry, as does the main railway line from Glasgow/Edinburgh to Inverness. From here the B8019 connects to the B846 west to Rannoch Moor or south to Aberfeldy.

ESSENTIALS

Visitor Information Pitlochry (⊠ *22 Atholl Rd.* ☎ *01796/472215* ⊕ *www. perthshire.co.uk*).

EXPLORING

Most Scottish dams have salmon passes or ladders of some kind, enabling the fish to swim upstream to their spawning grounds. The **Pitlochry Dam and Fish Ladder,** just behind the main street, leads into a glass-paneled pipe that allows the fish to observe the visitors. ⊠ *Off A9* ☎ *01796/473152* ☐ *£3* ☉ *Apr.–Oct., weekdays 10–5:30.*

If you have a whisky-tasting bent, visit **Edradour Distillery,** which claims to be the smallest single-malt distillery in Scotland (but then, so do others). There's a fun, informative tour of the distillery where you get to see how the whisky is made; you also get to savor a free dram at the end of the tour. ⊠ *A924, 2½ mi east of Pitlochry* ☎ *01796/472095* ⊕ *www.edradour.co.uk* ☐ *Tours £5* ☉ *Tours Mar.–Oct., Mon.–Sat. 9:30–5, Sun. noon–5; Nov. and Dec., Mon.–Sat. 10–4.*

The **Linn of Tummel,** a series of marked walks along the river and through tall, mature woodlands, is a little north of Pitlochry. Above the Linn, the A9 rises on stilts and gives an exciting view of the valley.

★ The **Pass of Killiecrankie,** set among the oak woods and rocky river just north of the Linn of Tummel, was the site of a famous battle won by the Jacobites in 1689. The National Trust for Scotland's **visitor center** at Killiecrankie explains the significance of this battle, which was the first attempt to restore the Stewart monarchy. The battle was noted for the death of the central Jacobite leader, John Graham of Claverhouse (1649–89), also known as Bonnie Dundee, who was hit by a stray bullet. The rebellion fizzled after Claverhouse's death. ⊠ *Off A9, 4 mi north of Pitlochry* ☎☎ *01796/473233* ⊕ *www.nts.org.uk/Visits* ☉ *Site daily 24 hrs; visitor center Apr.–Oct., daily 10–5:30.*

WHERE TO EAT AND STAY

£ ╳ **Moulin Hotel and Brewery.** The Moulin is a traditional pub with dark
BRITISH wooden interiors that serves standard Scottish fare in large quantities. Venison Braveheart, for example, is cooked in the brewery's own Braveheart beer, and the haggis with neeps and tatties is predictable but

good. There's also a table d'hôte menu (££££). This is a pleasant place, provided you are not too averse to the stuffed animals along the walls. The home-brewed beer is powerful, and you can visit the brewery, which is beside the hotel. ✉*A93* ☏*01796/472196* ▤*DC, MC, V.*

££££ ⊞ **Atholl Palace Hotel.** A grand hotel in the best Victorian style, the Atholl Palace is a 19th-century vision of what a medieval castle should look like. Built when the popularity of spas and water treatments was at its height, in the 1870s, it stands in its own 50-acre grounds with views of hills and valleys. Its fourth-floor suites, in the pointed towers, have circular sitting rooms with lovely

> ### LOCH RANNOCH
>
> With its shoreline of birch trees framed by dark pines, **Loch Rannoch** is the quintessential Highland loch. Fans of Robert Louis Stevenson (1850–94), especially of *Kidnapped* (1886), will not want to miss the last, lonely section of road. Stevenson describes the setting: "The mist rose and died away, and showed us that country lying as waste as the sea, only the moorfowl and the peewees crying upon it, and far over to the east a herd of deer, moving like dots." Loch Rannoch is off B846, 20 mi west of Pitlochry.

views (though it is quite a climb to reach them). The bedrooms are bright and luxurious; most have grand curtained beds and reproduction antique furniture. Bathrooms are spacious and unique. The hotel also boasts a genuinely interesting basement museum (£3 admission) that looks at working life and the visitor experience in the hotel over time. The elegant restaurant offers a prix-fixe (£26) and à la carte menu, as well as special menus and a separate seating area for children. There are gardens and woods to walk in, and a range of activities for guests who prefer not to lounge in the ample leather sofas in the lobby. **Pros:** lovely grounds; lots for kids to do; high comfort. **Cons:** old-fashioned feel; long anonymous corridors. ✉*A924* ☏*01796/472400* ⊕*www.athollpalace.com* ⤳*100 rooms* ⌂ *In-room: no a/c, Wi-Fi. In-hotel: restaurant, room service, bar, tennis court, pool, spa* ▤ *AE, DC, MC, V* ⦿❘ *BP.*

£££ ⊞ **Killiecrankie House Hotel.** This neat oasis is set amid the wooded hills and streams of the Pass, and just two minutes walk from the Soldier's Leap (where an escaping redcoat jumped 18 feet to avoid the pursuing Jacobites.) Located in what was once a manse (a priest's home), the hotel's clean lines are echoed in the simple, elegant rooms. The bathrooms have touches of luxury, with thick towels and multiple scents. The 5 acres of woodland around the hotel provide gentle walks, but it is also well situated for those with more ambitious walking or fishing. There is a lunch and early evening menu in the bar and a prix-fixe dinner menu. ✉*Near Pitlochry* ☏*01796/473220* ⊕*www.killiecrankiehotel.co.uk* ⤳*10 rooms* ⌂ *In-room: no a/c, Wi-Fi. In-hotel: restaurant, bar* ▤ *AE, DC, MC, V* ⦿❘*BP.*

£ ⊞ **Tir Aluinn Guest House.** Tir Aluinn (pronounced tiralin is a comfortable, bright, and friendly B&B that looks down over the town of Pitlochry and the valley beyond. The house is stone built with a large garden. The bedrooms are simple and unpretentious, and most have clear views; en-suite shower rooms are bright and clean. There is ample parking available. **Pros:** friendly attentive owners; good views; bright decor. **Cons:** slightly outside the town; good but basic furnishings. ⊠ *10 Higher Oakfield* ☎ *01796/473811* ⊕ *www.tiraluinn.co.uk* ↻ *4 rooms* ↻ *In-room: no a/c, Wi-Fi. In-hotel: Wi-Fi hotspot* ⊟ *D, DC, MC, V* ⦿ *BP.*

NIGHTLIFE AND THE ARTS

Pitlochry Festival Theatre (☎ *01796/484626 box office, 01796/484600 general inquiries* ⊕ *www.pitlochry.org.uk*) presents six plays each season, hosts eight Sunday concerts, and holds art exhibitions. It also has a café and restaurant overlooking the River Tummel.

BLAIR ATHOLL

10 mi north of Pitlochry.

GETTING HERE AND AROUND

Popular Blair Castle is just off the A9 Pitlochry-to-Inverness road, beyond the village of Blair Atholl. The village has a railway station that is on the main Inverness line.

EXPLORING

Fodor'sChoice ★ Thanks to its historic contents and war-torn past, **Blair Castle** is one of Scotland's most highly rated sights. The turreted white castle was home to successive dukes of Atholl and their families, the Murrays, until the death of the 10th duke. One of the castle's fascinating details is a preserved piece of floor still bearing marks of the red-hot shot fired through the roof during the 1745 Jacobite rebellion—the last occasion in Scottish history that a castle was besieged. The castle holds not only military artifacts—historically, the duke was allowed to keep a private army, the Atholl Highlanders—but also a rich collection of furniture, china, and paintings. The Hercules Gardens is a 9-acre Victorian walled garden, and the extensive grounds have woodland and river walks. ⊠ *A9 (Pitlochry-to-Inverness road), Blair Atholl* ☎ *01796/481207* ⊕ *www.blair-castle.co.uk* ⊠ *Castle and grounds £8.25, grounds only £4* ⦿ *Apr.–Oct., daily 9:30–4:30; last admission at 3:30.*

SHOPPING

The **House of Bruar** (⊠ *A9, just north of Blair Atholl* ☎ *01796/483236*) is an upscale shopping complex with a heavy emphasis on traditional tweeds and cashmeres. A large food supermarket here sells local produce and food, as well as a range of international delicatessen foods. When you're done shopping, take a walk up the path that crosses the Bruar Falls, accessed at the back of the shopping complex.

ABERFELDY

15 mi southwest of Pitlochry, 25 mi southwest of Blair Castle.

The most dramatic thing about Aberfeldy is the high hump-backed bridge into the town, built by William Adam in 1733 and commissioned by General Wade, who marched through Scotland suppressing local resistance after the Jacobite rebellion. The town itself is rather sleepy, but this is a popular base for exploring the region. It's Scotland's first fair-trade town, and a water mill here produces delicious stone-ground oatmeal. There's also a whisky distillery and plenty of local golf courses.

GETTING HERE AND AROUND
You can reach Aberfeldy from Dunkeld via the A9 and the A827. The town is also served by regular buses from Perth and Pitlochry.

ESSENTIALS
Visitor Information **Aberfeldy Tourist Information Centre** (⊠ *The Square* ☎ *01887/820276* ⊕ *www.visitscotland.com*).

EXPLORING

Dewar's World of Whisky. This established distillery has a whisky museum and a tour that demonstrates how whisky is made (with a tasting at the end, of course). There's also a nature trail on the grounds as well as a café restaurant. ⊠ *Aberfeldy* ☎ *01887/822010* ⊕ *www.dewars. com* ☑ *£6.50* ☉ *Apr.–Oct., weekdays 10–6, Sun. noon–4; Nov.–Mar., Mon.–Sat. noon–4.*

Castle Menzies, a 16th-century fortified tower house, contains the **Clan Menzies Museum,** which displays many relics of the clan's history. Beside the castle is an old byre that's been converted into a craft shop, winery, and café complex. The castle stands west of Aberfeldy, on the opposite bank of the River Tay. ⊠ *Weem, near Aberfeldy* ☎ *01887/820982* ☑ *£4* ☉ *Apr.–Oct., Mon. 10:30–5, Sun. 2–5.*

You can reach **Glen Lyon** traveling north from Aberfeldy on the B846 or by a high road from Loch Tay: take the A827 to Fearnan, then turn north to Fortingall, a small hamlet of pretty thatched cottages unusual in southern Scotland. Its famous yew **tree,** in the churchyard near the Fortingall Hotel, is thought to be more than 3,000 years old. Legend has it that Pontius Pilate was born beside it, when his father was serving as a Roman legionnaire in Scotland. Turn west into the glen, one of central Scotland's most attractive glens, and one of its longest at 34 mi. It has a rushing river, thick forests, and the typical big *hoose* (house) hidden on private grounds. There's a dam at the head of the loch, a reminder that little of Scotland's scenic beauty is unadulterated. The winding road lends itself to an unrushed, leisurely drive, past the visitor center at the access to Ben Lawers, a popular climb, and on to Killin. ⊠ *A827, 15 mi north of Aberfeldy via Fortingall and Fearnan.*

OFF THE BEATEN PATH

Scottish Crannog Centre. Here's your chance to travel back 5,000 years to a time when the local inhabitants of this area, in common with others across Scotland and Ireland, started building defensive homesteads, known as *crannogs,* on wooden piles standing in lochs. They were approachable only by narrow bridges that could be easily defended. This practice continued until as late as the 17th century. Archaeologists have found many remains of crannogs in lochs throughout Scotland. One of the best preserved was found several feet under the surface of Loch Tay, off the north shore at Fearnan, and it's now possible to visit an accurate replica built on the south shore. An exhibition gives details about crannog construction and the way of life in and around crannogs. The Crannog Centre is just west of Aberfeldy, on the southern shore of Loch Tay. ⊠ *Kenmore, South Loch Tay* ☎ *01887/830583* ⊕ *www.*

crannog.co.uk ✉ *£6.25* ⊙ *Apr.–Oct., daily 10–5:30; Nov., weekends 10–4; last entry 1 hr before closing.*

SHOPPING

Aberfeldy Water Mill (✉ *Mill St.* ☎ *01887/822896*) is a bookshop, gallery, and café complex in the center of town.

SPORTS AND THE OUTDOORS

Highland Safaris (✉ *Aberfeldy* ☎ *01887/820071* ⊕ *www.highlandsafaris. net*) offers a full range of off-road activities for cyclists, drivers, and walkers.

BOATING

Loch Tay Boating Centre (✉ *Pier Rd., Kenmore* ☎ *01887/830291*) rents cabin cruisers, speedboats, fishing boats, and canoes. It's open from April through mid-October daily from 9 AM to 7 PM. The **National Kayak School** (✉ *Weem* ☎ *01887/820498* ⊕ *www.nationalkayakschool.co.uk*), near Aberfeldy, offers a range of courses.

KILLIN

24 mi southwest of Aberfeldy, 39 mi north of Stirling, 45 mi west of Perth.

Killin's setting near the Breadalbane Mountains at the end of Loch Tay (where the Falls of Dochart rush into the lake) gives the village an almost alpine flavor. You'll find a surprisingly diverse selection of crafts and woolen shops here, as well as a plethora of B&Bs.

GETTING HERE AND AROUND

Killin can be reached from Stirling via the A85 and A827, or from Aberfeldy via the A827, the winding road beside Loch Tay.

ESSENTIALS

Visitor Information Killin Tourist Information Office (✉ *Breadalbane Folklore Centre, Falls of Dochart* ☎ *01567/820254*).

EXPLORING

The **Falls of Dochart,** white-water rapids overlooked by a pine-clad islet, are at the west end of the village. ✉ *Off A827.*

The **Breadalbane Folklore Centre,** by the Falls of Dochart, focuses on the area's heritage and folk tales. The most curious of these are the "Healing Stones of St. Fillan"—water-worn stones that have been looked after for centuries, valued for their supposed curative powers. ✉ *Falls of Dochart* ☎ *01567/820254* ✉ *£2.95* ⊙ *Apr.–Oct., daily 10–4*

Across the River Dochart and near the golf course sit the ruins of **Finlarig Castle,** built by Black Duncan of the Cowl, a notorious Campbell laird. The castle grounds can be visited at any time. ✉ *Off A827.*

BICYCLING

If you want to explore the north end of the Glasgow–Killin cycleway, rent a mountain bike from **Killin Outdoor Centre and Mountain Shop** (✉ *Main St.* ☎ *01567/820652*). Also available are canoes, crampons, skis, and ice axes.

CRIEFF

25 mi southwest of Killin.

A spa and market town in the foothills of the Grampians, Crieff still retains the prosperous air of its Victorian heyday. Its central square, where local farmers may once have gathered to trade, is still a lively center. For a very different view of the town, you could climb Knock Hill, which is signposted from the town center.

GETTING HERE AND AROUND

Crieff once prospered because of the arrival of the railway. There is no station here today, but there are regular buses from Stirling and Glasgow. By car, take the A85 from Perth, or the A9 after Dunblane.

ESSENTIALS

Visitor Information Crieff (✉ *Town Hall, High St.* ☎ *01764/653418* ⊕ *www. visitscotland.com*).

EXPLORING

If you wish to discover the delights of whisky distilling, sign up for the **Famous Grouse Experience** at the Glenturret Distillery. A guide takes you through the distillery and to the Pavilion Bar where you can have a glass of Famous Grouse Finest (a blended, not a single-malt whisky) and try your skill at "nosing." Here you learn how whisky is made and why time, water, soil, and air are so important to the taste. You might cap your tour with lunch or dinner at either of the two Scottish restaurants. Signs lead to the distillery on the west side of the town. ✉ *Off A822* ☎ *01764/656565* ⊕ *www.famousgrouse.co.uk/experience* 🎟 *£6.95* ⊙ *Mar.–Dec., daily 9–6, last tour at 4:30; Jan. and Feb., daily 10–4:30, last tour at 3.*

Drummond Castle Garden is a large, formal Victorian parterre celebrating family and Scottish heraldry. The flower beds are planted and trimmed in the shapes of various heraldic symbols, such as a lion rampant and a checkerboard, associated with the coat of arms of the family that owns the castle and the Scottish Royal Coat of Arms. It's regarded as one of the finest of its kind in Europe, and it even made an appearance in the film *Rob Roy*. ✉ *Off A822, 6 mi southwest of Crieff* ☎ *01764/681433* ⊕ *www.drummondcastlegardens.co.uk* 🎟 *£5* ⊙ *Easter weekend and May–Oct., daily 1–6; last admission at 5.*

WHERE TO STAY

£££ 🏨 **Crieff Hydro.** One of the great Victorian hydropathy centers scattered across central Scotland, this grand, old-fashioned hotel has been owned and run by the same family for over a hundred years. Its modernized rooms are of a standard design and some are fairly cramped, but most have king-size beds. The hotel appeals to families, and there's a wide range of activities for children both in hotel and on the extensive 900-acre grounds. More a resort than a hotel, it offers golf, tennis, riding, and off-road driving; there's also a gym and an extensive spa. The on-site Meikle restaurant is formal and offers a prix-fixe menu (££££). **Pros:** fine, extensive grounds; variety of activities; particularly good for children. **Cons:** rooms are rather dull; some activities are quite expensive. ✉ *Off A85* ☎ *01764/655555* ⊕ *www.crieffhydro.com* 🛏 *216*

6

rooms ⅛ *In-room: no a/c, Wi-Fi. In-hotel: gym, spa, golf, tennis, children's activities* 🟰 *AE, DC, MC, V* 🍴*FAP.*

SHOPPING

Crieff is a center for china and glassware. **Stuart Crystal** (✉ *Muthill Rd.* ☎ *01764/654004*), a factory shop, sells not only its own Stuart crystal but also Waterford, Dartington, and Wedgwood wares.

AUCHTERARDER

11 mi southeast of Crieff.

Famous for the Gleneagles Hotel and nearby golf courses, Auchterarder also has a flock of tiny antiques shops to amuse Gleneagles's golf widows and widowers.

GETTING HERE AND AROUND

Gleneagles Station is on the main Inverness line, while the A9 gives direct access to Gleneagles and Auchterarder via the A823.

ESSENTIALS

Visitor Information Auchterarder (✉ *90 High St.* ☎ *01764/663450* ⊕ *www. perthshire.co.uk*).

WHERE TO STAY

££££££

Fodor's Choice
★

Gleneagles Hotel. One of Britain's most famous hotels, Gleneagles is the very essence of modern grandeur. Like a vast, secret palace, it stands hidden in breathtaking countryside amid its world-famous golf courses. The rooms are elegant, hung with indulgent draperies and filled with soft leather furniture. All the details are here, from fluffy bathrobes hanging behind the door to freshly cut flowers in every room. For the most celebrated Scottish dining experience, enjoy Andrew Fairlie's signature dishes of lobster smoked over whisky barrels, and black truffle gnocchi. Recreation facilities are nearly endless: a shopping arcade, a spa, an equestrian center, a falconry center, and more. **Pros:** numerous amenities; the three courses are a golfer's paradise. **Cons:** luxury comes at steep price. ✉ *Off A823* ☎ *01764/662231* ⊕ *www.gleneagles.com* ↪*216 rooms, 13 suites* ⅛ *In-room: no a/c, refrigerator, Wi-Fi. In-hotel: 4 restaurants, room service, golf courses, tennis courts, pools, gym, spa, bicycles, children's programs (ages 4–10)* 🟰 *AE, DC, MC, V* 🍴*BP.*

Aberdeen and the Northeast

WORD OF MOUTH

"In Dufftown you will find Glenfiddich distillery. Probably one of the best sellers in the world and almost certainly the best tour. In Aberlour you are in the heart of Speyside on the Whisky Trail. If you have a favorite distillery, ask at a tourist office if they do a tour and just go along."

—Sheila

"Near Castle Fraser is Drum Castle and Garden, and it's likely to have fewer visitors than many others. It was home to the Irvines (gifted by Robert the Bruce) until the National Trust for Scotland took over. It's a wonderful mixture of medieval, Jacobean, and Victorian architecture, with an ancient tower. Well worth a visit."

—historytraveler

Updated by
Shona Main

Here, in this granite shoulder of Grampian, are some of Scotland's most enduring travel icons: Royal Deeside, the countryside that Queen Victoria made her own; the Castle Country route, where fortresses stand hard against the hills; and the Malt Whisky Trail, where peaty streams embrace the country's greatest concentration of distilleries. The region's gateway is the city of Aberdeen, constructed of granite and now aglitter with new wealth and new blood drawn together by North Sea oil.

Because of its isolation, Aberdeen has historically been a fairly autonomous place. Even now it's perceived by many U.K. inhabitants as lying almost out of reach in the northeast. In reality, it's 90-minutes' flying time from London or a little more than two hours by car from Edinburgh. Its magnificent 18th- and early-19th-century city center amply rewards exploration. Yet even if this popular base for travelers vanished from the map, an extensive portion of the northeast would still remain at the top of many travelers' wish lists.

Balmoral, the Scottish baronial–style house built for Queen Victoria as a retreat, is merely the most famous castle in the area, and certainly not the oldest. There are so many others that in one part of the region a Castle Trail has been established, leading you to such fortresses as the ruined medieval Kildrummy Castle, which once controlled the strategic routes through the valley of the River Don. In later structures, such as Castle Fraser, you can trace the changing styles and tastes of each of its owners over the centuries. Grand mansions such as 18th-century Haddo House, with its symmetrical facade and elegant interior, surrender any defensive role entirely.

A trail leading to a more ephemeral kind of pleasure can be found south of Elgin and Banff, where the glens embrace Scotland's greatest concentration of malt-whisky distilleries. With so many in Morayshire, where the distilling is centered in the valley of the River Spey and its tributaries, there's now a Whisky Trail. Follow it to experience a surprising wealth of flavors, considering that whisky is made of three basic ingredients.

The northeast's chief attraction lies in the gradual transition from high mountain plateau—by a series of gentle steps through hill, forest, and farmland—to the Moray Firth and North Sea coast, where the word "unadulterated" is redefined. Here you'll find some of the United Kingdom's most perfect wild shorelines, both sandy and sheer cliff, and breezy fishing villages like Cullen on the Banffshire coat and Stonehaven, south of Aberdeen. The Grampian Mountains, to the west, contain some of the highest ground in the nation, in the area of the Cairngorms. In recognition of this area's very special nature,

TOP REASONS TO GO

■ **Glorious castles:** With more than 75 castles, some Victorian and others dating back to the 13th century, this area has everything from ravaged ruins like Dunnottar to opulent Fyvie Castle. They still evoke the power, grandeur, and sometimes the cruelty of Scotland's past.

■ **Distilleries on the Whisky Trail:** The valley of the River Spey is famous for its single-malt distilleries, nine of which are connected by the signposted Malt Whisky Trail. You can choose from bigger operations such as Glenfiddich to the iconic Strathisla.

■ **Seaside cities and towns:** The fishing industry may be in decline, but the big-city port of Abderdeen and the colorful smaller fishing towns of Stonehaven and Cullen in the northeast are great (and very different) places to soak up the seagoing atmosphere—and some seafood.

■ **Great walking:** There are all types of walking for all kinds of walkers, from the bracing but spectacular inclines of the Grampian Hills, to the wooded gardens and grounds of Balmoral and Haddo House, to breath-stealing golden sands near towns such as Cullen.

■ **Superb golf:** The northeast has more than 50 golf clubs, some of which have championship courses. Less-famous clubs, both inland and by the sea, have some amazing courses as well.

Cairngorms National Park (Scotland's second, after Loch Lomond and the Trossachs National Park) was created in early 2003. The Grampian hills also have shaped the character of the folk who live in the northeast. In earlier times the massif made communication with the south somewhat difficult. As a result, native northeasterners still speak the richest Lowland Scottish.

ORIENTATION AND PLANNING

GETTING ORIENTED

Aberdeen, on the North Sea in the eastern part of the region, is Scotland's third-largest city; many people start a trip here. Once you have spent time in the city, you may be inclined to venture west into rural Deeside, with its royal connections and looming mountain backdrop. To the north of Deeside is Castle Country, with many ancient fortresses. Speyside and the Whisky Trail lie at the western edge of the region, and are equally accessible from Inverness. From Speyside you might travel back east along the pristine coastline at Scotland's northeasternmost tip.

Aberdeen. Family connections or Royal Deeside often take travelers to this part of Scotland, but many are surprised by how grand and rich in history Aberdeen is. The august granite-turreted buildings and rose-lined roads make this a surprisingly pleasant city to explore; don't miss Old Aberdeen in particular.

Royal Deeside and Castle Country. When Prince Albert designed Balmoral Castle for Queen Victoria, so began the Royal family's love affair with Deeside—and Deeside's love affair with it. However, this area has long been the retreat or the fortress of distinguished families, as the clutter of castles throughout the region shows. The majesty of the countryside also guarantees a superlative stop for everyone interested in history and romance.

The Northeast and the Malt Whisky Trail. For lovers of whisky, this is a favored part of Scotland to visit. Unique in their architecture, their ingredients and the end product, the distilleries of Speyside are keen to share with you their passion for "the water of life." This region also has rolling hills and, to the north, the beautiful, wild coastline of the North Sea.

PLANNING

WHEN TO GO

May and June are probably the loveliest times to visit, but many travelers arrive from late spring to early fall. Because the National Trust for Scotland tends to close its properties in winter, many of the northeast's castles are not suitable for off-season travel, though you can always see them from the outside. The distilleries are open much of the year.

PLANNING YOUR TIME

How you allocate your time may depend on your special interests—whether it's castles or whisky, for example. But even if you can only manage a morning or an afternoon, do not miss a walk around the granite streets of Old Aberdeen, and take in Aberdeen Art Gallery, St. Nicholas Kirk, and a pint in the Prince of Wales pub. A trip southward to the fishing town of Stonehaven and the breathtaking cliff-top fortress of Dunnottar makes a rewarding afternoon. Royal Deeside, with a good sprinkling of castles and grandeur, needs a good two days; even this might be tight for those who want to lap up every moment of majesty at Balmoral, Crathes, Fraser and Fyvie, the best of the bunch. A tour of malt whisky country should include tours of Glenfiddich, Glenfarclas, Glenlivet, and Glen Grant distilleries, and although it's not technically a maker of malt whisky, Strathisla. Real enthusiasts should allot two days for the distilleries, and they shouldn't pass up a visit to Speyside Cooperage, one of the few remaining cooperages in the Scotland. Cullen and Duff House gallery in Banff, on the coast, can be done in a day before returning to Aberdeen.

GETTING HERE AND AROUND

AIR TRAVEL

Aberdeen Airport is the region's major airport; there's good service to other parts of Britain and to Europe. *For more information, see Getting Here and Around in Aberdeen, below.*

BOAT AND FERRY TRAVEL

There's ferry service between Aberdeen, Lerwick (Shetland), and Kirkwall (Orkney) operated by Northlink Ferries.

Boat and Ferry Contacts Northlink Ferries (✉ *Jamieson's Quay, Aberdeen* ☎ *0845/600–0449* ⊕ *www.northlinkferries.co.uk*).

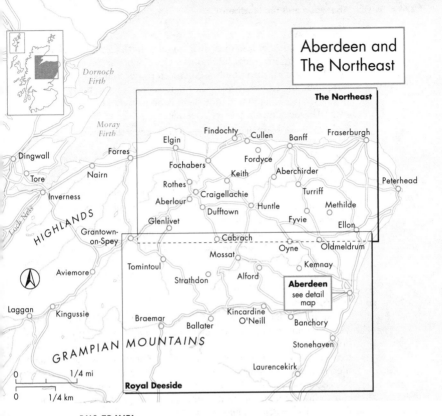

The Northeast

Dornoch Firth

Moray Firth

Dingwall
Tore
Inverness
Nairn
Forres
Elgin
Findochty
Cullen
Banff
Fraserburgh
Fordyce
Fochabers
Keith
Aberchirder
Peterhead
Rothes
Craigellachie
Turriff
Aberlour
Dufftown
Huntle
Methilde
Glenlivet
Fyvie
Ellon
Grantown-on-Spey
Cabrach
Oyne
Oldmeldrum
Mossat
Kemnay
Tomintoul
Aviemore
Strathdon
Alford
Aberdeen see detail map
Laggan
Kingussie
Braemar
Kincardine O'Neill
Banchory
Ballater
Stonehaven
GRAMPIAN MOUNTAINS
Laurencekirk

HIGHLANDS

Loch Ness

0   1/4 mi
0   1/4 km

Royal Deeside

BUS TRAVEL

Long-distance buses run to Aberdeen and from most parts of Scotland, England, and Wales. Contact National Express for bus connections with English towns. Contact Scottish Citylink for bus connections with Scottish towns. There's a network of local buses throughout the northeast run by Stagecoach (formerly by Bluebird), but they can take a long time and connections are not always well timed.

Bus Contacts National Express (☎ 08705/808080 ⊕ www.nationalexpress. com). **Scottish Citylink** (☎ 08705/505050 ⊕ www.citylink.co.uk). **Stagecoach** (☎ 0871/200–2233 ⊕ www.stagecoachbus.com/bluebird).

CAR TRAVEL

A car is the best way to see the northeast. If you are coming from the south, take the A90, continuing on from the M90 (from Edinburgh) or the M9/A9 (from Glasgow), which both stop at Perth. The coastal route, the A92, is a more leisurely alternative, with its interesting resorts and fishing villages. The most scenic route, however, is the A93 from Perth, north to Blairgowrie and into Glen Shee. The A93 then goes over the Cairnwell Pass, the highest main road in the United Kingdom. This route isn't recommended in winter, when snow can make driving difficult.

Around the northeast roads can be busy, with speeding and erratic driving a problem on the main A roads.

TRAIN TRAVEL

You can reach Aberdeen directly from Edinburgh (2½ hours), Glasgow (3 hours), and Inverness (2½ hours). Get a ScotRail timetable for full details. There are also London–Aberdeen routes that go through Edinburgh and the east-coast main line connecting Aberdeen to all corners of the United Kingdom. Sadly, there is no longer a train line running from Aberdeen through Royal Deeside.

Train Contacts **ScotRail** (☎ 08457/550033 ⊕ www.scotrail.co.uk).

RESTAURANTS

Partly in response to the demands of workers in the oil industry, restaurants have cropped up all over Aberdeen, and the quality of the food improves yearly. As in the rest of Scotland, this region is rediscovering the quality and versatility of the local produce. Juicy Aberdeen Angus steaks, lean lamb, and humanely reared pork appear on local menus, but despite this being the center of the fishing industry, most seafood available is still of the fish-and-chips variety. Restaurants like the Silver Darling in Aberdeen are spearheading a new interest in fish dishes, though, and old standards like Cullen skink (a creamy smoked fish soup) are increasingly on every menu.

HOTELS

The northeast has some splendid country hotels with log fires and old Victorian furnishings, where you can also be sure of eating well. Many hotels in Aberdeen are in older buildings that have a baronial feel. The trend for serviced apartments has caught on here, with some extremely modish and good-value options for those who want a bit more privacy. It's also now heading, fortunatley, into Deeside: it's notoriously difficult to find good accommodation beyond some country-house hotels, despite this being a popular tourist spot.

WHAT IT COSTS IN POUNDS					
	£	££	£££	££££	£££££
RESTAURANTS	under £10	£10–£14	£15–£19	£20–£25	over £25
HOTELS	under £70	£70–£120	£121–£160	£161–£220	over £220

Restaurant prices are for a main course at dinner. Hotel prices are for two people in a standard double room in high season, generally including the 17.5% V.A.T.

VISITOR INFORMATION

The tourist information center in Aberdeen has a currency exchange, Internet access, and supplies information on all of Scotland's northeast. There are also year-round tourist information offices in Braemar and Elgin. In summer, also look for tourist information centers in Alford, Ballater, Banchory, Braemar, Dufftown, Elgin, and Stonehaven.

Contacts **Aberdeen** (✉ 23 Union St. ☎ 01224/288828 ⊕ www.aberdeen-grampian.com).

ABERDEEN

As a gateway to Royal Deeside and the Malt Whisky Trail, Aberdeen attracts visitors, though many are eager to get out into the countryside. Today, though, the city's unique history is finally being recognized as more impressive than many Scots had previously realized, and the city is being rediscovered. Distinctive architecture, some fine museums, universities, and good restaurants, nightlife, and shopping add to the appeal of Scotland's third-largest city (population 202,000). Union Street is the heart of the city, but take time to explore the university and the pretty streets of Old Aberdeen.

In the 18th century, local granite quarrying produced a durable silver stone that would be used boldly in the glittering blocks, spires, columns, and parapets of Victorian-era Aberdonian structures. The city remains one of the United Kingdom's most distinctive, although some would say it depends on the weather and the brightness of the day. The mica chips embedded in the rock look like a million mirrors in the sunshine. In rain (and there is a fair amount of driving rain from the North Sea) and heavy clouds, however, their sparkle is snuffed out.

The city lies between the Dee and Don rivers, with a working harbor that has access to the sea; it has been a major fishing port and is the main commercial port in northern Scotland. The North Sea has always been important to Aberdeen. In the 1850s the city was famed for its sleek, fast clippers that sailed to India for cargoes of tea. In the late 1960s the course of Aberdeen's history was unequivocally altered when oil and gas were discovered offshore, sparking rapid growth, prosperity, and further industrialization.

GETTING HERE AND AROUND

AIR TRAVEL The city is easy to reach from other parts of the United Kingdom as well as Europe. British Airways, bmi, EasyJet, and Flybe are some of the airlines with service to other parts of Britain. Aberdeen Airport—serving both international and domestic flights—is in Dyce, 7 mi west of the city center on the A96 (Inverness). The drive to the center of Aberdeen is easy via the A96 (which can be busy during rush hour).

First Aberdeen Bus 27 operates between the airport terminal and Union Street in the center of Aberdeen. Buses (£2) run frequently at peak times, less often at midday and in the evening; the journey time is approximately 40 minutes.

Dyce is on ScotRail's Inverness–Aberdeen route. The rail station is a short taxi ride from the terminal building. The ride takes 12 minutes, and trains run approximately every two hours. If you intend to visit the western region first, you can travel northwest, from Aberdeen, by rail, direct to Elgin via Inverurie, Insch, Huntly, and Keith.

BUS TRAVEL First Aberdeen has easy and reliable service within the city of Aberdeen. Timetables are available from the tourist information center at St. Nicholas House.

CAR TRAVEL Aberdeen is a compact city with good signage. Its center is Union Street, the main thoroughfare running east–west, which tends to get crowded with traffic. Anderson Drive is an efficient ring road on the city's west side; be extra careful on its many traffic circles. It's best to leave your car in one of the parking garages (arrive early to get a space) and walk around, or use the convenient park-and-ride stop at the Bridge of Don, north of the city. Street maps are available from the tourist information center, newsdealers, and booksellers.

TAXI TRAVEL   You can find taxi stands throughout the center of Aberdeen: along Union Street, at the railway station at Guild Street, at Back Wynd, and at Regent Quay. The taxis have meters and might be saloon cars or black cabs. They are great ways to travel between neighborhoods.

TRAIN TRAVEL   Aberdeen has good ScotRail service. *See Getting Here and Around in Orientation and Planning, above.*

ESSENTIALS

Airport and Transfer Contacts Aberdeen Airport (☎ 0870/040–0006 ⊕ www.baa.co.uk). **First Aberdeen** (☎ 01224/650000 ⊕ www.firstaberdeen.co.uk). **ScotRail** (☎ 08457/550033 ⊕ www.scotrail.co.uk).

Bus Contacts First Aberdeen (☎ 01224/650000 ⊕ www.firstaberdeen.co.uk).

Visitor and Tour Information Aberdeen (✉ 23 Union St. ☎ 01224/288828 ⊕ www.aberdeen-grampian.com).

AROUND UNION STREET

Aberdeen centers on Union Street, with its many fine survivors of the Victorian and Edwardian streetscape. Marischal College, dating from the late 16th century, has many grand buildings that are worth exploring.

TIMING

You can explore the center of Aberdeen in half a day, but you'll probably want to devote a full day to poking around its interesting old buildings.

TOP ATTRACTIONS

❻ ★ **Aberdeen Art Gallery.** Housed in a 19th-century neoclassical building, the museum contains excellent paintings, prints, and drawings, sculpture, porcelain, costumes, and much else—from 18th-century art to major contemporary British works by Lucien Freud and Henry Moore. Scottish artists are well represented. Local stone has been used in interior walls, pillars, and the central fountain, designed by the acclaimed British sculptor Barbara Hepworth. ■ TIP➜ Look for the unique collection of Aberdeen silver on the ground floor. The museum also has a bustling café. ✉ *Schoolhill* ☎ *01224/523700* ⊕ *www.aagm.co.uk* 🎫 *Free* ⊙ *Tues.–Sat. 10–5, Sun. 2–5.*

▮ NEED A BREAK?   **The Beautiful Mountain** (✉ 11–13 Belmont St. ☎ 01224/ 645353) is a simple, good-natured café full of life and banter. Stop for a well-filled sandwich and a cup of tea, or perhaps a cake or two.

❿ ⏱ ★ **Aberdeen Maritime Museum.** This excellent museum, which incorporates the 1593 Provost Ross's House, tells the story of the city's involvement with the sea, from early inshore fisheries to tea clippers and the North Sea oil boom. It's a fascinating place for kids and adults, with its ship models, paintings, and equipment associated with the fishing,

Aberdeen

River Don

Beach Esplanade

Don St.

King St.

Seaton Park

OLD ABERDEEN

Kings

Links

Golf

Course

Tillydrone Rd.

Tillydrone Ave.

Portal Ter.

St. Machar's Dr.

Powis Crescent

Bedford Rd.

Sunnyside

Bedford Pl.

Sunnybank Rd.

Chanonry

Don St.

Dunbar St.

High St.

College Bounds

Spital

Kings Cr.

Seaton Pl. E.

School Rd.

School Dr.

Regent Walk

King St.

University Rd.

Orchard St.

Linksfield Stadium

Linksfield Rd.

Pittodrie Pl.

Pittodrie St.

Merkland Rd.

Golf Rd.

Elmbank Ter.

Froghall Ter.

Powis Pl.

Causeway End

Seaforth Rd.

Urquhart Rd.

Park Rd.

Nelson St.

George St.

Hutcheson St.

Skene Sq.

Maberly St.

Rosemount Pl.

John St.

St.Andrew

Schoolhill

Rosemount Viaduct

Union Ter.

Belmont St.

George St.

Gal150wgate

W. North St.

King St.

Park Rd.

Constitution St.

Beach Blvd.

Cotton St.

Castle St.

Miller St.

Justice St.

Marischal St.

Regent Quay

Victoria Dock

Blaikies Quay

Commercial Quay

Albert Basin

Upper Dock

Upper Kirkgate

Broad St.

Ship Row

St. Nicholas House

His Majesty's Theatre

The Green

Guild St.

S. College St.

Railway Station

Bus Station

TO DUTHIE PARK
↓

Market St.

0   1/4 mile

0   1/4 kilometer

6 **7** **8** **9** **1** **5** **4** **2** **3** **10**

13 **14** **12** **11** **15**

shipbuilding, and oil and gas industries. ⊠ *Ship Row* ☎ *01224/337700* ⊕ *www.aagm.co.uk* ▢ *Free* ☉ *Tues.–Sat. 10–5, Sun. noon–3.*

❺ Provost Skene's House. Now a museum portraying civic life, the house has restored, furnished period rooms and a painted chapel. Steeply gabled and built from rubble, it dates in part from 1545. The house was originally a mayor's domestic dwelling (*provost* is Scottish for "mayor"). Its costume gallery displays colorful exhibitions of fashions from different centuries. ⊠ *Guestrow off Broad St.* ☎ *01224/641086* ⊕ *www.aagm.co.uk* ▢ *Free* ☉ *Mon.–Sat. 10–5.*

❾ St. Nicholas Kirk. The original burgh church, the Mither Kirk, as this edifice is known, is not within the bounds of the early town settlement; that was to the east, near the end of present-day Union Street. During the 12th century the port of Aberdeen flourished, and there wasn't room for the church within the settlement. Its earliest features are its pillars—supporting a tower built much later—and its clerestory windows: both date from the 12th century. St. Nicholas was divided into east and west kirks at the Reformation, followed by a substantial amount of renovation from 1741 on. ▪ TIP➔ **In the chapel, look for two books: one contains the names of the victims of an oil-rig disaster in 1989; the second is empty, a reminder the many others who have lost their lives in the oil industry in the North Sea.** ⊠ *Union St.* ☎ *01224/643494* ⊕ *www.kirk-of-st-nicholas.org.uk* ▢ *Free, but donations welcome* ☉ *Weekdays noon–4.*

WORTH NOTING

OFF THE
BEATEN ☺
PATH

Duthie Park Winter Gardens. A great place to feed the ducks, Duthie Park also has a boating pond and trampolines, carved wooden animals, and playgrounds. In the attractive Winter Gardens (tropical and arid conservatories) are fish in ponds, free-flying birds, and turtles and terrapins among the luxuriant foliage and flowers. The park lies close beside Aberdeen's other river, the Dee. ⊠ *Polmuir Rd., Riverside Dr., about 1 mi south of city center* ▢ *Free* ☉ *Gardens daily 10–sunset.*

❹ Marischal College. Founded in 1593 by the Earl Marischal (the earls Marischal held hereditary office as keepers of the king's mares), Marischal College was a Protestant alternative to the Catholic King's College in Old Aberdeen. The two joined to form the University of Aberdeen in 1860. The spectacularly ornate work of the main university building is set off by the gilded flags, and this turn-of-the-20th-century creation is still the world's second-largest granite building. Only El Escorial, outside Madrid, is larger. The building, no longer needed by the university, will become the new headquarters for the city council by early 2011. The interior will be rebuilt, with the old materials recycled and used in buildings around the city. Though it's currently a building site, you can admire its spires and vast proportions from the street. ⊠ *Broad St.*

❸ Mercat Cross. Built in 1686 and restored in 1820, the Mercat Cross (the term stems from "marketplace"), always the symbolic center of a Scottish medieval burgh, stands just beyond King Street. Along its parapet are 12 portrait panels of the Stewart monarchs. ⊠ *Justice and Marischal Sts.*

A GOOD WALK IN DOWNTOWN ABERDEEN

For a lovely stroll downtown, start at the east end of Union Street, east of Marischal Street. Here within the original old town is a square called Castlegate. The actual castle once stood somewhere behind the Salvation Army Citadel (1896), an imposing baronial granite tower whose design was inspired by Balmoral Castle. On the north side of Castle Street stands the 17th-century Tolbooth, a reminder of Aberdeen's earliest days. The impressive Mercat Cross is near King Street. Turn north down Broad Street to reach the main Marischal College building with its granite frontage; it is being converted to a government building.

A survivor from an earlier Aberdeen can be found opposite Marischal College, beyond the concrete supports of St. Nicholas House (which houses the tourist information center): Provost Skene's House was once part of a closely packed area of town houses and is now a museum portraying civic life. Just around the corner on Upperkirkgate, at the lowest point, are two modern shopping malls—the St. Nicholas Centre on the left, the Bon-Accord Centre on the right.

7 **Rosemount Viaduct.** Three silvery, handsome buildings on this bridge are collectively known by all Aberdonians as Education, Salvation, and Damnation. The **Central Library** and **St. Mark's Church** date from the last decade of the 19th century, and **His Majesty's Theatre** (1904–08) has been restored inside to its full Edwardian splendor. If you're taking photographs, you can choose an angle that includes the statue of Scotland's first freedom fighter, Sir William Wallace (1270–1305), in the foreground pointing majestically to Damnation.

2 **Tolbooth.** The city was governed from this 17th-century building, which was also the burgh court and jail, for 200 years. Now a museum of crime and punishment, it is as amusing as it is stomach churning— making it a must-see for older kids. ⊠ *Castle St.* ☎ *01224/621167* ⊕ *www.aagm.co.uk* ▣ *Free* ☉ *Tues.–Sat. 10–12:30 and 1:30–5, Sun. 12:30–3:30.*

1 **Union Street.** This great thoroughfare is to Aberdeen what Princes Street is to Edinburgh: the central pivot of the city plan and the product of a wave of enthusiasm to rebuild the city in a contemporary style in the early 19th century.

8 **Union Terrace.** In the 19th-century development of Union Terrace stands a statue of Robert Burns (1759–96) addressing a daisy. Behind Burns are the **Union Terrace Gardens,** faintly echoing Edinburgh's Princes Street Gardens in that both separate the older part of the city, to the east, from the 19th-century development to the west. Most buildings around the grand-looking Caledonian Hotel are late Victorian.

OLD ABERDEEN

Old Aberdeen is very much a separate area of the city, north of the modern center and clustered around St. Machar's Cathedral and the many fine buildings of the University of Aberdeen. Take a stroll on College

Bounds; handsome 18th- and 19th-century houses line this cobbled street in the oldest part of the city.

TIMING

The neighborhood is a 20- to 30-minute walk north of the center of town; it's also easily reachable by First Aberdeen bus numbers 1 and 20 from Union Street. The ride takes 5 to 15 minutes. Old Aberdeen is a compact area, and will take you no more than a few hours to explore.

TOP ATTRACTIONS

⑭ Cruickshank Botanic Gardens. Built on land bequeathed by Miss Anne Crickshank in memory of her beloved brother Alexander, the small, 11-acre Cruickshank Botanic Garden has a peaceful water garden and lush greens ideal for lounging around on—when the weather allows—and beautifully tended subtropical and alpine collections. ⊠ *St. Machar Dr. at the Chanonry* ☎ *01224/272704* ⊕ *www.abdn.ac.uk* ⊠ *Free* ☾ *May–Sept., Mon.–Thurs. 9–4:30, Fri. 9–3:30, weekends 2–5; Oct.–Apr., Mon.–Thurs. 9–4:30, Fri. 9–3:30.*

⑪ King's College. Founded in 1494, King's College is now part of the University of Aberdeen. Its **chapel,** built around 1500, has an unmistakable

Fodor's Choice
★

flying (or crown) spire. That it has survived at all was because of the zeal of the principal, who defended his church against the destructive fanaticism that swept through Scotland during the Reformation, when the building was less than a century old. Today the renovated chapel plays an important role in university life. ■ TIP→ **Don't miss the tall oak screen that separates the nave from the choir, the ribbed wooden ceiling, and the stalls, as it constitutes the finest medieval wood carvings found anywhere in Scotland.** The **King's College Centre** has more information about the university. ⊠ *High St.* ☎ *01224/272660* ⊕ *www.abdn.ac.uk* ☾ *Weekdays 9:30–5, Sat. 11–4.*

▌ NEED A
BREAK?

St. Machar Bar (⊠ *97 High St.* ☎ *01224/483079*) is a small, vibrant pub in the middle of the university campus, selling not just pints but also *stovies* (a hot potato-based stew). This is a great place to warm up or pass away the time with a newspaper if the weather is unbecoming.

⑫ Old Town House. Now owned by Aberdeen University and operating as a gateway to the campus, this plain but handsome Georgian building is a great starting point at which to learn about the University and explore the grounds of this celebrated, ancient seat of learning. The building was the center of all trading activity in the city before it became a grammar school, a Masonic lodge, and then a library. Check out the walking tours of the campus on the Web site. ⊠ *High St., Old Aberdeen* ☎ *01224/273650* ⊕ *www.abdn.ac.uk/oldtownhouse* ⊠ *Free* ☾ *Mon.–Sat. 9–5.*

⑬ St. Machar's Cathedral. Rich in history, this cathedral is worth a look. It's said that St. Machar was sent by St. Columba to build a church on a grassy platform near the sea, where a river flowed in the shape of a shepherd's crook. This spot fit the bill. Although the cathedral was founded in AD 580, most of the existing building dates from the 15th and 16th centuries. The central tower collapsed in 1688, reducing the building to half its original length. The nave is thought to have been rebuilt in red sandstone in 1370, but the final renovation was completed in granite by the middle of the 15th century. Along with the nave ceiling, the twin octagonal spires were finished in time to take a battering in the Reformation, when the barons of the Mearns stripped the lead off the roof of St. Machar's and stole the bells. The cathedral suffered further mistreatment until it was fully restored in the 19th century. ⊠ *Chanonry* ☎ *01224/485988* ⊕ *www.stmachar.com* ⊙ *Daily 9–5.*

WORTH NOTING

🅕 **Brig o'Balgownie.** Until 1827 the only way out of Aberdeen going north was over the River Don on this single-arch bridge. It dates from 1314 and is thought to have been built by Richard Cementarius, Aberdeen's first provost. ⊠ *Seaton Park.*

WHERE TO EAT

£   ✕ **Ashvale.** Ask anyone about this long-established place and the
BRITISH   response will probably be overwhelmingly positive. Fish-and-chips are undoubtedly the specialty here. Attempt the Whale—a gigantic 1-pound fillet of battered cod—and you'll be rewarded with a free dessert. This may be the priciest fish-and-chips you've ever ordered, but the fresh fish and secret-recipe batter are now the stuff of legend. Decor is simple and minimal; you don't come for the ambience. ⊠ *42–48 Great Western Rd.* ☎ *01224/596981* ⊕ *theashvale.co.uk* ⊟ *AE, MC, V.*

££   ✕ **Café 52.** Right in the historic Grassmarket, this café-restaurant has
BRITISH   taken a few years to find its niche but now serves up lovely homemade dishes at pocket-friendly prices until 9:30. Roast beetroot soup, pork and sage meatloaf, and bramble panna cotta are just some of the quirky options; local produce stars in all. The restaurant is in a handsome silvery granite building with exposed stone walls, huge windows, and shiny black tables. ⊠ *52 The Green* ☎ *01224/590094* ⊕ *www.cafe52. net* ⊟ *MC, V* ⊙ *No dinner Sun.*

£££   ✕ **Foyer Restaurant and Gallery.** In this splendid restaurant in a former
BRITISH   church, curving lines, pale woods, and touches of bright color strike a
★   modern note—a good background for changing art exhibitions. Foyer has a feel-good factor, too: not only are the lunch and dinner offerings exceptional, but all profits support work with the city's unemployed and homeless. Soups, sandwiches, and hot mains make up lunch; the dinner menu has steaks as well as seafood chowder and roast saddle of venison. Helpings are ample. The same group also runs the café at His Majesty's Theatre on Rosemount Viaduct; the three-course fixed-price dinner is a good value at £18.50. ⊠ *82A Crown St.* ☎ *01224/582277* ⊕ *www.foyerrestaurant.com* ⊟ *MC, V.*

££££   ✕ **Silver Darling.** Huge windows overlook the harbor and beach at this
SEAFOOD   quayside favorite in a former customs house, long one of Aberdeen's
Fodor's Choice   most acclaimed restaurants. It specializes, as the name suggests, in fish;
★   a silver darling is a herring. Try the panfried langoustine with beetroot and celeriac risotto for a starter, and steamed wild halibut with tomato-and-red-pepper tagliatelle or poached turbot in Beaujolais. The wine list is a good match for the food. Stark white tablecloths and white walls add a hint of sophistication; flowers throw in a dash of color. ⊠ *Pocra*

7

Quay, Footdee ☎ *01224/576229* ⊕ *www.silverdarlingrestaurant.co. uk* ⚓ *Reservations essential* ▭ *AE, DC, MC, V* ⊘ *Closed Sun. No lunch Sat.*

WHERE TO STAY

££   ▦ **Atholl Hotel.** With its many turrets and gables, this granite hotel recalls a bygone era but has modern amenities. It's in the middle of a leafy residential area about five minutes west of the city center. Rooms are done in rich, dark colors but have contemporary furnishings; if space is more important than a view, opt for a room on the first floor. **Pros:** clean and friendly; very pleasant staff. **Cons:** food in restaurant is well prepared but unimaginative; some rooms look a little dated. ⊠ *54 Kings Gate* ☎ *01224/323505* ⊕ *www.atholl-aberdeen.com* ⇗ *34 rooms* ⟁ *In-room: no a/c, Wi-Fi. In-hotel: restaurant, bar, Internet terminal, laundry service* ▭ *AE, DC, MC, V* ¶◎¶ *BP.*

£££   ▦ **City Wharf.** With one- to four-bedroom apartments in three city-center sites and more in the pipeline, City Wharf offers fuss-free stays of any length in luxury settings. All apartments have daily maid service, washers and driers, and are kitted out with quality furnishings, providing the perfect base for anyone who wants space and privacy. A welcome hamper includes some food basics to get you started. **Pros:** feels brand spanking new; all mod cons; guest can use a nearby gym. **Cons:** no porters to help you with your bags; no restaurant. ⊠ *47 Regent Quay* ☎ *01224/589282* ⊕ *www.citywharfapartments.co.uk* ⇗ *22 apartments* ⟁ *In-room: no a/c, kitchen, DVD, Wi-Fi. In-hotel: laundry facilities, Wi-Fi hotspot* ▭ *AE, MC, V* ¶◎¶ *CP.*

££   ▦ **Craibstone Suites.** Right on one of Aberdeen's greenest, most attractive
★   squares, these modish but comfortable serviced suites in several sizes come with fully equipped kitchens and a fridge with goodies for breakfast. They are well designed, with LCD TVs and king beds as pluses. **Pros:** great central location; no "vacate-your-room-by-10" rule, allowing those who need it to sleep in. **Cons:** executive suites are small: go for the grand or superior if you need to swing a cat. ⊠ *15 Bon Accord Sq.* ☎ *01224/857950* ⊕ *www.craibstone-suites.co.uk* ⇗ *15 suites* ⟁ *In-room: no a/c, kitchen, refrigerator, DVD, Wi-Fi* ▭ *MC, V* ¶◎¶ *CP.*

££   ▦ **The Jays Guest House.** Alice Jennings or her husband George will greet you at the front door of this granite house, a homey bed-and-breakfast. The warmth and friendliness of your hosts, who are pleased to recommend local restaurants or help plan trips out of town, makes for a memorable stay. The spacious rooms are impeccably clean. Breakfasts may include scrumptious oatcakes, savory omelets, or your own special request. **Pros:** immaculate rooms; expert advice on city's sites; near shops and restaurants. **Cons:** no public areas; not all rooms have en-suite bathrooms. ⊠ *422 King St.* ☎ *01224/638295* ⊕ *www.jaysguesthouse. co.uk* ⇗ *10 rooms, 2 with shared bath* ⟁ *In-room: no a/c, no phone, Wi-Fi. In-hotel: Wi-Fi hotspot* ▭ *MC, V* ¶◎¶ *BP.*

£££££   ▦ **Marcliffe Hotel and Spa.** Set on 11 wooded acres, this spacious, elegant country-house hotel combines old and new to impressive effect. Some of the individually decorated rooms have reproduction antique furnishings, whereas others are more modern. Pampering touches are plentiful, from fresh fruit to 24-hour room service. The restaurant (££££) serves fresh local seafood and top-quality Aberdeen Angus beef, and you can choose from more than 400 wines. Since it opened in 1993, this faux château has hosted such dignitaries as Prince Charles, former prime minister Tony Blair, the Sultan of Brunei, and actor Charlton Heston. **Pros:** lush gardens; a country pace near the city; good spa. **Cons:** a little out of town; restaurant is pricey. ⊠ *N. Deeside Rd., Pitfodels* ☎ *01224/861000* ⊕ *www.marcliffe.com* ↩ *35 rooms, 7 suites* ⇩ *In-room: no a/c, refrigerator, Wi-Fi. In-hotel: restaurant, room service, bar, spa, laundry service* ⊟ *AE, DC, MC, V* ⊚ *BP.*

NIGHTLIFE AND THE ARTS

Aberdeen has a fairly lively nightlife scene revolving around pubs and clubs. Theaters, concert halls, arts centers, and cinemas are also well represented. The principal newspapers—the *Press and Journal* and the *Evening Express*—and *Aberdeen Leopard* magazine can fill you in on what's going on anywhere in the northeast. Aberdeen's tourist information center has a monthly publication with an events calendar.

THE ARTS

Aberdeen is a rich city, both financially and culturally. August sees the world-renowned **Aberdeen International Youth Festival** (*Box office* ⊠ *Custom House, 35 Regent Quay* ☎ *01224/213800* ⊕ *www.aiyf.org*), which attracts youth orchestras, choirs, dance troupes, and theater companies from many countries. During the festival some companies take their productions to other venues in the northeast.

ARTS CENTERS **Aberdeen Arts Centre** (⊠ *33 King St.* ☎ *01224/635208* ⊕ *www.* ★ *aberdeenartscentre.org.uk*) hosts experimental plays, poetry readings, and exhibitions by local and Scottish artists. The **Lemon Tree** (⊠ *5 W. North St.* ☎ *01224/642230* ⊕ *www.boxofficeaberdeen.com*) has an innovative and international program of dance, stand-up comedy, puppet theater, and folk, jazz, and rock-and-roll music. **Peacock Visual Arts** (⊠ *21 Castle St.* ☎ *01224/639539* ⊕ *www.peacockvisualarts.com*) displays photographic, video, and slide exhibits of contemporary art and architecture.

About 20 mi north of Aberdeen, **Haddo House** (⊠ *Off B999 near Tarves* ☎ *01651/851440* ⊕ *www.nts.org.uk*) offers a mixed bag of events, from opera and ballet to Shakespeare, Scots-language plays, and puppetry from spring through fall.

CONCERT The Edwardian **His Majesty's Theatre** (⊠ *Rosemount Viaduct* ☎ *01224/* HALLS *641122*) hosts performances on par with those in some of the world's biggest cities. It's a regular venue for musicals and operas, as well as classical and modern dance. The **Music Hall** (⊠ *Union St.* ☎ *01224/641122*) presents seasonal programs of concerts by the Scottish National Orchestra, the Scottish Chamber Orchestra, and other major groups. Events also include folk concerts, crafts fairs, and exhibitions.

FILM **The Belmont** (⊠ *49 Belmont St.* ☎ *01224/343536*) screens independent and classic films. **Cineworld** (⊠ *Queen's Link Leisure Park, Links Rd.* ☎ *0871/200–2000*) shows recent releases.

NIGHTLIFE

With a greater club-to-clubber ratio than either Edinburgh or Glasgow, loud music and dancing dominate a night out in Aberdeen. There are also plenty of pubs and pool halls for those with two left feet. Pubs close at midnight on weekdays and 1 AM on weekends; clubs go until 2 or 3 AM.

BARS AND PUBS
The old-fashioned **Illicit Still** (⊠ *Guest Row, Broad St.* ☎ *01224/623123*) is named after the 18th-century practice of brewing your own beer to avoid the malt tax. A beautifully fitted drinking establishment, it serves up hearty pub grub. Drawing a slightly older crowd, the traditional **Old Blackfriars** (⊠ *52 Castle St.* ☎ *01224/581922*) enjoys a nice location at the end of Union Street. The lighting is dim and the big fireplace warms things up on a chilly evening. This cask ale pub has a great selection— Belhaven St. Andrews Ale and Caledonian 80 top the list.

Fodor's Choice ★
Dating from 1850, **The Prince of Wales** (⊠ *7 St. Nicholas La.* ☎ *01224/640597*) has retained its paneled walls and wooden tables. Here you can belly up to the longest bar in Aberdeen. Good-quality food and reasonable prices draw lunchtime crowds. **Soul** (⊠ *333 Union St.* ☎ *01224/211150*), in a converted church, has private booths with stained-glass windows and ecclesiastical furnishings. The eclectic menu includes everything from chicken satay and mussels. It's the most interesting of the Union Street hangouts.

DANCE CLUBS
People tend to dress up a bit to go clubbing, and jeans or sneakers might get you turned away at the door. Clubs are open until 2 AM during the week and until 3 AM on Friday and Saturday nights.

Pop and dance music take the floor at **Liquid & Envy** (⊠ *5 Bridge Pl.* ☎ *01224/595239*), which merges two clubs in one. Liquid thumps with more commercial music, and Envy plays a retro soundtrack. **Club Snafu** (⊠ *1 Union St.* ☎ *01224/596111*), a boutique club, hosts all manner of specialty nights, from comedy to electronica.

SPORTS AND THE OUTDOORS

BICYCLING

Alpine Bikes (⊠ *64–70 Holburn St.* ☎ *01224/211455*) rents mountain bikes from June to August. The staff will give you good advice on scenic routes around and outside the city, including near Aberdeen Beach.

GOLF

Northeast Scotland is known for good golf *(see Chapter 12 for more top courses)*, and it might get even better. Donald Trump wants to turn the Menie Estate, just north of Aberdeen and the Ythan estuary, and bordering on a protected dune system, into an expensive haven for Pringle-wearing putters. Despite environmental concerns, the government has given a go-ahead and work has begun; visit ⊕ *www.trumpgolfscotland* for updates. Just south of Aberdeen, Jack Nicklaus has been lined up to design a championship course at Ury Castle. The financial climate has delayed the project, though.

You can expect to pay £15 to £100 per round at the golf courses in and around Aberdeen. Make reservations at least 24 hours in advance. Some private courses restrict tee times for visiting golfers to certain days or hours during the week, so be sure to check that the course you wish to play is open when you want to play it. *For more courses, including Balgownie, see Chapter 12.*

★ **Murcar.** Sea views and a variety of rugged terrain—from sand dunes to tinkling burns—are the highlights of this course, founded in 1909. It's most famous for breathtaking vistas at the seventh hole, appropriately called the Serpentine. Designer Archibald Simpson considered this course to be one of his finest. ⊠ *Bridge of Don* ☎ *01224/704354* ⊕ *www. murcarlinks.com* ⚑ *18 holes, 6,314 yds, SSS 72* ⛳ *£70 per round.*

Westhill. This parkland course, founded in 1977, overlooks Royal Deeside. It's the most inexpensive in the area. ⊠ *Westhill Heights* ☎ *01224/749124* ⊕ *www.westhillgolfclub.co.uk* ⚑ *18 holes, 5,849 yds, SSS 69* ⛳ *£20 per round.*

SHOPPING

You can find most of the large national department stores in the Bon Accord, St. Nicholas, and Trinity shopping malls or along Union Street, but Aberdeen has some good specialty shops as well.

SPECIALTY SHOPS

The constantly changing crafts and jewelry at the **Aberdeen Art Gallery Shop** (⊠ *Schoolhill* ☎ *01224/523695*) always have something of interest, and there are pretty postcards of the city from times gone by. At the **Aberdeen Family History Society Shop** (⊠ *158–164 King St.* ☎ *01224/646323*) you can browse through publications related to local history and genealogical research. ■ TIP→ For a small fee the Aberdeen & North-East Scotland Family History Society will undertake some research on your behalf.

For Scottish kilts, tartans, crests, and other traditionally Scottish clothes, a good place to start is **Alex Scott & Co** (⊠ *43 Schoolhill* ☎ *01224/643924*). The **Books and Beans** (⊠ *22 Belmont St.* ☎ *01224/646438*) is a secondhand bookshop with its own little café. You're welcome to browse and sip at the same time. **Candle Close Gallery** (⊠ *123 Gallowgate* ☎ *01224/624940*) has some strange and wonderful mirrors, clocks, ceramics, and jewelry that you're unlikely to see elsewhere or ever again. **Colin Wood** (⊠ *25 Rose St.* ☎ *01224/643019*) is the place to go for small antiques, prints, and regional maps. **Nova** (⊠ *18–20 Chapel St.* ☎ *01224/641270*), where the locals go for gifts, stocks Scottish silver jewelry and scarves. You can also find major U.K. brand names, such as Neal's Yard, Dartington Glass, and Crabtree and Evelyn.

ROYAL DEESIDE AND CASTLE COUNTRY

Deeside, the valley running west from Aberdeen down which the River Dee flows, earned its "royal" appellation when discovered by Queen Victoria. To this day, where royalty goes, lesser aristocracy and freshly minted millionaires follow. Many still aspire to own a grand shooting estate in Deeside, and you may appreciate this yearning when you see how the piney hill slope, purple moor, and blue river intermingle tastefully here. Royal Deeside's gradual scenic change adds a grow-ing sense of excitement as you travel deeper into the Grampian Mountains.

There are castles along the Dee as well as to the north in Castle Country, a region that also illustrates the gradual geological change in the north-east: uplands lapped by a tide of farms. All the Donside and Deeside castles are picturesquely sited, with most fitted out with tall slender turrets, winding stairs, and crooked chambers that epitomize Scottish baronial style. All have tales of ghosts and bloodshed, siege and tor-ture. Many were tidied up and "domesticated" during the 19th century. Although best toured by car, much of this area is accessible either by public transportation or on tours from Aberdeen.

STONEHAVEN

15 mi south of Aberdeen.

This historic town near splendid Dunnottar Castle was once a popu-lar holiday destination, with Robert Burns enjoying walks along the golden sands. The surrounding red-clay fields were made famous by Lewis Grassic Gibbon (real name James Leslie Mitchell) who attended school in the town and who wrote the seminal Scottish trilogy, *A Scots Quair,* about the people, the land, and the impact of World War I. The decline of the fishing industry emptied the harbor, but the town, being so close to Aberdeen, has begun to thrive again. It's now famous for its Hogmanay (New Year) celebrations, where local men swing huge balls of fire on chains before tossing them into the harbor.

GETTING HERE AND AROUND

Stagecoach Bluebird runs a number of buses to Stonehaven from Aberdeen, but numbers 107 and 109 are the fastest (50 minutes). Most trains heading south from Aberdeen stop at Stonehaven; there's at least one per hour making the 15-minute trip. Drivers should take A90 south and turn off at A957.

ESSENTIALS

Visitor Information **Stonehaven** (✉ *66 Allardyce St.* ☎ *01569/762806* ⊕ *www. aberdeen-grampian.com* ☉ *Apr.–Oct.*).

EXPLORING

Fodor's Choice
★

It's hard to beat the magnificent, cliff-top ruins of **Dunnottar Castle**, which straddles a headland overlooking Stonehaven and has panoramic views of the North Sea. Building began in the 14th century, when Sir William Keith, Marischal of Scotland (keeper of the king's mares and one of the king's right-hand men), decided to build a tower house to demon-strate his power. Subsequent generations added on to the structure over the centuries, and important visitors included Mary, Queen of Scots. The castle is most famous for holding out for eight months against Oliver Cromwell's army in 1651–52, and thereby saving the Scottish crown jewels, which had been stored here for safekeeping. Reach the castle via the A90; take the Stonehaven turnoff and follow the signs. ■ TIP➜ **Wear sensible shoes to investigate the ruins; allow about two hours.** ✉ *Stonehaven* ☎ *01569/860223* ⊕ *www.dunnottarcastle.co.uk*

📷 *£5* ⏱ *Easter–June and Oct., Mon.–Sat. 9–6, Sun. 2–5; July–Sept., daily 9–6; Nov.–Easter, Fri.–Mon. 9–sunset.*

They were extremely popular in the 1930s, but the **Stonehaven Open-Air Swimming Pool**, an art deco gem, is one of only a few remaining outdoor heated pools in Scotland. Salty water from the North Sea is pumped in and heated to a toasty 28°C (82°F). Run by a local trust, this place is perfect for families. ■ TIP➡ **Ask about Wednesday's midnight swims, when you can float under the stars.** ✉ *Queen Elizabeth Park, off A90* ☎ *01569/762134* ⊕ *www.stonehavenopenairpool.co.uk* 📷*£4.60* ⏱ *June and mid-Aug.–mid-Sept., weekdays 1–7:30, weekends 10–6; July and Aug., weekdays 10–7:30, weekends 10–6.*

WHERE TO EAT AND STAY

£££   ✕ **Carron Art Deco Restaurant.** For an outstanding meal of classic Scot-
BRITISH tish dishes served in the most splendid surroundings, try this longtime favorite. Evoking the style and class of the 1930s, it's a must for both architecture- and food lovers. Look out for the rather risqué figure of a woman etched onto a mirror between two dazzlingly tiled columns. The cuisine is not diminished by the surroundings: try the chicken breast cooked in white wine and covered with smoked salmon or the Aberdeen Angus roast beef with a Drambuie (a honey-flavored whisky liqueur) gravy. ✉ *Cameron St.* ☎ *01569/760460* 🍽 *AE, MC, V.*

££   🏨 **Bayview B&B.** Sitting right on the beach but just down the lane from
★   the town square, this newly built bed-and-breakfast couldn't be in a more convenient location—or have better views. There are standard rooms on the lower level and an executive suite (£150 per night) and a penthouse (£175 per night) on the upper levels. Each room is individually designed with original artwork, fascinating knickknacks, and modern furnishings. Huge, healthy breakfasts will fortify you against the northeast winds. **Pros:** spick-and-span rooms; walk to restaurants and shops; eccentric, colorful design. **Cons:** standard rooms are smallish; breakfast room is windowless. ✉ *Beachgate La.* ☎ *01569/766933* ⊕ *www.bayviewbandb.co.uk* 🛏 *3 rooms, 2 suites* 🍴 *In-room: no a/c, Wi-Fi. In hotel: Internet terminal* 🍽 *AE, MC, V* 🍽 *BP.*

BANCHORY

15 mi west of Stonehaven, 19 mi west of Aberdeen.

Banchory is an immaculate town filled with pinkish granite buildings. It's usually bustling with ice-cream-eating strollers, out on a day trip from Aberdeen. Nearby are Crathes and Drum castles.

GETTING HERE AND AROUND
A car is by far the best way to get around the area; A93 is one of the main roads connecting the towns.

For those reliant on public transport, Stagecoach buses operate a number of services for towns along or just off A93 (Drum Castle, Banchory, Kincardine, Aboyne, Ballater, Balmoral, and Braemar).

ESSENTIALS
Visitor Information Banchory (✉ *Bridge St.* ☎ *013308/22000* ⊕ *www.aberdeen-grampian.com* ⏱ *Apr.–Oct.).*

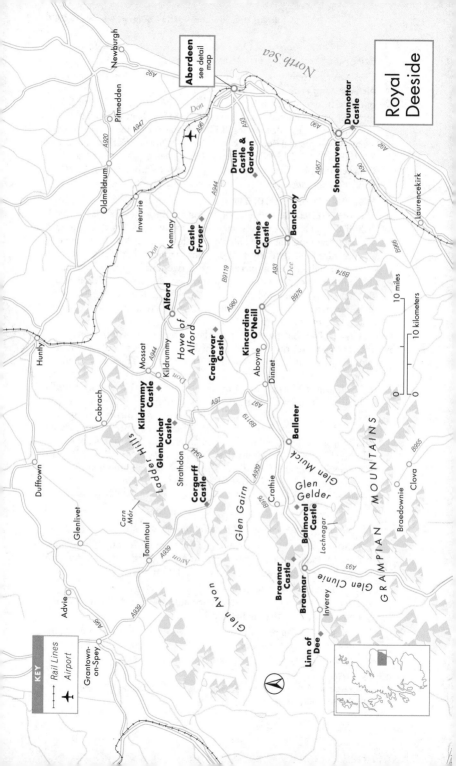

Royal Deeside

North Sea

Newburgh

Aberdeen
see detail
map

Pitmedden

A947

A920

A96

Oldmeldrum

Don

A90

A92

Dunnottar
Castle

A957

Stonehaven

Drum
Castle &
Garden

A944

B966

Laurencekirk

Inverurie

Kemnay

Castle
Fraser

Crathes
Castle

Banchory

Don

B9119

A93

Dee

B974

Alford

A980

A944

Howe of
Alford

Kincardine
O'Neill

B976

Huntly

Mossat

Kildrummy

Kildrummy
Castle

Craigievar
Castle

Aboyne

Dinnet

10 miles

10 kilometers

Cabrach

Don

A97

A97

Ballater

Glenbuchat
Castle

Strathdon

A944

B9119

A939

Glen Muick

B995

Dufftown

Ladder Hills

Corgarff
Castle

Glen Gairn

Crathie

Glen
Gelder

Clova

Glenlivet

Carn
Mór

Balmoral
Castle

Braedownie

Tomintoul

A939

Avon

Lochnagar

GRAMPIAN MOUNTAINS

Advie

A95

Braemar
Castle

Braemar

A93

Glen Clunie

Grantown-
on-Spey

A95

Glen Avon

Inverey

Linn of
Dee

KEY

Rail Lines

Airport

CLOSE UP

Which Castle Is Right for You?

We admit it—there are almost too many castles in this part of Scotland. Since it's nearly impossible to see all of them, we've noted the prime characteristics of each to help you decide which you'd most like to visit.

■ **Balmoral:** The Queen's home, this is where Queen Victoria and the Royal Family fell in love with Scotland and all things Scottish. Expect baronial largesse and groomed grounds, though you don't see much inside.

■ **Balvenie:** This ruined castle is known for its indomitable bearing and verdant surroundings, right in the midst of the Malt Whisky Trail.

■ **Braemar:** Offering memorable insight into the lives of the Scottish landed gentry, this recently restored castle heaves with memorabilia and mementos of the fascinating Farquharsons, who still hold their clan gathering here.

■ **Corgarff:** You'll find a sober solitude out on the moorland, as well as 18th-century graffiti and the reconstructed barracks used by Jacobite troops in 1746 as they retreated north.

■ **Craigievar:** Highlights of this 17th-century castle are a magical forest and fairy-tale turrets. The painstaking restoration of its exterior walls is due to be completed by summer 2010.

■ **Crathes:** Expect tight quarters, notable family portraits, and a network of walled gardens at this well-preserved seat of the Burnett family.

■ **Dunnottar:** The dramatic, scene-stealing clifftop location of Mel Gibson's *Hamlet* (1991), the ruins of this 14th-century tower house by the sea are unbeatable.

■ **Drum:** A fusion of architectural styles and some historic roses are notable at this castle, but it's the medieval chapel that stirs the senses.

■ **Fraser:** Considered the grandest castle in Aberdeenshire, Castle Fraser has opulent period furnishings and woodland walks that make for a rewarding day.

■ **Fyvie:** This 14th-century castle underwent a luxurious Edwardian makeover. Come here for an awesome art collection, rich interiors, and haunting history.

■ **Kildrummy:** This is the place for evocative ruins, some from the 13th century, and tales of a treacherous past. Its austere but poignant chapel is a must-see.

7

EXPLORING

If you visit in autumn and have time to spare, drive for a mile along the B974 south of Banchory to the **Brig o'Feuch** (pronounced *fyooch*, the *ch* as in loch). The area around this bridge is pleasant: salmon leap in season, and the fall colors and foaming waters make for an attractive scene.

Crathes Castle, 16 mi west of Aberdeen, was once the home of the Burnett family and is one of the best-preserved castles in Britain. Keepers of the Forest of Drum for generations, the family acquired lands here by marriage and later built a castle, completed in 1596. The National Trust for Scotland cares for the castle, which is furnished with many original pieces and family portraits. Outside are grand gardens with calculated symmetry and clipped yew hedges. Make sure you browse the Horsemill bookshop and sample the tasty home baking in the tearoom. ⊠ *Off A93, 3½ mi east of Banchory* ☎ *0844/493–2166* ⊕ *www.nts.org. uk* 🎟 *Garden £8, castle and garden £10.50* ☉ *Castle June, Sept., and Oct., daily 10–4:30; July and Aug., daily 10–4:30; last admission 45 min before closing. Gardens daily 9* AM*–sunset.*

Drum Castle and Garden is a foursquare tower with an evocative medieval chapel that dates from the 13th century; like many other castles, it also has later additions up to Victorian times. Note the tower's rounded corners, said to make battering-ram attacks more difficult. Nearby, fragments of the ancient Forest of Drum still stand, dating from the days when Scotland was covered by great stands of oak and pine. The Garden of Historic Roses, open from April to October, lays claim to some old-fashioned roses not commonly seen today. Drum Castle is 8 mi east of Banchory and 11 mi west of Aberdeen. ⊠ *Off A93* ☎ *0844/493–2161* ⊕ *www.nts.org.uk* 🎟 *Garden £2.50, castle and garden £8.50* ☉ *Castle Apr., May, and Sept., daily 12:30–5; June–Aug., daily 10–5. Grounds daily 9:30–sunset.*

WHERE TO STAY

£££   🏠 **Inchmarlo.** Beautifully designed, the fully serviced cottages and apartments here benefit hugely from the amenities on site. An 18-hole golf course is the big pull for visitors, but other outdoor activities are available. The more sedate can just enjoy their private terrace or the enormous sofas, cushy furnishings, and king-size beds. The well-run Gillies restaurant offers three meals a day at reasonable prices. **Pros:** luxe for less; pristine accommodation; fine dining but informal. **Cons:** occasionally hosts corporate groups of golfers; all apartments sleep four so the extra bedroom may be wasted. ⊠ *Glassel Rd., off A93* ☎ *01330/826424* ⊕ *www.inchmarlo.com* 🛏 *34 villas, 8 apartments* ♿ *In-room: kitchen, refrigerator, DVD, Wi-Fi. In-hotel: restaurant, bar, golf course, laundry facilities* 🖃 *AE, DC, MC, V* ⫶◯⫶ *CP.*

£££   🏠 **Raemoir House Hotel.** With portions dating from the 16th to 19th centuries, this baronial former home 2 mi north of Banchory evokes the past. Guest rooms—a number of which have four-poster beds—have a genteel period charm and large, modern bathrooms. The restaurant (£££££; fixed-price menu), in an oval ballroom, has a solid reputation based on exquisite Scottish fare created with seasonal local produce. And the morning room, despite its name, is the perfect place to nurse a wee nip of whisky before bed. You can take some lovely walks on the estate's 3,500 acres of hillock and woodland. **Pros:** charming old building with extensive grounds; staff is informal and efficient. **Cons:** pricey; some rooms are faded and rather old-fashioned. ⊠ *Off A980, Raemoir* ☎ *01330/824884* ⊕ *www.raemoir.com* 🛏 *17 rooms, 3 suites* ♿ *In-room: no a/c, Wi-Fi. In-hotel: restaurant, bar* 🖃 *AE, DC, MC, V* ⫶◯⫶ *BP.*

OFF THE BEATEN PATH

Kincardine O'Neill. The ruined kirk in this little village 9 mi west of Banchory on A93 was built in 1233 and once sheltered travelers: it was the last hospice before the Mounth, the name given to the massif that shuts off the south side of the Dee Valley. Beyond Banchory (and

CLOSE UP

Language and the Scots

"Much," said Doctor Johnson, "may be made of a Scotchman if he be caught young." This quote sums up, even today, the attitude of some English people—confident in their English, the language of parliament and much of the media—toward the Scots language. The Scots have long been made to feel uncomfortable about their mother tongue, and until the 1970s (and in some private schools, even today) they were encouraged to mimic the dialect of the Thames Valley ("standard English") in order to "get on" in life.

LOWLAND SCOTS

The Scots language (that is, Lowland Scots, not Gaelic) was a northern form of Middle English and in its day was the language used in the court and in literature. It borrowed from Scandinavian, Dutch, French, and Gaelic. After a series of historical blows—such as the decamping of the Scottish court to England after 1603 and the printing of the King James Bible in English but not in Scots—it declined as a literary or official language. It survives in various forms but is virtually an underground language, spoken among ordinary folk, especially in its heartland, in the northeast.

You may even find yourself exporting a few useful words, such as *dreich* (gloomy), *glaikit* (acting and looking foolish), or *dinna fash* (don't worry), all of which are much more expressive than their English equivalents.

Some Scottish words are used and understood across the entire country (and world), such as *wee* (small), *aye* (yes), *lassie* (girl), and *bonny* (pretty). Regional variations are evident even in the simplest of greetings. When you meet someone in the Borders, *Whit*

fettle? (What state are you in?) or *Hou ye lestin?* (How are you lasting?) may throw you for a loop; elsewhere you could hear *Hou's yer dous?* (How are your pigeons?). If a group of Scots take a fancy to you at the pub, you may be asked to *Come intil the body o the kirk,* and if all goes well, your departure may be met with a jovial farewell, *haste ye back* (return soon).

GAELIC

Scottish Gaelic, an entirely different language, is still spoken across the Highlands and Hebrides. There's also a large Gaelic-speaking population in Glasgow as a result of the Celtic diaspora—islanders migrating to Glasgow in search of jobs in the 19th century. Speakers of Gaelic in Scotland were once persecuted, after the failure of the 18th-century Jacobite rebellions. Official persecution has now turned to guilt-tinged support, as the promoters of Gaelic now lobby for substantial public funds to underwrite television programming and language classes for new learners.

One of the joys of Scottish television is watching Gaelic news programs to see how the ancient language copes with such topics as nuclear energy, the Internet, and the latest band to hit the charts. A number of Gaelic words have been absorbed into English: *banshee* (a wailing female spirit), *galore* (plenty), *slob* (a slovenly person), and *brat* (a spoiled or unruly child).

To experience Gaelic language and culture in all its glory, you can attend the Royal National Mod—a competition-based festival with speeches, drama, and music, all in Gaelic—held in a different location every year.

7

the B974), no motor roads run south until you reach Braemar (A93), though the Mounth is crossed by a network of tracks once used by Scottish soldiers, invading armies (including the Romans), and cattle drovers. Photography buffs won't want to miss the bridge at Potarch, just to the east.

Queen's View. To reach one of the most spectacular vistas in northeast Scotland—stretching across the Howe of Cromar to Lochnagar—take the B9094 due north from Aboyne, then turn left onto the B9119 for 6 mi.

BALLATER AND BALMORAL CASTLE

22 mi west of Kincardine O'Neill, 43 mi west of Aberdeen.

The handsome holiday resort of Ballater, once noted for the curative properties of its waters, has profited from the proximity of the royals, nearby at Balmoral Castle. You might be amused by the array of BY ROYAL APPOINTMENT signs proudly hanging from many of its various shops (even monarchs need bakers and butchers). Take time to stroll around this well-laid-out community. The railway station houses the tourist information center and a display on the glories of the Great North of Scotland branch railway line, closed in the 1960s along with so many others in this country.

The locals have long taken the town's royal connection in stride. To this day, the hundreds who line the road when the queen and her family arrive for services at the family's parish church at Crathie are invariably visitors to Deeside—one of Balmoral's attractions for the monarch has always been the villagers' respect for royal privacy.

GETTING HERE AND AROUND
There's good train service to Aberdeen, but you'll need to catch a bus to get to this and other towns near A93. Stagecoach Bluebird buses numbers 201 and 202 operate hourly to all the main towns, including Ballater. Otherwise, it's an easy car trip.

ESSENTIALS
Visitor Information **Ballater** (✉ *Old Royal Station, Station Sq.* ☎ *013397/55306*).

EXPLORING
As long as you have your own car, you can capture the feel of the eastern Highlands yet still be close to town. Start your expedition into **Glen Muick** (Gaelic for pig, pronounced mick) by crossing the River Dee and heading west on the B976. When the road forks, you'll take the unnamed single-track road that runs along the River Muick. The native red deer are quite common throughout the Scottish Highlands, but the flat valley floor here is one of the best places to see them. Beyond the lower glen, the prospect opens to reveal fine views of the battlement of cliffs edging the mountain called Lochnagar.

★   The enormous parking lot is indicative of the popularity of **Balmoral Castle**, one of Queen Elizabeth II's favorite family retreats. Balmoral's visiting hours depend on whether the royals are in residence. In truth, there are more interesting and historic buildings to explore, as the only part of the castle on view is the ballroom, with an exhibition of royal artifacts. The

Carriage Hall has displays of commemorative china, carriages, and native wildlife. Thanks to Victoria and Albert, who built the house to Prince Albert's design, stags' heads abounded, the bagpipes wailed incessantly, and the garish Stuart tartan was used for every item of furnishings, from carpets to chair covers. A more somber Duff tartan, black and green to blend with the environment, was later adopted. Queen Elizabeth II follows her predecessors' routine in spending a holiday of about six weeks in Deeside, usually from mid-August to the end of September. During this time Balmoral is closed to visitors, including the grounds. You can take a guided tour in November and December; if the weather is crisp and bright, the estate is at its most dramatic and romantic.

Around and about Balmoral, which is 7 mi west of Ballater, are some notable spots—Cairn O'Mount, Cambus O'May, and the Cairngorms from the Linn of Dee—and some of them may be seen on pony-trekking expeditions, which use Balmoral stalking ponies and go around the grounds and estate.

Tempted by the setting? Balmoral Castle has five cottages (some very large) for rent by the week at certain times. They are atmospheric but can be basic. Check the Web site for details, though you must contact the properties directly for specifics.

✉ *A93* ☎ *013397/42534* ⊕ *www.balmoralcastle.com* 🎫 *£8* ⊙ *Apr.– July, daily 10–5; last admission 1 hr before closing. Guided tours on certain dates in Nov. and Dec.*

WHERE TO EAT AND STAY

££££ ✕ **The Green Inn.** A family affair, this restaurant with rooms is run by a
MODERN BRITISH couple who take great pleasure in looking after their guests. Their son—
★ trained by the great celebrity chef Raymond Blanc—serves sophisticated food that many consider to be the best in the northeast. The tables are laid with heavy china and polished cutlery, and you can dine in the bright conservatory or the red-walled dining room. A prix-fixe dinner (£38) might include lasagna of rabbit and mushrooms or panfried sea bass with fennel and lobster bisque. You can extend your stay in one of the three very well-appointed guest rooms. ✉ *Victoria Rd.* ☎ *01339/55701* ⊕ *www.green-inn.com* ▭ *AE, DC, MC, V* ⊙ *No lunch.*

££ 🏠 **Auld Kirk.** A striking renovation of an old church into a contemporary bed-and-breakfast makes for an interesting stay. Guest rooms are simply furnished but functional and have fair-size, high-quality showers. Breakfast is served in the calm of the Minister's Room, and you can opt for a dinner of good, updated Scottish fare in the stark but stylish Spirit Restaurant. The Kirk Bar—an oxymoron if ever there was one, considering the Calvinist views of the church—is a modish lounge with a bar made from the old pews and tables outside for balmier evenings. **Pros:** helpful team looks after you; pin-tidy bedrooms and public rooms. **Cons:** bar is popular with the locals so can get noisy. ✉ *Braemar Rd.* ☎ *01339/733762* ⊕ *www.theauldkirk.com* 🛏 *6 rooms* 🛎 *In-room: no a/c, Wi-Fi (some). In-hotel: restaurant, bar, Internet terminal* ▭ *MC, V* ⊙| *BP.*

££ 🏠 **Hilton Craigendarroch.** This grand old country house was, in its day,
☾ considered a luxury retreat for the oil-rich Aberdonians. Now a little

CLOSE UP

Balmoral, Queen Victoria's Retreat

Some credit Sir Walter Scott with having opened up Scotland for tourism through his poems and novels. But it was probably Queen Victoria (1819–1901) who gave Scottish tourism its real momentum when, in 1842, she first came to Scotland and when, in 1847—on orders of a doctor, who thought the relatively dry climate of upper Deeside would suit her—she bought Balmoral. The pretty little castle was knocked down to make room for a much grander house in full-flown Scottish baronial style, designed by her husband, Prince Albert (1819–61), in 1855. It had a veritable rash of tartanitis. Before long the entire Deeside and the region north were dotted with country houses and mock-baronial châteaux.

"It seems like a dream to be here in our dear Highland Home again," Queen Victoria wrote. "Every year my heart becomes more fixed in this dear Paradise."

Victoria loved Balmoral more for its setting than its house, so be sure to take in its pleasant gardens. Year by year Victoria and Albert added to the estate, taking over neighboring houses, securing the forest and moorland around it, and developing deer stalking and grouse shooting here.

In consequence, Balmoral is now a large property, with grounds that run 12 mi along the Deeside road. Its privacy is protected by belts of pinewood, and the only view of the castle from the A93 is a partial one, from a point near Inver, 2 mi west of the gates.

There's an excellent bird's-eye view of Balmoral from an old military road, now the A939, which climbs out of Crathie, northbound for Cockbridge and the Don Valley. This view embraces the summit of Lochnagar, in whose *corries* (hollows) the snow lies year-round and whose boulder fields the current Prince of Wales, Charles Windsor, so fondly and so frequently treads.

---

weary and certainly not for those seeking lavish splendor, it does offer a good, woodsy location and excellent food (in both the Oaks Restaurant and the Club House) that keep many of its guests coming back. The rooms can be small and suffer from generic hotel decor, but all are clean and well-aired. **Pros:** a great pool and decent gym facilities; good amenities for kids; leafy location in Cairngorm National Park. **Cons:** some rooms are yet to be upgraded; if there's a conference, nonattending guests can feel lost among the crowds. ⊠ *Braemar Rd.* ☎ *01339/755558* ⊕ *www.hilton.co.uk/craigendarroch* ⇨ *40 rooms, 11 suites* ⚿ *In-room: no a/c, Wi-Fi. In-hotel: 2 restaurants, room service, bar, tennis court, pool, gym, spa, laundry service* ⊟ *AE, DC, MC, V* ⊺◎⊺ *BP.*

££   🏠 **Schoolhouse B&B.** In an old schoolhouse just out of the center of
★   town, this solid, dependable B&B offers superior accommodation that's a bit unusual for Aberdeenshire. Renovated and reimagined using ideas picked up from the owners' travels in Sri Lanka and India, the huge rooms provide flexibility for families and groups, or just extra space for couples. Bedrooms have tasteful maple and bamboo floors, Sri Lankan wall hangings, and large beds with the softest sheets; the lounge has a

vast fireplace and oversize sofas. Cathy, the owner, can also prepare evening meals; she is a well-known storyteller in the region, so prepare to be entertained and enthralled. **Pros:** low priced luxury; meticulously clean. **Cons:** TV has only four channels. ⊠ *Anderson Rd.* ☎ *01339/756333* ⊕ *www.school-house.eu* ➾ *4 rooms* ☾ *In-room: no a/c, Wi-Fi. In-hotel: laundry service, Wi-Fi hotspot.* ═ *AE, DC, MC, V* ◉ *CP.*

SHOPPING

Byzantium (⊠ *1–3 Bridge St.* ☎ *013397/55055*) is a boutique and gift shop with an eclectic, fashionable mix of clothing and accessories; even if you don't buy, you will be inspired. At either location of **Countrywear** (⊠ *15 and 35 Bridge St.* ☎ *013397/55453*), you can find everything you need for Highland country living, including fishing tackle, natty tweeds, and that flexible garment popular in Scotland between seasons: the body warmer. For a low-cost gift you could always see what's being boiled up at **Dee Valley Confectioners** (⊠ *Station Sq.* ☎ *013397/55499*). The **McEwan Gallery** (⊠ *On A939, 1 mi west of Ballater* ☎ *013397/55429*) displays fine paintings, watercolors, prints, and books (many with a Scottish or golf theme) in an unusual house built by the Swiss artist Rudolphe Christen in 1902.

EN ROUTE As you continue west into Highland scenery past Balmoral Castle, further pine-framed glimpses appear of the "steep frowning glories of dark Lochnagar," as it was described by the poet Lord Byron (1788–1824). Lochnagar (3,786 feet) was made known to an audience wider than hill walkers by the Prince of Wales, who published a children's story, *The Old Man of Lochnagar.*

BRAEMAR

17 mi west of Ballater, 60 mi west of Aberdeen, 51 mi north of Perth via A93.

Synonymous with the British monarchy, due to its closeness to Balmoral, and with the famous Highland games, this village is popular year round as a base for walkers and climbers enjoying the Grampian Mountains. There isn't really much else going on in Braemar, although the castle is well worth a couple of hours.

GETTING HERE AND AROUND

The town is on A93; there's bus service here as to other towns on the road, but the closest train station is Aberdeen.

ESSENTIALS

Visitor Information Braemar (⊠ *The Mews, Mar Rd.* ☎ *013397/41600* ⊕ *www. braemarscotland.co.uk*).

EXPLORING

The village of Braemar is associated with the **Braemar Highland Gathering** (⊕ *www.braemargathering.org*), held the first Saturday in September. Although there are many such gatherings celebrated throughout Scotland, this one is distinguished by the presence of the royal family. Competitions and events include hammer throwing, caber tossing, running races, Highland dancing, and bagpipe playing. If you plan to attend, book accommodations months in advance and be flexible; you may have to travel a good distance. You can get tickets about six months in advance; they do sell out.

You can find out more about the highland games at the **Braemar Highland Heritage Centre,** in a converted stable block in the middle of town. The center tells the history of the village with displays and a film, and it also has a gift shop. The tourist office is here, too. ⊠ *The Mews, Mar Rd.* ☎ *013397/41944* 🖃 *Free* ☉ *Jan.–May, Nov., and Dec., Mon.–Sat. 10:30–1:30 and 2–5, Sun. 1–4; June, Sept., and Oct., daily 9–5; July and Aug., daily 9–6.*

★ **Braemar Castle,** on the northern outskirts of town, has been restored by a local trust to show how the Farquahrson family would have lived. The castle dates from the 17th century, although its defensive walls, in the shape of a pointed star, came later. At Braemar (the *braes,* or slopes, of the district of Mar) the standard, or rebel flag, was first raised at the start of the unsuccessful Jacobite Rebellion of 1715. Thirty years later, during the last Jacobite rebellion, Braemar Castle was strengthened and garrisoned by Hanoverian (government) troops. From the early 1800s the castle was the clan seat of the Farquharsons, who hold their clan reunion here every summer. Thanks to the commitment of local volunteers, a remarkable 2008 renovation has restored Braemar back to the home it would have been in the early 20th century, complete with all the necessary comforts and family memorabilia. Twelve rooms are on view, including the Lairds's day room with a plush day bed and the kitchen. ⊠ *Off A93* ☎ *013397/41219* ⊕ *www.braemarcastle.co.uk* 🖃 *£5* ☉ *Apr.–June, Sept., and Oct., weekends 11-4; July and Aug., Wed. and weekends 11–4.*

OFF THE
BEATEN
PATH

Linn of Dee. Although the main A93 slinks off to the south from Braemar, a little unmarked road will take you farther west into the hilly heartland. In fact, even if you do not have your own car, you can still explore this area by catching the post bus that leaves from the Braemar post office once a day. The road offers views over the winding River Dee and the blue hills before passing through the tiny hamlet of Inverey and crossing a bridge at the Linn of Dee. *Linn* is a Scots word meaning "rocky narrows," and the river's gash here is deep and roaring. Park beyond the bridge and walk back to admire the sylvan setting.

WHERE TO EAT

£ ✕ **Taste.** It's strangely difficult to eat like a queen in Braemar, but this
CAFÉ simple, clean café serves her subjects and visitors well, with the tastiest, freshest soups and sandwiches (Scottish cheddar and homemade meatloaf are two options) and moist cakes. You can get your latte here, too. ⊠ *Auchendryne Sq.* ☎ *01339/741425* 🖃 *No credit cards* ☉ *No dinner. Closed Tues. and Wed.*

GOLF

The tricky 18-hole **Braemar Golf Course,** founded in 1902, is laden with foaming waters. Erratic duffers take note: the compassionate course managers have installed, near the water, poles with little nets on the end for those occasional shots that may go awry. The cost for a round is £25 during the week, £30 on weekends. ⊠ *Cluny Bank Rd.* ☎ *013397/41618* ⊕ *www.braemargolfclub.co.uk* 🏌 *18 holes, 4,916 yds, SSS 64.*

CORGARFF CASTLE

23 mi northeast of Braemar, 14 mi northwest of Ballater.

GETTING HERE AND AROUND

By car, take A939 and then follow signs. From May to September, the Heather Hopper Bus runs twice daily from Ballater; it stops at Strathdon and Corgarff (☎ *01224/664584*).

EXPLORING

Eighteenth-century soldiers paved a military highway, now the A939, north from Ballater to **Corgarff Castle**, an isolated tower house on the moorland with a star-shape defensive wall—a curious replica of Braemar Castle. Corgarff was built as a hunting lodge for the earls of Mar in the 16th century. After an eventful history that included the wife of a later laird being burned alive in a family dispute, the castle ended its career as a garrison for Hanoverian troops. The troops were responsible for preventing illegal whisky distilling. Reconstructed barracks show what the castle must have been like when the redcoats arrived in 1746. ⊠ *Signposted off A939* ☎ *01975/651460* ⊕ *www.historic-scotland.gov. uk* ☜ *£4.70* ☉ *Apr.–Sept., daily 9:30–6:30; Oct., daily 9:30-4:30; Nov.– Mar., weekends 9:30–4:30; last admission 30 mins before closing.*

EN ROUTE If you return east from Corgarff Castle to the A939/A944 junction and make a left onto the A944, the thorough castle signposting indicates you're on the **Castle Trail.** The A944 meanders along the River Don to the village of Strathdon, where a great mound by the roadside—on the left—turns out to be a *motte*, or the base of a wooden castle, built in the late 12th century. Although it takes considerable imagination to become enthusiastic about a great grass-covered heap, surviving mottes have contributed greatly to the understanding of the history of Scottish castles. The A944 then joins the A97 (go left), and a few minutes later a sign points to **Glenbuchat Castle**, a plain Z-plan tower house.

KILDRUMMY CASTLE

18 mi northeast of Corgarff, 23 mi north of Ballater, 22 mi north of Aboyne.

GETTING HERE AND AROUND

By car, take A97 off A93 (or the A980 if you're coming direct from Banchory). Be wary of the sign for Kildrummy Castle Garden and Hotel. You want the turn after this for Kildrummy Castle itself.

EXPLORING

Kildrummy Castle, although in ruins, is significant because it dates to the 13th century and has ties to the mainstream medieval traditions of European castle building. It shares features with Harlech and Caernarfon, in Wales, as well as with Château de Coucy, near Laon, France. Kildrummy underwent several expansions at the hands of England's King Edward I (1239–1307); the castle was back in Scottish hands in 1306, when it was besieged by King Edward I's son. The defenders were betrayed by Osbarn the Smith, who was promised a large amount of gold by the English forces. They gave it to him after the castle fell, pouring it molten down his throat, or so the ghoulish story goes.

Kildrummy's prominence ended after the collapse of the 1715 Jacobite uprising. It had been the rebel headquarters and was consequently dismantled. Although the castle is almost completely ruined, its unadorned yet strangely moving chapel remains intact. ⊠ *A97* ☎ *019755/71331* ⊕ *www.historic-scotland.gov.uk* ⌑ *£3.50* ☉ *Apr.–Sept., daily 9:30– 5:30; Oct., daily 9:30–4:30.*

The **Kildrummy Castle Gardens,** behind the castle and with a separate entrance from the main road, are built in what was the original quarry for the castle. This sheltered bowl within the woodlands has a broad range of shrubs and alpine plants and a notable water garden. ⊠ *A97* ☎ *019755/71203* ⊕ *www.kildrummy-castle-gardens. co.uk* ⌑ *£3.50* ☉ *Apr.–Sept., daily 9:30–5:30; call to confirm opening times late in season.*

WHERE TO STAY

££££ 🏨 **Kildrummy Castle Hotel.** A grand late-Victorian country house, this elegant lodging offers a peaceful stay and attentive service. Hand-carved oak paneling, elaborate plasterwork, and gentle color schemes create a serene environment, enhanced by the views of nearby Kildrummy Castle Gardens. The Scottish cuisine served in the excellent restaurant (£££££) uses local game as well as seafood. **Pros:** fabulous old hunting lodge; great views. **Cons:** rather pricey (including restaurant); there's no elevator, and you may need to go up a fair number of steps. ⊠ *A97, Kildrummy* ☎ *019755/71288* ⊕ *www.kildrummycastlehotel.co.uk* 🛏 *16 rooms* △ *In-room: no a/c, Wi-Fi. In-hotel: restaurant, bar, laundry service, some pets allowed* ▭ *MC, V* ☉ *Closed Jan.* ⌑⌒*BP.*

ALFORD

9 mi east of Kildrummy, 28 mi west of Aberdeen.

A plain and sturdy settlement in the Howe (Hollow) of Alford, this town gives those who have grown somewhat weary of castle-hopping a break: it has a museum instead. Craigievar Castle and Castle Fraser are nearby, though.

GETTING HERE AND AROUND
The town is on A944.

ESSENTIALS
Visitor Information Alford (⊠ *Old Station Yard, Main St.* ☎ *019755/62052* ⊕ *www.aberdeen-grampian.com* ☉ *Apr.–Sept.*).

EXPLORING

★ The entertaining **Grampian Transport Museum** specializes in road-based means of locomotion, backed up by an archives and library. Its collection of buses is second to none, but the Craigievar Express, a steam-driven creation invented by the local postman to deliver mail more efficiently, is the most unusual. ⊠ *Montgarrie Rd.* ☎ *019755/62292* ⊕ *www.gtm.org.uk* ⌑ *£6* ☉ *Apr.–Sept., daily 10–5; Oct., daily 10–4.*

Craigievar Castle is much as the stonemasons left it in 1626, with pepper-pot turrets and towers that make it an outstanding example of a tower house. Striking and well preserved, it has many family furnishings, and the lovely grounds are worth exploring, too. Craigievar was built in relatively peaceful times by William Forbes, a successful merchant in trade with the Baltic Sea ports (he was also known as Danzig Willie). Closed for conservation work at the time of this writing, the castle is due to reopen in summer 2010; call ahead to check. ⊠ *5 mi south of Alford on A980* ☎ *0844/493–2174* ⊕ *www.nts.org.uk.*

The massive **Castle Fraser**, 8 mi southeast of Alford, is the ancestral home of the Frasers and one of the largest of the castles of Mar; it's certainly a contender as one of the grandest castles in the northeast. Although the well-furnished building shows a variety of styles reflecting the taste of its owners from the 15th through the 19th centuries, its design is typical of the cavalcade of castles in the region, and for good reason. This—along with many others, including Midmar, Craigievar, Crathes, and Glenbuchat—was designed by a family of master masons called Bell. There are plenty of family items, but don't miss the two Turret Rooms—one of which is the trophy room—and Major Smiley's Room. He married into the family but is famous for having been one of the escapees from Colditz (a high-security POW camp) during World War II. The walled garden includes a 19th-century knot garden, with colorful flowerbeds, box hedging, gravel paths, and splendid herbaceous borders. Have lunch in the tearoom or the picnic area. ⊠ *Off A944* ☎ *0844/493–2164* ⊕ *www.nts.org.uk* ⌑ *£8.50* ☉ *Easter–June, Sept., and Oct., Thurs.–Sun. noon–5; July and Aug., daily 11–5; last admission 45 min before closing.*

THE NORTHEAST AND THE MALT WHISKY TRAIL

North of Deeside another popular area of this region lies inland, toward Speyside—the valley, or strath, of the River Spey—famed for its whisky distilleries, some of which it promotes in another signposted trail. Distilling scotch is not an intrinsically spectacular process. It involves pure water, malted barley, and sometimes peat smoke, then a lot of bubbling and fermentation, all of which cause a number of odd smells. The result is a prestigious product with a fascinating range of flavors that you may either enjoy immensely or not at all.

Instead of closely following the Malt Whisky Trail, dip into it and blend visits to distilleries with some other aspects of the county of Moray, particularly its coastline. Whisky notwithstanding, Moray's scenic qualities, low rainfall, and other reassuring weather statistics are worth remembering. The suggested route also allows you to sample the northeastern seaboard, including some of the best but least-known coastal scenery in Scotland.

DUFFTOWN

54 mi west of Aberdeen.

On one of the Spey tributaries, Dufftown was planned in 1817 by the earl of Fife. Its simple cross layout with a square and a large clock tower (originally from Banff and now the site of the visitor center) is typical of a small Scottish town built in the 19th century. Its simplicity is made all the more stark by the brooding, heather-clad hills that rise around it. Dufftown is convenient to a number of distilleries.

GETTING HERE AND AROUND

To get here from Aberdeen, drive west on A96 and A920; then turn west at Huntly. It's not easy or quick, but you can take the train to Elgin or Keith and then the bus to Dufftown

ESSENTIALS

Visitor Information **Dufftown** (⊠ *The Square* ☎ *01340/820501* ⊙ *Apr.–Oct.*).

EXPLORING

Many make **Glenfiddich Distillery,** ½ mi north of Dufftown, their first stop on the Malt Whisky Trail. The independent company of William Grant and Sons Limited was the first to realize the tourist potential of the distilling process. The company began offering tours around the typical pagoda-roof malting buildings and subsequently built an entertaining visitor center. Besides a free 20-minute tour of the distillery that you can supplement with audiovisual displays, there is a two-hour in-depth Connoisseurs' Tour (£20; reserve ahead in summer) that includes a special nosing and tasting session. Check out the Glenfiddich Distillery Art Gallery, showing the work of international artists who have completed a residency at the distillery. It's open Thursday to Sunday 12:30 to 5:30. ⊠ *A941* ☎ *01340/820373* ⊕ *www.glenfiddich.com* 🖂 *Free, Connoisseurs' Tour £20* ⊙ *Easter–mid-Oct., Mon.–Sat. 9:30–4:30, Sun. noon–4:30; mid-Oct.–Easter, weekdays 9:30–4:30.*

On a mound just above the Glenfiddich Distillery is a grim, gray, and squat curtain-walled castle, **Balvenie.** This ruined fortress, which dates from the 13th century, once commanded the glens and passes toward Speyside and Elgin. The Balvenie Distillery is next to the castle; it's open for tours. ⊠ *A941* ☎ *01340/820121* ⊕ *www.historic-scotland.gov. uk* 🖂 *£3.70* ⊙ *Apr.–Sept., daily 9:30–5:30; Oct., daily 9:30-4:30; last entry ½ hr before closing.*

Mortlach Church, set in a hollow by the Dullan Water, is thought to be one of Scotland's oldest Christian sites, perhaps founded by St. Luag, a contemporary of St. Columba, as early as AD 566. Note the weathered Pictish cross in the churchyard and the even older stone under cover in the vestibule, with a strange Pictish elephantlike beast carved on it. Though much of the church was rebuilt after 1876, some early work survives, including three lancet windows from the 13th century and a leper's squint (a hole extended to the outside of the church so that lepers could hear the service but be kept away from the rest of the congregation). ⊠ *Church St.*

WHERE TO EAT AND STAY

££££ ╳ **La Faisanderie.** Gourmands from around the northeast come to Dufftown for a truly French gastronomic experience. A large, distillery-

FRENCH inspired fresco in the plain dining room adds some panache to the tall windows, wood floors, and white tablecloths. The French and English owners use the freshest local beef, game, and seafood, creating classic dishes with smooth, glossy but not too heavy sauces; everything comes

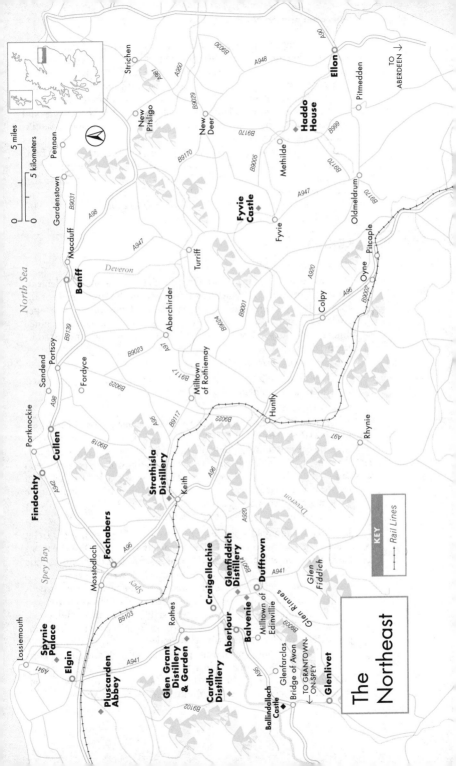

artfully arranged on the plate. Iced whisky with chestnut puree is perhaps the ultimate way for a sweet-toothed whisky lover to enjoy a tipple. ⊠ *2 Balvenie St.* ☎ *01340/821273* ▭ *AE, MC, V* ☺ *Closed Tues.*

£   🏠 **Tannochbrae.** It's great when places move with the times, and Dufftown is finally catching up with this stylish B&B. There are six bedrooms upstairs, individual in style but all with simple color schemes and tactile throws. The restaurant downstairs goes by the name of Scott's; it's rather expensive (three courses for £26) but serves modern dishes such as tender young venison with a fragrant blueberry sauce. **Pros:** Dufftown is beautiful; cozy but cramped whisky bar. **Cons:** pricey restaurant; two rooms (and their bathrooms) are not as well decorated as the others. ⊠ *22 Fife St.* ☎ *01340/820541* ⊕ *www.tannochbrae.co.uk* 🛏 *6 rooms* ⌂ *In-room: no a/c. In-hotel: restaurant, bar* ▭ *AE, MC, V* ⦿ *BP.*

CRAIGELLACHIE

4 mi northwest of Dufftown via A941.

Renowned as an angling resort, Craigellachie, like so many settlements on the River Spey, is sometimes enveloped in the malty reek of the local industry. Glen Grant is one of the distilleries nearby. The Spey itself is crossed by a handsome suspension bridge, designed by noted engineer Thomas Telford (1757–1834) in 1814 and now bypassed by the modern road.

GETTING HERE AND AROUND

The town is on A491; it's best to drive here, as public transportation is infrequent and complicated.

EXPLORING

★   Just before the village is the huge **Speyside Cooperage and Visitor Centre,** a major stop on the Malt Whisky Trail and a must for all whisky fans. Making casks is a surprisingly physical and dramatic process that uses the same tools and skills employed for hundreds of years. Inside you can watch highly skilled coopers make and repair oak barrels used in the local whisky industry. The Acorn to Cask exhibit tells all about the ancient craft of coopering. ⊠ *Dufftown Rd.* ☎ *01340/871108* ⊕ *www.speysidecooperage.co.uk* 🎟 *£3.30* ☺ *Weekdays 9–4.*

James Grant founded a distillery in 1840 when he was only 25, and it
★   was the first in the country to be electrically powered. **Glen Grant Distillery & Garden** will come as a welcome relief to less-than-enthusiastic companions of dedicated Malt Whisky Trail followers, because in addition to the distillery there's a large and beautiful garden. The gardens are planted and tended as Grant planned them, with orchards and woodland walks, log bridges over waterfalls, a magnificent lily pond, and azaleas and rhododendrons in profusion. Now owned by Campari, Glen Grant produces a distinctive pale-gold, clear whisky, with an almost floral or fruity finish, using peculiarly tall stills and special purifiers that follow a design introduced over a century ago. You'll see these on your tour. ⊠ *A941, Rothes* ☎ *09785/3548–6454* ⊕ *www.glengrant.com* 🎟 *£3.50* ☺ *Feb.–Dec., Mon.–Sat. 9:30–4, Sun. noon–4.*

CLOSE UP

Whisky, the Water of Life

Conjured from an innocuous mix of malted barley, water, and yeast, malt whisky is for many synonymous with Scotland. Clans produced whisky for hundreds of years before it emerged as Scotland's national drink and major export. Today those centuries of expertise result in a sublimely subtle drink with many different layers of flavor. Each distillery produces a malt with—to the expert—instantly identifiable, predominant notes peculiarly its own.

WHISKY TYPES AND STYLES

There are two types of whisky: malt and grain. Malt whisky, generally acknowledged to have a more sophisticated bouquet and flavor, is made with malted barley—barley that is soaked in water until the grains germinate and then is dried to halt the germination, all of which adds extra flavor and a touch of sweetness to the brew. Grain whisky also contains malted barley, but with the addition of unmalted barley and maize.

Blended whiskies, which make up many of the leading brands, usually balance malt- and grain-whisky distillations; deluxe blends contain a higher percentage of malts. Blends that contain several malt whiskies are called "vatted malts." Whisky connoisseurs

often prefer to taste the single malts: the unblended whisky from a single distillery.

In simple terms, malt whiskies may be classified into "eastern" and "western" in style, with the whisky made in the east of Scotland, for example in Speyside, being lighter and sweeter than the products of the western isles, which often have a taste of peat smoke or even iodine.

The production process is, by comparison, relatively straightforward: just malt your barley, mash it, ferment it and distill it, then mature to perfection. To find out the details, join a distillery tour, and be rewarded with a dram. Check out ⊕ www.scotlandwhisky.com for more information.

TASTING WHISKY

When tasting whisky, follow these simple steps. First, pour a dram. Turn and tilt the glass to coat the sides. Smell the whisky, "nosing" to inhale the heady aromas. If you want, you can add a little water and turn the glass gently to watch it "marry" with the whisky, nosing as you go. Take a wee sip and swirl it over your tongue and sense what connoisseurs call the "mouthfeel." Swallow and admire the finish. Repeat until convinced it's a good malt!

7

WHERE TO STAY

££ 🏨 **Highlander Inn.** Don't be fooled by the rather Alpine exterior: this very Scottish hotel prides itself on its whisky bar and its friendliness. The good-size guest rooms are nothing fancy, but there is a high standard of upkeep, especially in the bathrooms. A restaurant serves straightforward Scottish meals like haggis, neeps (turnips), and tatties. However, you are sure to gravitate toward the bar, a belt-and-braces affair that stocks 180 malts: the barman will happily talk you through each and every one of them. **Pros:** simple accommodation; a warm welcome. **Cons:** bar meals could be more exciting. ✉ *Victoria St.* ☎ *01340/881446*

CHOOSING A DISTILLERY TOUR

Like whiskies, distillery tours are not the same, though you'll usually spend about an hour or two at each place. The company's history, size, and commercial savvy create different experiences. You should also investigate any special in-depth tours if you're willing to pay extra and spend more time. Here's a cheat sheet to help you choose a tour or two on the Malt Whisky Trail.

Cardhu: Architecturally, the stocky buildings and proud towers of Cardhu, formerly an illicit still, seem to have a grim defiance. The tour gives you a great understanding of whisky's simple ingredients, including locally sourced springwater, and the process they undergo.

Glen Grant: The distillery tour is good, but the gardens of Major Grant are sublime. He traveled the world collecting species and created a Victorian garden that has been gloriously restored.

Glenfarclas: This proud family-owned still may not provide the slickness of the Glenfiddich tour, but the quiet passion of the still workers

and their belief in their whisky is more powerful than a dram of the stuff.

Glenfiddich: Owned by the same family since day one, this distillery offers both entry-level and enthusiasts' tours that cover the older, more atmospheric buildings and the swankier visitor center.

Glenlivet: It's a beautiful drive to this, the first licensed distillery in the Highlands. You'll learn the fascinating story of Glenlivet's founder, George Smith.

Speyside Cooperage: Although this isn't a distillery, real whisky enthusiasts shouldn't miss a visit to one of the few remaining cooperages in the Scotland. Watch the coopers at work and see just how much craft goes into making and treating these precious barrels.

Strathisla: Home of Chivas, not a malt but a fine blended whisky, this is perhaps one of the prettiest and most compact distilleries in the northeast and is delightfully situated on the River Isla.

⊕ *www.whiskyinn.com* ↜ *5 rooms* ⚘ *In-room: no a/c, Wi-Fi (some). In-hotel: restaurant, bar, bicycles* ▭ *MC, V* ⦿⎮ *BP.*

ABERLOUR

2 mi southwest of Craigellachie.

Aberlour, often listed as Charlestown of Aberlour on maps, is a handsome little burgh, essentially Victorian in style, though actually founded in 1812 by the local landowner. The names of the noted local whisky stills are Cragganmore, Aberlour, and Glenfarclas; Glenlivet and Cardhu are also nearby. Also in Aberlour is Walkers, famous for producing shortbread, tins of buttery, crumbly goodness, since 1898.

GETTING HERE AND AROUND

Aberlour is on A95; public transportation here is infrequent.

EXPLORING

In an age when most small distilleries have been taken over by multi-nationals, **Glenfarclas** remains family owned, passed down from father to son since 1865. That link to the past is most visible among its low buildings, where the retired still sits outside: if you didn't know what it was, you could mistake it for part of a submarine. The tours end with tastings in the superlative Ship Room, the intact lounge of an ocean liner called the *Empress of Australia*. An in-depth Ambassador's Tour and tasting is available for £15. ⊠ *Off A95, Ballindalloch* ☎ *01807/500257* ⊕ *www.glenfarclas.co.uk* 🎫 *£3.50* 🕙 *Apr.–June, weekdays 10–5; July–Sept., weekdays 10–5, Sun. 10–4; Oct.–Mar., weekdays 10–4.*

★ The famous **Glenlivet** was the first licensed distillery in the Highlands, founded in 1824 by George Smith. Today it produces one of the best-known 12-year-old single malts in the world. Take the free distillery tour for a chance to see inside the huge bonded warehouse where the whisky steeps in oak casks. The tour has two aspects: the Spirit of the Glen examines how unique factors come together to make this nectar, and the Glenlivet Legacy looks at the dream of the distillery's founder. There's a coffee shop with home baking and, of course, a whisky shop. Glenlivet is 10 mi southwest of Aberlour via A95 and B9008. ⊠ *Glenlivet, Ballindalloch* ☎ *01340/821720* ⊕ *www.glenlivet.com* 🎫 *Free* 🕙 *Apr.–Oct., Mon.–Sat. 10–4, Sun. 12:30–4.*

The striking outline of **Cardhu Distillery,** whose main product lies at the heart of Johnnie Walker Blends, is set among the heather-clad Mannoch hills. Established by John and Helen Cumming in 1811, it was officially founded in 1824, after distilling was made legal by the Excise Act of 1823. Today Cardhu is owned by the superbrewer Diageo (who tried to rename it Cardow, although the single malt is still known as Cardhu). Guided tours take you to the mashing, fermenting, and distilling halls, and they explain the malting process that now takes place at Burghead on the coast. Take time to walk around the attractive grounds or picnic there. Cardhu is 10 mi north of Glenlivet via B9008, A95, and B9102; it's 7 mi west of Aberlour. ⊠ *B1902, Knockando* ☎ *01340/875635* ⊕ *www.scotlandwhisky.com* 🎫 *£4* 🕙 *Dec.–Feb., weekdays 11–3; Mar.–June and Nov., weekdays 10–5; July–Sept., Mon.–Sat. 10–5, Sun. noon–4; last tour 1 hr before closing.*

WHERE TO EAT AND STAY

£ ✕ **Old Pantry.** This pleasantly rustic corner restaurant and gift shop over-
BRITISH looks Aberlour's tree-shaded central square. The kitchen serves every-thing from a cup of coffee with a sticky cake at teatime to a three-course spread of soup, roast meat, and traditional pudding. ⊠ *The Square* ☎ *01340/871617* 🍽 *MC, V* 🕙 *No dinner Oct.–May.*

£ 🏨 **Mash Tun.** Curvy yet sturdy, this former station hotel harks back to
★ a time when Aberlour was a busy holiday destination on the Aberdeen to Aviemore train line. Now a smart B&B and popular restaurant, it is once again the heart of the village. The bedrooms, named after local distilleries, are bold and fresh, decorated with deep hues and an abundance of snow white pillows and duvets. If you want to work up an appetite or work off the splendid food in the restaurant (try the haggis or venison), the Speyside Way walk along the alder-, oak-,

7

and rowan tree–lined river is just a few moments away. **Pros:** superb accommodation; great atmosphere in the restaurant and bar. **Cons:** book well ahead in summer; those who like an early night might find the bar disturbs them. ✉ *8 Broom-field Sq.* ☎ *01340/88171* ⊕ *www. mashtun-aberlour.com* ⇄ *4 rooms, 1 suite* � *In-room:, no a/c, Wi-Fi. In-hotel: restaurant, bar* ▭ *AE, MC, V* ❘◎❘ *BP.*

SHOPPING

A couple of miles west of Aberlour and just south of the Glenfarclas Distillery, look for **Speyside Pottery** (✉ *A95, Ballindalloch* ☎ *01807/500338*), where Thomas and Anne Gough produce domestic stoneware in satisfying, sturdy traditional shapes. Call ahead November through March, as hours are limited.

> **FISHING SPOT**
>
> The Spey is one of Scotland's most popular rivers for anglers. **Ballindalloch Castle** (✉ *Off A95, between Craigellachie and Grant-own on Spey* ☎ *01807/500205* ⊕ *www.ballindallochcastle.co.uk*), the family home of the Macpher-son-Grants since 1546, offers a limited number of permits for fishing on the banks of the Spey and the Avon. It's 10 mi southwest of Craigellachie.

ELGIN

15 mi north of Craigellachie, 69 mi northwest of Aberdeen, 41 mi east of Inverness.

As the center of the fertile Laigh (low-lying lands) of Moray, Elgin has been of local importance for centuries. Sheltered by great hills to the south, the city lies between two major rivers, the Spey and the Findhorn. Beginning in the 13th century, Elgin became an important religious center, a cathedral city with a walled town growing up around the cathedral and adjacent to the original settlement.

Elgin prospered, and by the early 18th century it became a mini-Edinburgh of the north and a place where country gentlemen spent their winters. It even echoed Edinburgh in carrying out wide-scale reconstruction in the 18th century. Many fine neoclassical buildings survive today despite much misguided demolition in the late 20th century for better traffic flow. However, the central main-street plan and some of the older little streets and *wynds* (alleyways) remain. You can also see Elgin's past in the arcaded shop fronts—some of which date from the late-17th century—on the main shopping street.

GETTING HERE AND AROUND

Elgin is on the A96 road from Aberdeen to Inverness. The A941 runs north from the distillery area to the city. There's a train stop here on the line that links Aberdeen and Inverness: Aberdeen is 90 minutes away.

ESSENTIALS

Visitor Information Elgin (✉ *17 High St.* ☎ *01343/542666*).

EXPLORING

At the center of Elgin, the most conspicuous structure is **St. Giles Church**, which divides High Street. The grand foursquare building constructed in 1828 exhibits the Greek Revival style: note the columns, the pilasters, and the top of the spire, surmounted by a representation of the Lysi-crates Monument. ⊠ *High St.*

Cooper Park contains a magnificent ruin, the **Elgin Cathedral,** consecrated in 1224. Its eventful story included devastation by fire: a 1390 act of retaliation by Alexander Stewart (circa 1343–1405), the Wolf of Badenoch. The illegitimate-son-turned-bandit of King David II (1324–71) had sought revenge for his excommunication by the bishop of Moray. The cathedral was rebuilt but finally fell into disuse after the Reformation in 1560. By 1567 the highest authority in the land, the regent earl of Moray, had stripped the lead from the roof to pay for his army. Thus ended the career of the religious seat known as the Lamp of the North. Some traces of the cathedral settlement survive—the gateway Pann's Port and the Bishop's Palace—although they've been drastically altered. Cooper Park is a five-minute walk northeast of Elgin Museum (at 1 High Street), across the bypass road. ⊠ *Cooper Park* ☎ *01343/547171* ⊕ *www.historic-scotland.gov.uk* ▣ *£4.70; £6.20 with Spynie Palace* ⊙ *Apr.–Sept., daily 9:30–6:30; Oct.–Mar., Sat.–Wed. 9:30–4:30; last admission ½ hr before closing.*

Just north of Elgin is **Spynie Palace,** the impressive 15th-century former headquarters of the bishops of Moray. It has now fallen into ruin, though the top of the tower has good views over the Laigh of Moray. Find it by turning right off the main A941 Elgin–Lossiemouth road. *Off A941* ☎ *01343/546358* ⊕ *www.historic-scotland.gov.uk* ▣ *£3.70; £6.20 with Elgin Cathedral* ⊙ *Apr.–Sept., daily 9:30–6:30; Oct., daily 9:30–4:30; Nov.–Mar., weekends 9:30–4:30; last admission ½ hr before closing.*

OFF THE
BEATEN
PATH

Pluscarden Abbey. Given the general destruction caused by the 16th-century upheaval of the Reformation, abbeys in Scotland tend to be ruinous and deserted, but at Pluscarden Abbey the monks' way of life continues. Originally a 13th-century structure, the abbey was abandoned by the religious community after the Reformation. Monks from Prinknash Abbey near Gloucester, England, returned here in 1948, and the abbey is now a Benedictine community. ⊠ *Off B9010, 6 mi south-west of Elgin* ⊕ *www.pluscardenabbey.org* ▣ *Free* ⊙ *Daily 9–5.*

SHOPPING

Gordon and MacPhail (⊠ *58–60 South St.* ☎ *01343/545110*), an outstanding delicatessen and wine merchant, also stocks rare malt whiskies. This is a good place to shop for gifts for those foodies among your friends. **Johnstons of Elgin** (⊠ *Newmill* ☎ *01343/554099*) is a woolen mill with a worldwide reputation for its luxury fabrics, especially cashmere. The bold color range is particularly appealing. The large shop stocks not only the firm's own products but also top-quality Scottish crafts and giftware. There's a coffee shop on the premises.

FOCHABERS

9 mi east of Elgin.

With its hanging baskets of fuchsia in summer and its perfectly mowed village square, Fochabers has a cared-for charm that makes you want to stop here, even just to stretch your legs. Lying just to the south of the

River Spey, the former market town was founded in 1776 by the Duke of Gordon. The duke moved the village from its original site because it was too close to Gordon Castle. Famous today for being home to the Baxters brand of soups and jams, Fochabers is near some of the best berry fields: come and pick your own in the summer months.

GETTING HERE AND AROUND

Fochabers is not on the Inverness to Aberdeen train line, but there is an hourly bus service (Stagecoach Bluebird number 10) from Fochabers to Elgin. It's near the junction of A98 and A96.

EXPLORING

Just a mile west of the center of Fochabers, you can see the works of a major local employer, Baxters of Fochabers. From Tokyo to New York, upmarket stores stock the company's soups, jams, chutneys, and other gourmet products—all of which are made here, close to the River Spey. Take home a can of Royal Game Soup, a favorite of the late Queen Mum. The **Baxters Highland Village** presents a video, *Baxters Experience,* about the history of the business, plus interactive exhibits and cooking demonstrations. You can have a look at a re-creation of the Baxters' first grocery shop, a real shop that stocks Baxters' goods, and a shop called the Best of Scotland, specializing all kinds of Scottish products. A restaurant serves up an assortment of delectables. ⊠ *A96* ☎ *01343/820666* ⊕ *www.baxters.com* ⊠ *Free* ☉ *Daily 10–5.*

Once over the Spey Bridge and past the cricket ground (a very unusual sight in Scotland), you can find the symmetrical, 18th-century Fochabers village square lined with antiques dealers. Through one of these shops, Pringle Antiques, you can enter the **Fochabers Folk Museum,** a converted church with a fine collection of items relating to past life in the village and surrounding area. Exhibits include carts and carriages, farm implements, and Victorian toys. ⊠ *High St.* ☎ *01343/821204* ⊕ *www.fochabers-heritage.org.uk* ⊠ *Free* ☉ *Easter–Oct., Tues.–Fri. 11–4, weekends 2–4.*

One of the village's lesser-known treasures is the **Gordon Chapel** (⊠ *Castle St., just off the Square*), which has an exceptional set of stained-glass windows by Pre-Raphaelite artist Sir Edward Burne-Jones.

★ Whisky lovers should take the A96 10 mi (15 minutes) southeast from Fochabers to see one of Scotland's most iconic distilleries, the **Strathisla Distillery,** with its cobblestone courtyard and famous double pagoda roofs. Stretching over the picturesque River Isla, the Strathisla Distillery was built in 1786 and now produces the main component of the Chivas Regal blend. Guided tours take you to the mash house, tun room, and still house—all pretty much the same as they were when production began. The tour ends with a tasting session. ⊠ *Seafield Ave., Keith* ☎ *01542/783044* ⊕ *www.chivas.com* ⊠ *£5* ☉ *Apr.–Oct., Mon.–Sat. 9:30–4, Sun. noon–4.*

SHOPPING

Art and Antiques (⊠ *33–35 High St.* ☎ *01343/829104*) combines an unusual mix of original art by the owners with ceramic, glassware, and small pieces of furniture. **Watts Antiques** (⊠ *45 High St.* ☎ *01343/820077*) has small collectibles, jewelry, ornaments, and china.

If you're interested in works by local artists, head to **Just Art** (⊠ *64 High St.* ☎*01343/820500*), a fine gallery with high-quality contemporary ceramics and paintings. At **the Quaich** (⊠ *85 High St.* ☎*01343/820981*) you can stock up on cards and small gifts, then sit with a cup of tea and a home-baked snack.

EN ROUTE

Ten miles east of Fochabers, along the A942 coastal road, **Findochty** (pronounced Fin-echty) has residents who take the art of house painting to a new level. Some even paint the mortar between the stonework a different color from the exterior. The harbor, with many colorful small sailing boats tied up to the quay, has a faint echo of the Mediterranean about it. A drive east from Findochty takes you past a string of salty little fishing villages. They make a colorful scene with their gabled houses and fishing nets set out to dry amid the rocky shoreline.

CULLEN

★ *13 mi east of Fochabers, 3 mi east of Findochty.*

Look for some wonderfully painted homes at Cullen, in the old fishing town below the railway viaduct. The real attractions of this charming little seaside resort, however, are its white-sand beach (the water is quite cold, though) and the fine view west toward the aptly named Bowfiddle Rock. In summer Cullen bustles with families carrying buckets and spades and eating ice cream and chips.

A stroll past the small but once busy harbor reveals numerous fishers' cottages, huddled together with small yards where they dried their nets. Beyond these, the vast stretch of beach curves gently round the bay. Above is the disused Victorian viaduct—formerly the Peterhead train line—and the 18th-century town.

GETTING HERE AND AROUND
Cullen is on A98, on Cullen Bay.

EXPLORING
The town has a fine mercat (market) cross and one main street—**Seafield Street**—that splits the town. It holds numerous specialty shops—antiques and gift stores, an ironmonger, a baker, a pharmacy, and a locally famous ice-cream shop among them—as well as several cafés.

In summer it can seem as if everyone you see in Cullen is licking a cone from the **Ice Cream Shop** (⊠ *40 Seafield St.* ☎*01542/840484*). It sells just a handful of flavors but they are all made on-site.

NEED A BREAK?

Cullen Chip Shop (⊠ *47 Seafield St.* ☎ *01542/841004*) serves the freshest fish, landed in nearby Buckie and cooked to melt-in-your-mouth perfection. There are no seats inside, but walk down the hill and head toward the harbor for some benches with sweeping views.

WHERE TO EAT AND STAY
£ ✕ **Puddleduck Patch.** The name suggests something child or duck related,
CAFÉ but this place is a cheery café and gift shop as well as a spiritual home to northeast quilt makers. Uncomplicated and fresh lunches include chunky sandwiches oozing tasty filings, as well as Cullen skink (a

popular soup made from smoked fish), and there is always a mountain of cakes to choose from. At dinner, expect Scottish standards like stews and haddock fishcakes. Puddleduck is just five minutes from the square (and the best parking). Plans are under way to offer B&B in later in 2010, so check. ⊠ *Seafield St.* ☎ *01542/841888* ⊟ *AE, MC, V* ⊘ *No dinner Sun.–Tues.*

££ ⛺ **Academy House.** Ten minutes from the seaside town of Cullen, this
★   bed-and-breakfast in a handsome Victorian house was once the head-master's house for the local secondary school. Well-chosen antiques decorate the spacious rooms. Evening meals are served on request at £22 per person. The village of Fordyce, with narrow streets that follow a medieval plan, lies among the barley fields of Banffshire like a small slice of rural England gone far adrift. You can stroll by the churchyard or picnic on the old bleaching green (a notice board explains everything). **Pros:** good home cooking; delightful setting. **Cons:** rooms book up fast; there's little to do in Fordyce. ⊠ *School Rd., Fordyce* ☎ *01261/842743* ⊕ *www.fordyceaccommodation.com* ⤴ *2 rooms* ⌂ *In-room: no a/c, no phone, Wi-Fi. In-hotel: some pets allowed* ⊟ *No credit cards* ⦿ *BP.*

SHOPPING
Abra Antiques (⊠ *6 Seafield St.* ☎ *01542/840605*) overflows with all kinds of trinkets, Victoriana, antiquarian books, and Scottish miscellany, but at surprisingly pleasing prices.

BANFF

36 mi east of Elgin, 47 mi north of Aberdeen.

Midway along the northeast coast, overlooking Moray Firth and the estuary of the River Deveron, Banff is a fishing town of considerable elegance that feels as though it's a million miles from tartan-clad Scotland. Part Georgian, like Edinburgh's New Town, and part 16th-century small burgh, like Culross, Banff is an exemplary east-coast salty town, with a tiny harbor and fine architecture. It's also within easy reach of plenty of unspoiled coastline—cliff and rock to the east, at Gardenstown (known as Gamrie) and Pennan, or beautiful little sandy beaches westward toward Sandend and Cullen.

GETTING HERE AND AROUND
Banff is on the A98 coastal road and at the end of the tree-lined A947 to Aberdeen. If you are relying on public transportation, Bus 325 from Aberdeen Bus Station takes two hours and gets you into Low Street, just five minutes from Duff House.

ESSENTIALS
Visitor Information Banff (⊠ *Collie Lodge, Low St.* ☎ *01261/812419* ⊘ *Apr.–Sept.*).

EXPLORING
★ The jewel in Banff's crown is the grand mansion of **Duff House,** a splendid William Adam–designed (1689–1748) Georgian mansion. Restored as an outstation of the National Galleries of Scotland, it exhibits many fine paintings, including works by El Greco, Sir Henry Raeburn, and Thomas Gainsborough, in rooms furnished to reflect the days when the

dukes of Fife occupied the house. A good tearoom and a shop are in the basement. ⊠ *Off A98* ☎ *01261/818181* ⊕ *www.duffhouse.org.uk* 🖾 *£6.40* ⊙ *Apr.–Oct., daily 11–5; Nov.–Mar., Thurs.–Sun. 11–4.*

Across the river in Banff's twin town, Macduff, on the shore east of the harbor, stands the conical **Macduff Marine Aquarium.** A 250,000-gallon central tank and many smaller display areas and touch pools show the sea life of the Moray Firth and North Atlantic. Between 2 and 3:30 on most afternoons there are feeding, diving (they hand feed the fish), and rock pool displays. ⊠ *11 High Shore* ☎ *01261/833369* ⊕ *www. macduff-aquarium.org.uk* 🖾 *£5.50* ⊙ *Daily 10–5.*

FYVIE CASTLE

18 mi south of Banff, 18 mi northwest of Ellon.

GETTING HERE AND AROUND
If you're driving from Banff, take the A947 south for 20 minutes or so until you see the turnoff.

EXPLORING
In an area rich with castles, **Fyvie Castle** stands out as the most complex. Five great towers built by five successive powerful families turned a 13th-century foursquare castle into an opulent Edwardian statement of wealth. Some superb paintings are on view, including 12 works by Sir Henry Raeburn, and there are myriad sumptuous interiors; you can also explore many walks on the castle grounds. A former lady of the house, Lillia Drummond, was apparently starved to death by her husband, who entombed her body inside the walls of a secret room. In the 1920s when the bones were disrupted during renovations, a string of such terrible misfortunes followed that they were quickly returned and the room sealed off. Her name is carved into the windowsill of the Drummond Room. ⊠ *Off A947, between Oldmeldrum and Turriff* ☎ *0844/4932182* ⊕ *www.nts.org.uk* 🖾 *£10.50* ⊙ *Apr.–June and Sept., Sat.–Tues. noon–5; July and Aug., daily 11–5; last admission 45 mins before closing.*

ELLON

32 mi southwest of Banff, 14 mi north of Aberdeen.

Formerly a market center on what was then the lowest bridging point of the River Ythan, Ellon, a bedroom suburb of Aberdeen, is a small town at the center of a rural hinterland. It's also well placed for visiting Fyvie Castle and Haddo House.

GETTING HERE AND AROUND
To get to Ellon, take the A947 from Banff or the A90 from Aberdeen; both routes take half an hour.

EXPLORING
Fodor's Choice ★ Created as the home of the Gordon family, earls and marquesses of Aberdeen, **Haddo House**—designed by William Adam—is now cared for by the National Trust for Scotland. Built in 1732, the elegant mansion has a light and graceful Georgian design, with curving wings on

either side of a harmonious, symmetrical facade. The interior is late-Victorian ornate, filled with magnificent paintings (including works by Pompeo Batoni and Sir Thomas Lawrence) and plenty of objets d'art. Pre-Raphaelite stained-glass windows by Sir Edward Burne-Jones grace the chapel. Outside is a terrace garden with a fountain, and few yards farther is Haddo Country Park, which has walking trails leading to memorials about the Gordon family. Visits are by prebooked tour only. The house is 8 mi northwest of Ellon. ⊠ *Off B999, Methlick, Ellon* ☎ *0844/493–2179* ⊕ *www.nts.org.uk* ☞ *£8.50* ⊘ *July and Aug., guided tours daily at 11:30, 1:30, and 3:30; Sept. and Oct., guided tours Fri.–Mon. at 11 and 4:30. Tours must be prebooked.*

Argyll and the Isles

WORD OF MOUTH

"My favorite has to be Iona. It's a tiny, cut-off island with a beautiful deserted beach on the back side of it. It also has an incredible old church and abbey. There isn't much to do on the island, but it's very peaceful if you want long windswept walks and to relax together."

—michael_eire

"On Islay, the Laphroaig distillery has a malting floor. Laphroaig has a great visitor experience (although, like you, I prefer Lagavulin whisky). They're only about a mile apart, so you can go for a walk at Lagavulin and do your tour at Laphroaig."

—Sheila

Updated
by Mike
Gonzalez

Argyll's rocky seaboard looks out on to islands that were once part of a single prehistoric landmass. The Atlantic breaks against the islands' wild western coasts, bringing the rain that waters inland forests of the Argyll and the Kintyre Peninsula. Here narrow roads wind around natural obstacles, slowing travel but forcing you to see and admire the lochs, the woods, and the ruins that hint at the region's dramatic past. Distances are relatively small, but the stark contrasts on the journey are often unexpected and moving.

Divided in two by the long peninsula of Kintyre, western Scotland has a complicated, splintered coastline. Looking out on to the islands and the Atlantic Sea beyond, it is breathtakingly beautiful, though it often catches extremely wet ocean weather. Locals say that you can experience four seasons in a single day, and cliffs and woods can suddenly and dramatically disappear and re-emerge from sea mist. Oak woods and bracken-covered hillsides dot the region, and the everywhere you'll encounter the bright interplay of sea, loch, and rugged green peninsula.

Ruined ancient castles like Dunstaffnage, Kilchurn, and the towers on the islands of Loch Awe give testimony to the region's past importance. The stone circles, carved stones, and Bronze- and Iron Age burial mounds around Kilmartin and on Islay are reminders of even earlier periods, when the region was already occupied. More recent grand houses, like Inveraray Castle and Brodick Castle on the island of Arran, guard their own historic interiors, with treasure troves of art and antique furniture. Their grounds, nourished by the temperate west coast climate, hold great gardens that are the pride of Argyll. Crarae, south of Inveraray, has winding paths through plantings of magnolias and azaleas, and Ardkinglas Woodland Garden holds an outstanding conifer collection. And at Kilmartin, prehistoric peoples have left their mark in stone circles.

The working people of Glasgow traditionally spent their family holidays on the Clyde estuary, taking day trips to Dunoon or Rothesay on the Isle of Bute. Carrick Castle and Benmore Garden are a short trip from Dunoon. From Ardrossan, further down the coast, ferries cruise to the prosperous and varied Isle of Arran.

Western Scotland's small islands have jagged cliffs or tongues of rock, long white sand beaches, fertile pastures where sheep and cattle graze, fortresses, and shared memories of clan wars and mysterious beasts. Their cliff paths and loch-side byways are a paradise for walkers and cyclists, and their whisky the ideal reward after a long day outside. While the islands' western coasts are dramatic, their more sheltered eastern seaboards are the location for the pretty harbor towns like the

TOP REASONS TO GO

Whisky, whisky, whisky: Take the "whisky trail" in Port Ellen on the Isle of Islay; it's a leisurely 3-mi stroll passing Ardbeg, Laphroaig, and Lagavulin distilleries, whose whiskies share the distinct flavors of peat, seaweed, and iodine. Arran, Oban, and Jura have their own unique distilleries. All have plenty of local character and provide an intimate visiting experience.

Seaside biking: Oban and Arran are two great cycling destinations. Biking along the coast provides breathtaking scenery; just keep in mind that it rains a lot in this part of the country, so bring rain gear.

Iona and its abbey: Maybe it's the remoteness—especially if you explore beyond the abbey—that adds to the almost mystical sense of history here, but a visit to this early center of Scottish Christianity is a magical experience. This was also the burial place of Scottish kings until the 11th century.

Fantastic fishing and golf: The largest skate in Britain are found in the waters off the Isle of Mull. There are 20 coastal settlements suited to sea angling where charter-boat companies offer trips. If it's loch and river sites you're after, there are 50 for game fishing that yield salmon, trout, and other fish. Prefer to tee off? Western Scotland has about two dozen golf courses, notably some fine coastal links. Machrihanish, near Campbeltown, is the best known.

Glorious gardens: Plants flourish in the mild Gulf Steam that brushes against this broken, western coastline. For vivid flowers, trees, birds and butterflies, visit Crarae Garden, southwest of Inveraray. The Achamore House Gardens on the Isle of Gigha are another colorful extravaganza.

8

brightly painted Tobermory on Mull or Port Ellen, with its neat rows of low whitewashed houses, on Islay. Arran is often said to be Scotland in miniature, the rich green fields of the southern part of the island giving way to the challenging Goat Fell in the north.

ORIENTATION AND PLANNING

GETTING ORIENTED

With long sea lochs carved into its hilly, wooded interior, Argyll is a beguiling interweaving of water and land. The Kintyre Peninsula stretches between the islands of the Firth of Clyde (including Arran) and the islands of the Inner Hebrides. Ferry services allow all kinds of interisland tours and can shorten mainland trips as well.

On land, you can take the A85 to Oban (convenient for the ferry to Mull) past barren hills and into the forest of Argyll after Loch Lomond (and the A82) ends. The roads grow narrower as they wind around the banks of Loch Awe and Loch Etive. Alternatively, you can turn off the A82 at Arrochar and trace the longer route around Loch Fyne, once an active fishing center, to Inveraray and down to Campbeltown. Along the way you'll pass Kennacraig, where ferries sail to Isay and Jura.

Argyll. The twin peninsulas of Kintyre are thickly wooded areas broken up by long pretty lochs. From Inverarary at the head of Loch Fyne, you can take in Auchindrain's re-created fishing village on the way to the Arran ferry. Or turn west toward Crinan and the pre historic sites around Kilmartin, then travel northwards toward Loch Awe and its intriguing island ruins. A short drive away is Oban, the busy resort where you catch the island ferries.

Arran. Touring this island will give you a glimpse of the whole of Scotland in a day or two. In the north, the forbidding Goat Fell is a challenge that draws walkers and climbers. The island's wilder west coast attracts birdwatchers and naturalists, while t he fertile south of the island contains nine lovely golf courses, leisurely walks, and Brodick Castle.

Islay and Jura. The smell of peat that hangs in the air on Islay is bottled in its famous whiskies. Aside from distilleries, the island's historical sites evoke a past in which these islands—now so remote—were once the heart of an empire. The whitewashed cottages along its coast line clean and beautiful beaches, many of them visited by a variety of wildlife.

Iona and the Isle of Mull. The pretty harbor of Tobermory, with its painted houses, is a relaxing base from which to explore the varied and beautiful island of Mull. Along Mull's west coast, spectacular cliffs and rocky beaches look out on to the Atlantic. From Craignure, the road crosses the sweeping green valleys of the Ross of Mull to Fionnhport and the ferry to the history-filled island Iona.

The Smaller Islands. These islands seem closer to the remoter Outer Hebrides than to the greener pastures of Mull or Arran. Abandoned by many of their original inhabitants, they are havens for birdlife, particularly Coll's giant dunes or the cliffs of Tiree. Colonsay's Kiloran Bay is open to the Atlantic's breakers, while Tiree's waves draw surfers from around the world.

PLANNING

WHEN TO GO

This part of the mainland is close enough to Glasgow that it's convenient to reach year-round. Oban is just over two hours from the city by car (three hours by bus), but getting to the isles via ferries takes longer. You can take advantage of quiet roads and plentiful accommodations in early spring and late autumn. The summer months of July and August can get very busy indeed; book accommodations and restaurants in advance during high season, or you'll miss out. In winter, short daylight hours and winds can make island stays rather bleak.

This is a coastal region, buffeted by Atlantic winds and rains. The climate is erratic, and locals take a curious pride in the fact that the area often experiences several seasons in a single day. Come prepared with adequate clothing for the changing weather, including good walking shoes, waterproof outerwear, and sunscreen.

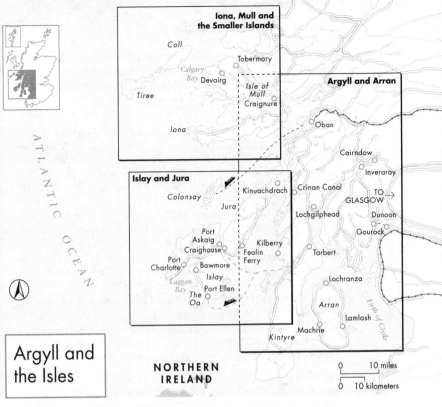

Argyll and
the Isles

PLANNING YOUR TIME

You could easily spend a week exploring the islands alone, so consider
spending at least a few nights in this region. Argyll and some island
excursions make pleasant and easy side trips from Glasgow and Loch
Lomond. Driving anywhere here takes a little longer than you'd think,
so allow ample travel time. A leisurely day will take you to Inveraray,
its castle, and the surrounding gardens (don't miss the folk museum at
Auchindrain). From there you can drive on to Ardrossan and take the
ferry to Arran. Spend the night and see the gardens and Brodick Castle
before returning to Kennacraig to take the ferry for Islay and Jura.
Two or three days here will give you a sense of the history and varied
landscapes of these stunning islands—and time for a distillery or two.
If time is a constraint, begin in Oban and sail to Mull, returning the
same day or the next to take in the Sea Life Centre. And if you can,
drive around Loch Awe on your way back to Glasgow.

Plan ahead: ferries fill up in the summer months, and some of the smaller
islands are served only once or twice a week. Bear in mind that it is not
easy to find places to eat after 8:30 PM at any time of year—though you
can usually find a place that will sell you a whisky.

GETTING HERE AND AROUND

AIR TRAVEL

Flybe operates flights from Glasgow to Campbeltown, Islay, Tiree, and Mull. Highland Airways flies from Oban to the islands.

Air Travel Contacts **Flybe** (☎ 08717/002000 ⊕ www.flybe.com). **Highland Airways** (☎ 08454/502245 ⊕ www.highlandairways.co.uk).

BOAT AND FERRY TRAVEL

Caledonian MacBrayne (CalMac) operates car-ferry services to and from the main islands; timetables can be accessed from its Web page. It is important to plan ahead when traveling to the islands in order to coordinate the connecting ferries; CalMac can advise you on this. Multiple island tickets are available and can significantly reduce the cost of island-hopping.

CalMac ferries run from Oban to Mull, Lismore, Coll, and Tiree; from Kennacraig to Islay, Jura, and Gigha; and from Ardrossan to Arran as well as a number of shorter routes. Western Ferries operate between Dunoon, in Argyll, and Gourock, west of Glasgow. The ferry passage between Dunoon and Gourock is one frequented by locals; it saves a lot of time, and you can take your car across as well.

Ferry reservations are needed if you have a car; passengers traveling by foot do not need to make reservations.

Boat and Ferry Travel Contacts **Caledonian MacBrayne** (*CalMac* ✉ *Ferry terminal, Gourock* ☎ 08705/650000 ⊕ www.calmac.co.uk). **Western Ferries** ✉ *Hunter's Quay, Dunoon* ☎ 01369/704452 ⊕ www.western-ferries.co.uk).

BUS TRAVEL

You can travel throughout the region by bus, but service here tends to be less frequent than elsewhere in Scotland. Scottish Citylink runs daily service from Glasgow's Buchanan Street Station to the mid-Argyll region and Kintyre; the trip to Oban takes about three hours. Several other companies provide local service within the region.

Bus Contacts **B. Mundell Ltd** (☎ 01496/840273). **Bowman's Tours** (☎ 01631/563221 ⊕ www.bowmanscoaches.co.uk). **Islay Coaches** (☎ 01496/840273). **Royal Mail** (☎ 08457/740740). **Scottish Citylink** (☎ 08705/505050 ⊕ www.citylink.co.uk). **Stagecoach West Scotland** (☎ 08712/002233 ⊕ www.stagecoach-westscotland.co.uk). **West Coast Motors** (☎ 01586/552319 ⊕ www.westcoastmotors.co.uk).

CAR TRAVEL

Negotiating this area is easy except in July and August, when the roads around Oban may be congested. There are some single-lane roads, especially on the east side of the Kintyre Peninsula and on the islands. You'll probably have to board a ferry at some point during your trip; nearly all ferries take cars as well as pedestrians.

From Glasgow, you can take the A85 to Oban, the main ferry terminal for Mull (about two-and-a-half hours by car). The A83 rounds Loch Fyne to Inveraray; from there you can take the A819 from Inveraray around Loch Awe and rejoin the Glasgow–Oban road. Alternatively, you can stay on the A83 and head down Kintyre to Kennacraig, the

SIGHTSEEING TOURS

BOAT TOURS

Getting out on the water is a wonderful way to see the landscape of the islands and also sealife.

Gordon Grant Tours leads an excursion from Oban to Mull, Iona, and Staffa and leaves Mull on other trips to Treshnish Isles and Staffa. From Taynuilt, near Oban, boat trips are available from Loch Etive Cruises. Sea Life Surveys offers four- and six-hour whale-watching and wildlife day trips from Tobermory, on the Isle of Mull.

Turas-Mara runs daily excursions in summer from Oban and Mull to Staffa, Iona, and the Treshnish Isles and specializes in wildlife tours. On a daylong trip to the Treshnish islands, you might see puffins, seals, otters, and, at certain times of year, dolphins and the occasional whale. Staffa is the site of Fingal's Cave, immortalized by Mendelssohn's overture.

Boat Tour Contacts Gordon Grant Tours (✉ *Railway Pier, Oban* ☎ *01631/562842* ⊕ *www.fingals-cave-staffa.co.uk*). **Loch Etive Cruises** (*Kelly's Pier, Lochandhu Rd., Aynuilt* ☎ *01866/822430*). **Sea Life Surveys** (✉ *Taigh Solais, Ledaig, Tobermory, Isle of Mull* ☎ *01688/302916*). **Turas-Mara** (✉ *Penmore Mill, Dervaig, Isle of Mull* ☎ *01688/400242* ⊕ *www.turasmara.com*).

BUS TOURS

Many of the bus companies listed in Bus Travel (⇨ see Getting Here and Around, above) arrange sightseeing tours. Bowman's Tours runs trips from Oban.

Bus Tour Contacts Bowman's Tours ✉ *Waterfront, Railway Pier Oban* ☎ *01631/563221* ⊕ *www.bowmanstours.co.uk*).

ferry terminal for Islay. Farther down the A83 is Tayinloan, the ferry port for Gigha. You can reach Brodick on Arran by ferry from Ardrossan, on the Clyde coast (M8/A78 from Glasgow); in summer, you can travel to Lochranza from Claonaig on the Kintyre Peninsula.

TRAIN TRAVEL

Oban and Ardrossan are the main rail stations; it's a three-hour trip from Glasgow to Oban. For information call ScotRail. All trains connect with ferries.

Trail Contacts ScotRail (☎ *08457/550033* ⊕ *www.scotrail.co.uk*).

RESTAURANTS

Until recently this part of Scotland had few restaurants of distinction. Today, though, more and more quality restaurants are opening and using the excellent local produce—fine fish and shellfish, lamb, and excellent venison, as well as game of many kinds. Most hotels and many guesthouses offer evening meals, though the quality can vary. Bear in mind that most restaurants and pubs stop serving food by nine in the evening; lunch usually ends at 2:30.

HOTELS

Accommodations in Argyll and on the isles range from country house hotels—once home to landowning families—to homes and farms offering bed and breakfast. Most small traditional provincial hotels in coastal resorts have updated and modernized (while still retaining personalized service). And though hotels often have a restaurant offering evening meals, the norm for bed-and-breakfasts is to offer breakfast only.

WHAT IT COSTS IN POUNDS					
	£	££	£££	££££	£££££
RESTAURANTS	under £10	£10–£14	£15–£19	£20–£25	over £25
HOTELS	under £70	£70–£120	£121–£160	£161–£220	over £220

Restaurant prices are for a main course at dinner. Hotel prices are for two people in a standard double room in high season, generally including the 17.5% V.A.T.

VISITOR INFORMATION

The tourist offices in Lochgilphead, Tarbert, and Tobermory (Mull) are open April through October only; other offices are open year-round.

Contacts Visit Scottish Hearlands (⊕ www.visitscottishheartlands.com).

AROUND ARGYLL

Topographical grandeur and rocky shores are what make Argyll special. Try to take to the water at least once, even if your time is limited. The sea and the sea lochs have played a vital role in the history of western Scotland since the time of the war galleys of the clans. Oban is the major ferry gateway and transport hub, with a main road leading south into the Kintyre Peninsula.

OBAN

96 mi northwest of Glasgow, 125 mi northwest of Edinburgh, 50 mi south of Fort William, 118 mi southwest of Inverness.

It's almost impossible to avoid Oban when touring the west. Its waterfront has some character, but the town's main role is as a launch point for excursions into Argyll and for ferry trips to the islands. A traditional Scottish resort town, Oban has many music festivals, *ceilidhs* with Highland dancing, as well as all the usual tartan kitsch and late-night revelry in pubs and hotel bars. Still, there are more exciting destinations just over the horizon, on the islands and down Kintyre.

GETTING HERE AND AROUND

From Glasgow, the A82 along Loch Lomond meets the A85 at Crianlarich. Turn left and continue to Oban. In summer the center of Oban can become gridlocked with ferry traffic, so leave yourself time for the wait. Alternatively, the A816 from Lochgilphead enters Oban from the less crowded south. Train services run from Glasgow to Oban (ScotRail); bus services from Glasgow to Oban by Scottish Citylink run several times a day.

ESSENTIALS

Visitor Information Oban (✉ *Argyll Sq.* ☎ *08707/200630* ⊕ *www.visitscotland. com*).

EXPLORING

Four miles north of Oban stands **Dunstaffnage Castle,** an important stronghold of the MacDougall clan in the 13th century. From the ramparts you have outstanding views across the **Sound of Mull** and the **Firth of Lorne,** a nautical crossroads of sorts, once watched over by Dunstaffnage Castle and commanded by the galleys (*birlinn* in Gaelic) of the Lords of the Isles. ✉ *Off A85* ☎ *01631/562465* ⊕ *www.historic-scotland.gov.uk/places* 🎟 *£3.70* ⊙ *Apr.–Sept., daily 9:30–5:30; Oct., daily 9:30–4:30; Nov.–Mar., Sat.–Wed. 9:30–4:30.*

⟳ At the **Scottish Sealife Sanctuary** kids and adults love the outstanding display of marine life, including shoals of herring, sharks, rays, catfish, otters, and seals. Many of the animals at the sanctuary have been rescued, and this is where they receive rehabilitation before being released into the wild. There is also a beautiful aquarium, and kids will appreciate the adventure playground and gift shop. The restaurant serves morning coffee, plus a full lunch menu and afternoon tea. To get here, drive north from Oban for 10 mi on the A828; West Coast Motors also provide a regular bus service. ✉ *Barcaldine, Connel* ☎ *08714/232110* ⊕ *www.sealsanctuary.co.uk* 🎟 *£12* ⊙ *Jan.–mid-Feb., weekends 10–4; Mar.–Oct., daily 10–5; last admission 1 hr before closing.*

WHERE TO EAT

£££ ✕ **Ee-usk.** This restaurant's name means "fish" in Gaelic, and it has
BRITISH earned quite a reputation for serving excellent seafood dishes made with the freshest fish and shellfish delivered directly from Oban's harbor. Its signature dishes use plain sauces; try oven-baked wild halibut with creamed leeks. On clear days, there are nice views of the islands. ✉ *North Pier* ☎ *01631/565666* ⊕ *www.eeusk.com* ▭ *MC, V.*

££ ✕ **Kitchen Garden.** This delicatessen directly across the road from the
CAFÉ ferry port serves good home made soups, panini, and sandwiches as well as fresh cakes. Service is sometimes a little slow; prices are reasonable and the location is quite convenient. ✉ *14 George St. North Pier* ☎ *01631/566332* ▭ *MC, V* ⊙ *No dinner.*

WHERE TO STAY

££ ▥ **Dungrianach.** In Gaelic, *dungrianach* means "the sunny house on the
★ hill," and this late Victorian house is set high in a wooded area with superb views of the islands. Although it feels quite isolated, it's only a few minutes' walk from the center of Oban and the ferry piers. Guest rooms are filled with antique and reproduction furniture. **Pros:** plenty of space for your car; great views. **Cons:** credit cards are not accepted. ✉ *Pulpit Hill* ▥▥ *01631/562840* 🛏 *2 rooms* ⚷ *In-room: no a/c, no phone. In-hotel: bar* ▭ *No credit cards* ⊙ *Closed Oct.–Mar.* ⦿| *BP.*

££ ▥ **Kilchrenan House.** Just a few minutes' walk from the town center, this Victorian-era stone house has been fully refurbished and transformed into a lovely bed-and-breakfast. Many of the comfortable rooms—individually furnished in neutral tones with clean-lined, light-wood pieces and some antiques—overlook the sea and the islands. **Pros:** great sea

8

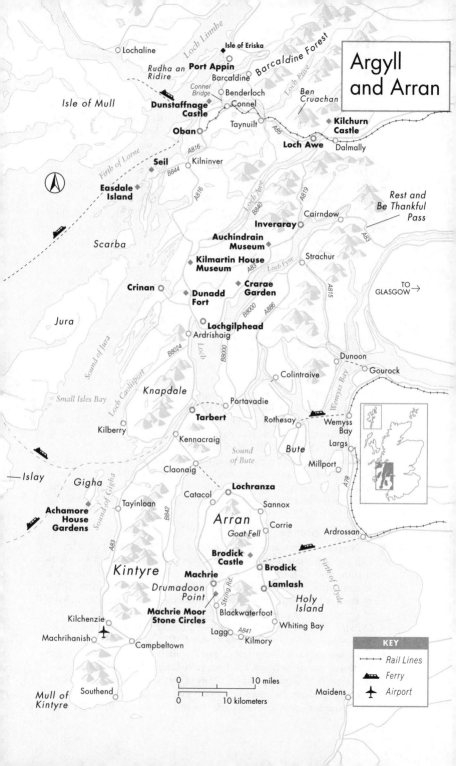

Argyll and Arran

Lochaline

Loch Linnhe

Isle of Eriska

Port Appin

Barcaldine

Barcaldine Forest

Rudha an Ridire

Connel Bridge

Benderloch

Loch Etive

Dunstaffnage Castle

Connel

Ben Cruachan

Isle of Mull

Taynuilt

A85

Kilchurn Castle

Oban

Loch Awe

Dalmally

A816

Firth of Lorne

Kilninver

Seil

B844

A819

A816

Easdale Island

B840

Cairndow

Rest and Be Thankful Pass

Scarba

Loch Awe

Inveraray

A83

Auchindrain Museum

Strachur

Loch Fyne

Kilmartin House Museum

A815

Crinan

Crarae Garden

TO GLASGOW →

Jura

Dunadd Fort

B8000

A886

Lochgilphead

Ardrishaig

B8024

Loch

B8000

Dunoon

Sound of Jura

Colintraive

Gourock

Small Isles Bay

Knapdale

Portavadie

Wemyss Bay

Loch Caolisport

Rothesay

Wemyss Bay

Islay

Kilberry

Tarbert

Largs

Kennacraig

Sound of Bute

Bute

Millport

Gigha

Claonaig

A78

Achamore House Gardens

Tayinloan

Catacol

Lochranza

Sound of Gigha

B842

Sannox

Ardrossan

A83

Arran

Corrie

Goat Fell

Kintyre

Brodick Castle

Machrie

Brodick

Firth of Clyde

Drumadoon Point

String Rd.

Lamlash

Machrie Moor Stone Circles

Blackwaterfoot

Holy Island

Kilchenzie

Lagg

A841

Whiting Bay

Machrihanish

Kilmory

Campbeltown

0   10 miles

0   10 kilometers

Mull of Kintyre

Southend

Maidens

KEY

+—+ *Rail Lines*

⛴ *Ferry*

✈ *Airport*

views; tasteful attention to detail. **Cons:** some bedrooms on the top floor have a slanting roof that can be irritating. ✉ *Corran Esplanade* 🕾🕾 *01631/562663* ⊕ *www.kilchrenanhouse.co.uk* 🛏 *14 rooms* 🜚 *In-room: no a/c. In-hotel: bar* ▭ *DC, MC, V* ⊙ *Closed Dec. and Jan.* ▮◎▮ *BP.*

£££   🕍 **Manor House Hotel.** On the coast near Oban, this 1780 stone house—once the home of the duke of Argyll—has wonderful sea views. Public areas are furnished with antiques, and the bedrooms are filled with lovely reproductions. The restaurant (£££££) serves a five-course prix-fixe dinner of Scottish and French dishes—including local seafood and game in season—complemented by a carefully selected wine list. The house is within walking distance of the center of the city and the bus, train, and ferry terminals. **Pros:** excellent restaurant; location near all necessary amenities. **Cons:** smallish bedrooms. ✉ *Gallanach Rd.* 🕾 *01631/562087* ⊕ *www.manorhouseoban.com* 🛏 *11 rooms* 🜚 *In-room: no a/c, Wi-Fi. In-hotel: restaurant, bar, Wi-Fi hotspot, no kids under 12* ▭ *AE, MC, V* ▮◎▮ *BP.*

££   🕍 **Ronebhal Guest House.** You can see Loch Etive and the mountains beyond from this stone house 5 mi east of Oban (in Connel), set back within its own lovely grounds. Rooms are light and modern, and some have expansive bay windows. The front bedrooms have the best views of the loch. **Pros:** nice library; good breakfast. **Cons:** some slightly worn decor; not good for families with young children. ✉ *A85, Connel* 🕾 *01631/710310* ⊕ *www.ronebhal.co.uk* 🛏 *6 rooms, 4 with bath* 🜚 *In-room: no a/c, no phone. In-hotel: bar, no kids under 7* ▭ *MC, V* ⊙ *Closed Dec. and Jan.* ▮◎▮ *BP.*

SPORTS AND THE OUTDOORS

BICYCLING   You can rent bicycles from **Oban Cycles** ✉ *29 Lochside St.* 🕾 *01631/566996*), whose shopkeepers will give you advice on waterside routes as far out as Ganavan Bay and Dunstaffnage Castle.

FISHING   The **Gannet** ✉ *3 Kiel Croft, Benderloch* 🕾🕾 *01631/720262*), a charter-fishing company run by Adrian Lauder, offers full-day sea-angling trips for £500 a day for up to 10 passengers (so that would be £50 per person); a light lunch is included. Fishing parties are limited to 10 people (8 for skate-fishing).

APPIN

The little peninsula of Appin, some 20-minutes' drive from Oban, is a charming, well-kept secret. Just 2 mi along a narrow road from the main Fort William route (A828), the bay opens to Lismore and the sea. Castle Stalker, a privately owned castle on the water, sits magnificently in the center of the picture, a symbol of ancient coastal Scotland. This is an excellent, uncrowded base for walking, fishing, water sports, and cycling. The Appin Rocks, on the headland, are frequently visited by seals.

GETTING HERE AND AROUND

From Oban, follow the A828 around Loch Creran and take the left turn to Port Appin just beyond Tynribbie. Continue for just over 2 mi to the old pier. From the port, the passenger ferry runs to the island of Lismore throughout the year; steamers once plied the waters of Loch

Linnhe, but today the largest boats here are those taking workers to the quarries of Kingairloch.

WHERE TO STAY

££££   🏨 **Airds Hotel.** The old ferry inn for travelers visiting Lismore now houses
★   this luxurious small hotel. Rooms are stylish and restrained, with superb views either toward the sea or the woods behind. There is a sense of quiet grandeur here, with comfortable-but-elegant public rooms. The hotel will organize fishing, walking, sailing, and other outdoor activities in the area. The exquisite restaurant's prix-fixe menu (£55; but included in the price for overnight guests) uses local produce, seafood, and game in highly imaginative ways. **Pros:** fabulous views from the breakfast room; spare boots for the unprepared; beautiful location. **Cons:** a very expensive option. ✉ *A828, Port Appin* ☎ *01631/730236* ⊕ *www.airds-hotel.com* ➪ *9 rooms, 2 suites, 1 cottage* ⌂ *In-room: DVD, Wi-Fi. In-hotel: restaurant, room service, bar, some pets allowed* ⊟ *AE, D, MC, V* ⦿ *MAP.*

£££££   🏨 **Isle of Eriska.** A severe, baronial-style granite facade belies the sense of welcome within this hotel, set on its own island 10 mi north of Oban and accessible by a bridge from the mainland (off the A828 Fort William road outside the village of Benderloch). The rooms are individual and luxurious in their detail, and a range of outdoor activities are available, as are pools and gyms—all contained within the island. Be sure to take a stroll to watch seals and otters offshore and herons and badgers on the grounds. The restaurant (£££££) serves innovative Scottish cuisine made with local ingredients: try the scallop and zucchini timbale with lobster, artichoke, and champagne-butter sauce. **Pros:** exceptional food, service, and peace and quiet. **Cons:** you're in the middle of nowhere, so you don't have a lot of choice when it comes to dining out. ✉ *Ledaig, by Oban* ☎ *01631/720371* ⊕ *www.eriska-hotel. co.uk* ➪ *25 rooms* ⌂ *In-room: no a/c. In-hotel: restaurant, golf course, tennis court, spa, pool, gym, Wi-Fi hotspot* ⊟ *AE, MC, V* ⦿ *MAP.*

£££   🏨 **Pierhouse Hotel.** The twin round towers of the old pier mark the entrance to this hotel, built on the water's edge beside the Port Appin jetty. It's a good base for exploring the region, but it's also a nice place to simply relax and watch the changing moods of the loch. The public bar is pleasantly animated, filled with walkers and water sports enthusiasts en route to or from Lismore. Rooms are quite small, but clean and comfortable. The seafood restaurant (£35) serves the freshest seafood; try its signature Pierhouse platter of lobster (caught at the pier's edge), scallops, mussels, and langoustine (£22.95). **Pros:** breathtaking view across the loch; lively warm atmosphere. **Cons:** rooms are a little small; not all rooms have views over the water. ✉ *Port Appin* ☎ *01631/730302* ⊕ *www.pierhousehotel.co.uk* ➪ *12 rooms* ⌂ *In-room: no a/c, Wi-Fi. In-hotel: restaurant, bar, Wi-Fi hotspot, parking (free), some pets allowed* ⊟ *AE, DC* ⦿ *BP.*

LOCH AWE

18 mi east of Oban.

At more than 25 mi long, Loch Awe is Scotland's longest stretch of fresh water. Its northwest shore is quiet; forest walks crisscross the Inverliever Forest here. At the loch's northern end tiny islands, many with ruins, pepper the water. One, Inishail, is home to a 13th-century chapel.

GETTING HERE AND AROUND

From Oban the A85 will bring you to the head of Loch Awe and the small town of the same name. Turn onto the B845 at Taynuilt to reach the loch's the northern shore, or continue through the forbidding Pass of Brander and turn onto the A819 to get to the southern shore. From here you can continue on to Invararay, or drive along the loch on the B840.

EXPLORING

★ **Kilchurn Castle**, a ruined fortress at the north eastern end of Loch Awe, was built in the 15th century by Sir Colin Campbell (d. 1493) of Glenorchy, and rebuilt in the 17th century. Airy vantage points amid the towers have fine panoramas of the surrounding highlands and loch. It is accessible by boat from Loch Awe pier, or by land along an old railway line. ✉ *A85, 1 mi northeast of Loch Awe* ☎ *01866/833333* ⊕ *www. historic-scotland.gov.uk/places* 🎫 *Free* ☉ *Daily 24 hrs.*

The **Duncan Ban Macintyre Monument** was erected in honor of this Gaelic poet (1724–1812), sometimes referred to as the Robert Burns of the Highlands. ■TIP→ **The view from here is one of the finest in Argyll, taking in Ben Cruachan and the other peaks nearby, as well as Loch Awe and its scattering of islands.** To find the monument from Dalmally, just east of Loch Awe, follow an old road running southwest toward the banks of the loch. You can see the round, granite structure from the road's highest point, often called Monument Hill.

WHERE TO STAY

£££££ 🏨 **Taychreggan Hotel.** Once a drover's inn, this beautiful country house on the shores of Loch Awe has spectacular views. A good base for walking (or simply relaxing), the elegant inn's recently refurbished rooms are decorated in floral style. A prix-fixe dinner menu (£44) features local food, particularly shellfish and venison; the menu changes daily. **Pros:** lovely setting; high level of comfort. **Cons:** slightly fussy decor; a little isolated. ✉ *By Taynuilt* ☎ *01866/833211* ⊕ *www.taychregganhotel. co.uk* 🛏 *18 rooms* ⚬ *In-room: no a/c, Wi-Fi (some). In-hotel: restaurant, room service, bar, Wi-Fi hotspot, parking (free), some pets allowed* 🍴 *AE, D, DC, MC, V* ⚍ *BP*

EN ROUTE The A819 south to Inveraray initially runs alongside Loch Awe, but soon leaves these pleasant banks to turn east and join the A83, which carries traffic from Glasgow and Loch Lomond by way of the high **Rest and Be Thankful** pass. This quasi-alpine pass, set among high green slopes and gray rocks, is one of the most scenic points along the road.

8

INVERARAY

★ *21 mi south of Loch Awe, 61 mi north of Glasgow, 29 mi west of Loch Lomond.*

On the approaches to Inveraray, note the ornate 18th-century bridge-work that carries the road along the loch side. This is your first sign that Inveraray is not just a jumble of houses; in fact, much of it was designed as a planned town for the third duke of Argyll in the mid-18th century. The town is a sparkling fishing village with cute shops, attractions, and the haunted Campbell Castle all within walking distance. There are lovely views of the water and plenty of fishing boats to watch. Several worthwhile gardens and museums are nearby, too.

GETTING HERE AND AROUND

If you're driving from Oban, take the A85 and the A819 beyond Loch Awe (the village). From Glasgow, take the A82, turn on to the A83 at Arrochar, and make the long drive around Loch Fyne.

ESSENTIALS

Visitor Information Inveraray (✉ *Front St.* ☎ *01499/302063* ⊕ *www. visitscotland.com).*

EXPLORING

TOP ATTRACTIONS

Ardkinglas Woodland Garden. One of Britain's finest collections of conifers is set off by rhododendron blossoms in early summer. You'll find it around the head of Loch Fyne, about 10 mi east of Inveraray. ✉ *A83, Cairndow* ☎ *01499/600261* ⊕ *www.ardkinglas.com* 🎫 *£3.50* ⊙ *Daily sunrise–sunset.*

★ **Auchindrain Museum.** Step a few centuries back in time at this open-air museum, a rare surviving example of an 18th-century communal tenancy farm. The old bracken-thatch and iron-roof buildings, about 20 in all, give you a feel for early farming life in the Highlands, and the interpretation center explains it all. Among the furnished buildings are cottages, longhouses, and barns. The museum is 5 mi south of Inveraray. ✉ *Off A83* ☎ *01499/500235* ⊕ *www.auchindrain-museum.org.uk* 🎫 *£4.50* ⊙ *Apr.–Oct., daily 10–5, last admission 4.*

★ **Crarae Garden.** Well worth a visit for plant lovers is this 100-acre garden, where magnolias, azaleas, and rhododendrons flourish in the moist, lush environment around Crarae Burn (a small stream). A rocky gorge and waterfalls add appeal, and the flowers and trees attract several different species of birds and butterflies. The gardens are 10 mi southwest of Inveraray. ✉ *Off A83* ☎ *01546/886614* ⊕ *www.nts.org.uk/Visits* 🎫 *£5.50* ⊙ *Garden daily 9:30–sunset; visitor center Apr.–Oct., daily 10–5.*

Inveraray Castle. The current seat of the Campbell duke is a smart, grayish-green turreted stone house with a self-satisfied air, visible through trees from the town itself. Spires on the four corner turrets give it a vaguely French look. Like the town, the castle was begun around 1743. Tours of the interior convey the history of the powerful Campbell family. There is a tearoom for snacks and light lunches. You can hike around the estate grounds, but wear sturdy footwear. ✉ *Off A83*

☏ 01499/302203 ⊕ *www.inveraray-castle.com* 🎫 *£6.80* ☉ *Apr.–Oct., daily 10–5:45, last admission at 5.*

WORTH NOTING

Arctic Penguin. This 1911 lightship is a rare example of a riveted iron vessel. It now houses exhibits on the maritime heritage of the River Clyde and the rest of Scotland's west coast. Beside it sits the "puffer" *Eilean Eisdeal,* a tiny interisland freight boat. ✉ *Inveraray Pier* ☏ *01499/ 302213* ⊕ *www.inveraraypier.com* 🎫 *£3.80* ☉ *Daily 10–5.*

☺ **Inveraray Jail.** In this old jail, realistic courtroom scenes, carefully recreated cells, and other paraphernalia give you a glimpse of life behind bars in Victorian times—and today. The site includes a Scottish crafts shop. Visitors to the Jail who also visit the Arctic Penguin get a 20% discount. ✉ *Inveraray* ☏ *01499/302381* ⊕ *www.inverarayjail.co.uk* 🎫 *£7.95* ☉ *Apr.–Oct., daily 9:30–6; Nov.–Mar., daily 10–5; last admission 1 hr before closing.*

Loch Fyne Oysters. About 10 mi northeast of Inveraray, you can stop at the shop here to purchase these delicious shellfish to go, or order them to be shipped. You can also consume a dozen with a glass of wine at Loch Fyne Oysters Restaurant. ✉ *A83, Clachan Farm, Cairndow* ☏ *01499/600236* ⊕ *www.lochfyne.com* ☉ *Daily 9–7.*

WHERE TO EAT AND STAY

££ ✕ **Loch Fyne Oysters.** The well-regarded seafood restaurant at the head
SEAFOOD of Loch Fyne has beautiful views; it's often crowded, so reservations are a good idea. The menu features a range of seafood dishes, served in simple and unpretentious ways. A good option is the seafood platter (£18). ✉ *A83, Clachan Farm, Cairndow* ☏ *01499/600264* ⊕ *www. lochfyne.com* ▭ *AE, DC, MC, V* ☉ *No dinner Oct.–Mar.*

££ 🏨 **The George Hotel.** The Clark family has run this 18th-century former
Fodor'sChoice coaching inn at the heart of Inveraray town for six generations, and
★ the warmth of the welcome reflects the benefit of continuity. Roaring log fires invite repose in the common rooms, and antiques and oil paintings in the individually decorated rooms make you feel as though you were in another, slower-paced era. Rooms vary in price substantially based on size and amenities; the most expensive have whirlpool tubs. Locals fill the restaurant (££) to sample the excellent food, such as king scallop and bacon kebabs with lemon basil and shallots. **Pros:** excellent restaurant; atmospheric stone-floored bars; hotel Scottish in every way. **Cons:** too much tartan for some; small, unattractive reception area; some old mattresses. ✉ *Main St. E* ☏ *01499/302111* ⊕ *www. thegeorgehotel.co.uk* 🛏 *17 rooms* ᗱ *In-room: no a/c. In-hotel: restaurant, 2 bars* ▭ *MC, V* ⑩ *BP.*

LOCHGILPHEAD

26 mi south of Inveraray.

Lochgilphead, the largest town in this region, looks best when the tide is in, as Loch Gilp (really a bite out of Loch Fyne) reveals a muddy shoreline at low tide. With a series of well-kept, colorful buildings along its main street, this neat little town is worth a look.

GETTING HERE AND AROUND
From Inveraray continue south for 24 mi along the A83, which follows the bank of the Loch Fyne.

HORSEBACK RIDING
Castle Riding Centre and Argyll Trail Riding (✉ *Brenfield Farm, Ardrishaig* ☎ *01546/603274*), south of Lochgilphead, offers guided rides along routes throughout Argyll and the West Highlands.

SHOPPING
The factory shop at the **Highbank Collection** (✉ *Highbank Industrial Estate* ☎ *01546/602044*) sells hand-painted pottery and glassware, colorful ceramics, and model wooden boats.

CRINAN

1 mi north of Lochgilphead.

Crinan is synonymous with its canal, the reason for this tiny community's existence and its mainstay. The narrow road beside the Crinan Hotel bustles with yachting types waiting to pass through the locks, bringing a surprisingly cosmopolitan feel to such an out-of-the-way corner of Scotland. Also accessible from Crinan is the worthwhile Kilmartin House Museum.

GETTING HERE AND AROUND
To reach Crinan, take the A816 Oban road north from Lochgilphead for about a mile, then turn left at Cairnbaan.

EXPLORING
The **Crinan Canal** opened in 1801 to let fishing vessels reach Hebridean fishing grounds without making the long haul south around the Kintyre Peninsula. At its western end the canal drops to the sea in a series of locks.

★ For an exceptional encounter with early Scottish history, visit the **Kilmartin House Museum,** about 8 mi north of Crinan. The museum explores more than 300 ancient monuments, all within a 6-mi radius of the village of Kilmartin. Learn about the stone circles and avenues, burial mounds, and carved stones dating from the Bronze Age and earlier that are scattered thickly around this neighborhood, and then go out and explore them. Nearby **Dunadd Fort,** a rocky hump rising out of the level ground between Crinan and Kilmartin, was once the capital of the early kingdom of Dalriada, founded by the first wave of Scots who migrated from Ireland around AD 500. Clamber up the rock to see a basin, a footprint, and an outline of a boar carved on the smooth upper face of the knoll. ✉ *A816, Kilmartin* ☎ *01546/510278* ⊕ *www.kilmartin.org* ☐ *£4.60* ⊙ *Mar.–Oct., daily 10–5:30.*

WHERE TO STAY
££ ⊡ **Allt-Na-Craig.** This large stone Victorian house, 4 mi south of Lochgilphead, is set in lovely gardens overlooking Loch Fyne on the edge of the
★ village. It was once the home of *Wind in the Willows* author Kenneth Grahame. Nearby is the yacht-filled eastern basin of the Crinan Canal. Charlotte Nicol's hearty home cooking (£££) using local ingredients is well worth a stay, whether you are a meat lover or a vegetarian. The

cottage has a kitchen and can be rented by the week. **Pros:** atmospheric; good food and views. **Cons:** you're pretty isolated, so it helps to have a car. ⊠ *Tarbert Rd., Ardrishaig* ☎ *01546/603245* ⊕ *www.allt-na-craig. co.uk* ♥ *5 rooms, 1 cottage* ♿ *In-room: no a/c. In-hotel: restaurant, Wi-Fi hotspot* ▭ *MC, V* ⦿ *BP.*

KINTYRE PENINSULA

52 mi south of Lochgilphead (to Campbeltown).

Rivers and streams crisscross this long, narrow strip of green pasture-lands and hills stretching south from Lochgilphead.

GETTING HERE AND AROUND

Continue south on the A83 (the road to Campbeltown) to Tarbert. Some four mi further along the A83, just beyond Kennacraig, is the pier at Tayinloan; Calmac ferries run from here.

ESSENTIALS

Air Travel Contacts Campbeltown Airport (☎ *01667/462445* ⊕ *www.hial. co.uk*).

Visitor Information Campbeltown (⊠ *Mackinnon House, at the pier* ☎ *01586/552056* ⊕ *www.visitscotland.com*). **Tarbert, Loch Fyne** (⊠ *Harbour St.* ☎ *08452/255121* ⊕ *www.visitscotland.com*).

EXPLORING

Tarbert, a name that appears throughout the Highlands, is the Gaelic word for "place of portage," and a glance at the map tells you why it was given to this little town with a workaday waterfront: Tarbert sits on the narrow neck of land between East and West Loch Tarbert, where long ago boats were actually carried across the land to avoid looping all the way around the peninsula.

The **Isle of Gigha,** barely 5 mi long, is sheltered in a frost-free, sea-warmed climate between Kintyre and Islay. The island was long favored by British aristocrats as a summer destination.

One relic of the Isle of Gigha's aristocratic legacy is the **Achamore House Gardens,** which produce lush shrubberies with spectacular azalea displays in late spring. For a nimble day trip, take the 20-minute ferry to Gigha from Tayinloan and walk right over to the gardens. You may not want to take your car, as the walk is fairly easy. ☎ *01583/505267* ⊕ *www.isle-of-gigha.co.uk* ⦿ *Gardens £2, ferry £4.50 per person plus £15.80 per car* ⦿ *Gardens daily sunrise–sunset. Ferry Mon.–Sat. 9–5, Sun. at 11, 2, and 3.*

GOLF

You can play **Machrihanish Golf Club's** perfectly manicured 18 holes warmed by Gulf Stream breezes. U.S. Navy Seal teams-in-training have been known to drop from the air into a chilly nearby loch. £60 per round. ⊠ *Campbeltown* ☎ *01586/810213* ⊕ *www.machgolf.com* ⛳ *18 holes, 6,228 yds, par 70.*

8

ARRAN

Approaching Arran by sea, you'll first see the forbidding Goat Fell (2,868 feet) in the north, then the green fields of the south. It is this contrast and varied geography that has led visitors to describe Arran as "Scotland in Miniature." Arran's temperate climate allows tropical plants to grow, and this relative warmth probably attracted the ancient cultures whose stone circles still stand on the island. Arran's weather also explains why it has long been a favorite resort getaway for Glasgow's residents, who come here to walk, climb Goat Fell, play golf on Arran's nine courses, observe the rich bird life, and simply enjoy the sea.

GETTING HERE AND AROUND

Caledonian MacBrayne runs regular car and passenger ferries cross the Firth of Clyde from Ardrossan (near Saltcoats) to Brodick throughout the year (crossing takes just under an hour). There is also a small ferry from Claonaig on the Kintyre Peninsula in summer to Lochranza during the summer months.

Connecting trains run here from Glasgow's Queen Street station. Stagecoach runs regular local bus services xploring the island by car is easy, as the A841 road circles it.

BRODICK

1 hr by ferry from Ardrossan.

Arran's largest village, Brodick, has a main street that is set back from the promenade and the lovely bay beyond. Other than its accommodation, there is little to keep the visitor here before exploring the island.

GETTING HERE AND AROUND

You can reach Brodick from Ardrossan by ferry. From Brodick the A841 circles the island; head south to reach Lamlash, north to reach Lochranza. The String Road crosses the island between Brodick and Machrie.

ESSENTIALS

Visitor Information Brodick, Arran (⊠ *The pier* ☎ *01770/303776* ⊕ *www. visitscotland.com*).

EXPLORING

The **Isle of Arran Heritage Museum** documents life on the island from ancient times to the present. Several buildings, including a cottage and *smiddy* (smithy), have period furnishings as well as displays on prehistoric life, farming, fishing, and other aspects of the island's social history. ⊠ *Rosaburn* ☎ *01770/302636* ⊕ *www.arranmuseum.co.uk* ⊠ *£3* ⊙ *Apr.–Oct., daily 10:30–4:30.*

In **Glen Rosa** you can stroll through a long glen glimpsing the wild ridges that beckon so many outdoors enthusiasts. To get here from Brodick, pass the Isle of Arran Heritage Museum and find the junction where the String Road cuts across the island. Drive a short way up the String Road and turn right at the signpost into the glen. The road soon becomes undrivable; park the car and wander on foot.

★ Arran's biggest cultural draw is **Brodick Castle,** on the north side of Brodick Bay. This red-sandstone structure—parts of which date back to the 13th century—is surrounded by lush woods and parkland. Several rooms are open to the public, both in the original 16th-century section and in the Victorian additions (which illustrate the Hamilton family's opulent lifestyle). The large downstairs kitchen gives a contrasting impression—showing how servants lived—and the 87 stag's heads on the stairs are a slightly disturbing reminder of how the aristocracy spent their leisure time. There is a guide in each room with all the information you need. The vast gardens, open all year, are filled with rhododendrons and azalea. The café in the Servants' Hall serves morning coffee and homemade cakes as well as a light lunch menu. ✉ *1 mi north of Brodick Pier* ☎ *01770/302202* 🌐 *www.nts.org.uk* 🎫 *Castle and gardens £12* ⏲ *Castle and restaurant Easter–Oct., daily 11–4:30. Reception center, shop, and walled garden Easter–Oct., daily 10–4:30; Nov. and Dec. 21, Fri.–Sun. 10–3:30.*

WHERE TO EAT AND STAY

££ ITALIAN ✕ **Eilean-Mor Bar Bistro.** Painted bright red, this small unpretentious Italian style bar-bistro has friendly and attentive staff. The pastas, pizzas, and burgers are substantial and well made—even the haggis ravioli in whisky sauce is startlingly tasty. ✉ *Shore Rd.* ☎ *01770/302579* 💳 *AE, DC, MC, V.*

££ 🏨 **Glencloy Farmhouse.** Surrounded by colorful gardens, this 19th-century sandstone house nestles in a peaceful valley. Brodick and views of the hills and sea are a few minutes' walk away. Breakfast is a treat, with organic eggs, homemade jam, and fresh-baked bread and muffins. **Pros:** outstanding breakfast; lovely location. **Cons:** plenty of the owners' personal decorations all around; access road has many potholes. ✉ *Brodick* ☎ *01770/302251* 🛏 *5 rooms, 2 with bath* 🛎 *In-room: no a/c, no phone* 💳 *MC, V* ⏲ *Closed Nov.–Feb.* 🍽 *BP.*

BICYCLING

You can rent bicycles at **Arran Adventure Centre** (✉ *Shore Rd., Brodick* ☎ *01770/302244*).

SHOPPING

Arran's shops are well stocked with locally produced goods. The Home Farm is a popular shopping area with several shops and a small restaurant. **Creelers Smokery and Restaurant** (✉ *The Home Farm* ☎ *01770/302810*) is a restaurant with an adjoining smokehouse selling fish, smoked and otherwise. The **Duchess Court Shops** (✉ *The Home Farm* ☎ *01770/302831*) include Bear Necessities, with everything bear-themed; the Nature Shop, with nature-oriented books and gifts; and Arran Aromatics, one of Scotland's top makers of toiletries. The **Island Cheese Company** (✉ *The Home Farm* ☎ *01770/302788*) stocks Arran blue cheese among other handmade Scottish cheeses.

LAMLASH

4 mi south of Brodick.

With views offshore to Holy Island, which is now a Buddhist retreat, Lamlash has a breezy seaside-holiday atmosphere. To reach the highest point accessible by car, go through the village and turn right beside the bridge onto Ross Road, which climbs steeply from a thickly planted valley, **Glen Scorrodale,** and yields fine views of Lamlash Bay. From Lamlash you can explore the southern part of Arran: 4 mi to the southwest, **Whiting Bay** has a pleasant well-kept waterfront and a range of hotels and guesthouses. If you travel another 6 mi, you'll reach the little community of **Lagg,** which sits peacefully by the banks of the Kilmory Water.

GETTING HERE AND AROUND

You can reach Lamlash by driving south from Brodick on the A841. The town is also served by Stagecoach buses.

WHERE TO STAY

££   **Lagg Hotel.** Arran's oldest inn is an 18th-century lodge with fire-
★   places in the common rooms and 11 acres of gardens and grounds that meander down to the river. Each room is quiet and bright, if a little flowery in its decor, and many overlook the riverside flower beds or woodland. Hearty but elegant home cooking in the restaurant (£££) focuses on entrées such as lemon tagliatelle with butternut squash. The friendly locals in the bar help make a stay here a fine evening. The inn is 12 mi southwest of Lamlash, beyond Kilmory. **Pros:** beautiful gardens; warming fireplaces; good-size rooms. **Cons:** floral designs everywhere. ✉ *Kilmory, Isle of Arran* ☎ *01770/870255* 🖙 *13 rooms* ⚘ *In-room: no a/c. In-hotel: restaurant, bars* ▭ *MC, V* ⦾ *BP.*

SHOPPING

Patterson Arran (✉ *The Old Mill* ☎ *01770/600606*) is famous for its preserves and marmalades, as well as its mustards.

MACHRIE

10 mi west of Brodick, 11 mi north of Lagg.

The area surrounding Machrie, home to a popular beach, is littered with prehistoric sites: chambered cairns, hut circles, and standing stones dating from the Bronze Age.

GETTING HERE AND AROUND

The quick route to Machrie is via the String Road (B880) from Brodick; turn off onto the Machrie Road 5 mi outside Brodick. A much longer but stunning journey will take you from Brodick, north to Lochranza, around the island to Machrie, and down the island's dramatic west coast, a distance of some 28 mi.

EXPLORING

From Machrie, a well-surfaced track takes you to a grassy moor by a
★   ruined farm, where you can see the **Machrie Moor Stone Circles:** small, rounded granite-boulder circles and much taller, eerie red-sandstone monoliths. Out on the bare moor, the lost and lonely stones are very evocative, well worth a walk to see if you like the feeling of solitude.

The stones are about 1 mi outside of Machrie; just follow the HISTORIC SCOTLAND sign pointing the way.

HORSEBACK RIDING

Even novices can enjoy a guided ride on a mount from **Cairnhouse Riding Centre** (⊠ *A84, 2 mi south of Machrie, Blackwaterfoot* ☎ *01770/ 860466*).

SHOPPING

The **Old Byre Showroom** (⊠ *A841, 2 mi north of Machrie* ☎ *01770/840227*) sells sheepskin goods, hand-knit sweaters, designer knitwear, leather goods, and rugs. The store is at Auchencar Farm.

EN ROUTE Continuing south to Blackwaterfoot, you can return to Brodick via the String Road: from the Kinloch Hotel, head up the hill. As you drive, there are more fine views of the granite complexities of Arran's hills: gray-notched ridges beyond brown moors and, past the watershed, a vista of Brodick Bay.

LOCHRANZA

11 mi north of Brodick.

The road from Blackwaterfoot to Lochranza exposes another face of Arran: muddy, rocky beaches line one side, while the other has views of the sweeping slopes up to Goat Fell and Caisteal Abhail (2,735 feet), whose stark granite peaks dominate the skyline of the north of the island. The variety of bird life here is striking, which is why ornithologists flock to Arran in the off-season.

Arran's only distillery, the sparkling Isle of Arran Distillery, is in Lochranza, nestled in the hills overlooking Lochranza Bay.

8

GETTING HERE AND AROUND

Lochranza is 11 mi from Brodick via the A841.

EXPLORING

The ruined **Lochranza Castle,** set on a low sand spit on the mud flats of the bay, is quite picturesque, and you'll often see deer grazing nearby. This is said to have been the landing place of Robert the Bruce when he returned from Rathlin Island in 1307 to start the campaign that won Scotland's independence. A sign indicates where you can pick up the key to get in. ⊠ *Off A841* ☎ *0131/668–8800* ⊕ *www.historic-scotland.gov.uk* ⊠ *Free* ☉ *Apr.–Sept., daily 9:30–5:30; Oct.–Mar., daily 9:30–4:30.*

WHERE TO STAY

££ **Apple Lodge.** A charming whitewashed house that was once the manse (or pastor's house), Apple Lodge sits beneath the hills at the edge of Lochranza, close to the brewery. It has elegant landscaped gardens and a reputation for good home cooking. Rooms are comfortably old-fashioned, reflecting the origins of the house. **Pros:** lovely setting; charming gardens. **Cons:** on the outskirts of Lochranza; dinner not always available. ⊠ *Lochranza* ☎ *01770/830229* ⇆ *4 rooms* ⌂ *In-room: no a/c, no phone. In-hotel: restaurant, no kids under 12* ▭ *No credit cards* ⍾⍾ *FAP.*

ISLAY AND JURA

Islay has a character distinct from that of the rest of the islands that make up the Hebrides. In contrast to areas where most residents live on crofts (small plots generally worked by people in their spare time), Islay's western half in particular has large, self-sustaining farms. Many of the island's wildlife preserves, historical sites, and beautiful beaches are also on the western side of the island. It's dangerous to swim at the coastal beaches, but the white sand beaches around Loch Indaal are safe and clean. The southeast, by contrast, is mainly an extension of the island of Jura's inhospitable quartzite hills. Islay is particularly known for its birds, including the rare chough (a crow with red legs and beak) and, in winter, its barnacle geese. Several distilleries produce Islay's characteristically peaty malt whiskies, and most welcome visitors. Some charge a small fee for a tour, which you can usually credit toward any whiskey purchases.

Although it's possible to meet an Islay native in a local pub, such an event is less likely on Jura, given the island's one road, one distillery, one hotel, and six sporting estates. In fact, you have a better chance of bumping into one of the island's red deer, which outnumber the human population by at least 20 to 1. The island is more rugged than Islay, with its profiles of the Paps of Jura, a hill range at its most impressive when basking in the rays of a west-coast sunset.

BOWMORE

On Islay: 11 mi north of Port Ellen.

Compact Bowmore, on Islay, is about the same size (population 1,000) as Port Ellen, but it works slightly better as a base for touring because it's central to Islay's main routes. Sharing its name with the whisky made in the distillery by the shore, Bowmore is a tidy town, its grid pattern having been laid out in 1768 by the local landowner Daniel Campbell, of Shawfield. Main Street stretches from the pier head to the commanding parish church, built in 1767 in an unusual circular design—so the devil could not hide in a corner.

GETTING HERE AND AROUND

Flybe flights from Glasgow to Islay take forty minutes. The trip by CalMac ferry from Kennacraig to Port Ellen takes about two-and-a-half hours; ferries also travel less frequently to Port Askaig. From Port Ellen, you'll need to travel 10 mi on the A846 to reach Bowmore; drivers should use caution during the first mile out of Port Ellen, as the road is filled with sharp turns. The rest of the route is straight but very bumpy, since the road is laid across peat bog. The ferry to Feolin on Jura departs from Port Askaig; the crossing takes five minutes.

Bus service is available through Islay Coaches and Royal Mail; comprehensive timetables are available from the tourist information center.

ESSENTIALS

Air Travel Contacts Glenegadale Airport, Islay (☎ *01667/462445* ⊕ *www. hial.co.uk*).

Visitor Information **Bowmore, Islay**
(✉ *The Square* ☎ *08707/200617*
⊕ *www.visitscotland.com*).

EXPLORING

You can purchase whisky and take a tour at **Bowmore Distillery** (✉ *School St.* ☎ *01496/810671*), which was founded in 1779. You can visit Monday through Saturday; call ahead for opening hours and tour times.

★ The **Islay Woollen Mill,** in a wooded hollow by the river, has a fascinating array of working machinery; proud owner Gordon will take you on a personal tour. The shop sells high-quality products that were woven on-site. Beyond the usual tweed there's a distinctive selection of hats, caps, and clothing made from the mill's own cloth. All the tartans and tweeds worn in the film *Braveheart* were woven here. The mill is on the A846 between Bridgend and Port Askaig, 3 mi outside Bridgend. ✉ *Off A846* ☎ *01496/810563* ⊕ *www.islaywoollenmill.co.uk* 💲 *Free* ⊗ *Mon.–Sat. 10–5.*

> ## THE WHISKY COAST
>
> Scotland likes trails for travelers, whether castles or whiskies are being pursued. The country's dramatic west coast, from the Isle of Skye in the north to Islay and Arran in the south, has plenty of distinguished distilleries. The **Whisky Coast** (⊕ *www. whiskycoast.co.uk*) is a consortium of distilleries, hotels, restaurants, golf courses, and tour operators created to make planning a trip around the area easier. The Web site is one starting point if you're dreaming of touring this part of the country in search of the perfect dram.

WHERE TO STAY

££ 🏨 **Harbour Inn.** The cheerfully noisy bar of this harborside inn is frequented by off-duty distillery workers who are happy to rub elbows with travelers and exchange island gossip. The superb restaurant (£££), which has expansive views over the water, serves morning coffee, lunch, and dinner. Menus highlight local lobster, crab, and prawns, as well as island lamb and beef. The bedrooms are bright and contemporary, with simple wood or velvet-upholstered furniture; some have water views. **Pros:** great location and restaurant. **Cons:** restaurant service can be slow; bedroom linens could be a bit nicer for the price. ✉ *The Square* ☎ *01496/810330* ⊕ *www.harbour-inn.com* 🛏 *7 rooms* ⚙ *In-room: no a/c. In-hotel: restaurant, bar* 🖃 *MC, V* ⦿ *BP.*

PORT CHARLOTTE

On Islay: 11 mi west of Bowmore.

A delightful conservation village at the head of Loch Indaal on Islay, Port Charlotte is home to the Museum of Islay Life, the lovely Natural History Trust, and safe, sandy beaches.

GETTING HERE AND AROUND

To reach Port Charlotte from Bowmore, take the A846 via Bridgend and then the A847, Portnahaven Road. Islay Coaches and Royal Mail buses also travel here from Bowmore.

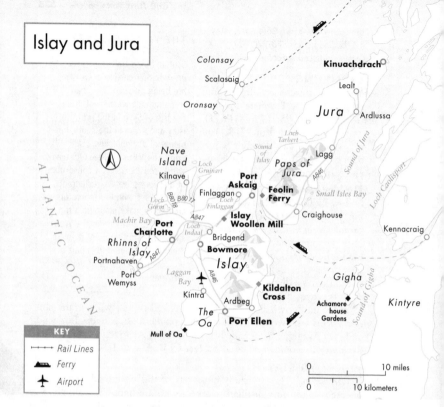

Islay and Jura

Colonsay
Scalasaig
Oronsay
Kinuachdrach
Lealt
Jura
Ardlussa

Nave
Island
Kilnave

Loch
Gruinart
Loch
Tarbert
Sound
of
Islay
Lagg
Paps of
Jura

Port
Askaig
Finlaggan
Feolin
Ferry
Small Isles Bay

Loch
Finlaggan
Loch
Gorm
B80
B80
Machir Bay
A847
Islay
Woollen Mill
Craighouse

Port
Charlotte
Loch
Indaal
Bridgend
Kennacraig

Rhinns of
Islay
A847
Bowmore
Islay
Portnahaven
Port
Wemyss
Laggan
Bay
Gigha
Kintyre

Kintra
Kildalton
Cross
Achamore
house
Gardens

The
Oa
Ardbeg
Port Ellen

Mull of Oa

ATLANTIC OCEAN

Sound of Jura
Loch Caolisport
Sound of Gigha

KEY

+—+—+	Rail Lines
🚢	Ferry
✈	Airport

0   10 miles
0   10 kilometers

EXPLORING

Above the road on the north side in a converted kirk (church) is the **Museum of Islay Life,** a haphazard but authentic collection of local artifacts, photographs, and memorabilia. ✉ *A847* ☎ *01496/850358* ⊕ *www.islaymuseum.org* 🎫 *£3* ⊙ *Apr.–Oct., Mon.–Sat. 10–5.*

The **Natural History Visitor Centre** has a comprehensive exhibition of Islay wildlife, with lots of hands-on activities for children. It's a great stop on rainy days. ✉ *Main St.* ☎ *01496/850288* ⊕ *www.islaynaturalhistory.org* 🎫 *£3* ⊙ *May–Oct, daily 10–4.*

South of Port Charlotte, the A847 continues along the wild landscape of the **Rhinns of Islay**. The road ends at **Portnahaven** and its twin, **Port Wemyss**, where pretty white cottages built in a crescent around the headland belie the harsh lives of the fisher families who live and work here. Return to Port Charlotte via the bleak, unclassified road that loops north and east, passing by the recumbent stone circle at Coultoon and the ruined chapel at Kilchiaran along the way. The strange whooping sound you may hear as you turn away from Portnahaven comes from Scotland's first wave-powered generator, sucking and blowing as it supplies electricity for both villages. It's well worth the climb down to the shore to see it in action.

WHERE TO STAY

£££ ⊞ **Port Charlotte Hotel.** A whitewashed building looking over a white sandy beach, this restored Victorian hotel is warm and bright, its walls decorated with the owners' interesting contemporary art collection. Rooms are simple but comfortable (if slightly cramped), and most have a view of Loch Indaal and, on a clear day, Bowmore, beyond. There is a comfortable and spacious guest lounge next to the hotel's elegant restaurant (£££), which features local food and a menu that changes daily. (The lively bar also has an excellent menu.) **Pros:** beautiful location in a conservation village. **Cons:** slightly expensive; rooms are quite small. ⊠ *Main St.* ☎ *01496/850360* ⊕ *www.milford.co.uk* ⤶ *10 rooms* ⌂ *In-room: no a/c, Wi-Fi. In-hotel: restaurant, bar, Wi-Fi hotspot, parking (free), some pets allowed* ⊟ *D, DC, MC, V* ⊧❋ *BP.*

PORT ELLEN

On Islay: 11 mi south of Bowmore.

Islay's sturdy community of Port Ellen was founded in the 1820s, and much of its architecture dates from the following decades. It has a harbor (ferries stop here), a few shops, and a handful of inns. The road traveling east from Port Ellen (the A846 to Ardbeg) passes three top distilleries and makes a pleasant afternoon's "whisky walk." Tours are free at all three distilleries, but you must call ahead for an appointment; there may be no tours on weekends at times.

GETTING HERE AND AROUND

It is likely that Port Ellen will be your port of arrival on Islay. From here you can travel north to Bowmore, along the A846 before turning northwest towards Bridgend and Port Askaig.

8

EXPLORING

Ardbeg Distillery (☎ *01496/302244* ⊕ *www.ardbeg.com*) is the farthest from Port Ellen. It closed in 1981, but whisky aficionados cheered when the malt flowed again in 1997.

Laphroaig Distillery (☎ *01496/302418* ⊕ *www.laphroaig.com*) is a little less than 1 mi from Port Ellen toward Ardbeg. The whisky it produces is one of the most distinctive in the Western Isles, with a tangy, peaty, seaweed-and-iodine flavor.

Lagavulin Distillery (☎ *01496/302400* ⊕ *www.discovering-distilleries. com/lagavulin*) has the whisky with the strongest iodine scent of all the island malts.

About 8 mi northeast of Port Ellen is one of the highlights of Scotland's Celtic heritage. After passing through a pleasantly rolling, partly wooded landscape, take a narrow road (it's signposted KILDALTON CROSS) from Ardbeg. This leads to a ruined chapel with surrounding kirkyard, in which stands the finest carved cross anywhere in Scotland: the 8th-century **Kildalton Cross.** Carved from a single slab of epidiorite rock, the ringed cross is encrusted on both sides with elaborate designs in the style of the Iona school. The surrounding grave slabs date as far back as the 12th and 13th centuries. ⊕ *www.historic-scotland.gov.uk.*

★

The southern **Oa Peninsula,** west of Port Ellen, is a region of caves that's rich in smuggling lore. At its tip, the Mull of Oa, is a monument recalling the 650 men who lost their lives in 1918 when the British ships *Tuscania* and *Otranto* sank nearby. Bring good, strong walking shoes.

SPORTS AND THE OUTDOORS

GOLF **Machrie Golf Links** would be a lot more crowded if it were a little more accessible. The course was designed in 1891, and except for minor changes in the 1970s, has changed little. Watch out for the sand dunes! £55 per round. ⊠ *1 mi from airport, 4 mi from Port Ellen* ☎ *01496/302310* ⊕ *www.machrie.com* ⚐ *18 holes, 5,894 yds, par 71.*

HORSEBACK RIDING **Ballivicar Pony Trekking** (⊠ *Ballivicar Farm* ☎ *01496/302251*) leads trips on nearby beaches and into the surrounding countryside.

PORT ASKAIG

On Islay: 11 mi northeast of Bowmore.

Serving as the ferry port for Jura and receiving ferries from Kennacraig, Port Askaig is a mere cluster of cottages. Uphill, just outside the village, a side road travels along the coast, giving impressive views of Jura on the way. There are distilleries near here, too; make appointments for tours.

GETTING HERE AND AROUND

Traveling from Bowmore, you can reach Port Asakaig (where the road ends) via A846. The village is also served by local buses.

EXPLORING

At road's end, the **Bunnahabhain Distillery** (☎ *01496/840646* ⊕ *www.bunnahabhain.com*) sits on the shore. It was established in 1881.

You can also purchase whisky at the **Caol Ila Distillery** (☎ *01496/840207* ⊕ *www.islayinfo.com/islay_caolila_distillery.html*), which filled its first bottle in 1846.

JURA

5 mins by ferry from Port Askaig.

The rugged, mountainous landscape of the island of Jura—home to only about 200 people—looms immediately east of Port Askaig, across the Sound of Islay. Jura has only one single-track road (the A846), which begins at Feolin, the ferry pier. It climbs across moorland, providing scenic views of the island's most striking feature, the Paps of Jura, three beastlike rounded peaks. The ruined Claig Castle, on an island just offshore, was built by the Lords of the Isles to control the Sound.

Jura House lies between Feolin and Craighouse, the island's only village, some 8 mi away (its walled gardens are open to the public for part of the year). Jura's solitude attracted George Orwell to the remote farmhouse at Barnhill, where completed his famous novel, *1984.*

GETTING HERE AND AROUND

The Port Askaig–Feolin car ferry takes five minutes to cross the Sound of Islay. Buses service is also available from Craighouse and Inverlussa.

EXPLORING

The community of Craighouse has the island's only distillery, the **Isle of Jura Distillery** (✉ *A846* ☎ *01496/820240* ⊕ *www.isleofjura.com*), producing malt whisky since 1810. Phone ahead to reserve your place on a tour.

The settlement of **Kinuachdrach** once served as a crossing point to Scarba and the mainland. To get to Kinuachdrach after crossing the river at Lealt, follow the track beyond the surface road for 5 mi. The coastal footpath to Corryvreckan lies beyond, over the bare moors. This area has two enticements: the first is the house at **Barnhill** (not open to the public) where George Orwell wrote *1984*; the second, for wilderness enthusiasts, is the whirlpool of the **Gulf of Corryvreckan** and the unspoiled coastal scenery.

WHERE TO STAY

££ 🏨 **Jura Hotel.** In spite of its monopoly on Jura, this hotel surrounded by pleasant gardens can be relied on for adequate accommodations. Rooms are simple and a bit old-fashioned. The restaurant (££) serves good, satisfying food prepared with local ingredients. **Pros:** good views across the bay; spacious rooms; next door to distillery. **Cons:** room decor is tired, to say the least; you may have to share a bathroom. ✉ *Craighouse* ☎ *01496/820243* ⊕ *www.jurahotel.co.uk* ⇆ *18 rooms, 11 with bath* ⚒ *In-room: no a/c, no phone, no TV. In-hotel: restaurant, bar* ⊟ *AE, DC, MC, V* ⏸ *BP.*

ISLE OF MULL AND IONA

8

Though its economy has historically been built on agriculture, fishing, and whisky distilling, today the Isle of Mull relies on tourism dollars—which makes sense, since there are many wonderful things to see here. The landscapes range from the pretty harbor of Tobermory and the gentle slopes around Dervaig to the dramatic Atlantic beaches on the west. In the south, the long road past the sweeping green slopes of the Ross of Mull leads to Iona, a year-round attraction.

GETTING HERE AND AROUND

Ferries to Mull are run by the ubiquitous Caledonian MacBrayne. Their most frequent and shortest car ferry route to Mull is from Oban to Craignure (45 minutes). Two shorter routes are from Lochaline on the Morvern Peninsula to Fishnula (15 minutes), or Kilchoan (on the Adrnamurchan Peninsula) to Tobermory (15 minutes). The ferries do not accept bookings, and the Lochaline ferry does not run on Sunday. Bowman's Coaches serve the east coast, running between Tobermory, Craignure, and Fionnphort (for the ferry to Iona).

CRAIGNURE

On Mull: 40-min ferry crossing from Oban, 15-min ferry crossing to Fishnish (5 mi northwest of Craignure) from Lochaline.

Craignure, little more than a pier and some houses, is close to the Isle of Mull's two best-known castles, Torosay and Duart. Reservations for the year-round ferries that travel from Oban to Craignure are advisable

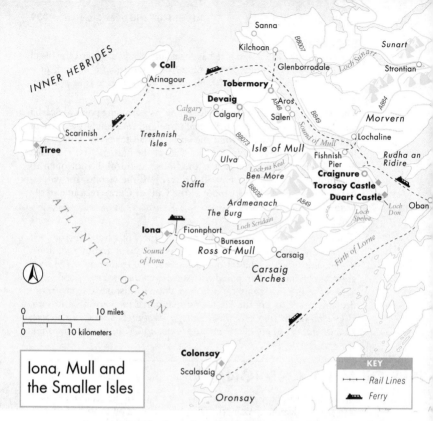

0   10 miles
0   10 kilometers

in summer. The ferry from Lochaline to Fishnish, just northwest of Craignure, does not accept reservations and does not run on Sunday.

GETTING HERE AND AROUND

The arrival point for the 40-minute ferry crossing from Oban, Craignure is the starting point for further travel on Mull northwest toward Salen and Tobermory, or towards Fionnphort and the Iona ferry to the southwest.

ESSENTIALS

Visitor Information Craignure, Mull (✉ *The Pierhead* ☎ *01680/812377* ⊕ *www.visitscotland.com*).

EXPLORING

★ A trip to **Torosay Castle** can include the novelty of steam-and-diesel service on a narrow-gauge railway, which takes 20 minutes to run from the pier at Craignure to the grounds of Torosay (about ½ mi, £4.75). Scottish baronial in style, the turreted mid-19th-century country house has a friendly air. You're free to wander round the principal rooms, which include the front hall dominated by a collection of red deer-stag antlers. The castle's gardens are home to blue poppies and many other rare plants. ✉ *Off A849, about 1 mi southeast of Craignure* ☎ *01680/812421* ⊕ *www.torosay.com* 🎫 *Castle, garden, play park, tearoom/gallery £6.50, garden, play park, tearoom/gallery £4.75*

⊘ *Castle Easter–Oct., daily 10:30–5; last admission at 4:30. Gardens daily 9–sunset.*

The 13th-century **Duart Castle,** ancient seat of the Macleans, was ruined by the Campbells in 1691 but purchased and restored by Sir Fitzroy Maclean in 1911. It stands dramatically on a cliff top overlooking the Sound of Mull. Inside, one display depicts the wreck of the *Swan,* a Cromwellian vessel sunk offshore in 1653 and excavated in the 1990s by marine archaeologists. Outside you can visit nearby **Millennium Wood,** planted with groups of Mull's indigenous trees. You can walk 4 mi along the shore from Torosay to Duart Castle; if you have less energy, you can drive from Craignure. To reach Duart by car, take the A849 and turn left around the shore of Duart Bay. For buses to the castle from Craignure call the castle in advance. ⊠ *3 mi southeast of Craignure* ☎ *01680/812309* ⊕ *www.duartcastle.com* ☎ *£5.30* ⊘ *Apr., Sun.–Thurs. 11–4; May–mid-Oct., daily 10:30–5:30.*

WHERE TO STAY

££ ☷ **Craignure Inn.** This 18th-century whitewashed drover's inn, a short walk from the ferry pier, has a lively bar that often hosts local musicians. Hearty, home-cooked meals (£) include staples such as shepherd's pie and fish-and-chips. The rooms are warm and snug, with polished-wood furniture, exposed beams, and views of the Sound of Mull. **Pros:** lively bar scene; hearty local foods. **Cons:** live music can get loud. ⊠ *Near the ferry pier* ☎ *01680/812305* ⊕ *www.craignure-inn.co.uk* ⤴ *3 rooms* ♿ *In-room: no a/c. In-hotel: restaurant, bar* ⊟ *MC, V* ☷ *BP.*

DERVAIG

On Mull: 27 mi northwest of Craignure, 60 mi north of Fionnphort.

A pretty riverside village, Dervaig has a circular, pointed church tower that is reminiscent of the Irish-Celtic style of the 8th and 9th centuries. The Bellart is a good trout- and salmon-fishing river, and Calgary Bay, 5 mi away, has one of the best beaches on Mull.

GETTING HERE AND AROUND

You can reach Dervaig from Craignure via the A849. From Salen, take the B8073, and from Tobermory, take the B8073.

EXPLORING

At the **Old Byre Heritage Centre,** an audiovisual presentation on the history of the region plays hourly. The tearoom's wholesome fare, particularly the homemade soup, is a boon to travelers. There's also a craft shop here. You'll see signs for the center on the B8073, just before Dervaig. ⊠ *Off B8073* ☎ *01688/400229* ⊕ *www.old-byre.co.uk* ☎ *£4* ⊘ *Easter–Oct., Wed.–Sun. 10:30–6:30; last admission at 5:30.*

WHERE TO STAY

££ ☷ **Calgary Hotel.** In a small wooded valley overlooking the beautiful sandy bay, this former farmhouse feels quite secluded. Rooms have colorful quilts and drapes, and some have views over the woods to Calgary Bay. The hotel also rents several apartments by the week. The hotel sponsors the Art in Nature project, sculptures in natural settings; some work in metal by owner Matthew Reade also decorates the hotel.

The restaurant (£16), in a converted dovecote, serves sophisticated Scottish fare; there is also a tearoom open during the day. **Pros:** excellent staff; south-facing rooms have lovely bay views; lots of polished wood. **Cons:** not for those who want a remote location. ⊠ *Calgary, by Dervaig* ☎ *01688/400256* ⊕ *www.calgary.co.uk* ⊅ *9 rooms, 2 apartments* ⌂ *In-room: no a/c. In-hotel: restaurant, bar* ⊟ *MC, V* ⊗ *Closed Dec.–Feb.* †◎† *BP.*

TOBERMORY

5 mi northeast of Dervaig, 21 mi north of Craignure.

Founded as a fishing station, Tobermory is now a lively tourist center and a base for exploring Mull. The town is famous for its crescent of brightly painted houses around the harbor.

GETTING HERE AND AROUND

The most frequent service to Mull is via the Oban-Craignure ferry. Tobermory is 21 mi from Craignure along the A849/848 (via Salen). Bowman's coaches run services between Tobermory and Craignure.

ESSENTIALS

Visitor Information **Tobermory, Mull** (⊠ *Main St.* ☎ *01688/302182* ⊕ *www. visitscotland.com*).

WHERE TO EAT AND STAY

££
SEAFOOD
✕ **Café Fish.** The location of this newish restaurant has certainly contributed to its success. Perched on the pier at the end of Tobermory and overlooking the bay beyond, Café Fish prides itself on the freshness of its fish (the owners have their own boat land their own shellfish daily). Fish is served simply, grilled with a slice of lemon, to let the natural flavors speak for themselves. Diver-harvested scallops are served with vermouth and orange juice over rice. ⊠ *The pier, Tobermory* ☎ *01688/301253* ⊟ *MC, V* ⊗ *Closed Jan.–mid-Mar.*

£££
⌂ **Highland Cottage.** This elegant family-run hotel prides itself on the detail of its rooms and its fine dining. Set on the hill above the harbor, the upstairs rooms have sea views. The small restaurant offers a fixed price menu (£45) of imaginative dishes prepared by owner Josephine Currie, typically using fine local venison, lamb, and seafood. **Pros:** comfortable hotel with attentive owners; high-quality dining. **Cons:** rooms are a bit small. ⊠ *Breadalbane St.* ☎ *01688/302030* ⊕ *www.highlandcottage. co.uk* ⊅ *6 rooms* ⌂ *In-room: no a/c, Wi-Fi. In-hotel: restaurant, room service, Wi-Fi hotspot, parking (free), some pets allowed* ⊟ *AE, D, DC, MC, V* †◎† *BP.*

££
⌂ **Tobermory Hotel.** Made up of five former fishermen's cottages, this lodging on Tobermory's waterfront has a warm, intimate feel. Some rooms have a view of the bay, and several have nice touches like a four-poster bed, but all are modest in size and have minimal furniture. Using local produce, the Water's Edge restaurant (£27 prix-fixe) prepares traditional dishes with a twist: for example, the spiced-salmon fillet is served over a haddock-and-prawn roll and topped with lemon-and-coriander cream. **Pros:** adorable cottage setting with fireplace; toys for children. **Cons:** small rooms and bathrooms. ⊠ *Main St.* ☎ *01688/302091* ⊕ *www.*

thetobermoryhotel.com ⤳ *16 rooms* ⬠ *In-room: no a/c, Wi-Fi, no phone. In-hotel: restaurant, bar* ▭ *D, DC, MC, V* ⊘ *Closed Jan.* ⊪ *BP.*

£££ ⊞ **Western Isles Hotel.** Like an elderly dowager, the Western Isles Hotel looks down on Tobermory from its wonderful location overlooking the Sound of Mull. A grand hotel from the Victorian era, it suffered a period of neglect but is now being refurbished and restored to its former state. The glorious views from its huge windows and its large high-ceilinged rooms make it an attractive place to stay. Bedrooms are very comfortable and roomy; the more expensive ones have sea views. The hotel has a lovely outside terrace and a bar in a large conservatory, as well as reassuringly old-fashioned lounges. The restaurant serves a very good £27.50 prix-fixe dinner. **Pros:** the view; spacious public rooms; great food. **Cons:** outmoded plumbing; occasional lack of hot water; still being renovated. ✉ *Isle of Mull* ☎ *01688/302012* ⊕ *www. westernisleshotel.co.uk* ⤳ *26 rooms* ⬠ *In-room: no a/c. In-hotel: 2 restaurants, bar, Wi-Fi hotspot* ▭ *AE, D, MC, V* ⊪ *BP.*

THE ARTS

The renowned **Mull Theatre** (✉ *Druimfin* ☎ *01688/302828*) —once the Mull Little Theatre, the smallest in the U.K.—has now grown into the new Druimfin centre. Its productions tour the islands, so it is essential to consult the Web site and book ahead.

EN ROUTE

Between Craignure and Fionnphort at the end of the Ross of Mull, the double-lane road narrows as it heads southwest, touched by sea inlets at Lochs Don and Spelve. Inland, vivid grass and high rock faces in Glen More make gray and green the prevalent hues. These stepped-rock faces reach their highest point in Ben More, the only island *munro* (a Scottish mountain more than 3,000 feet high) outside Skye. Stay on the A849 for a pleasant drive the length of the Ross of Mull, a wide promontory with scattered settlements. The National Trust for Scotland cares for the rugged stretch of coast, known as the Burg. The A849 eventually ends in a long parking lot opposite the houses of Fionnphort.

IONA

5 mins by ferry from Fionnphort (Mull), which is 36 mi west of Craignure.

The ruined abbey on Iona gives little hint that this was once one of the most important Christian religious centers in the land. The priceless Book of Keils (now in Dublin) was illustrated here, and it was the monks of Iona who spread Christian ideas across Scotland and the north. The abbey was founded in the year 563 by the fiery and argumentative Columba (circa 521–97) after his expulsion from Ireland. Until the 11th century, many of Scotland's kings and rulers were buried here, their tombstones still visible inside the abbey. While few visitors venture beyond the pier and the abbey, there are several tranquil paths.

GETTING HERE AND AROUND

Caledonian MacBrayne's ferry from Fionnphort departs at regular intervals throughout the year (£4.50 round-trip). Timetables are available on the Caledonian MacBrayne Web site. Note that cars are not permitted; there's a parking lot by the ferry at Fionnphort.

EXPLORING

Iona Abbey survived repeated Norse sackings but finally fell into disuse around the time of the Reformation. Restoration work began at the turn of the 20th century. In 1938 the **Iona Community** (☎ *01681/700404* ⊕ *www.iona.org.uk*), an ecumenical religious group, was founded. It was involved in rebuilding the abbey and now offers multiday programs at several buildings on the island. Today the restored buildings, including the abbey, serve as a spiritual center under the jurisdiction of the Church of Scotland. Guided tours, run by the Iona Community, are every half hour in summer and on demand in winter. ☎ *01681/700793* ⊕ *www.historic-scotland.gov.uk/places* 🎟 *£4.70* ⊙ *Apr.–Sept., daily 9:30–5:30; Oct.–Mar., daily 9:30–4:30.*

WHERE TO STAY

£££   📷 **St. Columba Hotel.** Rooms in this 1846 former manse are very simple, but all front rooms have glorious views across the Sound of Iona to Mull. Chefs in the restaurant (£££) serve exceptional three-course meals using organic ingredients. **Pros:** eco-minded; this place is all about what's good for the earth and soul; nice log fires. **Cons:** no TV in hotel; rooms minimal in style. ⊠ *Next to cathedral, about ¼ mi from the ferry pier* ☎ *01681/700304* ⊕ *www.stcolumba-hotel.co.uk* 🛏 *27 rooms* ⚒ *In-room: no a/c, no TV. In-hotel: restaurant, bar, Wi-Fi hotspot* ▤ *MC, V* ⊙ *Closed mid-Oct.–Easter* ❢ *BP.*

SHOPPING

Iona has a few pleasant surprises for shoppers, the biggest of which is the **Old Printing Press Bookshop** (⊠ *Beside St. Columba Hotel* ☎ *01681/ 70069*), an excellent antiquarian bookstore. The **Iona Community Shop** (⊠ *Across from Iona Abbey* ☎ *01681/700404*) carries Celtic-inspired gift items, as well as sheet music and songbooks, and CDs and tapes.

THE SMALLER ISLANDS

The smaller islands, sometimes known as the Southern Hebrides, may seem quite remote but were once important centers of power and production. Successively depopulated by force or by emigration to Glasgow's industries or the promise of the Americas, the islands still survive on fishing, cattle- and sheep raising, and, of course, whisky production. Their Gaelic language is vibrant once again, but their populations remain small. For the visitor, the experience is one of open, often barely populated landscapes and a slightly brooding sense of history.

TIREE

4-hr sail from Oban, via Coll.

GETTING HERE AND AROUND

Caledonian MacBrayne runs ferries to Tiree via Coll, four times a week (Tuesday, Thursday, Saturday, and Sunday). You can also fly here from Glasgow on Flybe or from Oban on Highland Airways. On Tiree, the Royal Mail postbus (which carries mail and passengers) runs an infrequent service around the island; there is a shared taxi service (☎ 01879/220311), which you should book ahead of your arrival. An alternative is to rent a bike from **Skerryvore House** (☎ 01879/220268).

ESSENTIALS

Air Travel Contacts Tiree Airport (☎ 01667/462445 ⊕ www.hial.co.uk).

EXPLORING

A fertile, low-lying island with its own microclimate, **Tiree** is windswept, but has more hours of sunshine per year than any other part of the British Isles. Long, rolling Atlantic swells attract surfers, and summer visitors can raise the population to the nearly 4,500 it supported in the 1830s. Among Tiree's several archaeological sites are a large boulder near Vaul covered with more than 50 Bronze Age cup marks, and an excavated *broch* (stone tower) at Dun Mor Vaul.

COLL

8

3-hr sail from Oban.

Unlike their neighbors in Tiree, Coll's residents were not forced to leave the island in the 19th century. Today half of the island's sparse population lives in its only village, Arinagour. Its coasts offer extraordinarily rich bird life, particularly along the beautiful sandy beaches of its southwest.

GETTING HERE AND AROUND

Caledonian MacBrayne runs ferries to Coll on Tuesday, Thursday, Saturday, and Sunday. You can also fly here from Oban on Highland Airways. There is no public transportation on Coll, but you can rent a bike (☎ 01879/230333) or use the island's one taxi (☎ 01879/230402).

EXPLORING

Near Tiree, **Coll** is even lower lying but also rockier and less fertile. The island is rich in archaeology, with standing stones at Totronald, a cairn at Annagour, and the remains of several Iron Age forts around the island.

The keep of **Breachacha Castle,** on the south end of the island, dates to 1450. A former stronghold of the Maclean clan, the castle is very similar to Kisimul Castle on the Isle of Barra. Today the castle is privately owned, but you may view it from the road near Uig.

COLONSAY

2½-hr sail from Oban.

Less bleak than Coll and Tiree, Colonsay is one of Scotland's quietest, mo st unspoiled, and least populated islands. It is partly wooded, with a fine quasi-tropical garden at Colonsay House and a great variety of wildlife.

GETTING HERE AND AROUND

CalMac ferries run to Colonsay on Monday, Wednesday, Friday, and Sunday. The island of Oronsay lies half a mile away and can be reached at certain times across a natural causeway. There is a limited postbus service on the island; bikes can be rented from **A. McConnel** (☎ *01951/200355*).

EXPLORING

Colonsay is one of Scotland's quietest, most unspoiled, and least populous islands. The beautiful beach at Kiloran Bay is an utterly peaceful place even at the height of summer. The standing stones at Kilchattan Farm are known as Fingal's Limpet Hammers. Fingal, or Finn, MacCoul is a warrior of massive size and strength in Celtic mythology. Standing before the stones, you can imagine Fingal wielding them like hammers to cull equally large limpets from Scotland's rocky coast. The island's social life revolves around the bar at the 19th-century Colonsay Hotel, 100 yards from the ferry pier. The adjacent island of Oronsay with its ruined cloister can be reached at low tide in a 1½-mi wade across a sandy sound.

Around the Great Glen

WORD OF MOUTH

"The funicular CairnGorm Mountain Railway is a very scenic trip, and besides the stunning views, an excellent restaurant awaits you at the top."
—HollydaleK

"We went to Fort Augustus for lunch. It's a lovely town. We grabbed a quick sandwich and rushed over to see the boats on the Caledonian Canal, which came right by where we were parked. It's part of a canal system that runs from Fort William on the western side of Scotland, to Inverness on the eastern side. There is a lock (not loch) right in the middle of town and we were able to see boats locking through."
—sallyky

Updated by
Elizabeth
Reeder

The ancient rift valley of the Great Glen is a dramatic feature on the map of Scotland, giving the impression that the top half of the country has slid southwest. Geologists confirm that this actually occurred, after matching granite from Strontian, west of Fort William, with the same type of rock found at Foyers, on the east side of Loch Ness, some 65 mi away. No map can convey the area's brilliant purple and emerald moorland, its forests and astonishingly varied wildlife (mountain hares, red deer, golden eagles), or the courtesy of its soft-spoken inhabitants and their sense of history.

Though it's the capital of the Highlands, Inverness has the flavor of a Lowland town, its winds blowing in a sea-salt air from the Moray Firth. Inverness is also home to one of the world's most famous monster myths: in 1933, during a quiet news week, the editor of a local paper decided to run a story about a sighting of something splashing about in nearby Loch Ness. The story lives on, and the dubious Loch Ness phenomenon continues to keep cameras trained on the deep waters.

Fort William, without a monster on its doorstep, makes do with Ben Nevis and the Road to the Isles, a title sometimes applied to the breathtaking scenic route to Mallaig. This is best seen by rail, since the road to Mallaig is still narrow, winding, and single track in places, and meeting an oncoming bus can be alarming—especially if you're distracted by the view. On the way, road and rail routes pass Loch Morar, the country's deepest body of water, which lays claim to its own monster, Morag. Away from the Great Glen to the north lie the heartlands of Scotland, a bare backbone of remote mountains.

The great hills that loom to the southeast form the border of Strathspey, the broad valley of the fast-flowing River Spey. This area, commonly called Speyside, is known as one of Scotland's main whisky-distilling areas and is traversed by the Malt Whisky Trail.

Impressive castles are also on the agenda in the Great Glen. Perhaps one of the best known of which is ruined Urquhart Castle, a favorite haunt of Nessie-watchers because of its location halfway down Loch Ness. To the east are two top-of-the-list castles that are still inhabited: Cawdor Castle, with its happy marriage of different furnishings—modern and ancient, mellow and brightly colored—and Brodie Castle, with its magnificent library and a collection of paintings that extend well into the 20th century.

TOP REASONS TO GO

Castles, fortresses, and battle-fields: Hear stories of the Highland people and famous figures like Bonnie Prince Charlie, and absorb the atmosphere of castles and battlefields, at Culloden Moor, Cawdor and Brodie castles, Fort George, and Glencoe.

Hill walking and outdoor activities: The Great Glen is renowned for its hill walking. Some of the best routes are around Glen Nevis, Glencoe, and on Ben Nevis, the highest mountain in Britain. It's not just hiking: Glenmore Lodge in the Cairngorms offers everything from kayaking to ice climbing.

Wild landscapes and rare wildlife: Spot rare plants and beasts including tiny least willow trees and golden eagles in the near-arctic tundra of Cairngorms National Park.

Whisky Trail: The two westernmost distilleries on the Malt Whisky Trail are in Forres. Benromach is the smallest distillery in Moray and has excellent tours; Dallas Dhu is preserved as a museum. You can strike out from here to nearby distilleries in Speyside (⇨ *see Chapter 7*).

Stunning beaches: The west coast may not have tropical temperatures, but it has untouched white-sand beaches with clear waters. The coastline between Morar and Arisaig is lined with miles upon miles of them.

Boat trips: There are many ferries to the small isles (or to Skye) from Arisaig and Mallaig. You can also go Nessie-watching on Loch Ness or hire a small boat and travel the Caledonian Canal.

ORIENTATION AND PLANNING

GETTING ORIENTED

Experiencing the whole of the Great Glen requires quite a bit of travel. The road from Fort William northwest to Mallaig (A830), though narrow and winding, is one of the classic routes of Scottish touring and is popularly known as the Road to the Isles. Similarly, the road from Fort William northeast to Inverness (A82) is a vital coast-to-coast link. If you are heading to Mallaig, you'll definitely want to venture over to the Isle of Skye *(see Chapter 10)* or perhaps to the Small Isles.

Speyside and Loch Ness. Speyside is best known for its whisky distilleries, and those who enjoy a good dram often follow the Whiskey Trail. A visit to Loch Ness is on most itineraries, but you will then want to see places more wild and dramatic than Scotland's most famous loch. There are long, walkable beaches at Nairn, and Findhorn. Inverness, a small city, is an excellent base for exploring the area, though it's not a prime attraction by itself.

Toward the Small Isles. An area known for larger-than-life figures both old (the Bonnie Prince) and new (Harry Potter), the Road to the Isles gives you classic views across water to rocky islands perched on blue seas. Base yourself at Fort William so that you can take in the spectacular scenery of Glencoe and Glen Nevis and also get a glimpse of the western seaboard toward Mallaig.

PLANNING

WHEN TO GO

Late spring to early autumn is the best time to visit the Great Glen. If you catch good weather in summer, the days can be glorious. Summer is also when you might encounter midges (biting insects: keep walking, as they can't move very fast). Winter can bring a damp chill, gusty winds, and snow-blocked roads, although many Scots value the open fires and the warming whisky that make the off-season so appealing.

PLANNING YOUR TIME

The Great Glen is an enormous area that can easily be broken into two separate trips. The first would be based in or near Inverness, allowing an exploration of Speyside, the Cairngorms, Cawdor and Brodie castles, and perhaps a few whisky distillery tours. The second, based in Fort Williams, moves through the moody Rannoch Moor to the nearly always cloud-laden Glencoe and toward the Road to the Isles.

For those with more time, a trip around the Great Glen could be combined with forays north into the Northern Highlands, east toward Aberdeen and the rest of the Malt Whisky Trail, southeastward to the Central Highlands, or south to Argyll.

GETTING HERE AND AROUND
AIR TRAVEL

Inverness Airport has flights from London, Edinburgh, and Glasgow. Domestic flights covering the Highlands and islands are operated by British Airways (⊕ *www.britishairways.com*), Servisair ⊕ *www.servisair.com*), easyJet (⊕ *www.easyjet.com*), Eastern Airways (⊕ *www.easternairways.com*), and Highland Airways (⊕ *www.highlandairways.co.uk*). Fort William has bus and train connections with Glasgow, so Glasgow Airport can be a good access point.

BUS TRAVEL

A long-distance Scottish Citylink service connects Glasgow and Fort William. Inverness is also well served from the central belt of Scotland. For bargain-priced coach transport between the main cities of Glasgow, Edinburgh, Perth, Dundee, Aberdeen, and Inverness, contact Megabus (book online to avoid phone charges).

There's limited service available within the Great Glen area and some local service running from Fort William. Highland Country Buses serves the Great Glen and around Fort William. A number of postbus services will help get you to the more remote corners of the area. A timetable is available from Royal Mail Post Buses.

Bus Contacts Highland Country Buses (☏ *01397/702373* ⊕ *www.rapsons.com*). **Megabus** (☏ *08705/505050* ⊕ *www.megabus.com*). **Royal Mail Post Buses** (☏ *01463/256273* ⊕ *www.royalmail.com*). **Scottish Citylink** (☏ *08705/505050* ⊕ *www.citylink.co.uk*).

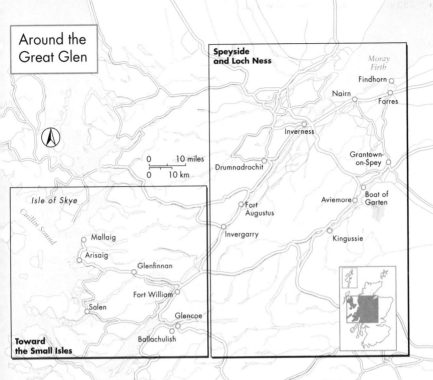

Speyside and Loch Ness

Moray Firth

Findhorn

Nairn

Farres

Inverness

Grantown-on-Spey

Drumnadrochit

Aviemore

Boat of Garten

Fort Augustus

Isle of Skye

Cuillin Sound

Invergarry

Kingussie

Mallaig

Arisaig

Glenfinnan

Fort William

Salen

Glencoe

Ballachulish

Toward the Small Isles

0   10 miles
0   10 km

CAR TRAVEL

The fast A9 brings you to Inverness in roughly three hours from Glasgow or Edinburgh, even if you take your time.

As in all areas of rural Scotland, a car is a great asset for exploring the Great Glen and Speyside, especially since the best of the area is away from the main roads. You can use the main A82 from Inverness to Fort William, or use the smaller B862/B852 roads to explore the much quieter east side of Loch Ness. The same applies to Speyside, where several options open up away from the A9, especially through the pinewoods by Coylumbridge and Feshiebridge, east of the main road. Mallaig, west of Fort William, is reached via a new road, but there are still a few narrow and winding sections. In Morvern, the area across Loch Linnhe southwest of Fort William, you may encounter single-lane roads, which require slower speeds and concentration.

TRAIN TRAVEL

ScotRail has connections from London to Inverness and Fort William (including overnight sleeper service), as well as reliable links from Glasgow and Edinburgh. There's train service between Glasgow (Queen Street) and Inverness, via Aviemore, which gives access to the heart of Speyside.

Although there's no rail connection among towns within the Great Glen, this area has the West Highland Line, which links Fort William to Mallaig. This train, run by ScotRail, remains the most enjoyable way to experience the rugged hills and loch scenery between these two places. The Jacobite Steam Train is an exciting summer (mid-May–mid-October) option on the same route.

Train Contacts ScotRail (☎ *08457/484950* ⊕ *www.scotrail. co.uk*). **Jacobite Steam Train** (☎ *01524/737751* ⊕ *www.westcoastrailway.co.uk*).

RESTAURANTS

Inverness, Fort William, and Aviemore have plenty of cafés and restaurants in all price ranges. Fort William has a particularly good seafood restaurant. Outside of the towns, there are many country-house hotels serving superb meals.

HOTELS

In the Great Glen, cities have a range of accommodations ranging from cozy inns to expansive hotels; in more remote areas your choice will usually be limited to smaller establishments. Because this is an established vacation area, you should have no trouble finding a room for a night; however, the area is quite busy in the peak season and the best places book up early. In Inverness, you may find it more appealing to stay outside the city center or in the nearby, very pretty countryside.

SIGHTSEEING TOURS

Inverness Tours runs the occasional boat cruise but is mainly known for tours around the Highlands in well-equipped vehicles, which are led by expert guides and heritage enthusiasts. James Johnstone, a personal guide, is based in Inverness but will drive you anywhere; he has a particularly good knowledge of the Highlands and islands, including the Outer Isles.

Tour Contacts Inverness Tours (☎ *01456/450168* ⊕ *www. invernesstours.com*). **James Johnstone** (☎ *01463/798372* ⊕ *www. jajcd.com*).

WHAT IT COSTS IN POUNDS					
	£	££	£££	££££	£££££
RESTAURANTS	Under £10	£10–£14	£15–£19	£20–£25	over £25
HOTELS	Under £70	£70–£120	£121–£160	£161–£220	over £220

Restaurant prices are for a main course at dinner. Hotel prices are for two people in a standard double room in high season, generally including the 17.5% V.A.T.

VISITOR INFORMATION

Aviemore, Fort William, and Inverness have year-round tourist offices. Other tourist centers, open seasonally, include those at Fort Augustus, Grantown-on-Spey, Kingussie, Mallaig, and Nairn.

Visitor Information Visit Highlands (⊕ *www.visithighlands.com*).

SPEYSIDE AND LOCH NESS

Because Jacobite tales are interwoven with landmarks throughout this entire area, you should first learn something about this thorny but colorful period of Scottish history in which the Jacobites tried to restore the exiled Stuarts to the British monarchy. One of the best places to do this is at Culloden, just east of Inverness, where a major battle in 1746 ended in final, catastrophic defeat for the Jacobites. Inverness itself is not really a town in which to linger, unless you need to do some shopping. Other areas to concentrate on are the inner Moray Firth moving down into Speyside, with its famous distilleries and great salmon fishing, before moving west into the Great Glen. Loch Ness is just one of the attractions hereabouts. In the Great Glen and Speyside, the best sights are often hidden from the main road, an excellent reason to favor peaceful rural byways and to avoid as far as possible the busy A82 (down Loch Ness's western shore), as well as the A96 and A9, which carry much of the traffic in the area.

INVERNESS

176 mi north of Glasgow, 109 mi northwest of Aberdeen, 161 mi northwest of Edinburgh.

Inverness seems designed for the tourist, with its ever-expanding range of restaurants, excellent pubs, and well-equipped visitor center. Compared with other Scottish towns, however, Inverness has less to offer visitors who have a keen interest in Scottish history. Throughout its past, Inverness was burned and ravaged by the restive Highland clans competing for dominance. Thus, a decorative wall panel here and a fragment of tower there are all that remain.

But Inverness makes a great base for exploring the region, and you can fan out in almost any direction for interesting day trips: east to Moray and the distilleries near Forres, south to Loch Ness, and southeast to the Cairngorms. You can even head north to the Northern Highlands *(see Chapter 10).*

9

GETTING HERE AND AROUND

You can easily fly into Inverness Airport, as there are daily flights from London, Edinburgh, and Glasgow. However, there are also easy train and bus connections from Glasgow Airport. Scottish Citylink has service here, and Megabus has long-distance bus service from Edinburgh and Glasgow. ScotRail runs trains here from London, Edinburgh, Glasgow, and other cities.

Once you're here, you can explore much of the city by foot. A rental car makes exploring the surrounding area much easier. But if you don't have a car, there are bus and boat tours from the city center to a number of places in the Great Glen.

ESSENTIALS

Airport Contacts Inverness Airport (✉ *Dalcross* ☎ *01667/462445* ⊕ *www. hial.co.uk*).

Bus Contacts Inverness Coach Station (✉ *Academy St.* ☎ *01463/233371*).

Visitor Information **Inverness** (⊠ *Castle Wynd* ☎ *01463/234353* ⊕ *www. inverness-scotland.com*).

EXPLORING

One of Inverness's few historic landmarks is reddish sandstone **Inverness Castle** (now the local Sheriff Court), nestled above the river off Castle Road on Castle Hill. The current structure is Victorian, built after a former fort was blown up by the Jacobites in the 1745 campaign.

⟳ The excellent, although small, **Inverness Museum and Art Gallery** covers archaeology, art, local history, and the natural environment in its lively displays. ⊠ *Castle Wynd* ☎ *01463/237114* ⊕ *www.invernessmuseum. com* 🎫 *Free* ⊙ *Mon.–Sat. 10–5.*

Inverness Dolphin Cruises (☎ *01463/717900* ⊕ *www.inverness-dolphin-cruises.co.uk*) provides trips by boat from Inverness harbor into the Moray Firth, offering you the chance to see dolphins in their breeding area.

An unusual option from Inverness is a day trip to Orkney: **John o'Groats Ferries** (☎ *01955/611353* ⊕ *www.jogferry.co.uk*) runs day tours from Inverness to Orkney, daily from May through August.

WHERE TO EAT

££   ✕ **Riva.** With views over the River Ness towards Inverness Castle, Riva
ITALIAN   has a great location; try and get a window seat. The dining room has elegantly lighted deep-red walls lined with black-and-white photographs of Italian cityscapes. Tasty Italian dishes include pasta carbonara (with eggs, cream, and bacon), as well as more unusual concoctions like *ravioli alla granchio* (crab and tiger prawn ravioli on a salad of rocket and garden peas with a chervil olive oil). ⊠ *4–6 Ness Walk* ☎ *01463/237377* 🖱 *MC, V* ⊙ *No lunch Sun.*

£££   ✕ **RocPool Restaurant.** Highly recommended by locals, the RocPool has a
BRASSERIE   calming mix of dark and light woods and cream and pale mint furnishings that creates a welcoming ambience. The frequently changing menus may include items such as sweet-pea-and-spinach risotto for lunch and loin of venison with creamed parsnips and wild mushrooms for dinner. ⊠ *1 Ness Walk* ☎ *01463/717274* 🖱 *MC, V* ⊙ *Closed Sun.*

WHERE TO STAY

There are many places to stay in Inverness, but if your goal is to explore the countryside, a hotel outside the center may be a good choice.

£–££   🏠 **Atholdene House.** This family-run stone villa dating from 1879 extends
★   a warm welcome with a roaring fire. Rooms are simply decorated with pine furniture. Downtown Inverness is a short walk away. **Pros:** reasonably priced; family friendly; quality produce at breakfast. **Cons:** rooms can get a little noisy. ⊠ *20 Southside Rd.* ☎ *01463/233565* ⊕ *www. atholdene.com* 🛏 *9 rooms* 🛋 *In-room: no a/c, no phone. In-hotel: Wi-Fi hotspot* 🖱 *MC, V* ⊙❍ *BP, CP.*

££   🏠 **Daviot Lodge.** Built in Highland-lodge style, the rooms are decorated in bold colors and have vibrant artwork. On room has a four-poster canopy bed and bay windows overlooking verdant pastures. Enthusiastic members of the fair-trade movement, the management serves locally sourced produce at breakfast. Daviot Lodge is 5 mi south of Inverness.

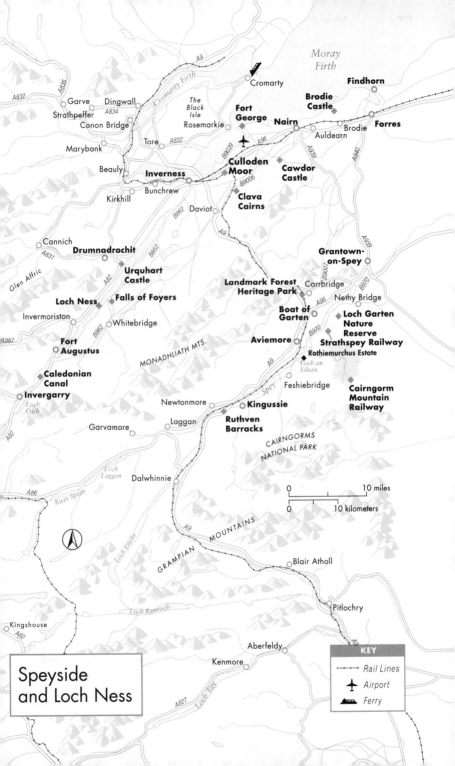

Moray
Firth

A9
Cromarty
A832
Garve   Dingwall
Strathpeffer   A834
Conon Bridge
A836

The
Black
Isle
Rosemarkie

Brodie
Castle
Nairn
Auldearn   Brodie   Forres
A939

A832   Tore
Marybank
Beauly
Kirkhill   Bunchrew
Inverness
Daviot

Fort
George
A96
Culloden
Moor
B9006
Clava
Cairns

Cawdor
Castle
A940
A939

B862

A9

A831
Cannich
Drumnadrochit

Glen Affric
A82

Loch Ness
Invermoristen
B862

Urquhart
Castle
Falls of Foyers
Whitebridge

Grantown-
on-Spey
A939
Carrbridge   B970
Nethy Bridge
A95
Boat of
Garten
B970
Loch Garten
Nature
Reserve
Strathspey Railway

Landmark Forest
Heritage Park

A887
Fort
Augustus
Caledonian
Canal
Invergarry
Loch
Oich
A82

MONADHLIATH MTS.

Aviemore
Rothiemurchus Estate
Loch an
Eilean
Spey
Feshiebridge
A9

Cairngorm
Mountain
Railway

Newtonmore   Kingussie
Laggan   Ruthven
Barracks
Garvamore

CAIRNGORMS
NATIONAL PARK

A86
Dalwhinnie
Loch
Laggan
River Spey

Loch Ericht

A9   MOUNTAINS

0   10 miles
0   10 kilometers

GRAMPIAN

Blair Atholl

Kingshouse
A82
Loch Rannoch

Pitlochry

Aberfeldy
Kenmore
A827
Loch Tay
A9

Speyside
and Loch Ness

Pros: excellent value; pastures grazed by cows and sheep; wheelchair access. **Cons:** dated decor. ⊠ *A9* ☎ *01463/772215* ⊕ *www. daviotlodge.co.uk* ⟿ *7 rooms* ⟨ *In-room: no a/c, DVD, Wi-Fi* ⊟ *MC, V* ⓧ *BP.*

£££   ⌂ **Dunain Park Hotel.** It's not difficult to relax at this atmospheric 18th-century mansion on 6 acres of wooded gardens. An open fire awaits you in the living room, a good place to sip a drink and browse through books and magazines. Antiques and traditional touches make the bedrooms equally cozy and attractive. The restaurant serves French-influenced Scottish dishes including upscale fish-and-chips: marinated scallops and butternut squash chips. The hotel is 2½ mi southwest of Inverness. **Pros:** attractive Victorian gardens; lounges full of country-house charm. **Cons:** quality of service can be inconsistent; not ideal for families with young children. ⊠ *A82, Dunain* ☎ *01463/230512* ⊕ *www.dunainparkhotel. co.uk* ⟿ *11 rooms, 2 cottages* ⟨ *In-room: no a/c. In-hotel: restaurant, laundry service, Internet terminal* ⊟ *AE, MC, V* ⓧ *BP.*

£££   ⌂ **Glendruidh House Hotel.** This former dower house (a dwelling given to the widow on an estate) exudes character from its turreted exterior to its circular drawing room warmed by open fires. Guest rooms have antique furnishings and look onto tranquil, mature gardens frequented by birds and badgers. Book in advance to sample fine food featuring local produce in the intimate dining room (for guests only). The hotel is 2 mi south of the heart of the city. **Pros:** quiet location; peaceful gardens. **Cons:** brief breakfast hours; outside city center. ⊠ *Old Edinburgh Rd. S* ☎ *01463/226499* ⊕ *www.cozzee-nessie-bed.co.uk* ⟿ *5 rooms* ⟨ *In-room: no a/c, Wi-Fi. In-hotel: bar, laundry service* ⊟ *AE, DC, MC, V* ⓧ *BP.*

££££   ⌂ **Glenmoriston Town House.** Great food and excellent fishing distinguish
★   this stylish hotel with exclusive rights to a stretch of the River Nairn. Most of the guest rooms are decorated in unfussy and calming hues, a good choice because they're generally on the small side. However, it's the restaurant, Abstract, which wins the plaudits: chef Gordon Ramsay helped transform it into one of the best in the region. The French-influenced cuisine, including dishes such as roasted scallops on a pea puree and sea bream with an oyster-and-citrus tartar, has garnered numerous awards. The bar may be the most sophisticated-looking place in town to sample a malt or two—indeed, there are nearly 200 to choose from and a decent cocktail list to boot. **Pros:** fabulous restaurant; comfortable beds. **Cons:** cramped rooms; lacks decent soundproofing. ⊠ *20 Ness Bank* ☎ *01463/223777* ⊕ *www.glenmoristontownhouse. com* ⟿ *30 rooms* ⟨ *In-room: no a/c, Wi-Fi. In-hotel: restaurant, room service, bar, laundry service* ⊟ *AE, DC, MC, V* ⓧ *BP.*

FISHING

The Great Glen is laced with rivers and lochs where you can fly-fish for salmon and trout. The fishing seasons are as follows: salmon, from early February through September or early October (depending on the area); brown trout, from March 15 to September 30; sea trout, from May through September or early October; rainbow trout. Sea angling from shore or boat is also possible. Tourist centers can provide information on locations, permits, and fishing rights.

££ 🏠 **Moyness House.** Scottish author Neil M. Gunn (1891–1973), known for short stories and novels that evoke images of the Highlands, such as *Morning Tide, Highland River,* and *Butcher's Broom,* once lived in this lovely Victorian villa. On a quiet residential street with well-trimmed hedges, it's a few minutes' walk from downtown Inverness. Careful decorative touches grace each subtly decorated room. The friendly owners provide excellent service and sound sightseeing advice. **Pros:** relaxing interiors; lovely garden; great location near the river. **Cons:** public rooms a bit fussy for some; books up quickly. ⊠ *6 Bruce GardensIV3 5EN* ☎ *01463/233836* ⊕ *www.moyness.co.uk* 🛏 *7 rooms* ♿ *In-room: no a/c, DVD, Wi-Fi* ⊟ *AE, MC, V* ⏐⚏⏐ *BP.*

££ 🏠 **Trafford Bank.** A 15-minute walk from downtown Inverness, this former manse is the perfect place to base yourself. Lorraine Freel has a talent for interior design and pays attentions to details like bespoke chairs in the dining room and handmade wallpaper in some of the rooms. Homemade scones often accompany breakfast, and the coffee is excellent. **Pros:** welcoming atmosphere; stylish rooms; relaxing vibe. **Cons:** rooms on the small side. ⊠ *96 Fairfield Rd.* ☎ *0143/241414* ⊕ *www. traffordbankguesthouse.co.uk* 🛏 *5 rooms* ♿ *In-room: no a/c, DVD, Wi-Fi* ⊟ *AE, DC, MC, V* ⏐⚏⏐ *BP.*

NIGHTLIFE AND THE ARTS

BARS AND LOUNGES **Blackfriars Pub** (⊠ *93–95 Academy St.* ☎ *01463/233881*) prides itself on its cask-conditioned ales. You can enjoy one to the accompaniment of regular live entertainment including jazz nights and *ceilidhs* (a mix of country dancing, music, and song; pronounced *kay*-lees) and poetry readings. **Gellion's Bar** (⊠ *14 Bridge St.* ☎ *01463/233648*) claims to be Inverness's oldest pub, dating from 1841. It hosts live music nightly, with ceilidhs on Saturday and the occasional Wednesday from 5 to 8 PM. **Hootenany** (⊠ *67 Church St.* ☎ *01463/233651*) is an odd combination of Scottish pub, concert hall, and Thai restaurant. The food is highly recommended by locals.

THEATER There's plenty of drama at the **Eden Court Theatre** (⊠ *Bishops Rd.* ★ ☎ *01463/234234* ⊕ *www.eden-court.co.uk*), but the varied program includes movies, music, comedy, ballet, pantomime, and musicals. Check out the art gallery and the brightly lighted café, and take a walk around the magnificent Bishop's Palace.

GOLF

Inverness Golf Club, established in 1883, welcomes visitors to its parkland course 1 mi from downtown. ⊠ *Culcabock Rd.* ☎ *01463/239882* ⊕ *www.invernessgolfclub.co.uk* 🏌 *18 holes, 6,256 yds, par 69.*

Torvean Golf Course is a municipal course with one of the longest par-5s (565 yards) in the north of Scotland. ⊠ *Glenurquhart Rd.* ☎ *01463/ 225651* ⊕ *www.torveangolfclub.co.uk* 🏌 *18 holes, 5,784 yds, par 68.*

SHOPPING

Although Inverness has the usual indoor shopping malls and department stores—including Marks and Spencer—the most interesting goods are in the specialty outlets in and around town. Don't miss the atmospheric indoor **Victorian Market** (✉ *Academy St.*), built in 1870, which houses more than 40 privately owned specialty shops.

BOOKSTORES **Leakey's Secondhand Bookshop** (✉ *Greyfriars Hall, Church St.* ☎ *01463/239947*) claims to be the biggest secondhand bookstore in Scotland. When you get tired of leafing through some of the 100,000 or so titles and maps, climb to the mezzanine café and study the cavernous church interior. Antique prints are housed on the balcony.

CLOTHING **Duncan Chisholm and Sons** (✉ *47–51 Castle St.* ☎ *01463/234599*) specializes in Highland dress and tartans. Mail-order and made-to-measure services are available.

GALLERIES The **Castle Gallery** (✉ *43 Castle St.* ☎ *01463/729512*) sells contemporary paintings, sculpture, prints and crafts. It occasionally hosts exhibitions by up and coming artists. The **Riverside Gallery** (✉ *11 Bank St.* ☎ *01463/224781*) sells paintings, etchings, and prints of Highland landscapes, as well as abstract and representational contemporary work by Highland artists.

LOCAL SPECIALTIES At **Moniack Castle** (✉ *A862, 7 mi west of Inverness toward Beauly, Kirkhill* ☎ *01463/831283*) you can tour the castle and buy wines produced from Scottish ingredients, such as birch sap. The company also makes jams, marmalade, and other preserves.

CULLODEN MOOR

8 mi east of Inverness.

GETTING HERE AND AROUND

Driving along the B9006 from Inverness is the easiest way to Culloden Moor, and there's a generous car park to handle many visitors. Local buses also run from Inverness to the battlefield.

EXPLORING

Culloden Moor was the scene of the last major battle fought on British soil—to this day considered one of the most infamous and tragic of all. Here, on a cold April day in 1746, the outnumbered, fatigued Jacobite forces of Bonnie Prince Charlie were destroyed by the superior firepower of George II's army. The victorious commander, the duke of Cumberland (George II's son), earned the name of the "Butcher" of Cumberland for the bloody reprisals carried out by his men on Highland families, Jacobite or not, caught in the vicinity. In the battle itself, the duke's army—greatly outnumbering the Scots—killed more than 1,000 soldiers. The National Trust for Scotland has re-created a slightly eerie version of the battlefield as it looked in 1746 that you can explore with a guided audio tour. An innovative visitor center enables you to get closer to the sights and sounds of the battle and to interact with the characters involved. Academic research and technology have helped re-create the Gaelic dialect, song, and music of the time. The excellent on-site café serves homemade soups, sandwiches, and cakes. ✉ *B9006* ☎ *0844/4932159* ⊕ *www.nts.org.uk/Culloden* 💷 *£10* ☼ *Nov.–Dec. and Feb.–Mar., daily 10–4; Apr.–Oct., daily 9–6; last entry half hr before closing.*

CLOSE UP

Bonnie Prince Charlie

His life became the stuff of legends. Charles Edward Louis John Casimir Silvester Maria Stuart, better known as Bonnie Prince Charlie or the Young Pretender, was born in Rome in 1720. The grandson of ousted King James II of England, Scotland, and Ireland (King James VII of Scotland) and son of James Stuart, the Old Pretender, he was the focus of Jacobite hopes to reclaim the throne of Scotland. Charles was charming and attractive, and he enjoyed more than the occasional drink.

In 1745 Charles led a Scottish uprising to restore his father to the throne. He sailed to the Outer Hebrides with only a few men but with promised support from France. When that support failed to arrive, he sought help from the Jacobite supporters, many from the Highland clans, who were faithful to his family. With 6,000 men behind him, Charles saw victory in Prestonpans and Falkirk, but the tide turned when he lied to his men about additional Jacobite troops waiting south of the border. When these fictitious troops did not materialize, his army retreated to Culloden where, on the April 16, 1746, they were massacred.

Charles escaped to the Isle of Benbecula where he met and is rumored to have fallen in love with Flora MacDonald. After he had hidden there for a week, Flora dressed him as her maid and brought him to sympathizers on the Isle of Skye. They helped him escape to France.

Scotland endured harsh reprisals from the government after the rebellion. As for Charles, he spent the rest of his life in drunken exile, taking the title count of Albany. In 1772 he married Princess Louise of Stolberg-Gedern, only to separate from her eight years later. He died a broken man in Rome in 1788.

—by Fiona G. Parrott

Not far from Culloden, on a narrow road southeast of the battlefield, are the **Clava Cairns**, dating from the Bronze Age. In a cluster among the trees, these stones and monuments form a large ring with passage graves, which consist of a central chamber below a cairn, reached via a tunnel. Placards explain the graves' significance. ⊠ *B851*.

NAIRN

12 mi east of Culloden Moor, 17 mi east of Inverness, 92 mi west of Aberdeen.

This once-prosperous fishing village has something of a split personality. King James VI (1566–1625) once boasted of a town so large the residents at either end spoke different languages. This was a reference to Nairn, whose fisherfolk, living by the sea, spoke Lowland Scots, whereas its uptown farmers and crofters spoke Gaelic. Nearby is Nairn Castle, loaded with history. East of Nairn pier is a long beach, great for a stroll.

GETTING HERE AND AROUND

A car gives you the most flexibility, but Nairn is close to Inverness (via B9006/B9091) and regular local buses service the town.

EXPLORING

The fishing boats have moved to larger ports, but Nairn's historic flavor has been preserved at the **Nairn Museum,** in a handsome Georgian building in the center of town. Exhibits emphasize artifacts, photographs, and model boats relating to the town's fishing past. A genealogy service is also offered, and there are occasional craft demonstrations. A library in the same building has a strong local history section. ⊠ *Viewfield House, Viewfield Dr.* ☎ *01667/456791* ⊕ *www.nairnmuseum.co.uk* ⊠ *£3* ⊗ *Apr.–Oct., weekdays 10–4:30, Sat. 10–1.*

⊗
Fodor's Choice
★
Shakespeare's (1564–1616) Macbeth was Thane of Cawdor, but the sense of history that exists within the turreted walls of **Cawdor Castle** is more than fictional. Cawdor is a lived-in castle, not an abandoned, decaying structure. The earliest part of the castle is the 14th-century central tower; the rooms contain family portraits, tapestries, fine furniture, and paraphernalia reflecting 600 years of history. Outside the castle walls are sheltered gardens and woodland walks. Children will have a ball exploring the lush and mysterious Big Wood, with its wildflowers and varied wildlife. There are lots of creepy stories and fantastic tales amid the dank dungeons and drawbridges. If you like it here, the estate has cottages to rent. ⊠ *B9090, 5 mi southwest of Nairn, Cawdor* ☎ *01667/404401* ⊕ *www.cawdorcastle.com* ⊠ *Grounds £4.50; castle £8* ⊗ *May–mid-Oct., daily 10–5.*

WHERE TO STAY

£££££ ⊞ **Boath House.** An elegant Regency survivor, this stunning 1820s manor house is surrounded by 20 acres of lovingly nurtured gardens. There's a 400-year-old walled garden you're welcome to explore. The spacious rooms have unique touches like the pair of cast iron tubs in the huge bathroom of Room 3. In the entrance hall, numerous awards boast of the restaurant's culinary skill; even if you do not stay here, you may want to come here for a special meal. Guests can choose to include dinner in the room rate. The house is a registered art gallery, so many of the oil paintings that grace the walls are for sale. An Aveda spa on the lower level provides additional rest and relaxation. **Pros:** excellent dining; well-kept grounds; relaxed atmosphere. **Cons:** rooms may have quirks; expensive rate; airplane noise can puncture the silence. ⊠ *A96, Auldearn* ☎ *01667/454896* ⊕ *www.boath-house.com* ⌕ *8 rooms* ♿ *In-room: no a/c. In-hotel: restaurant, spa* ⊟ *AE, MC, V* ❙⊘❙ *BP.*

GOLF

Nairn's courses are highly regarded by golfers and are very popular, so book far in advance. **Nairn Dunbar Golf Club,** founded in 1899, is a difficult course with gorse-lined fairways and lovely sea views. ⊠ *Lochloy Rd.* ☎ *01667/452741* ⊕ *www.nairndunbar.com* ⚑ *18 holes, 6,765 yds, par 72.*

★ **Nairn Golf Club,** founded in 1887, hosted the 1999 Walker Cup on its Championship Course, a traditional Scottish coastal golf links with what are claimed to be the finest greens in Scotland. ⊠ *Seabank Rd. OV12 5AE* ☎ *01667/453208* ⊕ *www.nairngolfclub.co.uk* ⚑ *18 holes, 6,721 yds, par 72.*

SHOPPING

At **Auldearn Antiques** (✉ *Dalmore Manse, Lethen Rd., Auldearn* ☎ *01667/453087*), 3 mi east of Nairn, it's easy to spend an hour wandering around the old church filled with furniture, fireplaces, architectural antiques, and linens, and the converted farmsteads, with their tempting antique (or just old) chinaware and textiles.

Visit **Brodie Countryfare** (✉ *A96, Brodie* ☎ *01309/641555*), 6 mi east of Nairn, only if you're feeling flush: you may covet the unusual knitwear, quality designer clothing and shoes, gifts, and toys, but they are *not* cheap. The excellent restaurant, on the other hand, is quite inexpensive.

FORT GEORGE

10 mi west of Nairn.

GETTING HERE AND AROUND

Off the A96, the main road running east from Inverness, Fort George is most easily reached by car; turn north on the B90060.

EXPLORING

★ As a direct result of the battle at Culloden, the nervous government in London ordered the construction of a large fort on a promontory reaching into the Moray Firth: **Fort George** was started in 1748 and completed some 20 years later. It's perhaps the best-preserved 18th-century military fortification in Europe. A visitor center and tableaux at the fort portray the 18th-century Scottish soldier's way of life. The on-site **Highlanders Museum** (☎ *0131/3108701* ☐ *Free* ☉ *Apr.–Sept., daily 9:30–5:15; Oct.–Mar., weekdays10–4*) gives you a glimpse of the fort's history. ✉ *B9006, Ardersier* ☎ *01667/460232* ⊕ *www.historic-scotland.gov.uk* ☐ *£6.70* ☉ *Apr.–Sept., daily 9:30–5:30; Oct.–Mar., daily 9:30–4:30; last admission 45 mins before closing.*

FORRES

10 mi east of Nairn.

The burgh of Forres is everything a Scottish medieval town should be, with a handsome tolbooth (the former courthouse and prison) as its centerpiece. It's remarkable how well the old buildings have adapted to their modern retail uses. With two distilleries—one still operating, the other preserved as a museum—Forres is a key point on the Malt Whisky Trail; Brodie Castle is also nearby.

GETTING HERE AND AROUND

Forres is easy to reach by car from Inverness on the A96. Daily ScotRail trains run here from Inverness and Aberdeen.

EXPLORING

At the eastern end of town, don't miss **Sueno's Stone,** a soaring pillar of stone carved with ranks of cavalry, foot soldiers, and dying victims. The stone is said to commemorate a 10th-century victory.

Benromach Distillery is the smallest distillery in Moray and was founded in 1898. It's now owned by whisky specialist Gordon and MacPhail, who stocks a vast range of malts. An informative hourly tour ends with a tutored nosing and tasting. ✉ *Invererne Rd.* ☎ *01309/675968* ⊕ *www. benromach.com* 💷 *£3.50* ⊙ *Oct.–Apr., weekdays 10–4; May–Sept., Mon.–Sat. 9:30–5; Sun. noon–4.*

Dallas Dhu Historic Distillery, the last port of call on the Malt Whisky Trail, was the last distillery built in the 19th century. No longer a working distillery, the entire structure is open to visitors. An audiovisual presentation tells the story of Scotch whisky. ✉ *Mannachie Rd.* ☎ *01309/ 676548* 💷 *£5.20* ⊙ *Apr.–Sept., daily 9:30–6:30; Oct.–Mar., Sat.–Wed. 9:30–4:30.*

At **Brodie Castle,** 2 mi west of Forres, the original medieval castle was rebuilt and extended in the 17th and 19th centuries. Fine examples of late-17th-century plasterwork are preserved in the Dining Room and Blue Sitting Room; an impressive library and a superb collection of pictures extend into the 20th century. Brodie Castle is in the care of the National Trust for Scotland. ✉ *A96, Brodie* ☎ *0844/493–2156* ⊕ *www. nts.org.uks* 💷 *Grounds free, castle £8.50* ⊙ *Grounds daily 10:30– sunset. Castle Apr., July, and Aug., daily 10:30–4:30; May and Sept.– Mar., Sun.–Wed. 10:30–4:30.*

FINDHORN

6 mi north of Forres, 26 mi east of Inverness.

Findhorn stretches along the edge of the semi-enclosed Findhorn Bay, which is excellent bird-watching territory.

GETTING HERE AND AROUND

It's easy to get here from Inverness by taking the A96 to the B9011. Without a car, take a train or bus to Forres and get a taxi to Findhorn.

EXPLORING

The **Findhorn Ecovillage,** just 6 mi from Forres, is an education center dedicated to developing "new ways of living infused with spiritual values." Drawing power from their own wind turbines, village inhabitants farm and garden to sustain themselves through direct connection with the earth. A visit—check in at Visitor Reception for information—affords a thought-provoking glimpse into the lives of the ultra-independent villagers. See homes made out of whisky barrels, and the Universal Hall, made of wood and beautiful engraved glass. The Phoenix Shop sells organic foodstuffs and handmade crafts, and the Blue Angel Café serves organic and vegetarian fare. ✉ *The Park* ☎ *01309/690311* ⊕ *www. findhorn.org* 💷 *Eco village free, tour £3* ⊙ *Dec.–Feb., weekdays 10–5; Mar., Apr., Oct., and Nov., weekdays 10–5, Sat. 1–4; May–Sept., weekdays 10–5, weekends 1–4.*

GRANTOWN-ON-SPEY

24 mi south of Forres, 14 mi northeast of Aviemore.

The sturdy settlement of Grantown-on-Spey, set amid tall pines that flank the River Spey, is a classic Scottish planned town. The community was laid out by the local landowner, in this case Sir James Grant, in 1776.

Today it's a center for sports, including fishing. It has handsome buildings in silver granite and some good shopping for locally made crafts.

GETTING HERE AND AROUND

If you don't have a car, the easiest way to get to Grantown-on-Spey is taking the train to Carrbridge and connecting via a local bus. By car, take the A940 and A939 from Forres or the A9 and A95 from Aviemore.

WHERE TO STAY

£££ ★ ⚏ **The Pines Hotel.** Grantown's elegant and relaxing 19th-century atmosphere is encapsulated at this well-run small hotel within walking distance of the center as well as woodlands. Flower borders and immaculate lawns surround the handsome country house, which is full of interesting antiques, artwork, and curios. After a day's outdoor pursuits, guests can unwind with a malt whisky in the cozy lounges or play genteel parlor games. The rooms have character and comfort, with well-chosen artworks and quality bed linens. A fine restaurant serves innovative Scots fare in dishes such as Scottish salmon with pistachio served on a bed of olive oil mashed potatoes with red pepper and corn salsa. **Pros:** gardens with a pond and resident red squirrels; lovely library. **Cons:** meals are pricey. ⊠ *Woodside Ave.,* ☎ *01479/872092* ⊕ *www.thepinesgrantown. co.uk* ⬫ *5 rooms* ⬫ *In-room: no a/c. In-hotel: restaurant* ▭ *DC, MC, V* ⊗ *Closed Nov.–Mar.* †◎† *BP, MAP.*

SHOPPING

Ewe and Me (⊠ *82 High St.* ☎ *01479/872911*) is a well-stocked gift shop with silver jewelry, glassware, Highland Stoneware platters and jugs, stuffed toys, and greeting cards.

Speyside Heather Centre (⊠ *Skye of Curr Rd.* ☎ *01479/851359*) has 200 to 300 varieties of heather for sale. Of course there's a demonstration about the uses of heather. Should you need sustenance, head to the center's Clootie Dumpling restaurant.

BOAT OF GARTEN

11 mi southwest of Grantown-on-Spey; 6 mi northeast of Aviemore.

In the peaceful village of Boat of Garten, the scent of pine trees mingles with an equally evocative smell—that of steam trains. You can take a nostalgic steam train trip on the Strathspey Steam Railway between Aviemore and Boat of Garden.

GETTING HERE AND AROUND

This charming town is an easy drive from Inverness or Aviemore via the A9 and the A95 and from Grantown via the B970. It's also serviced by local buses, and some people travel here on the Strathspey Steam Train.

EXPLORING

↻ In Boat of Garten you can hop aboard the **Strathspey Steam Railway** (☎ *01479/810725* ⊕ *www.strathspeyrailway.co.uk*). The oily scent of smoke and steam hangs faintly in the air near the authentically preserved train station. Travel in old-fashioned style and enjoy superb views of the high and often white domes of the Cairngorm Mountains. Breakfasts, lunches, and special dinners are served on board from March to mid-September.

Set in the heart of Abernethy Forest, the **Loch Garten Nature Reserve** offers a glimpse of the osprey, a large fishing bird that come here to breed. The reserve, one of the last stands of ancient Scots pines in Scotland, attracts a host of birds, including the bright crossbill and the crested tit. You might also spot the rarely seen red squirrel. The sanctuary, about 1 mi east of Boat of Garten via the B970, is administered by the Royal Society for the Protection of Birds. ⊠ *B970* ☏ *01479/831476* ⊕ *www.rspb.org.uk* ✉ *£3* ☉ *Apr.– Aug., daily 10–6.*

☾ **Landmark Forest Theme Park,** 4 mi northwest of Boat of Garten, has entertainments such as a Timber Trail with a fire tower you can climb, a steam-powered sawmill, and a Clydesdale horse that hauls the logs. At the forestry workshop, you can try out crosscut sawing. Kids will want to check out the Wild Forest Maze, terrifyingly steep waterslides, a climbing wall, miniature cars and trucks, and an adventure playground. ■TIP➔ **Plan on spending about three to five hours here.** To get to Carrbridge, take the quiet B9153, rather than the crowded A9. ⊠ *B9153, Carrbridge* ☏ *0800/7313446* ⊕ *www.landmark-centre.co.uk* ✉ *£10.55* ☉ *Apr.–mid-July, daily 10–6; mid-July and Aug., daily 10–7; Sept.–Mar., daily 10–5; last admission 1 hr before closing.*

AVIEMORE

6 mi southwest of Boat of Garten, 30 mi south of Inverness.

Once a quiet junction on the Highland Railway, Aviemore now has all the brashness and concrete boxiness of a year-round holiday resort. It's near some lovely country that's perfect for walking and kayaking in summer and skiing in winter.

■TIP➔ **Be forewarned: this region can get very cold above 3,000 feet, and weather conditions can change rapidly, even in the middle of summer.**

GETTING HERE AND AROUND

The A9, Scotland's major north–south artery, runs past Aviemore. From Boat of Garten, take the B970. The town is serviced by regular trains and buses from Inverness.

ESSENTIALS

Visitor Information Aviemore (⊠ *Grampian Rd.* ☏ *0845/2255121* ⊕ *www. visitaviemore.com*).

EXPLORING

★ **Cairngorms National Park,** a rugged wilderness of mountains, moorlands, glens, and lochs, is the country's second oldest national park. Past Loch Morlich at the high parking lot on the exposed shoulders of the Cairngorm Mountains are dozens of trails for hiking and cycling. The park is especially popular with birding enthusiasts, as it's the best place to see the Scottish crossbill, the only bird unique to Britain. Weather conditions in the park change abruptly, so be sure to have the proper gear or seek out many of the guided options. This is a massive park, but a good place to start exploring is the visitor center in Aviemore. ⊠ *Aviemore* ☎ *01479/873535* ⊕ *www.cairngorms.co.uk.*

The **CairnGorm Mountain Railway,** a funicular railway to the top of Cairn Gorm (the mountain that gives its name to the Cairngorms), operates both during and after the ski season and affords extensive views of the broad valley of the Spey. At the top is a visitor center and restaurant. Prebooking is recommended. ⊠ *B970* ☎ *01479/861261* ⊕ *www. cairngormmountain.co.uk* ⊡ *£9.50* ⊙ *Daily 10–4:30.*

☾ On the high slopes of the Cairngorms, you may see the reindeer herd that was introduced here in the 1950s. Inquire at the **Cairngorm Reindeer Centre,** 6 mi east of Aviemore by Loch Morlich, about accompanying the herders on their daily rounds. Daily visits from May to September depart at 11 and 2:30. The reindeer are docile creatures and seem to enjoy human company. Be sure to wear waterproof gear, as conditions can be wet and muddy. ⊠ *B970, Loch Morlich, Glen More Forest Park* ☎ *01479/861228* ⊕ *www.reindeer-company.demon.co.uk* ⊡ *£8* ⊙ *Feb.–Dec., daily 10–5.*

★ The place that best sums up Speyside's piney ambience is probably a nature reserve called **Loch an Eilean.** There are great low-level paths around the tree-rimmed loch (perfect for bikes) or longer trails to Glen Einich. A converted cottage beside Loch an Eilean serves as a visitor center. The lake is on the **Rothiemurchus Estate,** which offers several diversions, including hiking, biking, fly-fishing for salmon and trout, dogsledding, clay-pigeon shooting, and farm-shop tastings of estate-produced beef, venison, and trout. ⊠ *B970* ☎ *01479/812345* ⊕ *www. rothiemurchus.net* ⊡ *Free* ⊙ *Daily 9:30–4:30.*

9

WHERE TO EAT

£ ✕ **Mountain Cafe.** On the main street in Aviemore, Mountain Café is
CAFÉ a down-to-earth find in this touristy town. It's known for hearty all-day breakfasts, well-seasoned sandwiches and burgers, and rich coffee. Leave room for the cakes, which are made on the premises. Service can be slow at peak times, meaning you may have to wait for a table. There are great views of the Cairngorms from the dining room. ⊠ *111 Grampian Rd.* ☎ *01479 812 473* ⊕ *www.mountaincafe-aviemore.co.uk* ⊟ *MC, V* ⊙ *No dinner.*

SPORTS AND THE OUTDOORS

★ Scotland's National Outdoor Training Centre, **Glenmore Lodge** (⊠ *B970* ☎ *01479/861256*), 6 mi east of Aviemore in Cairngorms National Park, is your best bet for trying a new activity or enhancing your outdoor skills. Take your pick from the impressive courses (many are multiday)

CLOSE UP

Cairngorms National Park

Britain's newest national park is also its largest, covering nearly 1,400 square mi of countryside. At its heart is a wild arctic landscape that sits on a granite plateau. Five of Scotland's nine 4,000-feet-high mountains are found in this range, and there are 13 more over 3,000 feet. These rounded mountains, including Cairn Gorm (meaning "blue hill" in Gaelic) and Ben Macdui, the second highest in Britain at 4,295 feet, were formed at the end of the last ice age. The Larig Ghru Pass, a stunning U-shape glen, was formed by the retreating glacier.

Hikers, underestimate this landscape at your peril: the fierce conditions often found on the Cairngorms plateau have claimed many lives. If you venture out into it, make sure you are well-prepared and have informed someone of your planned route and estimated return time.

The environment supports rare arctic-alpine and tundra plant and animal species (a quarter of Britain's threatened species) including flora such as the least willow and alpine blue-sow thistle, and birds such as the ptarmigan, Scottish crossbill, and dotterel. Lower down the slopes, terrain that was once filled with woodland is now characterized by heather, cotton grass, and sphagnum moss. This open expanse allows visitors to glimpse wild animals such as the golden eagle, roe deer, or red deer.

Fragments of the ancient Caledonian forest (largely Scots pine, birch, and rowan) remain and are home to pine martins, red squirrels, and capercaillie (a large grouse). Studding these forests are dramatic glens and the rivers Spey, Don, and Dee, which are home to Atlantic salmon, otters, and freshwater pearl mussels.

on rock and ice climbing, hiking, kayaking, open boating, ski touring, mountain biking, and more. Some classes are for kids over 14. There's basic accommodation and equipment rental at the center, along with superb facilities such as an indoor climbing wall.

KINGUSSIE

13 mi southwest of Aviemore.

Set in a wide glen, Kinguissie is a pretty town east of the Monadhliadh Mountains. The town has great distant views of the Cairngorms.

GETTING HERE AND AROUND

From Aviemore, Kingussie is easy to reach by car via the A9 and the A86.

EXPLORING

In Newtonmore, the **Highland Folk Museum** allows you to explore reconstructed Highland buildings, including a Victorian-era schoolhouse, and watch tailors, clockmakers, and joiners demonstrating their trades. Walking paths (or an old-fashioned bus) take you to an 18th-century township that includes a feal house (made of turf) and a weaver's house. Throughout the museum there are hands-on exhibitions like a working quern stone for grinding grain, making this a great outing for kids. ⊠ *Kinguissie Rd., Newton-more* ☎ *01540/673551* ⊕ *www. highlandfolk.com* 🖙 *Free* ⊙ *Apr.– Aug., daily 10:30–5:30; Sept.–Oct., daily 11–4:30.*

Ruthven Barracks, which from a distance looks like a ruined castle on a mound, is redolent with tales of "the '45" (as the last Jacobite rebellion is often called). The defeated Jacobite forces rallied here after the battle at Culloden, but then abandoned and blew up the government outpost they had earlier captured. You'll see its crumbling yet imposing stone outline as you approach Kingussie. ⊠ *B970, ½ mi south of Kingussie* ☎ *01667/ 460232* ⊕ *www.historic-scotland. gov.uk* 🖙 *Free* ⊙ *Daily 24 hrs.*

BIKING THE GLEN

A dedicated bicycle path, created by Scotland's National Cycle Networks, runs from Glasgow to Inverness, passing through Fort William and Kingussie. Additionally, a good network of back roads snakes around Inverness and toward Nairn. The B862/B852, which runs by the southeast side of Loch Ness, has little traffic and is a good bet for cyclists. Stay off the A9, however, as it's busy with vehicular traffic on both sides of Aviemore. The very busy A82 main road, along the northwest bank of Loch Ness via Drumnadrochit, is for the same reason not recommended for cyclists.

WHERE TO EAT AND STAY

££   ✕ **Blasta.** On Newtonmore's nar-
BRITISH   row main street, this restaurant is in the town's old post office and still utilizes the chunky oak counter. Dark wood floors, light walls and well-chosen art provide a great backdrop for the generous dishes, which may include the unlikely but delicious vegetarian moussaka (layered with eggplant and vegetarian haggis), Creag Meagaidh venison, and sage-and-sea-salt potatoes. Order a perfect espresso to end the meal. ⊠ *Main St., Newtonmore* ☎ *01540/673231* ⊕ *www.blasta-restaurant. co.uk* 🖃 *MC, V* ⊙ *No lunch. No dinner Sun. and Mon.*

£££££   ✕ **The Cross.** This former tweed mill, with a burn (a narrow river) run-
BRITISH   ning alongside its stone walls, is set in 4 acres of woodlands. The inti-
★   mate dining room, where the stone walls have been painted a creamy white, is warmed by a crackling fireplace. The food here is smart and bold, with dishes such as baked Scrabster brill, slow-roasted Ayrshire pork, and honey-baked apricots. Each dish reveals an intimate knowledge of textures and flavors. If you like it here so much you don't want to leave, you'll be glad to know that there are also rooms for rent. ⊠ *Tweed Mill Brae, Ardbroilach Rd.* ☎ *01540/661166* ⊕ *www.thecross. co.uk* 🖃 *AE, MC, V* ⊙ *Closed Jan. No dinner Sun. and Mon.*

££   🛏 **Coig Na Shee.** This century-old Highland lodge has a warm and cozy atmosphere. Each bedroom is unique, with well-chosen furnishings and soothing colors schemes. The property is surrounded by trees, providing lots of privacy. The Cairngorms are visible from some rooms, reminding you just how close you are to the mountains. The location is near several great dinner options. **Pros:** excellent rooms; quiet location; great walks from house. **Cons:** a bit out of the way. ⊠ *Laggan Rd., Newtonmore* ☎ *01540/670109* ⊕ *www.coignashee.co.uk* 🛏 *5 rooms* 🖏 *In-room: no a/c, no phone, DVD, Wi-Fi* 🖃 *AE, DC, MC, V* 🍴 *BP.*

9

EN ROUTE A stretch of the A86, quite narrow in some places, hugs the western shore of Loch Laggan. It has superb views of the mountainous heartlands to the north, and, over the silvery spine of hills known as the Grey Corries, culminates with views of Ben Nevis to the south. Halfway along the loch is the **Creag Meagaidh Nature Reserve,** a sublime picnic spot and a good base for walks into the restored woodland below the spectacular ice-carved crags of Coire Ardair. ⊠ *Aberarder, Kinlochlaggan* ☎ *01528/544265* ⊕ *www.nnr-scotland.org.uk.*

INVERGARRY AND THE CALEDONIAN CANAL

54 mi west of Kingussie.

Traveling north up the Great Glen takes you parallel to Loch Lochy (on the eastern shore) and over the Caledonian Canal at Laggan Locks, north of Invergarry. From this beautiful spot, which offers stunning vistas of lochs, mountains, and glens in all directions, you can look back on the impressive profile of Ben Nevis.

The canal, which links the lochs of the Great Glen—Loch Lochy, Loch Oich, and Loch Ness—owes its origins to a combination of military as well as political pressures that emerged at the time of the Napoleonic Wars with France: for the most part, the British needed a better and faster way to get naval vessels from one side of Scotland to the other. The great Scottish engineer Thomas Telford (1757–1834) surveyed the route in 1803. The canal, which took 19 years to complete, has 29 locks and 42 gates. Telford ingeniously took advantage of the three lochs that lie in the Great Glen, which have a combined length of 45 mi, so that only 22 mi of canal had to be constructed to connect the lochs and complete the waterway from coast to coast.

GETTING HERE AND AROUND

A car is by far the best way to get here, either from Inverness on the A82 or from Kingussie on A86 and A82. Buses run here, but not frequently enough to make them a convenient way to travel.

WHERE TO STAY

£££ 🔠 **Glengarry Castle Hotel.** This rambling Victorian baronial mansion, ★ tucked away in Invergarry, makes a good base for touring the area; the village is just south of Loch Ness and within easy reach of the Great Glen's most popular sights. The alluringly old-fashioned rooms have traditional Victorian decor; some more expensive rooms have superb views over Loch Oich. Try the restaurant for classic Scottish fare with a contemporary twist, such as fillet of Angus beef with whisky and tarragon sauce or oak-smoked salmon parcels filled with chive-scented scrambled eggs. On the grounds are the ruins of Invergarry Castle, a seat of the MacDonnell clan. The hotel entrance is south of the A82–A87 road junction. **Pros:** atmospheric building and gardens; good-value takeout lunches; family rooms available. **Cons:** showers not always piping hot; steps to climb. ⊠ *A82* ☎ *01809/501254* ⊕ *www.glengarry. net* ⤴ *26 rooms* ⚐ *In-room: no a/c, Wi-Fi. In-hotel: restaurant, tennis court, water sports, Wi-Fi hotspot* ▭ *MC, V* ⊗ *Closed mid-Nov.–mid-Mar.* ⦿ *BP.*

FORT AUGUSTUS AND LOCH NESS

7 mi north of Invergarry, 33 mi south of Inverness.

A bustling small town at the head of the Caledonian Canal and on the banks of Loch Ness, Fort Augustus is a great place to begin walking and cycling excursions, or to sit by the canal locks watching boats sail between Loch Ness and Loch Laggan.

GETTING HERE AND AROUND

Fort Augustus is an easy drive from Inverness or Invergarry on the A82. Buses run frequently, as this is a busy tourist destination.

ESSENTIALS

Visitor Information **Caledonian Canal Visitor Centre** (✉ *Ardchattan House, Canalside* ☎ *01320/366493* ⊕ *www.scottishcanals.co.uk*).

EXPLORING

The best place to see the locks of the Caledonian Canal in action is at **Fort Augustus,** at the southern tip of Loch Ness. In the village center considerable canal activity takes place at a series of locks that rise from Loch Ness. Fort Augustus itself was captured by the Jacobite clans during the 1745 Rebellion. Later the fort was rebuilt as a Benedictine abbey, but the monks no longer live here.

The **Clansman Centre** (✉ *Canalside, Fort Augustus* ☎ *01320/366444* ⊕ *www.scottish-swords.com*) in a handsome Victorian building, tells some stirring tales about life in this region. The gift shop sells Celtic jewelry, traditional Highland garb, and ceremonial armor.

From the B862, just east of Fort Augustus, you can get your first good long view of the formidable and famous **Loch Ness,** which has a greater volume of water than any other Scottish loch, a maximum depth of more than 800 feet, and its own monster—at least according to popular myth. Early travelers who passed this way included English lexicographer Dr. Samuel Johnson (1709–84) and his guide and biographer, James Boswell (1740–95), who were on their way to the Hebrides in 1783. They remarked at the time about the poor condition of the population and the squalor of their homes. Another early travel writer and naturalist, Thomas Pennant (1726–98), noted that the loch kept the locality frost-free in winter. Even General Wade came here, his troops blasting and digging a road up much of the eastern shore. None of these observant early travelers ever made mention of a monster. Clearly, they had not read the local guidebooks.

EN ROUTE A more leisurely alternative to the fast-moving traffic on the busy A82 to Inverness, and one that combines monster-watching with peaceful road touring, is to take the **B862** from Fort Augustus and follow the east bank of Loch Ness; join the B852 just beyond Whitebridge and take the opportunity to view the waterfalls at Foyers. The B862 runs around the end of Loch Ness, then climbs into moorland and forestry plantation. The half-hidden track beside the road is a remnant of the military road built by General Wade. Loch Ness quickly drops out of sight but is soon replaced by the peaceful, reedy Loch Tarff.

9

DRUMNADROCHIT

21 mi north of Fort Augustus, 14 mi south of Inverness.

A tourist hub at the curve of the road, Drumnadrochit is not known for its style or culture, but it does seem to attract people interested in mythical monsters. There aren't many good restaurants, but there are some solid hotels.

GETTING HERE AND AROUND

It's easy to get here from Fort Augustus or Inverness via the A82, either by car or by local bus.

EXPLORING

If you're in search of the infamous beast Nessie, head to Drumnadrochit and the **Loch Ness Exhibition Centre,** which explores the facts and the fakes, the photographs, the unexplained sonar contacts, and the sincere testimony of eyewitnesses. You'll have to make up your own mind on Nessie. All that's really known is that Loch Ness's huge volume of water has a warming effect on the local weather, making the loch conducive to mirages in still, warm conditions. Whether or not the *bestia aquatilis* lurks in the depths is more than ever in doubt since 1994, when the man who took one of the most convincing photos of Nessie, confessed on his deathbed that it was a fake. You can take a cruise of the loch from the center, too. ⊠ *A82* ☎ *01456/450573* ⊕ *www.loch-ness-scotland.com* 🖼 *£6.50* ⊗ *Easter–May and Oct., daily 9:30–5; June–Sept., daily 9–6; Nov.–Easter, daily 10–3:30; last admission ½ hr before closing.*

Urquhart Castle, 2 mi southeast of Drumnadrochit, is a favorite Loch Ness monster–watching spot. This weary fortress stands on a promontory overlooking the loch, as it has since the Middle Ages. Because of its central and strategic position in the Great Glen line of communication, the castle has a complex history involving military offense and defense, as well as its own destruction and renovation. The castle was begun in the 13th century and was destroyed before the end of the 17th century to prevent its use by the Jacobites. The ruins of what was one of the largest castles in Scotland were then plundered for building material. A visitor center relates these events and gives an idea of what life was like here in medieval times. ⊠ *A82* ☎ *01456/450551* ⊕ *www.historic-scotland.gov.uk/places* 🖼 *£7* ⊗ *Apr.–Sept., daily 9:30–6; Oct 9:30–5; Nov.–Mar., daily 9:30–4; last admission 45 mins before closing.*

Jacobite Cruises (⊠ *Clansman Harbour* ☎ *01463/233999* ⊕ *www.jacobite.co.uk*) runs morning and afternoon cruises on Loch Ness to Urquhart Castle and other destinations throughout the region. The harbor is 5 mi northeast of Drumnadochit via the A82.

WHERE TO STAY

££££   **Loch Ness Lodge.** Run by siblings Scott and Iona Sutherland, Loch Ness Lodge is an exquisite place: opulent, classy, and welcoming. The owners keep the formalities to a minimum while making you feel pampered with nice touches like the small decanter of sherry that awaits you upon arrival. Rooms are spacious, and all but one have views of Loch Ness. The decor makes good use of dusky and deep colors, realized in crushed velvets and raw silks. They've even created sublime lighting in the large bathrooms. Make sure to reserve a table for the five-course dinner, which includes delicate, perfectly prepared dishes such as roasted breast of wild partridge. There's a small spa with a hot tub and sauna. **Pros:** excellent staff; superb views; near Inverness. **Cons:** pricey rates; near a busy road. ⊠ *A82, Brachla* ☎ *01456/459469* ⊕ *www.loch-ness-lodge. com* 🕾 *7 rooms* ♻ *In-room: no a/c, DVD, Wi-Fi. In-hotel: restaurant, spa* ⊟ *AE, DC, MC, V* 🍴 *BP.*

TOWARD THE SMALL ISLES

Travelers drive through this region to experience the landscape, which changes at nearly every turn. It's a brooding, haunting area that's worth a visit in any season. The desolate moors and lochans of Rannoch Moor stretch before the dark, cloud-laden mountains of Glencoe.

From Fort William—(an excellent, if uninspiring base—the A830, known as the Road to the Isles, leads to the coastal towns of Arisaig, Morar and Mallaig, with access to the small isles of Rum, Eigg, Canna, and Muck. From here you can also visit Skye *(see Chapter 10)* via the ferry at Mallaig.

GLENCOE

Fodor'sChoice *92 mi north of Glasgow, 44 mi northwest of Edinburgh.*
★

Glencoe is both a small town and a region of awesome beauty, with high peaks and secluded glens. The area, where wild, craggy buttresses loom darkly over the road, has a special place in the folk memory of Scotland: the glen was the site of an infamous massacre in 1692, still remembered in the Highlands for the treachery with which soldiers of the Campbell clan, acting as a government militia, treated their hosts, the MacDonalds. According to Highland code, in his own home a clansman should give shelter even to his sworn enemy. In the face of bitter weather, the Campbells were accepted as guests by the MacDonalds. Apparently acting on orders from the British government, the Campbells turned on their hosts.

GETTING HERE AND AROUND

Glencoe is easily accessed by car via the A82. ScotRail trains and regional buses arrive from most of Scotland's major cities.

EXPLORING

The National Trust for Scotland's **Visitor Center at Glencoe** (at the west end of the glen, 1 mi east of Glencoe village) tells the story of the MacDonald massacre and has an excellent display on mountaineering. You can also get advice about walking. ⊠ *A82* ☎ *01855/811307* ⊕ *www. glencoe-nts.org.uk* 🕾 *Exhibition £5* ⊗ *Nov.–Easter, Thurs.–Sun 10–4; Easter–Aug., daily 10–5:30; Sept., daily 10–5.*

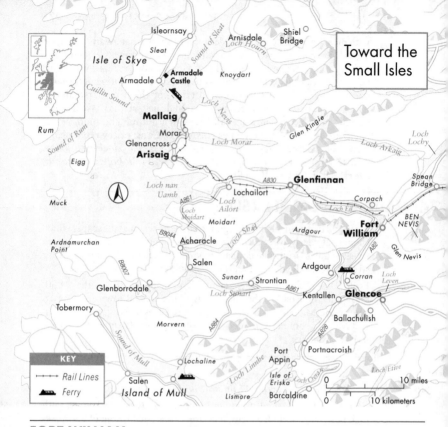

KEY

┄┄┄→ Rail Lines

⛴ Ferry

FORT WILLIAM

15 mi north of Glencoe, 69 mi southwest of Inverness, 108 mi north-west of Glasgow, 138 mi northwest of Edinburgh.

As its name suggests, Fort William originated as a military outpost, first established by Oliver Cromwell's General Monk in 1655 and refortified by George I (1660–1727) in 1715 to help combat an uprising by the turbulent Jacobite clans. It remains the southern gateway to the Great Glen and the far west, and it's a busy, commercial, tourist-oriented place with plenty of places to eat, stay, and shop.

GETTING HERE AND AROUND

From Glasgow (to the south) and Inverness (to the north), the A82 takes you the entire way. From Edinburgh, take the M9 to the A84. This empties into the A85, which connects to the A82 that takes you to Fort William. Roads around Fort William are well maintained, but mostly one lane in each direction. They can be very busy in summer.

A long-distance Scottish Citylink bus connects Glasgow and Fort William. ScotRail has trains from London, as well as connections from Glasgow and Edinburgh. It also operates a diesel train on the line between Fort William and Mallaig. Many travelers use it to shuttle back and forth between these towns.

ESSENTIALS

Visitor Information **Fort William** (✉ *Cameron Centre, Cameron Sq.* ☎ *08452/ 255121* ⊕ *www.visitscotland.com*).

EXPLORING

The **West Highland Museum**, in the town center, explores the history of Prince Charles Edward Stuart and the 1745 Rebellion. Included in the museum's folk exhibits are a costume and tartan display and a famous collection of Jacobite relics. ✉ *Cameron Sq.* ☎ *01397/702169* ⊕ *www.westhighlandmuseum.org.uk* ✐ *£3* ☉ *June and Sept., Mon.– Sat. 10–5; July and Aug., Mon.–Sat. 10–5, Sun. 2–5; Oct.–May, Mon.– Sat. 10–4.*

Great Britain's highest mountain, the 4,406-foot **Ben Nevis,** looms over Fort William, less than 4 mi from Loch Linnhe. A trek to its summit is a rewarding experience, but you should be fit and well prepared—food and water, map and compass, first-aid kit, whistle, hat, gloves, and warm clothing (yes, even in summer) for starters—as the unpredict-able weather can make it a hazardous hike. Ask for advice at the local tourist office before you begin.

★ The most relaxing way to take in the landscape of birch- and bracken-covered wild slopes is by rail. The best ride is on the **Jacobite Steam Train** (☎ *01524/737751* ⊕ *www.westcoastrailway.co.uk*), a famously scenic 84-mi round-trip that runs between Fort William and Mallaig from mid-May through mid-October; cost is £30. You'll see mountains, lochs, beaches, and islands along the way.

WHERE TO EAT AND STAY

£££   ✕ **Crannog Seafood Restaurant.** With its reputation for quality and sim-
SEAFOOD   plicity, this restaurant on the town pier has single-handedly transformed
★   the local dining scene. The sight of a fishing boat drawing up on the shores of Loch Linnhe to take its catch straight to the kitchen says it all about the freshness of the fish. The chef's capable touch ensures the fresh flavors are not overwhelmed. From the window seats you can watch the sun setting on the far side of the loch. The eatery runs four daily cruises between March and October. ✉ *The Pier* ☎ *01397/705589* ⊟ *MC, V.*

££   ⊞ **Crolinnhe.** An elegant Victorian house with colorful gardens, this exceptionally comfortable B&B overlooks Loch Linnhe yet is only a 10-minute walk from town. Antique and reproduction furniture in the rooms is set off by pastel walls and boldly colored drapes. Ask for the Superior Room, which has its own hot tub. The cooked-to-order breakfasts are first-rate. **Pros:** stunning loch views; helpful host. **Cons:** furnishings may be a bit fussy for some. ✉ *Grange Rd.* ☎ *01397/702709* ⊕ *www.crolinnhe.co.uk* ✐ *3 rooms* ⌂ *In-room: no a/c, no phone, Wi-Fi* ⊟ *No credit cards* ☉ *Closed Nov.–Easter* ⦿ *BP.*

££   ⊞ **The Grange.** A delightful confection of a Victorian villa stands in pretty
Fodor'sChoice   gardens a 10-minute walk from downtown. Interesting antiques in each
★   room, fresh flowers, log fires, and views of Loch Linnhe make this B&B quite special. The owners delight in giving sightseeing advice, and the bountiful breakfasts are first-rate. **Pros:** lots of little extras; great atten-tion to detail; elegant lounge with plenty of books. **Cons:** not suitable

9

for families with younger children. ⊠ *Grange Rd.* ☎ *01397/705516* ⊕ *www.thegrange-scotland.co.uk* ⌖ *4 rooms* ♿ *In-room: no a/c, no phone, Wi-Fi. In-hotel: no kids under 12* ⊟ *MC, V* ⊘ *Closed Oct.–Mar.* ⟋⊘︎ *BP.*

£££££   ⊟ **Inverlochy Castle Hotel.** A red-granite Victorian mansion, Inverlochy Castle stands on 50 acres of woodlands in the shadow of Ben Nevis, with striking Highland landscape visible on every side. Dating from 1863, the hotel retains all the splendor of its period, with a fine fresco ceiling, crystal chandeliers, and a handsome staircase in the Great Hall. The bedrooms, traditional in style, are plush and comfortable. An excellent restaurant serves local specialties like Isle of Skye crab and venison. The hotel is 3 mi northeast of Fort William. **Pros:** relaxing public rooms; sublime views. **Cons:** pricey rates; bland bathrooms. ⊠ *A82* ☎ *01397/702177* ⊕ *www.inverlochycastlehotel.com* ⌖ *14 rooms, 3 suites* ♿ *In-room: no a/c, Wi-Fi. In-hotel: restaurant, tennis court* ⊟ *AE, MC, V* ⊘ *Closed Jan. and Feb.* ⟋⊘︎ *BP.*

SPORTS AND THE OUTDOORS

BICYCLING   For a thrilling ride down Ben Nevis, take the gondola up to the beginning of the **Nevis Range Mountain Bike Track** (⊠ *A82* ☎ *01397/705825*) and then shoot off on a 2,000-foot descent. The lift costs £11.50. It's open May to September, weather permitting. Bike rentals are available near the gondola.

GOLF   The **Fort William Golf Course** has spectacular views of Ben Nevis and welcomes visitors. ⊠ *Torlundy, Fort William* PH33 6SQ ☎ *01397/704464* 🏌 *18 holes, 6,217 yds, par 70.*

HIKING   This area—especially around Glen Nevis, Glencoe, and Ben Nevis—is popular with hikers; however, routes are not well-marked, so contact the Fort William tourist information center before you go. The center will provide you with route advice based on your interests, level of fitness, and hiking experience. **Ben Nevis** is a large and dangerous mountain, where snow can fall on the summit plateau any time of the year. Several excellent guides are available locally; they should be consulted for high-altitude routes.

For a walk in **Glen Nevis,** drive north from Fort William on the A82 toward Fort Augustus. On the outskirts of town, just before the bridge over the River Nevis, turn right up the unclassified road signposted Glen Nevis. Drive about 6 mi, past a youth hostel, a campground, and a few houses, and cross the River Nevis over the bridge at Achriabhach (Lower Falls). Notice the southern flanks of Ben Nevis rising steeply to the east and the Mamores Mountains to the west. Park at a parking lot about 2½ mi from the bridge. Starting here, a footpath leads to waterfalls and a steel-cabled bridge (1 mi), and then to Steall, a ruined croft beside a boulder-strewn stream (a good picnic place). You can continue up the glen for some distance without danger of becoming lost, so long as you stay on the path and keep the river to your right. Watch your step going through the tree-lined gorge. The return route is back the way you came.

SKIING **Nevis Range** (☎ *01397/705825*), a modern development on the flanks of Aonach Mor, 7 mi north of Fort William, has good and varied skiing, as well as views of Ben Nevis. There's a gondola system and runs for all skill levels. Skiing gets under way, adequate snowfall permitting, at the end of December. The season normally continues until early April. Daily ski passes are £28.

SHOPPING

The majority of shops here are along High Street, which in summer attracts bustling crowds intent on stocking up for excursions to the west.

★ **Nevisport** (✉ *High St.* ☎ *01397/704921*) has been selling outdoor supplies, maps, and travel books for more than 30 years from its flagship store. **Ellis Brigham Mountain Sports** (✉ *St. Marys Hall, Belford Rd.* ☎ *01397/706220*) can help you get kitted out for your outdoor adventures. The **Scottish Crafts and Whisky Centre** (✉ *135–139 High St.* ☎ *01397/ 704406*) has lots of crafts and souvenirs, as well as homemade chocolates and a vast range of malt whiskies, including miniatures and limited-edition bottlings.

GLENFINNAN

10 mi west of Fort William, 26 mi southeast of Mallaig.

Perhaps the most visitor-oriented stop on the route between Arisaig or Mallaig and Fort William, Glenfinnan has much to offer if you're interested in Scottish history. Here the National Trust for Scotland has capitalized on the romance surrounding the story of the Jacobites and their intention of returning a Stuart monarch and the Roman Catholic religion to a country that had become staunchly Protestant. In Glenfinnan in 1745, the sometimes-reluctant clans joined forces and rallied to Prince Charles Edward Stuart's cause.

GETTING HERE AND AROUND

If you're driving here from Fort William, head here via the A830. For great views, take a ride in the Jacobite Steam Train, which you can catch in Fort William.

EXPLORING

The raising of the prince's standard is commemorated by the **Glenfinnan Monument,** an unusual tower on the banks of Loch Shiel; the story of his campaign is told in the nearby visitor center. Note that the figure at the top of the monument is of a Highlander, not the prince. ■ **TIP→ The view down Loch Shiel from the Glenfinnan Monument is one of the most photographed in Scotland.** ✉ *A830* ☎ *08444/932221* ⊕ *www.nts.org.uk* 🎟️ *£3* ⊙ *Monument daily 24 hrs. Visitor center Apr.–June, Sept., and Oct., daily 10–5; July and Aug., daily 9:30–5:30.*

As impressive as the Glenfinnan Monument is, the curving railway viaduct that stretches across the green slopes behind the monument is even more so. The **Glenfinnan Viaduct,** 1,248 feet long, was in its time the wonder of the Highlands. The railway's contractor, Robert MacAlpine, known as Concrete Bob by the locals, pioneered the use of concrete for bridges when his company built the Mallaig extension, which opened in 1901. The viaduct is famous again, this time for its appearance in the *Harry Potter* films. *For information about riding the Jacobite Steam Train across the viaduct, see Fort William, above.*

WHERE TO STAY

£££ ⧠ **Glenfinnan House.** This high-ceilinged hotel was built in the 18th cen-
★ tury as the home of Alexander MacDonald VII of Glenaladale, who was wounded fighting for Bonnie Prince Charlie, and was transformed into an even grander mansion in the mid-19th century. Today you can discover the dark-wood interiors from this period in the simply furnished, serene guest rooms. From many rooms there are stunning loch-side views of Ben Nevis. Scottish fare with a contemporary twist is served in the stately dining room. Expect top-notch service from the cosmopolitan staff. **Pros:** fabulous setting; atmospheric dining experience. **Cons:** driveway not well maintained some guest rooms look a little tired. ⊠ *A830* ☎ *01397/722235* ⊕ *www.glenfinnanhouse.com* ⤴ *13 rooms* ⚭ *In-room: no a/c, no TV. In-hotel: restaurant, bar, Wi-Fi hotspot* ⊟ *MC, V* ☯ *Closed mid-Nov.–mid-Mar.* ⦿ *BP.*

EN ROUTE As you get closer to Arisaig along A830, you'll be able to spot Eigg, a low island marked by the dramatic black peak of An Sgurr. Beyond Eigg is the larger Rum, with its range of hills and the Norse-named, cloud-capped Rum Coullin looming over the island. The breathtaking seaward views should continue to distract you from the road beside Loch nan Uamh (from Gaelic, meaning "cave" and pronounced oo-am). This loch is associated with Prince Charles Edward Stuart's nine-month stay on the mainland, during which he gathered a small army, marched as far south as Derby in England, alarmed the king, retreated to unavoidable defeat at Culloden in the spring, and then spent a few months as a fugitive in the Highlands. A cairn by the shore marks the spot where the prince was picked up by a French ship; he never returned to Scotland.

ARISAIG

15 mi west of Glenfinnan.

Considering its small size, Arisaig, gateway to the **Small Isles,** offers a surprising choice of high-quality options for dining and lodging. To the north of Arisaig, the road cuts across a headland to reach a stretch of coastline where silver sands glitter with the mica in the local rock; clear water, blue sky, and white sand lend a tropical flavor to the beaches—when the sun is shining.

From Arisaig try to visit a couple of the Small Isles: **Rum, Eigg, Muck,** and **Canna,** each tiny and with few or no inhabitants. Rum serves as a wildlife reserve.

GETTING HERE AND AROUND

From Glenfinnan, you reach Arisaig on the A830, the only road leading west. The Fort William–Mallaig train also stops here.

EXPLORING

Arisaig Marine (⊠ *Arisaig Harbour* ☎ *01687/450224* ⊕ *www.arisaig. co.uk*) runs a boat service from the harbor at Arisaig to the islands at Easter and from May to September, daily at 11. The MV *Shearwater* delivers supplies and sometimes visitors to the tiny island communities. Arisaig Marine also operates day cruises for whale-, seal-, and bird-watching. Available for charter from Arisaig Marine is a fast twin-engine motor yacht, which can take up to 12 passengers around the Small Isles and farther afield.

WHERE TO STAY AND EAT

££££   ✕ **Old Library.** On the waterfront, this 1722 barn has been converted
FRENCH   into a fine, reasonably priced restaurant. Local fish and other fare is prepared in a French-bistro style and served in the whitewashed, airy dining room. Six cozy rooms with contemporary furnishings are available as well. ⊠ *Road to the Isles* ☎ *01687/450651* ▭ *AE, MC, V.*

££   ⊡ **Arisaig Hotel.** A 1720 former coaching inn, this hotel is close to the water and has magnificent views of the Small Isles. The inn has retained its provinciality with simple furnishings, and its restaurant is renowned for its home cooking. High-quality local ingredients are used to good advantage: haddock, salmon, and scallops are specialties, as are "puds" (puddings) such as sticky ginger pudding. **Pros:** good-value restaurant; lots of life and music in the bar. **Cons:** dated furnishings; the main bar may be noisy for some. ⊠ *A830* ☎ *01687/450210* ⊕ *www.arisaighotel. co.uk* ⌫ *13 rooms* ⌂ *In-room: no a/c, Wi-Fi. In-hotel: restaurant, bar* ▭ *MC, V* ⧄ *BP.*

MALLAIG

8 mi north of Arisaig, 44 mi northwest of Fort William.

After the approach along the coast, the workaday fishing port of Mallaig itself is anticlimactic. It has a few shops, and there's some bustle by the quayside when fishing boats unload or the Skye ferry departs: this is the departure point for the southern ferry connection to the Isle of Skye, the largest island of the Inner Hebrides *(see Chapter 10).*

Mallaig is also the starting point for day cruises up the Sound of Sleat, which separates Skye from the mainland. The sound offers views into the rugged Knoydart region and its long, fjordlike sea lochs: Lochs Nevis and Hourn. The area to the immediate north and west beyond Loch Nevis, one of the most remote in Scotland, is often referred to as the Rough Bounds of Knoydart.

GETTING HERE AND AROUND

The Fort William–Mallaig train is by far the best way to travel to Mallaig, because you can relax and enjoy the stunning views. But road improvements on the A830 beyond Fort William makes the drive far less taxing and time consuming than it used to be.

EXPLORING

★   For year-round cruises to Loch Nevis, Inverie, and Tarbet, contact **Bruce Watt Sea Cruises** (☎ *01687/462320* ⊕ *www.knoydart-ferry.co.uk*).

Caledonian MacBrayne (☎ *01475/650100* ⊕ *www.calmac.co.uk*) runs scheduled service and cruises from Mallaig to Skye, the Small Isles, and Mull.

9

A small, unnamed side road just south of Mallaig leads east to an even smaller road that will bring you to **Loch Morar,** the deepest of all the Scottish lochs (more than 1,000 feet); the next deepest point is miles out into the Atlantic, beyond the continental shelf. The loch is said to have a resident monster, Morag, which undoubtedly gets less recognition than its famous cousin Nessie.

The Northern Highlands and the Western Isles

WORD OF MOUTH

"There are parts of Skye I would describe as stark and barren, but the scenery is more varied than that. The area around Armadale is very lush, and I second the recommendation of visiting the castle ruins and gardens. Even a single day on Skye is better than nothing; we just loved it!"

— Barbara_in_FL

"On Skye, we drove up the winding, steep, single-track road into the Quirang, which was outstanding! The views of this otherworldly area are amazing. Sunlight and clouds highlighted the green-covered landscape, making for surreal surroundings. The road made some hairpin turns, revealing more and more majesty."

—twina49

www.fodors.com/community

Updated by
Elizabeth
Reeder

Much of the romance of "Caledonia stern and wild"—the splendid and tranquil landscape, the Highland clans, red deer and golden eagles, Celtic mists and legends—is concentrated in this northern region. This is where you can find Eilean Donan, the most romantic of Scottish castles; the land's end at John o'Groats; and Skye, the mysterious island immortalized by the exploits of Bonnie Prince Charlie.

The rugged landscape means twisted, undulating roads that demand you shift down a gear, pause to let others pass, and take the time to do less and see more of the rough-hewn beauty. Much of Sutherland and Wester Ross in the far north of the country are made up of a rocky platform of Lewisian gneiss, some of the oldest rock in the world. On top of this rolling moorland sit strangely shaped quartzite-capped sandstone mountains, eroded and pinnacled. Take a walk here and the Ice Age doesn't seem so far away. One of the region's leitmotifs is the sea lochs that thrust watery fingers into the loneliest landscapes in Scotland, carrying the Atlantic's salty tang among the moors and deep forests. Solitary peaks rear up out of the heather, and if you're lucky, you may sight a golden or sea eagle soaring overhead.

Many place-names in this region reflect its early links with Scandinavia. Sutherland was once the southernmost land belonging to the Vikings. Cape Wrath got its name from the Viking word *hvarth* (turning point), and Laxford, Suilven, and dozens of other names in the area have Norse rather than Gaelic derivations.

The islands of Skye and the Outer Hebrides, which are now often referred to as the Western Isles, are the stronghold of the Gaelic language. Skye, famous for the misty Cuillin Moutains, has a surprisingly wide variety of landscape, considering its relatively small size. The more undulating southern end of the island gives way to dramatic mountains and steep cliffs that define the coasts.

ORIENTATION AND PLANNING

GETTING ORIENTED

Moving north and west from Inverness toward land's end at John o'Groats, this rugged land includes the old counties of Ross and Cromarty (sometimes called Easter and Wester Ross), Sutherland, and Caithness and together they constitute the most northern portion of mainland Scotland. To the west, to get to Skye, you can travel from Kyle of Lochalsh across the Skye Bridge or take a short summer ferry ride from Mallaig to Armadale. From Skye you can hop from island to island, taking in the Isles of Lewis, Harris, and the Uists.

TOP REASONS TO GO

Explore Skye, the misty island:
The landscape ranges from the lush,
undulating hills and coastal tracks
of Sleat in the Garden of Skye to
the deep glens that cut into the
saw-toothed peaks of the Cuillin
Mountains. Farther north are stunning geological features like the Old
Man of Storr and Kilt Rock.

Tuck into some seafood: Amazing
regional specialties abound. Sample
Bracadale crab, Dunvegan Bay langoustines, and Sconser king scallops,
as well as the local smoked salmon,
lobster, scallops, and oysters. Finish
up with Stornoway black pudding.

**Walk the coast in the Outer Heb-
rides:** There are no wilder places
in Britain to enjoy an invigorating
coastal walk than on the islands
of Lewis and the Uists. Expect vast
swaths of golden sand set against

blue bays, or—when the weather is
rough—giant waves crashing against
the rocks.

Get close to nature: Seals, deer,
otters, as well as an abundance of
birdlife can be seen throughout the
Northern Highlands and Western
Isles. Don't miss a boating foray to
the Handa Island bird reserve, off
Scourie.

Drive a single-track road: In the
Northern Highlands, take a drive on
single-track roads like Destitution
Road, north of Gairloch, which lead
through the most dramatic scenery
in Britain. The area is a primeval
landscape where strange craggy
mountains, with Gaelic and Nordic
names like An Teallach, Suilven, and
Stac Pollaidh, jut out of vast, desolate bog lands dotted with lochans.

The Northern Landscapes. North of Inverness, northwest Scotland is
known for its dramatic coastlines and desolate landscapes. It's no
wonder that this part of the country has been designated as Scotland's
first UNESCO Geopark. You'll want to explore Storr Lighthouse, the
beaches north of Lochinver, and islandlike hills such as Suilven.

Torridon. An hour's drive west of Inverness, Torridon has cool glens, mysterious lochs, impressive mountains, and tantalizing glimpses across to
the Isle of Skye. Single-track roads lead to lighthouses on promontories
battered by the sea. Glen Torridon is worth a visit.

Isle of Skye. Scotland's most famous island is home to the Cuillin Mountains, the quiet gardens of Sleat, and the dramatic peninsulas of Waternish and Trotternish. You can take a day trip to Skye, but it's worth
spending a few days exploring its shores. Skye is often called Scotland in
miniature, as the terrain varies from lush valleys in the south to craggy
mountains in the north.

The Outer Hebrides. Extending about 130 mi from north to south, this
archipelago is reached by ferry from the mainland and from the Isle
of Skye. Lewis has wonderful historic attractions, such as the Calanais
Standing Stones, and sandy beaches. The Uists are dotted with old
cairns and ruined forts and chapels. Barra is so small you can walk
from one end to the other without breaking a sweat.

10

PLANNING

WHEN TO GO

The Northern Highlands and islands are best seen from May to September. The earlier in the spring or later in the autumn you go, the greater the chances of your encountering the elements in their extreme form, and the fewer attractions and accommodations you will find open. Even tourist-friendly Skye closes down almost completely by the end of October. As a final deciding factor, you may not want to take a western sea passage in a gale, a frequent occurrence in the winter months.

PLANNING YOUR TIME

The Highlands and Islands, as this region is sometimes called, is not a place you can rush through. Single-track roadways, undulating landscapes, and eye-popping views will slow you down. For exploring the mainland, base yourself in Ullapool or one of the other towns, or perhaps in one of the excellent B&Bs in the countryside. (The villages here have less appeal than in the Lowlands.) If you have limited time, head directly to the Isle of Skye and the other islands off the coast. They attract hoards of tourists, and for good reason, yet you don't have to walk far to find yourself in lovely landscapes, often in solitude.

You could easily combine a trip to the Northern Highlands with forays into the Great Glen (including Inverness and Loch Ness) or even up to Orkney and the Shetland Islands.

GETTING HERE AND AROUND

AIR TRAVEL

On a map, this area may seem far from major urban centers, but it's easy to reach. Inverness has an airport with direct links to London, Edinburgh, Glasgow, and Amsterdam.

The main airports for the Northern Highlands are Inverness and Wick (both on the mainland). Loganair (⊕ *www.loganair.co.uk*) has direct air service from Edinburgh and Glasgow to Inverness and from Edinburgh to Wick. You can fly from London Gatwick, Luton Airport (near London), or Bristol to Inverness on one of the daily easyJet (⊕ *www. easyjet.com*) flights. British Airways (⊕ *www.britishairways.com*) also has a service from Gatwick. Loganair operates flights among the islands of Barra, Benbecula, and Lewis in the Outer Hebrides (weekdays only). Highland Airways (⊕ *www.highlandairways.co.uk*) operates flights from Inverness to Stornoway and Benbecula.

Airport Contacts Inverness Airport (☏ 01667/462445 ⊕ www.hial.co.uk/inverness-airport.html).

BOAT AND FERRY TRAVEL

Ferry services are generally reliable, weather permitting. Ferries run from Ullapool to Stornoway, from Oban to Castlebay and Lochboisdale, and from Uig (on the Isle of Skye) to Tarbert and Lochmaddy. Causeways link North Uist, Benbecula, and South Uist. The Island Hopscotch planned-route ticket and the Island Rover pass, both offered by Caledonian MacBrayne (called CalMac) give considerable reductions on interisland ferry fares. Various tickets are available, including the

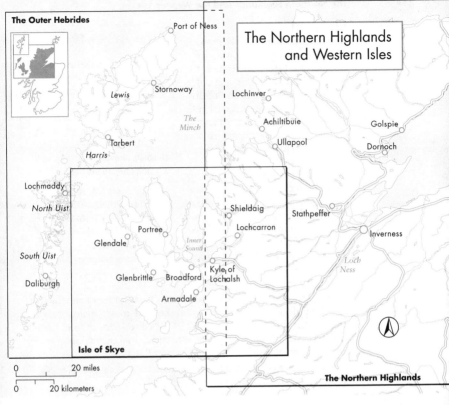

The Outer Hebrides

The Northern Highlands and Western Isles

Port of Ness

Lewis

Stornoway

The Minch

Tarbert

Harris

Lochmaddy

North Uist

South Uist

Daliburgh

Glendale

Portree

Glenbrittle Broadford

Armadale

Isle of Skye

Lochinver

Achiltibuie

Ullapool

Golspie

Dornoch

Shieldaig

Lochcarron

Stathpeffer

Inverness

Kyle of Lochalsh

Inner Sound

Loch Ness

The Northern Highlands

0   20 miles

0   20 kilometers

Hopscotch 12 (connecting Skye, Harris, Lewis, and the Uists), which costs £36 per person.

Boat and Ferry Contacts Caledonian MacBrayne (☎ 08000/665000 ⊕ www.calmac.co.uk).

BUS TRAVEL

Scottish Citylink and National Express run buses to Inverness, Ullapool, Thurso, Scrabster, and Wick. There are also coach connections between the ferry ports of Tarbert and Stornoway; consult the local tourist information center for details. Buses are a reliable way to see this region, but they often don't run frequently.

Highland Country Buses provides bus service in the Highlands area, often under the name Stagecoach. On the Outer Hebrides several small operators run regular routes to most towns and villages. The post-bus service—which also delivers mail—becomes increasingly important in remote areas. It supplements the regular bus service, which runs only a few times per week. A full timetable of services for the Northern Highlands (and the rest of Scotland) is available from the Royal Mail.

Bus Contacts Highland Country Buses (☎ 08712/002233 ⊕ www.rapsons.com). **National Express** (☎ 08705/808080 ⊕ www.nationalexpress.co.uk). **Royal Mail Post Buses** (☎ 0845/7740740 ⊕ www.royalmail.com/postbus). **Scottish Citylink** (☎ 08705/505050 ⊕ www.citylink.co.uk).

10

CAR TRAVEL

Because of the infrequent bus services and sparse railway stations, a car is definitely the best way to explore this region. The twisting, winding single-lane roads demand a degree of driving dexterity, however. Local rules of the road require that when two cars meet, whichever driver reaches a passing place first must stop and allow the oncoming car to continue. Small cars tend to yield to large commercial vehicles. Never park in passing places, and remember that these sections of the road can also be used to allow traffic behind you to pass. Note that in this sparsely populated area, distances between gas stations can be considerable.

SIGHTSEEING TOURS

J.A. Johnstone Chauffeur Drive will escort you anywhere and gives a lot of information about the Highlands and islands, including the Outer Hebrides. Raasay Outdoor Centre organizes courses in kayaking, sailing, windsurfing, climbing, rappelling, archery, walking, and navigation skills.

Tour Contacts J. A. Johnstone **Chauffeur Drive** (☎ 01463/ 798372). **Raasay Outdoor Centre** (☎ 01478/660266 ⊕ www. raasay-house.co.uk).

TRAIN TRAVEL

Main railway stations in the area include Oban (for Barra and the Uists) and Kyle of Lochalsh (for Skye), on the west coast, or Inverness (for points north to Thurso and Wick). There's direct service from London to Inverness and connecting service from Edinburgh and Glasgow. For information contact National Rail or ScotRail.

Train Contacts **National Rail** (☎ 08457/484950 ⊕ www.nationalrail.co.uk). **ScotRail** (☎ 08457/550033 ⊕ www.scotrail.co.uk).

RESTAURANTS

Northern Scotland has many excellent restaurants where talented chefs use locally grown produce. Most country-house inns (a good choice if you're looking for a restaurant) and pubs serve reliable, hearty, seafood, and meat-and-potatoes meals. The Isle of Skye has the most, and the most expensive, restaurants, many of them quite good. But you can find good meals almost everywhere, which wasn't the case a few years ago. In the more remote regions you may have to drive some distance to find them, however.

HOTELS

Charming, earthy, inexpensive inns and a few excellent luxury hotels will welcome you after a day of touring the Highlands. Check out hotel restaurants in this area, as they can be a fine option.

WHAT IT COSTS IN POUNDS					
	£	££	£££	££££	£££££
RESTAURANTS	under £10	£10–£14	£15–£19	£20–£25	over £25
HOTELS	under £70	£70–£120	£121–£160	£161–£220	over £220

Restaurant prices are for a main course at dinner. Hotel prices are for two people in a standard double room in high season, generally including the 17.5% V.A.T.

VISITOR INFORMATION

The tourist information centers at Dornoch, Dunvegan, Durness, Portree, Stornoway, Tarbert, and Ullapool are open year-round, with limited winter hours at Dunvegan, Durness, and Ullapool.

Seasonal tourist information centers are at Bettyhill, Broadford (Skye), Castlebay (Barra, Outer Hebrides), Gairloch, Helmsdale, John o'Groats, Kyle of Lochalsh, Lairg, Lochboisdale (South Uist, Outer Hebrides), Lochcarron, Lochinver, Lochmaddy (North Uist, Outer Hebrides), North Kessock, Shiel Bridge, Strathpeffer, Thurso, and Uig.

Information **Highlands of Scotland Tourist Board** (☎ *08452/255121* ⊕ *www. visithighlands.com*).

THE NORTHERN LANDSCAPES

Wester Ross and Sutherland, the northernmost part of Scotland, have some of the most distinctive mountain profiles and coastal stretches in all of Scotland. The rim roads around the wilds of Durness overlooking rocky shores and beaches are as dramatic as the awe-inspiring and desolate cross-country routes like Destitution Road in Wester Ross.

STRATHPEFFER

19 mi northwest of Inverness.

At the spa town of Strathpeffer you can take a walk to admire Victorian "holiday houses" and the Eagle Stone, a boulder carved with Pictish signs in the 7th century, now perched on a hill just outside the town. The Highland Museum of Childhood displays early Highlands toys in the former railway station.

GETTING HERE AND AROUND

Driving is the best way to get here; take A9, A835, and A834 from Inverness. Infrequent bus service, even in the summer, means you need to carefully check the schedule.

EXPLORING

10

The **Strathpeffer Spa Pavillion** (✉ *The Square* ☎ *01997/420124* ⊕ *www. strathpefferpavilion.org*) has been spruced up and now serves as a venue for artistic events including classical concerts, cabaret, and dance in period costumes.

Not far from Strathpeffer are the tumbling **Falls of Rogie** (signposted off the A835), where an interestingly bouncy suspension bridge presents you with a fine view of the waters below.

★ For a thrilling touch of vertigo, don't miss **Corrieshalloch Gorge**, 39 mi northwest of Strathpeffer on the way to Ullapool. Draining the high moors, the Falls of Measach plunge 150 feet into a 200-foot-deep, thickly wooded gorge. There's a suspension-bridge viewpoint and a heady atmosphere of romantic grandeur, like an old Scottish print come to life. A short walk leads from a parking area to the viewpoint.

WHERE TO STAY

££ ★ 🏠 **Craigvar.** Delightful host Margaret Scott stocks plenty of tourist leaflets to keep you busy at this pretty Georgian bed-and-breakfast. Idiosyncratic pictures—from 18th-century portraits to Japanese-style still lifes—hang on the walls. **Pros:** good location on town square; friendly owner. **Cons:** impractical carpets in the bathrooms; rooms get booked up early. ✉ *The Square* ☎ *01997/421622* ⊕ *www.craigvar.com* ⮐ *3 rooms* ᕀ *In-room: no a/c. In-hotel: bar* ▭ *MC, V* ⏸ *BP.*

ULLAPOOL

50 mi northwest of Strathpeffer, 238 mi north of Glasgow.

By the shores of salty Loch Broom, Ullapool was founded in 1788 as a fishing station to exploit the local herring stocks. There's still a smattering of fishing vessels, as well as visiting yachts and foreign ships. When their crews fill the pubs, the town has a cosmopolitan feel. The harbor area comes to life when the Lewis ferry arrives and departs. Ullapool is an ideal base for hiking throughout Sutherland and taking wildlife and nature cruises, especially to the Summer Isles.

GETTING HERE AND AROUND

A desolate but well-maintained stretch of the A835 takes you from Inverness to Ullapool.

ESSENTIALS

Visitor Information Ullapool (✉ *Argyll St.* ☎ *01854/612135* ⊕ *www. visithighlands.com*).

EXPLORING

The town's cultural focal point is **Ceilidh Place,** an excellent venue for music and literary events throughout the year. It started out as a small café, and over the years has added space for performers and a handful of rooms for those who want to spend the night. ✉ *14 W. Argyle St.* ☎ *01854/612103* ⊕ *www.theceilidhplace.com.*

In the **Ullapool Museum,** films, photographs, and audiovisual displays tell the story of the area from the ice age to modern times. ✉ *7–8 W. Argyle St.* ☎ *01854/612987* ⊕ *www.ullapoolmuseum.co.uk* 🎫 *£3* ⊙ *Apr.–Oct., Mon.–Sat. 10–5.*

WHERE TO STAY

££ ★ 🏠 **The Royal Hotel.** Sitting atop a hill above Ullapool, the Royal has fabulous views over the harbor and Loch Broom. The curvy 1960s facade was added to a 19th-century coaching inn. Guest rooms are bright and spacious. The clientele is diverse, especially during late September's Loopallu music festival. ■**TIP**➡ **Ask for a room with balcony and views of the loch. Pros:** stunning views from balconies; a short walk to Ullapool; good breakfasts. **Cons:** restaurant is uneven; some rooms have older mattresses. ✉ *Garve Rd.* ☎ *01854/612181* ⊕ *www.royalhotel-ullapool. com* ⮐ *52 rooms* ᕀ *In-room: no a/c. In-hotel: restaurant, bar* ▭ *AE, DC, V* ⏸ *BP.*

EN ROUTE Drive north of Ullapool on the A835 into **Coigach and Assynt,** and you enter a different kind of landscape. Here you won't find the broad flanks of great hills that hem you in, as you would in the Great Glen

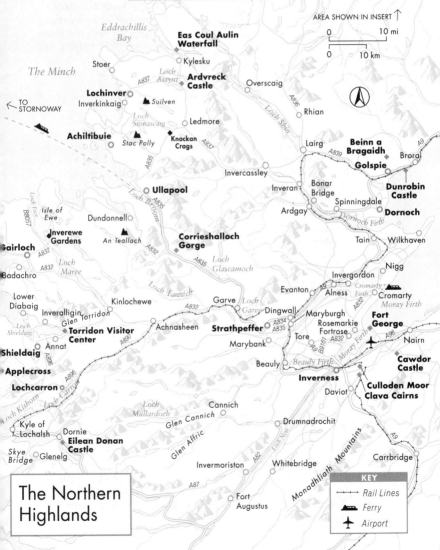

or Glencoe. Instead, in Wester Ross the mountains rear out of the hummocky terrain and seem to shift their position, hiding behind one another. Even their names seem different from those of the *bens* (mountain peaks or high hills) elsewhere: Cul Mor, Cul Beag, Stac Polly, Canisp, Suilven. Some owe their origins to Norse words rather than to Gaelic—a reminder that Vikings used to sail this northern seaboard. Much of this area lies within the Inverpolly National Nature Reserve, now encompassed within the North West Highlands Geopark.

> **GET HOOKED IN THE HIGHLANDS**
>
> The possibilities for fishing are endless in Sutherland, as a glance at the loch-covered map suggests. Brown trout and salmon are abundant. You can fish from the banks of Loch Garve, 4 mi west of Strathpeffer, or Loch Assynt, 5 mi east of Lochinver, from March to October. Boat fishing is popular on Loch Maree, southeast of Gairloch and north of Poolewe, from May to October. Fishing permits are available at local post offices, shops, and hotels.

ACHILTIBUIE

25 mi northwest of Ullapool.

Achiltibuie is a small farming community set in magnificent mountain and coastal scenery. Offshore are the attractive **Summer Isles,** whose history dates back to Viking raids. Cruises from Ullapool visit the largest and only inhabited island, Tanera Mhor, where you can buy special Summer Isle stamps—Tanera Mhor is the only Scottish island to have a private postal service.

The town has become a bit of a foodie haven thanks to businesses like the Achiltibuie Smokehouse and also the Summer Isles Hotel. At the time of this writing, an organic farm called Achiltibuie Gardens was set to open by summer 2010.

GETTING HERE AND AROUND
Achiltibuie is a two-hour drive from Inverness, much of it on the quick A835, with the last 15 mi on an occasionally daunting single-track road.

EXPLORING
At the **Achiltibuie Smokehouse,** Summer Isles Foods deliciously smokes all sorts of fish—salmon, haddock, eel, and trout—which can be purchased in the small shop; mail order is available. ⌂ *Altandhu* ☎ *01854/622353* ⊕ *www.summerislesfoods.com* ☺ *Easter–Oct., daily 9:30–5.*

LOCHINVER

18 mi north of Achiltibuie, 38 mi north of Ullapool.

Lochinver is a quiet shoreside community of whitewashed cottages, with a harbor used by the west-coast-fishing fleet, and a couple of dining and lodging options. Behind the town the mountain Suilven rises abruptly. Take the cul-de-sac, **Baddidarroch Road,** for a great photo opportunity.

GETTING HERE AND AROUND

To get to Lochinver, take A835/A837 north from Ullapool.

ESSENTIALS

Visitor Information **Assynt Visitor Centre** (✉ *Main St.* ☎ *01571/844373* ⊕ *www.assynt.info*).

EXPLORING

Bold souls spending time at Lochinver may enjoy the interesting single-track B869 **Drumbeg Loop** to the north of Lochinver—it has several challenging hairpin turns along with breathtaking views. (The junction is on the north side of the River Inver bridge on the outskirts of the village, signposted as STOER and CLASHNESSIE.) Just beyond the scattered community of Stoer, a road leads west to **Stoer Point Lighthouse.** If you're an energetic walker, you can hike across the short turf and heather along the cliff top for fine views east toward the profiles of the northwest mountains. There's also a red-sandstone sea stack: the **Old Man of Stoer.** This makes a pleasant excursion on a long summer evening.

DRIVING TIPS

In the Northern Highlands you'll encounter plenty of single-track roads wide enough only for just one car. When you meet an oncoming vehicle, or when a faster one wants to pass, pull into a passing place (always pull to the left, into the passing place or into the space on the road beside it). Drivers always wave, as a courtesy and as a genuine greeting. On bad days, you encounter trucks at the most awkward of spots. On good days, single-track driving can be relaxing, with a lovely pace of stopping, waving, moving on.

WHERE TO STAY

£ 🛏 **Davar.** The light-filled rooms at this modern, comfortable B&B have views over Lochinver Bay. Green carpets set off pastel walls, and the bedrooms are simple but spacious. **Pros:** lounge filled with books and games; wonderful mountain views. **Cons:** decor is a little busy; too small for some travelers. ✉ *A837* ☎ *01571/844501* ⊕ *www.davar-lochinver.co.uk* 🛏 *3 rooms* ♿ *In-room: no a/c, no phone* ⊟ *No credit cards* ⊘ *Closed Dec.–Mar.* ⵯ *BP.*

££££ 🛏 **Inver Lodge Hotel.** On a hillside above Lochinver, this modern hotel has stunning views of the sea. Floral fabrics and traditional mahogany furniture decorate the smart guest rooms. The restaurant makes the most of fresh, local seafood on its Scottish menu; try the lobster, straight from the sea the day you dine. Anglers feel especially at home here, with three salmon rivers and many trout lochs within easy reach. **Pros:** cozy public room with a fireplace; refreshing sauna; great fishing nearby. **Cons:** drab exterior; not good for families with children. ✉ *Iolaire Rd.* ☎ *01571/844496* ⊕ *www.inverlodge.com* 🛏 *20 rooms* ♿ *In-room: no a/c, Wi-Fi. In-hotel: restaurant, room service, no kids under 10* ⊟ *AE, DC, MC, V* ⵯ *BP.*

SHOPPING

At Inverkirkaig, just south of Lochinver, don't miss **Achins Book & Craft Shop** (✉ *Inverkirkaig* ☎ *01571/844262*). The shop is a great place for Scottish books on natural history, hill walking, and trout fishing. It also sells craft items—knitwear, tweeds, and pottery—along with works by

10

local artists and recordings of traditional music. The shop and pleasant café are open daily from 10 to 5 between Easter and October.

Highland Stoneware (⊠ *Baddidarroch* ☎ *01571/844376*) manufactures tableware and decorative items with hand-painted designs of Highland wildflowers, animals, and landscapes, all for sale in its showroom.

SCOURIE

28 mi north of Lochinver.

Scourie is a small settlement catering to visitors—fisherfolk especially—with a range of accommodations. The bayside town makes a good base for a trip to the bird sanctuary on the island of Handa.

GETTING HERE AND AROUND

From Lochinver, take the A837, which becomes the A894 as you turn north.

> **RULE OF THREE**
>
> Scourie has a trio of attractions not found together anywhere else on the globe: Highland cattle, red- and black-throated divers, and palm trees. There is reputedly a reward for anyone who can capture all three in a photograph. Your best bet to do so is from the shore of Scourie Bay.

EXPLORING

★ Just off the coast of Scourie is **Handa Island,** a bird sanctuary that shelters huge seabird colonies, especially impressive at nesting time in spring and early summer. Visitors can gaze on more than 200,000 birds nesting on spectacular cliffs, including guillemots, razorbills, great skuas, kittiwakes, and even the odd puffin from the towering sandstone vantage point of Stack an Seabhaig (Hawk's Stack). This remarkable park, administered by the Scottish Wildlife Trust, is open only in spring and summer. It can be reached by a small open boat from Tarbet; contact the tourist information center in Lochinver or Durness for details. ■ TIP → **Sturdy boots, a waterproof jacket, and a degree of fitness are needed to walk the path around the island.**

WHERE TO STAY

££ 🏨 **Eddrachilles Hotel.** This longtime favorite has one of the best views of any lodging in Scotland—across the islands of Eddrachilles Bay. (If you're entranced, you can explore them by boat.) The hotel sits on 320 acres of private moorland and is just south of the Handa Island bird sanctuary. The bedrooms are modern and comfortable, with chandeliers hanging above and photographs on the walls. In the restaurant, the chef uses local produce to prepare meals in straightforward Scottish style, with the emphasis on fish and game; try the poached salmon or the saddle of venison. **Pros:** attractive garden; stunning shoreline nearby; close to bird sanctuary. **Cons:** restaurant's quality can vary; service sometimes disappoints. ⊠ *Badcall Bay* ☎ *01971/502080* ⊕ *www.eddrachilles.com* ↷ *11 rooms* ⚙ *In-room: no a/c. In-hotel: restaurant, bar, Wi-Fi hotspot* ☐ *MC, V* ☉ *Closed early Oct.–mid-Mar.* ¹⊙¹ *BP.*

DURNESS

27 mi north of Scourie, 55 mi north of Lochinver.

The sudden patches of green surrounding the village of Durness, on the north coast, are caused by the richer limestone outcrops among the acid moorlands. Here you'll find the country's highest peak, Clo Mor.

GETTING HERE AND AROUND

Past Scourie, the A894 becomes the A838 as you head north. The road to Durness is often a single lane in each direction.

ESSENTIALS

Visitor Information Durness (✉ *Sango* ☎ *01971/511368* ⊕ *www.durness.org*).

EXPLORING

The limestone's most spectacular feature is **Smoo Cave,** hollowed out of the rock by rushing water. Access is via a steep cliff path. Also worth exploring are the wonderful near white-sand beaches, especially the one at Sango Bay. Boat tours around the Kyle of Durness run daily from April through September.

If you've made it this far north, you'll probably want to go all the way to **Cape Wrath,** a rugged headland at the northwest tip of Scotland. The white-sand beaches, impressive dunes covered in marram grass, and crashing seas of nearby Balnakeil Bay make it an exhilarating place to visit. You can't drive your own vehicle, however. From May through September, a small boat (☎ *07719/678792*) ferries people here from Keoldale, 2 mi outside Durness; once you're across the sea inlet called the Kyle of Durness, a minibus (☎ *01971/511287*) will then take you to the lighthouse. Check departure times on the board at the jetty.

The highest mainland cliffs in Scotland, including **Clo Mor,** at 920 feet, lie between the Kyle and Cape Wrath.

SHOPPING

★ Artisans sell pottery, leather, weavings, paintings, and more from their studios at **Balnakeil Craft Village** (☎ *01971/511777*). This crafty complex, on an unnamed road leading northwest from Durness, is open April through October. Hours at the studios vary, but most shops stay open daily from 10 to 5, and even later on summer evenings. Cocoa Mountain is a must for those with a sweet tooth; its "chocolate bar" serves up world-class truffles and hot chocolate.

10

THURSO

74 mi east of Durness.

The town of Thurso is quite substantial for a community so far north. In town are the Thurso Heritage Museum and Old St. Peter's Kirk, which dates back to the 12th century. There are also fine beaches, particularly at Dunnet Bay, and great seabird watching at Dunnet Head. With several restaurants and hotels, Thurso is one of the few towns that make a good starting point for exploring the far north. The town was the site of Britain's first nuclear-power plant, which is now in the process of being decommissioned.

GETTING HERE AND AROUND

A car remains the best way to see this region, although local buses and the post bus run on most days. At Tongue, the A838 becomes the A836.

ESSENTIALS

Visitor Information Thurso (✉ *Riverside Rd.* ☎ *01847/893155* ⊕ *www. visithighlands.com*).

EXPLORING

Many people make the trip to the northernmost point of mainland Britain, which is at **Dunnet Head,** with its fine views over the sea to Orkney. Dunnet Head Lighthouse, built in 1831, still stands here.

WHERE TO STAY

££ **Forss Country House Hotel.** Don't be fooled by the stark exterior, as this house dating from 1810 is a charming place to stay. It's surrounded by woodland and plenty of places to fish (guide service and instruction provided). Spare, dark-wood antique and reproduction furniture fill the simple rooms. Log fires and sturdy Scottish cuisine add to the appeal. Prix-fixe meals at the restaurant might include haggis-stuffed sirloin with Glenmorangie whisky sauce. The hotel is about 4 mi west of Thurso. **Pros:** large guest rooms; lots of outdoor activities; hearty meals. **Cons:** heavy old doors make a racket. ✉ *A836* ☎ *01847/861201* ⊕ *www.forsshousehotel.co.uk* ⤳ *14 rooms* ⌂ *In-room: no a/c, DVD. In-hotel: restaurant, bar* ⊟ *AE, DC, MC, V.*

££ **Murray House.** In the center of Thurso, this Victorian town house is convenient to the Orkney ferry. Floral wallpaper and bedding decorate the rooms. You may sit in the garden or watch a film in the lounge. **Pros:** near the railway station and the ferry. **Cons:** smallish rooms; dated decor; minimum stay in high season. ✉ *1 Campbell St.* ☎ *01847/895759* ⊕ *www.murrayhousebb.com* ⤳ *5 rooms* ⌂ *In-room: no a/c. In-hotel: bar* ⊟ *No credit cards* ⏍ *BP.*

BICYCLING

At the **Wheels Cycle Shop** (✉ *35 High St.* ☎ *01847/896124*), the staff rents bikes and gives advice on the best routes.

JOHN O'GROATS

21 mi east of Thurso.

The windswept little outpost of John o'Groats is usually taken to be the most northern community on the Scottish mainland, though that is not strictly accurate, as an exploration of the network of roads between Dunnet Head and John o'Groats will confirm. A crafts center has a few high-quality shops selling knitwear, candles, and gifts.

GETTING HERE AND AROUND

Traveling east from Thurso, take the coast-hugging A836.

EXPLORING

Head east to **Duncansby Head** for spectacular views of cliffs and sea stacks by the lighthouse—and puffins, too.

John o'Groats Ferries (☎ *01955/611353* ⊕ *www.jogferry.co.uk*) operates wildlife cruises from John o'Groats Harbor. The 1½-hour trip takes you past spectacular cliff scenery and bird life into the Pentland Firth, to Duncansby Stacks, and to the island of Stroma. Cruises cost £15 and are available daily at 2:30 between June and August. Between May and September the company also offers day trips to Orkney for £44 per person.

THE ARTS

The **Lyth Arts Centre** (✉ *Unmarked road, 4 mi off A9, Lyth* ☎ *01955/ 641270*), between Wick and John o'Groats, is in a Victorian-era school building. From April through November each year, it hosts performances by professional touring music and theater companies, as well as exhibitions of contemporary fine art. Check local papers or information centers for opening times, schedules, and fees.

WICK

17 mi south of John o'Groats, 22 mi southeast of Thurso.

Wick is a substantial town that was built on its fishing industry. The town itself is not very appealing, but it does have the gaunt, bleak ruins of **Castle Sinclair** and **Castle Girnigoe** teetering on a cliff top 3 mi north of the town.

GETTING HERE AND AROUND

From Thurso, the A836 follows the coast to John o'Groats and becomes the A99 as you head south. An alternative route, the A882, cuts away from the coast.

EXPLORING

To learn how this town grew, visit the **Wick Heritage Centre**—the local people who run it are real enthusiasts. The center is the largest museum in the Northern Highlands and has on display a restored fisherman's house, a fish kiln, and a blacksmith's shop, as well as collections of everything from fossils to 19th-century toys. An art gallery and terraced gardens overlooking the town round out the offerings. ✉ *18–27 Bank Row* ☎ *01955/605393* ⊕ *www.wickheritage.org* 💷 *£3* ⊙ *Easter–Oct., Mon.–Sat. 10–3:45.*

10

EN ROUTE Signposted west off the A9 about 10 mi south of Wick are the extraordinary **Grey Cairns of Camster,** two Neolithic chambered cairns, dating from 4000 BC to 3000 BC, that are among the best preserved in Britain. **Camster Round Cairn** is 20 yards in diameter and 13 yards high, and **Camster Long Cairn** reaches nearly 77 yards in length. Nineteenth-century excavations revealed skeletons, pottery, and flint tools in the round cairn's internal chamber. If you don't mind dirty knees, you can crawl into the chambers in both cairns.

DUNBEATH

21 mi south of Wick.

A tiny coast village, Dunbeath is bordered by moors on one side, the sea on the other. A few interesting museums make it worth a stop.

GETTING HERE AND AROUND

South of Wick, Dunbeath can be reached via the A9. This coast-hugging route, crowded with Orkney ferry traffic, can be quite daunting because the steep drop-offs when heading south.

EXPLORING

The moors of Caithness roll down to the sea at Dunbeath, where you find the **Dunbeath Heritage Centre** in a former school. Inside are photographs and domestic and crofting artifacts that relay the area's history from the Bronze Age to the oil age. It's particularly helpful to those researching family histories. ⊠ *Off A9* ☎ *01593/731233* ⊕ *www.dunbeath-heritage.org.uk* ⌑ *£2* ☉ *Mar.–Oct., daily 10–5; Nov.–Apr., weekdays 11–3.*

> ### A BRUTAL DUKE
>
> Traveling south on the A9 from Helmsdale to Golspie, you can see the controversial statue of the first Duke of Sutherland, looking like some Eastern Bloc despot. He's perched on Beinn a Bragaidh (Ben Braggie), the hilltop to the west. Many people want to remove the statue, as the "improvement" policies of the duke were ultimately responsible for the brutality of the Sutherland Clearances of 1810–20, which removed people from their farms so there would be more room for sheep to graze.

HELMSDALE

15 mi south of Dunbeath.

Helmsdale is a fascinating fishing village with a checkered past. It was a busy Viking settlement and then the scene of an aristocratic poisoning plot before it was transformed into a 19th-century village to house some of the people removed from their land to make way for sheep. These "clearances," perpetrated by the Duke of Sutherland, were among the area's most inhumane.

GETTING HERE AND AROUND

Helmsdale is one of the only towns on this part of the coast that has a daily train service from Inverness. However, a car will allow you to see more in the surrounding area. Get here via the coastal A9 or the inland A897.

EXPLORING

☾ ★ The **Timespan Heritage Centre,** a thought-provoking mix of displays, artifacts, and audiovisual materials, portrays the history of the area from the Stone Age to the 1869 gold rush in the Strath of Kildonan. There's a geology exhibit in the garden and a tour of the Kildonan gold rush site. The complex also includes a café and an art gallery with changing exhibitions. ⊠ *Dunrobin St.* ☎ *01431/821327* ⊕ *www.timespan. org.uk* ⌑ *£4* ☉ *Easter–Oct., Mon.–Sat. 10–5, Sun. 2–5; last admission 1 hr before closing.*

GOLSPIE

18 mi south of Helmsdale.

The little coastal town of Golspie is worth a stop if you're heading for Dunrobin Castle. It has a number of shops and accommodations.

GETTING HERE AND AROUND

Golspie can be reached by train from Inverness, and in summer the train also stops at Dunrobin Castle. Drivers should use the the A9.

EXPLORING

The Scottish home of the dukes of Sutherland is flamboyant **Dunrobin Castle,** an ancient seat developed by the first duke into a 19th-century white-turreted behemoth. As well as lavish interiors, there are falconry demonstrations and Versailles-inspired gardens. Trains so fascinated the duke that he built his own railroad in the park and staffed it with his servants. ⊠ *Off A9* ☎ *01408/633177* 🗐 *£8* ⊙ *Apr.–May, Sept., and early Oct., daily 10:30–4:30; June–Aug., Mon.–Sat. 10:30–5:30; Sun. 12:30–4:30; last entry 30 mins before closing.*

SHOPPING

The **Orcadian Stone Company** (⊠ *Main St.* ☎ *01408/633483*) makes stone products—some crafted from local Caithness slate—such as incised plaques. There's also a geological exhibition. The shop is open from Easter to October and for three weeks before Christmas.

DORNOCH

10 mi south of Golspie, 40 mi north of Inverness.

A town of sandstone houses, tiny rose-filled gardens, and a 13th-century cathedral with stunning traditional and modern stained-glass windows, Dornoch is well worth a visit. It's noted for its links: you may hear it referred to as the St. Andrews of the North, but because of the town's location so far north, the golf courses here are delightfully uncrowded. Royal Dornoch is the jewel in its crown, praised by the world's top golfers.

GETTING HERE AND AROUND

From Inverness, take the A9 north to Dornoch. Be cautious, as it's often busy with ferry traffic.

ESSENTIALS

Visitor Information Dornoch (⊠ *Sheriff Court House, Castle St.* ☎ *08452/255121* ⊕ *www.visithighlands.com*).

WHERE TO STAY

££ 🛏 **Dornoch Castle Hotel.** A genuine late-15th-century castle, once sheltering the bishops of Caithness, this hotel blends the quite old and the more modern. The lounge is a relaxing room of soft green and cream, and bedrooms wear pastel stripes and floral fabrics. It's clean and comfortable, with a friendly staff and satisfying, well-cooked Scottish food in the restaurant. Try the steak rolled in crushed peppercorns and wrapped in Parma ham. **Pros:** grand exterior; lovely gardens; friendly hotel staff. **Cons:** a few rooms still need a lick of paint. ⊠ *Castle St.* ☎ *01862/810216* ⊕ *www.dornochcastlehotel.com* 🛏 *24 rooms* ⚘ *In-room: no a/c. In-hotel: restaurant, room service, Wi-Fi hotspot* 🖃 *AE, MC, V* 🍴❙ *BP.*

10

GOLF

★ Were it not for its remote location, **Royal Dornoch** would undoubtedly be a candidate for the British Open Championship. It's a superb, breezy, challenging links course. ✉ *Golf Rd.* ☎ *01862/810219* ⊕ *www. royaldornoch.com* ⛳ *18 holes, 6,200 yds, par 70.*

TORRIDON

Torridon has a grand, rugged, and wild air that feels especially remote, yet it doesn't take much more than an hour's drive west from Inverness before you reach Kinlochewe, near the east end of Glen Torridon. The western side is equally spectacular. Walking trails and mountain panoramas abound. Torridon is a wonderful place to visit if you want to tackle one of the legendary peaks here—Beinn Alligin, Liathach, and Beinn Eighe—or if you enjoy outdoor activities like kayaking, climbing, or mountain biking. The A890, which runs from the A832 into the heart of Torridon, is a single-lane road in some stretches, with plenty of open vistas across the deserted heart of northern Scotland.

LOCHCARRON

66 mi west of Inverness.

Strung along the shore, the village of Lochcarron has some attractive croft buildings, a couple of churches (one an 18th-century ruin set in a graveyard), a golf club, and some handy shops.

GETTING HERE AND AROUND

To drive here from Inverness, take the A9 as it becomes the A835, A832, and then the A890. The single-track road skirts both steep mountains and lochs.

SHOPPING

At **Lochcarron Weavers** (✉ *Mid Strome* ☎ *01520/722212*) you can observe a weaver at work, producing pure-wool worsted tartans that can be bought here or at the firm's other outlets in the area.

SHIELDAIG

16 mi northwest of Lochcarron.

Just west of the southern coast of Upper Loch Torridon is Shieldaig, a village that sits in an attractive crescent overlooking a loch of its own, Loch Shieldaig. For an atmospheric evening foray, walk north toward Loch Torridon, at the northern end of the village by the church. The path—fairly well made, though hiking shoes are recommended—leads to exquisite views and tiny rocky beaches.

GETTING HERE AND AROUND

★ The scenic spectacle of **Glen Torridon** lies east of Shieldaig. Some say that Glen Torridon has the finest mountain scenery in Scotland. It consists mainly of the long gray quartzite flanks of **Beinn Eighe** (rhymes with *say*) and **Liathach** (*leea*-gach), with its distinct ridge profile that looks like the keel of an upturned boat. The National Trust for Scotland operates a **visitor center** that explains the ecology and geology of the area. A small deer museum has displays on these quintessentially Scottish beasts. ✉ *A896* ☎ *01445/791368* ⊕ *www.nts.org.uk/visits* 🎫 *£3* ⊘ *Visitor center Easter–Sept., daily 10–6; deer museum year-round, daily 9–5.*

OFF THE BEATEN PATH

Applecross. The tame way to reach this small community facing Skye is by a coastal road from near Shieldaig. The exciting route turns west off the A896 a few miles farther south and then a series of hairpin turns corkscrews up the steep wall at the head of a corrie (a glacier-cut mountain valley), over the **Bealach na Ba** (Pass of the Cattle). There are spectacular views of Skye from the bare plateau on top, and you can brag afterward that you've been on what is probably Scotland's highest drivable road.

WHERE TO STAY

£££ 🏨 **The Torridon and Torridon Inn.** The Victorian Gothic turrets of this former hunting lodge promise atmosphere and grandeur. Log fires, handsome plasterwork ceilings, mounted stag heads, and traditional furnishings set the mood downstairs, and bedrooms are decorated in restrained pastel shades with antique mahogany furniture. The Torridon Inn annex offers more modest contemporary-style accommodation. The four-course dinner may include seafood, beef, lamb, and game, and the cellar has many fine wines. ■ TIP➔ Ask for a room with loch views. **Pros:** breathtaking location; center for outdoor activities; bar has more than 300 malts. **Cons:** isolated location; modern wing lacks character; rather pricey. ✉ *A896, Annat* ☎ *01445/791242* ⊕ *www.thetorridon.com* 🛏 *19 rooms* ⚒ *In-room: no a/c. In-hotel: restaurant, bar, laundry service* ⊟ *AE, DC, MC, V* ⎟⊙⎟ *BP.*

GAIRLOCH

38 mi north of Shieldaig.

Aside from its restaurants and lodgings, peaceful Gairloch has one further advantage: lying just a short way from the mountains of the interior, this small oasis often escapes the rain clouds that can cling to the high summits. You can enjoy a round of golf here and perhaps stay dry, even when the nearby Torridon Hills are deluged.

10

GETTING HERE AND AROUND
From Ullapool, this coastal town can be reached via A832.

EXPLORING
In the village is the **Gairloch Heritage Museum,** with exhibitions covering prehistoric times to the present. ✉ *Junction of A832 and B8031* ☎ *01445/712287* ⊕ *www.gairlochheritagemuseum.org.uk* 🎫 *£3* ⊘ *Easter–Sept., Mon.–Sat. 10–5; Oct., weekdays 10–1:30; Nov.–Mar. by appointment.*

Fodor's Choice ★ Southeast of Gairloch stretches one of Scotland's most scenic lochs, **Loch Maree.** Its harmonious environs, with tall Scots pines and the mountain Slioch looming as a backdrop, witnessed the destruction of much of the tree cover in the 18th century. Iron ore was shipped in and smelted using local oak to feed the furnaces. Oak now grows here only on the northern limits of the range. Scottish Natural Heritage has an **informa-tion center** and nature trails by the loch and in the Beinn Eighe Nature Reserve. Red-deer sightings are virtually guaranteed; locals say the best place to spot another local denizen, the endangered pine marten (a member of the weasel family), is around the trash containers in the parking turnoffs.

★ A highlight of this area is **Inverewe Gardens**, 6 mi northeast of Gairloch. The main attraction lies in the contrast between the bleak coastal headlands and thin-soiled moors, and the lush plantings of the garden behind its dense shelterbelts. These are proof of the efficacy of the warm North Atlantic Drift, part of the Gulf Stream, which takes the edge off winter frosts. Inverewe is sometimes described as subtropical, but this inaccuracy irritates the head gardener; do not expect coconuts and palm trees here. Instead, look for rarities like the blue Himalayan poppy. ✉ *A832, Poolewe* ☎ *01445/781200* ⊕ *www.nts.org.uk* ✉ *£8* ⊘ *Easter–Oct., daily 9:30–9; Jan.–Easter, daily 9:30–4.*

WHERE TO STAY

££ 🏨 **Dundonnell Hotel.** This family-run hotel, set on the roadside by Little Loch Broom, 30 mi northeast of Gairloch, has cultivated a solid repu-tation for its hospitality. A floral theme in the guest rooms and public rooms gives them an old-fashioned feel. Many have stunning views of pristine hills and lochs. The restaurant serves homemade soups and fresh seafood, including sea bass, monkfish, and salmon. ■**TIP➔ Ask for a room with loch views. Pros:** fabulous scenery; plenty of outdoor activities; good dining options. **Cons:** bland exterior; decor not to every-one's taste. ✉ *A832, Dundonnell IV23 2QR* ☎ *01854/633204* ⊕ *www.dundonnellhotel.com* ⮡ *32 rooms* ⌂ *In-room: no a/c. In-hotel: restau-rant, bar, Wi-Fi hotspot* ▭ *AE, MC, V* ⊘⌷ *BP.*

£ 🏨 **Mountain Coffee Company & Hillbillies Bookstore.** A café, lodge, and book shop all rolled into one, this property is a center of activity in Gairloch. Guest rooms are cozy, and one even has a four-poster bed. The café has a conservatory with a sweeping view over the sea. Fresh-baked scones, both savory and sweet, are excellent for breakfast and lunch. Books on all subjects are everywhere, spilling over from the shop into the res-taurant. Mountaineering memorabilia decorate the walls. **Pros:** good dining options; great for spotting wildlife like porpoises and seals. **Cons:** dated decor; gets booked up quickly. ✉ *Strath Sq.* ☎ *01445/712316* ⮡ *3 rooms* ⌂ *In-room: no a/c. In-hotel: restaurant* ▭ *MC, V* ⊘ *Closed Jan.–Mar.* ⌷⌷ *CP.*

GOLF

Gairloch Golf Club is one of the few on this stretch of coast. ☎ *01445/712407* ⊕ *www.gairlochgolfclub.com* ⚑ *18 holes, 2,072 yds, SSS 62.*

EN ROUTE The road between Gairloch and the Corrieshalloch Gorge initially heads north and passes coastal scenery with views of Gruinard Bay and its white beaches, then woodlands around Dundonnell and Loch Broom. Soon the route traverses wild country: the toothed ramparts of the mountain An Teallach (pronounced *tyel*-lack) are visible on the horizon. The moorland route you travel is known chillingly as **Destitution Road.** At Corrieshalloch the road, A832, joins the A835 for Inverness.

ISLE OF SKYE

The misty isle, Skye is full of romance and myth, lovely gardens and steep, magnetic mountains (a compass is useless in the Cuillin Mountains). It ranks near the top of most visitors' must-see lists: the romance of Prince Charles Edward Stuart (1720–88), known as Bonnie Prince Charlie, combined with the Cuillin Mountains and their proximity to the mainland, all contribute to its popularity. Today Skye remains fey, mysterious, and mountainous, an island of sunsets that linger brilliantly until late at night, and of beautiful, magical mists. Much photographed are the really old crofts, one or two of which are still inhabited, with their thick stone walls and thatch roofs.

From the gentle, lush terrain of the Garden of Skye to the wild Cuillin Mountains, Skye has abundant beauty and memorable vistas aplenty. It also has as an increasingly impressive range of accommodations and some excellent restaurants that show off the best in the island's produce and culinary talent.

To reach Skye, you can cross over the bridge spanning the narrow channel of Kyle Akin, between Kyle of Lochalsh and Kyleakin, or in summer you can take the more romantic trip via ferries between Mallaig and Armadale or between Glenelg and Kylerea. You can tour comfortably around the island in two or three days, but a bit longer would allow time for some hiking or some sea-kayaking. Orientation is easy: follow the only roads around the loops on the northern part of the island and enjoy the road running the length of the Sleat Peninsula in southern Skye. There are some stretches of single-lane road, but with attention and care none pose a problem.

KYLE OF LOCHALSH

55 mi west of Inverness, 120 mi northwest of Glasgow.

This little town is the mainland gateway to Skye. Opened in 1995, the bridge transformed not only travel to Skye but the very seascape itself. The most noticeable attraction, though (in fact, almost a cliché), is not in Kyle at all, but 8 mi farther east at Dornie—Eilean Donan Castle.

GETTING HERE AND AROUND

From the north, you reach Kyle of Lochalsh via the A890 or A896; from the south, take the A87. Trains travel here from Inverness, but the journey requires changing trains several times.

EXPLORING

Fodor's Choice ★ Guarding the confluence of lochs Long, Alsh, and Duich stands that most picturesque of all Scottish castles, **Eilean Donan Castle,** perched on an islet connected to the mainland by a stone-arched bridge. Dating from the 14th century, this romantic icon has all the massive stone walls, timber ceilings, and winding stairs that you could ask for. Empty and neglected for years after being bombarded by frigates of the Royal Navy during an abortive Spanish-Jacobite landing in 1719, it was almost entirely rebuilt from a ruin in the early 20th century. The kitchen re-creates the busy scene before a grand banquet. Now the hero of travel

10

brochures, Eilean Donan has appeared in many Hollywood movies and TV shows. ⊠ *A87, Dornie* ☎ *01599/555202* ⊕ *www.eileandonancastle.com* 🎫 *£5.50* ⏱ *Mid-Mar.–Oct., daily 10–6; last admission at 5.*

BROADFORD

8 mi west of Kyle of Lochalsh via Skye Bridge.

One of the larger of Skye's settlements, Broadford lies along the shore of Broadford Bay, which has on occasion welcomed whales to its sheltered waters.

GETTING HERE AND AROUND

Broadford is on the main road crossing the Isle of Skye, the A87.

ESSENTIALS

Visitor Information Broadford (⊠ *Car park* ☎ *8452/255121* ⊕ *www.visithighlands.com*).

EXPLORING

🔆 You can observe and handle snakes, frogs, lizards, and tortoises at the **Serpentarium**, in the town center. It's also a refuge for wayward, worldly reptiles. ⊠ *The Old Mill* ☎ *01471/822209* ⊕ *www.skyeserpentarium.org.uk* 🎫 *£3.50* ⏱ *Easter–June, Sept., and Oct., Mon.–Sat. 10–5; July and Aug., daily 10–5.*

For fantastic views of the Cuillin Mountains, seabirds, abundant sea life, and the Inner Hebrides, book a place on one of the **Misty Isle Boat Trips** (⊠ Elgol jetty, *Elgol* ☎ *01471/866288* ⊕ *www.mistyisleboattrips. co.uk*). The expansive scenery around Loch Coruisk is some of the most spectacular in Scotland. From April to October, round-trip journeys depart from the nearby town of Elgol Monday to Saturday at 9, 11, 2:15, and 5:30. Private charters are also available.

OFF THE BEATEN PATH

The Road to Elgol. The B8083 leads from Broadford to one of the finest views in Scotland. This road passes through **Strath Suardal** and little **Loch Cill Chriosd** (Kilchrist) by a ruined church. You can appreciate breathtaking views of the mountain called **Bla Bheinn** as the A881 continues to Elgol, a gathering of crofts along this road that descends to a pier. Admire the heart-stopping profile of the Cuillin peaks from the shore, or, at a point about halfway down the hill, you can find the path that goes toward them across the rough grasslands. For even better views, take a boat trip on the **Bella Jane** (⊠ *Elgol jetty, Elgol* ☎ *0800/731–3089* ⊕ *www.bellajane.co.uk*) from the Elgol jetty toward Loch Coruisk; you'll be able to see seals and land and walk up to the loch itself. The roundtrip excursion, available April to October, costs £20 per person.

WHERE TO STAY

£££ **Broadford Hotel.** Extensive renovations (still in progress at this writing) have transformed the interior of this imposing 17th-century building into a modern hotel. Sparsely furnished and modern in style, the guest rooms are done up in the strong Drambuie tartan colors, softened a bit by more relaxing hues. The restaurant offers such dishes as fettuccine in a woodland-mushroom cream sauce, and locally caught langoustines. Dark wood in the bar adds warmth, and a glass conservatory looks across to the Inner Sound. **Pros:** good restaurant; innovative drinks in the bar. **Cons:** not for those who want traditional decor; some noise from ongoing renovations. ⊠ *Torrin Rd.* ☎ *01471/822204* ⊕ *www.broadfordhotel.co.uk* ⇄ *11 rooms* ⚐ *In-room: no a/c, Wi-Fi. In-hotel: restaurant, bar* ⊟ *AE, MC, V* ⊺⊙⊦ *BP.*

BICYCLING

If you want to explore the country roads **Fairwinds Bicycle Hire** (⊠ *Elgol Rd.* ☎ *01471/822270* rents bicycles year-round.

10

ARMADALE

17 mi south of Broadford, 43 mi south of Portree, 5 mi (ferry crossing) west of Mallaig.

Rolling moorlands, scattered with rivers and lochans, give way to enchanting hidden coves and scattered waterside communities here in **Sleat,** the southernmost part of Skye.

GETTING HERE AND AROUND

The Mallaig-Armadale ferry arrives here. There's a short (and beautiful) road to the southwest, while the main road heads east following the stunning coast.

EXPLORING

Walk the lush, extensive gardens at **Armadale Castle Gardens and the Museum of the Isles** and you take in magnificent view across the Sound of Sleat to Knoydart and the Mallaig Pennisula. The Clan Donald Centre tells the story of the Macdonalds and their proud title—the Lords of the Isles—with the help of an excellent audiovisual presentation. In the 15th century the clan was powerful enough to threaten the authority of the Stuart monarchs of Scotland. There's a gift shop, restaurant, library, and center for genealogy research. Also on the grounds are high-quality accommodations in seven cottages with kitchen facilities. ⊠ ½ mi north of Armadale Pier ☎ 01471/844305 ⊕ www.clandonald.com ✉ £6 ☉ Apr.–Oct., daily 9:30–5:30; last entry 30 mins before closing.

WHERE TO STAY

£££££ ⬚ **Duisdale House Hotel.** Set in 35 acres of mature woodlands and gardens, this former mansion has a lovely hillside location with views to the sea. Guest rooms have individual touches like corner bathtubs or four-poster bed. The seafood restaurant attracts visiting yachters. The anti-midge machine will help you enjoy the deck and hot tub. Join the daily sailings on the owner's yacht. **Pros:** nicely refurbished rooms; expansive views; excellent staff. **Cons:** nautical decor might not suit everyone. ⊠ Off A851, Sleat ☎ 01471/833202 ⊕ www.duisdale.com ⬚ 17 rooms ⬚ In-room: no a/c, DVD (some), Wi-Fi. In-hotel: restaurant, bar ⊟ DC, MC, V ⎟⊙⎟ BP.

££££ ⬚ **Hotel Eilean Iarmain.** Built on a small peninsula with a quiet lighthouse on the point, this hotel has an unforgettable location. The Isle Ornsay Hotel (as it's sometimes known) has an enchanting collection of wood paneling, chintz fabrics, and country-style antiques. The mix-and-match furniture in the rooms has genuine charm, while the newer pine bathrooms are less successful. The menu in the restaurant changes daily, and the bar serves inexpensive fare to locals and travelers. There's a whisky shop and art gallery on the premises. **Pros:** wonderful waterfront location; plenty of sporting activities, superb wine list. **Cons:** some unattractive renovations. ⊠ Off A851, Isle Ornsay ☎ 01471/833332 ⊕ www.eileaniarmain.co.uk ⬚ 12 rooms, 4 suites ⬚ In-room: no a/c, no TV (some). In-hotel: restaurant, bar ⊟ AE, MC, V ⎟⊙⎟BP.

£££££ ⬚ **Kinloch Lodge.** Overlooking the tidal Loch na Dal, this historic lodge has buildings that date from the 17th century. The newer South House has the best views and has been solidly built with comfort and relaxation in mind. You're welcomed with a glass of champagne by friendly, professional staff. Guest rooms, decorated with antiques, fine fabrics, and quilted bedspreads, have views over the water, the hills, or the grounds. The dining room serves up confidently prepared food—everything down to the shortbread is made on the premises. A small shop carries great kitchen gadgets as well as jams made by the owner, Lady Claire Macdonald. If you like the food, you can take cooking classes with her or award-winning chef Marcello Tully. **Pros:** historic property; interior full of character; great afternoon tea. **Cons:** rooms are pricey. ⊠ Off A851, Sleat ☎ 01471/833214 ⊕ www.kinloch-lodge.co.uk ⬚ 14 rooms ⬚ In-room: no a/c. In-hotel: restaurant, bars ⊟ AE, MC, V ⎟⊙⎟MAP.

SHOPPING

★ **Ragamuffin** (✉ *Armadale Pier* ☎ *01471/844217*) specializes in designer knitwear. In winter the friendly staff might make you a cup of coffee while you browse, then mail your purchases back home for you.

PORTREE

43 mi north of Armadale.

Portree, the population center of the island, is a pleasant place clustered around a small and sheltered bay. Although not overburdened by historical features, it's a good touring base with a number of good shops, and an excellent bakery.

GETTING HERE AND AROUND

The biggest town on Skye, Portree is well served by local buses and by a well-maintained road, the A87.

ESSENTIALS

Visitor Information Portree (✉ *Bayfield House, Bayfield Rd.* ☎ *01478/612137* ⊕ *www.visithighlands.com*).

EXPORING

On the outskirts of town is **Tigh na Coille: Aros** (*tigh na coille* is Gaelic for "house of the forest," and *aros* means "home" or "homestead"), a museum that provides an excellent account of Skye's often turbulent history over the centuries. It's also a great place to peep at the island's abundant wildlife. Park rangers regularly enthrall visitors by revealing the lives of Skye's sea eagles and sparrow hawks by way of nifty nest cams. ✉ *Viewfield Rd.* ☎ *01478/613649* ⊕ *www.aros.co.uk* 🖭 *£4* 🕙 *Daily 10–5.*

WHERE TO EAT AND STAY

££
BRITISH
✕ **Café Arriba.** Up a steep flight of stairs, the laid-back café has window seats with great views over Portree Harbour. Using only local produce ("whatever is fresh, local, and available"), this is a good option for no-frills eating. Good choices include locally caught scallops, creamy summer risotto, and, on the lighter side, salad with freshly baked bread. ✉ *Quay Brae* ☎ *01478/611830* ▤ *DC, MC, V.*

£££££ 🏨 **Cuillin Hills Hotel.** Just outside Portree, this Victorian-era hunting lodge has many rooms with views over Portree Bay. Bold floral patterns enliven the bedrooms. The seafood dishes in the restaurant are especially good: try the local prawns, lobster, or scallops. ■TIP→ **Ask for a room with views of the harbor and Cuillins beyond.** Pros: Portree is a short stroll away; good breakfast menu; attentive service. **Cons:** rooms at back overpriced; restaurant can get very busy. ✉ *A855* ☎ *01478/612003* ⊕ *www.cuillinhills-hotel-skye.co.uk* 🛏 *27 rooms* 🛁 *In-room: no a/c, Wi-Fi. In-hotel: restaurant, bar, laundry service* ▤ *AE, MC, V* ⦿ *BP.*

££ 🏨 **Rosedale Hotel.** The higgledy-piggledy 19th-century buildings that make up this harbor-front hotel contain clean and comfortable rooms are done in pastels and florals. Ask for a room at the front for views of the water. **Pros:** friendly staff; first-class location. **Cons:** dated decor in many rooms; tricky parking. ✉ *The Harbour* ☎ *01478/613131* ⊕ *www.*

10

Clans and Tartans

CLOSE UP

Whatever the origins of the clans—some with Norman roots, intermarried into Celtic society; some of Norse origin, the product of Viking raids on Scotland; others traceable to the monastic system; yet others possibly descended from Pictish tribes—by the 13th century the clan system was at the heart of Gaelic tribal culture. By the 15th century the clan chiefs of the Scottish Highlands were a threat even to the authority of the Stewart monarchs.

The word *clann* means "family" or "children" in Gaelic, and it was the custom for clan chiefs to board out their sons among nearby families, a practice that helped to bond the clan unit and create strong allegiances: the chief became "father" of the tribe and was owed loyalty by lesser chiefs and ordinary clansmen.

THE CLAN SYSTEM

The clan chiefs' need for strong men-at-arms, fast-running messengers, and bards for entertainment and the preservation of clan genealogy was the probable origin of the Highland Games, still celebrated in many Highland communities each year, and which are an otherwise rather inexplicable mix of sports, music, and dance.

Gradually, by the 18th century, increasing knowledge of Lowland agricultural improvements, and better roads into the Highlands that improved communication of ideas and "southern" ways, began to weaken the clan system. After Culloden, as more modern economic influences took hold, those on the "wrong" side lost all; many chiefs lost their lands, tartan was banned, and clan culture withered.

TARTAN REVIVAL

Tartan's own origins as a part of the clan system are disputed; the Gaelic word for striped cloth is *breacan*—piebald or spotted—so even the word itself is not Highland. However, when cloth was locally spun, woven, and dyed using plant derivatives, each neighborhood would have different dyestuffs. In this way, particular combinations of colors and favorite patterns of the local weavers could become associated with a particular area and therefore clan.

Between 1746 and 1782 the wearing of tartan was generally prohibited. By the time the ban was lifted, many recipes for dyes and weaving patterns had been forgotten.

It took the influence of Sir Walter Scott, with his romantic (and fashionable) view of Highland history, to create the "modern myth" of clans and tartan. Sir Walter engineered George IV's visit to Scotland in 1822, which turned into a tartan extravaganza. The idea of one tartan or group of tartans "belonging" to one particular clan was created at this time—literally created, with new patterns and color ways dreamed up and "assigned" to particular clans. Queen Victoria and Prince Albert reinforced the tartan culture later in the century.

It's considered "proper" in some circles to wear the "right" tartan, that is, that of your clan. You may be able to find a clan connection with expertise such as that available at the **Clan Tartan Centre** (✉ *70–74 Bangor Rd., Leith, Edinburgh* ☎ *0131/553–5161*).

rosedalehotelskye.co.uk ⬚ *24 rooms* ⬚ *In-room: no a/c. In-hotel: restaurant, bar* ⬚ *MC, V* ☺ *Closed Dec.–Mar.* ⬚ *BP.*

££ ⬚ **The Spoons.** After 13 years running a luxury estate for others, Marie
★ and Ian Lewis put their considerable talents to work at The Spoons. Ian built the house, set on a working farm. Marie designed and decorated each room, selecting furniture that includes restored antiques). Look for elegant touches like brass or ceramic light fixtures, original artwork, and locally made tweed doorstops. The comfortable beds are heaven after a day of exploring. Marie offers tea and baked goods when you arrive; the breakfast is superb, with fresh fruit, homemade crepes, and eggs from the property. **Pros:** top-notch breakfasts; perfect base for exploring. **Cons:** books up quickly. ⬚ *75 Aird Bernisdale* ⬚ *01470/532217* ⬚ *www.thespoonsonskye.com* ⬚ *3 rooms* ⬚ *In-room: no a/c, DVD (some), Wi-Fi (some)* ⬚ *AE, D, DC, MC, V* ⬚ *BP.*

SHOPPING

Isle of Skye Soap Company (⬚ *Somerled Sq.IV51 9EH* ⬚ *1478/611350)* stocks soaps, essential oils, and other nice-smelling gifts. The **Tartan Company** (⬚ *The Green* ⬚ *0845/1259749* chooses its stock well, including innovative tartan items like tweed doorstops.

TROTTERNISH PENINSULA

16 mi north of Portree.

As A855, the main road, goes north from Portree, cliffs rise to the left. They're actually the edge of an ancient lava flow, set back from the road and running for miles. Fossilized dinosaur bones have been uncovered at the base of these cliffs. Don't forget to look up in case you spot a sea eagle, identifiable by its flash of a white tail.

GETTING HERE AND AROUND

From Portree, take the twisting, undulating A855 as it follows the coast.

EXPLORING

In some places along the A855, the hardened lava has created spectacular features, including a curious pinnacle called the **Old Man of Storr.**

10

From Portree, the A855 travels past neat white croft houses and forestry plantings to **Kilt Rock.** Everyone on the Skye tour circuit stops here to peep over the cliffs (there's a safe viewing platform) for a look at the geology of the cliff edge: columns of two types (and colors) of rock create a folded, pleated effect, just like a kilt.

Staffin Museum. Built on the foundations of an 1840s schoolhouse, this single-room museum is a labor of love of builder Dugald Ross, who first saw the fossilized dinosaur prints as a boy and as an adult saved them from rough seas. ⬚ *Off A855,Staffin* ⬚ *Free* ☺ *Daily, call for hrs.*

The spectacular **Quiraing** dominates the horizon 5 mi past Kilt Rock. For a closer view of this area's strange pinnacles and rock forms, make a left onto a small road at Brogaig by Staffin Bay. There's a parking lot near the point where this road breaches the ever-present cliff line. The trail is on uneven, stony ground, and it's a steep scramble up to the rock formations. In ages past, stolen cattle were hidden deep within the Quiraing's rocky jaws.

The A855 reaches around the top end of Trotternish, to the **Skye Museum of Island Life** at Kilmuir, where you can see the old crofting ways brought to life. Included in the displays and exhibits are documents and photographs, reconstructed interiors, and implements. Flora Macdonald, who assisted Bonnie Prince Charlie, is buried nearby. ⊠ *A855, Kilmuir* ☎ *01470/552206* ⊕ *www.skyemuseum.co.uk* 🎫 *£2.50* ⊘ *Easter–Oct., daily 9–5.*

WHERE TO STAY

££££   🏠 **Flodigarry Country House Hotel.** Close links with Flora Macdonald, Prince Charles Edward Stuart's helpmate, are not the least of the attractions at this country-house hotel, which is well placed for exploring the north and west of Skye. Yes, you can actually have a room in Flora's own cottage, adjacent to the hotel, where six of her children were born. The main hotel is a bit grander, and serves excellent seafood in the dining room. There are no TVs in the rooms, but you can ask to borrow a portable. **Pros:** the chance to stay within historic walls; stunning views of the Quiraing. **Cons:** some beds are on the small side; erratic customer service. ⊠ *A855, Staffin* ☎ *01470/552203* ⊕ *www.flodigarry. co.uk* 🛏 *18 rooms* ⚐ *In-room: no a/c, no TV. In-hotel: restaurant, bar* 🗖 *MC, V* ⓄⓁ *BP.*

WATERNISH PENINSULA

20 mi northwest of Portree.

The northwest corner of Skye has scattered crofting communities, magnificent coastal views, and a few good restaurants well worth the trip in themselves. In the Hallin area look westward for an islet-scattered sea loch with small cliffs rising from the water—and looking like miniature models of full-size islands.

GETTING HERE AND AROUND

From Portree, follow the A850 to the Waternish Pennisula.

EXPLORING

Stoneware pottery is fired in a wood-fired kiln at the **Edinbane Pottery Workshop and Gallery.** You can watch the potters work, then buy from the showroom. ⊠ *Off A850, Edinbane* ☎ *01470/582234* ⊕ *www. edinbane-pottery.co.uk* ⊘ *Easter–Oct., daily 9–6; Nov.–Easter, weekdays 9–6.*

Skye Skyns (⊠ *17 Lochbay, Waternish* ☎ *01470/592237*) sells hand-tanned sheepskins above a working tannery. A tour of the tannery takes 10 minutes and gives excellent insight into the process of salting, washing, and preparing the skins. You'll learn the source of phrases such as "on tenterhooks" and "stretched to the limits."

WHERE TO EAT AND STAY

££££   ✕ **Loch Bay Seafood Restaurant.** On the waterfront in the village of Stein
★   stands a distinctive black-and-white restaurant. This relaxed place is
SEAFOOD where the island's top chefs unwind on their nights off, so you know the food must be good. The seafood is freshly caught and simply prepared,

the goal being to enhance the natural flavors of the ingredients rather than overwhelm the senses with extraneous sauces. ✉ *Near fishing jetty, Stein* ☎ *01470/592235* ▤ *MC, V* ⊘ *Closed Nov.–Easter, weekends Nov.–June, and Sun. July–Oct.*

£££££ ⊡ **Greshornish House.** Set above a sea loch, this pretty white house stands among mature trees and beside a nurtured, but not tame, walled garden filled with raspberries, currents, and gooseberries. The kitchen turns out good Scottish fare. It's a family house, with rules that create a slightly more restrained tone, but there's surely comfort to be found here. **Pros:** ideal setting; lovely gardens; great walks at the doorstep. **Cons:** reserved welcome may not suit everyone. ✉ *Greshornish* ☎ *01470/582266* ⊕ *www.greshornishhouse.com* ⮌ *8 rooms* ⌂ *In-room: no a/c. In-hotel: restaurant* ▤ *AE, MC, V* ⦿ *MAP.*

GLENDALE

2 mi south of Dunvegan.

The Glendale Visitor Route, a signed driving trail off the A863 through the westernmost area of northwest Skye, leads past crafts outlets, museums, and other attractions. Dunvegan Castle is at the eastern edge of the area.

GETTING HERE AND AROUND

Traveling south from Dunvegan, the B884 road twists and curves along the coast. It can feel quite isolated in bad weather or after dark.

EXPLORING

In a commanding position above a sea loch, **Dunvegan Castle** has been the seat of the chiefs of Clan MacLeod for more than 700 years. Though the structure has been greatly changed over the centuries, a gloomy ambience prevails, and there's plenty of family history on display, notably the Fairy Flag—a silk banner, thought to be originally from Rhodes or Syria and believed to have magically saved the clan from danger. The banner's powers are said to suffice for only one more use. Make time to visit the gardens, with their water garden and falls, fern house, a walled garden, and various viewing points. Dunvegan Sea Cruises runs a boat trip from the castle to the nearby seal colony. The castle is 22 mi west of Portree: follow A850. ✉ *Junction of A850 and A863, Dunvegan* ☎ *01470/521206* ⊕ *www.dunvegancastle.com* ▣ *Garden £5.50, castle and garden £7.50* ⊘ *Apr.–Oct., daily 10–5:30; Nov.–Mar., daily 11–4; last entry 30 mins before closing.*

10

The **Toy Museum,** has a remarkable collection of dolls, trains, games, puzzles, and books that transports visitors back to their childhoods. ✉ *B884* ☎ *01470/511240* ⊕ *www.toy-museum.co.uk* ▣ *£3* ⊘ *Mon.– Sat. 10–6.*

The fascinating **Borreraig Park Museum**—rightly described by the owner as "a unique gallimaufry for your delight and edification"—includes a detailed series of panels on the making of bagpipes and on the history of the MacCrimmons, hereditary pipers to the Clan MacLeod. A superb gift shop stocks unique island-made sweaters (the exact sheep can be named), bagpipes, silver and gold jewelry in Celtic designs, and recordings of traditional music. ⊠ *Borreraig Park* ☎ *01470/511311* ▭ *£2.50* ⊙ *Daily 10–6.*

WHERE TO EAT AND STAY

££££   ✕ **Three Chimneys.** On Loch Dunvegan, this old building with thick stone
Fodor's Choice   walls holds a restaurant that has become a top destination for serious
★   foodies. The kitchen serves consistently daring, well-crafted food, and
MODERN BRITISH   the chef's belief in Scottish ingredients is clear in what is on offer: Glendale salad leaves, Broadford smoked haddock, and grilled Mallaig cod
with a pine kernel crust. If you love the food so much you want to stay
here, there are six comfortable rooms at the nearby House Over-By.
Reservations are suggested; this place is well known. ⊠ *B884, Colbost*
☎ *01470/511258* ▭ *AE, MC, V* ⊙ *No lunch Sun.*

££   🖼 **Roskhill House.** A 19th-century croft house that once housed the local
post office in its dining room, this pretty white hotel feels like a home
away from home. Bold colors decorate the bedrooms, and the lounge
is filled with books and games. Stone walls, stick-back chairs, and a
scarlet carpet lend the dining room a publike air. In the morning, the
breakfast options are a change from the usual heavy fare. This B&B
is 3 mi south of Dunvegan. **Pros:** great breakfasts; genuinely friendly
and helpful hosts; cozy lounge with fireplace. **Cons:** very small place;
books up well in advance. ⊠ *A863, Roskhill* ☎ *01470/521317* ⊕ *www.
roskhillhouse.co.uk* ⇨ *5 rooms* ⌂ *In-room: no a/c, no phone, no TV.
In-hotel: Internet terminal* ▭ *MC, V* ⦿ *BP.*

SHOPPING

Skye Silver (⊠ *The Old School, Colbost* ☎ *01470/511263*) designs gold
and silver jewelry with Celtic themes. More unusual pieces that reflect
the natural forms of the seashore and countryside: silver-coral earrings,
silver-leaf pendants, and starfish earrings. It's near Dunvegan.

GLEN BRITTLE AND THE CUILLIN MOUNTAINS

28 mi southeast of Glendale.

GETTING HERE AND AROUND

Glen Brittle extends off the A863/B8009 on the west side of the
island.

EXPLORING

★   You can safely enjoy spectacular mountain scenery in **Glen Brittle**, with
some fine views of the Cuillin Mountains (which are not for the casual
walker, as there are many steep and dangerous cliff faces). The drive
from Carbost along a single-track road is one of the most dramatic in
Scotland and draws outdoorsy types from throughout the world. At the
southern end of the glen is a murky-color beach, a campground, and
the chance for a gentle stroll amid the foothills.

THE OUTER HEBRIDES

The Outer Hebrides—the Western Isles in common parlance—stretch
about 130 mi from end to end and lie about 50 mi from the Scottish
mainland. This splintered archipelago extends from the Butt of Lewis

in the north to the 600-foot Barra Head on Berneray in the south, whose lighthouse has the greatest arc of visibility in the world. In the Hebrides, clouds cling to the hills, and rain comes in squalls. Any trip here requires protection from the weather and a conviction that a great holiday does not require the sun.

The Isle of Lewis and Harris is the northernmost and largest of the group. The island's only major town, Stornoway, is on a nearly land-locked harbor on the east coast of Lewis; it's probably the most convenient starting point for a driving tour of the islands if you're approaching the Western Isles from the Northern Highlands. Lewis has some fine historic attractions, including the Calanais Standing Stones—a truly magical place. The Uists are known for their rare, plentiful wildlife.

Just south of the Sound of Harris is the Isle of North Uist, rich in monoliths, chambered cairns, and other reminders of a prehistoric past. Benbecula, sandwiched between North and South Uist, is in fact less bare and neglected-looking than its bigger neighbors to the north. The Isle of South Uist, once a refuge of the old Catholic faith, is dotted with ruined forts and chapels; in summer its wild gardens burst with alpine and rock plants. Eriskay Island and a scattering of islets almost block the 6-mi strait between South Uist and Barra, an isle you can walk across in an hour.

Harris tweed is available at many outlets on the islands, including some of the weavers' homes; keep an eye out for signs directing you to weavers' workshops. Sunday on the islands is observed as a day of rest, and nearly all shops and visitor attractions are closed.

STORNOWAY

On Lewis; 2½-hr ferry trip from Ullapool.

The port capital for the Outer Hebrides is Stornoway, the only major town on Lewis. The island's cultural center, it has an increasing number of good restaurants.

GETTING HERE AND AROUND

The ferry docks at Stornoway, and there's an airport. It's best to have a car to explore the island, but there are also infrequent local buses.

ESSENTIALS

Airport Contact Stornoway Airport (☎ 01851/702256 ⊕ www.hial.co.uk/stornoway-airport.html).

Visitor Information Stornoway (✉ 26 Cromwell St. ☎ 01851/703088 ⊕ www.visithebrides.com).

EXPLORING

★ The fabulous **An Lanntair Arts Centre** has exhibitions of contemporary and traditional art, as well as a cinema, a gift shop, and a restaurant serving international and Scottish fare. There are frequent traditional musical and theatrical events in the impressive auditorium. ✉ *Kenneth St.* ☎ *01851/703307* ⊕ *www.lanntair.com* 🎟 *Free* ☉ *Mon.–Sat. 10* AM–8 PM.

10

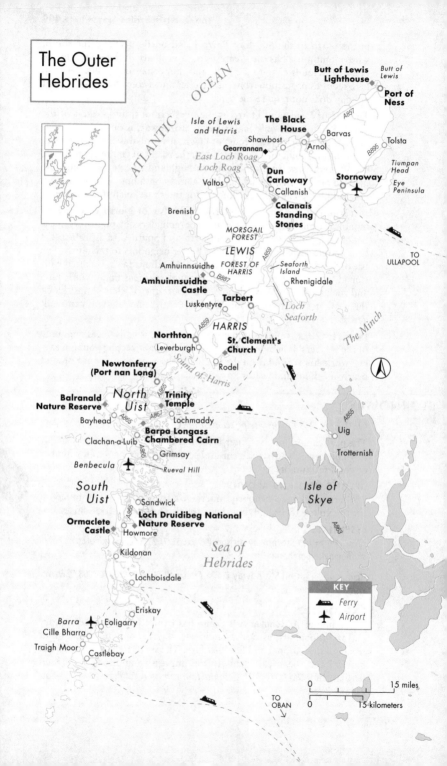

The Outer Hebrides

ATLANTIC OCEAN

Isle of Lewis and Harris

East Loch Roag
Loch Roag

Butt of Lewis Lighthouse · Butt of Lewis
Port of Ness

The Black House · Barvas
Shawbost
Arnol
Tolsta

Gearrannan
Dun Carloway
Valtos
Callanish
Stornoway · Tiumpan Head
Eye Peninsula

Brenish
Calanais Standing Stones

MORSGAIL FOREST

LEWIS

TO ULLAPOOL

Amhuinnsuidhe
FOREST OF HARRIS
Seaforth Island
Rhenigidale

Amhuinnsuidhe Castle
Tarbert
Luskentyre
Loch Seaforth

HARRIS

Northton
Leverburgh
St. Clement's Church
Rodel

Sound of Harris

The Minch

Newtonferry (Port nan Long)
Trinity Temple

Balranald Nature Reserve
North Uist
Bayhead
Lochmaddy

Barpa Longass Chambered Cairn
Clachan-a-Luib
Grimsay

Benbecula
Rueval Hill

Uig
Trotternish

South Uist
Sandwick

Isle of Skye

Ormaclete Castle
Loch Druidibeg National Nature Reserve
Howmore

Kildonan

Sea of Hebrides

Lochboisdale

Eriskay

Barra
Cille Bharra
Eoligarry

Traigh Moor
Castlebay

TO OBAN

KEY
Ferry
Airport

0 — 15 miles
0 — 15 kilometers

WHERE TO STAY AND EAT

££ ✕ **Digby Chick.** This local favorite is a great destination on a rainy night.

BRITISH The solid wood floors and white table clothes brighten the spirits. The seasonal food is hearty even in the middle of summer, with scallops and pea puree, duck breast with citrus syrup, and sweet-toothed desserts like the iced honeycomb meringue tart. ⊠ *5 Bank St.* ☎ *01851/700026* ▭ *MC, V.*

££££ ▦ **Broad Bay House.** About 7 mi north of Stornoway, Broad Bay House has great views over the bay. It's not in town, but you won't miss the hustle and bustle. Besides, it's a perfect base for walking or touring. Meticulously designed and constructed, the hotel pampers you with many small details, like the stereo system and weather predictor in your room. Solid oak defines the floors and the furniture, and the walls are decorated in colors that conjure earth, wind, and water. Exquisite evening meals are served in a dining room that is mostly windows. **Pros:** pure luxury; great coastal walks; fantastic evening meals. **Cons:** no kids; only one room has sea views; need a car. ⊠ *B895* ☎ *01851/820990* ⊕ *www.broadbayhouse.co.uk* ⟲ *4 rooms* ☖ *In-room: DVD, Internet, Wi-Fi. In-hotel: restaurant, beachfront, bicycles, laundry facilities, laundry service* ▭ *AE, DC, MC, V* ⦿ *BP.*

££ ▦ **Park Guest House and Restaurant.** This handsome Victorian-era house has retained many of its original features, including the grand fireplaces. Expect an interesting mix of tourists and people traveling for business. The restaurant, open to the public, serves lamb, seafood, and wild game. For breakfast you can choose traditional dishes like Stornoway kippers and black pudding. ■**TIP→** **Cooks should look into the on-site cooking classes.** **Pros:** excellent restaurant; on-site cookery courses. **Cons:** rooms facing the main road can be noisy; some rooms need refurbishment; service can be indifferent. ⊠ *30 James St.* ☎ *01851/702485* ⊕ *www.theparkguesthouse.co.uk* ⟲ *8 rooms* ☖ *In-room: no a/c. In-hotel: restaurant, bar* ▭ *AE, MC, V* ⦿ *BP.*

SHOPPING

The **Harris Tweed Artisans Cooperative** (⊠ *40 Point St.* ☎ *No phone*) sells stylish and quirky hand-crafted tweed clothing, hats, accessories, all made by artists belonging to the cooperative.

BICYCLING

Alex Dan Cycle Centre (⊠ *67 Kenneth St.* ☎ *01851/704025*) rents bicycles and can give you advice on where to ride, including a route to Tolsta that takes in five stunning beaches before reaching the edge of moorland.

10

PORT OF NESS

On Lewis; 30 mi north of Stornoway.

The stark, windswept community of Port of Ness cradles a small harbor squeezed in among the rocks.

GETTING HERE AND AROUND

From Stornoway, take the A857 to the Port of Ness.

EXPLORING

At the northernmost point of Lewis stands the **Butt of Lewis Lighthouse,** designed by David and Thomas Stevenson (of the prominent engineering family whose best-known member was not an engineer at all: the novelist Robert Louis Stevenson). The structure was first lighted in 1862. The adjacent cliffs provide a good vantage point for viewing seabirds, whales, and porpoises. The lighthouse is northwest of Port of Ness along the B8014.

In the small community of Arnol, 21 mi southwest of Port of Ness, look for signs off the A858 for the **Black House,** a well-preserved example of an increasingly rare type of traditional Hebridean home. Once common throughout the islands—even into the 1950s—these dwellings were built without mortar and thatched on a timber framework without eaves. Other characteristic features include an open central peat hearth and the absence of a chimney—hence the soot and the designation *black.* On display inside are many of the house's original furnishings. To reach Arnol from Port of Ness, go back south on the A857 and pick up the A858 at Barvas. ⊠ *Follow signs off A858, Arnol* ☎ *01851/710395* ⊕ *www.historic-scotland.gov.uk* 💷 *£2.50* ☉ *Apr.–Sept., Mon.–Sat. 9:30–5:30; Oct.–Mar., Mon.–Sat. 9:30–4.*

SHOPPING

At **Borgh Pottery** (⊠ *Fivepenny House, Borve, on road to Ness* ☎ *01851/ 850345*), open from Monday to Saturday 9:30 to 6, you can buy attractive hand-thrown studio pottery made on the premises, including lamps, vases, mugs, and dishes.

EN ROUTE

The journey along the A857 takes you past several interesting sights.

Dun Carloway (⊠ *Off A857*), one of the best-preserved Iron Age *brochs* (circular stone towers) in Scotland, dominates the scattered community of Carloway. The mysterious tower was probably built around 2,000 years ago as protection against seaborne raiders. The Dun Broch Centre explains more about the broch and its setting.

Up a side road north from Carloway at the community of **Gearrannan** (☎ *01851/643416* ⊕ *www.gearrannan.com*) an old black-house village has been brought back to life with a museum screening excellent short films on peat cutting and weaving. Groups can rent the restored houses here, too, for a unique experience.

CALANAIS STANDING STONES

On Lewis; 15 mi west of Stornoway.

GETTING HERE AND AROUND

Take the A858 to reach Calanais.

EXPLORING

★ The **Calanais Standing Stones** are actually part of a cluster of several different archeological sites in this area. Probably positioned in several stages between 3000 BC and 1500 BC, this impressive grouping consists of an avenue of 19 monoliths extending northward from a circle of 13 stones, with other rows leading south, east, and west. Ruins of a cairn sit within the circle on the east side. Researchers believe they may have been used for astronomical observations, but you can create your own explanations. The visitor center has an exhibit on the stones, a gift shop, and a tearoom. ⊠ *On an unmarked road off A858, Calanais* ☎ *01851/621422* ⊕ *www.historic-scotland.gov.uk* 🖃*£1.95* ⊙ *Visitor center Apr.–Sept., Mon.–Sat. 9:30–5:30; Oct.–Mar., Wed.–Sat. 9:30–4:30.*

TARBERT

On Harris; 47 mi south of Calanais.

The main port of Harris, Tarbert has some good shops and a few worthwhile sights. **Traigh Luskentyre,** roughly 5 mi southwest of Tarbert, is a spectacular example of Harris's tidy selection of beaches—2 mi of yellow sands adjacent to **Traigh Seilebost** beach, with superb views northward to the hills of the Forest of Harris.

GETTING HERE AND AROUND
The ferry from Uig arrives at Tarbert once or twice daily. Having a car makes travel on Harris much easier, but with careful planning local buses can make for an excellent trip.

ESSENTIALS
Visitor Information Tarbert (⊠ *Pier Rd.* ☎ *01859/502011* ⊕ *www. visithighlands.com*).

EXPLORING
Turreted **Amhuinnsuidhe Castle** (pronounced avun-*shooee*) was built in the 1860s by the earls of Dunmore as a base for fishing and hunting in the North Harris deer forest. The castle stands about 10 mi northwest of Tarbert on the B887, and you can view it from the outside only.

Caledonian MacBrayne (☎ *08705/650000* ⊕ *www.calmac.co.uk*) runs one or two ferries a day beween Tarbert and Uig on Skye.

WHERE TO EAT
££££ ✕ **Scarista House.** Hearty, well-seasoned food (three courses for £40) is
SEAFOOD what you'll find here, particularly local catches like Sound of Harris langoustine and perfectly pitched desserts like tarte tartin. Stunning views from the dining room extend across a sloping golf course to the sea. An older building, previously a manse, is made cozy with heavy curtains, sturdy sofas and chairs, and an open fire. Rooms and cottages are for rent here. ⊠ *Sgarasta Gheag, 15 mi south of Tarbert* ☎ *01859/550238* ⊟*DC, MC, V.*

LEVERBURGH

On Harris; 21 mi south of Tarbert.

At Leverburgh you can take the ferry to North Uist. Nearby Northton has several attractions; St. Clement's Church at Rodel is particularly worth a visit.

GETTING HERE AND AROUND
Leverburgh is on the A859 between Tarbert and Rodel.

10

EXPLORING

Located in a round building over-looking the bay, the **MacGillivray Centre** gives insight into the life and work of William MacGillivray (1796–1852), a noted naturalist with strong links to Harris. MacGillivray authored the five-volume *History of British Birds*. This is a great location for a picnic (there are tables for just such a purpose). A walk to a ruined church starts at the parking lot. ⊠ *A859, Northton* ☎ *01859/502011* ☜ *Donations accepted* ⊙ *Mon.–Sat. 9–9.*

The **Seallam! Visitor Centre and Co Leis Thu? Genealogical Research Centre** is where you can trace your Western Isles ancestry. Photographs and interpretive signs describe the history of Harris and its people. The

THE BONNIE PRINCE

At the Battle of Culloden, George II's army outnumbered that of Prince Charles Edward Stuart. After the battle, Bonnie Prince Charlie wandered over the Highlands. He escaped to the isles of Harris and South Uist, where he met Flora Macdonald (1722–90), the woman who took him, disguised as her maid, "over the sea to Skye." *Will ye no' come back again... Speed, bonnie boat... Charlie is my darling...* The tunes and lyrics of Lady Nairn, jaunty or mournful, composed long after the events, are as good an epitaph as any adventurer could wish for.

owners organize guided walks and cultural evenings weekly between May and September. ⊠ *Off A859, Northton HS3 3JA* ☎ *01859/520258* ⊕ *www.seallam.com* ☜ *£3* ⊙ *Mon.–Sat. 9–5.*

At the southernmost point of Harris is the community of Rodel, where you can find **St. Clement's Church**, a cruciform church standing on a hillock. This is the most impressive pre-Reformation church in the Outer Hebrides; it was built around 1500 and contains the magnificently sculptured tomb (1528) of the church's builder, Alasdair Crotach, MacLeod chief of Dunvegan Castle. Rodel is 3 mi south of Leverburgh and 21 mi south of Tarbert. ⊠ *A859.*

NORTH UIST

8 mi south of Rodel via ferry from Leverburgh.

Lovely coastal scenery and ancient ruins are the main draws on the isle of North Uist. Throughout the island you'll find art everywhere: at the end of roads or paths or on the shore, only visible from a boat. Be sure to visit the camera obscura (an old-fashioned projector) just beyond the ferry terminal. Its watery images are evocative and a bit eerie.

GETTING HERE AND AROUND

You can get to North Uist by ferry, either from Harris, the Isle of Skye, or from one of the other islands. Public transport is infrequent, so a car (or a bike) is the most reliable way to travel.

EXPLORING

At **Newtonferry (Port nan Long)**, by Otternish and the ferry pier for the Leverburgh (Harris) ferry service, stand the remains of what was reputed to be the last inhabited broch in North Uist, **Dun an Sticar**. This defensive tower, reached by a causeway over the loch, was home to

Hugh Macdonald, a descendant of Macdonald of Sleat, until 1602.

You can explore the ruins of **Trinity Temple (Teampull na Trionaid),** a medieval college and monastery said to have been founded in the 13th century by Beathag, daughter of Somerled, the progenitor of the Clan Donald. The ruins stand 8 mi southwest of Lochmaddy, off the A865.

The **Barpa Langass Chambered Cairn,** dating from the 3rd millennium BC, is the only chambered cairn in the Western Isles known to have retained its inner chamber fully intact. You can peek inside, but don't venture too far without a light. It sits close to the A867 between Lochmaddy and Clachen.

> ### RIDING THE FERRY
>
> Rumor has it that a dentist in Scotland covered his ceilings with pictures of Caledonian MacBrayne Ferries to relax his patients. Locals call them CalMac Ferries, and for some travelers they're the best part of a trip to Scotland. Imagine the slow rolling of the boat on the waves, storm petrels in the distance, seagulls and gannets nearer the boat. Some locals sleep through the often-blustery trip, but hearty folk don their rain slickers and look for whales and dolphins from the deck.

The **Balranald Nature Reserve,** administered by the Royal Society for the Protection of Birds, shelters large numbers of waders and seabirds. It's on the west side of North Uist. ✉ *Off A865, 3 mi northwest of Bayhead* ☎ *01876/560287* ⊕ *www.rspb.org* 🎫 *Free* ⊙ *Daily 24 hrs.*

SOUTH UIST

34 mi south of Newtonferry (on North Uist) via Grimsay, Benbecula, and three causeways.

Carpets of wildflowers in spring and early summer, superb deserted beaches, and historical connections to Flora Macdonald and Bonnie Prince Charlie head the list of reasons to visit this island.

GETTING HERE AND AROUND

You can travel the length of South Uist along Route A865, making short treks off this main road on your way to Lochboisdale, on the southeast coast of the island. At Lochboisdale you can catch ferries to Barra, the southernmost principal island of the Outer Hebrides, or to Oban, on the mainland.

WHERE TO STAY

££ 🏠 **Polochar Inn.** With its own standing stone surviving the rough winds off the sea, the Polochar Inn sits at the southern end of South Uist. Run by Morag and Margaret MacKinnon since 2005, the inn is a charming work in progress. Inexpensive smaller rooms (as befits the 300-year-old historic building) are simply decorated. The bathrooms are a bit old, but they're clean, and the owners are steadily upgrading everything. Off the beaten track, the hotel is near Eriskay and the ferry to Barra, with sea views and paths through the countryside. **Pros:** wild and remote location. **Cons:** some rooms smaller than others. ✉ *A865, Lochboisdale* ☎ *01878/700215* ⊕ *www.polocharinn.com* 🛏 *11 rooms* 🔓 *In-room:*

10

no a/c, DVD (some), Wi-Fi. In-hotel: restaurant, bar, beachfront ▭ *DC, MC, V* †◎| *BP*

EXPLORING

One of only two remaining British native—that is, nonmigrating—populations of greylag geese make their home at **Loch Druidibeg National Nature Reserve** in a fresh and brackish loch environment. Stop at the warden's office for information about access and nature trails. ⊠ *Off A865* ☎ *01870/620–0238.*

The **Kildonan Museum and Heritage Centre** houses South Uist artifacts collected in the 1950s and 1960s by Father John Morrison, a local priest. On your left when you enter is a simple exhibition with concise and unsentimental descriptions of living on South Uists that reads, "However we interpret it there is nothing surer than history has as much to do with the present as the past." The simple details, like how people filled their mattresses or the names for the tools they used in their houses are what makes this place interesting. ⊠ *A865, Kildonan* ☎ *01878/710343* ▭ *£2* ⊙ *Easter–Oct., Mon.–Sat. 10–5, Sun. 2–5.*

SHOPPING

Hebridean Jewellery (⊠ *Garrieganichy, Iochdar* ☎ *01870/610288*) sells local and Scottish crafts, and much of the jewelry is made in the workshop which you can tour. A café serves excellent espresso, rich cakes, and tasty soups and panini.

Orkney and Shetland Islands

Updated by
Shona Main

A Scandinavian heritage gives the 170 islets that make up Orkney and Shetland a history and an ambience different from that of any other region of Scotland. Both Orkney and Shetland are essentially austere and bleak, but they have awe-inspiring seascapes, fascinating seabirds, remarkable ancient ruins, and genuinely warm, friendly people. Although a trip requires time and effort, your reward will be a unique and memorable experience.

An Orcadian has been defined as a farmer with a boat, whereas a Shetlander has been called a fisherman with a croft (small farm). Orkney, the southern archipelago, is greener and is rich with artifacts that testify to the many centuries of continuous settlement here: stone circles, burial chambers, ancient settlements, and fortifications. UNESCO has recognized the key remains as a World Heritage Site called the Heart of Neolithic Orkney.

North of Orkney, Shetland, with its ocean views and sparse landscapes—trees are a rarity because of ever-present wind—seems even more remote. However, don't let Shetland's desolate countryside fool you: it has a wealth of historic interest and is far from being a backwater. Oil money from local mineral resources and its position as a crossroads in the northern seas for centuries have helped make Shetland a busy thriving community that wants for little.

For mainland Scots, visiting these islands is a little like traveling abroad without having to worry about a different language or currency. Neither has yet been overrun by tourism, but the people of Orkney and Shetland will be delighted that you have come so far to see their islands and learn a little of their extraordinary past.

ORIENTATION AND PLANNING

GETTING ORIENTED

Just 10 mi from Caithness in Scotland, Orkney is made up of 70 islands, of which 10 are inhabited. A number of ferries travel to ports on the Mainland, the main island of Orkney, including its administrative center, Kirkwall, where an airport serves Scotland's larger cities. The primary road is essentially a loop that passes near the key historic sites. The Mainland is linked to the southern island of South Ronaldsay by way of the Barricades. About 125 mi north of Orkney lies the spiney outline of Shetland, comprising 100 islands. Sumburgh has the main airport, and 25 mi north is Lerwick, the island's "capital" and a port linking the island to Scotland and Orkney. South Mainland, half an hour from Lerwick, has prehistoric sites. Less than an hour north of Lerwick are

TOP REASONS TO GO

Standing stones and ancient sites: Among the many Neolithic treasures in Orkney are the Ring of Brodgar, a 3,000-year old circle of standing stones, and Skara Brae, the remarkable remains of a village uncovered in the grounds of delightful Skaill House. In Shetland, Jarlshof has been the home to different societies since the Bronze Age. Don't miss Mousa Broch and Clickimin Broch in Shetland, two Iron Age towers.

Music and arts festivals: The Shetland Folk Festival in May is a fiddly-diddly shindig that attracts musicians and revelers from around the world. Orkney's St. Magnus Festival is less of a pub-crawl and more of a highbrow celebration of classical music, poetry, and performance.

Seabirds, seals, and more: These islands have some of the planet's most important colonies of seabirds, with millions clinging to colossal cliffs. You're guaranteed to see seals and may spot dolphins, orcas, or porpoises. In Shetland, Noss and Eshaness nature reserves are prime spots, or you can check out the puffins by Sumburgh Head.

Pure relaxation: There's a much more laid-back approach to life on these islands than on the mainland. Shetlanders are particularly renowned for their hospitality and are often happy to share stories and tips that will enrich your adventure.

Outdoor activities by the coast and ocean: The rugged terrain, beautiful beaches, and unspoiled waters make a perfect backdrop for invigorating strolls, sea fishing, diving, or exploring the coastline and sea lochs by boat.

dramatic landscapes such as Eshaness. Ferries go beyond the mainland to Yell and Unst, the latter Britain's most northerly point.

Around Orkney. The towns of Stomness and Kirkwall have sights and museums testifying to Orkney's rich past, including Kirkwall's Norman St. Magnus Cathedral. For many people, though, they're a prelude to impressive Neolithic sites around the Mainland: Maes Howe, Skara Brae, the Ring of Brodgar, and others. Beyond the Mainland, explore sights such as Scapa Flow on Hoy, which reveals the islands' role in two world wars.

Around Shetland. A descent at Sumburgh's airport provides stunning views of a shining white lighthouse, bird-crammed cliffs, and golden bays. Lerwick has the excellent Shetland Museum, and nearby on the South Mainland are the prehistoric sites of Jarlshof, Old Scatness, and Mousa Broch. Worth exploring to the north are the lunarlike Ronas Hill and wave-lashed Eshaness. Unst, the island farthest north, is worth the journey for wide-open ocean views and superb bird-watching at Hermaness National Nature Reserve.

PLANNING

WHEN TO GO

Although shivering, wind-flattened winter visitors braving Orkney and Shetland's winter are not unheard of, the travel season doesn't really start until May, and it runs until September. June is one of the most popular months for both islands. The bird colonies are at their most lively in early summer, which is also when the long northern daylight hours allow you plenty of sightseeing time. Shetland's northerly position means that it has only four or five hours or darkness around the summer solstice, and on a clear night it doesn't seem to get dark at all. Beware the changeable weather even in summer: it could be 75°F one day and then hail the next. Many sights close in September, and by October wilder gales will be mixed with hail one minute and glorious sunshine the next. If you are determined to brave the elements, take into account that there are only six hours of daylight in winter months.

Shetland's festival of fire, Up-Helly-Aa is held the last Tuesday of each January. The spectacle of Lerwick overrun by Vikings, with torches aflame and a huge Viking longship, has become increasingly popular. Book a year in advance if you want to get a bed for the night.

PLANNING YOUR TIME

Orkney and Shetland require at least a couple of days each if you're to do more than just scratch the surface. Since getting to Shetland isn't easy, you may want to spend three or four days here. The isles generate their own laid-back approach to life, and once here, you may want to take it slowly. A good clutch of the key sites of Mainland Orkney can be seen in a day, if you have a car and are disciplined, but to really get the most out of them, take two days. You can do the Kirkwall sights in a morning before heading to the Italian Chapel on South Ronaldsay in the afternoon. This allows a whole day for Stomness, a town caught in the most poignant of time warps, and the archaeological sites of Maes Howe, the Ring of Brodgar, Skara Brae, and Skaill House and Gurness Broch. To include Birsay, plan your day round the tides.

In Shetland, the sites on the South Mainland—Jarlshof, Scatness, the Crofhouse Museum, St. Ninian's Isle, and Mousa Broch—take the best part of a day, although sailing times for Mousa must be factored in to your schedule. Lerwick and its lanes and spectacular museum is a good day, and can be supplemented with a trip to the Bonhoga Gallery in Weisdale. It's a good idea to take a whole day to explore the north of the islands, including Eshaness and Tangwick Haa, although a car or a guide who drives will be necessary. Ferry times allow for a mad dash round the northern islands of Yell and Unst, but you will see more if you book an overnight stay.

GETTING HERE AND AROUND

AIR TRAVEL

Flybe provides regular service to Sumburgh in Shetland and Kirkwall in Orkney from Edinburgh, Glasgow, Aberdeen, and Inverness. Because of the isolation of Orkney and Shetland, there's also a network of interisland flights, through Directflight in Shetland and Loganair in Orkney.

Airline Contacts **Directflight** (☎ *01595/840246* ⊕ *www.directflight.co.uk*).
Flybe (☎ *01392/268529* ⊕ *www.flybe.com*). **Loganair** (☎ *01856/872494*
⊕ *www.loganair.co.uk*).

BOAT AND FERRY TRAVEL

Northlink operates ferries from Aberdeen to Kirkwall in Orkney and
Lerwick in Shetland. These leave Aberdeen harbor each evening (or
every second night for Kirkwall), arriving at Kikwall at 11 PM and Lerwick at 7:30 AM the next day. These top-notch services have recliner
seats for the budget traveler or clean, compact cabins in single, double,
or four-berth combinations. There's a shop, a cinema, two bars and two
restaurants (one self-service and one table service) on each boat.

If you're arriving in Aberdeen on Sunday morning and plan on meeting a train, note that the station does not open until 9 AM. Northlink
allows you to stay in your cabin or the restaurant until 9:30 AM. Contact
Northlink Ferries for reservations.

An alternate way of reaching Orkney is the ferry from John o'Groats to
Burwick, operated by John o'Groats Ferries. There are up to four daily
departures May through September. The ferry from Gills Bay, Caithness, to St. Margaret's Hope on Orkney, operated by Pentland Ferries,
has three daily departures.

In both Orkney and Shetland, the local council runs the interisland
ferry networks (Orkney Ferries and Shetland Island Ferries) to the outer
islands. Northlink Ferries has service between Lerwick on Shetland and
Kirkwall on Orkney. ■ TIP→ **Always book ferry tickets in advance.**

Ferry Contacts **John o'Groats Ferries** (☎ *01955/611353* ⊕ *www.jogferry.
co.uk*). **Orkney Ferries** (☎ *01856/872044* ⊕ *www.orkneyferries.co.uk*). **Northlink Ferries** (☎ *0845/6000449* ⊕ *www.northlinkferries.co.uk*). **Pentland Ferries**
(☎ *01856/831226* ⊕ *www.pentlandferries.co.uk*). **Shetland Island Ferries**
(☎ *01595/743970* ⊕ *www.shetland.gov.uk/transport*).

BUS TRAVEL

Scottish Citylink and National Express operate buses to Aberdeen
where you can get a plane, ferry, or connecting bus to the ferries at
John o'Groats, Gills Bay, or Scrabster. John o'Groats Ferries operates
the Orkney Bus, a direct express coach from Inverness to Kirkwall (via
ferry) that runs daily from June to early September.

The main bus service on Orkney is operated by Orkney Coaches and
on Shetland, by ZetTrans (although buses are also run by small operators). Shetland Islands Council provides information on all bus routes
and timetables on its Web site.

Bus Contacts **John o'Groats Ferries** (☎ *01955/611353* ⊕ *www.jogferry.
co.uk*). **National Express** (☎ *08705/808080* ⊕ *www.nationalexpress.co.uk*).
Orkney Coaches (☎ *01856/870555* ⊕ *www.rapsons.co.uk*). **Scottish Citylink**
(☎ *08705/505050* ⊕ *www.citylink.co.uk*). **ZetTrans** (☎ *01595/744868* ⊕ *www.
zettrans.org.uk*).

CAR TRAVEL

The most convenient way of getting around these islands is by car, especially if your time is limited. Roads are well maintained and traffic is nearly nonexistent, although speeding cars can be a problem Orkney has causeways—the Barricades—connecting some of the islands, but in some cases using these roads take fairly roundabout routes.

You can transport your rental car from Aberdeen, but for fewer than five days it's usually cheaper to rent a car from one of Shetland and Orkney's agencies. Most are based in Lerwick, Shetland, and Kirkwall, Orkney.

Local Car Rental Contacts Bolts Car and Minibus Hire (⊠ 26 North Rd., Lerwick ☎ 01595/693636 ⊕ www.boltscarhire.co.uk). **James D. Peace & Co.** (⊠ Junction Rd., Kirkwall ☎ 01856/872866 ⊕ www.orkneycarhire.co.uk). **Star Rent-a-Car** (⊠ 22 Commercial Rd., Lerwick ☎ 01595/692075 ⊕ www.starrentacar.co.uk). **W. R. Tullock** (⊠ Terminal Bldg., Kirkwall Airport, Kirkwall ☎ 01856/875500 ⊕ www.orkneycarrental.co.uk).

TRAIN TRAVEL

There are no trains on Orkney or Shetland, but you can take the train to Aberdeen or Thurso and then take a ferry to the islands. For information, contact ScotRail.

Train Contacts ScotRail (☎ 08457/484950 ⊕ www.scotrail.co.uk).

RESTAURANTS

Kirkwall has an increasing number of good cafés and restaurants, as does Lerwick, but both islands now have memorable spots beyond the main towns, from cafés and fish-and-chips spots to some fancier restaurants. Orkney and Shetland have first-class seafood, and in pastoral Orkney the beef is lauded and in Shetland the heather- or seaweed-fed lamb. Orkney is famous for its cheese and its fudge; a glug of its Highland Park malt whisky or some Skull Splitter Ale is also worth trying. Shetlanders are beginning to make much more of their natural edible resources, making ice cream and smoking fish in a variety of ways. Some bakeries create their own version of bannocks—a scone-type baked item you eat with salt beef, mutton, or jam—but Johnson and Wood of Voe (available in shops across the islands) takes the biscuit.

HOTELS

Accommodations in Orkney and Shetland are on par with mainland Scotland, with a growing range of stylish bed-and-breakfasts that might suit some travelers better than the bigger hotels that rely and therefore focus on business customers. Although standards are improving, the islands still do not offer luxury accommodations. To experience a simpler stay, check out the unique "camping bods" in Shetland—old cottages providing inexpensive, basic lodging (log fires, cold water, and sometimes no electricity). For details, contact the Shetland Tourist Information Centre.

SIGHTSEEING TOURS

Orkney Coaches runs general tours of Orkney, and John Leask & Son arranges tours of Shetland and Orkney. These companies can also tailor tours to your interests. Michael Hartley, an accredited tour guide in Orkney, runs Wildabout; call for details on minibus tours that combine sightseeing of archaeological sites and the folklore, flora, and fauna of the islands.

In Shetland, Island Trails offers excellent tours enriched by the many myths, customs, and folklore of the islanders, as told by Shetland storyteller Elma Johnson. To visit the outlying islands of Shetland, such as the mist-capped Foula and the once-inhabited Hildasay, take a Cycharters day or afternoon trip on their boat,

the Cyfish; the company also offers private charters. Seabirds and Seals tours take you on board their cruiser *Dunter III* to tour Bressay and the island of Noss, a national nature reserve and bird sanctuary, weather permitting.

Tour Contacts Cycharters (☎ 01595/696598 ⊕ www. cycharters.co.uk). **Island Trails** (☎ 01950/422408 ⊕ www. island-trails.co.uk). **J. Leask** (☎ 01595/693162 ⊕ www. leaskstravel.co.uk). **Orkney Coaches** (☎ 01856/870555 ⊕ www. rapsons.co.uk). **Seabirds and Seals** (☎ 07595/540224 ⊕ www. seabirds-and-seals.com). **Wild-about** (☎ 01856/851011 ⊕ www. wildaboutorkney.com).

WHAT IT COSTS IN POUNDS					
	£	££	£££	££££	£££££
RESTAURANTS	under £10	£10–£14	£15–£19	£20–£25	over £25
HOTELS	under £70	£70–£120	£121–£160	£161–£220	over £220

Restaurant prices are for a main course at dinner. Hotel prices are for two people in a standard double room in high season, generally including the 17.5% V.A.T.

VISITOR INFORMATION
The Orkney visitor center in Kirkwall, and the Shetland visitor center, in Lerwick, are open year-round.

Visitor Information Orkney (✉ West Castle St., Kirkwall ☎ 01856/872856 ⊕ www.visitorkney.com). **Shetland** (✉ Market Cross, Lerwick ☎ 01595/999440 ⊕ www.visitshetland.com ✉ Sumburgh Airport Terminal, Sumburgh ☎ 08701/999440).

AROUND ORKNEY

If you're touring the north of Scotland, the short boat trip to Orkney offers the chance to step outside the Scottish history you've experienced on the mainland. Prehistoric sites such as the Ring of Brodgar, and the remnants of Orkney's Viking-influenced past, are in dramatic contrast to that of the mainland. The Orkney Islands may have a population of just 20,000, but a visit reveals the islands' cultural richness. In addition,

Orkney's continued reliance on farming and fishing reminds you how things stay the same despite technological advances. At Maes Howe, for example, it becomes evident that graffiti is not solely an expression of today's youths: the Vikings left their marks here way back in the 12th century. ■TIP→ You can purchase the Historic Scotland joint-entry ticket at the first site you visit; the ticket costs less than paying separately for entry into each site.

STROMNESS AND THE NEOLITHIC SITES

1¾ hrs north of Thurso on Scotland's mainland, via ferry from Scrabster.

On the southwest of the Mainland, on the shore of Hamnavoe, is Stromness, a remarkably attractive fishing town seemingly so unsullied by modernity that it evokes an uncomplicated way of life long gone. Walk past the old-fashioned shops and austere cottages that line the main street and you'll understand why local poet and novelist George Mackay Brown (1921–96) was inspired and moved by its sober beauty.

With its ferry connection to Scrabster in Caithness, Stromness makes a good base for visiting the western parts of Orkney, and the town holds several points of interest. It was once a key trading port for the Hudson Bay company, and the Stromness Museum displays artifacts from those days. Nearby are three spectacular ancient sites, the Ring of Brodgar, Maes Howe, and Skara Brae at Skaill House.

GETTING HERE AND AROUND

Stromness is at the end of the A965 and can be reached by one of the many buses from Kirkwall.

Orkney Coaches numbers T10 and T8 links Kirkwall, the Ring of Brodgar, and Skara Brae and Skaill House with Kirkwall. Altogether there are three bus services there and three back per day, so plan accordingly.

ESSENTIALS

Visitor Information **Stromness** (✉ *Pier Head* ☎ *01856/850716* ⊕ *www. visitorkney.com* ⊗ *Mar.–Oct., daily 9–5*).

EXPLORING

At the strikingly renovated **Pier Arts Centre,** a gallery in a former merchant's house and adjoining buildings, huge sheets of glass offer tranquil harborside views and combine with space-maximizing design to make the best use of every shard of natural light and inch of wall to display the superb permanent collection. The more than 100 20th- and 21st-century paintings and sculptures include works by Barbara Hepworth and Douglas Gordon, and edgy temporary exhibitions showcase international contemporary artists. A chic shop sells design products and art books. ✉ *28–30 Victoria St.* ☎ *01856/850209* ⊕ *www.pierartscentre. com* ⊠ *Free* ⊗ *Sept.–May, Mon.–Sat. 10:30–5; June–Aug., Mon.–Sat. 10:30–5, Sun. noon–4*

Ⓒ
Fodor's Choice
★

The enchanting **Stromness Museum** has the feel of some grand Victorian's private collection but has, in fact, been community-owned since it opened in 1837. Its crammed but utterly fascinating exhibits on fishing, shipping, and whaling are full of interesting trinkets from all over

The Orkney Islands

ATLANTIC OCEAN

Seal Skerry
North Ronaldsay
Hollandstoun

Papa
Westray
Holland
Pierowall
Westray
Rapness
Calfsound

The North
Sound

North
Ronaldsay
Firth

Northwall
Burness
Sanday
Kettletoft
Braeswick

Sanday
Sound

Westray
Firth

Rousay
Wasbister
Eday
Backaland
Whitehall
Aith
Stronsay

Brough of
Birsay
Birsay
**Marwick Head
Nature Reserve**
Marwick
Bay
Skara Brae
Mainland
A965
Dounby
A986
Finstown
Brinyan
**Gurness
Broch**
**Unstan
Chambered
Tomb**
Balfour
Shapinsay
Stronsay
Firth
Whitehall

Ring of Brodgar
Stromness
Stenness
**Maes
Howe**
A965
St. Ola
Kirkwall
Skaill

**Orphir
Church**
Orphir
Houton
Moness
Scapa
Flow
St. Mary's
A961
A960
Copinsay

Rackwick
**Scapa Flow
Visitor Centre**
B9047
Lyness
Hoy
St. Margaret's
Hope
**Italian
Chapel**
Lambholm
South
Ronaldsay
Burwick
Old Head

Pentland Firth
A964

Scrabster
Thurso
A836
Gills
John o'
Groats
Pentland
Skerries

TO →
SCALLOWAY

KEY	
🚢	Ferry
✈	Airport

0 ——— 10 miles
0 ——— 10 kilometers

the world that found their way to this small Orcadian town because of its connections with the Hudson Bay Shipping Company. The company recruited workers in Stromness between the late 18th and 19th centuries as they were considered more sober and therefore reliable than other Scots. Also here are model ships and displays on the German fleet that was scuttled on Scapa Flow in 1919. Upstairs, don't miss the beguiling, traditionally presented collection of birds and butterflies that are native to the British Isles. ⊠ *52 Alfred St.* ☎ *01856/850025* 🖃 *£3.50* ⊗ *Oct.–Mar., Mon.–Sat. 11–5; Apr.–Sept., Mon.–Sat. 10–5, Sun. 10–12:30 and 1:30–5.*

NEED A BREAK?

Julia's Café Bistro (⊠ *Ferry St. KW16 3AE* ☎ *01856/850904*) is right on the quayside and serves the kinds of cakes that make you conveniently forget the existence of calories. Expect huge slices of lemon drizzle, coffee layer, raspberry cream, and other cakes, as well as scones and shortbreads. Baked potatoes, quirky salads, and quiches round out the savory side of the menu.

★ The **Ring of Brodgar,** 5 mi northeast of Stromness, is a magnificent circle of 36 Neolithic standing stones (originally 60) surrounded by a henge, or deep ditch. When the fog descends over the stones—a frequent occurrence—their looming shapes seem to come alive. The site dates to between 2500 and 2000 BC. Though the original use of the circle is uncertain, it's not hard to imagine strange rituals taking place here in the misty past. The stones stand between Loch of Harray and Loch of Stenness. ⊠ *B9055* ☎ *01856/841815* ⊕ *www.historic-scotland.gov.uk* 🖃 *Free* ⊗ *Year-round.*

★ The huge burial mound of **Maes Howe** (circa 2500 BC) measures 115 feet in diameter and contains an enormous burial chamber. It was raided by Vikings in the 12th century, and Norse crusaders found shelter here, leaving a rich collection of runic inscriptions. Outside you see a large, grassy mound; the stunning interior of the chambered tomb has remarkably sophisticated stonework. This site is 6 mi northeast of Stromness and 1 mi from the Ring of Brodgar. You must call Tormiston Hill visitor center (across the road) early on the desired day of your visit to reserve a tour spot. ⊠ *A965* ☎ *01856/761606 for reservations* ⊕ *www.historic-scotland.gov.uk* 🖃 *£5.20* ⊗ *Apr.–Sept., daily 9:30–5; Oct.–Mar., daily 9:30–4. Tours (prebooked) begin at 10 and run hourly with the last at 4.*

Fodor's Choice ★ After a fierce storm in 1850, the laird of Breckness, William Graham Watt, discovered **Skara Brae,** a cluster of Neolithic houses, at the bottom of his garden. The houses, first occupied around 3000 BC and containing stone beds, fireplaces, dressers, and cupboards, are the most extensive of their kind in northern Europe and provide real insight into this ancient civilization. A reconstruction of one house can be seen in the excellent visitor center, which displays artifacts from the site. Skara Brae stands on the grounds of **Skaill House**, a splendid, intriguing mansion built by the bishop of Orkney in the 1600s. His descendants, the lairds of Breckness, along with the various ladies of the manor, added to the house and to the eclectic furnishings. These sites offer a joint ticket well worth the price: the juxtaposition of different societies thousands of years apart that shared the same corner of Orkney makes a fascinating visit. Skara Brae is 8 mi north of Stromness. ⊠ *B9056* ☎ *01856/841815* ⊕ *www.historic-scotland.gov.uk* 🖃 *£6.70 Apr.–Sept. Skara Brae and Skaill House; £5.70 Oct.–Mar. Skara Brae only* ☉ *Skara Brae Apr.–Sept., daily 9:30–5:30; Oct.–Mar., daily 9:30–4:30. Skaill House Apr.–Sept., daily 9:30–5:30.*

WHERE TO STAY

££ 🖼 **Mill of Eyrland.** White-painted stone walls, country antiques, and the rippling sound of a stream running beneath the windows make for a pleasant stay at this bed-and breakfast in a former mill dating from 1861. The old machinery can still be seen, and attractive gardens surround the house. Evening meals are available on request. This makes a good base for visiting nearby archaeological sites. Two bedrooms are suites (good for families), but another has no bathroom. **Pros:** lovely original features in public rooms; beautiful views out to Scapa Flow. **Cons:** difficult to find (call ahead for detailed directions); breakfast is served at one big table, so be prepared to be sociable. ⊠ *Stenness* ☎ *01856/850136* ⊕ *www.millofeyrland.co.uk* 🛏 *4 rooms, 3 with bath* ⚒ *In-room: no a/c, no phone. In-hotel: bar* ▭ *No credit cards* ⊠ *BP.*

SPORTS AND THE OUTDOORS

DIVING The cool, clear waters of Scapa Flow and eight sunken ships that were part of Germany's fleet during World War I make for an unparalleled diving experience. Several companies organize trips to Scapa Flow and other nearby dive sites, including **Scapa Scuba** (⊠ *Lifeboat House Stromness* ☎ *01856/851218*).

BIRSAY

12 mi north of Stromness, 25 mi northwest of Kirkwall.

Birsay itself is a small collection of houses, but some interesting historic and natural sitees are nearby.

GETTING HERE AND AROUND

The village is on A966; a car is the easiest way to see the nearby sites.

EXPLORING

A Romanesque church can be seen at the **Brough of Birsay,** a tidal island with the remains of an early Pictish and then Norse settlement. (*Brough* is another word for burgh.) The collection of roofless stone structures on the tiny island, close to Birsay, are accessible only at low tide by means of a concrete path that winds across the seaweed-strewn bay. ■TIP→ **To ensure you won't be swept away, check the tides with the tourism office in Kirkwall or Stromness before setting out.** ⊠ *A966* ☎ *01856/841815 (Skara Brae)* ⊕ *www.historic-scotland.gov.uk* 🖃 *£3.20* ☉ *June–Sept., daily 9:30–5:30 (tide permitting).*

The Royal Society for the Protection of Birds tends the remote **Marwick Head Nature Reserve,** where cliffs are home in spring and summer to thousands of nesting seabirds, including cormorants, kittiwakes, and guillemots. The Kitchener Memorial, recalling the 1916 sinking of the cruiser HMS *Hampshire* with Lord Kitchener aboard, sits atop a cliff.

Access to the reserve, which is unstaffed, is along a path north from Marwick Bay. Take care near cliff edges. The reserve is 4 mi south of Birsay and 11 mi north of Stromness. ☒ *Off B9056* ☎ *01856/850176* ⊕ *www.rspb.org.uk* ☞ *Free* ⊗ *Daily 24 hrs.*

Gurness Broch, an Iron Age tower built between 500 BC and 200 BC, stands more than 10 feet high and is surrounded by stone huts, indicating that this was a village. The tower's foundations and dimensions suggest that it was one of the biggest brochs in Scotland, and the remains of the surrounding houses are well preserved. The site is along the coast about 8 mi east of Birsay. ☒ *A966, Aikerness* ☎ *01856/751414* ⊕ *www. historic-scotland.gov.uk* ☞ *£4.70* ⊗ *Apr.–Sept., daily 9:30–5:30.*

KIRKWALL

16 mi east of Stromness.

In bustling Kirkwall, the main town on Orkney, there's plenty to see in the narrow, winding streets extending from the harbor. The cathedral and some museums are highlights.

GETTING HERE AND AROUND
Kirkwall is a ferry port and also near Orkney's main airport. Its sights are all near one other. Visitors to the Highland Park Distillery might want to hop on the T11 Kirkwall Circular or get a taxi (about £4).

ESSENTIALS
Visitor Information Orkney (☒ *West Castle St., Kirkwall* ☎ *01856/872856* ⊕ *www.visitorkney.com*).

EXPLORING
TOP ATTRACTIONS

OFF THE
BEATEN
PATH

Italian Chapel. During World War II, 550 Italian prisoners of war were captured in North Africa and sent to Orkney to assist with the building of the Churchill Barriers, four causeways that blocked entry into Scapa Flow, Orkney's great natural harbor. Using two corrugated-iron Nissan huts, the prisoners, led by Domenico Chiocchetti, a painter-decorator from the Dolomites, constructed this beautiful and inspiring chapel in memory of their homeland. The elaborate interior frescoes were painted with whatever came to hand—bits of metal, colorful stones, leftover paints. The chapel is 7 mi south of Kirkwall and just across from the first of the Churchill Barriers. ☒ *A961, Lambholm* ☞ *Free* ⊗ *Apr.–Sept., daily 9 AM–10 PM; Oct.–Mar., daily 9–4:30.*

⊗ **Orkney Museum.** From the Neolithic period and then on to the Picts, the Vikings, medieval times, farming in the18th century, and right up to the 1960s, this museum in Tankerness House (a former residence) has the entire history of Orkney crammed into a rabbit warren of rooms; it's not easily accessible for those with disabilities. The setup may be old-fashioned, but some artifacts are riveting. Lovely gardens around the back provide a spot to recoup after a history lesson. ☒ *Broad St.* ☎ *01856/873191* ☞ *Free* ⊗ *May–Sept., Mon.–Sat. 10:30–5; Oct.–Apr., Mon.–Sat. 10:30–12:30 and 1:30–5.*

Orkney Wireless Museum. The lifetime collection of Jim MacDonald, a radio operative during World War II, tells the story of wartime communications at Scapa Flow, where thousands of servicemen and servicewomen were stationed; they used the equipment displayed to protect the Home Fleet. The museum also contains many handsome 1930s wireless radios and examples of the handicrafts produced by Italian prisoners of war. ⊠ *Kiln Corner, Junction Rd.* ☎ *01856/871400* ⊕ *www. owm.org.uk* ▣ *£3* ⏱ *Apr.–Sept., Mon.–Sat. 1–4:30, Sun. 2–4.30.*

★ **St. Magnus Cathedral.** Founded by the Norse earl Jarl Rognvald in 1137 and named for his uncle, the cathedral was mostly finished by 1200, although more work was carried out during the following 300 years. The cathedral is still in use and contains some fine examples of Norman architecture, although traces of later styles are found here and there. The ornamentation on some of the tombstones in the church is particularly striking. At the far end to the left is the tomb of Dr. John Rae, the Victorian-era Orcadian adventurer who discovered the final section of the Northwest Passage in Canada. Also worth seeing is the memorable Martyrdom of Magnus as painted by schoolchildren from the Isle of Arran. ⊠ *Broad St.* ☎ *01856/874894* ⊕ *www.stmagnus.org* ⏱ *Mon.–Sat. 9–6, Sun. 2–6.*

WORTH NOTING

Bishop's Palace. The palace dates to the 12th century when St. Magnus Cathedral was built. In 1253 this was the site of King Hakon IV of Norway's death, marking the end of Norwegian rule over Sudreyjar (the Southern Hebrides). It was rebuilt in the late15th century, and a round tower was added in the 16th century. ⊠ *Palace Rd.* ☎ *01856/ 871918* ⊕ *www.historic-scotland.gov.uk* ▣ *£3.70, includes Earl's Palace* ⏱ *Apr.–Sept., daily 9:30–6.*

Earl's Palace. Perhaps the best surviving example of Renaissance architecture in Scotland, this grand, ruined palace was built in 1607 by Patrick Stewart, the much despised (yes, still) Earl of Orkney and Lord of Shetland. There are no tours, so you can explore the palace ruins, including the Great Hall with its large fireplace, at your own pace. ⊠ *Palace Rd.* ☎ *01856/871918* ⊕ *www.historic-scotland.gov.uk* ▣ *£3.70, includes Bishop's Palace* ⏱ *Apr.–Sept., daily 9:30–6.*

Highland Park Distillery. After shopping and exploring Kirkwall, you'll have earned a dram of the local single malt at Scotland's northernmost distillery. The distillery tour takes you through the essential aspects of this near-sacred process, from the ingredients, to the hand turning of the malt, the peating in the peat kilns, the mashing, the distillation, and finally the maturation in oak casks. This smoky sweet malt can be purchased all over Orkney as well as from the distillery itself. ⊠ *Holm Rd.* ☎ *01856/874619* ⊕ *www.highlandpark.co.uk* ▣ *£6* ⏱ *Apr. and Sept., weekdays 10–5; May–Aug., Mon.–Sat. 10–5, Sun. noon–5; Oct.–Mar., weekdays 1–5; call to confirm tour times.*

OFF THE BEATEN PATH

Orkneyinga Saga Centre. A good starting point for an exploration of Orkney's Norse heritage, the center examines the Orkneyinga Saga, an oral history first written down in the 13th century that tells of the Norse conquest of Orkney, with murders and battles galore. Panels discuss the saga and Viking life (with, rather amusingly, Hollywood hunks pasted in to the Norse family tree). Exhibits include the remains of the

12th-century Orphir Church, Scotland's only circular medieval church, and the outline of a Viking drinking hall. The center is 8 mi southwest of Kirkwall. There's an Orkneyinga trail (⊕ *orkneyvikingtrail.com*) with other panels around the island at Viking sites associated with the saga. ⊠ *Off A964, Orphir* ☏ *01856/811319* 🖼 *Free* ☉ *Daily 9–5.*

Unstan Chambered Tomb. This intriguing burial chamber lies within a 5,000-year-old cairn. Access to the tomb can be awkward for those with mobility problems. ⊠ *A964, 7½ mi west of Kirkwall* ☏ *01856/841815* ⊕ *www.historic-scotland.gov.uk* 🖼 *Free* ☉ *Apr.–Sept., daily 9:30–5:30; Oct.–Mar., daily 9:30–4:30.*

WHERE TO EAT AND STAY

£££
★
MODERN BRITISH

✕ **The Creel.** This outstanding "restaurant with rooms" with a glowing reputation sits right on the waterfront 13 mi south of Kirkwall (a 20-minute drive) on the island of South Ronaldsay. The inn's charm lies partly in the fuss-free approach to hospitality that makes everyone, from the local farmer to a visiting business executive, feel welcome. Imaginative modern Scottish cuisine uses the freshest Orcadian seafood, seaweed-fed lamb, and locally grown vegetables. Three simple guest rooms overlook St. Margaret's Hope Bay. ⊠ *Front Rd., St. Margaret's Hope* ☏ *01856/831311* ⊕ *www.thecreel.co.uk* ⚓ *Reservations essential* ▤ *MC, V* ☉ *Closed Oct.–Mar.*

££

▦ **Foveran Hotel.** Thirty-four acres of grounds surround this modern, ranch-style hotel overlooking Scapa Flow, about 3 mi southwest of Kirkwall. The Foveran has an attractive light-wood, Scandinavian-style dining room, as well as a sitting room with a fireplace. Rooms are simply furnished, with firm beds and well-maintained baths. The dinner-only restaurant—worth a stop—serves homemade soups, fresh seafood, wondrously gooey fried Orkney cheese, and a sweet Orkney-fudge cheesecake. **Pros:** friendly, efficient service; local produce well priced and simply cooked to perfection. **Cons:** exterior looks a bit institutional; you must book the popular restaurant ahead. ⊠ *Off A964, St. Ola* ☏ *01856/872389* ⊕ *www.foveranhotel.co.uk* ➴ *8 rooms* ⚅ *In-room: no a/c, Internet. In-hotel: restaurant, bar* ▤ *MC, V* ⑪ *BP.*

££

▦ **Merkister Hotel.** On the edge of Loch Harray, this hotel is an angler's dream. Experienced ghillies (guides) lead experts to the choicest spots and provide instruction for novices. Left your rod at home? You can rent all the equipment you need, including boats. The comfortable, old-fashioned rooms encourage a good night's sleep after a hard day on the water. Skerries, the hotel's restaurant, serves superior Scottish cuisine that includes local seafood and Aberdeen Angus beef. Halfway between Kirkwall and Stromness, the Merkister makes a good base for touring the region. **Pros:** great loch side location; "trust bar" where you tell them what you drank and then pay for it; notable restaurant. **Cons:** some small rooms; decor a bit dated. ⊠ *A965, Harray* ☏ *01856/771366* ⊕ *www.merkister.com* ➴ *16 rooms* ⚅ *In-room: no a/c. In-hotel: restaurant, public Wi-Fi* ▤ *AE, MC, V* ⑪ *BP.*

££

▦ **Miller's House and Harbourside Guest House.** Built by a naval lieutenant, James Miller, this old house dates to before 1660 and now serves as a comfortable bed-and-breakfast. Guest rooms are not fancy but are fresh, simple, and spotless. Breakfast is the high point of a stay, with the kippers, Orkney salmon, homemade bread, and smooth creamy porridge all worth trying. A two-bedroom apartment with a kitchen is nearby. **Pros:** great value for the money; near the ferry. **Cons:** not easy to find; books up well in advance. ⊠ *13 John St.* ☎ *01856/851969* ⊕ *www. millershouseorkney.com* ⟿ *6 rooms, 1 apartment* ♿ *In-room: no a/c. In-hotel: laundry facilities* ⊟ *MC, V* ⎟◎⎟ *BP.*

££ 🖥 **The Shore.** Right on the harbor, this place has always been a hotel but has been pleasantly upgraded with amenities such as large beds, big TVs, bathrobes, and modish bathrooms that make you want to linger. The look is modern, neutral, and minimal. A rear-facing room help you avoid street noise. Two bars downstairs sell pub grub, and a restaurant specializes in seafood. **Pros:** clean and well-maintained bedrooms; friendly waitstaff. **Cons:** breakfast costs an extra £7.50; bars have a somewhat cheesy faux-cocktail-bar feel; cars tearing up the main road outside may disturb sleep. ⊠ *Shore St.* ☎ *01856/872200* ⊕ *www.theshore.co.uk* ⟿ *10 rooms* ♿ *In-room: no a/c, Wi-Fi. In-hotel: restaurant, bars, laundry service* ⊟ *MC, V.*

THE ARTS
The region's cultural highlight is Kirkwall's **St. Magnus Festival** (☎ *01856/ 871445* ⊕ *www.stmagnusfestival.com*), usually held the third week in June. Its impressive program includes distinguished orchestral, operatic, and choral artists. Orkney also hosts an annual folk festival at the end of May.

SPORTS AND THE OUTDOORS
BICYCLING Bicycles can be rented from **Cycle Orkney** (⊠ *Tankerness La.* ☎ *01856/ 875777*), open year-round, for £10 a day.

FISHING The **Merkister Hotel** (⊠ *A965, Harray* ☎ *01856/771366*), on Loch Harray, arranges fishing packages, with all equipment, including boats, available to rent.

SHOPPING
Kirkwall is Orkney's main shopping hub. At **Judith Glue** (⊠ *25 Broad St.* ☎ *01856/874225*) you can purchase designer knitwear with traditional patterns, as well as handmade crafts and hampers of local produce. Don't miss **The Longship** (⊠ *11 Broad St.* ☎ *01856/873251*), which sells a huge array of Ola Gorrie's original designs in gold and silver jewelry with Celtic and Norse themes. **Ortak** (⊠ *Albert St.* ☎ *01856/873536*) stocks Celtic-theme jewelry and has exhibits and jewelry-making demonstrations.

SCAPA FLOW VISITOR CENTRE

On Hoy, 14 mi southwest of Kirkwall, 6 mi south of Stromness.

GETTING HERE AND AROUND
The car ferry from Houton (7 mi east of Stromness) takes 25 minutes to reach Lyness on Hoy and the visitor center. The ferry costs around £22 round-trip for a regular-size car and £7 round-trip per passenger.

ESSENTIALS
Ferry Contacts **Orkney Ferries** (☎ *01856/872044* ⊕ *www.orkneyferries.co.uk*).

CLOSE UP | Island Festivals

Islanders know how to celebrate their unique heritage and the performing arts. Joining one of the island festivals can be a memorable part of any trip. Some festivals are very popular, so plan ahead.

Shetland has quite a strong cultural identity, thanks to its Scandinavian heritage. There are, for instance, books of local dialect verse, a whole folklore and identification system for lost fishermen contained in knitting patterns, and a strong tradition of fiddle playing.

In the middle of the long winter, at the end of January, Shetlanders celebrate their Viking culture with the **Up-Helly-Aa Festival,** which—for the men—involves dressing up as Vikings, parading with flaming torches, and then burning of a replica of a Viking longship, followed by one or sometimes two nights of carousing. Women play hostess in the halls, feeding and quenching the thirsts of those involved, and dancing with them. The **Shetland Folk Festival,** held in April, and October's **Shetland Accordion and Fiddle Festival** both attract large numbers of visitors.

Orkney's **St. Magnus Festival,** a celebration focusing on classical music, is based in Kirkwall and is usually held the third week in June. Orkney also hosts a jazz festival in April, an annual folk festival at the end of May, the unique Boys' Ploughing Match in mid-August, and The Ba' (ball; street rugby-football played by the Uppies and Doonies residents of Kirkwall) on Christmas and New Year's Day.

On a smaller scale, throughout summer, both islands run mini-festivals and events for lovers of literature, films, food, art, music and, in Shetland, even bannocks! Information about these can be found in the visitor centers.

EXPLORING

On the beautiful island of Hoy, **Scapa Flow Visitor Centre** explores the strategic and dramatic role that this sheltered anchorage played in two world wars. It displays military vehicles and guns, as well as equipment salvaged from the German boats scuttled off the coast. In the plain but poignant graveyard here, British and German personnel both rest in peace. ■TIP→ **If you want to take your car over to Hoy, book well in advance with Orkney Ferries, as this is a popular route.** The visitor center is a short walk from the ferry terminal. ⊠ *Off B9047, Lyness* ☎ *01856/791300* 🖃 *Free* ☯ *June–Sept., Mon.–Sat. 9–4, Sun. 10–4; Oct.–May, weekdays 9–4.*

AROUND SHETLAND

The Shetland coastline is an incredible 900 mi because of the rugged geology and many inlets; there isn't a point on the islands farther than 3 mi from the sea. Lerwick is the primary town, but the population of 22,000 is scattered across the 15 inhabited islands. The oil boom means that communities are well cared for: no one in Shetland lives more than 20 minutes away from a publicly run swimming pool.

In general, the prehistoric treasures such as Jarlshof and Mousa Broch are in the South Mainland. For the geological marvels of the islands, Ronas Hill and Eshaness, visit the North Mainland. The social history of the islands is told most comprehensively in the Shetland Museum and in the lanes of Lerwick. Wherever your interest, you'll see and hear an island that buzzes with music, life, and history.

LERWICK

14 hrs by ferry from Aberdeen.

Founded by Dutch fishermen in the 17th century, Lerwick today is a busy town and administrative center. Handsome stone buildings—known as lodberries—line the harbor; they provided loading bays for goods, some of them illegal. The town's twisting flagstone lanes and harbor once heaved with activity, and Lerwick still an active port today. This is also where most visitors to Shetland dock, spilling out of cruise ships, allowing passengers to walk around the town.

GETTING HERE AND AROUND

If you arrive on the ferry from Aberdeen, the town centre of Lerwick is 1 mi south of Holmsgarth, the ferry terminal. You can get a bus from Holmsgarth to the center or to the bus station for travel to Sumburgh or Scalloway. Car rentals can be arranged to meet you at the ferry terminal. Lerwick is a small and compact town, but ZetTrans offers an hourly bus services around town.

ESSENTIALS

Transportation Contacts Boddam Cabs (☎ *01950/460111).* **ZetTrans** (☎ *01595/744868* ⊕ *www.zettrans.org.uk)*

Visitor Information Lerwick (✉ *Market Cross* ☎ *08701/999440* ⊕ *www. visitshetland.com).*

EXPLORING

Fodor'sChoice On the last remaining stretch of the old waterfront at the restored Hay's Dock, the striking **Shetland Museum** building, with its sail-like tower, is Shetland's cultural hub and a stimulating introduction to local culture. The spaces are filled with displays about archaeology, art and textiles, island culture, and contemporary art. Standout exhibits include depictions of the minutiae of everyday Shetland life across the centuries, the last remaining *sixareen* (a kind of fishing boat), and the Monk's Stone, a carving depicting the Irish monks who introduced Christianity to the people of Shetland. The museum is also a wonderful place to hang out; look for vintage vessels moored in the dock and seals that pop up to observe everyone checking out the scene from the glass-fronted café-restaurant terrace. ✉ *Hay's Dock* ☎ *01595/695057* ⊕ *www.shetland-museum.org.uk* 🖼 *Free* ☺ *Weekdays 10–5:30, Sat. 10–5, Sun. noon–5.*

Fort Charlotte, an artillery fort, was built in 1665 to protect the Sound of Bressay from the invading Dutch. They seized it in 1673 and razed the fort to the ground. They were soon chased out of Shetland and the fort was rebuilt in 1781. ✉ *Market St.* ☎ *01856/841815* 🖼 *Free* ☺ *Apr.–Sept., daily 9:30–6:30; Oct.–Mar., daily 9:30–4:30.*

The Shetland Islands

Hermaness   *Muckle Flugga*

Hermaness National Nature Reserve   *Unst*

Burrafirth   ◆ Saxa Vord

Haroldswick

Baltasound

Bluemull Sound

A968

Uyeasound

Gloup   B9082   **Keen of Hamar**

Yell   **Muness Castle**

Gutcher

Fetlar

Mid Yell   Funzie

Isbister   Otterswick

Yell Sound   A968   B9081

Ronas Hill   A970

Ulsta   *Colgrave Sound*

Burravoe

Eshaness   B9078   Hillswick   Toft

Out Skerries

Tangwick Ha Museum   *Ura Firth*   Hamnavoe

Whalsay

Mavis Grind   B9076

Brae   *Brough*

St. Magnus Bay   *Muckle Roe*   Symbister

Papa Stour   B9071   Voe   Laxo

A970

Sandness   *Mainland*

A971   Bixter   B9075   B9075

Walls   **Weisdale**

Culswick   A971

Island of Bressay

Lerwick   **Noss National Nature Reserve** ◆

Scalloway   *Isle of Noss*

TO   **Clickimin Broch**

← KIRKWALL, ORKNEY   Quarff

South Mainland   A970

Sandwick

St. Ninian's Isle   **Mousa Broch**

Bigton   Levenwick

Loch of Spiggie   B9122

Shetland Croft House Museum

Fitful Head   **Old Scatness**

TO ABERDEEN

Jarlshof   Sumburgh

TO FAIR ISLE ↓   ✈ Sumburgh Head

Sumburgh Roost

KEY
🚢 Ferry
✈ Airport

0 — 5 miles
0 — 5 kilometers

Clickimin Broch, a stone tower on the site of what was originally an Iron Age fortification, makes a good introduction to these mysterious Pictish buildings. It was possibly intended as a place of retreat and protection in the event of attack. South of the broch are vivid views of the cliffs at the south end of the island of Bressay, which shelters Lerwick Harbor. ✉ *Off A970, 1 mi south of Lerwick* ☎ *01856/ 841815* ⊕ *www.historic-scotland. gov.uk* 🎫 *Free* 🕙 *Daily 24 hrs.*

OFF THE BEATEN PATH

Noss National Nature Reserve. The island of Noss (which means "nose" in old Norse) rises to a point called the Noup. The smell and noise of the birds that make their homes on the vertiginous cliffs can be a violent assault on the senses. Residents nest in orderly fashion: black and white guillemots (45,000 pairs) and razorbills at the bottom; gulls, gannets, cormorants, and kittiwake in the middle; fulmars and puffins at the top. If you get too close to their chicks, some will dive-bomb from above. To get here, take a ferry from Lerwick to Bressay, then an inflatable boat to Noss; call the reserve office, managed by Scottish Natural Heritage, for boat schedules. ■TIP→ Be sure to wear waterproof clothing and sensible shoes; mid-May to mid-July is the best time to view breeding birds. ✉ *Bressay* ☎ *01595/693345* ⊕ *www.nnr-scotland.org.uk* 🎫 *£3* 🕙 *Mid-May–Aug., Tues., Wed., and Fri.–Sun. 10–5, weather permitting.*

> **TROWS AND TALES**
>
> The Shetlands have a tradition of folk tales, many with Norse origins. Speak to Elma Johnson, a storyteller and spellbinding tour guide, and you may believe the place is teeming with trows, cousins of Scandinavian trolls. There's a cavelike dwelling in the Shetland Museum—the Trowie Knowe—and a fantastical device—the Trowie Detector—that may help track down these elusive characters. To enter the world of Shetlandic history and folklore, book a trip or an evening of storytelling with **Island Trails** (☎ *01950/422408* ⊕ *www.island-trails.co.uk*).

WHERE TO EAT

££
★

BRITISH

✕ **Hay's Dock.** The airy, glass-fronted café-restaurant serving coffee, lunch, and dinners in the Shetland Museum has proved very popular. Chunky wooden tables fitted with glass panels allow you to see the artwork featured on top of each table. Good picks are the seafood chowder and salt beef with bannocks (a savory scone) or, in the evening, tagliatelle with scallops and monkfish in a vanilla cream sauce. ✉ *Hay's Dock* ☎ *01595/741569* ⊕ *www.haysdock.co.uk* ⚭ *Reservations essential* ▤ *MC, V* 🕙 *No dinner Sun.–Wed.*

£
CAFÉ

✕ **The Peerie Shop Cafe.** Who would believe you could get such good cappuccino at 60 degrees north? Round the back of the popular Lerwick knitwear shop is a modish, consistently good café that sells filled sponge cakes, lip-smackingly good soups, and, yes, the best coffee on the islands. It's always busy and Shetlanders do like to talk, so be prepared to hang around for a table during lunchtime. Alas, the café closes at 6. ✉ *Esplanade* ☎ *01595/692816* ⊕ *www.peerieshopcafe.com* ▤ *MC, V* 🕙 *Closed Sun. No dinner.*

WHERE TO STAY

£   🏠 **Alder Lodge Guest House.** Occupying a solid, 1830s-built former bank building, this guesthouse is on a quiet street within easy reach of Lerwick's harbor, shops, pubs, and attractions. Spacious guest rooms have orthopedic beds and well-looked-after bathrooms. The lounge is a cozy place to unwind, and there's an eccentrically adorned patio to relax in when the weather is fine. **Pros:** comfortable beds; superb location; child friendly. **Con:** breakfasts may be too greasy for some; breakfast room is in a '70s time warp. ⊠ *8 Clairmont Pl.ZE1 0BR* ☎ *01595/695705* ⊕ *www.alder-lodge.co.uk* ⤵ *8 rooms* ♿ *In-room: refrigerator, no a/c. In-hotel: laundry service* ☰ *No credit cards* �'◎' *BP.*

££   🏠 **Westhall Bed & Breakfast.** Two miles south of the city center, this grand
★   stone Victorian mansion overlooks the otter-populated water of Sound. The owners were born to run a B&B and have thought carefully about what makes a good stay. Plain but quality decor, good solid furniture, and a comfortable lounge with an open fire provide creature comforts, and firm beds help assure a good night's sleep. Breakfast is a mouth-watering spread of Shetland smoked salmon, porridge, and homemade jam. **Pros:** splendid comforts; easygoing hosts; cooked breakfasts with not a greasy sausage in sight. **Cons:** car is necessary unless you're happy walking or willing to pay for taxis. ⊠ *Lower Sound ZE1 0RN* ☎ *01595/694247* ⊕ *www.bedandbreakfastlerwick.co.uk* ⤵ *3 rooms* ♿ *In-room: no a/c, no phone, no TV, Wi-Fi* ☰ *MC, V* �'◎' *BP.*

BICYCLING

Eric Brown Cycles (⊠ *Grantfield Garage, North Rd.* ☎ *01595/692709*), open year-round, rents bikes for the jolly decent price of £5 a day.

SHOPPING

Anderson & Co. (⊠ *60–62 Commercial St.* ☎ *01595/693714*) carries handmade knitwear and souvenirs. **J. G. Rae Limited** (⊠ *92 Commercial St.* ☎ *01595/693686*) stocks gold and silver jewelry with Norse and Celtic motifs. **Ninian** (⊠ *110 Commercial St.* ☎ *01595/696655*) sells traditional and funky handmade scarves, clothing, and throws, all using Shetland wool. The **Peerie Shop** (⊠ *Esplanade* ☎ *01595/692816*) sells a colorful mix of knitwear, cards, ceramics and books. **Shetland Times** (⊠ *Commercial St.* ☎ *01595/695531*) is the best bookshop within a radius of about 250 mi, stocking a good selection of travel guides and local history titles.

THE SOUTH MAINLAND

14 to 25 mi south of Lerwick via A970.

The narrow 3- or 4-mi-wide stretch of land that reaches south from Lerwick to Sumburgh Head has a number of fascinating ancient sites (and an airport) as well as farmland, wild landscapes, and dramatic ocean views.

GETTING HERE AND AROUND

Arriving in Sumburgh by plane offers stunning views of Sumburgh Head and its golden sands. A fairly regular bus makes the hour-long trip between the airport and Lerwick, and it's also easy to drive here if you're based in Lerwick. You can hire a car from the airport or take a taxi. Jarlshof and Scatness are both within walking distance of the terminal.

ESSENTIALS

Visitor Information Sumburgh
(⊠ *Sumburgh Airport Terminal* ☎ *08701/999440* ⊕ *www.visitshetland. com* ⊗ *Weekdays 7:15 AM–7:45 PM, Sat. 10:15–5:15, Sun. 12:45–7:45*).

EXPLORING

Sandwick, 14 mi south of Lerwick via A970, is the departure point for the passenger ferry to the tiny isle of Mousa, where you can see

★ **Mousa Broch,** a fortified Iron Age stone tower about 40 feet high. The massive walls give a real sense of security, which must have been reassuring for islanders subject to

---

SHETLAND PONIES

The endearingly squat and shaggy Shetland pony has been a common sight for more than 12 centuries. Roaming wild over the hills, the pony evolved its long mane and dense winter coat. The animals stand between 28 and 42 inches tall, which made them ideal for working in cramped coalmine tunnels in the 1850s, when child labor was restricted. They became a popular pet in the late 19th century; many believe this has helped save the breed. Today a studbook society protects the purity of the stock, and you'll see plenty of ponies at equine events as well as near dry-stone walls.

---

attacks from ship-borne raiders. Exploring this beautifully preserved, curved-stone structure, standing on what feels like an untouched island, makes you feel as if you're back in 100 BC. From May to July the ferry also takes bookings for night trips (£12) to see the bewitching sight and sound of thousands of storm petrels returning home after a day at sea. ⊠ *Mousa* ☎ *01950/431367 ferry* ⊕ *www.mousaboattrips.co.uk* ⊠ *Site free; ferry round-trip £12.50* ⊗ *Site daily; ferry Apr.–Sept., once or twice daily in afternoon.*

⊗ The **Shetland Croft House Museum,** a 19th-century thatched house, re-
★ creates the way of life of the rural Shetlander, which the traditionally attired attendant will be delighted to discuss with you. The peat fire casts a glow on the box bed, the resting chair, and the wealth of domestic implements, including a hand mill for preparing meal and a willow basket for carrying peat. The upturned boat in the field outside is used for storing and drying fish and mutton. Huts like this inspired the design of the new Scottish Parliament. If you're lucky, the museum's curator may be making bannocks from his homegrown and home-milled flour. The museum is 7 mi south of Sandwick. ⊠ *East of A970, on unmarked road, South Voe* ☎ *01595/695057* ⊕ *www.shetland-museum.org.uk* ⊠ *Donations welcome* ⊗ *May–Sept., daily 10–1 and 2–5.*

⊗ Ongoing excavations at **Old Scatness** have uncovered the remains of an
★ Iron Age village, including one building that still has a roof. The digs continue, but enthusiastic and entertaining guides, most in costume, tell stories that breathe life into the stones and the middens. They also show how the former residents made their clothes and cooked their food, including their staple dish: the ghastly seaweed porridge. Call ahead for hours. ⊠ *Off A970, Virkie* ☎ *01595/694688* ⊕ *www.shetland-heritage. co.uk/amenitytrust* ⊠ *£3* ⊗ *June–Sept., hrs vary.*

Jarlshof is one of Shetland's archaeological highlights. In 1897 a huge storm blew away 4,000 years of sand to expose the extensive remains of Norse buildings, prehistoric wheelhouses, and earth houses that represented thousands of years of continuous settlement. It's a large and complex site, and you can roam the remains freely. The small visitor center is packed with facts and figures, and illustrates Jarlshof's more recent history as a medieval farmstead and home of the 16th-century Earl of Orkney and Shetland, "cruel" Patrick Stewart, who enslaved the men of Scalloway to build Scalloway Castle. ⊠ *Sumburgh Head, off A970* ☎ *01950/460112* ⊕ *www. historic-scotland.gov.uk* ⊡ *£4.70* ☺ *Apr.–Sept., daily 9:30–5:30.*

> ## PUFFINS AND MORE
>
> Every summer more than a million birds alight on the cliff faces in Shetland to nest, feeding on the coastal fish and sand eels. Bird-watchers can spot more than 20 species, from tiny storm petrels to gannets with 6-foot wingspans. Popular with visitors are the puffins, with their short necks, striped beaks, and comical orange feet. Look for them on the cliffs at Sumburgh Head near the lighthouse, 2 mi south of Sumburgh Airport. It's a steep climb to the viewing areas. The visitor center in Lerwick has leaflets about nesting sites.

It was on **St. Ninian's Isle** that a schoolboy helping archaeologists excavate the ruins of a 12th-century church discovered the St. Ninian treasure, a collection of 28 silver objects dating from the 8th century. This Celtic silver is housed in the Museum of Scotland in Edinburgh (a point causing some controversy), but good replicas are in the Shetland Museum in Lerwick. Although you can't see the silver, walking over the causeway of golden sand (called a tombolo) that joins St. Ninian's Isle to the mainland is an unforgettable experience. The island is 8 mi north of Sumburgh via A970 and B9122; then turn left at Skelberry.

WHERE TO STAY

£ ⊞ **Hayhoull B&B.** Built in 2009, this restful place is the shining realization
★ of the owners' dream of running a bed-and-breakfast. Rooms are simple and well designed, and the dining room and lounge have beautiful views of St. Ninian's Isle and Foula. Breakfast can be whatever you want, and packed lunches and hearty evening meals (£15 for two courses) can be provided with notice. Children are welcomed with games and DVDs at their disposal. **Pros:** right next to the bus stop for Lerwick; in friendly village next to the magical St Ninian's Isle. **Cons:** 4 mi to the nearest pub or restaurant. ⊠ *Off B9122, Bigton* ☎ *01950/422206* ⊕ *www.hayhoull. co.uk* ◻ *3 rooms* ⌂ *In-room: no a/c, no phone, Wi-Fi. In-hotel: laundry facilities* ▤ *MC, V* ⓘ◎ *BP*

SCALLOWAY

6 mi west of Lerwick, 21 mi north of St. Ninian's Isle.

On the west coast of Mainland Island is Scalloway, which preceded Lerwick as the capital of the region. During World War II, Scalloway was the port for the "Shetland Bus," a secret fleet of boats that carried British agents to Norway to perform acts of sabotage against the Germans, who were occupying the country. On the return trips, the boats would carry refugees back to Shetland. Look for the information board just off A970, which overlooks the settlement and its castle.

GETTING HERE AND AROUND

The town is just 10 minutes by car from Lerwick, or you can get one of the fairly regular buses or even a taxi (£8).

EXPLORING

Scalloway Castle, on the harbor, was built in 1600 by Patrick Stewart, earl of Orkney and Shetland. He was hanged in 1615 for his cruelty and misdeeds, and the castle was never used again. To enter the castle, you must retrieve the key from the shopkeeper at Shetland Woollen Company, or, on Sunday, from the host at the Scalloway Hotel. You may explore the castle ruins to your heart's content; unsafe areas are fenced off. ⊠ *A970* ☎ *01856/841815* ⊕ *www.historic-scotland.gov.uk* 🖾 *Free* ☉ *Daily.*

SHOPPING

The **Shetland Woollen Company** (⊠ *Castle St.* ☎ *01595/880243*), open Monday to Saturday 9:30 to 5, is one of many purveyors in Scalloway with a selection of Shetland knitwear.

WEISDALE

9 mi north of Lerwick.

This tiny place is less a village than a group of houses, but it does have a worthwhile gallery.

GETTING HERE AND AROUND

Take A971 from Lerwick. The number 9 bus runs weekdays runs three times a day; the trip from Lerwick is 20 minutes.

EXPLORING

Built in 1855 using stones from the Kergord estate's "cleared" (forcibly evicted) crofts and converted to a museum in 1994, Weisdale Mill is now the **Bonhoga Gallery,** a contemporary art space showing quirky exhibitions by local, national, and international artists. Other forms of art are represented in programs of films, poetry, and more. Downstairs is a well-appreciated café that looks over the Weisdale burn; try the excellent coffee and snacks. ⊠ *B9075* ☎ *01595/830400* ⊕ *www.shetlandarts.org* ☉ *Tues.–Sat. 10:30–4:30, Sun. noon–4:30.*

SHOPPING

Shetland Jewellery (⊠ *Sound Side* ☎ *01595/830275*) sells gold and silver Celtic-inspired jewelry.

BRAE

15 mi north of Weisdale, 24 mi north of Lerwick.

A thriving community, Brae is where you can see the spoils of Shetland's oil money. The rugged moorland and tranquil *voes* (inlets) of Brae are the home of Busta House, one of the best hotels on the island.

GETTING HERE AND AROUND

There are buses from Lerwick to Brae, but the spread-out sights make it impossible to really see this area without a car. A970 is the main road, and B9078 will take you through Hillswick and to Eshaness.

EXPLORING

North of Brae the A970 meanders past **Mavis Grind,** a strip of land so narrow you can throw a stone—if you're strong—from the Atlantic, in one inlet, to the North Sea, in another. Keep an eye out for sea otters, who sometimes cross here.

OFF THE
BEATEN
PATH

Eshaness and Ronas Hill. About 15 mi north of Brae are the rugged, forbidding cliffs around **Eshaness;** drive north and then turn left onto B9078. On the way, look for the striking sandstone stacks or pillars (known as the Drongs) in the bay that resemble a Viking galley under sail. After viewing the cliffs at Eshaness, call in at **Tangwick Haa Museum** (⊠ *Off B9078, Tangwick* ☎ *01806/503389*), a former laird's house filled with a collection of photographs from the turn of the last century. Then return to join the A970 at Hillswick and follow an ancillary road from the head of Ura Firth. This road provides vistas of rounded, bare **Ronas Hill,** the highest hill in Shetland. Though only 1,468 feet high, it's noted for its arctic-alpine flora. If you want to gain a bit of height but haven't the shoes or time to walk, drive up Collafirth Hill, just off A970. It has the remains of an early NATO communications station on the top and a landscape strewn with huge red granite boulders.

WHERE TO EAT AND STAY

£

BRITISH

✕ **Braewick Café.** The café's stunning position overlooking Eshaness's seastacks (columns of rock in the sea), and the wholesome fare that uses the owners' produce attract Shetlanders and visitors by word of mouth. Browse the local craft creations in the shop while waiting for a crispy battered-fish supper, or just sit back in the sofas by the huge picture window and watch the dramatic sea and sky. Don't pass up the many tempting home-baked desserts like sponges, cheesecakes, and giant scones. This is also one of the best-equipped sites for camping in Shetland. ⊠ *Eshaness* ☎ *01806/503345* ☰ *AE, MC, V.*

£
★

BRITISH

✕ **Frankie's Fish & Chip Cafe.** Proudly claiming to be the northernmost fish-and-chip shop in Britain, this casual spot is also the best of its kind on the islands. The combination of super-fresh fish—skate wings, squid, and crab legs—light and crispy batter, and value for your money means Frankie's is everything a chip shop could be. Try the juicy fresh mussels, too. There's a lovely dining room with views toward Busta Voe, and you can sit on the deck in finer weather. ⊠ *A970* ☎ *01806/522700* ☰ *MC, V* ☉ *No lunch Sun.*

££££

🏠 **Busta House.** Surrounded by terraced grounds, Busta House dates in part from the 16th century and has a restrained, austere elegance that tells you something of the Gifford family that lived here in the 18th century—ask the current owners about the Gifford family's ill-starred history. All the rooms are different (ask about size, location, and possible noise when you book) and are prettily furnished, many with antique headboards. The 16th-century Long Room is a delightful place to sample a selection of malt whiskies beside a peat fire. The restaurant serves four-course dinners (£40 prix-fixe), and the bar has a less expensive (around £10 for a main courses) menu. This is a good place to get away from it all. **Pros:** truly haunting atmosphere; atmospheric public rooms; lovely grounds. **Cons:** noisy plumbing; lack of soundproofing; some dishes in the restaurant come smothered in sauce. ⊠ *Off A970* ☎ *01806/522506* ⊕ *www.bustahouse.com* ↪ *22 rooms* ♨ *In-room: no a/c. In-hotel: restaurant, bar, Wi-Fi, Internet terminal* ▤ *AE, DC, MC, V* ⫚ *BP.*

YELL

11 mi northeast of Brae, 31 mi north of Lerwick.

A desolate-looking blanket bog cloaks two-thirds of the island of Yell, creating an atmospheric landscape to pass through on the way to Unst to the north.

GETTING HERE AND AROUND

Although you will see the odd walker or cyclist, a car is needed to explore the northern isles. To get to Yell, take A970 or B9076 and catch the ferry from Toft to Ulsta. On Yell, B9081 runs through Burravoe and up the east side and joins the A968, which leads to Gutcher and the ferry to Unst.

EXPLORING

Burravoe's **Old Haa** *(hall)*, the oldest building on the island, is known for its crow-stepped gables (the stepped effect on the ends of the roofs), typical of an early-18th-century Shetland-merchant's house. There's an earnest memorial to Bobby Tulloch, the great Shetland naturalist (1929–96), and the displays in the upstairs museum tell the story of the wrecking of the German ship, the *Bohus*, in 1924. A copy of the ship's figurehead is displayed outside the building; the original remains at the shipwreck, overlooking Otterswick along the coast on B9081. The Old Haa serves light meals with home-baked buns, cakes, and other goodies and also acts as a kind of unofficial information center. A crafts shop is on the premises, too. ⊠ *Burravoe* ☎ *01957/722339* ⫚ *Free* ⊙ *Late Apr.–Sept., Tues.–Thurs. and Sat. 10–4, Sun. 2–5.*

UNST

49 mi north of Lerwick.

Unst is the northernmost inhabited island in Scotland, a remote and special place, especially for nature lovers. On a long summer evening, views north to Muckle Flugga, with only the ocean beyond, are incomparable. If you're a bird-watcher, head to the Hermaness and Keen of Hamar nature reserves.

GETTING HERE AND AROUND

A ferry (take the A968 at Mid Yell to Gutcher) crosses the Bluemull Sound to Unst. A car is best for exploring, though there is limited bus service, including from Lerwick; taxis are an option. The island has some B&B and house-rental options if you choose to linger.

EXPLORING

Muness Castle, Scotland's northernmost castle, was built just before the end of the 16th century and has circular corner towers. It is a ruin but has notable architectural details; you can visit when you wish. To get here from the A968, turn right onto the B9084. ⊠ *B9084* 🕾 *No phone* ⊕ *www.historic-scotland.gov.uk* ⌐ *Free* ⊙ *Daily 24 hrs.*

Just to the north of Muness Castle is the **Keen of Hamar National Nature Reserve,** off A968, with subarctic flora and arctic terns.

In the far north of Unst is the town of **Haroldswick,** with its post office, proud of its status as the most northerly one, and heritage center. Named after King Harold of Norway, it was at this sheltered bay that the Norwegians landed in AD 875 to claim the islands. Also here is **Unst Boat Haven,** displaying a collection of traditional small fishing and sailing boats reflecting Shetland's maritime heritage. ⊠ *haroldswick* 🕾 *01957/711528* ⊕ *www.unst.org* ⌐ *£3* ⊙ *May–Sept., daily 11–5.*

★   The **Hermaness National Nature Reserve,** a bleak moorland ending in rocky cliffs, is prime bird-watching territory. About half the world's population (6,000 pairs) of great skuas, called "bonxies" by locals, are found here. ■ TIP→ **These sky pirates attack anything that strays near their nests, including humans, so keep to the paths.** Thousands of other seabirds, including more than 50,000 puffins, nest in spectacular pro-fusion on the cliffs, about one hour's walk from the reserve entrance. Hermaness is not just about birds—gray seals gather in caves at the foot of the cliffs in fall, and offshore, dolphins and occasionally whales (including orcas) can be seen on calm days. The flora includes the insect-eating butterwort and sundew, purple field gentians, orchids, and red campion. The visitor center at the lighthouse has leaflets that outline a walk; mid-May to mid-July is the best time to visit. To get here from Haroldswick, follow the B9086 around the head of Burra Firth, a sea inlet. ⊠ *B9086, Shore Station, Burra Firth* 🕾 *01957/711278* ⊕ *www. nnr-scotland.org.uk* ⌐ *Free* ⊙ *Mid-Apr.–mid-Sept., daily 9–5.*

A path in the Hermaness National Nature Reserve (on B9086) mean-ders across moorland and climbs up a gentle hill, from which you can see, to the north, a series of tilting offshore rocks; the largest of these sea-battered protrusions is **Muckle Flugga,** meaning "big, steep-sided island," on which stands a lighthouse. This is the northernmost point in Scotland—the sea rolls out on three sides, and no land lies beyond.

WHERE TO EAT

££   ✕ **Saxa Vord.** This restaurant is set among the former homes of person-
BRITISH nel from the now-decommissioned Royal Air Force radar station. It's part of an odd collection of buildings strewn around the edge of an eye-wateringly—that's the wind—gorgeous peninsula that is being turned into a remote resort with cottages for rent (from £300 per week) and a hostel (£37 per double room). The tidy, well-run, and informal eatery serves lunches and dinners as fresh and good for you as the Unst air. Try local scallops, Shetland smoked salmon, and lamb hot pot. You can retire to the bar to chat with the locals and sip a tasty real ale such as Auld Wife or Simmer Dim. ⊠ *Off A968, Valsgarth* 🕾 *01957/711711* ⊕ *www.saxavord.com* ⊟ *MC, V* ⊙ *Closed Mon. Oct.–Apr.*

A Golfer's Country

WORD OF MOUTH

"I consider the Prestwick/Troon area to be the best spot for a short trip incorporating the top courses — it's at least on a par with St. Andrews. Play Prestwick (a bit outdated for the modern game, but birthplace of the Open and proud home of the first dozen championships); Royal Troon (expensive but with a new, more visitor-friendly booking policy and rate structure); Turnberry, the Pebble Beach of Scotland; and little-known gem Western Gailes. These are four top courses, three with British Open pedigree, all within a 45-minute drive of each other. They may lack the ambience of the town of St. Andrews, but this is great golf in the middle of Robert Burns country."

—ClarkB

Updated
by Duncan
Forgan

There are some 550 golf courses in Scotland and only 5.1 million residents, so the country has probably the highest ratio of courses to people anywhere in the world. If you're coming to Scotland, you'll probably want to play the "famous names" sometime in your career.

So, by all means, play the championship courses such as the Old Course at St. Andrews, but remember they *are* championship courses and you may enjoy the game itself much more at a less challenging course. Remember, too, that everyone else wants to play the big names, so booking can be a problem at peak times in summer. Booking three to four months ahead is not too far for the famous courses, although you may be able to get a time up to a month (or even a week) in advance if you are relaxed about your timing. If you're staying in a hotel attached to a course, get them to book for you.

Happily, golf has always had a peculiar classlessness in Scotland. It's a game for everyone, and for centuries Scottish towns and cities have maintained golf courses for the enjoyment of their citizens. Admittedly, a few clubs have always been noted for their exclusive air, and some newer golf courses are losing touch with the game's inclusive origins, but these are exceptions to the tradition of recreation for all. Golf here is usually a democratic game, played by ordinary folk as well as the wealthy.

TIPS ABOUT PLAYING IN SCOTLAND

Golf courses are everywhere in Scotland. Most courses welcome visitors with a minimum of formalities, and some at a surprisingly low cost. Other courses are very expensive, but a lot of great golf can be played for between about £30 to £100 a round. Online booking at many courses has made arranging a golf tour easier, too.

Be aware of the topography of a course. Scotland is where the distinction between "links" and "parkland" courses was first made. Links courses are by the sea and are subject to the attendant sea breezes—some quite bracing—and mists, which can make them trickier to play. The natural topography of sand dunes and long, coarse grasses can add to the challenge of playing, too. Invariably, a parkland course is in a wooded area and its terrain is more obviously landscaped. A "moorland" course is found in an upland area.

Here are three pieces of advice, particularly for North Americans: 1) in Scotland the game is usually played fairly quickly, so don't dawdle if others are waiting; 2) caddy carts are hand-pulled carts for your clubs and driven golf carts are rarely available; and 3) when they say "rough," they really mean "rough."

Unless specified otherwise, course-playing hours are generally sunrise to sundown, which in June can be as late as 10 PM. Note that some courses advertise the SSS, "standard scratch score," instead of par (which may be different). This is the score a scratch golfer could achieve under perfect conditions. Clubs, balls, and other golfing gear are generally for rent from clubhouses, except at the most basic municipal courses. Don't get caught by the dress codes enforced at many golfing establishments: in general, untailored shorts, round-neck shirts, jeans, and sneakers are frowned upon. The prestigious courses may ask for evidence of your golf skills by way of a handicap certificate; it's rare, but check in advance and carry this with you.

Many courses will lower their rates before and after the peak season—at the end of September, for example. It's worth asking about this.

■ TIP → **Some areas offer regional golf passes that are a great way to save money. Check with the local tourist board.**

For a complete list of courses, contact local tourist offices or Visit-Scotland's official and comprehensive golf Web site, ⊕ *http://golf. visitscotland.com*. It has information about the country's golf courses and special golf trails, a course search, links to golf course and regional golf Web sites, lists of special golfing events and tour operators, and updates on golf passes as well as on accommodations convenient to the courses. Another site, ⊕ *www.uk-golfguide.com*, has a handy feature that allows you to see the courses via Google Earth. *For information about good regional courses, also see individual chapters; see Tours in Travel Smart Scotland for some golf tour operators.*

THE STEWARTRY

At the very southern border, the Stewartry is a delightful part of Scotland set in the rich farmlands around Dumfries, a golfing vacation area since Victorian times. There are also several fine 9-hole courses in the area.

Powfoot. A pleasant mix of links and parkland holes and views south over the Solway Firth to distract you make this lesser-known gem designed by James Braid a pleasure to play. ⊠ *Powfoot Golf Club, Cummertrees, Annan* ☎ *01461/204100* ⊕ *www.powfootgolfclub.com* ⚑ *18 holes, 6,255 yds, SSS 71* ✉ *Weekdays £37 per round, £48 per day; weekends £43 per round, £60 per day* ☉ *Daily.*

Southerness. Mackenzie Ross designed this course, the first built in Scotland after World War II, in 1947. Southerness is a long course, played over extensive links with fine views southward over the Solway Firth. The greens are hard and fast, and the frequent winds make for some testing golf. ⊠ *Southerness Golf Club, Southerness, Kirkbean* ☎ *01387/880677* ⊕ *www.southernessgolfclub.com* ⚑ *Reservations essential* ⚑ *18 holes, 6,566 yds, par 69* ✉ *Weekdays £50 per round, £65 per day; weekends £60 per round, £75 per day* ☉ *Daily.*

AYRSHIRE AND THE CLYDE COAST

An hour south of Glasgow, Ayrshire and the Clyde Coast have been a holiday area for Glaswegians for generations. Few golfers need an introduction to the names of Turnberry, Royal Troon, Prestwick, or Western Gailes—all challenging links courses along this coast. There are at least 20 other courses in the area within an hour's drive.

Girvan. This is an old, established course that plays along a narrow coastal strip and a more lush inland section next to the Water of

Girvan—a river that constitutes a particular hazard at the 15th, unless you're a big hitter. The course is scenic, with good views of Ailsa Craig and the Clyde Estuary. ✉ *40 Golf Course Rd., Girvan* ☎ *01465/714346* ⊕ *www.golfsouthayrshire.com* ⛳ *18 holes, 5,064 yds, par 64* 🍽 *Weekdays £16 per round, £24 per day; weekends £19 per round, £33 per day* ⊘ *Daily.*

Prestwick. Tom Morris was involved in designing this challenging Ayrshire coastal links course, which saw the birth of the British Open Championship in 1860. Prestwick has excellent, fast rail links with Glasgow. ✉ *2 Links Rd., Prestwick* ☎ *01292/477404* ⊕ *www.prestwickgc.co.uk* ⛳ *18 holes, 6,544 yds, par 71* 🍽 *Weekdays £120 per round, £175 per day; Sun. £145 per round* ⊘ *Sun.–Fri. Limited number of tee times on Saturday afternoons.*

Royal Troon. Of the two courses at Royal Troon, it's the Old Course—a traditional links course with superb sea views—that is used for the British Open Championship. You can buy a day ticket for one round on each course, which is a good value, as the ticket includes an excellent lunch. ✉ *Craigend Rd., Troon* ☎ *01292/311555* ⊕ *www.royaltroon. com* ⛳ *Old Course: 18 holes, 7,150 yds, SSS 74; Portland Course: 18 holes, 6,289 yds, SSS 70* 🍽 *Old Course: £160 per round; Portland Course: £60 per round; one round on each course (lunch included): £220 per day* ⊘ *Mon., Tues., and Thurs.*

Turnberry. The Ailsa Course at Turnberry is one of the most famous links courses in Scotland. Right on the seashore, the course is open to the elements, and the ninth hole requires you to hit the ball over the open sea. The British Open was staged here in 1977, 1986, 1994, and 2009. A second course, the Kintyre, is more compact than the Ailsa, with tricky sloped greens. Five of the holes have sea views; the rest are more inland. ✉ *Turnberry Resort, off A719 Turnberry* ☎ *01655/331000* ⊕ *www. luxurycollection.com/turnberry* ⛳ *Ailsa Course: 18 holes, 7,204 yds, SSS 70; Kintyre Course: 18 holes, 6,853 yds, SSS 72* 🍽 *Ailsa Course: £170 per round for hotel guests, £210 per round for nonguests; Kintyre Course: £120 per round for hotel guests, £140 per round for nonguests* ⊘ *Daily.*

★ **Western Gailes.** Known as the finest natural links course in Scotland, Western Gailes is entirely nature-made, and the greens are kept in truly magnificent condition. This is the final qualifying course when the British Open is held at Troon or Turnberry. Tom Watson lists the par-5 sixth as one of his favorite holes. ✉ *Gailes Rd., Irvine* ☎ *01294/311649* ⊕ *www.westerngailes.com* ⛳ *18 holes, 6,700 yds, par 71* 🍽 *Mon., Wed., Fri. £115 per round, £165 double round (lunch included); Sat. 3:30–4:30 (May–Sept.) £100 per round; Sun. afternoon £125 per round* ⊘ *Mon., Wed., Fri., and weekend afternoons.*

ARGYLL

The lochs and glens of Argyll in the west of Scotland have provided the scenic backdrop for family outings for generations. The string of courses north from the Mull of Kintyre all offer golf in a relaxed environment, with sea, beach, and hills not far away.

Machrihanish, by Campbeltown. Many enthusiasts discuss this course in hushed tones—it's a kind of out-of-the-way golfers' Shangri-la, though developments are now being built around it. It was laid out in 1876 by Tom Morris on the links around the sandy Machrihanish Bay. The drive off the first tee is across the beach to reach the green—an intimidating start to a memorable series of individual holes. Consider flying from Glasgow to nearby Campbeltown if time is short. The new Machrihanish Dunes course, adjacent to this course opened in 2009 to rave reviews. ⊠ *Machrihanish, near Campbeltown* ☎ *01586/810277* ⊕ *www.machgolf.com* ⌂ *Reservations essential* ⅃ *18 holes, 6,225 yds, par 70* ⌂ *Weekdays and Sun. £50 per round, £80 per day; Sat. £60 per round, £90 per day* ☉ *Daily.*

GLASGOW

Most of Glasgow's old golf clubs have moved out to the suburbs—you can tee off from at least 30 different courses less than an hour from the city center. Remember: in addition to these, all the Ayrshire courses are just down the road.

Douglas Park. North of the city near Milngavie (pronounced mul-*gai*), Douglas Park is an attractive course set among birch and pine trees where masses of rhododendrons bloom in early summer. The Campsie Fells form a pleasant backdrop. ⊠ *Milngavie Rd., Hillfoot, Bearsden* ☎ *0141/942–0985* ⊕ *www.douglasparkgolfclub.co.uk* ⅃ *18 holes, 5,962 yds, par 69* ⌂ *£30 per round* ☉ *On request.*

Gailes. The Glasgow Golf Club originally played on Glasgow Green in the heart of the ancient city center, but as the pressure for space grew, the club moved north to the leafy suburb of Bearsden, on the road to Loch Lomond. Killermont, the club's home course, is not open to visitors, but you can play the club's other course at Gailes, near Irvine on the Firth of Clyde. The Glasgow Club's Tennant Cup, in June, is the oldest open amateur tournament in the world. ⊠ *Gailes* ✛ *Near Irvine* ☎ *0141/942–2011* ⊕ *www.glasgowgailes-golf.com* ⅃ *18 holes, 6,535 yds, SSS 72* ⌂ *Weekdays £75 per round, £90 per day (includes a two-course lunch); weekends £80 per round (after 2:30)* ☉ *Daily.*

EAST LOTHIAN

The sand dunes that stretch eastward from Edinburgh along the southern shore of the Firth of Forth made an ideal location for some of the world's earliest golf courses. Muirfield is perhaps the most famous course in the area, but around it are more than a dozen others. All are links courses, many with views to the islands of the Firth of Forth and northward to Fife. If you weary of the East Lothian courses, try one of the nearly 30 courses within the city boundaries of Edinburgh, 20 mi or so to the west.

Dunbar. This ancient golfing site by the sea was founded in 1794 and has a lighthouse at the ninth hole. It's a good choice for experiencing a typical east-coast links course in a seaside town but within easy reach of Edinburgh. There are stunning views of the Firth of Forth and May Island. ⊠ *East Links, Dunbar* ☎ *01368/862086* ⊕ *www.dunbargolfclub.co.uk* ⌂ *Reservations essential* ⅃ *18 holes, 6,597 yds, par 71*

Great Golf
Courses

North Sea

GRAMPIAN MOUNTAINS

HIGHLANDS

INNER HEBRIDES

The Minch

The Little Minch

North Channel

12

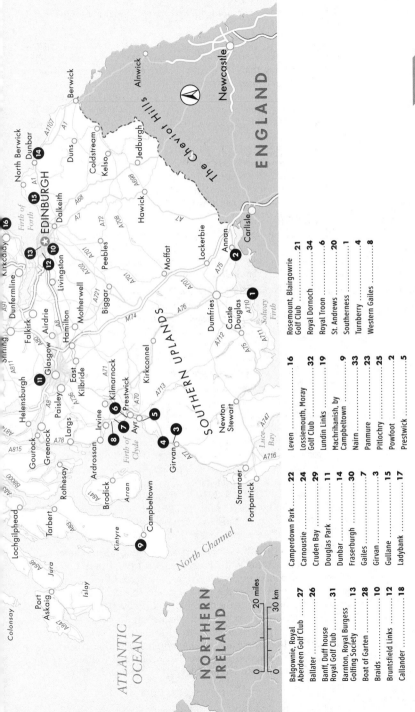

Balgownie, Royal Aberdeen Golf Club	**27**
Ballater	**26**
Banff, Duff house Royal Golf Club	**31**
Banton, Royal Burgess Golfing Society	**13**
Boat of Garten	**28**
Braids	**10**
Bruntsfield Links	**12**
Callander	**18**
Camperdown Park	**22**
Carnoustie	**24**
Cruden Bay	**29**
Douglas Park	**11**
Dunbar	**14**
Fraserburgh	**30**
Gailes	**7**
Girvan	**3**
Gullane	**15**
Ladybank	**17**
Leven	**16**
Lossiemouth, Moray Golf Club	**32**
Lundin Links	**19**
Machrihanish, by Campbeltown	**9**
Nairn	**33**
Panmure	**23**
Pitlochry	**25**
Powfoot	**2**
Prestwick	**5**
Rosemount, Blairgowrie Golf Club	**21**
Royal Dornoch	**34**
Royal Troon	**6**
St. Andrews	**20**
Southerness	**1**
Turnberry	**4**
Western Gailes	**8**

⌨ *Weekdays £55 per round, £70 per day; weekends £70 per round, £90 per day* ⊙ *Fri.–Wed.*

Gullane. Often overshadowed by its more famous neighbor, Muirfield, Gullane provides an equally authentic links experience and a far more effusive welcome than its slightly snooty counterpart just along the road. The three courses here crisscross Gullane hill and all command outstanding views of the Firth of Forth. No. 1 is the toughest test, but No. 2 and No. 3 offer up equally compelling sport. ⊠ *West Links Rd., Gullane* ☎ *01620/842123* ⊕ *www.gullanegolfclub.com* ⌖ *Reservations essential* ⅀. *No 1. Course: 18 holes, 6,466 yds, par 71; No 2. Course: 18 holes, 5,868 yds, par 71; No 3. Course: 18 holes, 5,259 yds, par 68* ⌨ *No 1. Course: weekdays £85 per round, £120 per day; weekends £100 per round. No 2. Course: weekdays £40 per round, £50 per day; weekends £45 per round, £65 per day. No 3. Course: weekdays £30 per day; weekends £40 per day* ⊙ *Daily.*

EDINBURGH

Scotland's capital has nearly 30 golf courses within its boundaries. Most are parkland courses, though some of the hillier layouts are more moorland in character. Some are used by private clubs and offer visitors limited access; others that belong to the city are more accessible.

Barnton, Royal Burgess Golfing Society. Dating to 1735, this is one of the world's oldest golf clubs. Its members originally played on Bruntsfield Links; now they and their guests play on elegantly manicured parkland in the city's northwestern suburbs. It's a testing course with fine greens. ⊠ *181 Whitehouse Rd., Barnton* ☎ *0131/339–2075* ⊕ *www. royalburgess.co.uk* ⌖ *Reservations essential* ⅀. *18 holes, 6,111 yds, par 68* ⌨ *Weekdays £60 per day; weekends £75 per day* ⊙ *Daily.*

Braids. Braids (no connection with James Braid) is beautifully laid out over a rugged range of small hills in the southern suburbs. The views to the south and the Pentland Hills and north over the Edinburgh skyline towards the Firth of Forth are worth a visit in themselves. The city built this course at the turn of the 20th century after urban development forced golfers out of the city center. The 9-hole Princes Course was completed in 2003. Reservations are recommended for weekend play. ⊠ *The Braids, 27 Braids Hill Approach, Edinburgh* ☎ *0131/447–6666 for Braids, 0131/666–2210 for Princes* ⊕ *www.edinburghleisure. co.uk/detail-74* ⅀. *Braids: 18 holes, 5,865 yds, par 70; Princes: 9 holes* ⌨ *Braids: weekdays £19 per round, weekends £23 per round; Princes: weekdays £7.50 per round, weekends £9.50 per round* ⊙ *Daily.*

Bruntsfield Links. The British Seniors and several other championship games are held at this Willie Park–designed 1898 course 3 mi west of the city. The course meanders among 155 acres of mature parkland and has fine views over the Firth of Forth to Fife. Bruntsfield takes its name from one of the oldest golf links in Scotland, in the center of Edinburgh—now just a 9-hole pitch-and-putt course—where the club used to play. ⊠ *32 Barnton Ave., Davidson's Mains, Edinburgh* ☎ *0131/336–1479* ⊕ *www.sol.co.uk/b/bruntsfieldlinks* ⌖ *Reservations essential* ⅀. *18 holes, 6,407 yds, par 71* ⌨ *Weekdays £57.50 per round, £85 per day; weekends £70 per round, £90 per day* ⊙ *Daily.*

FIFE

The presence of St. Andrews makes this an important area—a pilgrimage center, even—for fans of the sport, but Fife has other courses, too. Along the north shores of the Firth of Forth is a string of ancient villages, each with its harbor, ancient red-roof buildings, and golf course. In all, there are about 30 courses in the area.

Ladybank. Fife is known for its coastal courses, but this one is an interesting inland contrast. Although Ladybank, designed by Tom Morris in 1876, is laid out on fairly level ground, the fir woods, birches, and heathery rough give it a Highland flavor among the gentle Lowland fields. Qualifying rounds of the British Open are played here when the main championship is played at St. Andrews. ⊠ *A92, Annsmuir, Ladybank* ☎ *01337/830814* ⊕ *www.ladybankgolf.co.uk* ⌲ *Reservations essential* ⚑ *18 holes, 6,580 yds, par 71* ⛳ *May–Sept., weekdays £50 per round, £75 per day; weekends £60 per round. Oct. and Apr., weekdays £40 per round, £65 per day; weekends £50 per round. Nov.–Mar., weekdays £22 per round; weekends £25 per round* ☉ *Daily.*

Leven. A fine Fife course that has been used as a British Open qualifier, this links course feels like the more famous St. Andrews, with hummocky terrain and a tang of salt in the air. The 1st and 18th share the same fairway, and the 18th green has a creek running by it. ⊠ *The Promenade, Leven* ☎ *01333/428859* ⊕ *www.leven-links.com* ⌲ *Reservations essential* ⚑ *18 holes, 6,450 yds, par 71* ⛳ *Weekdays £45 per round, £55 per day; Sun. £50 per round, £60 per day* ☉ *Sun.–Fri.*

Lundin Links. One of a string of fantastic links courses stretching from Leven all the way round the Fife coast to Scotscraig on the Firth of Tay, Lundin Links is a worthy addition to any Scottish golfing itinerary. Designed by the great James Braid, the course is always in prime condition and the greens are a joy to putt on. The pick of the holes is the 14th, a par-3 hole played from an elevated tee back toward the sea. ⊠ *Golf Rd., Lundin Links* ☎ *01333/320051* ⊕ *www.lundingolfclub.co.uk* ⚑ *18 holes, 6,138 yards, par 71* ⛳ *Weekdays £52 per round, £75 per day; weekends £60 per round* ☉ *Daily.*

St. Andrews. Few would dispute the claim of St. Andrews to be the home of golf, holding as it does the Royal & Ancient, the organization that governs the sport worldwide. Golf has been played here since the 15th century, and to play in Fife is for most golfers a cherished ambition. St. Andrews itself has six other 18-hole courses besides the famous 15th-century Old Course. *For full details, see St. Andrews in Chapter 5.*

PERTHSHIRE

Perthshire has several attractive country courses developed specifically for visiting golfers. Gleneagles Hotel (*see Chapter 6*) is, with its outstanding facilities, the most famous of these golf resorts. But several courses in the area, set on the edges of beautiful Highland scenery, will delight any golfer.

Callander. Designed by Tom Morris in 1890 and extended to 18 holes in 1913 by Willie Fernie, Callander has a scenic upland feel in a town well prepared for visitors. Pine and birch woods and hilly fairways afford fine views, especially toward Ben Ledi, and the tricky moorland

CLOSE UP

The Evolution of Golf

The matter of who invented golf has been long debated, but there's no doubt that its development into one of the most popular games in the world stems from Scotland. The first written reference to golf, variously spelled as "gowf" or "goff," was in 1457, when James II (1430–60) of Scotland declared that both golf and football (soccer) should be *"utterly cryit doune and nocht usit"* (publicly criticized and prohibited) because they distracted his subjects from archery practice. Mary, Queen of Scots (1542–87), was fond of golf. When in Edinburgh in 1567, she played on Leith Links and on Bruntsfield Links. When in Fife, she played at Falkland and at St. Andrews itself.

GOLF EXPANDS
Golf clubs (i.e., organizations) arose in the middle of the 18th century. The Honourable Company of Edinburgh Golfers, now residing at Muirfield, was founded in 1744. From then on, clubs sprang up all over Scotland: Royal Aberdeen (1780), Crail Golfing Society (1786), Dunbar (1794), and the Royal Perth Golfing Society (1824).

By the early 19th century, clubs had been set up in England, and the game was being carried all over the world by enthusiastic Scots. These golf missionaries spread their knowledge not only of the sport, but also of the courses. Large parts of the Scottish coast are natural golf courses; indeed,

the origins of bunkers and the word *links* (courses) are found in the sand dunes of Scotland's shores. Willie Park of Musselburgh, James Braid, and C. K. Hutchison are some of the best known of Scotland's golf-course architects.

CHANGES IN THE GAME
Many of the important changes in the design and construction of balls and clubs were pioneered by the players who lived and worked around the town courses. The original balls, called *featheries*, were leather bags stuffed with boiled feathers and often lasted only one round. In 1848, the gutta-percha ball, called a *guttie*, was introduced. It was in general use until the invention of the rubber-core ball in 1901. Clubs were made of wood with shafts of ash (later hickory), and heads of thorn, apple, or pear. Heads were spliced, then bound to the shaft with twine. Later in the 19th century, manufacturers began to experiment with metal in clubfaces and shafts.

Caddies—the word comes from the French *cadet* (young boy)—carried the players' clubs, usually under the arm. Golf carts didn't come into fashion in Britain until the 1950s, and some people still consider them to be potentially injurious to the national health and moral fiber. The technology of golf continues to change, but its addictive qualities are timeless.

layout demands accurate hitting off the tee. ⊠ *Callander Golf Club, Aveland Rd., Callander* ☎ *01877/330090* ⊕ *www.callandergolfclub. co.uk* ⚑ *18 holes, 4,431 yds, par 63* ▱ *Weekdays £25 per round, £35 per day; weekends £35 per round, £45 per day* ☼ *Daily.*

Pitlochry. A decent degree of stamina is needed for the first three holes at Pitlochry where steep climbs are involved. The reward is magnificent Highland scenery that can make the golf seem like something of an afterthought. Don't get too distracted, however, because despite its relatively short length, this beautiful course has more than its fair share of testing surprises. ⊠ *Golf Club Rd., Pitlochry* ☎ *01796/472792* ⊕ *www.pitlochrygolf.co.uk* ⚘. *18 holes, 5,695 yds, par 70* ⚐ *Mar.–late May and Oct: weekdays £27 per round, £38 per day; weekends £36 per round. Late May–Sept.: weekdays £30 per round, £40 per day; weekends £38 per round, £40 per day* ☼ *Daily.*

12

★ **Rosemount, Blairgowrie Golf Club.** Well-known to native golfers looking for a challenge, Rosemount's 18 (James Braid, 1934) are laid out on rolling land in the pine, birch, and fir woods, which bring a wild air to the scene. There are, however, wide fairways and at least some large greens. The club is open daily, but visitor play may be restricted depending on tournament and match schedules. If you can't manage a game on Rosemount itself, you can play on Lansdowne, another 18-hole course, or Wee, a 9-hole course. A handicap certificate may be required to play here. ⊠ *Golf Course Rd., Blairgowrie* ☎ *01250/872622* ⊕ *www.theblairgowriegolfclub.co.uk* ⚘. *Rosemount: 18 holes, 6,689 yds, par 72. Lansdowne: 18 holes, 7,007 yds, par 72. Wee: 9 holes, 2,352 yds, par 32* ⚐ *Rosemount: £70 per round; Lansdowne: £50 per round; Wee: £15 per round. £90 per day (includes 1 round on Rosemount and 1 on Lansdowne)* ☼ *Daily.*

ANGUS

East of Perthshire, near the city of Dundee, lies a string of demanding courses along the shores of the North Sea and inland into the foothills of the Grampian Mountains. The most famous course in Angus is probably Carnoustie, one of several British Open Championship venues in Scotland. Golfers who excel in windy conditions particularly enjoy the breezes blowing eastward from the sea. Inland Edzell, Forfar, Brechin, and Kirriemuir all have courses nestling in the Strathmore farmlands.

Camperdown Park. For an alternative to the wild and windy east-coast links courses, try this magnificent municipal parkland golf challenge on the outskirts of Dundee. You can enjoy a game amid tree-lined fairways near the imposing Camperdown House and wildlife park. ⊠ *Camperdown Park, Coupar Angus Rd., Dundee* ☎ *01382/431820* ⊕ *www.dundeecity.gov.uk/golf* ⚘. *18 holes, 6,548 yards, par 71* ⚐ *Weekdays £26 per round, weekends £31 per day* ☼ *Daily.*

Carnoustie. The venue for the British Open Championship in 1999 and 2007, the coastal links around Carnoustie have been played since at least 1527. Open winners here have included Armour, Hogan, Cotton, Player, and Watson. The choice Burnside course is full of historical snippets and local color, as well as being tough and interesting. The Buddon course, designed by Peter Allis and Dave Thomas, is recommended for links novices. ⊠ *20 Links Parade, Carnoustie* ☎ *01241/802270* ⊕ *www.carnoustiegolflinks.co.uk* ⚑ *Reservations essential* ⚘. *Championship course: 18 holes, 6,941 yds, par 72; Burnside: 18 holes, 6,028 yds, par 68; Buddon: 18 holes, 5,420 yds, par 66* ⚐ *Championship: Apr.–Oct., £130 per round; Burnside: £35 per round; Buddon: £30 per round; combined ticket for all 3 courses: £150* ☼ *Daily.*

Panmure. Down the road from the famous Carnoustie club, this traditional links course offers an excellent challenge with its seaside climate, undulating greens, and sometimes excruciating—but always entertaining—burrows. The signature sixth is named after British Open Championship winner Ben Hogan, who practiced here prior to his triumphant tournament at Carnoustie in 1953. ⊠ *Burnside Rd., off Station Rd.,Carnoustie* ☎ *01241/855120* ⊕ *www.panmuregolfclub. co.uk* ⌂ *Reservations essential* ⚑ *18 holes, 6,317 yds, par 70* ☞ *£68 per round, £88 per day* ☉ *Daily.*

ABERDEENSHIRE

Aberdeen, Scotland's third-largest city, is known for its sparkling granite buildings and amazing displays of roses each summer. Within the city there are six courses, and to the north, as far as Fraserburgh and Peterhead, there are five others, including the popular Cruden Bay.

Balgownie, Royal Aberdeen Golf Club. This old club, founded in 1780, is the archetypal Scottish links course: long and testing over uneven ground, with the frequently added hazard of a sea breeze. Prickly gorse is inclined to close in and form an additional hurdle. The two courses are tucked behind the rough, grassy sand dunes, and there are surprisingly few views of the sea. One historical note: in 1783 this club originated the five-minute-search rule for a lost ball. A handicap certificate or letter of introduction is required. ⊠ *Links Rd., Bridge of Don, Aberdeen* ☎ *01224/702571* ⊕ *www.royalaberdeengolf.com* ⌂ *Reservations essential* ⚑ *Balgownie: 18 holes, 6,530 yds, par 71; Silverburn: 18 holes, 4,021 yds, par 64* ☞ *Balgownie: weekdays £100 per round, £150 per day; weekends £120 per round. Silverburn: weekdays £50 per round, £75 per day; weekends £60 per round* ☉ *Balgownie: tee off weekdays 10–11:30 and 2–3:30, weekends after 3:30; Silverburn: daily.*

Ballater. The mountains of Royal Deeside surround this course laid out along the sandy flats of the River Dee. Ideal for a relaxing round of golf, the course makes maximum use of the fine setting between river and woods. The club, originally opened in 1892, has a holiday atmosphere, and the shops and pleasant walks in nearby Ballater make this a good place for non-golfing partners. Reservations are advised. ⊠ *Victoria Rd., Ballater* ☎ *013397/55567* ⊕ *www.ballatergolfclub.co.uk* ⚑ *18 holes, 6,059 yds, par 70* ☞ *Weekdays £25 per round, £36 per day; weekends £28 per round, £45 per day* ☉ *Daily.*

Cruden Bay. An east-coast Lowland course sheltered behind extensive sand hills, Cruden Bay offers a typical Scottish golf experience. Runnels and valleys, among other hazards, on the challenging fairways ensure plenty of excitement, and some of the holes are rated among the country's finest. Like Gleneagles and Turnberry, this course owes its origins to an association with the grand railway hotels built in the heyday of steam. Unlike at the other two courses, however, Cruden Bay's railway hotel and the railway itself have gone, but the course remains in fine shape. ■ TIP→ **Weekend tee times are extremely limited; book months in advance.** ⊠ *Aulton Rd., Cruden Bay, Peterhead* ☎ *01779/812285* ⊕ *www.crudenbaygolfclub.co.uk* ⌂ *Reservations essential* ⚑ *Championship: 18 holes, 6,287 yds, par 70; St. Olaf: 9 holes, 2,463 yds, par*

32 ⌘ *Championship: weekdays £65 per round, £85 per day; weekends £75 per round. St. Olaf: weekdays £20 per day, weekends £30 per day* ☉ *Daily; limited weekend tee times.*

SPEYSIDE

On the main A9 road an hour south of Inverness amid the Cairngorm Mountains, the valley of the River Spey is one of Scotland's most attractive all-year sports centers, with winter skiing and fine golf the rest of the year. The area's main courses are Newtonmore, Grantown-on-Spey, and Boat of Garten, all fine inland courses with wonderful views of the surrounding mountains and challenging golf provided by the springy turf and the heather.

Boat of Garten. This is possibly one of Scotland's greatest "undiscovered" courses. Boat of Garten, which dates to the late 19th century, was redesigned and extended by James Braid in 1932, and each of its 18 holes is individual: some cut through birch wood and heathery rough; most have long views to the Cairngorms and a strong Highland feel. An unusual feature is the preserved steam railway that runs along part of the course. ⊠ *Nethybridge Rd., Boat of Garten* ☎ *01479/831282* ⊕ *www.boatgolf.com* ⌂ *Reservations essential* ⚑ *18 holes, 5,876 yds, par 70* ⌘ *Weekdays £34 per round, £44 per day; weekends £39 per round, £49 per day* ☉ *Daily.*

MORAY COAST

No one can say that the Lowlands have a monopoly on Scotland's fine seaside golf courses. The Moray Coast, stretching eastward from Inverness, has some spectacular sand dunes that have been adapted to create stimulating and exciting links courses. The two courses at Nairn have long been known to golfers.

Banff, Duff House Royal Golf Club. Just moments away from the sea, this club combines a coastal course with a parkland setting. It lies only minutes from Banff center, within the grounds of Duff House, a country-house art gallery in a William Adam–designed mansion. The club has inherited the ancient traditions of seaside play (golf records here go back to the 17th century). Mature trees and gentle slopes create a pleasant playing environment. ⊠ *The Barnyards, Banff* ☎ *01261/812075* ⊕ *www.theduffhouseroyalgolfclub.co.uk* ⌂ *Reservations essential* ⚑ *18 holes, 6,161 yds, par 68* ⌘ *Apr.–Sept. weekdays £30 per round, £40 per day; weekends £36 per round, £50 per day. Oct.–Mar. weekdays £15 per round, £20 per day; weekends £18 per round, £25 per day* ☉ *Daily.*

Fraserburgh. This northeast fishing town has extensive links and dunes that seem to have grown up around the course rather than the other way around. Be prepared for a hill climb and a tough finish. You can warm up on the extra nine holes (Rosehill). ⊠ *Philorth, Fraserburgh* ⊕ *At eastern end of town* ☎ *01346/516616* ⊕ *www.fraserburghgolfclub.org* ⚑ *18 holes, 6,200 yds, par 70* ⌘ *Weekdays £37 per round, weekends £42 per round* ☉ *Daily.*

Lossiemouth, Moray Golf Club. Discover the mild air of what's called the Moray Riviera, as Tom Morris did in 1889 when he was inspired by the lay of the natural links. The club has two courses plus a six-hole mini-course. There's lots of history here, with golfing memorabilia in the clubhouse. All other hazards on these testing courses are entirely natural, with the 18th hole providing a memorable finish. Handicap certificates are required for the Old Course. ⊠ *Stotfield Rd., Lossiemouth* ☎ *01343/813330* ⊕ *www.moraygolf.co.uk* ⅂. *Old Course: 18 holes, 6,572 yds, par 71; New Course: 18 holes, 6,068 yds, par 70* ✎ *Old Course: weekdays £45 per round, £65 per day; weekends £55 per round, £70 per day. New Course: weekdays £20 per round, £25 per day; weekends£30 per day. Joint ticket (1 round on each course) weekdays £60, weekends £70* ☉ *Daily.*

★ **Nairn.** Well regarded in golfing circles, Nairn dates from 1887 and is the regular home of Scotland's Northern Open. Huge greens, aggressive gorse, a beach hazard for five of the holes, a steady prevailing wind, and distracting views across the Moray Firth to the northern hills make play here unforgettable. The adjoining 9-hole Cameron Course is ideal for a warm-up or a fun round for the family. ⊠ *Seabank Rd., Nairn* ☎ *01667/453208* ⊕ *www.nairngolfclub.co.uk* ⌂ *Reservations essential* ⅂. *Championship: 18 holes, 6,721 yds, par 72; Cameron: 9 holes, 1,634 yds, par 29* ✎ *Championship: £85 per round, £125 for a two-round ticket that entitles you to a second round within 4 days of the first outing; Cameron: £15 per round* ☉ *Daily.*

DORNOCH FIRTH

The east coast north of Inverness is deeply indented with firths (the word is linked to the Norwegian *fjord*) that border some excellent, relatively unknown golf courses. Knowledgeable golfers have been making the northern pilgrimage to these courses for well over 100 years. There are half a dozen enjoyable links courses around Dornoch and Strathpeffer, an inland Victorian golfing holiday center.

Fodor's Choice **Royal Dornoch.** This course, laid out by Tom Morris in 1886 on a sort of
★ coastal shelf behind the shore, has matured to become one of the world's finest. Its location in the north of Scotland, though less than an hour's drive from Inverness Airport, means it's far from overrun even in peak season. The little town of Dornoch is sleepy and timeless. A handicap certificate may be required. The Royal Dornoch's Struie is a historic course that has been modified over the years. It's a challenging course with wonderful views of the Dornoch Firth and the mountains to the west. ⊠ *Golf Rd., Dornoch* ☎ *01862/810219* ⊕ *www.royaldornoch. com* ⌂ *Reservations essential* ⅂. *Championship Course: 18 holes, 6,222 yds, par 71; Struie Course: 18 holes, 5,721 yds, par 71* ✎ *Championship Course: weekdays £82 per round, weekends £92 per round; Struie Course: single round £35, day ticket £45; combined ticket: weekdays £97, weekends £107* ☉ *Daily.*

UNDERSTANDING SCOTLAND

SCOTLAND AT A GLANCE

FAST FACTS

Capital: Edinburgh

National anthem: "God Save the Queen"

Type of government: Scotland is part of the United Kingdom, which is a constitutional monarchy. It also has its own Parliament.

Administrative divisions: 32 council areas

Independence: April 6, 1320; the Declaration of Arbroath. Scottish nobles wrote Pope John XXII during the War of Independence and asked him to persuade the English king to stop his hostility toward the Scottish.

Constitution: There is no one document; it's a centuries-old accumulation of statutes as well as common law and practice.

Legal system: Scotland's system is organized separately from that of the rest of the United Kingdom. The two highest courts are the High Court of Justiciary (criminal) and the Court of Session (civil). Appeals to the British House of Lords may be made only from the Court of Session. The sheriff courts deal with less important civil and criminal cases.

Suffrage: 18 years of age

Legislature: Governed as an integral part of the United Kingdom's constitutional monarchy, Scotland is represented by 59 Members of Parliament in the House of Commons in London. On May 6, 1999, Scotland gained its own Parliament, located in Edinburgh, for the first time in nearly 300 years. Parliament has the power to pass Scottish laws; it's responsible for managing agriculture, education, health, and justice, and it can impose certain taxes within Scotland.

Population: 5,168,500

Population density: 66 persons per square km (171 persons per square mi)

Median age: male 37, female 39

Life expectancy: male 75, female 79.9

Literacy: 99%

Language: Predominantly English (fewer than 1,000 people speak only Gaelic, and fewer than 60,000 speak Gaelic in addition to English)

Ethnic groups: 98% of the population is Caucasian (88% of this is Scottish and 7.5% other British); Indian, Pakistani, Bangladeshi, and other South Asian groups are the largest ethnic minorities.

Religion: Residents identified their religion as follows: 42.4% Church of Scotland, 27.55% none, 15.88% Roman Catholic, 6.81% other Christian, 0.13% Buddhist, 0.11% Hindu, 0.13% Jewish, 0.84% Muslim, 0.13% Sikh, 0.53% another religion, 5.49% not answered

Discoveries and inventions: Steam engine (1765), postage stamp (1834), telephone (1876), television (1924), penicillin (1928), radar (1935)

We look to Scotland for all our ideas of civilization.

—Voltaire

GEOGRAPHY AND ENVIRONMENT

Land area: 78,722 square km (30,414 square mi)

Coastline: 3,680 km (2,280 mi)

Terrain: Scotland is divided into three distinct regions, roughly from north to south: the Highlands (characterized by mountains with deep ravines, valleys, cliffs, lakes, and sea lochs); the Central Lowlands (mainly hills and rivers); and the Southern Uplands (moorland plateaus, rolling valleys, and mountainous outcrops).

Islands: 790, of which 10% are inhabited. The largest groups are Shetland and Orkney to the north; and the Hebrides, including Lewis, Harris, Barra, Skye, and Mull, to the west.

Natural resources: Coal, petroleum, natural gas, zinc, iron ore, limestone, clay, silica, gold

Natural hazards: Winter windstorms, floods

Flora: Dominant flora: rowan (tree belonging to the rose family), oak, fir, pine, and larch trees; heather, ferns, mosses, grasses, saxifrage, and mountain willow

Fauna: Principal fauna: deer, hare, rabbit, otter, ermine, pine marten, wildcat, grouse, blackcock, ptarmigan, waterfowl, kite, osprey, golden eagle, salmon, trout, cod, haddock, herring, various types of shellfish

Environmental issues: Climate change, air pollution, wind farms, recycling, nuclear power

There are two seasons in Scotland: June and winter.

—Billy Connolly

ECONOMY

Currency: British pound (GBP)
Exchange rate: £1 = $1.60
GDP: £86 billion ($137 billion)
Per-capita income: £16,900 ($26,938)
Inflation: 1.8% in the United Kingdom
Unemployment: 6.6%
Workforce: 2,678,000 (services 79.1%; agriculture 1.4%; industry 19.5%)
Major industries: Aerospace, chemicals, construction, digital media and creative industries, energy, financial services, food and drink, life sciences, microelectronics and optoelectronics, textiles, and tourism
Agricultural products: Barley, wheat, oats, potatoes, livestock (sheep and cattle)
Exports: £17.5 billion ($27.9 billion)
Major export products: Office machinery, radio/TV/communication equipment, whisky, chemicals, manufactured machinery/equipment and transport equipment
Export partners: United States, Germany, France, Ireland, Netherlands
Imports: £57 billion ($90.9 billion)

We'll never know the worth of water till the well go dry.

—18th-century Scottish proverb

DID YOU KNOW?

■ Christmas was not celebrated as a festival in Scotland for about 250 years (from the end of the 17th century up to the 1950s) because the Protestant church believed Christmas to be a Catholic holiday and therefore banned it. Many Scots worked over Christmas and their winter solstice holiday took place at New Year or "hogmanay."

■ Kilts are not native to Scotland. They originated in France.

■ The first woman to play golf at St. Andrew's Golf Club was Mary, Queen of Scots, in 1552. She was the club's founder.

■ More redheads are born in Scotland than in any other country: 11% of the population has red hair.

■ Homer Simpson's catchphrase "Doh!" was based on the catchphrase of actor James Finlayson, who was born in Falkirk in 1887 and starred alongside Laurel and Hardy in many of their films.

■ Haggis may not be Scottish after all. In 2009 historian Catherine Brown found literary evidence that placed haggis in England 171 years before it showed up in any Scottish text. The book in question is the *English Hus-Wife* from 1615.

BOOKS AND MOVIES

Books

Scotland has always had a love and respect for books and learning, for poetry and song. From the poems of Robert Burns, which reflect his Ayrshire roots, to the "bothy ballads" of the northeast, with which the farmhands entertained each other after a hard day's work, from Sir Walter Scott's Borders sagas to Mairi Hedderwick's Katie Morag children's stories set in the Western Isles—all share the strong visual thread of their own Scottish landscapes. Whether written 200 or two years ago, these books and poems have much to tell visitors about the character of Scotland's hugely varied countryside and of the resilient, softhearted, yet sometimes dour Scottish people. Wherever you intend to travel in Scotland, there are books to read to set the scene beforehand. Dipping into some nonfiction, whether it's a guide to history or the landscape, can also enhance your visit.

Fiction

Edinburgh has inspired many writers. Muriel Spark's *The Prime of Miss Jean Brodie* was written in 1961 yet still has much to say about the importance of the city's private schools to the financial success and social life of Edinburgh's prim middle classes. Laura Hird's novel *Born Free* paints a more modern portrait of life in the Scottish capital through the various points of view of a very dysfunctional working-class family. Ian Rankin's famous Inspector Rebus crime thrillers cunningly contrast the architecture and wealth of Edinburgh's Old and New towns and the poverty of public-housing occupants. Among his best works are *Let It Bleed, Mortal Causes,* and *Black and Blue.* On the lighter side, Alexander McCall Smith's Isabel Dalhousie mysteries, including *The Sunday Philosophy Club,* are set in modern Edinburgh.

Glasgow, too, has its dark side, chronicled in Denise Mina's trilogy of contemporary detective novels: *Garnethill, Exile,* and *Resolution,* where the criminal underbelly of the city comes to life through reluctant detective Maureen O'Donnell. Mina's sharp eye for detail provides vivid views of the cityscape. Louise Welsh's protagonist, Rilke, travels around Glasgow's trendy West End district solving the mystery of some disturbing old photographs in Welsh's literary crime novel *The Cutting Room.* Christopher Brookmyre's Glasgow-based novels fall under the popular Scottish subgenre "tartan noir"; they involve murder, mystery, and plenty of sharp Scottish wit. The protagonist in five of his novels (*Quite Ugly One Morning, Country of the Blind, Boiling a Frog, Be My Enemy,* and *Attack of the Unsinkable Rubber Ducks*), is investigative journalist Jack Parlablane, who picks on local white-collar criminals.

James Kelman's deep, brooding characters, coupled with his use of urban Scots dialect, resonate Glasgow from beginning to end. His best book, *A Disaffection* (1989), was nominated for the prestigious Booker Prize. Like Kelman, Anne Donovan also writes in Scots; however, her characters and stories have a lighter, softer tone. Her debut novel, *Buddha Da,* unravels the story of Jimmy, a painter whose decision to become a Buddhist changes his family forever.

The novels of Lewis Grassic Gibbon (pseudonym of James Leslie Mitchell, 1901–35) are set in the bleak farmlands of Kincardineshire, in an area known as the Howe of Mearns, south of Stonehaven, where he grew up. *A Scots Quair, Sunset Song, Cloud Howe,* and *Grey Granite* incorporate the rhythms and cadences of speech in the northeast, which you can still hear today. The unremitting harshness of farming life, described in *A Scots Quair,* is still to some extent valid, despite the advent of modern machinery and farming practices. Nonetheless, the spare beauty of the landscape—with its patchwork of fields rising to higher ground and a coastline with towering cliffs and white-sand beaches—rewards those who visit the area.

Another writer and poet whose work is intimately related to his environment is George Mackay Brown (1921–96), born in Stromness, Orkney. His work reflects Orkney's rich heritage of prehistoric sites, its farming and fishing communities, and its religious history. *Greenvoe* vividly describes life in an imaginary Orkney village; you may also want to read *Fishermen with Ploughs* or his other books of poems.

Scotland's most famous poet and champion of the underdog was Robert Burns (1759–96), who found inspiration in the landscapes of his native Ayrshire in southwest Scotland. His poems and songs will never be far away during your visit, and indeed he has been translated into more languages than any other poet writing in English, including Shakespeare. The Burns Heritage Trail takes you to Alloway, where you can visit his birthplace; to Auld Alloway Kirk, where Tam o'Shanter saw the witches; and to the Tam o' Shanter Experience, a tourist attraction that brings the poem to life. Burns Night (January 25) is still a fixture on the Scottish calendar, with readings of "To a Haggis" and "The Selkirk Grace" being the highlights.

For a taste of life in the Scottish Hebridean islands before you arrive, read Mairi Hedderwick's delightful Katie Morag stories, set on a Hebridean island. Children's stories they may be, but for insights into life on the islands—positive and negative—they are hard to equal. Many teenagers on the islands still dream of their eventual escape to Glasgow or Edinburgh, just as they did 50 or 100 years ago, and Katie Morag's day-to-day life perhaps shows why: the islands are not rich in dance clubs, sports and entertainment centers, fashion boutiques, or Internet cafés. But they are rich in community spirit, tradition and music, and beauty of land and seascape, all of which comes across vividly both in Mairi Hedderwick's text and in the superb, amusingly detailed illustrations. *Katie Morag and the Big Boy Cousins* is a good title to start with.

Historical novels are a painless way to absorb some of Scotland's history. Mollie Hunter's work is geared toward teenagers; *Escape from Loch Leven* deals with Mary, Queen of Scots, and *The Ghosts of Glencoe* covers the Glencoe massacre. Eric Linklater's *The Prince in the Heather* tells of Bonnie Prince Charlie's efforts to escape after the failure of the 1745 Jacobite rebellion. D. K. Broster's *The Flight of the Heron* and its sequel, *The Dark Mile*, deal with the changes to the clan system effected by the defeat of the Jacobites at Culloden in the mid-18th century.

And then there are those quintessentially Scottish books that you're told to read. The novels and narrative poems of Sir Walter Scott (1771–1832) don't seem very accessible these days, and with their lengthy introductions, melodramatic plots, overpowering wealth of historical detail, and stately language, they offer no instant gratification. Still, Scott not only tells a great story, he is also historically accurate, and his settings among the hills and river valleys of southern Scotland are not so very different today. Try reading *Rob Roy* or *The Lady of the Lake* when traveling in the Trossachs, or *Redgauntlet* if you're in Dumfries and Galloway.

Another top storyteller, Robert Louis Stevenson (1850–94), was born in Edinburgh though destined to spend much of his life outside Scotland. Read *Kidnapped* and shiver amid the bleak expanse of Rannoch Moor. Then go and gaze across that very moor—its gray, brown, and watery wastes so accurately described by Stevenson—and imagine being a fugitive among its hummocks and pools.

The *Oxford Literary Guide to the British Isles,* edited by Dorothy Eagle and Hilary Carnell, *A Reader's Guide to Writers' Britain* by Sally Varlow, and *Scotland: A*

Literary Guide, by Alan Bold, can direct you to other literary landscapes in addition to those mentioned above. Edinburgh has been named the first UNESCO World City of Literature; Allan Foster's *Literary Traveler in Edinburgh* is an illustrated sightseeing guide to literary hot spots, including writers' homes and the settings for famous works.

Nonfiction

Scottish history is both extensive and absorbing. The most accessible book on the subject to date, Tom Devine's *The Scottish Nation,* examines the last three centuries from the Act of Union to the reestablishment of the Scottish Parliament. Another pivotal historical book is Neal Ascherson's *Stone Voices: The Search for Scotland,* in which archaeology, geology, myth, and travel combine to create an impressive image of Scotland as a nation. George Rosie's *Curious Scotland: Tales from a Hidden History* explores a more marginal historical timeline. If you're interested in facts such as why a Hebridean island was deliberately infested with anthrax, then it's the book to read. John Prebble's *The Highland Clearances* is an excellent commentary on the aftermath of the Battle of Culloden. For raw urban historical narrative, try Alexander McArthur and Herbert Kingsley Long's *No Mean City: A Story of the Glasgow Slum.*

For books on Scottish art and architecture, Duncan MacMillan's *Scottish Art in the 20th Century, 1890–2001* is a comprehensive guide to artists from Charles Rennie Mackintosh to Ken Currie. Jude Burkhauser's *Glasgow Girls: Women in Art and Design 1880–1920* is more narrow in scope but equally intriguing. Bella Bathurst's *The Lighthouse Stevensons* uniquely catalogs the engineering revolution of lighthouse building through the work of four generations of writer Robert Louis Stevenson's family. For good background information on castles, look for Damien Noonan's *Castles and Ancient Monuments of Scotland* and John G. Dunbar's *Scottish Royal Palaces.*

Football in Scotland is, in many respects, a religion. To find out more on the subject, read David Ross's passionate *The Roar of the Crowd: Following Scottish Football Down the Years.* Another important sport in Scotland is the game invented there: golf. A popular book on the subject, Malcolm Campbell's *Scottish Golf Book* will not only tell you where to putt but also will give you a thorough background on the game itself. Curtis Gillespie's memoir *Playing Through: A Year of Life and Links Along the Scottish Coast* takes a more personal approach to golf and its past through the year he spent with his family in Gullane, as does Lorne Rubenstein's *A Season in Dornoch: Golf and Life in the Scottish Highlands.*

Travel and landscape books on Scotland are almost as plentiful as the country's native thistle. Although initially published in 1779, the reflections and descriptions in Samuel Johnson and James Boswell's *Journey to the Hebrides* (reprinted in 1996) are just as relevant today. Kathleen Jamie's poetically told *Findings* will wet your taste buds for Scotland's picturesque countryside like no other. Cameron McNeish has written some excellent books; *The Munros: Scotland's Highest Mountains* is a carefully crafted guide to climbing those peaks. Colin Prior's impressive photography collection *Highland Wilderness* gives stunning panoramic views of the wild but wonderful north.

Movies

One quintessential "kilt movie" is *Rob Roy* (1995), with Liam Neeson and Jessica Lange—shot at and around Glen Nevis and Glencoe, the gardens of Drummond Castle, and Crichton Castle. Another is Mel Gibson's *Braveheart* (1995), the story of Scotland's first freedom fighter, Sir William Wallace (circa 1270–1305), which also uses the spectacular craggy scenery of Glen Nevis. Both films are great on atmosphere though not so hot on accurate historical detail; they do give a fine preview of Scotland's varied scenery. *Highlander* (1986), with Christopher Lambert and Sean Connery, also uses the spectacular crags of Glencoe, along with the prototypical Scottish castle Eilean Donan—almost a visual cliché in Scottish terms.

The movie of the Scottish classic tale by Muriel Spark, *The Prime of Miss Jean Brodie* (1969), starring Maggie Smith, was filmed in several locations around Edinburgh, as well as in London. In stark contrast *Trainspotting* (1996), directed by Danny Boyle and starring Ewan McGregor, is a commentary (based on the book by Irvine Welsh) on heroin addicts in a depressed Edinburgh housing project; however, filming took place in both Glasgow and Edinburgh. Danny Boyle's first feature film, *Shallow Grave* (1994), which also stars Ewan McGregor, is a highly entertaining suspense thriller about money, friends, and murder. Because the film was shot almost entirely in Edinburgh, it gives viewers a much better sense of the city. *Festival*, a 2005 film written and directed by Annie Griffin, takes a humorous look behind the scenes of Edinburgh's Festival Fringe.

Award-winning director Ken Loach has set several films in Glasgow. His gritty portrayals of extreme Glaswegian life are captured in the unofficial trilogy *My Name Is Joe* (1998), *Sweet Sixteen* (2002), and *Ae Fond Kiss* (2004). Because of the strong local dialects used, all three films have English subtitles. On a more uplifting note, the well-received, must-see *American Cousins* (2003) tells the warmhearted story of two American mafiosi taking refuge with their Scottish cousin in his Glasgow fish-and-chips shop. The well-received *Red Road* (2006) stars Kate Dickie in a dark drama about a CCTV operator who becomes obsessed with a man she sees on one of her screens.

To get a good sense of the Scottish landscape, watch *Restless Natives* (1985), a road-trip comedy about two guys from Edinburgh who travel the countryside holding up tour buses. For a hilarious peek into island life, see *Whisky Galore!* (1949), set on the Outer Hebridean island of Todday. The cult film *The Wicker Man* (1973), starring Christopher Lee, is shot in various locations from Skye to Culzean Castle. Its chilling plot of a secret island society, wanton lust, and pagan blasphemy has inspired an annual musical festival.

For English films set in Scotland, *Her Majesty, Mrs. Brown* (1997), known in Scotland as *Mrs. Brown*, and starring Dame Judi Dench and Billy Connolly, tells the tender story of Queen Victoria and John Brown, her favorite gillie (servant). It was filmed at locations in the Borders and the Highlands, with the Ardverikie Estate near Dalwhinnie standing in for Balmoral. Another entertaining, albeit extremely different kind of film, is *Monty Python and the Holy Grail* (1975). Glencoe, Rannoch Moor, Doune Castle, Arnhall Castle, Duke's Pass, Loch Tay, Sheriffmuir, and Castle Stalker all make magnificent appearances.

For more information on movies filmed in Scotland, you can buy *The Pocket Scottish Movie Book* by Brian Pendreigh, or you can visit the Scotland the Movie Guide Web site (⊕ *www.scotlandthe-movie.com*).

CHRONOLOGY

7000 BC   Hunter-gatherers move north into Scotland after the ice sheets of the last Ice Age recede; these travelers leave arrowheads and bone implements as testimony to their passing.

ca. 6000 BC   First settlers arrive, bringing farming methods with them.

ca. 3000 BC   Neolithic migration from Mediterranean: "chambered cairn" people in north (such as the Grey Cairns of Camster), "beaker people" in southeast.

ca. 300 BC   Iron Age: infusion of Celtic peoples from the south and from Ireland; "Gallic forts" and "brochs" (towers) built.

AD 79–89   Julius Agricola (AD 40–93), Roman governor of Britain, invades Scotland; Scots tribes defeated at the battle of Mons Graupius (thought to be somewhere in the Grampians). Roman forts built at Inchtuthil and Ardoch.

142   Emperor Antoninus Pius (86–161) orders the defensive Antonine Wall built between the Firths of Forth and Clyde.

185   Antonine Wall abandoned.

392   St. Ninian's (ca. 360–432) mission to the Picts sets out from the first Christian chapel at Whitehorn.

400–500   Tribes of Celtic origin, including the Scotti, emigrate from Ireland to present-day Argyllshire and establish the kingdom of Dalriada.

400–843   Four kingdoms exist in Scotland: Dalriada (Argyllshire), the kingdom of the Picts (Aberdeenshire down to Fife and the Highlands excepting Argyllshire), Strathclyde (southwest Scotland), and the Lothians (Edinburgh and the Borders).

563   Columba (ca. 521–97) establishes monastery at Iona.

843   Kenneth MacAlpin, king of Dalriada, unites with the Picts while remaining king. In this way the embryonic Kingdom of Scotland is born, with its capital at Scone.

780–1065   Scandinavian invasions; Hebrides remain Norse until 1263, Orkney and Shetland until 1472.

1018   Malcolm II (ca. 953–1034) brings the Lothians into the Kingdom of Scotland and (temporarily) repels the English.

1034   Duncan (d. 1040), king of Strathclyde, ascends the throne of Scotland and unification is complete.

1040   Duncan is slain by his rival, Macbeth (d. 1057), whose wife has a claim to the throne.

HOUSE OF CANMORE

1057   Malcolm III (ca. 1031–93), known as Canmore (Big Head), murders Macbeth and assumes the throne.

1093   Death of Malcolm's queen, St. Margaret (1046–93), who brought Roman Catholicism to Scotland.

1099   Donald III becomes the last king of Scots to be buried on the island of Iona.

1124–53   David I (ca. 1082–1153), *sair sanct* (sore saint), builds the abbeys of Jedburgh (1118), Kelso (1128), Melrose (1136), and Dryburgh (1150) and brings Norman culture to Scotland.

1250   Queen Margaret, wife of Malcolm III, is canonized, becoming Scotland's first (and only) royal saint.

1290   Death of Alexander III, great-great-grandson of David I. The heir is his granddaughter, Margaret, Maid of Norway (1283–90). She dies at sea on her way from Norway to claim the Scottish throne and marry the future Edward II (1284–1327), son of Edward I of England (1239–1307). The Scots naively ask Edward I, subsequently known as the Hammer of the Scots, to arbitrate between the remaining 13 claimants to the throne. Edward's choice, John Balliol (1249–1315), is known as Toom Tabard (Empty Coat).

1295   Under continued threat from England, Scotland signs its first treaty of the "auld alliance" with France. Wine trade flourishes.

1297   Revolutionary William Wallace (ca. 1270–1305), immortalized by Burns, leads the Scots against the English.

1305   Wallace captured by the English and executed.

1306–29   Reign of Robert the Bruce (1274–1329), later to become King Robert I. Defeats Edward II (1284–1327) at Bannockburn, 1314; Treaty of Northampton, 1328, recognizes Scottish sovereignty.

1349   The first cases of the Black Death are recorded in Scotland.

HOUSE OF STEWART

1371   Robert II (1316–90), the first Stewart monarch and son of Robert the Bruce's daughter Marjorie and Walter the Steward, is crowned. Struggle (dramatized in Scott's novels) between the crown and Scottish barons over control of the barons' land ensues for the next century, punctuated by sporadic warfare with England.

1383   Bishop Wardlaw of Glasgow is the first Scot to be made a cardinal.

1411   University of St. Andrews founded.

1451   University of Glasgow founded.

1488–1513   Reign of James IV (1473–1513). The Renaissance reaches Scotland. The Golden Age of Scots poetry includes Robert Henryson (ca. 1425–1508), William Dunbar (ca. 1460–1530), Gavin Douglas (1474–1522), and the king himself.

1495   University of Aberdeen founded.

1507   Andrew Myllar and Walter Chapman set up first Scots printing press in Edinburgh.

1513   After invading England in support of the French, James IV is slain at Flodden.

1542   Henry VIII (1491–1547) defeats James V (1512–42) at Solway Moss; the dying James, hearing of the birth of his daughter, Mary, declares: "It came with a lass [Marjorie Bruce] and it will pass with a lass."

1542–67   Reign of Mary, Queen of Scots (1542–87); Mary's mother is appointed regent. Romantic, Catholic, and with an excellent claim to the English throne, Mary proved to be no match for her barons, John Knox (1513–72), or her cousin Elizabeth I (1533–1603) of England.

1560   Mary returns to Scotland from France after the death of her husband, Francis II of France, at the same time that Catholicism is abolished in favor of Protestantism. The spelling "Stuart" adopted instead of "Stewart."

1565   Mary marries Lord Darnley (1545–67), a Catholic.

1567   Darnley is murdered at Kirk o' Field; Mary marries one of the conspirators, the earl of Bothwell (ca. 1535–78). Driven from Scotland, she appeals to Elizabeth, who imprisons her. Mary's son, James (1566–1625), is crowned James VI of Scotland.

1582   University of Edinburgh is founded.

1587   Elizabeth orders the execution of Mary.

1600   Charles I is born in Scotland.

1603   Elizabeth dies without issue; James VI is crowned James I of England. Parliaments remain separate for another century.

1638   National Covenant challenges Charles I's personal rule.

1639–41   Crisis. The Scots and then the English parliaments revolt against Charles I (1600–49).

1643   Solemn League and Covenant establishes Presbyterianism as the Church of Scotland (the Kirk). Civil War in England.

1649   Charles I beheaded. Oliver Cromwell (1599–1658) made Protector.

1650–52   Cromwell roots out Scots royalists.

1658   The first Edinburgh–London coach is established. The journey takes two weeks.

1660   Restoration of Charles II (1630–85). Episcopalianism reestablished in Scotland; Covenanters persecuted.

1688   The unpopular James VII of Scotland (and II of England, Scotland, and Ireland) flees to France.

1688–89   Glorious Revolution; James VII and II (1633–1701), a Catholic, deposed in favor of his daughter Mary (1662–94) and her husband, William of Orange (1650–1702). Supporters of James (known as Jacobites) defeated at Killiecrankie. Presbyterianism reestablished.

1692 Highlanders who were late in taking oath to William and Mary massacred at Glencoe.

1695 The first bank in Scotland, the Bank of Scotland, is founded.

1698–1700 Attempted Scottish colony at Darien (on the Isthmus of Panama) fails. Many of the Scottish nobility face bankruptcy, and are therefore open to overtures from an English government anxious to unite the Scottish and English parliaments.

1707 Union of English and Scots parliaments under Queen Anne (1665–1714), the last Stuart monarch; deprived of French wine trade, Scots turn to whisky.

HOUSE OF HANOVER

1714 Queen Anne dies; George I (1660–1727) of Hanover, descended from a daughter of James VI and I, crowned.

1715 First Jacobite Rebellion. James II's son, James Edward Stuart, agrees to undertake an invasion of England. His supporter, the earl of Mar (1675–1732), is defeated.

1730–90 Scottish Enlightenment. The Edinburgh Medical School is the best in Europe; David Hume (1711–76) and Adam Smith (1723–90) redefine philosophy and economics. In the arts, Allan Ramsay the elder (1686–1758) and Robert Burns (1759–96) refine Scottish poetry; Allan Ramsay the younger (1713–84) and Henry Raeburn (1756–1823) rank among the finest painters of the era. Edinburgh's New Town, begun in the 1770s by the brothers Adam (Robert, 1728–92; brother James, 1730–94; father William 1689–1748), provides a fitting setting.

1736 The first public theater in Scotland is opened in Carruber's Close in Edinburgh.

1745–46 Last Jacobite Rebellion. Bonnie Prince Charlie (1720–88), grandson of James II, is defeated at Culloden and eventually escapes back to France; wearing of the kilt is forbidden until 1782. James Watt (1736–1819), born in Greenock, is granted a patent for his steam engine.

1760 Thomas Braidwood (1715–1806) opens the first school for the deaf and dumb in Great Britain, in Edinburgh.

1771 Birth of Walter Scott (1771–1832), Romantic novelist.

1778 First cotton mill, at Rothesay.

1788 Death of Bonnie Prince Charlie in Rome.

1790 Forth and Clyde Canal opened.

1800–50 Highland Clearances: increased rents, and conversion of farms to sheep pasture lead to mass migration, sometimes forced, to North America and elsewhere. Meanwhile, the Lowlands industrialize; Catholic Irish immigrate to factories of Glasgow and the southwest.

1807 The first museum in Scotland, the Hunterian Museum, is founded.

1822 Visit of George IV to Scotland, the first British monarch to make such a trip since Charles I. Sir Walter Scott orchestrates the visit, and almost single-handedly invents Scotland's national costume: the formal kilt, tartan plaid, and jacket.

1831 The first passenger rail service in Scotland opens on the line between Glasgow and Garnkirk.

1832 Parliamentary Reform Act expands the franchise, redistributes seats.

1837 Victoria (1819–1901) ascends to the British throne.

1842 Edinburgh–Glasgow railroad opened.

1846 Edinburgh–London railroad opened.

1848 Queen Victoria buys estate at Balmoral as her Scottish residence. Andrew Carnegie emigrates from Dunfermline to Pittsburgh.

1860 The first British Open golf championship is held in Scotland, at Prestwick.

1884–85 Gladstone's Reform Act gives the majority of men 21 and older the right to vote. Office of Secretary for Scotland authorized.

1886 Scottish Home Rule Association founded.

1890 Forth Rail Bridge opened.

1901 Death of Queen Victoria.

HOUSE OF WINDSOR

1928 Equal Franchise Act gives the vote to women. Scottish Office established as governmental department in Edinburgh. Scottish National Party founded.

1931 Depression hits industrialized Scotland severely.

1939 The first German air raids of World War II on Scotland are made on the Forth Estuary.

1945 Two Scottish Nationalists elected to parliament.

1947 The Edinburgh International Festival, with events in all the performing arts, is launched.

1959 Finnart Oil Terminal, Chapelcross Nuclear Power Station, and Dounreay Fast Breeder Reactor opened.

1964 Forth Road Bridge opened.

1970 British Petroleum strikes oil in the North Sea; revives economy of northeast.

1973   Britain becomes a member of the European Economic Community (formerly known as the Common Market).

1974   Eleven Scottish Nationalists elected as members of Parliament. Old counties reorganized and renamed as new regions and districts.

1979   Referendum on devolution—the creation of a separate Scotland: 33% in favor, 31% against; 36% don't vote.

1981   Europe's largest oil terminal opens at Sullom Voe, Shetland.

1992   Increasing attention focused on Scotland's dissatisfaction with rule from London. Poll shows 50% of Scots want independence.

1997   The Labour Party wins the general election in May. A referendum in Scotland votes in favor of the establishment of a Scottish parliament (with restricted powers). The first successful cloning of an animal in the world is achieved with the birth of Dolly the Sheep at the Roslin Institute in Edinburgh.

1999   Scotland elects its first parliament in 300 years.

2002   The Millennium Link—the restoration of the canal link between Glasgow and Edinburgh—is completed at a cost of £78 million. It includes the Falkirk Wheel, the world's only rotating boat lift.

2004   The Scottish Parliament Building opens for business.

2007   Alex Salmond, leader of the Scottish National Party, becomes the First Minister of Scotland heading a minority government. Scotland wins its bid for the 2014 Commonwealth Games; Glasgow is the host city.

2009   The country endures recession as part of the international economic upheaval. Scotland invokes compassionate release and sends the ailing Lockerbie bomber, convicted in the attack on Pan Am Flight 103 in 1988, back to Libya. Singer Susan Boyle attracts attention around the world on the TV show *Britain's Got Talent*. Discussion continues about a referendum about Scotish independence.

Travel Smart
Scotland

WORD OF MOUTH

"Driving conditions are good, but you have to assume that you won't average more than 30 mph in the Highlands because the roads are winding, there are sheep, and you will be stopping often to take pictures. So try to concentrate on one area and don't try to see everything. You also have to assume that there will be a lot of rain and so proper waterproof clothing and boots are mandatory, even if you do only easy hikes."

—mbgg

GETTING HERE AND AROUND

▌ AIR TRAVEL

Scotland's main hubs are Glasgow, Prestwick (near Glasgow), Edinburgh, Inverness, and Aberdeen. Glasgow and Prestwick are the gateways to the west and southwest, Edinburgh the east and southeast, Aberdeen and Inverness the north. All of these cities have excellent bus and train transportation services and well-maintained roads that link them with each other and other cities within Scotland. Taxis are also an efficient and reliable option, but they are three to four times the cost of going by public transport.

Traveling by air is straightforward in Scotland; you shouldn't encounter any surprises. Security is heavy but efficient. You can often breeze through check-in lines by using your airline's online check-in option, but confirm this ahead of time.

Flying time to Glasgow (and to Aberdeen) is 6½ hours from New York, 7½ hours from Chicago, 9½ hours from Dallas, 10 hours from Los Angeles, and 21½ hours from Sydney. Flying time to Edinburgh is 7 hours from New York, 8 hours from Chicago, 10 hours from Dallas, 10½ hours from Los Angeles and 22 hours from Sydney. Not all airlines offer direct flights to Scotland; many go via London. For those flights allow an extra four to five hours of travel (two to three for the layover in London plus an addition hour or two for the duration of the flight).

Smoking is prohibited on all flights.

Airline-Security Issues Transportation Security Administration (⊕ www.tsa.gov).

AIRPORTS

The major international gateway to Scotland is Glasgow Airport (GLA), about 7 mi outside Glasgow. Edinburgh Airport (EDI), 7 mi from the city, has limited transatlantic flights (Continental and Delta have services from New York, and there's service to Toronto), but does offer connections for dozens of European cities and hourly flights to London's Gatwick (LGW) and Heathrow (LHR) airports. It's also possible to fly into Glasgow and then take bus or train service to Edinburgh in less than two hours. Aberdeen Airport (ABZ) has direct flights to most major European cities. Prestwick (PIK) has direct flights to most major British and European cities at discounted rates. Inverness (INV) offers direct flights in and around the United Kingdom.

Airport tax is included in the price of your ticket. Generally the tax for economy tickets within the United Kingdom from European Union countries is £5. For all other flights it is £20. For first- and club class flights from the United Kingdom and European Union the tax is £10; for all other destinations it's £40.

All Scottish airports offer typical modern amenities: restaurants, cafés, shopping (from clothes to food to tourist trinkets), sandwich and salad bars, pubs, pharmacies, bookshops, and newsstands; some even have spas and hair salons. Glasgow is the largest, most interesting airport when it comes to a delayed flight. Good food and shopping options about—try Tartan Plus for Scottish-inspired goods—and if you're in need of some tranquillity, head for the Relaxation Station for a clothed massage, no reservation necessary.

There are plenty of hotels near all airports, and all airports also have Internet access.

Airport Information Aberdeen Airport (☎ 0844/481–6666 ⊕ www.aberdeenairport. com). **Edinburgh Airport** (☎ 0844/481–8989 ⊕ www.edinburghairport.com). **Glasgow Airport** (☎ 0844/481–5555 ⊕ www. glasgowairport.com).**Glasgow Prestwick Airport** (☎ 0871/223–0700 ⊕ www.gpia.co.uk). **Inverness Airport** (☎ 01667/464000 ⊕ www. hial.co.uk).

GROUND TRANSPORTATION

The best way to get to and from the airport based on speed and convenience is by taxi. All airport taxi stands are just outside the airport's front doors and are well marked with clear signs; ask one of the airport porters for help if you can't find the stand. Most taxis have a set price when going to and from the airport to the city center but will turn on the meter at your request. Ask the driver to turn on the meter to confirm the flat-rate price.

If you're traveling with a large party, you can request a people carrier to transport everyone, luggage included. Luggage is included in the taxi fare; you should not be charged extra for it. If you're traveling alone, a more economical transfer option is public transportation. Buses travel between city centers and Glasgow, Edinburgh, Aberdeen, and Inverness airports. Trains go direct to Prestwick Airport. All are fast, inexpensive, and reliable. *For more information and specific contacts, refer to the Orientation and Planning sections at the beginning of chapters.*

TRANSFERS BETWEEN AIRPORTS

Scottish airports are relatively close to one another and all are connected by a series of buses and trains. Flights between airports add hours to your journey and are very expensive (between £200 and £400). The best way to travel from one airport to another is by bus, train, car, or taxi. Normally you must take a combination of bus and train, which is easy and—if you travel light—quite enjoyable.

From Edinburgh Airport you can take a bus to the city center (£3.50) and then a train to Glasgow city center (£9.80) and a bus to Glasgow Airport (£3.50). This journey should take you less than two hours. Taxis are fast but costly. The price of a taxi from Edinburgh Airport to Glasgow Airport is around £50, a good choice if you're traveling with a few people. Renting a car would be a good choice if you want to get from Edinburgh to, say, Aberdeen Airport and you're traveling with a few people. Otherwise, take a bus to the city center and then take a train. Public transportation is excellent in Scotland. *For specific information, see the Orientation and Planning section at the start of appropriate chapters.*

FLIGHTS

Scotland has a significant air network for a small country. Contact British Airways or British Airways Express for details on flights from London's Heathrow Airport or from Glasgow, Edinburgh, Aberdeen, and Inverness to the farthest corners of the Scottish mainland and to the islands. *See individual chapters for information on flying to various islands.*

Among the low-cost carriers, Ryanair flies from London Stansted to Prestwick; bmibaby has service from Heathrow; and easyJet flies from London Luton/Gatwick/Stansted to and between Glasgow, Edinburgh, Aberdeen, and Inverness, plus to and from Belfast. Flybe has services to Inverness from Bristol, Exeter, Manchester, and Southampton.

Major Airline Contacts British Airways (☎ 800/247–9297 in U.S., 0844/493–0787 in U.K. ⊕ www.britishairways.com). **Continental Airlines** (☎ 800/523–3273 in U.S., 0845/607–6760 in U.K. ⊕ www.continental. com). **Delta Airlines** (☎ 800/221–1212 in U.S., 0845/600–0950 in U.K. ⊕ www.delta.com). **KLM** (☎ 866/434–0320 in U.S., 0871/222–7740 in U.K. ⊕ www.klm.com). **United Airlines** (☎ 800/864–8331 in U.S., 0845/844–4777 in U.K. ⊕ www.united.com). **US Airways** (☎ 800/428–4322 in U.S., 0845/600–3300 in U.K. ⊕ www.usairways.com). **Virgin Atlantic** (☎ 800/821–5438 in U.S., 0844/209–7777 in U.K. ⊕ www.virgin-atlantic.com).

From London to Edinburgh and Glasgow bmibaby/British Midland (☎ 0870/264–2229 in U.K. ⊕ www.bmibaby.com). **British Airways** (☎ 0870/850–9850 in U.K. ⊕ www. britishairways.com). **easyJet** (☎ 0871/244–2366 in U.K. ⊕ www.easyjet.com). **Ryanair** (☎ 0871/246–0000 in U.K. ⊕ www.ryanair.com).

Within Scotland British Airways (☎ 0870/850–9850 in U.K. ⊕ www.britishairways.com). **easyJet** (☎ 0871/244-2366 in U.K. ⊕ www.

easyjet.com). **Flybe** (☎ *011–44–1392–268513 from U.S., 0871/700–2000 from U.K.* ⊕ *www. flybe.com).*

AIRLINE TICKETS

The least expensive airfares to Scotland are often priced for round-trip travel and must usually be purchased in advance. Airlines generally allow you to change your return date for a fee; most low-fare tickets, however, are nonrefundable.

If you intend to fly to Scotland from London, take advantage of the current fare wars on internal routes—notably among London's four airports and between Glasgow and Edinburgh. Among the cheapest fares are those on Ryanair between London Stansted (with its excellent rail links from London's Liverpool Street Station) and Glasgow Prestwick; easyJet offers bargain fares from London Luton/Gatwick/Stansted (all with good rail links from central London) to Glasgow, Edinburgh, Aberdeen, and Inverness. Even British Airways now offers competitive fares on some flights.

AIR PASSES

The Discover Europe Airpass from bmi is available on the airline's British and European flights. The pass is valid for up to 90 days and allows passengers to travel to a combination of European cities for reduced fares. The Europe Pass from British Airways offers travelers a way to choose from the airline's and its partners' networks. You must purchase these passes before you leave home through the companies' Web sites. In Britain the best place to search for consolidator tickets, or so-called bucket-shop tickets, is through Cheap Flights, a Web site that pools all flights available and then directs you to a phone number or site to purchase tickets.

Air Pass Information **bmi** (☎ *800/788– 0555, 0870/607–0555 in U.K.* ⊕ *www.flybmi. com).* **British Airways** (☎ *800/247–9297, 0870/850–9850 in U.K.* ⊕ *www.britishairways. com).***Cheap Flights** (☎ *no phone number* ⊕ *www.cheapflights.co.uk).* **easyJet** (☎ *0870/600–0000 in U.K.* ⊕ *www.easyjet.*

com). **FlightPass** (*EuropebyAir* ☎ *888/321– 4737 in U.S.* ⊕ *www.europebyair.com).*

▮ BIKE TRAVEL

Bicycling in Scotland is variable. The best months for cycling are May, June, and September, when the roads are often quieter and the weather is usually better. Winds are predominantly from the southwest, so plan your route accordingly.

Because Scotland's main roads are continually being upgraded, bicyclists can easily reach the network of quieter rural roads in southern and much of eastern Scotland, especially Grampian. Still, be careful getting from town centers to rural riding areas; if in doubt, ask a local. In a few areas of the Highlands, notably in northwestern Scotland, the rugged terrain and limited population have resulted in the lack of side roads, making it difficult—sometimes impossible—to plan a minor-road route in these areas.

Several agencies now promote "safe routes" for recreational cyclists. These routes are signposted, and agencies have produced maps or leaflets showing where they run. Perhaps best known is the Glasgow–Loch Lomond–Killin Cycleway, which uses former railway track beds, forest trails, quiet rural side roads, and some main roads. VisitScotland has advice on a site dedicated to cycling.

TRANSPORTING BIKES

Although some rural bus services will transport cycles if space is available, don't count on getting your bike on a bus. Be sure to check well in advance with the appropriate bus company.

You can take bicycles on car and passenger ferries in Scotland, and it's not generally necessary to book in advance. Check cycles on car ferries early so that they can be loaded through the car entrance.

ScotRail strongly advises that you make a train reservation for you and your bike at least one month in advance. On several trains reservations are compulsory.

BIKING ORGANIZATIONS

The Cyclists' Touring Club publishes a members' magazine, route maps, and guides. Sustrans Ltd. is a nonprofit organization dedicated to providing environmentally friendly routes for cyclists, notably in and around cities.

Bike Maps and Information Cyclists' Touring Club (☎ 0844/736–8450 ⊕ www.ctc.org. uk). Sustrans (☎ 0131/539–8122 ⊕ www. sustrans.org.uk). VisitScotland (☎ 0845/225–5121 ⊕ http://cycling.visitscotland.com).

▌ BOAT AND FERRY TRAVEL

Because Scotland has so many islands, plus the great Firth of Clyde waterway, ferry services are of paramount importance. Most ferries transport vehicles as well as foot passengers, although a few smaller ones are for passengers only.

It's a good idea to make a reservation ahead of time, although reservations are not absolutely necessary. Most travelers show up on the day of departure and buy their tickets from the stations at the ports. Keep in mind that these are working ferries, not tourist boats. Although journeys are scenic, most people use these ferries as their daily means of public transportation to and from their hometowns.

The main operator is Caledonian MacBrayne, known generally as CalMac. Services extend from the Firth of Clyde in the south, where there's an extensive network, right up to the northwest of Scotland and all of the Hebrides. CalMac sells an Island Rover runabout ticket, which is ideal for touring holidays in the islands, as well as an island-hopping scheme called Island Hopscotch. Fares can range from £4 for a short trip to almost £50 for a longer trip with several legs.

The Dunoon–Gourock route on the Clyde is served by Western Ferries.

The Falkirk Wheel in Tamfourhill, about halfway between Glasgow and Edinburgh, is an attraction as much as a form of transportation. The only rotating boat lift in the world, it carries tour boats from the Forth and Clyde Canal over to the Union Canal, and back again.

Northlink Ferries operates a car ferry for Orkney between Scrabster, near Thurso, and Stromness, on the main island of Orkney; and between Aberdeen and Kirkwall, which is also on Mainland, Orkney. Northlink also runs ferries for Shetland between Aberdeen and Lerwick.

For fares and schedules, contact ferry companies directly. Traveler's checks (in pounds), cash, and major credit cards are accepted for payment. *See the Orientation and Planning sections of each chapter for more details about ferry services.*

Information Caledonian MacBrayne (☎ 01475/650100, 08705/650000 reservations, 01475/650288 brochure hotline ⊕ www. calmac.co.uk). Falkirk Wheel (✉ Lime Rd., Tamfourhill ☎ 01324/619888, 08700/500208 reservations ⊕ www.thefalkirkwheel.co.uk). Northlink Ferries (☎ 0845/600–0449 ⊕ www. northlinkferries.co.uk). Western Ferries (☎ 01369/704452 ⊕ www.western-ferries. co.uk).

▌ BUS TRAVEL

Long-distance buses usually provide the cheapest way to travel between England and Scotland; fares may be as little as a third of the rail fares for comparable trips and are cheaper if you buy in advance. However, the trip is not as comfortable as by train (no dining cart or carriage, smaller bathrooms, less spacious seats), and travel takes longer. Glasgow to London by bus (nonstop) takes 8 hours, 45 minutes; by train it takes about 5 hours, 30 minutes.

Scotland's bus (short-haul) and coach (long-distance) network is extensive. Bus service is comprehensive in cities, less so in country districts—something to consider if you want to explore really rural areas. Express service links main cities and towns, connecting, for example, Glasgow and Edinburgh to Inverness, Aberdeen,

Perth, Skye, Ayr, Dumfries, and Carlisle; or Inverness with Aberdeen, Wick, Thurso, and Fort William. These express services are very fast, and fares are reasonable. Scottish Citylink, National Express, and Megabus are some of the main operators; there are about 20 in all.

The London terminal is Victoria Coach Station for National Express and the London Victoria Greenline Coach Station for Megabus.

There is one class of service, and all buses are nonsmoking.

DISCOUNTS AND DEALS

On Scottish Citylink, the Explorer Passes offer complete freedom of travel on all services throughout Scotland. Three permutations give three days of consecutive travel, any 5 days of travel out of 10, or any 8 days of travel in a 16-day period. They're available from Scottish Citylink offices, and cost £35 to £79.

National Express offers discounted seats on buses from London to more than 50 cities in the United Kingdom, including Glasgow and Aberdeen. Tickets range from £8 to £15, but only when purchased online. Megabus (order tickets online), a discount service, has similarly competitive prices between major cities throughout Scotland, including Aberdeen, Dundee, Glasgow, Inverness, and Perth.

Those travelers ages 16 to 26 are eligible for 30% reductions with the National Express Coachcard (£10).

FARES AND SCHEDULES

Contact Traveline Scotland for information on all public transportation and timetables.

For town, suburban, or short-distance journeys, you buy your ticket on the bus, from a pay box, or from the driver. You need exact change. For longer journeys— for example, Glasgow–Inverness—it's usual (and a good idea; busy routes and times can book up) to reserve a seat and pay at the bus station booking office.

PAYING

Credit cards and traveler's checks are accepted at most bus stations.

Bus Information **Traveline Scotland** (☎ *0871/200–2233* ⊕ *www.travelinescotland. com*).

Bus Lines **Megabus** (☎ *08705/505050* ⊕ *www.megabus.co.uk*). **National Express** (☎ *08705/808080 or 8717/818181* ⊕ *www. nationalexpress.com*). **Scottish Citylink** (☎ *08705/505050* ⊕ *www.citylink.co.uk*).

▌ CAR TRAVEL

If you plan to stick mostly to the cities, you will not need a car. All cities in Scotland are either so compact that most attractions are within easy walking distance of each other (Aberdeen, Dundee, Edinburgh, Inverness, and Stirling) or are accessible by an excellent local public transport system (Glasgow). And there is often good train and/or bus service from major cities to nearby day-trip destinations. Bus tours are also a good option for a day trip out of town; from Inverness, you can even catch a (quick) glance at the isles of Orkney this way.

Once you leave Edinburgh, Glasgow, and the other major cities, a car will make journeys faster and much more enjoyable than trying to work out public-transportation connections to the farther-flung reaches of Scotland (though it's possible to see much of the country by public transportation). A car allows you to set your own pace and visit off-the-beaten-path towns and sights most easily.

In Scotland your own driver's license is acceptable. International driving permits (IDPs) are available from the American Automobile Association and, in the United Kingdom, from the Automobile Association and Royal Automobile Club. These international permits, valid only in conjunction with your regular driver's license, are universally recognized; having one may save you a problem with local authorities.

GASOLINE

Expect to pay a lot more for gasoline, about £7 a gallon (£1.04 a liter) for unleaded—up to 10p a gallon higher in remote rural locations. The British imperial gallon is about 20% more in volume than the U.S. gallon—approximately 4.5 liters. Pumps dispense in liters, not gallons. Most gas stations are self-service and stock unleaded, super unleaded, and LRP (replacing four-star) plus diesel; all accept major credit cards.

PARKING

On-street parking is a bit of a lottery in Scotland. Depending on the location and time of day, the streets can be packed or empty of cars. In the cities, you must pay for your on-street parking by getting a sticker from a parking machine; these machines are clearly marked with a large P. Make sure you have the exact change; it's normally around £2 for four hours but can vary. Put the parking sticker on the inside of your front windshield and make sure the time expiration is clearly visible for parking attendants. Parking lots are scattered throughout urban areas and tend to be more or less the same price as on-street parking. Most parking lots are near shopping malls or busy financial districts.

The local penalty for illegally parked cars is £25, and parking regulations are strictly enforced.

ROAD CONDITIONS

A good network of superhighways, known as motorways, and divided highways, known as dual carriageways, extends throughout Britain. In the remoter areas of Scotland where the motorway hasn't penetrated, travel is noticeably slower. Motorways shown with the prefix M are mainly two or three lanes in each direction, without any right-hand turns. These are the roads to use to cover long distances, though inevitably you'll see less of the countryside. Service areas are at most about an hour apart.

Dual carriageways, usually shown on a map as a thick red line (often with a black line in the center) and the prefix A followed by a number perhaps with a bracketed T (for example, A304[T]), are similar to motorways, except that right turns are sometimes permitted, and you'll find both traffic lights and traffic circles on them.

The vast network of other main roads, which typical maps show as either single red A roads, or narrower brown B roads, also numbered, are for the most part the old coach and turnpike roads built originally for horses and carriages. Travel along these roads is slower than on motorways, and passing is more difficult. On the other hand, you'll see much more of Scotland.

Minor roads (shown as yellow or white on most maps, unlettered and unnumbered) are the ancient lanes and byways of Britain, roads that are not only living history but a superb way of discovering hidden parts of Scotland. You have to drive along them slowly and carefully. On single-track (one-lane) roads, found in the north and west of Scotland, there's no room for two vehicles to pass, and you must use a passing place if you meet an oncoming car or tractor, or if a car behind wishes to overtake you. Never hold up traffic on single-track roads.

For some typical driving times, see the Scotland Planner in Chapter 1.

ROADSIDE EMERGENCIES

For aid if your car breaks down, contact the 24-hour rescue numbers of either the Automobile Association or the Royal Automobile Club. If you're a member of the AAA (American Automobile Association) or another association, check your membership details before you travel; reciprocal agreements may give you free roadside aid.

Emergency Contacts in the U.K. **Automobile Association** (*AA* ☎ *08705/500600* ⊕ *www.theaa.co.uk*). **Royal Automobile Club** (*RAC* ☎ *08705/722722* ⊕ *www.rac.co.uk*).

Emergency Contacts in the U.S. **American Automobile Association** (*AAA* ☎ *800/564–6222* ⊕ *www.aaa.com*).

RULES OF THE ROAD

The most noticeable difference for most visitors is that when in Britain, you drive on the left and steer the car on the right. Give yourself time to adjust to driving on the left—especially if you pick up your car at the airport. One of the most complicated questions facing visitors to Britain is that of speed limits. In urban areas, it's generally 30 mph, but it's 40 mph on some main roads, as indicated by circular red-rimmed signs. In rural areas the official limit is 60 mph on ordinary roads and 70 mph on divided highways and motorways—and traffic police can be hard on speeders, especially in urban areas. Driving while using a cell phone is illegal, and the use of seat belts is mandatory for passengers in front and back seats. Service stations and newsstands sell copies of the Highway Code (£2.50), which lists driving rules and has pictures of signs. It's also online (for £2.50) at ⊕ *www.direct.gov.uk.*

Drunk-driving laws are strictly enforced. It's safer to avoid alcohol if you're driving.

CAR RENTAL

If you're going beyond the major cities, having a car makes traveling much easier in Scotland. Public transportation is good but you need your own vehicle to reach the more isolated areas. You can rent any type of car you desire; however, in Scotland cars tend to be on the smaller side. Many roads are narrow, and a smaller car saves money on gas. Common models are the Nissan Micra, Renault Clio, Ford Focus, and Peugeot 407 SW. Four-wheel-drive vehicles aren't a necessity. Most cars are manual, not automatic, and come with air-conditioning, although you rarely need it in Scotland. If you want an automatic, always reserve ahead. The cars are in very good condition and must pass a series of inspections and tests before they are rented out. When you're returning the car, allow an extra hour to drop it off and sort out any paperwork.

If you're traveling to more than one country, make sure your rental contract permits you to take the car across borders and that the insurance policy covers you in every country you visit. British cars have the steering wheel on the right, so you may want to leave your rented car in Britain and pick up a left-side drive when you cross the Channel.

Rates in Glasgow begin at £25 a day and £140 a week for an economy car with a manual transmission and unlimited mileage. This does not include tax on car rentals, which is 17.5%. The busiest months are June through August, when rates may go up 30%. During this time, book at least two to four weeks in advance. Online booking is fine.

Companies frequently restrict rentals to people over age 23 and under age 75. If you are over 70, some companies require you to have your own insurance. If you are under 25, a surcharge of £11 per day plus V.A.T. will apply

Child car seats usually cost about £24 extra; you must ask for a car seat when you book, at least 48 hours in advance. The same is true for GPS. Adding one extra driver is usually included in the original rental price.

Local Agencies Arnold Clark (☎ *0141/847–8602* ⊕ *www.arnoldclarkrental.co.uk*).

Major Rental Agencies Avis (☎ *0870/608–6338* ⊕ *www.avis.com*). **Budget** (☎ *0844/544–4604* ⊕ *www.budget.com*). **Hertz** (☎ *0870/846–0007* ⊕ *www.hertz.com*). **National Car Rental** (☎ *0141/887–8134* ⊕ *www.nationalcar.com*).

Wholesalers Auto Europe (☎ *800/223–5555* ⊕ *www.autoeurope.com*). **Europe by Car** (☎ *212/581–3040 in U.S, 0141/887–0414 in Glasgow* ⊕ *www.europebycar.com*). **Eurovacations** (☎ *877/471–3876 in U.S.* ⊕ *www.eurovacations.com*). **Kemwel** (☎ *877/820–0668 in U.S.* ⊕ *www.kemwel.com*).

▌TAXI TRAVEL

In Edinburgh, Glasgow, and the larger cities, black hackney taxis—similar to those in London—with their TAXI sign illuminated can be hailed on the street, or booked by phone (free of charge). If you call a private hire taxi from the phone book, expect a regular-looking car to pick you up. The only distinctions are that these private hire taxis have a special sign attached to their license plate indicating that they have a taxi license and they have a meter stuck on the dashboard, along with an ID card for the driver. Private hire taxis are cheaper than black hackney taxis and will pick you up only from a specific location. They will not pick you up off the street.

Scottish taxis are reliable, safe, and metered. Meters begin at £2 and should increase in 50p intervals. Beyond the larger cities, most communities of any size have a taxi service; your hotel will be able to supply telephone numbers. Very often you can find an advertisement for the local taxi service in public phone booths, online, or in the phone book.

▌TRAIN TRAVEL

Train service within Scotland is generally run by ScotRail, one of the most efficient of Britain's service providers. Trains are modern, clean, and comfortable. Long-distance services carry buffet and refreshment cars. Scotland's rail network extends all the way to Thurso and Wick, the most northerly stations in the British Isles. Lowland services, most of which originate in Glasgow or Edinburgh, are generally fast and reliable. A shuttle makes the 50-minute trip between Glasgow and Edinburgh every half hour. It's a scenic trip with plenty of rolling fields, livestock, and traditional houses to view along the way. One word of caution: there are very few trains in the Highlands on Sunday and services throughout the country are generally limited on Sunday.

CLASSES

Most trains have first-class and standard-class coaches. First-class coaches are always less crowded; they have wider seats and are often cleaner and less well-worn than standard-class cars, and they're a lot more expensive. However, on weekends you can often upgrade from standard- to first class for a small fee (often £10 to £20)—ask at the time of booking.

FARES AND SCHEDULES

The best way to find out which train to take, which station to catch it at, and what times trains travel to your destination is to call National Rail Enquiries. It's a helpful, comprehensive, free service that covers all Britain's rail lines. National Rail will help you choose the best train to take, and then connects you with the ticket office for that train company so that you can buy tickets.

Train fares vary according to class of ticket purchased and distance traveled.

Before you buy your ticket, stop at the Information Office/Travel Centre and request the lowest fare to your destination and information about any special offers. There's often little difference between the cost of a one-way and round-trip ticket. So if you're planning on departing from and returning to the same destination, buy a round-trip fare upon your departure, rather than purchasing two separate one-way tickets.

It's much cheaper to buy a one-way or round-trip ticket in advance than on the day of your trip (except for commuter services); the closer to the date of travel, the more expensive the ticket will be. Try to purchase tickets at least eight weeks in advance during peak season summer travel to save money and reserve good seats. Check train Web sites for deals. You can also check the trainline, which sells discounted advance-purchase tickets from all train companies to all destinations in Britain. It's worthwhile to compare several sites.

Information **National Rail Enquiries** (☎ *0845/748–4950* ⊕ *www.nationalrail. co.uk).* **ScotRail** (☎ *08457/550033* ⊕ *www. scotrail.co.uk)* **the trainline**(☎ *0871/244–1545* ⊕ *www.thetrainline.com).*

PAYING

All major credit cards and cash are accepted for train fares paid both in person and by phone.

RESERVATIONS

Reserving your ticket in advance is always recommended.

Tickets and rail passes do not guarantee seats on the trains. For that you need a seat reservation, which if made at the time of ticket purchase is usually included in the ticket price, or if booked separately, must be paid for at a cost of £1 *per train* on your itinerary. You also need a reservation if you purchase overnight sleeping accommodations.

TRAIN PASSES

To save money, look into rail passes. But be aware that if you don't plan to cover many miles, you may come out ahead by buying individual tickets. If you plan to travel by train in Scotland, consider purchasing a BritRail Pass, which also allows travel in England and Wales. All BritRail passes must be purchased in your home country; they're sold by travel agents as well as BritRail or Rail Europe. Rail passes do not guarantee seats on the trains, so be sure to reserve ahead. Remember that Eurail Passes aren't honored in Great Britain.

The cost of an unlimited BritRail adult pass for 4 days is $263/$393 (standard/first class); for 8 days, $373/$549; for 15 days, $549/$813; for 22 days, $689/$1,029; and for a month, $809/$1,209. The Youth Pass, for ages 16 to 25, costs $213/$319 for 4 days, $299/$439 for 8 days, $439/$653 for 15 days, $553/$823 for 22 days, and $649/$969 for one month. The Senior Pass, for passengers over 60, costs $263/$333 for 4 days, $373/$469 for 8 days, $549/$693 for 15 days, $689/$873 for 22 days, and $809/$1029 for one

month. Another option is a Flexipass, which allows a particular number of days of travel within a given period: for example, 4 days in 2 months for $479.

The Scottish Freedom Pass allows transportation on all Caledonian MacBrayne and Strathclyde ferries in addition to major bus links and the Glasgow underground. You can travel any 4 days in an 8-day period for $249 or any 8 days in a 15-day period for $329.

Information **ACP Rail International** (☎ *886/ 274–7245* ⊕ *www.acprail.com).* **BritRail Travel** (☎ *886/274–7245* ⊕ *www.britrail.com).* **DER Travel Services** (☎ *888/660–5300* ⊕ *www.der. com).* **Rail Europe** (☎ *800/622–8600* ⊕ *www. raileurope.com).*

FROM ENGLAND

There are two main rail routes to Scotland from the south of England. The first, the west-coast main line, runs from London Euston to Glasgow Central; it takes 5½ hours to make the 400-mi trip to central Scotland, and service is frequent and reliable. Useful for daytime travel to the Scottish Highlands is the direct train to Stirling and Aviemore, terminating at Inverness. For a restful route to the Scottish Highlands, take the overnight sleeper service, with soundproof sleeping carriages. It runs from London Euston, departing in late evening, to Perth, Stirling, Aviemore, and Inverness, where it arrives the following morning.

The east-coast main line from London King's Cross to Edinburgh provides the quickest trip to the Scottish capital. Between 8 AM and 6 PM there are 16 trains to Edinburgh, three of them through to Aberdeen. Limited-stop expresses like the Flying Scotsman make the 393-mi London-to-Edinburgh journey in around four hours. Connecting services to most parts of Scotland—particularly the Western Highlands—are often better from Edinburgh than from Glasgow.

Trains from elsewhere in England are good: regular service connects Birmingham, Manchester, Liverpool, and Bristol with Glasgow and Edinburgh. From Harwich (the port of call for ships from Holland, Germany, and Denmark), you can travel to Glasgow via Manchester. But it's faster to change at Peterborough for the east-coast main line to Edinburgh.

SCENIC ROUTES

Although many routes in Scotland run through extremely attractive countryside, several stand out: from Glasgow to Oban via Loch Lomond; to Fort William and Mallaig via Rannoch (ferry connection to Skye); from Edinburgh to Inverness via the Forth Bridge and Perth; from Inverness to Kyle of Lochalsh and to Wick; and from Inverness to Aberdeen.

A private train, the Royal Scotsman, does all-inclusive scenic tours, partly under steam power, with banquets en route. This is a luxury experience: some evenings require formal wear. You can choose itineraries from two nights ($3,610) to seven nights ($10,680) per person.

Train Tours **The Royal Scotsman** (☎ *0845/077-2222 or 800/524-2420* ⊕ *www. royalscotsman.com*).

ESSENTIALS

▮ ACCOMMODATIONS

Your choices in Scotland range from small, local B&Bs to large, elegant hotels—some of the chain variety. Bed-and-breakfasts tend to be less expensive than large hotels because many are spare rooms in spacious homes. Proprietors keep costs down and guests get something with a more personal, Scottish touch. One note: there is a ban on smoking in all indoor public spaces in Scotland, and this includes hotel rooms.

Accommodation can seem expensive because the pound has been strong against the dollar, but the economic downturn in 2009 has brought some special deals.

VisitScotland classifies and grades accommodations using simple star system. The greater the number of stars, the greater the number of facilities and the more luxurious they are.

If you're touring around, you're not likely to be stranded: even in the height of the season—July and August—hotel occupancy runs at about 80%. On the other hand, if you arrive in Edinburgh at festival time or some place where a big Highland Gathering or golf tournament is in progress, you'll have an extremely limited choice of accommodations, and your best bet will be to try for a room in a nearby village.

To secure your first choice, reserve in advance, either directly with the facility, or through local tourist information centers, making use of their "book-a-bed-ahead" services. Telephone bookings made from home should be confirmed by e-mail, fax, or letter. Country hotels expect you to turn up by about 6 PM.

Some hotels, B&Bs and guesthouses offer discounted rates for stays of two nights or longer.

Be sure you understand the hotel's cancellation policy. Some places allow you to cancel without any kind of penalty; others,

particularly B&Bs, require you to cancel a week in advance or penalize you.

Most hotels allow children under a certain age to stay in their parents' room at no extra charge, but others charge for them as extra adults; find out the cutoff age for discounts.

The lodgings we list are the cream of the crop in each price category. Properties are assigned price categories based on the price of a standard double room at high season (excluding holidays). Unless otherwise noted, all lodgings listed have a private bathroom, air-conditioning, a room phone, and a television. *Price charts appear at the start of each chapter or, for Edinburgh and Glasgow, in the Where to Stay section.*

We always list the facilities that are available, but we don't specify whether they cost extra; when pricing accommodations, always ask what's included. Many hotels and most guesthouses and B&Bs include a breakfast within the basic room rate. Meal-plan symbols appear at the end of a review.

CATEGORY	EDINBURGH AND GLASGOW	ELSEWHERE
£	under £70	under £70
££	£70–£120	£70–£120
£££	£121–£180	£121–£160
££££	£181–£250	£161–£220
£££££	over £250	over £220

Prices are for two people in a standard double room in high season, including V.A.T., and are given in pounds.

▮TIP➔ Assume that hotels operate on the European Plan (**EP**, no meals) unless we specify that they use the Breakfast Plan (**BP**, with full breakfast), Continental Plan (**CP**, continental breakfast), or Modified American Plan (**MAP**, breakfast and dinner).

APARTMENT AND HOUSE RENTALS

Rental houses and flats (apartments) are becoming more popular lodging choices for travelers visiting Scotland, particularly for those staying in one place for more than a few days. Some places may rent only by the week. Prices can work out to be cheaper than a hotel (though perhaps not than a bed-and-breakfast; this will depend on the number in your group), and the space and comfort are much better than what you'd find in a hotel or B&B.

In the country, your chances of finding a small house to rent are good; in the city you're more likely to find a flat (apartment) to let (rent). Either way, your best bet for finding these rentals is online. Individuals and large consortiums can own these properties, so it just depends on what you're looking for. The White House is a good, central place for rentals in Glasgow, and Scottish Apartment is a good source for apartments in Edinburgh. The National Trust for Scotland has many unique properties, from island cottages to castles, for rent.

International Agencies At Home Abroad (☎ 212/421-9165 ⊕ www.athomeabroadinc. com).

Barclay International Group (☎ 800/845-6636 ⊕ www.barclayweb.com). **Drawbridge to Europe** (☎ 541/482-7778 or 888/268-1148 ⊕ www.drawbridgetoeurope.com). **Forgetaway** (⊕ www.forgetaway.weather.com). **Home Away** (☎ 512/493-0382 ⊕ www.homeaway. com). **Interhome** (☎ 954/791-8282 or 800/882-6864 in U.S. ⊕ www.interhome.us). **Villas & Apartments Abroad** (☎ 212/213-6435, 800/433-3020 in U.S. ⊕ www.vaanyc. com).

Local Contacts National Trust for Scotland (☎ 0131/243-9331 ⊕ www.nts.org. uk). **Scottish Apartment** (☎ 0131/240-0080 ⊕ www.scottishapartment.com). **White House** (☎ 0141/339-9375 ⊕ www.whitehouse-apartments.com).

BED-AND-BREAKFASTS

B&Bs, common throughout Scotland, are a special British tradition and the backbone of budget travel, with an average price of £40 to £85 per night, depending on the region, time of year, and particular accommodation. They're usually in a family home, don't often have private bathrooms, and usually offer only breakfast. Guesthouses are a slightly larger, somewhat more luxurious version. More upscale B&Bs, along the line of American B&Bs or small inns, can be found in Edinburgh and Glasgow especially, but in other parts of Scotland as well. All provide a glimpse of everyday British life. Note that local tourist offices can book a B&B for you; there may be a small charge for this service.

Reservation Services BedandBreakfast. com (☎ 512/322-2710, 800/462-2632 in U.S. ⊕ www.bedandbreakfast.com). **Bed & Breakfast Scotland** (⊕ www. bedandbreakfastscotland.co.uk). **UK Bed and Breakfast Accommodation** (⊕ www. bedandbreakfasts.co.uk).

FARMHOUSE AND CROFTING HOLIDAYS

A popular option for families with children is a farmhouse holiday, combining the freedom of B&B accommodations with the hospitality of Scottish family life. You need a car if you're deep in the country, though. Information is available from VisitBritain or VisitScotland, from Scottish Farmhouse Holidays, and from the Farm Stay UK.

Contacts Farm Stay UK (☎ 024/7669-6909 ⊕ www.farmstayuk.co.uk). **Scottish Farmhouse Holidays** (☎ 01334/650233 ⊕ www. scotfarmhols.co.uk).

HOME EXCHANGES

With a direct home exchange you stay in someone else's home while they stay in yours. Some outfits also deal with vacation homes, so you're not actually staying in someone's full-time residence, just their vacant weekend place.

LOCAL DO'S AND TABOOS

GREETINGS

Although many Scots are fantastic talkers, they're less enthusiastic with greetings on the physical front. If you're in less familiar company, a handshake is more appreciated than a kiss or hug.

SIGHTSEEING

When you are visiting houses of worship, modest attire is appreciated, though you will see shorts and even bared midriffs. Photographs are welcome in churches, outside of services.

Shorts and other close-fitting attire are allowed just about anywhere at any time, weather permitting; these days locals tend not to cover up as much as they used to.

It's the same with food; Scots eat and drink just about anywhere, and much of the time they do it standing up or even walking.

ETIQUETTE

In Scotland it's rude to walk away from conversation, even if it's with someone you don't know. If you're at a pub, keep in mind that it's very important to buy a round of drinks if you're socializing with a group of people. You don't simply buy your own drink; you buy a drink for all of the people you're there with, and those people do the same. It can make for a very foggy evening and public drunkenness, especially on Friday and Saturday nights. Conversational topics that are considered taboo are money matters; the Scots are quite private about their finances.

You should give up your seats for elderly people or pregnant women without a second thought. Hold the door open for someone who is leaving or entering the same building as you. Don't let the door go in the person's face or you might have a small riot on your hands. Say please and thank you.

Polite driving etiquette is carefully observed, too; allow people to pass and be courteous. Jaywalking isn't rude or illegal, but it's much safer to cross with the lights, especially if traffic is coming from a direction you might not be used to.

As for waiting in lines and moving through crowds, be courteous. The Scots are very polite and you'll be noticed (and not in a good way) if you're not polite in return.

OUT ON THE TOWN

People may dress up for a special restaurant or for clubbing, but other people will be casual. Some restaurants and clubs frown on jeans and sneakers.

If you're visiting a family home, a simple bouquet of flowers is a welcome gift. If you're invited for a meal, bringing a bottle of wine is appropriate, if you wish, as is some candy for the children. To thank a host for hospitality, either a phone call or thank-you card is always appreciated.

DOING BUSINESS

Punctuality is of prime importance, so call ahead if you anticipate a late arrival. Spouses do not generally attend business dinners, unless specifically invited.

If you invite someone to dine, it's usually assumed that you'll pick up the tab. However, if you're the visitor, your host may insist on paying.

LANGUAGE

The Lowland Scots language, which borrows from Scandinavian, Dutch, French, and Gaelic, survives in various forms but is virtually an underground language, spoken at home among ordinary folk, especially in its heartland, in northeast Scotland. Gaelic, too, hangs on in spite of the Highlands depopulation.

Otherwise, Scots speak English often with a strong accent (which may be hard for non-native Brits and Americans to understand), but be patient and your ear will soon come to terms with it.

Exchange Clubs Home Exchange.com
(☎ 800/877–8723 ⊕ www.homeexchange.
com); $99.95 for a 1-year online listing.
HomeLink International (☎ 800/638–3841 in
U.S., 01962/886882 in U.K. ⊕ www.homelink.
org); $90 yearly for Web-only membership;
$140 includes Web access and two catalogs.
Intervac U.S. (☎ 800/756–4663 ⊕ www.
intervacus.com); has various online packages
ranging from $90 to $200.

HOTELS

Large hotels vary in style and price. Most
lean toward Scottish themes when it
comes to decoration, but you can expect
the same quality and service from a chain
hotel wherever you are in the world.
Keep in mind that hotel rooms in Scotland are smaller than what you'd find in
the United States. Today hotels of all sizes
are trying to be greener, and many newer
chains are striving for government environmental awards. Discounted rooms are
another trend, as are discounts for room
upgrades.

In the countryside, some older hotels are
former castles or converted, luxurious
country homes. These types of hotels are
full of character and charm but can be
very expensive. Normally they have all
the amenities, if not more, of their urban
counterparts. Their locations may be so
remote that you must eat on the premises,
which limits your options when it comes
to your wallet.

∎ COMMUNICATIONS

INTERNET

Make sure your laptop is dual-voltage;
most, but not all, laptops operate equally
well on 110 and 220 volts and so require
only an adapter. Never plug your computer into any socket without first asking
about surge protection: although Scotland is computer-friendly, few hotels and
B&Bs outside the major cities have built-
in current stabilizers. Electrical fluctua-
tions and surges can short your adapter
or even destroy your computer, so it's
worthwhile to purchase a surge protector

in the United Kingdom that plugs into the
socket.

All hotels and many B&Bs have facilities
for computer users, such as a dedicated
PC room or broadband and Wi-Fi services
for Internet access.

Contacts Cybercafes (⊕ www.cybercafes.
com) lists more than 4,000 Internet cafés
worldwide.

PHONES

The good news is that you can now make
a direct-dial telephone call from virtually any point on earth. The bad news?
You can't always do so cheaply. Calling
from a hotel is almost always the most
expensive option; hotels usually add huge
surcharges to all calls, particularly international ones.

When you're calling anywhere in Great
Britain from the United States, the country code is 44. When dialing a Scottish
or British number from abroad, drop
the initial 0 from the local area code.
For instance, if you're calling Edinburgh
Castle from New York City, dial 011 (the
international code), 44 (the Great Britain
country code), 131 (the Edinburgh city
code), and then 225–9846 (the number
proper).

CALLING WITHIN SCOTLAND

Cell phones are ubiquitous, but there are
three types of public pay phones: those
that accept only coins, those that accept
only phone cards, and those that take
British Telecom (BT) phone cards and

credit cards. For coin-only phones, insert coins *before* dialing (minimum charge is 10p). Sometimes phones have a "press on answer" (POA) button, which you press when the caller answers.

All calls are charged according to the time of day. Standard rate is weekdays 8 AM TO 6 PM; cheap rate is weekdays 6 PM TO 8 AM and all day on weekends, when it's even cheaper. A local call before 6 PM costs 15p, 30p from a pay phone for three minutes. A daytime call to the United States will cost 24p a minute on a regular phone (weekends are cheaper), 80p on a pay phone.

To call a number with the same area code as the number from which you are dialing, omit the area-code digits when you dial. For long-distance calls within Britain, dial the area code (which usually begins with 01), followed by the telephone number. In provincial areas the dialing codes for nearby towns are often posted in the booth.

To call the operator, dial 100; directory inquiries (information), 118–500; international directory inquiries, 118–505.

In Scotland cellular-phone numbers, the 0800 toll-free code, and local-rate 0345 numbers do not have a 1 after the initial 0, nor do many premium-rate numbers, for example 0891, and special-rate numbers, for example 08705.

Freephone (toll-free) numbers start with 0800 or 0808; national information numbers start with 0845. A word of warning: 0870 numbers are *not* toll-free numbers; in fact, numbers beginning with 0871 or the 0900 prefix are premium-rate numbers, and it costs extra to call them. The amount varies and is usually relatively small when dialed from within the country but can be excessive when dialed from outside the United Kingdom.

CALLING OUTSIDE SCOTLAND

The country code for the United States is 1.

To make international calls *from* Scotland, dial 00 + the country code + area code +

number. For the international operator, credit card, or collect calls, dial 155.

Access Codes **AT&T Direct** (☎ *0500/890011 for cable and wireless, 0800/890011 for British Telecom, 0800/0130011 for AT&T, 800/435–0812 for other areas*). **MCI World-Phone** (*In U.K.:* ☎ *0800/890222 to call U.S. via MCI, 800/444–4141 for other areas*). **Sprint International Access** (☎ *0500/890877 cable and wireless, 0800/890877 British Telecom, 800/877–4646 for other areas*).

CALLING CARDS

You can purchase BT (British Telecom) phone cards for use on public phones from shops, post offices, and newsstands. They're ideal for longer calls, are composed of units of 20p, and come in values of £2, £5, £10, and £20. An indicator panel on the phone shows the number of units you've used; at the end of your call the card is returned. Where credit cards are taken, slide the card through, as indicated. Beware of buying cards that require you to dial a free phone number; some of these are not legitimate. It's better to get a BT card.

MOBILE PHONES

If you have a multiband phone (some countries use different frequencies than what's used in the United States) and your service provider uses the world-standard GSM network (as do T-Mobile, Cingular, and Verizon), you can probably use your phone abroad. Roaming fees can be steep, however: 99¢ a minute is considered reasonable. And overseas you normally pay the toll charges for incoming calls. It's almost always cheaper to send a text message than to make a call, since text messages have a very low set fee (often less than 5¢).

If you just want to make local calls, consider buying a new SIM card (note that your provider may have to unlock your phone for you to use a different SIM card) and a prepaid-service plan in the destination. You'll then have a local number and can make local calls at local rates.

Cell phones are getting less and less expensive to buy; so much so that it's now cheaper to buy a new cell phone while abroad than it is to rent one. Rates run from as low as £20 a month for unlimited calls with a pay-as-you-go card. Visit or contact one of the cell-phone providers below for more information.

Contacts Cellular Abroad (☎ 800/287–5072 ⊕ www.cellularabroad.com). **Mobal** (☎ 888/888–9162 ⊕ www.mobalrental.com).

■ CUSTOMS AND DUTIES

You're always allowed to bring goods of a certain value back home without having to pay any duty or import tax. But there's a limit on the amount of tobacco and liquor you can bring back duty-free, and some countries have separate limits for perfumes; for exact figures, check with your customs department. The values of so-called "duty-free" goods are included in these amounts. When you shop abroad, save all your receipts, as customs inspectors may ask to see them as well as the items you purchased. If the total value of your goods is more than the duty-free limit, you'll have to pay a tax (most often a flat percentage) on the value of everything beyond that limit.

Check ahead with the Department for Environment, Food and Rural Affairs if you want to bring a pet into Scotland.

Information in Scotland Department for Environment, Food and Rural Affairs (☎ 08459/3355 77 ⊕ www.defra.gov.uk).

HM Revenue & Customs (☎ 0845/010–9000 ⊕ www.hmrc.gov.uk).

U.S. Information U.S. Customs and Border Protection (⊕ www.cbp.gov).

■ EATING OUT

The restaurants we review in this book are the cream of the crop in each price category. Today the traditional Scottish restaurant offers more than fish-and-chips, fried sausage, and black pudding; instead you'll find the freshest of scallops, organic salmon, wild duck, and free-range Angus beef as well as locally grown seasonal vegetables and fruits.

Whether you want to try traditional haggis (ground-up sheep's organs) or black pudding (made from congealed blood) is up to you. Just know that there are other, more tempting Scottish dishes for you to choose from, as well as a wide array of international restaurants: Chinese, French, Greek, Indian, Italian, Japanese, Mexican, Mongolian, and Russian (to name but a few) can be truly exceptional. There are a couple of vegetarian options on every menu and most restaurants, particularly pubs that serve food, welcome families with young children.

Places like Glasgow, Edinburgh, and Aberdeen have sophisticated restaurants at various price levels; of these, the more notable tend to open only in the evening. But it's not just the urban areas that will spoil you for choice; fabulous restaurants are popping up in the smaller villages as well. Dining in Scotland can be an experience for all the senses but it is rarely cheap, so don't forget your credit card.

City Scots usually take their midday meals in a pub, wine bar, sandwich bar/shop, bistro, or department-store restaurant (which might not serve alcohol). When traveling, Scots generally eat inexpensively and quickly at a country pub or village tearoom.

Note that most pubs do not have any waitstaff, and you're expected to go to the bar and order a beverage and your meal—this can be particularly disconcerting when you're seated in a "restaurant" upstairs but are still expected to go downstairs and get your own drinks and food. You're not expected to tip the bartender, but you are expected to tip restaurant waitstaff, by leaving 10% to 15% of the tab on the table.

Since 2007, smoking has been banned in pubs, clubs, and restaurants throughout Britain.

Properties are assigned price catego-ries based on dinner prices. Price charts appear at the start of each chapter or, for Edinburgh and Glasgow, in the Where to Eat section.

CATEGORY	COST
£	under £10
££	£10–£14
£££	£15–£19
££££	£20–£25
£££££	over £25

All prices are per person in pounds for a main course at dinner.

DISCOUNTS AND DEALS

Many city restaurants have very good pre-theater meal deals that last from 5 to 7 PM. Lunch deals can also save you money; some main courses can be nearly half the price of dinner entrées. All supermarkets, sell a large variety of high-quality sand-wiches, wraps, and salads at reasonable prices. If the weather's dry, opt for a mid-day picnic.

MEALS AND MEALTIMES

To start the day with a full stomach, try a traditional Scottish breakfast of bacon and fried eggs served with sausage, fried mushrooms, and tomatoes, and usually fried bread or potato scones. Most places also serve kippers (smoked herring). All this is in addition to juice, porridge, cereal, toast, and other bread products.

"All-day" meal places are becoming prev-alent. The normal lunch period, however, is 12:30 to 2:30. A few places serve high tea—masses of cakes, bread and butter, and jam, served with tea only, around 2:30 to 4:30. Typical dinner times are fairly early, around 5 to 8.

Familiar fast-food chains are often more expensive than a good home-cooked meal in a local café or pub, where large servings of British comfort food—fish-and-chips, stuffed baked potatoes, and sandwiches—are served. In more upscale restaurants, cutting costs can be as simple as requesting *tap* water; "water" means a bottle of mineral water that could cost up to £5.

Unless otherwise noted, the restaurants listed in this guide are open daily for lunch and dinner.

PAYING

Many restaurants exclude service charges from the printed menu (which the law obliges them to display outside), then add 10% to 15% to the check, or else stamp SERVICE NOT INCLUDED along the bottom, in which case you should add the 10% to 15% yourself. Just don't pay twice for service—unscrupulous restaurateurs have been known to add service but leave the total on the credit-card slip blank.

Credit cards are widely accepted at most types of restaurants.

For guidelines on tipping, see Tipping below.

PUBS

A common misconception among visitors to Scotland is that pubs are cozy bars. But pubs are also gathering places, con-versation zones, even restaurants. Pubs are, generally speaking, where people go to have a drink, meet their friends, and catch up on one another's lives. Tradition-ally pub hours are 11–11, with last orders called about 20 minutes before closing time, but pubs can choose to stay open until midnight or 1 AM, or later.

Some pubs are child-friendly, but others have restricted hours for children. If a pub serves food, it will generally allow children in during the day with adults. Some pubs are stricter than others, though, and will not admit anyone younger than 18. Some will allow children in during the day, but only until 6 PM. If you're in doubt, ask the bartender. Family-friendly pubs tend to be packed with kids, parents, and all of their accoutrements, so you can just use your common sense.

RESERVATIONS AND DRESS

It's a good idea to make a reservation if you can. We only mention them specifically when reservations are essential (there's no other way you'll ever get a table) or when they are not accepted. For popular restaurants, book as far ahead as you can (often 30 days), and reconfirm as soon as you arrive. (Large parties should always call ahead to check the reservations policy.) We mention dress only when men are required to wear a jacket or a jacket and tie.

Online-reservation services make it easy to book a table before you even leave home. Toptable has listings in many Scottish cities.

Contacts Toptable (⊕ *www.toptable.co.uk*).

WINES, BEER, AND SPIRITS

Bars and pubs typically sell two kinds of beer: lager is light in color, very carbonated, and served cold, and ale is dark, semicarbonated, and served just below room temperature. You may also come across a pub serving "real ales," which are hand-drawn, very flavorful beers from smaller breweries. These traditionally produced real ales have a fervent following; check out the Campaign for Real Ale's Web site, www.camra.org.uk.

You can order Scotland's most famous beverage—whisky (here, most definitely spelled without an *e*)—at any local pub. All pubs serve any number of single-malt and blended whiskies. It's also possible to tour numerous distilleries, where you can sample a dram and purchase a bottle for the trip home. Most distilleries are concentrated in Speyside and Islay.

The legal drinking age in Scotland is 18.

▌ ECOTOURISM

Ecotourism is an emerging trend in the United Kingdom. The Shetland Environmental Agency Ltd. runs the Green Tourism Business Scheme (GTBS), a program that evaluates sites and lodgings in England, Scotland, and Wales and gives

them a gold, silver, or bronze rating according to their sustainability. You can find a list of green hotels, B&Bs, apartments, and other properties on the GTBS Web site. Also check out the VisitBritain and Visit Scotland Web sites, which have information and tips about green travel in Britain.

Contact Green Tourism Business Scheme (☎ *01738/632162* ⊕ *www.green-business.co.uk*). **VisitBritain** (⊕ *www.visitbritain.us*). **VisitScotland** (⊕ *www.visitscotland.com*).

▌ ELECTRICITY

The electrical current in Scotland, as in the rest of Great Britain, is 220–240 volts (in line with the rest of Europe), 50 cycles alternating current (AC); wall outlets take three-pin plugs, and shaver sockets take two round, oversize prongs.

Consider making a small investment in a universal adapter, which has several types of plugs in one lightweight, compact unit. Most laptops and mobile-phone chargers are dual voltage (i.e., they operate equally well on 110 and 220 volts), so require only an adapter. These days the same is true of small appliances such as hair dryers. Always check labels and manufacturer instructions to be sure. Don't use 110-volt outlets marked FOR SHAVERS ONLY for high-wattage appliances such as hair dryers.

▌ EMERGENCIES

If you need to report an emergency, dial 999 for police, fire, or ambulance. Be prepared to give the telephone number you're calling from. You can get 24-hour treatment in Accident and Emergency at British hospitals, but depending on the urgency of your situation, as in any U.S. hospital, you should expect to wait for treatment. Treatment from the National Health Service is free to British citizens; as a foreigner, you will be billed after the fact for your care. (Prices are nowhere near what they are in the United States.)

General Emergency Contacts Ambulance, fire, police (☎ 999).

U.S. Embassies American Consulate General (✉ 3 Regent Terr., Calton, Edinburgh ☎ 0131/556–8315). **U.S. Embassy** (✉ 24 Grosvenor Sq., London ☎ 020/7499–9000); for passports go to the **U.S. Passport Unit** (✉ 55 Upper Brook St., London ☎ 020/7499–9000 ⊕ www.usembassy.org.uk).

▌ HEALTH

SPECIFIC ISSUES IN SCOTLAND

If you take prescription drugs, keep a supply in your carry-on luggage and make a list of all your prescriptions to keep on file at home while you are abroad. You will not be able to renew a U.S. prescription at a pharmacy in Britain. Prescriptions are accepted only if issued by a U.K.-registered physician.

If you're traveling in the Highlands and islands in summer, pack some midge repellent and antihistamine cream to reduce swelling: the Highland midge is a force to be reckoned with. Check ⊕ www.midgeforecast.co.uk for updates on these biting pests.

OVER-THE-COUNTER REMEDIES

Over-the-counter medications in Scotland are similar to those in the United States, with a few significant differences. Medications are sold in boxes rather than bottles, and are sold in very small amounts—usually no more than 12 pills per package. There are also fewer brands than you're likely to be used to—you can, for example, find aspirin, but usually only one kind in a store. You can buy generic ibuprofen or a popular European brand of ibuprofen, Nurofen, which is sold everywhere. Tylenol is not sold in the United Kingdom, but its main ingredient, acetaminophen, is—although, confusingly, it's called paracetamol.

Drugstores are generally called pharmacies, but sometimes referred to as chemists' shops. The biggest drugstore chain in the country is Boots, which has outlets everywhere, except for the smallest towns. If you're in a rural area, look for shops marked with a sign of a green cross; almost all small drugstores have one of these.

Supermarkets and newsagents all usually have a small supply of cold and headache medicines, often behind the cash register. As in the United States, large supermarkets will have a bigger supply.

MEDICAL INSURANCE AND ASSISTANCE

Consider buying trip insurance with medical-only coverage. Neither Medicare nor some private insurers cover medical expenses anywhere outside of the United States. Medical-only policies typically reimburse you for medical care (excluding that related to pre-existing conditions) and hospitalization abroad, and provide for evacuation. You still have to pay the bills and await reimbursement from the insurer, though.

Another option is to sign up with a medical-evacuation assistance company. A membership in one of these companies gets you doctor referrals, emergency evacuation or repatriation, 24-hour hotlines for medical consultation, and other assistance. International SOS Assistance Emergency and AirMed International provide evacuation services and medical referrals. MedjetAssist offers medical evacuation.

Medical Assistance Companies **AirMed International** (⊕ *www.airmed.com*). **International SOS Assistance Emergency** (⊕ *www.intsos.com*). **MedjetAssist** (⊕ *www. medjetassist.com*).

Medical-Only Insurers **International Medical Group** (☎ *800/628-4664* ⊕ *www.imglobal. com*). **International SOS** (⊕ *www.internationalsos.com*). **Wallach & Company** (☎ *800/237- 6615 or 540/687-3166* ⊕ *www.wallach.com*).

SHOTS AND MEDICATIONS

No particular shots are necessary for visiting Scotland from the United States.

Health Warnings **National Centers for Disease Control & Prevention** (*CDC* ☎ *877/394- 8747 international travelers' health line* ⊕ *wwwnc.cdc.gov/travel*). **World Health Organization** (*WHO* ⊕ *www.who.int*).

▌HOURS OF OPERATION

Banks are open weekdays 9 to 5. Some banks have extended hours on Thursday evening, and a few are open on Saturday morning. The major airports operate 24-hour banking services seven days a week.

Service stations are at regular intervals on motorways and are usually open 24 hours a day, though stations elsewhere usually close from 9 PM to 7 AM; in rural areas many close at 6 PM and Sunday.

Most museums in cities and larger towns are open daily, although some may be closed on Sunday morning. In smaller villages museums are often open when there are visitors around—even late on summer evenings—but closed in poor weather, when visitors are unlikely; there's often a contact phone number on the door.

Pharmacies (often called "chemists" in Scotland) usually open 9 to 5 or 5:30 Monday through Saturday, though most large towns and cities have either a large supermarket open extended hours, with a pharmacy on the premises, or have a rotation system for pharmacists on call (there will be a note displayed in the pharmacy's window with the number to call). In rural areas doctors often dispense medicines themselves. In an emergency the police should be able to locate a pharmacist.

Usual business hours are Monday through Saturday 9 to 5 or 5:30. In small villages many shops close for lunch. Department stores in large cities and many supermarkets even in smaller towns stay open for late-night shopping (usually until 7:30 or 8) one or more days a week. Apart from some newsstands and small food stores, many shops close Sunday except in larger towns and cities, where main shopping malls may open.

HOLIDAYS

The following days are public holidays in Scotland; note that the dates for England and Wales are slightly different. Ne'er Day and a day to recover (January 1–2), Good Friday, May Day (first Monday in May), Spring Bank Holiday (last Monday in May), Summer Bank Holiday (first Monday in August), and Christmas (December 25–26).

▌MAIL

Stamps may be bought from post offices (open weekdays 9 to 5:30, Saturday 9 to noon), from stamp machines outside post offices, and from news dealers' stores and newsstands. Mailboxes, known as post- or letter boxes, are painted bright red; large tubular ones are set on the edge of sidewalks, and smaller boxes are set into post-office walls. Allow at least four days for a letter or postcard to reach the United States by airmail. Surface mail service can take up to four or five weeks.

Airmail letters to the United States cost 62p (under 10 grams) or 90p (under 20 grams); postcards cost 62p. Within the United Kingdom first-class letters cost 39p, second-class letters and postcards 30p. The Royal Mail Web site is ⊕ *www. royalmail.com*.

If you're uncertain where you'll be staying, you can arrange to have your mail sent to American Express. The service is free to cardholders; all others pay a small fee. You can also collect letters at any post office by addressing them to poste restante at the post office you nominate. In Edinburgh a convenient central office is St. James Centre Post Office, St. James Centre, Edinburgh, EH1 3SR, Scotland.

SHIPPING PACKAGES

Most department stores and retail outlets can arrange to ship your goods home. You should check your insurance for coverage of possible damage. If you want to ship goods yourself, use one of the overnight postal services, such as Federal Express, DHL, or TNT.

To find the nearest branch providing overnight mail services, contact the following agencies.

Express Services DHL (☎ 0844/248–0844 ⊕ www.dhl.co.uk). **FedEx** (☎ 08456/070809 ⊕ www.fedex.com). **TNT** (☎ 0800/100600 ⊕ www.tnt.com).

▌ MEDIA

NEWSPAPERS AND MAGAZINES

Scotland's major newspapers include the *Scotsman*—a conservative sheet that also styles itself as the journal of record—and the moderate Glasgow-based *Herald,* along with the tabloid *Daily Record.* The *Sunday Post,* conservative in bent, is the country's leading Sunday paper; *Scotland on Sunday* competes directly with London's *Sunday Times* for clout north of the border; and the *Sunday Herald,* an offshoot of the *Glasgow Herald,* is another major title.

Scotland also has many regional publications; the *List,* a twice-monthly magazine with listings, covers the Glasgow and Edinburgh scenes. Many Scottish newsstands also feature editions of the leading London newspapers, such as the *London Times,* the *Evening Standard,* the *Independent,* and the *Guardian;* the *Sunday Telegraph* usually has the biggest Scotland coverage.

For magazines the selection is smaller and its purview is less sophisticated. *Heritage Scotland,* a publication of the National Trust, covers the historic preservation beat. *Scottish Homes and Interiors* is devoted to home design and style, and the *Scottish Field* covers matters dealing with the countryside. For more regional coverage check out the glossy *Scottish Life.*

RADIO AND TELEVISION

The Scotland offshoot of the British Broadcasting Corporation, BBC Scotland, is based in Glasgow and has a wide variety of Scotland-based TV programming. BBC Scotland usually feeds its programs into the various BBC channels, including BBC1 and BBC2, the latter considered the more eclectic and artsy, with a higher proportion of alternative humor, drama, and documentaries. Channel 3 is used by independent channels, which can change from region to region in Scotland: Grampian, the Borders, and Scottish are three channels that are regional in focus, with Grampian beamed into the north and west of Scotland and Scottish into the southern regions. Originating in England, Channel 4 is a mixture of mainstream and off-the-wall programming, whereas Channel 5 has more sports and films.

Satellite TV has brought dozens more channels to Britain including BBC 3 and BBC 4, which show more experimental, cutting-edge shows than BBC 1 and BBC 2.

Radio has seen a similar explosion for every taste, from 24-hour classics on Classic FM (100–102 MHz) to rock (Richard Branson's Virgin at 105.8 MHz). BBC Radio Scotland is a leading radio station, tops for local news and useful as it provides Scottish (rather than English) weather information. Originating from England—and therefore not always received in regions throughout Scotland—the BBC channels include Channel 1 (FM 97.6) for the young and hip; 2 (FM 88) for middle-of-the-roadsters; 3 (FM 90.2) for classics, jazz, and arts; 4 (FM 92.4) for news, current affairs, drama, and documentaries; and 5 Live (MW 693 kHz) for sports and news coverage, with listener phone-ins.

▌ MONEY

Prices can seem high in Scotland largely because of the exchange rate, though this has improved because of the economic downturn. However, travelers do get some breaks: national museums are free, and staying in a B&B or renting a city apartment brings down lodging costs. The chart below gives some ideas of the kinds of prices you can pay for day-to-day life.

ITEM	AVERAGE COST
Cup of Coffee	£1.50
Glass of Wine	£3.50
Pint of Beer	£3.50
Sandwich	£3
One-Mile Taxi Ride Edinburgh	£2.20
Newspaper	40p–60p

Prices throughout this guide are given for adults. Substantially reduced fees are almost always available for children, students, and senior citizens.

▌TIP→ Banks never have every foreign currency on hand, and it may take as long as a week to order. If you're planning to exchange funds before leaving home, don't wait until the last minute.

ATMS AND BANKS

ATMs are available throughout Scotland at banks and numerous other locations such as railway stations, gas stations, and department stores. Three banks with many branches are Lloyds, Halifax, and the Royal Bank of Scotland. PINs have four or fewer digits.

Your own bank will probably charge a fee for using ATMs abroad; the foreign bank you use may also charge a fee. Nevertheless, you'll usually get a better rate of exchange at an ATM than you will at a currency-exchange office or even when changing money in a bank. And extracting funds as you need them is a safer option than carrying around a large amount of cash.

▌TIP→ PINs with more than four digits are not recognized at ATMs in many countries. If yours has five or more, remember to change it before you leave.

ATM Locations Cirrus (☎ 800/424–7787 ⊕ www.mastercard.com). **Plus** (☎ 800/843–7587 ⊕ www.visa.com).

CREDIT CARDS

Credit cards are accepted almost everywhere and for everything (except for bus and taxi fares), as are debit cards. You shouldn't experience any problems using your Visa or MasterCard; however, it is a good idea to travel with picture ID in case you're asked for it. American Express and Diners Club are not as widely accepted.

Throughout this guide, the following abbreviations are used: **AE,** American Express; **DC,** Diners Club; **MC,** MasterCard; and **V,** Visa.

CURRENCY AND EXCHANGE

Britain's currency is the pound sterling, which is divided into 100 pence (100p). Bills (called notes) are issued in the values of £50, £20, £10, and £5. Coins are issued in the values of £2, £1, 50p, 20p, 10p, 5p, 2p, and 1p. Scottish coins are the same as English ones, but Scottish notes are issued by three banks: the Bank of Scotland, the Royal Bank of Scotland, and the Clydesdale Bank. They have the same face values as English notes, and English notes are interchangeable with them in Scotland.

At this writing, the exchange rate was U.S. $1.64 to the pound. Britain's entry into the European Union's currency—the euro—continues to be debated.

Google does currency conversion. Just type in the amount you want to convert and an explanation of how you want it converted (e.g., "14 Swiss francs in dollars"), and then voilà. **Oanda.com** also allows you to print out a handy table with the current day's conversion rates.

XE.com is another good currency conversion Web site.

Conversion Sites Google (⊕ *www.google. com*). **Oanda.com** (⊕ *www.oanda.com*). **XE.com** (⊕ *www.xe.com*).

PACKING

Travel light. Porters are more or less extinct these days (and very expensive where you can find them). Also, if you're traveling around the country by car, train, or bus, large, heavy luggage is more of a burden than anything else. Save a little packing space for things you might buy while traveling.

In Scotland casual clothes are the norm, and very few hotels or restaurants insist on jackets and ties for men in the evening. It is, however, handy to have something semi-dressy for going out to dinner or the theater. For summer, lightweight clothing is usually adequate, except in the evening, when you'll need a jacket or sweater. A waterproof coat or parka and an umbrella are essential at any time of year. You can't go wrong with comfortable walking shoes, especially when you're climbing Edinburgh's steep urban hills or visiting Glasgow's massive museums. Drip-dry and wrinkle-resistant fabrics are a good bet since only the most prestigious hotels have speedy laundering or dry-cleaning service. Bring insect repellent if you plan to hike.

Some visitors to Scotland appear to think it necessary to adopt Scottish dress. It's not unless you've been invited to a wedding, and even then it's optional. Scots themselves do not wear tartan ties or Balmoral "bunnets" (caps), and only an enthusiastic minority prefers the kilt for everyday wear.

▌ PASSPORTS AND VISAS

U.S. citizens need only a valid passport to enter Great Britain for stays of up to six months. Travelers should be prepared to show sufficient funds to support and accommodate themselves while in Britain (credit cards will usually suffice for this) and to show a return or onward ticket. If you're within six months of your passport's expiration date, renew it before you leave—nearly extinct passports are not strictly banned, but they make immigration officials anxious, and may cause you problems. Health certificates are not required for travel in Scotland.

If only one parent is traveling with a child under 17 and his or her last name differs from the child's, then he or she will need a signed and notarized letter from the parent with the same last name as the child authorizing permission to travel. Airlines, ferries, and trains have different policies for children traveling alone, so if your child must travel alone, make sure to check with the carrier prior to purchasing your child's ticket.

U.S. Passport Information U.S. Department of State (🕿 *877/487-2778* ⊕ *http://travel. state.gov/passport*).

▌ RESTROOMS

Most cities, towns, and villages have public restrooms, indicated by signposts to WC, TOILETS, or PUBLIC CONVENIENCES. They vary hugely in cleanliness. You'll often have to pay a small amount (usually 30p) to enter public conveniences; a request for payment usually indicates a high standard of cleanliness. Gas stations, called petrol stations, also usually have restrooms (to which the above comments also apply). In towns and cities, department stores, hotels, restaurants, and pubs are usually your best bets for at least reasonable standards of hygiene.

Find a Loo The Bathroom Diaries (⊕ *www. thebathroomdiaries.com*) is flush with unsanitized info on restrooms the world over—each one located, reviewed, and rated.

▌ SAFETY

Overall, Scotland is a very safe country to travel in, but be a cautious traveler and keep your cash, passport, credit cards, and tickets close to you or in a hotel safe. Don't agree to carry anything for strangers. It's a good idea to distribute your cash, credit cards, IDs, and other valuables between a deep front pocket, an inside jacket or vest pocket, and a hidden money pouch. Don't reach for the money pouch once you're in public. Otherwise, you need not avoid wearing jewelry or be wary of passing cyclists snatching your purse. Use common sense as your guide.

General Information and Warnings Transportation Security Administration (*TSA* ⊕ www.tsa.gov). **U.K. Foreign & Commonwealth Office** (⊕ www.fco.gov.uk/travel). **U.S. Department of State** (⊕ www.travel.state.gov).

▋ SHOPPING

Tartans, tweeds, and woolens may be a Scottish cliché, but nevertheless the selection and quality of these goods make them a must-have for many visitors, whether a made-to-measure traditional kilt outfit or a classy designer sweater from Skye. Particular bargains can be found in Scottish cashmere sweaters; look for Johnstons of Elgin and Ballantyne, two high-quality labels. Glasgow is great for designer wear, although prices may seem high.

Food items are another popular purchase: whether shortbread, smoked salmon, boiled sweets, *tablet* (a type of hard fudge), marmalade and raspberry jams, Dundee cake, or black bun, it's far too easy to eat your way around Scotland.

Unique jewelry is available all over Scotland but especially in some of the remote regions where get-away-from-it-all craftspeople have set up shop amid the idyllic scenery.

Scottish antique pottery and table silver make unusual, if sometimes pricey, souvenirs: a Wemyss-ware pig for the mantelpiece, perhaps, or Edinburgh silver candelabra for the dining table. Antique Scottish pebble jewelry is a unique style of jewelry popular in Scotland; several specialized antique jewelry shops can be found in Edinburgh and Glasgow. Antiques shops and one- or two-day antiques fairs held in hotels abound all over Scotland. In general, goods are reasonably priced: shops in small communities must deal fairly if they hope for repeat business. Most dealers will drop the price a little if asked, "What's your best price?"

▋ SIGHTSEEING PASSES

Discounted sightseeing passes are a great way to save money on visits to castles, gardens, and historic houses. Just check what the pass offers against your itinerary to be sure it's worthwhile.

The Scottish Explorer Ticket, available from any staffed Historic Scotland (HS) property and from many tourist information centers, allows visits to HS properties for 3 days in a 5-day period (£21), 7 days in a 14-day period (£30), or 10 days in a 30-day period (£35). The Trust Discovery Ticket, issued by the National Trust for Scotland, is available for 3 days (£12), 7 days (£17), or 14 days (£22) and allows access to all National Trust for Scotland properties. It's available to overseas visitors only and can be purchased from the National Trust for Scotland online and by phone, or at properties and some of the main tourist information centers.

The Great British Heritage Pass grants you access to sights administered by National Trust for Scotland and Historic Scotland as well as numerous other sights throughout Great Britain. A 7-day pass costs £54; 15-day (£72) and 30-day (£96) passes are also available.

Discount Passes **Great British Heritage Pass** (☎ 0870/242–9988 in U.K. ☎ +44 (0)1664/485020 outside U.K. ⊕ www. britishheritagepass.com). **Historic Scotland** (☎ 0131/668–8600 ⊕ www.historic-scotland. gov.uk/explorer). **National Trust for Scotland** (☎ 0844/493–2100 ⊕ www.nts.org.uk).

▌TAXES

An airport departure tax of £40 (£10 for within U.K. and EU countries) per person is included in the price of your ticket.

The British sales tax, V.A.T. (Value-Added Tax), is 17.5%. It's almost always included in quoted prices in shops, hotels, and restaurants. The most common exception is at high-end hotels, where prices often exclude V.A.T. Be sure to verify whether the quoted room price includes V.A.T.

Further details on how to get a V.A.T. refund and a list of stores offering tax-free shopping are available from VisitBritain.

When making a purchase, ask for a V.A.T.-refund form and find out whether the merchant gives refunds—not all stores do, nor are they required to. Have the form stamped by customs officials when you leave the country or, if you're visiting several European Union countries, when you leave the EU. After you're through passport control, take the form to a refund-service counter for an on-the-spot refund or mail it to the address on the form after you arrive home.

Global Refund is a Europe-wide service with 225,000 affiliated stores and more than 700 refund counters at major airports and border crossings. Its refund form, called a Tax Free Check, is the most common across the European continent.

V.A.T. Refunds Global Refund (☎ 800/566–9828 ⊕ www.globalrefund.com). **VisitBritain** (⊕ www.visitbritain.com).

▌TIME

Great Britain sets its clocks by Greenwich Mean Time, five hours ahead of the U.S. East Coast. British summer time (GMT plus one hour) requires an additional adjustment from about the end of March to the end of October.

Time Zones Timeanddate.com (⊕ www.timeanddate.com/worldclock) can help you figure out the correct time anywhere.

▌TIPPING

Tipping is done in Scotland as in the United States, but at a lower level. Some restaurants and hotels add a service charge of 10% to 15% to the bill. In this case you aren't expected to tip. Always check first. Taxi drivers, hairdressers, and barbers should also get 10% to 15%. You're not expected to tip theater- or movie theater ushers, or elevator operators.

TIPPING GUIDELINES FOR SCOTLAND	
Bartender	£1–£5 depending on the size of the round (in the more modern bars). It's common in traditional pubs to buy the bartender a drink as a tip.
Bellhop	£1–£3 per bag
Hotel Concierge	£10 or more, if he or she performs a service for you
Hotel Doorman	£2–£5 if he helps you get a cab
Hotel Maid	£2–£3 a day (either daily or at the end of your stay, in cash)
Hotel Room-Service Waiter	£1 to £2 per delivery, even if a service charge has been added
Porter at Airport or Train Station	£1 per bag
Skycap at Airport	£1 to £2 per bag checked
Taxi Driver	10%–15%, but round up the fare to the next pound amount
Tour Guide	10% of the cost of the tour, but optional
Valet Parking Attendant	£2–£3, but only when you get your car
Waiter	10%–15%, with 15% being the norm at high-end restaurants; nothing additional if a service charge is added to the bill
Other	Restroom attendants in more expensive restaurants expect some small change or £1. Tip coat-check personnel at least £1–£2 per item checked unless there's a fee, then nothing.

▌ TOURS

Many companies offer fully guided tours in Scotland. Most of these are full packages including hotels, all food, and transportation costs in one flat fee. Because each tour company has different specialties, do a bit of research—either on your own or through a travel agent—before booking. You'll want to know about the hotels you'll be staying in, how big your group is likely to be, precisely how your days will be structured, and who the other people are likely to be.

CIE Tours offers all-inclusive themed tours of Scotland; moderately priced tours by Globus cover Scotland and Great Britain. Heart of Scotland has a seven-day ultimate tour of Scotland that takes you through the lowlands, highlands, borders, and islands; the company also has many one-day tours that could be appealing for part of a trip.

Another option is Rabbie's Trail Burners, which offers small-group guided tours in and around Scotland, as well as handy day tours from Edinburgh and Glasgow. They have won numerous awards including the Scottish Thistle award for sustainable tourism.

Contacts CIE Tours (☎ 800/243–8687 ⊕ www.mycietour.com). **Globus** (☎ 866/755–8581 ⊕ www.globusjourneys.com). **Heart of Scotland Tours** (☎ 01828/627799 ⊕ www.heartofscotlandtours.co.uk). **Rabbie's Trail Burners** (☎ 0845/643–2248 ⊕ www.rabbies.com)

SPECIAL-INTEREST TOURS

You can find tours for many special interests. We recommend Celtic Dream Tours, which specializes in Celtic-inspired and Burns tours, as well as golf and whisky tours. The Wayfarers offers exciting walking tours through the countryside. Scottish Ancestral Trail does high-end genealogy tours.

Contacts Celtic Dream Tours (☎ 813/317–6039 ⊕ www.celticdreamtours.com). **Scottish Ancestral Trail** (☎ 01683/300389 ⊕ www.

scottish-ancestral-trail.co.uk). **The Wayfarers** (☎ 800/249–4420 ⊕ www.thewayfarers.com).

GOLF TOURS

Scotland has fabulous golf courses; a tour can help enthusiasts make the most of their time. VisitScotland has a dedicated golf Web site with a list of tour companies.

Contacts Golf Scotland (☎ 866/875–4653 ⊕ www.golfscotland.com). **Scotland for Golf** (☎ 01334/460762 ⊕ www.scotlandforgolf.co.uk). **Thistle Golf** (☎ 0141/942-4043⊕ www.thistlegolf.co.uk).

PRIVATE GUIDES

The Scottish Tourist Guides Association has members throughout Scotland who are fully qualified professional guides able to conduct walking tours in the major cities, half- or full-day tours or extended tours throughout Scotland, driving tours, and special study tours. Many guides speak at least one language in addition to English. Fees are negotiable with individual guides.

Contacts Scottish Tourist Guides Association (☎ 01786/447784 ⊕ www.stga.co.uk).

▌ TRIP INSURANCE

Comprehensive trip insurance is valuable if you're booking a very expensive or complicated trip (particularly to an isolated region) or if you're booking far in advance. Comprehensive policies typically cover trip-cancellation and interruption, letting you cancel or cut your trip short because of illness, or, in some cases, acts of terrorism in your destination. Such policies might also cover evacuation and medical care. (For trips abroad you should have at least medical-only coverage. *See Medical Insurance and Assistance under Health.*) Some also cover you for trip delays because of bad weather or mechanical problems as well as for lost or delayed luggage.

Another type of coverage to consider is financial default—that is, when your trip is disrupted because a tour operator, airline, or cruise line goes out of business. Generally you must buy this when you book your trip or shortly thereafter, and it's available to you only if your operator isn't on a list of excluded companies.

Always read the fine print of your policy to make sure that you're covered for the risks that most concern you. Compare several policies to be sure you're getting the best price and range of coverage available.

Insurance Comparison Information
InsureMyTrip.com (☎ 800/487–4722 ⊕ www. insuremytrip.com). **Squaremouth.com** (☎ 800/240–0369 ⊕ www.squaremouth.com).

Comprehensive Insurers Access America (☎ 800/284–8300 ⊕ www.accessamerica.com). **CSA Travel Protection** (☎ 800/711–1197 ⊕ www.csatravelprotection.com). **Travel Guard** (☎ 800/826–4919 ⊕ www.travelguard. com). **Travelex Insurance** (☎ 888/228–9792 ⊕ www.travelex-insurance.com). **Travel Insured International** (☎ 800/243–3174 ⊕ www.travelinsured.com).

▌ VISITOR INFORMATION

See the Orientation and Planning section at the start of each chapter for regional tourist information offices; look for Essentials sections in towns for local offices.

Contacts in Britain VisitScotland (✉ Ocean Point One, 94 Ocean Dr., Edinburgh ☎ 0845/225–5121 ⊕ www.visitscotland.com Drop-in visits only ✉ 19 Cockspur St., off Trafalgar Sq., London). **The Scotland Desk, Britain and London Visitor Centre** (*Drop-in visits* ✉ 1 Regent St., Piccadilly Circus, London).

Contacts in the U.S. VisitBritain (☎ 800/462–2748 ⊕ www.visitbritain.com).

ONLINE RESOURCES
VisitScotland is Scotland's official Web site and includes a number of special-interest sites on topics from golf to genealogy. VisitBritain, Great Britain's official site, has ample information on Scotland's sights, accommodations, and more.

Historic Scotland cares for the more than 300 historic properties described on its site. The National Trust for Scotland has information about stately homes, gardens, and castles. Both offer sightseeing passes *(see Sightseeing Passes above)*.

All About Scotland VisitScotland (⊕ www. visitscotland.com). **VisitBritain** (⊕ www. visitbritain.com).

Historic Sites Historic Scotland (⊕ www. historic-scotland.gov.uk). **National Trust for Scotland** (⊕ www.nts.org.uk).

INDEX

NOTES

NOTES

ABOUT OUR WRITERS

Duncan Forgan has traveled far and wide in his quest for stories and exotic food, but his native Scotland still retains a potent pull for him. He has written travel articles on the country for major publications including the *Sunday Times* and the *Scotsman,* and his inside knowledge of the cultural and culinary scenes has allowed him to provide insight for travel guides and magazines. Duncan updated the Edinburgh and the Lothians and golf chapters for this edition; bagging a birdie on the second hole at Lundin Links was a particular highlight of his research.

Mike Gonzalez is professor of Latin American Studies at Glasgow University and also writes regularly for the *Herald* and other publications on politics and culture. Mike's assignment for Fodor's was the Central Highlands and Argyll and the Isles chapters. His travels took him to places familiar and less familiar, and included exploring a tiny island on Islay whose houses were once an imperial center.

Shona Main grew up in Shetland; after moving to the mainland, she spent some informative years working on magazines for teenagers. She had a brief career in law and politics before she returned to writing. Now based in Dundee, Shona is a freelance contributor to newspapers and books and has just written her first work of fiction, which is based on a wind-flattened island community not unlike the one she grew up in. Her territory for this edition was Fife and Angus, Aberdeen and the Northeast, and Orkney and Shetland.

Fiona G. Parrott is a native of California who fell in love with Scotland in 1999 and made it her home. A freelance writer, she contributes regularly to publications on both sides of the Atlantic. She's been a veterinarian, actor, bartender, watermelon picker, latrine builder and university lecturer, but writing for Fodor's has been one of her most exciting jobs. She now divides her time between Scotland and California where she writes, teaches, and raises her family. Her contributions to this edition included updates of the Glasgow, Borders and the Southwest, and Travel Smart chapters; she also wrote pieces such as Flavors of Scotland for Experience Scotland. In recent years Fiona has also worked on Fodor's San Francisco.

Originally from Chicago, Elizabeth Reeder first visited Scotland while backpacking around Europe; after getting drenched in Glencoe and dried out on the sands of Morar, she was hooked. She has now lived in Scotland for more than fifteen years and writes essays, stories, and novels. Her work is regularly broadcast on BBC Radio 4, and she is a lecturer in the Creative Writing program at Glasgow University. Elizabeth's contributions included revising two chapters: the Northern Highlands and the Western Isles, and Around the Great Glen.